HANDBOOK OF
FINANCE RESEARCH IN KOREA

VOLUME 1

Edited by

Hee-Joon Ahn
Sungkyunkwan University, Seoul, Korea

The Korean Finance Association

Handbook of Finance Research in Korea (Volume 1)
Copyright © 2012 by the Korean Finance Association

Permissions may be sought from the Korean Finance Association, Korea by phone +82-2-2003-9641; fax +82-2003-9649; e-mail office@korfin.org

ISBN 978-89-968339-0-1 94320
ISBN 978-89-968339-1-8 (SET)

Notice
This handbook is a collection of survey articles that were originally published in Volume 24 of the *Asian Review of Financial Research*. A citation of any of the articles in this handbook must refer to the appropriate page or range of pages, issue, and volume of the Asian Review of Financial Research in which the article was published. The relevant page, issue, and volume information can be found on the cover page of each respective article.

Publisher
Seokchin Kim, President
The Korean Finance Association
KOFIA Building 11F
143, Uisadang-daero, Yeongdeungpo-gu
Seoul, 150-974, Korea

Published on February 29, 2012

Printed and bound in Seoul, Korea by Daesung Publishing Co.

FORWARD

The financial markets in Korea have grown dramatically over the past several decades. Korea now boasts several of the leading market sectors in the world. As of 2011, the Korea Exchange (KRX) has become the second largest in value of securitized derivatives among all world exchanges. In addition, the KRX maintains the pole position among world exchanges in terms of trading of stock index options and equity derivatives, with its KOSPI 200 index options being the world's most actively traded derivative product. Further, the KRX is globally the eighth most active market in equity trading and the sixth largest in term of total value of bonds traded.

Like the financial markets, the finance academia of Korea has also seen impressive growth in research activities over the past three decades. The vast literature it has accumulated to date and the abundance of the evidences that have been recorded merit a biblical compilation, calling for a need to develop a handbook. The *Handbook of Finance Research in Korea* is the first such attempt to bring together a systematic review of various research topics about the Korean financial markets. I hope that the Handbook will offer an invaluable knowledge base for researchers, professionals, and students in the finance area. I also hope that the Handbook becomes an effective vehicle for introducing academics outside of Korea to the empirical evidences on Korean financial markets that have been put forward by the finance academia in Korea.

I would like to express my appreciation to all the persons involved in creating this Handbook, particularly the contributors of the eleven articles contained in it. I would also like to give my gratitude to all the sponsors who provide generous support for the success of various academic activities carried out by the Korean Finance Association, including the publication of this Handbook.

December 2011

Sangsoo Park
President(2011), Korean Finance Association

PREFACE

The purpose of this Handbook is to provide academicians, practitioners, and doctoral-level graduate students with a comprehensive survey of research on the Korean financial markets. Written by a prominent group of financial economists in Korea, the Handbook is the first systematic survey of the finance literature that has been compiled from the Korean academia of the past several decades. The Handbook serves as a useful reference source for researchers who need a literature search on a specific topic or topics related to the Korean financial markets. It can also work as supplementary reading material for doctoral level courses in finance in Korea. It also has an important role to introduce those outside Korea to the knowledge base that has been built up by the finance academic society in Korea.

During the past three decades, finance research in Korea has evolved considerably, producing an extensive body of research in various areas. The increased interest in Korea's financial markets spurred by the growth of the country's economy, the increased availability of financial data, the emergence of advanced economic and statistical theories, and the growing population of finance academicians in the country all have contributed a fair share to the process. Yet, there has never been a single coordinated endeavor to put together the finance literature in Korea into accessible surveys. This is why the Korean Finance Association (KFA) launched the initiative 'The KFA Knowledge Database Project' to create a comprehensive reference source for professional researchers as well as graduate students who are interested in doing a research work on finance in Korea.

With the above-mentioned grand objective, the KFA Knowledge Database Project was initiated in 2010 by the then president of the association Hyuk Choe. A special committee was formed with the task of choosing topics to be covered by the survey and to select a group of scholars to contribute survey articles. Various factors went into the topic and author selection processes with the fundamental requirements being that the selected topics be of the greatest academic and practical importance and that the selected authors be leading researchers in relevant topics. Collectively, they form some of the best experts in the finance academia of Korea. While the authors were instructed to primarily concentrate on the Korean literature, they were also asked to present on literature from outside Korea, particularly that in the U.S., so that comprehensive comparisons between the existing literature inside and outside of Korea could be possible.

Upon the initial completion by the author or co-authors, each article went through a review process by two reviewers, also carefully selected for their authority in the knowledge of the pertinent topic. The articles, eleven in total, were then published over one year in 2011 in four different issues (issue 1 through 4) of Volume 23 of the *Asian Review of Financial Research*. This Handbook is a collection of the eleven articles that originally appeared in Volume 23 of the *Review*.

Out of the eleven articles in this Handbook, the first six deal with topics in the investment area. The first article by Dongcheol Kim surveys the studies on asset pricing in Korea over the past three decades. In the second article, Bong-Chan Kho focuses on the literature on foreign investors in Korea that has accumulated from the past two decades since the liberalization of the Korean capital markets. Kyong Shik Eom reviews the market microstructure area in the third article. The area of market microstructure has been one of the more prolific areas of finance in Korea due to the availability of comprehensive transaction-level datasets on the Korean equity and derivative markets. In the next article, Keunsoo Kim and Jinho Byun jointly explore the evidences compiled by the behavioral studies on Korean capital markets. Sukho Sonu and Hyungsuk Choi, meanwhile, survey the evidences on market anomalies in Korea in the fifth article. In the article that follows, Kwangsoo Ko offers a comprehensive summary of the literature on the mutual fund market in Korea, a market that has grown substantially during the second half of the last decade.

The next three articles address corporate finance topics. The seventh article, written by Mun-Soo Choi, addresses the topic of IPOs in Korea. In the next article, Sungmin Kim takes up the literature on payout policy in Korea. The subsequent article by Chae-Yeol Yang concentrates on the literature on corporate governance, an area which saw a significant amount of research work in Korea after the 1997 Asian financial crisis. The final two articles of the Handbook are concerned with the topics of derivative markets and foreign exchange markets, respectively. The review by In Joon Kim provides a comprehensive examination of the studies that have been carried out on the Korean derivative markets. Despite their short history, the derivative markets in Korea have grown explosively lately, igniting strong research interest. The survey by Daekeun Park covers issues and evidences related to exchange rates and foreign exchange markets and wraps up the Handbook.

While a significant effort went into having the Handbook cover as wide a range of research areas as possible, it is by no means complete. For example, the area of banking is not covered in this volume as neither is the topic of mergers and acquisitions. This is why we plan on providing a subsequent volume in the future.

Lastly, I wish to thank the authors for their overcoming enormous challenges and for producing excellent surveys in a limited amount of time. I am also grateful to the reviewers for contributing their precious time and effort to improve and enrich the contents of the articles. My thanks also go to the members of the editorial board of the *ARFR*, whose valuable advice greatly helped in shaping this Handbook, and to the members of the Academic Research Committee of the KFA in 2010, Jaeuk Khil (Committee Chair), J. M. Chung, Chung-Hun Hong, and Joon-Haeng Lee, who were involved in topic and author selections. The whole project would not have been possible without the leadership and continual support of the presidents of the KFA - Hyuk Choe, the former president in 2010, Sangsoo Park, the current president, and Seokchin Kim, the president elect for the 2012 term. I express my gratitude to all three of them. I also thank Timothy Smart, Hyung Chul Lee, Hee Jin Yang, and Jae-Myung Yoo, who provided much needed editorial help. Finally, my special thanks go to Jung-Ae Kim. None of this would have been accomplished without her invaluable administrative support.

December 2011

Hee-Joon Ahn
Editor

CONTRIBUTORS

Jinho Byun
Ewha Womans University

Hyungsuk Choi
Hongik University

Mun-Soo Choi
Soongsil University

Kyong Shik Eom
University of Seoul

Bong-Chan Kho
Seoul National University

Keunsoo Kim
Kyung Hee University

Sungmin Kim
Hanyang University

In Joon Kim
Yonsei University

Dongcheol Kim
Korea University

Kwangsoo Ko
Pusan National University

Daekeun Park
Hanyang University

Sukho Sonu
Hongik University

Chae-Yeol Yang
Chonnam National University

REVIEWERS

CONTENTS

Forward iii

Preface iv

Contributors vii

Reviewers viii

Chapter 1
Asset Pricing Models in the Korean Stock Markets: A Review
for the Period of 1980 ~ 2009

Dongcheol Kim 1

I.   Introduction 2

II. Capital Asset Pricing Model 4

    1. Time-Series Tests of the CAPM 5

    2. Cross-Sectional Regression Tests of the CAPM 9

    3. Mis-specification Issues in the CSR Tests 15

    4. Conditional Versions of the CAPM and GMM Tests 21

III. Arbitrage Pricing Theory (APT) 27

    1. APT Tests by Identifying Both Factors and Factor Loadings 29

    2. APT Tests by Identifying Factors from Macroeconomic
       Variables 30

    3. APT Tests through Constructing Factor Mimicking Portfolios 31

IV. The Consumption-Based Capital Asset Pricing Model
    (C-CAPM) 36

V. Intertemporal Capital Asset Pricing Model 37

VI. Summary and Concluding Remarks 43

References 45

Chapter 2
The Impact and Role of Foreign Investors in Korea

Bong-Chan Kho   63

I.   Introduction   64

II. The Recent Evolution of Foreign Equity Flows in Korea   66

III. The Benefits and Costs of Capital Market Liberalization   70

     1. The Measure and Degree of Capital Market Integration   70

     2. The Impacts of Capital Market Liberalizations on Returns
        and Volatility   76

     3. Foreign Portfolio Flows and Destabilization   80

     4. The Effects of Foreign Investment Restrictions on Stock
        Prices   84

IV. Financial Globalization, Governance, and Home Bias   87

V.   Information Asymmetries and Investment Performances   89

     1. Evidence for the Information Disadvantage of Foreign
        Investors   89

     2. Evidence for the Information Advantage of Foreign Investors   93

VI. Summary and Conclusions   96

References   99

Chapter 3
Market Microstructure in the Korean Financial Markets:
A Survey

Kyong Shik Eom   107

I.   Introduction   108

II. Micro Aspects of the Microstructure World: Orders and
     Trades, Basic Market Quality, Price Discovery, and
     Trading Mechanisms   112

     1. Orders and Trades   112

     2. Market Quality-Spread, Trading Volume, Volatility, Market
        Impact Cost, and Private-Information Risk   120

     3. Short-Term (Intraday) Return Predictability and Price
        Discovery   126

     4. Trading Mechanisms and Related Issues   128

III. Trading Protocols-Rules and Regulations Related to
      Trading   131

      1. Minimum Tick Size   132

      2. Liquidity Providers   134

      3. Price-Limit System   135

      4. Sidecar   137

      5. Short Sales Including Stock Lending and Credit Balance 138

IV.   Market Transparency   140

V.   Market Macrostructure   143

      1. Comparisons among Markets in the Korean Stock Market
         Hierarchy   144

      2. Cross-Listing between Domestic and Foreign Stock Markets 149

VI.   Expansion of Market Microstructure to the Fields of
      Investments and Corporate Finance   151

      1. Expansion to Investments   151

      2. Expansion to Corporate Finance   165

VII. Concluding Remarks   167

      References   170

Chapter 4
Studies on Korean Capital Markets from the Perspective of
Behavioral Finance

Keunsoo Kim and *Jinho Byun*   203

I.   Introduction   204

II.   Foundation of Behavioral Finance   206

      1. Beginning of Behavioral Finance   206

      2. Limits of Arbitrage   207

III. Prospect Theory and Empirical Results   210

      1. Prospect Theory   210

      2. Psychological Bias of Gamblers   213

      3. Disposition Effect   214

IV. Over-reaction and Under-reaction   221

    1. Over-reaction and Under-reaction Models   221

    2. Profitability of Contrarian Strategy in Korea   222

    3. Profitability of Momentum Strategy in Korea   229

    4. Other Anomalies Related to Over-reaction or Under-reaction   232

V. Trading and Return Behavior with Psychological Bias   236

    1. Investor Trading Behavior   236

    2. Corporate Behavioral Finance   242

    3. Investor Sentiment and Corporate Event   245

    4. Irrational Return Behavior   247

VI. Conclusion   250

References   254

Chapter 5
Capital Market Anomalies in Korea

Sukho Sonu and *Hyungsuk Choi*   271

I.   Introduction   272

II. Cross-sectional Empirical Regularities   274

    1. Size and Book-to-Market Effect   274

    2. Turn-of-the-Year Effect (January Effect)   279

    3. Weekend Effect   282

III. Time-Series Empirical Regularities   284

    1. Long-Term Reversal and Momentum Effect   284

    2. Short-Term Interest Rate and Dividend Yield   291

IV. Returns to Different Types of Markets   293

    1. IPO Markets   293

    2. SEO Markets   300

    3. M&A Markets   305

V. Implications for Market Efficiency and Corporate Finance   308

VI. Conclusions   309

References   312

Chapter 6

A Survey of Mutual Fund Studies: Implications for Korean
Markets

Kwangsoo Ko 325

  I.   Introduction 326

  II. Review of Mutual Fund Markets and Industry 328

       1. A Brief History of the U.S. Mutual Fund Markets and Industry 328

       2. The History of the Korean Mutual Fund Markets and Industry 330

  III. Overseas Mutual Fund Studies 334

       1. The Economics of Mutual Funds 339

       2. Agency Problems 351

       3. Other Issues 358

  IV. Mutual Fund Studies in Korea 369

       1. The Economics of Mutual Funds 373

       2. Agency Problems 377

       3. Other Issues 377

  V.   Concluding Remarks 380

  References 383

Chapter 7
Review of Empirical Studies on IPO Activity and Pricing
Behavior in Korea

Mun-Soo Choi 415

  I.   Introduction 416

  II. Evidence of IPO Underpricing in the Korean IPO Market 418

  III. Asymmetric Information Hypotheses 422

       1. Winner's Curse 422

       2. Ex Ante Uncertainty 423

       3. Partial Adjustment (Information Extraction) 426

       4. Information Spillover 428

       5. Certification Effect 429

IV. Price Stabilization 432

V. Hot Issue Markets 437

VI. Long-Run Performance 439

VII. Concluding Remarks 444

References 446

Chapter 8
Payout Policy in Korea: A Review of Empirical Evidence

Sungmin Kim 457

I. Introduction 458

II. Dividends: Empirical Evidences 467

    1. Dividend Irrelevance Theory 467

    2. The Impact of Market Imperfections on Dividend 468

    3. Dividend Types 480

    4. Survey Evidence on Dividends and Dividend Policy 485

III. Share Repurchases: Empirical Evidences 487

    1. Asymmetric Information 489

    2. Agency Costs and Free Cash Flow Hypothesis 491

    3. Managerial Incentive Hypothesis 492

    4. Takeover Deterrence Hypothesis 493

    5. Substitute Hypothesis 494

IV. Summary and Concluding Remarks 497

References 500

Chapter 9

A Survey of the Korean Literature on Corporate Governance

Chae-Yeol Yang 517

I. Introduction 518

II. The Effect of Corporate Governance Structure on
Corporate Policy 521

1. Perquisite Consumption 521

2. Investment 522

3. R&D 523

4. Cash Holdings 524

5. Wage Decisions 524

6. Chaebol and Internal Market: Tunneling/propping 525

7. Financing Decision 527

III. Corporate Governance and Firm Value 527

1. Ownership Structure and Firm Value with Ownership
   Measure as a LHS Variable 528

2. Ownership Structure and Firm Value with Corporate
   Governance Index as a LHS Variable 529

3. Ownership Structure and Accounting Profitability 530

4. Outside Director's Role, Blockholder's Holdings, etc. 531

5. Distribution of Shares and Firm Value 532

6. Disparity and Firm Value and Related Issues 532

IV. Market Discipline 533

1. Discipline in Debt Market 533

2. Discipline in Managerial Labor Market 534

3. Discipline in Product Market and M&A 535

4. Discipline in Capital Market: Security Offerings 536

5. Discipline in Insurance Markets 537

6. Distribution of Stock Returns 538

7. Governance Premium: Stock Returns 539

V. Determinants of Governance Structure 540

1. Managerial Compensation: Stock Options 540

2. Share Ownership, Outside Directors, and Holding Company ... 541

VI. Discussions and Conclusions 542

1. Problems in Research Design 543

2. Normative Issues: Policy Implications 544

3. Future Research Directions and Conclusion 545

References 547

Chapter 10
A Review of the Literature on Derivative Securities in Korea

In Joon Kim 561

I. Introduction 562

II. A Brief Overview of the Derivative Securities Markets in
Korea 563

III. The Literature on Derivative Securities in Korea 567

1. The Derivative Securities Markets 567

2. Valuation of Derivative Securities 580

3. Risk Management 590

IV. Concluding Remarks 594

References 598

Chapter 11
Empirical Studies in Exchange Rates and Foreign Exchange
Markets: A Survey

Daekeun Park 615

I. Introduction 616

II. Purchasing Power Parity and Real Exchange Rates 617

1. The Purchasing Power Parity 618

2. Equilibrium Real Exchange Rate 621

III. Studies on Nominal Exchange Rates 622

1. Models of Nominal Exchange Rates 622

2. The Effect of "News" on Nominal Exchange Rates 626

3. Exchange Rate Forecasting 627

IV. Studies on Foreign Exchange Markets 631

1. Foreign Exchange Market Efficiency 631

2. Foreign Exchange Market Intervention 636

3. Market Microstructure Approach   639

V. Exchange Rates and Corporate Finance   646

    1. Measuring and Managing Foreign Exchange Exposure of Firms   646

    2. International Portfolio Investment and Foreign Exchange Risk   650

    3. Optimal Hedge Ratio   652

VI. Conclusion   654

References   656

Any citation of this article must refer to the following: Kim, Dongcheol, "Asset Pricing Models in the Korean Stock Markets: A Review for the Period of 1980~2009", Asian Review of Financial Research, Vol. 24 (2011), No. 1, pp. 167-229.

Chapter 1

Asset Pricing Models in the Korean Stock Markets: A Review for the Period of 1980~2009

Dongcheol Kim*   Professor, Business School, Korea University

Abstract

This paper reviews 30 years of empirical research on asset pricing models in the Korean stock markets. The validity of the Capital Asset Pricing Model (CAPM) has been seriously challenged in Korea as in the other countries. The overall empirical results in Korea show, as they do in other countries, that the static CAPM fails to explain for stock returns in Korea. Contrary to the prediction of the CAPM, firm characteristic variables such as firm size, book-to-market, and earnings-to-price ratio have significant explanatory power for average stock returns in the Korean stock markets. Because of these CAPM-anomalous phenomena, various asset pricing models such as the types of Arbitrage Pricing Theory (APT), the Consumption-based Capital Asset Pricing Model (C-CAPM), and the types of the Intertemporal Capital Asset Pricing Model (I-CAPM) have been introduced and tested in the literature. The Fama and French(1993) three-factor model is arguably acceptable in explaining Korean stock returns. This paper also provides some explanations of various testing methodologies used in the literature for asset pricing models and discusses the related econometric issues.

Keywords   Asset Pricing Models, CAPM, Arbitrage Pricing Theory, Intertemporal CAPM, Consumption-based CAPM, Korean Stock Markets

---

* **Address:** Korea University, Anam-dong, Seongbuk-gu, Seoul 136-701, Korea; **E-mail:** kimdc@korea.ac.kr; **Tel:** 82-2-3290-2606.

The paper was accomplished as a part of the knowledge database project by the Korean Finance Association and was financially supported by the Korean Finance Association. The author thanks two referees, Bong-Chan Kho and one anonymous referee, and the Editor, Hee-Joon Ahn, for their helpful comments. The author also thanks Soon-Ho Kim for his excellent assistantship.

I. Introduction

Since the Capital Asset Pricing Model (CAPM) of Sharpe (1964), Lintner (1965), and Black (1972) was developed, this model has become a backbone of financial economics. The CAPM provides an easy and simple framework about how to measure risk and the relation between expected return and risk. Almost 45 years after its introduction, the CAPM is still widely used in the field in estimating cost of capital for firms and discount rates for project cash flows and evaluating the performance of managed portfolios, etc. (see the survey results by Graham and Harvey (2001) for the U.S.). Nonetheless, since its introduction, the validity of the CAPM has been seriously challenged in Korea as well as in other countries. In the unconditional model of the traditional Sharpe-Lintner-Black CAPM, expected returns and market betas are assumed constant. However, there is no justification for the idea that expected returns and betas should be constant. Since corporate investment and the financial decisions of a firm could affect investors' expected return of the firm and its systematic risk and since macroeconomic conditions change over time, betas and the market risk premium can be time-varying. In fact, numerous papers empirically show the time-varying behavior of market betas and the market risk premium. In order to capture this time-varying behavior (or non-stationarity) of market betas and the market risk premium, various versions of the conditional CAPM have been suggested in the literature.

The arbitrage pricing theory (APT), formulated by Ross (1976), is considered an alternative pricing model to the CAPM. The APT is less restrictive than the CAPM in that it applies in both single-period and multi-period settings. Further, it does not require that the market portfolio be mean-variance efficient, which is a critical condition for the CAPM. The APT requires an assumption that markets are perfectly competitive and investors' utility functions are monotonically increasing and concave. Although the APT seems more robust compared to the CAPM in many respects, it has two problems. First, the theory provides no clue as to the number of factors. Second, even though the number of factors is known, the daunting task of identifying the risk factors remains. Thus, many researchers attempt to estimate the number of factors and to empirically identify these factors. This paper reviews the various models of the APT suggested in the Korean literature.

One of the assumptions about the CAPM open to criticism is that the CAPM is a static single-period model. That is, all investors have the same holding period and maximize their expected utility of returns over a one-period planning horizon. This means that the trading horizon, the decision horizon, and the planning horizon are all assumed to be equal to each other and to be of the same length for all investors. Critics argue, however, that investors make their investment decisions intertemporally by maximizing their multi-period utility of lifetime consumption, rather than choosing their portfolios according to the Markowitz mean-variance criterion to maximize their single-period utility. Merton (1973) argues that if preferences and future investment opportunity sets are state dependent, investors need an equilibrium model accommodating portfolio selection behavior for intertemporal utility maximization. Merton suggests a multi-period version asset pricing model, called the Intertemporal Capital Asset Pricing Model (I-CAPM).

Rubinstein (1976), Lucas (1978), and Breeden (1979) employ a different approach to obtain investors' equilibrium expected return. These authors assume that investors maximize the expected value of a time-additive and state-independent lifetime utility function. In a situation in which an investor (or a representative agent) has the intertemporal choice problem of maximizing expected utility which depends only on current and future consumption, an asset's risk premium depends on the covariance between the asset's return and the aggregate consumption growth rate. This is the Consumption-based CAPM (C-CAPM). The above two intertemporal models (I-CAPM and C-CAPM) are different from the model for a single-period utility maximizer such as the CAPM.

This paper reviews 30 years of empirical research on the above-mentioned asset pricing models in the Korean stock markets. It provides some explanations of the testing methodologies used in the literature for the asset pricing models. It cites articles published in finance-related journals in Korea after 1990, since most of these articles report results covering the 1980's there are few articles on asset pricing models published prior to 1990. For the non-Korean stock markets (mostly the U.S. markets), I cite only the most important articles. However, I cite these articles only if they are needed to explain the asset pricing models and to review the Korean articles. Thus, I try to minimize the reference list of such articles.

This paper proceeds as follows: Section II reviews the literature on the CAPM, both unconditional and conditional, and explains the testing methodologies. Section III reviews the literature on the APT models, and Sections IV and V explain and review the published works on the C-CAPM and I-CAPM, respectively. Section IV sets forth a discussion and conclusions.

II. The Capital Asset Pricing Model (CAPM)

The CAPM implies that the expected return on asset i, $E(R_i)$, is a linear function of its systematic risk as represented by β_i. Equation (1) summarizes the CAPM more succinctly:

$$E(R_i) = r_f + [E(R_m) - r_f]\,\beta_i \tag{1}$$

where β_i is the market beta representing systematic risk of asset i, r_f is the riskless rate of return, and $E(R_m)$ is the expected return on the market portfolio. Note that when there is no riskless borrowing and lending, the riskless rate of return is substituted with the expected return on the zero-beta portfolio, which is unrelated to the market portfolio (Black 1972). Each expected return can be interpreted as the appropriate discount rate, cost of capital, or equilibrium rate of return that investors should expect for that amount of systematic risk.

The CAPM is a mathematically perfect model. However, as with all models, many unrealistic assumptions are used in its derivation. This is why the model must be tested against data. The following two sections explain two primary testing methodologies used in the literature: time-series regression and cross-sectional regression (CSR) tests.

1. Time-Series Tests of the CAPM

The ex post form of the CAPM in equation (1) can be represented as

$$R_{it} - r_{ft} = \alpha_i + \beta_i (R_{mt} - r_{ft}) + \epsilon_{it} \tag{2}$$

or $\qquad r_{it} = \alpha_i + \beta_i r_{mt} + \epsilon_{it} \tag{3}$

where $r_{it} = R_{it} - r_{ft}$ and $r_{mt} = R_{mt} - r_{ft}$ are returns in excess of the risk-free rate of return r_{ft} on asset i and the market portfolio m, respectively, and ϵ_{it} is the idiosyncratic term with mean zero and variance σ_{ei}^2. If the CAPM is valid, the intercept term α_i should be zero for all assets. The Sharpe-Lintner-Black version of the CAPM predicts that the market portfolio is mean-variance efficient. Therefore, the test for the validity of the CAPM is equivalent to the test for the mean-variance efficiency of the market portfolio.[1] In

---

1) According to Roll (1977), however, this hypothesis cannot be tested since the true market portfolio cannot be

this circumstance, the only practical empirical test of the CAPM is narrowed to a test of whether a given proxy for the market portfolio is a valid surrogate. That is, to test whether a given market proxy is mean-variance efficient. Therefore, the mean-variance efficiency test for a given market proxy is equivalent to testing the null hypothesis $H_0 : \alpha_i = 0$ for $i = 1, \cdots, N$, where N is the number of test assets.[2]

The first extensive study on the mean-variance efficiency of the Korean stock market indexes is conducted by Hwang and Lee (1991). These authors consider four Korean indexes: Korea Composite Stock Price Index (KOSPI), Hankyung-Dow Stock Index, the equally-weighted stock index, and the value-weighted stock index. They also use two sets of test assets: 14 industry portfolios and 20 beta-sorted portfolios. Over the test period from January 1981 through June 1988, they report individual t-test statistics of the intercept estimates of the test assets, $\hat{\alpha}_i$, for each of the four market indexes. When KOSPI and Hankyung-Dow Stock Index are used as a proxy for the market portfolio, 12 out of 14 industry portfolios have significantly different intercept estimates from zero. When the equally-weighted and value-weighted stock indexes are used, none of the intercept estimates are significant. Their testing procedure is based on Black, Jensen, and Scholes (1972).

Hwang and Lee's (1991) individual t-tests assume that the intercept estimates are independent across test assets. However, insofar as the same explanatory variable is used in estimating the intercept α_i, the independence assumption is not valid. To avoid this problem, Gibbons, Ross, and Shanken (GRS) (1989) suggest a joint test for the null hypothesis $H_0 : \alpha = (\alpha_1, \alpha_2, \cdots, \alpha_N)' = 0$.

---

observed. According to Roll (1977), only one potentially testable hypothesis associated with the CAPM is to examine if the true market portfolio is mean-variance efficient. All other hypotheses (such as there being a linear relationship between beta and expected return) can be shown to be redundant, given this main hypothesis.

2) To test the hypothesis, the estimation of parameters in asset pricing equations such as equation (2) or (3) is needed. The parameter estimation can be conducted by ordinary (or generalized) least squares (OLS or GLS), maximum likelihood estimation (MLE), or generalized method of moment (GMM) according to the form of the error term ϵ_{it}.

Assuming the error terms are jointly normally distributed with mean zero and nonsingular covariance matrix Σ, GRS suggest the following test statistic for the null hypothesis:

$$W = \left(\frac{T(T-N-1)}{N(T-2)} \right) \left[\frac{\hat{\alpha}' \hat{\Sigma}_\epsilon^{-1} \hat{\alpha}}{(1+\hat{\theta}^2)} \right] \sim F(N,\ T-N-1) \tag{4}$$

where $\hat{\Sigma}_\epsilon$ is the unbiased residual covariance matrix, θ is the ratio of average excess return on portfolio m to its standard deviation $(= \bar{r}_m / s_m)$, which is the Sharpe ratio of the given market proxy portfolio m, N is the number of assets, and T is the number of time-series return observations.[3] Hwang and Lee (1991) also employ the above GRS test statistic to test the mean-variance efficiency of the four Korean indexes. These authors conclude that the mean-variance efficiency of KOSPI and Hankyung-Dow Price Index is rejected, while that of the equally-weighted and value-weighted stock indexes is not rejected, which is consistent with their individual t-tests results.

Song and Lee (1997) report different results for the mean-variance efficiency of KOSPI from Hwang and Lee (1991). These authors report that all intercept estimates of 13 industry portfolios are insignificant for the test period $1980 \sim 1995$.[4] Kim, D. (2004) and Kim, D. and Shin (2006) also report test results for the mean-variance efficiency of KOSPI. Kim, D. (2004) presents test results over the period $1987 \sim 2002$. When 25 size and book-to-market portfo-

---

3) When there are K factor portfolios in an asset pricing equation like equation (2), the GRS test statistic of equation (4) can be generalized as follows:

$$W = \left[\frac{T(T-N-K)}{N(T-K-1)} \right] \left[\frac{\hat{\alpha}' \hat{\Sigma}_\epsilon^{-1} \hat{\alpha}}{(1+\hat{\theta}^2)} \right] \sim F(N,\ T-N-K),$$

where $\hat{\Sigma}_\epsilon$ is the unbiased residual covariance matrix, $\hat{\theta}^2 = \bar{F}' \hat{\Sigma}_F^{-1} \bar{F}$ ($\hat{\theta}$ is the Sharpe ratio), $\bar{F}$ is a $K \times 1$ vector of average returns of the factor portfolios $(= (1/T) \sum_{t=1}^{T} F_t)$, $\hat{\Sigma}_F$ is the covariance matrix of the factor portfolio returns, N is the number of test assets, and T is the number of time-series return observations.

4) They do not report the intercept estimates although they used 25 size and book-to-market portfolios as another set of test assets.

lios are used as test assets, 21 out of 25 intercept estimates are significant, and the GRS test also rejects the mean-variance efficiency of KOSPI. On the contrary, Kim, D. and Shin (2006) report [the test period is 1988. 1 to 2004. 12] that when 10 size portfolios are used as test assets, 2 out of 10 intercept estimates are significant, and the GRS test does not reject the mean-variance efficiency of KOSPI. Even though the test periods are similar, the reason that the opposite test results are obtained is that the CAPM test could be sensitive to the choice of test assets.

Kandel (1984) and Shanken (1985) also suggest a multivariate test for the validity of the Black (1972) zero-beta CAPM, assuming the error terms are normally distributed. By applying their test approach, Koo (1995) conducts the test for the mean-variance efficiency of the Korean market indexes, assuming that the riskless asset does not exist. This author reports that the mean-variance efficiency of KOSPI and Hankyung-Dow Price Index is rejected in that their average returns are even lower than the average return of the global minimum variance portfolio (GMVP). However, the equally-weighted market index has higher average return than that of the GMVP and its mean-variance efficiency is not rejected. Koo's results are consistent with Hwang and Lee (1991).

Several points should be noted. The GRS test is valid when the disturbance terms are jointly normally distributed. Put differently, conditional on returns of a given market index, returns of test assets are jointly normally distributed. Note that the multivariate normality assumption of the disturbance terms drives a multivariate normality of the intercept estimates, $\hat{\alpha}$. However, there is ample evidence that asset returns are not normally distributed in Korea (e.g., see Koo (1998) among others), as well as in other countries. As long as a distributional form of the disturbance terms is known, the parameters can be estimated through maximum likelihood methods. Since maximum likelihood estimates are asymptotically normal, the GRS test statistic follows asymptotically an *F*-distribution, although the disturbance terms are non-normal. Thus, if the disturbance terms are non-normal, the use of the GRS test is limited when sample size (*T*) is small. With large sample size, however, the GRS test can be used even when the disturbance terms are non-normal. Like other multivariate tests such as the Hansen-Jagannathan (1997) distance test using the inverse of the covariance matrix, the use of the GRS test is limited as well when the number of test assets (*N*) is large relative to the time-series sample size (T).

2. Cross-Sectional Regression Tests of the CAPM

The Sharpe-Lintner-Black version of the CAPM also implies that the difference in expected return across assets should be explained solely by the difference in market beta, but other variables, such as firm characteristic variables, should add no explanatory power for expected return. This implication is key in tests of the CAPM, and it leads to the CSR tests.

Unlike the implication of the CAPM, U.S. data shows that stock returns have a regular pattern across variables other than market beta. The most prominent firm characteristic variables that challenge the validity of the CAPM are firm size and book-to-market. Banz (1981) and Reinganum (1981) report that small firms earn considerably higher returns than large firms even after adjusting for beta risk. This phenomenon has since been dubbed "the size effect". This is cited as one of the strongest market anomalies against the CAPM. Stattman (1980), Rosenberg, Reid, and Lanstein (1985), and Fama and French (1992) report that firms with high book-to-market earn considerably higher risk-adjusted returns than firms with lower look-to-market. This phenomenon is also dubbed "the book-to-market effect."

To test the validity of the CAPM and the size and book-to-market effects, the following Fama and MacBeth's (1973) CSR model is estimated at time t:

$$r_{it} = \gamma_{0t} + \gamma_{1t}\, \hat{\beta}_{it-1} + \gamma_{2t}\, \ln \mathrm{ME}_{t-1} + \gamma_{3t}\, \ln \mathrm{BM}_{t-1} + \epsilon_{it} \tag{5}$$

where r_{it} denotes the excess return on asset i in month t, $\hat{\beta}_{it-1}$ is the market beta of asset i estimated from the first-pass market model by using return observations available up to month $t-1$, ME is the market capitalization of asset i (stock price per share times the number of common shares outstanding), and BM is the ratio of book value to market value of common equity. Note that time subscript $t-1$ does not necessarily mean precisely time period $t-1$. Rather, it means the period prior to the estimation time period t. One useful feature of this methodology is that the risk premiums (or gammas) are implicitly allowed to be time varying.

Each month over the test period, the CSR model of equation (5) is estimated. Thus, estimates of the CSR coefficients, $\hat{\gamma}_{0t}$, $\hat{\gamma}_{1t}$, $\hat{\gamma}_{2t}$, and $\hat{\gamma}_{3t}$, are obtained each month. Fama and MacBeth regard the averages of these estimated values ($\bar{\hat{\gamma}}_0$, $\bar{\hat{\gamma}}_1$, $\bar{\hat{\gamma}}_2$, and $\bar{\hat{\gamma}}_3$) as the ultimate estimates of the risk premia, γ_0, γ_1, γ_2, and γ_3, for the corresponding variables. In particular, $\hat{\gamma}_{1t}$ is regarded as the estimate of the market risk premium. The t-statistics for testing the null hypothesis that $\gamma_j = 0$ for $j = 0, 1, 2, 3$ are

$$t\left(\bar{\hat{\gamma}}_j\right) = \frac{\bar{\hat{\gamma}}_j}{S\left(\bar{\hat{\gamma}}_j\right)/\sqrt{T}} \tag{6}$$

where $S\left(\bar{\hat{\gamma}}_j\right)$ is the standard deviation of the estimated gamma coefficients $\hat{\gamma}_{jt}$, and T is the number of the estimated gamma coefficients. The null hypothesis for the validity of the CAPM is

$$H_0 : \gamma_1 > 0 \text{ and } \gamma_0 = \gamma_2 = \gamma_3 = 0 \tag{7}$$

In particular, of more interest is whether $\gamma_2 = \gamma_3 = 0$, since firm characteristics such as firm size and book-to-market should add no explanatory power for average stock returns when the market beta is in the model.

Most empirical studies in Korea show that market betas are generally insignificant in explaining average stock returns.[5] Several authors show that the market risk premium estimate, $\bar{\hat{\gamma}}_1$, is insignificantly different from zero.[6] Other studies show that it is even negatively significant.[7] One exception is Kim, D. (2004), which shows that market betas have a significant positive explanatory power for average stock returns after adjusting for structural shifts in market betas.

Contrary to the prediction of the CAPM, firm size and book-to-market have significant explanatory power for average stock returnsin the Korean stock markets. Empirical results in Korea are consistent with those in other countries. Kam (1997), Song (1999), Kim, S. P. and Yoon (1999), Kim, K. Y. and Kim, Y. B. (2001), Kim, D. (2004), and Yun, Ku, Eom, and Hahn (2009) and Paek (2000) report that firm size is negatively significant and book-to-market is positively significant.[8] Some researchers find somewhat weaker evidence for firm size.[9] For example, Kim, S. J. and Kim, J. Y.

---

5) Ahn (1999) divides the whole sample into a bull market (when the market excess return is positive) and a bear market (whenthe market excess return is negative) and estimates the beta risk price in each market. He reports that the beta risk estimate ($\hat{\gamma}_{1t}$) is significantly positive in the bull market, while it is significantly negative in the bear market.

6) See Kam (1997), Song (1999), Kim, S. P. and Yoon (1999), Kim, S. J. and Kim, J. Y. (2000), Kim, K. Y. and Kim, Y. B. (2001, 2006), Lee and Kim, Y. B. (2006), Yun et al. (2009), and Jung and Kim, D. (2010).

7) Since the Korea Composite Stock Price Index (KOSPI) began in 1980, I tried to cite more recent works rather than past works as long as the cited works cover the period starting from 1980, although there are many works published before the cited works. For example, Kam (1997), which is the oldest among the cited works, covers the sample period from 1980 to 1995 (its actual testing period starts at 1983 after excluding the estimation period).

8) Sunwoo et al. (1994), also report that firm size is prominent over all months (not necessarily in January) in the Korean stock markets over the period 1980-1992, even after controlling for market betas and other firm characteristics, such as the leverage ratio and price-to-earnings ratio (PER).

9) Hwang (1993) and Kim, K. J. et al. (1994), report that the choice of the market proxy can affect the results of firm size. For example, when the equally-weighted market returns are used instead of the rates of return on the KOSPI (which is the value-weighted index), firm size disappears for the period 1980~1990.

(2000) report that when newly listed stocks are added into their sample, firm size becomes insignificant, while book-to-market is robustly positively significant regardless of the addition of the new listings. Kim, K. Y. and Kim, Y. B. (2006) and Lee and Kim, Y. B. (2006) examine whether the explanatory power of market betas, firm size, and book-to-market is sensitive to market conditions. Market betas have a significantly negative relation with average stock returns in down markets, and firm size is negatively significant only when the market is less volatile, but is insignificant in highly volatile markets. These authors also report that book-to-market has a robustly positive relation with average stock returns. Jung and Kim, D. (2010) estimate the CSR model of equation (5) by using the factor loadings on SMB and HML, β_{SMB} and β_{HML}, rather than firm characteristic variables (ln ME and ln BM). These authors find that the risk premiums on β_{SMB} and β_{HML} are both positively significant.

<Table 1> summarizes the results of the CSR tests for market betas, firm size, and book-to-marketfor average stock returns in the Korean stock markets. Overall, the firm size and book-to-market effect are significant in the Korean stock markets.

Another firm characteristic variable that challenges the validity of the CAPM in Korea is Basu's (1983) price-to-earnings ratio (PER). Kim, D. S. and Kim, J. H. (1993), Oh (1994), Sunwoo, Yun, Kang, Kim, Lee, and Oh (1994), and Paek (2000) report a "PER effect" in which firms with lower PER earn higher returns than firms with high PER. Kim, D. S. and Kim, J. H. (1993) examine whether firm size and PER are prominent in Korea after controlling for the effect oneach other, and conclude that, by using CAPM-adjusted (and the market model-adjusted) abnormal returns, the PER effect is significant over the period 1982~1992 even after controlling for firm size, and firm size is also significant after controlling for PER.

〈Table 1〉 Results of Cross-Sectional Regression Tests for Market Betas, Firm Size, and Book-to-Market

Author(s)	Testing period	Market beta (β)	Firm size (ME)	Book-to-market (BM)	Test assets	Variables for Firm size or BM
Jung and Kim, D. [2010]	1995. 3~2008. 6	Insignificant	(+) risk premium	(+) risk premium	25 size/BM portfolios	Factor loadings
Yun et al. [2009]	1991. 7~2007. 6 non-financial	(−) significant	(−) significant	(+) insignificant	Individual stocks	Characteristic variable
Kim, K. Y. and Kim, Y. B. [2006] and Lee and Kim, Y. B. [2006]	1990. 1~2002. 12 and 1990. 1~2003. 12	(−) significant only for down markets	(−) significant conditioning on the market condition	(+) insignificant conditioning on the market condition	15 beta portfolios	Characteristic variable
Kim, D. [2004]	1982. 7~2002. 12	(+) significant after adjusting for structural shift	(−) significant	(+) significant	Individual stocks	Characteristic variable
Kim, K. Y. and Kim, Y. B [2001]	1982. 5~1997. 4 non-financial	Insignificant	(−) significant	(+) significant	15 size/beta portfolios	Characteristic variable
Kim, S. J. and Kim, J. Y. [2000]	1992. 1~1997. 12 non-financial	Insignificant	(−) significant, but insignificant with new listings	(+) significant	25 size/BM portfolios	Characteristic variable
Paek [2000]	1985~1996 non-financial	(−) significant	(−) significant	(+) insignificant	Individual stocks	Characteristic variable
Kim, S. P. and Yoon [1999]	1983. 4~1997. 3 non-financial	(+) significant	(−) significant	(+) significant	Individual stocks, 25 size/beta portfolios	Characteristic variable
Song [1999]	1988. 4~1995. 12	n.a.	(−) insignificant	(+) significant	Individual stocks,	Characteristic variable
Gam [1997]	1983. 4~1995. 12	(−) insignificant	(−) insignificant	(+) significant	25 size/BM portfolios	Characteristic variable

However, these effects tend to disappear over the long-term (at least a three-year horizon). By pointing out the bias caused by using the CAPM in computing abnormal returns, Oh (1993) computes abnormal returns by using a multi-factor model with the SUR approach and finds that PER is still significant but that firm size is prominent in January only. Sunwoo et al. (1994) also obtain the similar results with respect to the PER effect even after controlling for the capital structure of the firm.

In addition to the above-mentioned firm characteristic variables, seasonality in stock returns is also a notable variable that challenges the validity of the CAPM. It is well known that seasonality is particularly prominent in January in international stock markets. Many researchers also report the January effect in the Korean stock markets. Kim, K. H. (1991) reports that after adjusting for market beta risk, higher returns are observed in the first three calendar months (January, February, and March) over the period 1981~1989. This phenomenon is especially notable in small firms. However, Yun et al. (1994) report that higher risk-adjusted returns are observed only in January, not in the other calendar months. Their sample period is from 1980 to 1992, which is slightly different from that of Kim, K. H. (1991). Kim, D. and Shin (2006) also report that the January effect is prominent only in January by using more recent stock return data (from 1988 through 2004).

Overall, the empirical studies show that the explanatory power of market betas in the cross-section of stock returns is weak in the Korean stock markets, while firm characteristics such as firm size, book-to-market, and earnings-to-price ratio are significant. However, the results could be subject to many econometric issues in conducting the CSR test. Thus, it would be premature to conclude the rejection of the validity of the CAPM before these issues are resolved. The next section reviews these issues which are related to the test results.

3. Mis-specification Issues in the CSR Tests

3.1 The Errors-in-Variables Problem

The CSR tests performed within the traditional two-pass estimation framework are subject to the errors-in-variables (EIV) problem, since the true beta is unknown and the estimated beta is used instead. That is, in the first-pass, beta estimates are obtained from separate time-series regressions from the market model for each asset, and in the second-pass, these estimated betas are used in CSR's as a regressor. Therefore, the explanatory variable in the CSR is measured with error. The EIV problem is one of the most serious problems in the CSR. The EIV problem induces an underestimation of the price of beta risk (γ_{1t} in equation (5)) and an overestimation of the other CSR coefficients (γ_{2t} and γ_{3t} in equation (5)) associated with such idiosyncratic variables as firm size, book-to-market, and earnings-to-price ratio. The greater the correlation between the estimated beta and the idiosyncratic variable, the more downward bias in the estimate of the price of beta risk and the more upward bias in the estimate of the other CSR coefficients on the idiosyncratic variables (i.e., exaggeration of their explanatory power) [see Miller and Scholes (1972), Litzenberger and Ramaswamy (1979), Shanken (1992), and Kim, D. (1995, 1997)].

There are several approaches to mitigate the EIV problem. The first is to group stocks into portfolios. Since Black et al. (1972) and Fama and MacBeth (1973), it has been a standard practice to construct portfolios as test assets. Portfolios are formed by sorting individual stocks according to some characteristics of the stock, such as market beta from a previous period, firm size, book-to-market, or past returns. Portfolio betas have much smaller estimation errors than individual stock betas and hence, the use of portfolio betas mitigates the EIV problem. The advantage of this approach is simplicity. However, this approach has several disadvantages as well. The most serious is that the test results are sensitive to the portfolio formation method (i.e., how to sort stocks) and the number of portfolios. Another disadvantage of this approach is the potential loss of unique information about individual stocks by grouping them.

An alternative approach is to directly tackle the EIV problem.[10] Inferences of the two-pass methodology are based on the t-statistics of equation (6). Shanken (1992) provides an EIV-bias correction for the standard error of the estimate of the price of beta risk, and suggests an EIV-bias corrected t-statistic. On the other hand, Kim (1995, 1997) provides a direct EIV-bias correction for the estimate of the price of beta risk. In particular, the Kim correction is useful when individual stocks are used as test assets, since it can be directly applied to obtain the EIV-bias-corrected estimate of the price of beta risk itself. It appears that there are no significant articles that thoroughly examine the explanatory power of market betas in Korean stock markets that directly tackle the EIV bias.[11]

3.2 Non-Normal Distributions of Stock Returns

Multivariate tests of the mean-variance efficiency for a given market proxy based on the GRS statistic of equation (4) are valid only when the disturbance terms are jointly normally distributed. In the Fama and MacBeth (1973) CSR tests, the disturbance terms are assumed to be serially independent and homoskedastistic (in the OLS estimation). Thus, if the disturbance terms are non-normal, serially correlated, and heteroskedastistic, the estimation results from the previously-described methods may be biased and mislead the test

---

10) Gibbons (1982) suggests an iterative one-step Gauss-Newton method to estimate betas and argues that his method can avoid the EIV problem. As Shanken (1992) points out, however, the advantage of Gibbons's approach is apparently lost in linearizing the constraint that isvalid under the CAPM, and thus, the Gibbons estimates are still subject to the EIV bias.

11) Han (1994) employs a reverse regression approach to control the EIV problem. From the reverse regression estimation, Han obtains the results that the firm size effect disappeared in Korean stock markets.

results. For this circumstance, Hansen (1982) and Hansen and Singleton (1982) suggest a generalized method of moment (GMM) method. One of the advantages of the GMM method is that the distributional forms of asset returns and the error terms are not assumed, and it accommodatesempirical irregularities that are found in actual return data.

Jung and Kim, H. C. (1992) conduct a GMM test over the period 1977~ 1991 for the mean-variance efficiency of KOSPI by using 10 size portfolios and 10 industry portfolios, each a set of test assets. They report that the mean-variance efficiency of KOSPI is not rejected under the assumption of constant expected returns, but is rejected when expected returns are assumed to be time-varying.[12] Koo (1998) also conducts a GMM test by assuming non-normality of asset returns, but obtains results similar to those obtained by assuming normality of asset returns in his 1995 study (Koo; 1995). That is, the mean-variance efficiency of KOSPI and Hankyung- Dow Price Index is rejected, while the efficiencyof the equally-weighted market index is not rejected. It could be argued, based on the (GRS and GMM) tests, that the equally-weighted market index is more mean-variance efficient than the other Korean market indexes.

3.3 Mis-specification in Estimating Market Betas

The CAPM is an ex ante model. Therefore, ex antemarket betas should be used in cross-sectional tests of the CAPM. It is not possible, however, to know ax ante market betas. Instead, a proxy for the ex ante market beta is used. Since the use of the mis-estimated proxy of the ex ante market beta could mislead the CSR tests, mis-specification of the market beta can be a serious issue in the CSR test.

---

12) Lee and Nam (1992) estimate market betas through a GMM method, assuming that the error terms are serially correlated and their variance is auto-regressive conditional heteroskedastistic (ARCH). However, these authors do not perform tests for the mean-variance efficiency of the Korean market indexes.

The most popular proxy for the ex ante market beta is the beta estimate obtained from the market model using historical return observations (i.e., ex post market beta estimates). The implicit assumption behind estimating market betas is that market betas are stationary over time. Market betas are estimated using an arbitrarily chosen length of estimation period such as a five-year period, assuming that market betas are stationary over that period. However, most empirical studies do not support this assumption. In particular, the stationarity of the market beta over relatively long periods has been severely questioned in many empirical studies. Moreover, the capital structure theory shows that the levered firm's market beta is a function of the debt-equity ratio in a simple setting. Since the debt-equity ratio changes irregularly over time, the stationarity assumption of the market beta is hardly acceptable theoretically as well.

Sim et al. (1989) investigate the extent of beta nonstationarity over the period 1977~1986 and conclude that the stationarity of the market beta is not acceptable. They also investigate three different lengths of the estimation periods of 24, 36, and 48 months and conclude that 48 months may be the best estimation period among the three in that the nonstationarity of the market beta is the least severe. Kim, D. (2004) directly estimates the structural shift time points of the market beta of individual Korean firms by assuming that the market beta over the period between two beta shift points is stationary. He uses the market betas estimated over this stationary period in the CSR tests and finds that the explanatory power of market betas for average stock returns becomes significant. Kho and Yae (2005) employ thestochastic beta model of Ang and Chen (2003) and Jostova and Philipov (2005) in which the market beta is assumed to change at every time point. They show that the beta estimates obtained from the stochastic betamodel have stronger cross-sectional explanatory power for average stock returns than the other beta estimates.[13)]

Another approach to estimating ax ante market betas is to relate the market beta of a firm to macroeconomic variables. In other words, if the systematic risk changes over time, this approach attempts to determine which macroeconomic variables underlie the non-stationarity of the market beta and to identify a relationship between the market beta and the macroeconomic variables. Lee and Shin (1991) examine the relation between market betas and macroeconomic variables over the period 1975~1989. They find that the real growth rates of GNP and money supply, unexpected inflation rate, interest rate, the government fiscal deficit, and business cycle affect the market betas of Korean firms. In particular, the sign of each of the macroeconomic variables on the market beta depends on the magnitude of the market beta and the business cycle.[14)] Kang, Choi, and Lee (1996) relate rates of return on portfolios (10 firm size and 9 industry portfolio) to the following macroeconomic variables: three-year corporate bond yield, the term spread (three-year corporate bond yield minus call rate), rate of return on KOSPI, lagged growth rate of industrial production, growth rate of money supply, and the ratio of imports to exports. They find that among those variables, the term spread and the ratio of imports to exports significantly affect the market betas of the portfolio, but the extent of association differs by industry and firm size.

A similar approach to estimate ax ante market betas is to relate the market beta of a firm to the firm's fundamental variables which are mostly accounting variables. Lee et al. (1992) and Park (1993, 1999) show that the beta estimate containing firm accounting information has better predictive power for future risk of the firm than the historical beta estimate. Park (1993)

---

13) Han (1994) employs a reverse regression method to decrease the estimation error of the beta. He finds that the beta estimates from this method are able to explain the firm size effect in Korean markets.
14) Koo and Shin (1990) employs a similar approach and derive results similar to Lee and Shin (1991).

argues that firm size is the most prominent determinant of market beta among the firm fundamental variables considered.

The above approach of relating market betas to macroeconomic or fundamental variables is a conditional approach. In other words, market betas are represented as a linear combination of these variables, and thus, market betas are conditioned on the information contained in the given variables. Since macroeconomic or fundamental variables change over time, this approach in fact allows market betas to be time-varying. Rather than conditioning on macroeconomic or fundamental variables to capture the time-variation of market betas, their time-varying behavior can be directly (unconditionally) modeled. Ryu and Lee (2009) assume a first-order autoregressive process [AR(1)] to model the time-varying behavior of the market beta. After accommodating this unconditional time-varying behavior of market betas, they find that firm size becomes insignificant, while book-to-market is still significant.

3.4 Return Measurement Intervals

Another issue in the CSR test is the arbitrary choice of the return measurement interval in estimating market betas. The CAPM assumes that all investors are single-period expected-utility-of-terminal-wealth maximizers. There is no particular restriction on the length of the holding period (investment horizon) as long as it is the same for all investors. That is, the CAPM implicitly assumes that asset betas are invariant to the investment horizon. In empirical tests, the investment horizon is arbitrarily selected, since the "true" investment horizon is unknown. In reality, however, betas are sensitive to the investment horizon. The covariance of an asset's (buy-and-hold) return with the market return and the variance of the market return do not change proportionately according to the investment horizon (see Levhari and Levy 1977, and Handa, Kothari, and Wasley 1989). Kim, D. H. (1996) empirically shows that the beta estimates are sensitive to the length of the return measurement interval and the extent of the sensitivity differs according to the magnitude of the beta and firm size in Korea. That is, for firms with small market capitalization and low beta (with large market capitalization and high beta), the beta estimate tends to increase (decrease) with the return measurement interval.

The literature shows, in general, that the explanatory power of market betas in the cross-section of stock returns is weak in Korean stock markets. Most CSR tests are based on a return measurement interval of one month. It would be necessary, therefore, to re-examine the explanatory power of market betas in various return measurement intervals.[15]

4. Conditional Versions of the CAPM and GMM Tests

The Sharpe-Lintner-Mossin or Black CAPM is the static or the unconditional model. Tests of the unconditional version of the CAPM by Black et al. (1972), Fama and MacBeth (1973), Gibbons (1982), Stambaugh (1982), and Shanken (1985) are conducted by assuming that expected returns are constant and that asset betas are stationary over a fixed period of time. Thus, in the CSR tests, unconditional expected returns are regressed on unconditional betas. However, there is no reason to believe that expected returns and betas should be constant. Corporate investment and the financial decisions of a firm could affect investors' expected return of the firm and its systematic risk. Numerous papers show that betas change over time. According to changes inmacroeconomic conditions, the market risk premium is also affected. In this context, it would be rational to allow expected returns and betas to be time-varying. Furthermore, a number of papers sug-

---

15) Lee (2007) examines a continuous-time version of the CAPM by using returns measured over various intervals. Jo and Lee (2004) suggest a beta estimation method of considering the frequency of trades by using the Wavelet transform technique.

gest that the inability of the unconditional version of the CAPM to explain firm size, book-to-market (or value premium), the momentum phenomenon, and other market anomalies could be due to afailure to accommodate non-stationarity or time-variation of expected returns and market betas.

One convenient way to model the time-variation of expected returns and betas is to model them conditioned on some information set. If the information set changes over time, expected returns and betas also change since their values are conditioned on this information set. Let I_{t-1} be the information set available at time $t-1$. Then, the conditional version of the CAPM is stated as

$$E(r_{it} \mid I_{t-1}) = \beta_{it}(I_{t-1}) \; E(r_{mt} \mid I_{t-1}) \tag{8}$$

where

$$\beta_{it}(I_{t-1}) = \frac{\mathrm{Cov}(r_{it}, \, r_{mt} \mid I_{t-1})}{\mathrm{Var}(r_{mt} \mid I_{t-1})} \tag{9}$$

Since the true information set, I_{t-1}, is unavailable, expected returns and betas are conditioned on the observed information set, Z_{t-1}. We decompose the return on asset i and the market into their forecastable and unforecastable components as follows:

$$r_{it} = E(r_{it} \mid Z_{t-1}) + u_{it}, \quad i = 1, 2, \cdots, N \tag{10}$$

$$r_{mt} = E(r_{mt} \mid Z_{t-1}) + u_{mt} \tag{11}$$

where u_{it} and u_{mt} are the forecast errors with mean zero and are orthogonal to the information set Z_{t-1}.

There are many ways to formulate a test of the conditional CAPM of equation (8), according to the assumption on the right-hand side terms of equations (10) and (11). The first way is to use the instrumental variables to estimate the forecastable parts of equations (10) and (11). That is,

$$E(r_{it} \mid Z_{t-1}) = Z_{t-1}\,\delta_i, \qquad i = 1, 2, \cdots, N \tag{12}$$

$$E(r_{mt} \mid Z_{t-1}) = Z_{t-1}\,\delta_m \tag{13}$$

where Z_{t-1} is the vector of the l instrumental variables and δ_i (δ_m) is the $l \times 1$ coefficient vector for asset i (the market).[16] Thus, the unforecastable parts are denoted, respectively,

$$u_{it} = r_{it} - Z_{t-1}\,\delta_i, \qquad i = 1, 2, \cdots, N \tag{14}$$

$$u_{mt} = r_{mt} - Z_{t-1}\,\delta_m \tag{15}$$

We first consider a simpler version of the conditional CAPM of equation (8) by assuming that the reward-to-variance ratio of the market portfolio is constant. This implies that, for $i = 1, 2, \cdots, N$,

$$E(r_{it} \mid Z_{t-1}) = \lambda\,\mathrm{Cov}(r_{it}, r_{mt} \mid Z_{t-1}) \tag{16}$$

$$= \lambda E\{[r_{it} - E(r_{it} \mid Z_{t-1})][r_{mt} - E(r_{mt} \mid Z_{t-1})]\}$$

where $\lambda = E(r_{mt} \mid I_{t-1})/\mathrm{Var}(r_{mt} \mid I_{t-1})$ is the reward-to-variance ratio of the market portfolio. We define a disturbance term from equation (16) as

$$e_{it} = r_{it} - \lambda[r_{it} - E(r_{it} \mid Z_{t-1})][r_{mt} - E(r_{mt} \mid Z_{t-1})] \tag{17}$$

$$= r_{it} - \lambda(r_{it} - Z_{t-1}\,\delta_i)(r_{mt} - Z_{t-1}\,\delta_m)$$

The conditional mean of the three disturbance terms, $E(u_{it} \mid Z_{t-1})$, E

16) Here we assume that asset returns and the instrumental variables are jointly distributed and that their joint distribution falls into the class of spherically invariant distributions.

$(u_{mt} \mid Z_{t-1})$, and $E(e_{it} \mid Z_{t-1})$, are zero. In other words, these three disturbance terms are orthogonal to the predetermined instrumental variables, Z_{t-1}. Thus, we have the orthogonality condition $g = \text{vec}(\epsilon' Z)$, where ε is a vector of all stacked disturbance terms. Parameters δ_i, δ_m, and λ are estimated by minimizing the quadratic form, $g' W g$, where W is a symmetric weighting matrix that is defined as the metric to make the orthogonality condition g as close to zero as possible. This estimation is usually conducted through the Hansen (1982) generalized method of moments (GMM) method. Rather than assume the constant reward-to-variance ratio of the market portfolio, we can assume the time-varying reward-to-variance ratio as in equation (8). In this case, a disturbance term different from equation (17) is defined.[17] One advantage of this instrumental variables approach is that the EIV problem can be mitigated and the assumption on the distribution of the disturbance terms is not needed only the intertemporal independence of the disturbance terms is needed. However, the critical disadvantage of this approach is that the choice of instrumental variables is arbitrary and test results could be sensitive to their selection. Another disadvantage of this approach is that it cannot be applied when the number of test assets is large.

Nam and Lee (1995) conduct a GMM test for the conditional CAPM by choosing the constant, the difference between the corporate bond yield, and the bank deposit interest rate as instrumental variables. By using 10 size portfolios as test assets, these authors find that the conditional covariances, expected returns, and reward-to-variance ratio of the market portfolio are time-varying and they report a rejection of the conditional version of the CAPM. Cho (1996) chooses the constant, the January dummy, and the corporate bond yield as instrumental variables in the GMM tests and uses eight industry portfolios as test assets for the period from April 1980 to March 1995. Cho con-

---

17) See Harvey (1989) for more details.

cludes that the conditional CAPM explains well the returns of the test assets, which is opposite to the conclusions of Nam and Lee (1995).

The second way to formulate a test of the conditional CAPM of equation (8) is to model the time-series behavior of the disturbance terms of equations (10) and (11). The most commonly assumed model of such time-series behavior is the auto-regressive conditional heteroskedasticity (ARCH) model. Specific ARCH-type models are assumed for the conditional variance of each disturbance term and the conditional covariance between u_{it} and u_{mt}. Differently from the instrumental variables approach, this approach assumes the conditional variance (or covariance) as a function of past conditional variances (or covariances). By using ARCH-type models to formulate the conditional CAPM, Cho and Lee (1998) findthat the risk premium is time-varying but statistically insignificant and that the conditional CAPM also does not explain well the stock returns although their conditional version of the CAPM performs better than does the unconditional CAPM. Chang (1998) obtains similar results. This author finds that market risk premium estimates are insignificant and that the validity of the conditional version of the CAPM is rejected.

The third way to formulate a test of the conditional CAPM is the Jagannathan and Wang (1996) approach. According to these authors' arguments, the conditional expected return for each asset i at time t is linearly related to its conditional beta at time t-1. That is,

$$E(R_{it} \mid I_{t-1}) = \gamma_{0t-1} + \gamma_{1t-1} \beta_{1t-1} \tag{18}$$

where $\beta_{1t-1} = \mathrm{Cov}(R_{it}, R_{mt} \mid I_{t-1})/\mathrm{Var}(r_{mt} \mid I_{t-1})$ is the conditional beta, γ_{0t-1} is the conditional expected return on the zero-beta portfolio, and γ_{1t-1} is the conditional market risk premium. By taking the unconditional expectations on both sides of equation (18), the unconditional CAPM is obtained:

$$E(R_{it} = \gamma_0 + \gamma_1 \overline{\beta}_i + \mathrm{Cov}(\gamma_{1t-1}, \beta_{1t-1}) \qquad (19)$$

where $\gamma_0 = \mathrm{E}(\gamma_{0t-1})$ and $\gamma_1 = \mathrm{E}(\gamma_{1t-1})$ are the corresponding uncondi-tional expected returns, and $\overline{\beta}_i = \mathrm{E}(\beta_{1t-1})$ is the unconditional beta of asset i. If the covariance between the conditional beta of asset i and the conditional market risk premium, $\mathrm{Cov}(\gamma_{1t-1}, \beta_{1t-1})$, is zero, equation (19) becomes the static CAPM. Jagannathan and Wang (1996) argue, however, that the conditional betas and the expected market risk premium are time-varying and they are correlated. They also argue that the uncondi-tional expected return is not a linear function of the unconditional beta alone, since the last term in equation (19) is not zero in general.

Under certain circumstances, the unconditional expected return of equa-tion (19) becomes

$$E(R_{it}) = c_0 + c_m \beta_i + c_{\mathrm{prem}} \beta_i^{\mathrm{prem}} \qquad (20)$$

where $\beta_i = \mathrm{Cov}(R_{it}, R_{mt})/\mathrm{Var}(R_{mt})$ and $\beta_i^{\mathrm{prem}} = \mathrm{Cov}(R_{it}, \gamma_{1t-1})/\mathrm{Var}(\gamma_{1t-1})$, and c_m and c_{prem} are coefficients. To measure the prem-beta, β_i^{prem}, the condi-tional market risk premium (γ_{1t-1}) should be given. Jagannathan and Wang (1996) choose the default yield spread between Baa- and Aaa-rated bonds for (γ_{1t-1}). These authors use the sum of the value-weighted market index and human capital as a proxy for the true market portfolio, which is not observable. Thus, the return on the true market portfolio, R_{mt}, can be repre-sented as

$$R_{mt} = \phi_0 + \phi_{vw} R_t^{vw} + \phi_{labor} R_t^{labor} \qquad (21)$$

where R_t^{vw} is the return on the value-weighted market index and R_t^{labor}

is the growth rate in per capita labor income which is used to measure the return on human capital. Finally, the unconditional expected return of equation (20) can be represented as

$$E(R_{it}) = c_0 + c_m \beta_{\mathrm{i}}^{\mathrm{vw}} + c_{\mathrm{prem}} \beta_{\mathrm{i}}^{\mathrm{prem}} + c_{\mathrm{labor}} \beta_{\mathrm{i}}^{\mathrm{labor}} \tag{22}$$

Kook and Hahn (1999) perform the cross-sectional tests based on equation (22) and the GMM tests over the period 1984~1995. They report that the unconditional standard CAPM is also invalid and that the conditional CAPM performs better than the static CAPM. In particular, the human capital beta, $\beta_{\mathrm{i}}^{\mathrm{labor}}$, is statistically significant in explaining stock returns. However, they also report that firm size is still significant regardless of inclusion of human capital betas.

Ⅲ. Arbitrage Pricing Theory (APT)

As described in the previous section, the validity of the CAPM has been seriously challenged in Korea as well as in the other countries. Thus, its acceptance in academia as the premier asset pricing paradigm is less than universal, although it rather tends to be widely accepted in industry (see Graham and Harvey (2001)). The APT, formulated by Ross (1976), is considered as an alternative pricing model, together with the Breeden (1979) consumption-based CAPM and the Merton (1973) intertemporal CAPM.

The APT begins by assuming that asset returns are governed by a linear return-generating process similar to the multiple-index models. In particular, any asset i is assumed to have returns that are generated by the following process:

$$r_{it} = \alpha_i + \beta_{i1} r_{p_2, t} + \beta_{i2} r_{p_2, t} + \cdots + \beta_{iK} r_{pK, t} + \epsilon_{it} \tag{23}$$

where α_i is a constant for asset i, β_{ik} is the factor loading of asset i on the k-th factor $(k = 1, \cdots, K)$, $r_{p_k, t}$ denotes the return on the k-th factor portfolio, and ϵ_{it} is the mean-zero random error term for asset i that representsresidual or idiosyncratic risk. The error term satisfies the following conditions: $E(\epsilon_{it} \epsilon_{jt}) = 0$ for $i \neq j$ and $E(\epsilon_{it} r_{p_k, t}) = 0$. Taking the expected value of equation (23) yields

$$E(r_i) = \alpha_i + \beta_{i1} E(r_{p_1, t}) + \beta_{i2} E(r_{p_2, t}) + \cdots + \beta_{iK} E(r_{p_K, t}) \tag{24}$$

Subtracting equation (24) from equation (23) and rearranging results in

$$r_{it} = E(r_i) + \beta_{i1} f_{1t} + \beta_{i2} f_{2t} + \cdots + \beta_{iK} f_{Kt} + \epsilon_{it} \tag{25}$$

where $f_{kt} = r_{p_k, t} - E(r_{p_k, t})$ is a mean-zero common factor. Under no arbitrage conditions, the expected return on asset i is represented as a linear combination of the factor loadings;

$$E(r_i) r_f + \lambda_1 \beta_{i1} + \lambda_2 \beta_{i2} + \cdots + \lambda_K \beta_{iK} \tag{26}$$

where λ_k is the risk premium of the k-th risk factor which is measured by $E(r_{p_k, t}) - r_f$. Here, $E(r_{p_k, t})$ is the expected return on a portfolio that has unit sensitivity to the k-th factor and no sensitivity to all other factors.

The APT is less restrictive than the CAPM in that it applies in both the single-period and multi-period settings. Furthermore, the APT is based on fewer and more realistic assumptions. It requires only that markets are perfectly competitive and investors' utility functions are monotonically increasing and concave (i.e., only risk aversion is required). The CAPM assumptions of quadratic utility functions and/or normally distributed returns are not necessary in deriving the APT. The CAPM (to be valid) requires that the market portfolio be mean-variance efficient, while the APT requires nothing special from the market portfolio. However, although the APT seems more robust than the CAPM in many aspects, it has two critical problems. First, the theory contains no clue about the number of factors. Second, even if the number of factors is known, the task of identifying the risk factors is daunting.

There are roughly three approaches in empirical studies that test the APT pricing equation (26).

1. APT Tests by Identifying Both Factors and Factor Loadings

As in Roll and Ross (1980), the first approach is to test the APT pricing equation (26) without specifically identifying the factors. Rather, both the factor loading β's and the factor scores of each factor in equation (25) are simultaneously estimated at a given number of factors K by using the factor analysis or principal component analysis in which only the covariance matrix of test assets' returns is needed. By applying a searching method, the optimal number of factors is determined according to some criterion. The estimated factor loading β's are used as regressors in CSR tests.

By using factor analysis, Lee et al. (1984) report that there might be four common factors in the Korean stock markets over the period from January 1977 to August 1983. These authors also report that only one or two factor loadings among the four explain significantly the cross-section of average stock returns. Lee (1994) also employs factor analysis to find the number of significant factors. Lee argues that two or three factors are significant and that the most plausible macroeconomic variables for these factors are returns on KOSPI, industrial production, unemployment rate, and an index of firm size. Cho (1998) teststhe APT pricing equation in a dynamic setting by assuming that risk premia and factor loadings (or betas) are time varying. Time-varying factor loadings are estimated under the assumption that the variances of asset returns and factor returns follow an ARCH process. Cho confirms that the variances show conditional heteroskedastisticity. He extracts four factors from the covariance matrix of 17 industry portfolios' returns by using factor analysis. He later replaces the first factor with the equally-weighted market returns since their correlation coefficient is almost perfect; it is 99.45%.[18] By using the GMM estimation method, Cho reports that three among the four risk premia estimates are all significant. In particular, the risk premium of the first factor (i.e., the market return) is highly significant. By using the 11 industry portfolio returns from January 1980 to June 1997, Koo (1999) argues that the determination of the priced factors in Korea maybe meaningless, since the test results are similar and the validity of the APT pricing equation is not rejected in any number of assumed factors (2, 4, and 10 factors are assumed). Based on the above results, there may be at least two to three common factors in the Korean stock markets.

2. APT Tests by Identifying Factors from Macroeconomic Variables

The second approach of the APT test is to first identify the factors by relating macroeconomic variables to common factors. Chen, Roll, and Ross (1986) is most representative in this approach. After identifying the relevant factors, the typical testing procedure of the APT pricing equation is the Fama and MacBeth two-pass methodology. In the first-pass, betas are estimated by regressing returns of test assets on the identified macroeconomic variables, and, in the second-pass, risk premia are estimated in CSR's of excess returns of test assets on the estimated betas.

---

18) There is almost no ambiguity in other countries' literature as well that the first factor from factor analysis or principal component analysis represents the return on the market portfolio.

Kam (1991) chooses six macroeconomic variables and conducts CSR tests by using the estimated betas of the six variables. He finds that three among the six betas significantly explain the cross-section of average stock returns. After estimating seven factors through factor analysis, Cheong (1991) relates 73 available macroeconomic variables to the seven factors. By examining the correlation coefficients between each of the seven factor scores and each of the 73 macroeconomic variables, Jung identifies returns on KOSPI, unit labor cost, money supply, exporting price index, inventory index of manufacturing products, corporate bond yields, and corporate bond yield spread as the relevant factors in Korea. Jung also argues that the chosen seven factors are significantly priced in Korea. Further, Chi (1992) similarly investigates which variables are priced in Korea. This author reports that five macroeconomic variables are relevant: changes in foreign exchange rates, changes in industrial production, changes in unexpected risk premium, changes in money supply, and oil price changes. Since the macroeconomic variables are not factor portfolios, factor models containing macroeconomic variables cannot be used as pricing equations. In other words, the intercept α in equation (23) does not indicate pricing error.

3. APT Tests through Constructing Factor Mimicking Portfolios

The third approach of the APT test is to construct factor portfolios and include them in factor models such as equation (23). Unlike the second approach, the intercept α can be used as a measure of pricing error. Factor portfolios are usually estimated by constructing arbitrage portfolios by taking a long position in high risk-high return assets and a short position in low risk-low return assets. Fama and French (1993) is most representative of this approach. The literature shows that there are several market phenomena (so called *anomalies*) that the CAPM fails to explain. The most prominent such phenomena in international markets are firm size, book-to-market, momentum, liquidity, information quality, and information asymmetry. It is conjectured, therefore, that there might be systematic risks associated with these characteristics that market betas do not capture. In other words, since only the market portfolio may be insufficient to diversify away idiosyncratic risk, investors may need other portfolio(s) to hedge risks associated with these characteristics. This portfolio should be a well-diversified factor portfolio, and its returns should track innovations in the particular source of risk associated with the characteristic.

The most popular model in this approach is the three-factor model by Fama and French (1993). The three factors are the market portfolioand the factor portfolios associated with firm size and book-to-market, SMB and HML, respectively. Kam (1997) conducts time-series testsof the three-factor model over the period 1983~1995 by using 25 portfolios sorted by firm size and book-to-market as test assets. This author reports that the three-factor model explains well time-series variations of the test assets in thatall 25 intercept estimates are insignificant. Song and Lee (1997), Kim, S-J, and Kim, J-Y (2000), and Yun et al. (2009) also report similar results for Korea.[19] The above test results support the Fama and French (1993) three-factor model in Korea.

It is noteworthy, however, that the above test results may be naturally expected, since most tests employ the test assets from which the factors are generated. It is not surprising that these self-generated factors explain well returns of the same test assets. Kim, D. and Shin (2006) use a different set of test assets to test the performance of the three-factor model. Unlike the previous results, they report that the performance of the three-factor model is unsatisfactory. Three of the ten intercept estimates of 10 size-sorted portfo-

---

19) Song and Lee (1997) and Yun et al. (2009) argue that the explanatory power of HML is weak relatively to SMB.

lios are significantly different from zero. Chae and Yang (2008) use individual stocks to examine the explanatory ability of the following three asset pricing models: the CAPM, the Fama and French three-factor model, and the Carhart (1997) four-factor model. These authorsregress cross-sectionally the pricing errors produced from an asset pricing model on several idiosyncratic variables. The pricing error is defined as the difference between the expected return from an asset pricing model and the realized return. They find that the pricing errors from all three modelsare significantly related with transaction costs, investors' irrationality, and even firm size and book-to-market. Their resultsindicate that all three models fail to explain the cross-section of stock returns in Korea. Therefore, test results could be sensitive to the formation method of test assets and even the number of test portfolios. Further, the current literature in Korea shows that the reported average returns of the three factor portfolios are quite different depending on the sample period.[20] They are sometimes quite different even when the sample period does not differ much. Based on my observations of the literature on Korea, the test results may also be sensitive to the choice of the sample period.

Aside from therisk factors associated with firm size and book-to-market (i.e., SMB and HML), other risk factors are suggested. One risk factor that has recently drawn much interest in the literature is liquidity (or illiquidity). The literature suggests various measures (or proxies) for liquidity. Kwon and Park (1997) employ Roll's (1984) and George, Kaul, and Nimalendran's (1991)

---

[20] For example, Song and Lee (1997) report that the average monthly returns of the market portfolio, SMB, and HML are 0.11%, 0.64%, and 0.93%, respectively, over the period 1980-1995; Kim, D. and Shin (2006) report that they are 0.693%, 0.191%, and 1.065%, respectively, over the period 1988-2004; Yun et al. (2009), report that they are 0.26%, 0.99%, and 0.87%, respectively, over the period July 1991-June 2007; Kim, S-H, (2009) reports that they are -0.22% (after subtracting the risk-free return), 0.47%, and 0.68%, respectively, over the period January 1988-October 2007; and Jung and Kim, D. (2010) report that they are 0.41%, 1.11%, and 1.38%, respectively, over the period March 1995-December 2008. Overall, the average return of HML is relatively high in any period, which indicates that the value premium is strong in Korea relatively to the growth premium. The above-mentioned papers also report quite different correlation coefficients between SMB and HML. Kim, D. and Shin (2006), Yun et al. (2009), Kim, S-H (2009), and Jung and Kim (2010) report that the correlation coefficients between SMB and HML are -0.164, 0.641, 0.09, and 0.278, respectively.

liquidity costs as a measure of liquidity. In the CSR over the period 1986 ~ 1994, Kwon and Park find that the CSR coefficient estimate on the liquidity variable is positively significant even after adjusting for firm size and market betas. They argue that the liquidity risk premium is significant in Korea. Park and Eom (2008) also obtain similar results over amore recent period (1996 ~ 2006) in the CSR tests with controlling for market betas, firm size, book-to-market, and past returns. These authors also report that a significant liquidity risk premium is found in stocks traded on Korea Stock Exchange (KSE), but not found in stocks on Korean Securities Dealers Automated Quotations (KOSDAQ).[21] Yun et al. (2009) argue that a three-factor model including the market factor, SMB, and a liquidity factor better explains stock returns than the Fama and French three-factor model. Their liquidity factor is a mimicking portfolio of liquidity proxied by turnover ratio. By employing the Amihud (2002) illiquidity measure, Choe and Yang (2009) also report results supporting the role of liquidity; stocks with higher average illiquidity earn higher average returns. However, Nam, Park, and Eom (2005) report the irrelevance of liquidity in stock returns. Rather than using asset pricing models to examine the role of liquidity in Korea, these authors use principal component analysis to extract two common factors, one from liquidity data and the other from stock returns. They find that there is no significant relation between these two common factors, and conclude that the commonality of liquidity does not explain the commonality of stock returns.

Many other risk factors, such as foreign currency risk, earnings information uncertainty risk, and risk associated with information asymmetry and information quality, have also been considered in the literature. Kwon and Park (1999) examine whether foreign currency risk is priced in Korea. They

---

21) Park and Eom (2008) also report that in the time series tests, all of the intercept estimates (or Jensen's alpha) are insignificant only in the one-factor model with the liquidity factor, but not in the other multi-factor models although the liquidity factor is included.

report that foreign currency risk is not priced over the whole period from 1983~1996, but is weakly priced over the subsample period 1990~1996. By using the GMM method, Yu (2002) tests whether there exists a risk premium associated with foreign currency risk through a conditional asset pricing model and concludes that the risk premium exists in Korea.[22]

Kim, D. and Shin (2006) suggest a two-factor model containing the market factor and a risk factor associated with earnings information uncertainty, and argue that this two-factor model performs well in explaining firm size and the January effect. Choe and Yang (2007) examine whether information asymmetry affects systematically stock returns in Korea. They use three measures of information asymmetry; Glosten and Harris's (1998), Hasbrouck's (1991), and Easley, Hvidkjaer, and O'Hara's (2002) PIN (probability of informed trading). In particular, PIN has drawn much interest in the literature as a measure of information asymmetry. They report that the measures of Glosten and Harris (1998) and Hasbrouck (1991) support a positive relation between information asymmetry risk and stock returns, while PIN does not support the positive relation. They conclude that information asymmetry is a determinant of stock returns however, PIN is not useful as a measure of information asymmetry in Korea. Park and Eom (2008) also report that PIN is not useful, but that Duarte and Young's (2007) adjusted PIN is useful. An, Kim, J., and Kim, D. (2010) also examine whether information quality (or earnings quality) is priced in Korea. By using accruals qualityas a measure of information quality, they find that accruals quality is not priced. Note that accruals quality is priced in the U.S. markets (see Kim and Qi (2010)).

---

22) Yu (2000) reports that Korean firms are significantly exposed to a USD risk after the liberalization of capital flows in 1992. After controlling for Japanese yen and other macroeconomic variables, however, the USD risk exposure became insignificant.

IV. The Consumption-Based Capital Asset Pricing Model (C-CAPM)

By introducing the consumption beta, equation (27) can be rewritten as

$$E(r_{t+1}) = r_f + \lambda \beta_{c, t+1} \tag{28}$$

where $\lambda = \gamma \, \mathrm{Var}(g_{c, t+1})$ is the market price of consumption risk, and $\beta_{c, t+1} = \mathrm{Cov}(r_{t+1}, g_{c, t+1})/\mathrm{Var}(g_{c, t+1})$ is the consumption beta. This is the Consumption-based CAPM (C-CAPM).[23]

The intuition of the C-CAPM is that if an investor holds assets, he can sell some of the assets to finance consumption when his current income is low. Thus, an individual asset is more desirable if its return is expected to be high when consumption is low (since more can be invested). However, if its return is expected to be high when consumption is high (since less can be invested), the asset is less desirable and more risky, and thus, the investor demands a higher risk premium to hold it.

Empirical results on the validity of the C-CAPM in Korea are similar to those in the U.S. That is, the C-CAPM performs poorly empirically. By using 11 industry portfolios and the maximum likelihood estimation under the non-linear C-CAPM constraints, Koo (1992, 1993) tests whether there is a linear relation between stock returns and consumption betas and reports that the linearity is rejected over the sample period 1980~1990.[24] Choi and

---

23) The formulation of the C-CAPM can be generalized. If the utility is a function of an uncertain amount of total (market-wide) wealth instead of consumption, the C-CAPM of equation (28) becomes the standard CAPM, since the consumption growth rate is equivalent to the rate of return on the market portfolio. Cochrane (1991) also derives the production-based CAPM (P-CAPM) by using producers and production functions in the place of consumers and utility functions thatare used in deriving the consumption-based CAPM. The marginal rate of substitution of consumption is substituted as the marginal rate of transformation of capital. According to the reports from Koo (1993), Nam and Lee (1995), and Nam, Choi, and Kim (2003), the P-CAPM performs better in Korea than does the C-CAPM.

24) By using the same way, Koo (1992) reports that the linearity of the CAPM is valid over some subperiods.

Baik (1992) conduct a test for the validity of the C-CAPM over the period 1980~1990 through the Fama-MacBeth two-pass methodologyby using 27 industry portfolios. They report that (contemporaneous) consumption betas fail to explain the cross-section of average stock returns. By using a time-series analysis, they also report that stock returns are related more to changes in future consumption than changes in current or past consumption. Thus, Lee, Park, and Cho (1998) use forecasted future consumption betas (obtained from regressing returns at time t on the growth rate in consumption at time $t+k$, $k=1, 2, 3,$ and 4) rather than contemporaneous consumption betas. However, they report that future consumption betas also fail to explain the cross-section of average stock returns in Korea.

V. Intertemporal Capital Asset Pricing Model

Merton (1973) derives a version of the CAPM by assuming that trading in assets takes place continuously over time and that investors maximize their expected utility at each time for lifetime consumption. Merton argues that when there is stochastic variation in investment opportunities, there will be risk arising from unfavorable shifts in the investment opportunity set. Thus, this risk is associated with innovations in the state variables that describe the investment opportunities. One of the state variables that is directly observable is the interest rate. Under this circumstance, Merton argues that investors need another portfolio to hedge against this risk, in addition to the market portfolio. Investors will hold portfolios chosen from three funds: the risk-free asset, the market portfolio (m), and a hedge portfolio (N) whose return is perfectly negatively correlated with the stochastic risk-free rate of return. The first and second funds provide the service to investors of an instantaneously efficient risk-return frontier. The third fund (N) allows investors to hedge against risk caused by unfavorable intertemporal shifts in the efficient frontier (the investment opportunity set). All investors'optimal portfolios can be represented as a linear combination of the three mutual funds (portfolios). In this case, the equilibrium returns will satisfy

$$E(r_i) = r_f + [E(r_m) - r_f] \beta_i^{(m)} + [E(r_N) - r_f] \beta_i^{(N)} \tag{29}$$

where

$$\beta_i^{(m)} = \frac{\beta_{im} - \beta_{iN} \beta_{Nm}}{1 - \rho_{Nm}^2}, \quad \beta_i^{(N)} = \frac{\beta_{iN} - \beta_{im} \beta_{Nm}}{1 - \rho_{Nm}^2}, \quad \beta_{jk} = \frac{\mathrm{Cov}(r_j, \ r_k)}{\mathrm{Var}(r_k^2)}$$

This is the intertemporal capital asset pricing model (I-CAPM).

If there are S sources of uncertainty ("state variables") in the opportunity set rather than just the risk-free rate, these sources of uncertainty can influence the magnitude of the risk-return parameters of the assets and cause the investment opportunity set to shift intertemporally. In this case, investors need S hedging portfolios and Merton's two-factor I-CAPM can be extended to $(S+1)$ factor I-CAPM.[25]

It is difficult to construct factor portfolios (or hedging portfolios) tracking innovations in state variables. The firstapproach to construct factor portfolios is the economic tracking portfolio approach introduced by Lamont (2001). In this approach, economic tracking portfolios are designed to capture unexpected returns that are maximally correlated with unexpected components (or innovations) of a target macroeconomic variable. Future GDP growth (Vassalou; 2003), future labor income growth (Kim, Kim, and Min; 2010), and future money supply growth (Jung and Kim; 2010) are examples

---

25) Richard (1979) suggests the growth rate in the money supply, prices of industrial goods, disposable income, and wage rates as the state variables whose innovations are sources of uncertainty.

of such target macroeconomic variables. The second approach is to construct zero-investment portfolios by using firm characteristics such as Fama and French's (1993) SMB and HML and to attribute these factors to state variables that cause changes in investment opportunity sets. Fama and French (1992) state "examining relations between SMB and HML and economic variables that measure variations in business conditions might help expose the nature of the economic risks captured by size and book-to-market equity." In this approach, it would be ambiguous to empirically differentiate the I-CAPM from the APT-motivated models. The third approach is to determine macroeconomic factors that are most plausible to change investment opportunity sets. Campbell (1996) selects five state variables and suggests a five-factor model containing the market portfolio return, dividend yield, relative bill rate, yield spread, and real labor income growth rate.[26]

Most empirical research on the I-CAPM in Korea is quite recent. Son, Kim, and Yoon (2009), Kim, B. J. and Cho (2010), and Jung and Kim, D. (2010) compare the performance of pricing ability of several asset pricing models including the CAPM, several APT-motivated models, and the I-CAPM models such as the Campbell model. Their common model comparisons are conducted through the stochastic discount factor (SDF) approach by implementing the GMM method. Here, the SDF approach is briefly introduced.

In the circumstance in which the distributional form of the disturbance terms are unknown (or un-assumed), Hansen (1982) and Hansen and Singleton (1982) suggest a GMM method. It is well known that when there is no arbitrage, there exists a positive stochastic discount factor (SDF) (or pricing kernel) m_t such that

$$E(m_t R_t) = 1_N \tag{30}$$

---

26) The relative bill rate (RTB) is the difference between the 1-month Treasury bill rate and its 1-year backward moving average.

where R_t is a $(N \times 1)$ vector of gross returns; 1_N is an $(N \times 1)$ vector of ones; and N is the number of test assets. Since all asset pricing models under consideration are linear factor pricing models, the pricing kernel can be represented as a linear combination of the factors. That is,

$$m_t = b_0 + b_1' f_t \tag{31}$$

where f_t is a $(K \times 1)$ vector of factors; b_0 is an intercept; and b_1 is a $(K \times 1)$ coefficient vector. b_0 and b_1 are called the SDF loadings.

If the SDF m_t correctly prices the N portfolios (i.e., the test assets), the pricing error vector, $g(\theta)$, of the N portfolios should be zero. The pricing error vector is defined as

$$g(\theta) = E(m_t R_t) - 1_N \tag{32}$$

where $\theta = (b_0, b_1')$ is the set of parameters to be estimated. However, if m_t is misspecified, the pricing errors $g(\theta)$ are nonzero. When one of the factors (or a factor portfolio) in a factor model is not given but, rather, must be estimated, there occur orthogonality conditions. In this case, the or thogonality conditions are stacked in equation (32). The parameters are chosen to minimize the quadratic form

$$J_T = g(\theta)' W_g(\theta) \tag{33}$$

where W is an $(N \times N)$ weighting matrix. In order to compare the perform-ance of the pricing ability of the models, $E[RR']^{-1}$, which is the inverse of the second moments of asset returns, is used for the weighting matrix.[27]

---

27) The asymptotically optimal weighing matrix is adopted to compute Hansen's J-statistic of equation (33) on the overidentifying restrictions of the models. In this case, it is well known that the J-statistic is asymptotically χ^2

The advantage of using this weighting matrix is that it is invariant across competing asset pricing models. The Hansen-Jagannathan (1997) distance (HJ distance) is defined as

$$\text{HJ distancd} = \left[\underset{\theta}{\text{Min}} \, g(\theta)' \, W \, g(\theta) \right]^{1/2}$$

where $W = E[RR']^{-1}$. The HJ-distance can be interpreted as the maximum pricing error for the set of assets mis-priced by the model (Campbell and Cochrane, 2000). The disadvantage of using this weighting matrix is that the distribution of the HJ distance is difficult to find.

According to Cochrane (1996), the risk premia, λ, can be estimated in the SDF approach as follows

$$\lambda = -r_f \, Cov(f, f') \, b_1 \tag{35}$$

where r_f is the riskless return. If the SDF factor loading, b_1, is time-varying and its time-varying behavior is conditioned on instrumental variables, Z_{t-1}, then it can be represented as $b_1 = c_0 + c_1 + c_1 \, Z_{t-1}$. In this case, the model becomes a conditional model, and the parameters to be estimated are $\theta = (b_0, \, c_0, \, c_1')$. Of course, if c_1 is assumed to be zero, it is an unconditional model.

By using the SDF approach, Son, Kim, and Yoon (2009) compare four models over the period April 1991 through February 2009 by using 16 size-BM portfolios as test assets CAPM, the Fama and French three-factor model, the Fama and Frenchthree-factor model plus liquidity factor, and the Campbell (1996) five-factor model. These authors report that the Campbell model performs best in terms of the HJ distance and the Hansen J-test. Kim, B. J.

---

distribution with degrees of freedom equal to the number of moments minus the number of parameters.

and Cho (2010) also conductsimilar comparisons including the above four models plus the C-CAPM, the Jagannathan and Wang (1996) conditional CAPM, the Cochrane (1996) production-based CAPM. These authors report that the Jagannathan and Wang conditional CAPM, the Campbell model, and the Fama and French three-factor model perform best in terms of the HJ distance. Son, Kim, and Yoon (2009) and Kim, B. J. and Cho (2010) both report that when the models are conditioned on several instrumental variables, the performance of pricing ability is significantly improved.[28] By employing Lamont's (2001) economic tracking portfolio approach, Jung and Kim, D. (2010) construct a factor portfolio tracking innovations in future money sup-ply (as a state variable) and test whether it is priced by using the Fama and MacBeth CSR method and the SDF approach. Their test period is March 1995 through December 2008. These authors report that risks caused by in-novations in future money supply are priced. Also, they compare several mod-els and report that a four-factor model containing the Fama and French three factors plus the money supply factor performs best in terms of the HJ distance.

Recently, Kim, Kim, and Shin (2010) comprehensively evaluate and com-pare various asset pricing models in the Korean stock market over the period 1990～2009 by conducting time-series and cross-sectional tests based on individual *t*-tests, the GRS *F*-tests, the HJ distance, and the Kandel and Stambaugh (1995) R-squares. They report that the Fama and French (1993) five-factor model performs most satisfactorily amongthe asset pric-ing models considered in explaining the intertemporal and cross-sectional behavior of stock returns in Korea. The Fama and French three-factor model, the Chen, Novy-Marx, and Zhang (2010) three-factor model, and the Campbell (1996) model are next. They also report that over the two

---

28) As instrumental variables, Son, Kim, and Yoon (2009) employ term spread, default spread, and dividend yield, and Kim, B. J. and Cho (2010) employ industrial production and export. In particular, Kim, B. J. and Cho (2010) argue that the use of industrial production substantially improves the performance of the conditional models.

sub-periods before and after the Asian foreign currency crisis (1990~1998 and 1999~2009), the results are similar.

IV. Summary and Concluding Remarks

This paper reviews 30 years of empirical research on asset pricing models in the Korean stock markets. Asset pricing models reviewed include the CAPM (conditional and unconditional), APT, I-CAPM, and C-CAPM. This paper also provides explanations of the testing methodologies used in the literature for the asset pricing models: time-series tests, CSR tests, and tests by the SDF approach implemented by the GMM estimation method.

Since its introduction in 1964, the CAPM has become a backbone of financial economics. Nonetheless, the validity of the CAPM has been seriously challenged in Korea as well as in the other countries. The overall empirical results in Korea show, as they do in other countries, that the static CAPM fails to explain for stock returns in Korea. Contrary to the prediction of the CAPM, firm characteristic variables such as firm size, book-to-market, and earnings-to-price ratio have significant explanatory power for average stock returns in the Korean stock markets. However, the following points should be made regarding tests of the CAPM. The test results are subject to several econometric issues; the EIV problem in CSR tests, the use of mis-specified beta estimates, time-varying properties of market betas and risk premia, and arbitrary choice of the return measurement interval, among others. After resolving some of these issues, some papers report that the explanatory power of market betas for stock returns becomes stronger. It would be premature, therefore, to reject the validity of the CAPM before these issues are satisfactorily resolved.

Along with the above-mentioned econometric issues in the CAPM tests, the following points should also be considered. Many papers use returns on KOSPI. However, these returns do not include dividends. Thus, returns with dividends should be used as long as returns with dividends for individual stocks are used. Most papers use the yield of the government short-term bills as a proxy for the risk-free return. This yield is a promised (or ex ante) yield, not a realized (or ex post) yield. Insofar as realized stock returns are used in the tests, it is reasonable to use realized government bill yields for the risk-free return. Another issue is the sensitivity of portfolio formation to the test results. Many papers employ portfolios sorted by firm size and book-to-market as test assets. Since the test results could be sensitive to portfolio formation, it is necessary to consider various portfolios as test assets.

This paper also reviews the published works on testing various models of the APT-motivated models and the I-CAPM-motivated models. The Fama and French three-factor model is overall acceptable in the case of Korea. However, some papers report that other multi-factor models perform better in explaining stock returns than does the Fama and French three-factor model. Thus, a better multi-factor model should be pursued in future work.

References

Amihud, Y., "Illiquidity and Stock Return: Cross-Section and Time-Series Effect", *Journal of Financial Markets*, Vol. 5(2002), pp. 31-56.

An, Y. H., J. W. Kim, and D. Kim, "Is Accounting Information Quality Priced in the Korean Markets", *Korean Journal of Financial Studies*, Vol. 39, No. 1(2010), pp. 133-159.

Ang, A. and J. Chen, "CAPM over the Long Run: 1926~2001", *Journal of Empirical Finance*, Vol. 14(2003), pp. 1-40.

Banz, R. W., "The Relationship Between Return and Market Value of Common Stocks", *Journal of Financial Economics*, Vol. 9(1981), pp. 3-18.

Basu, S., "The Relationship Between Earnings Yield, Market Value, and Return for NYSE Common Stocks", *Journal of Financial Economics*, Vol. 12(1983), pp. 129-156.

Black, F., "Capital Market Equilibrium with Restricted Borrowing", *Journal of Business*, Vol. 45(1972), pp. 444-455.

Black, F., M. C. Jensen, and M. Scholes, "The Capital Asset Pricing Model: Some Empirical Tests", *Studies in the Theory of Capital Markets*, M. C. Jensen(ed.), New York: Praeger Publishers, Inc., 1972.

Breeden, D., "An Intertemporal Asset Pricing Model with Stochastic Consumption and Investment Opportunities", *Journal of Financial Economics*, Vol. 7(1979), pp. 265-296.

Campbell, J. Y., "Understanding Risk and Return", *Journal of Political Economy*, Vol. 104(1996), pp. 298-345.

Campbell, J. Y. and J. H. Cochrane, "Explaining the Poor Performance of Consumption-Based Asset Pricing Models", *Journal of Finance*, Vol. 55 (2000), pp. 2863-2878.

Carhart, M. M., "On Persistence in Mutual Fund Performance", *Journal of*

Finance, Vol. 52(1997), pp. 57-82.

Chae, J. and C. W. Yang, "Why Idiosyncratic Factors Can Explain the Pricing Errors from Asset Pricing Models in the Korean Stock Market?", *Asia-Pacific Journal of Financial Studies*, Vol. 37(2008), pp. 297-342.

Chang, K. H., "Conditional CAPM and Time-Varying Correlation: An Application of Multivariate GARCH-M Model", *Asia- Pacific Journal of Financial Studies*, Vol. 23, No. 1(1998), pp. 61-87(in Korean).
장국현, "다변량 GARCH-M 모형을 이용한 조건부CAPM의 검증과 시간가변적 상관관계에 관한 연구", 증권학회지, 제23권 제1호(1998), pp. 61-87.

Chen, L., R. Novy-Marx, and L. Zhang, "An Alternative Three-Factor Model", *Working Paper*, Ohio State University(2010).

Chen, N., R. Roll, and S. A. Ross, "Economic Forces and the Stock Market", *Journal of Business*, Vol. 59(1986), pp. 383-403.

Chi, H. J., "A Study on the Common Factors Explaining Systematic Risk Rewarded in the Stock Market", *Korean Management Review*, Vol. 21, No. 2(1992), pp. 139-164(in Korean).
지호준, "주식수익률을 결정하는 공통요인에 관한 연구", 경영학연구, 제21권 제2호(1992), pp. 139-164.

Cho, D., "Tests of CAPM under Conditional Heteroscedasticity", *Korean Journal of Finance*, Vol. 12(1996), pp. 51-76(in Korean).
조담, "조건부 이분산성을 고려한 자본자산가격결정모형의 실증적 검증", 재무연구, 제12권(1996), pp. 51-76.

Cho, D., "Empirical Tests of the Arbitrage Pricing Theory in a Dynamic Factor Structure", *Korean Journal of Financial Management*, Vol. 15, No. 1(1998), pp. 329-350(in Korean).
조담, "동태적 요인구조 하에서의 차익거래가격결정이론의 실증적 검증", 재무관리연구, 제15권 제1호(1998), pp. 329-350.

Cho, D. and C. H. Lee, "An Empirical Study on Time-Varying Market Price of Risk", *Korean Journal of Finance*, Vol. 15(1998), pp. 25-49(in Korean).

조담, 이창호, "위험의 시장가격의 시간가변성에 관한 실증적 연구", 재무연구, 제15권(1998), pp. 25-49.

Choe, H. and C. W. Yang, "Information Risk and Asset Returns in the Korean Stock Market", *Asia-Pacific Journal of Financial Studies*, Vol. 36, No. 4(2007), pp. 567-620(in Korean).

최혁, 양철원, "한국주식시장에서 정보위험과 수익률의 관계", 증권학회지, 제36권 제4호(2007), pp. 567-620.

Choe, H. and C. W. Yang, "Liquidity Risk and Asset Returns: The Case of the Korean Stock Markets", *Korean Journal of Financial Management*, Vol. 26, No. 4(2009), pp. 103-140.

Choi, W. Y. and Y. H. Baik, "A Study on the Relation Between Changes in Consumption and Stock Price", *Asia-Pacific Journal of Financial Studies*, Vol. 14(1992), pp. 401-424(in Korean).

최운열, 백용호, "주가변화와 소비변화의 관계에 대한 연구", 증권학회지, 제14권(1992), pp. 401-424.

Cochrane, J. H., "Production-Based Asset Pricing and the Link between Stock Returns and Economic Fluctuations", *Journal of Finance*, Vol. 46(1991), pp. 209-238.

Cochrane, J. H., "A Cross-Sectional Test of An Investment-Based Asset Pricing Model", *Journal of Political Economy*, Vol. 104(1996), pp. 572-621.

Chung, K. W., "Relations Between Macroeconomic Variables and Stock Price in Korea", *Korean Journal of Financial Management*, Vol. 8, No. 2(1991), pp. 111-129(in Korean).

정기웅, "거시경제변수와 주가 - 한국주식시장에서의 실증분석", 재무관리연구, 제8권 제2호(1991), pp. 111-129.

Duarte, J. and L. Young, "Why is PIN priced?", *Journal of Financial Economics*, Vol. 90(2009), pp. 119-138.

Easley, D., S. Hvidkjaer, and M. O'Hara, "Is Information Risk a Determinant of Asset Returns", *Journal of Finance*, Vol. 59(2002), pp. 2185-2221.

Fama, E. F. and K. R. French, "The Cross-Section of Expected Stock Returns", *Journal of Finance*, Vol. 47(1992), pp. 129-176.

Fama, E. F. and K. R. French, "Common Risk Factors in Returns on Stocks and Bonds", *Journal of Financial Economics*, Vol. 33(1993), pp. 3-56.

Fama, E. F. and J. D. MacBeth, "Risk, Return, and Equilibrium: Empirical Tests", *Journal of Political Economy*, Vol. 81(1973), pp. 607-636.

George, T. J., G. Kaul, and M. Nimalendran, "Estimation of the Bid-Ask Spread and Its Components: A New Approach", *Review of Financial Studies*, Vol. 4(1991), pp. 623-656.

Gibbons, M. R., S. A. Ross, and J. Shanken, "A Test of the Efficiency of a Given Portfolio", *Econometrica*, Vol. 57(1989), pp. 1121-1152.

Glosten, L. R. and L. E. Harris, "Estimating the Component of the Bid/Ask Spread", *Journal of Financial Economics*, Vol. 21(1988), pp. 123-142.

Graham, J. R. and C. R. Harvey, "The theory and practice of corporate finance: evidence from the field", *Journal of Financial Economics*, Vol. 60(2001), pp. 187-243.

Han, D., "A New Methodology for Measuring Abnormal Returns: Empirical Evidence on the Small Firm Effect and the Neglected Firm Effect in the Korean Stock Market", *Asia-Pacific Journal of Financial Studies*, Vol. 16(1994), pp. 315-337(in Korean).
한동, "초과수익률 측정을 위한 새로운 검증방법 : 소기업효과와 소외기업 효과 검증을 중심으로", 증권학회지, 제16권(1994), pp. 315-337.

Handa, P., S. P. Kothari, and C. Wasley, "The Relation Between the Return Interval and Betas: Implications for the Size Effect", *Journal of Financial Economics*, Vol. 23(1989), pp. 79-100.

Hansen, L. P., "Large Sample Properties of Generalized Methods of Moments Estimators", *Econometrica*, Vol. 50(1982), pp. 1029-1054.

Hansen, L. P. and R. Jagannathan, "Assessing specification errors in stochastic discount factor models", *Journal of Finance*, Vol. 52(1997), pp. 557-590.

Hansen, L. P. and K. J. Singleton, "Generalized Instrumental Variables Estimation of Nonlinear Rational Expectation Models", *Econometrica*, Vol. 50(1982), pp. 1269-1286.

Harvey, C. R., "Time-Varying Conditional Covariances in Tests of Asset Pricing Models", *Journal of Financial Economics*, Vol. 24(1989), pp. 289-317.

Hasbrouck, J., "Measuring the Information Content of Stock Trades", *Journal of Finance*, Vol. 46(1991), pp. 179-208.

Hwang, S. W., "An Empirical Study on the Tests of the Firm Size EffectConditional on the Choice of the Market Index in Korea", *Korean Journal of Financial Management*, Vol. 10, No. 2(1993), pp. 303-317(in Korean).
황선웅, "한국주식시장에서의 주가지수 선택에 따른 기업규모효과의 실증결과 비교분석", 재무관리연구, 제10권 제2호(1993), pp. 303-317.

Hwang, S. W. and I. K. Lee, "A Multivariate Test for the Efficiency of a Given Portfolio", *Asia-Pacific Journal of Financial Studies*, Vol. 13(1991), pp. 357-401(in Korean).
황선웅, 이일균, "자본자산 포트폴리오의 효율성에 대한 다변량 검증", 증권학회지, 제13권(1991), pp. 357-401.

Jagannathan, R. and Z. Wang, "The Conditional CAPM and the Cross-Section of Expected Returns", *Journal of Finance*, Vol. 51(1996), pp. 3-53.

Jo, H. H. and S. K. Lee, "The Study on the Scale-Dependence of CAPM's Beta by Using Wavelet", *Korean Journal of Finance*, Vol. 17, No. 1(2004), pp. 289-318(in Korean).
조하현, 이승국, "Wavelet기법을 이용한 CAPM의 베타추정에 대한 연구", 재무연구, 제17권 제1호(2004), pp. 289-318.

Jostova, G. and A. Philipov, "Bayesian Analysis of Stochastic Betas", *Journal of Financial and Quantitative Analysis*, Vol. 40(2005), pp. 747-778.

Jung, H. and D. Kim, "Innovations in the Future Money Growth and the Cross-Section of Stock Returns in Korea", *Asia-Pacific Journal of Financial Studies*, Vol. 40, No. 5(2011), pp. 683-709.

Jung, J. R. and H. C. Kim, "Tests for Mean-Variance Efficiency in the Korean Stock Markets", *Korean Journal of Finance*, Vol. 5(1992), pp. 277-303 (in Korean).

정종락, 김형찬, "한국주식시장의 평균-분산 효율성의 검증", 재무연구, 제5권(1992), pp. 277-303.

Kam, H. K., "An Empirical Study on the Determinants of Stock Prices", *Korean Journal of Financial Management*, Vol. 8, No. 2(1991), pp. 131-164 (in Korean).

감형규, "주식의 가격결정요인에 관한 실증적 연구", 재무관리연구, 제8권 제2호(1991), pp. 131-164.

Kam, H. K., "An Empirical Study on the Relation Between Fundamental Variables and Stock Returns", *Korean Journal of Financial Management*, Vol. 14, No. 2(1997), pp. 21-55(in Korean).

감형규, "기본적 변수와 주식수익률의 관계에 관한 실증적 연구", 재무관리연구, 제14권 제2호(1997), pp. 21-55.

Kandel, S., "On the Exclusion of Assets from Tests of the Mean Variance Efficiency of the Market Portfolio", *Journal of Finance*, Vol. 39(1984), pp. 63-75.

Kandel, S. and R. F. Stambaugh, "Portfolio Inefficiency and the Cross-Section of Expected Returns", *Journal of Finance,* Vol. 50(1995), pp. 157-184.

Kang, J. M., W. Y. Choi, and D. H. Lee, "An Analysis of the Relation Between Beta Changes and Macroeconomic Variables", *Korean Journal of Financial Management*, Vol. 13, No.1(1996), pp. 137-158(in Korean).

강종만, 최운렬, 이덕훈, "베타의 변화와 거시경제변수간의 관계 분석", 재무관리연구, 제13권 제1호(1996), pp. 137-158.

Kho, B. C. and S. M. Yae, "Bayesian Analysis of a Stochastic Beta Model in Korean Stock Markets", *Korean Journal of Financial Management*, Vol. 22, No.2(2005), pp. 43-69(in Korean).

고봉찬, 예승민, "확률베타모형의 베이지안 분석", 재무관리연구, 제22권 제2호(2005), pp. 43-69.

Kim, B. J. and J. H. Cho, "An Evaluation of Asset Pricing Models using the Minimum Distance Test", *Korean Journal of Financial Studies*, Vol. 39, No. 2(2010), pp. 267-305(in Korean).

김봉준, 조재호, "최소거리검정을 이용한 자산가격결정모형의 평가", 증권 학회지, 제39권 제2호(2010), pp. 267-305.

Kim, D., "The Errors-In-Variables Problem in the Cross-Section of Expected Stock Returns", *Journal of Finance*, Vol. 50(1995), pp. 1605-1634.

Kim, D., "A Reexamination of Firm Size, Book-to-Market, and Earnings-Price in the Cross-Section of Expected Stock Returns", *Journal of Financial and Quantitative Analysis*, Vol. 32(1997), pp. 463-489.

Kim, D., "Structural Shifts of Market Betas and Common Risk Factors in Korean Stock Returns", *Asia-Pacific Journal of Financial Studies*, Vol. 33, No. 4(2004), pp. 95-134(in Korean).

김동철, "시장위험의 구조적 변화와 주가수익률의 결정요인에 대한 재고 찰", 증권학회지, 제33권 제4호(2004), pp. 95-134.

Kim, D., S. Kim, and H. Shin, "Evaluating Asset pricing Models in the Korean Stock Market", *Pacific-Basin Finance Journal*, Forthcoming(2012).

Kim, D., T. S. Kim, and B. K. Min, "Future Labor Income Growth and the Cross Section of Equity Returns", *Journal of Banking and Finance*, Vol. 35, No. 1(2011), pp. 67-81.

Kim, D. and Y. Qi, "Accruals Quality, Stock Returns, and Macroeconomic Conditions", *The Accounting Review*, Vol. 85, No. 3(2010), pp. 937-978.

Kim, D. and S. H. Shin, "The Risk of Earnings Information Uncertainty and the January Effect in Korean Stock Markets", *Asia-Pacific Journal of Financial Studies*, Vol. 35, No. 4(2006), pp. 71-102(in Korean).

김동철, 신성호, "한국주식시장의 이익정보 불확실성 위험과 1월 효과", 증권학회지, 제35권 제4호(2006), pp. 71-102.

Kim, D. H., "Return Measurement Intervals and Betas", *Korean Journal of Financial Management*, Vol. 13, No. 2(1996), pp. 159-184(in Korean).
김동회, "수익률의 측정간격과 베타계수", 재무관리연구, 제13권 제1호(1996), pp. 159-184.

Kim, D. S. and J. H. Kim, "Effects of the Disclosure of Earnings Per Share and Firm Size on Stock Returns", *Journal of Money and Finance*, Vol. 7, No. 1(1993), pp. 1-46(in Korean).
김동순, 김진호, "주당순이익의 공표 및 기업규모가 주식수익률에 미치는 효과", 금융연구, 제7권 제1호(1993), pp. 1-46.

Kim, J. H. and Y. J. Hwang, "An Analysis on the Effect of Time Varying Risk to Stock Price Return: Non-Parametric Approach", *Journal of Money and Finance*, Vol. 1, No. 2(1996), pp. 153-170(in Korean).
김진호, 황윤재, "시간변동위험이 주가수익률에 미치는 영향분석 : 비모수적 접근", 금융학회지, 제1권 제2호(1996), pp. 153-170.

Kim, K. H., "A Study on Market Anomalies in the Korean Stock Markets", *Korean Journal of Financial Management*, Vol. 8, No. 2(1991), pp. 73-97(in Korean).
김기호, "한국증권시장의 주가이상반응에 관한 연구 : 1월 효과를 중심으로", 재무관리연구, 제8권 제2호(1991), pp. 73-97.

Kim, K. J., S. W. Hwang, and J. S. Kim, "Choice of Stock Index and Bias in Abnormal Return Estimates", *Asia-Pacific Journal of Financial Studies*, Vol. 16, No. 1(1994), pp. 467-511(in Korean).
김권중, 황선웅, 김진선, "지수수익률의 선택과 초과수익률 추정식의 편기", 증권학회지, 제16권 제1호(1994), pp. 467-511.

Kim, K. Y. and Y. B. Kim, "What Determines Expected Stock Returns in the Korean Stock Market?", *Asia-Pacific Journal of Financial Studies*, Vol. 28(2001), pp. 57-85(in Korean).

김규영, 김영빈, "한국 주식시장에서 기대수익률의 결정요인은 무엇인가?", 증권학회지, 제28권(2001), pp. 57-85.

Kim, K. Y. and Y. B. Kim, "The Conditional Relation Between Beta and Returns: An Empirical Analysis of the Korean Stock Market", *Journal of Industrial Economics and Business*, Vol. 19, No. 3(2006), pp. 1273-1290 (in Korean).
김규영, 김영빈, "베타와 주식수익률간의 조건부 관계 : 한국주식시장에서의 실증분석", 산업경제연구, 제19권 제3호(2006), pp. 1273-1290.

Kim, S. C. and J. Y. Kim, "Firm Size and Book-to-Market Factors in Korean Stock Returns", *Korean Journal of Finance*, Vol. 13, No. 2(2000), pp. 21-47(in Korean).
김석진, 김지영, "기업규모와 장부가/시가 비율과 주식수익률의 관계", 재무연구, 제13권 제2호(2000), pp. 21-47.

Kim, S. P. and Y. S. Yun, "Fundamental Variables, Macroeconomic Factors, Risk Characteristics and Equity Returns", *Korean Journal of Financial Management*, Vol. 16, No. 2(1999), pp. 179-213(in Korean).
김성표, 윤영섭, "기본적변수, 거시경제요인, 기업특성적 위험과 주식수익률", 재무관리연구, 제16권 제2호(1999), pp. 179-213.

Koo, M. H. and M. S. Shin, "Relations Between Systematic Risk of Common Stocks and Macroeconomic Variables", *Korean Journal of Financial Management*, Vol. 7, No. 2(1990), pp. 115-152(in Korean).
구맹회, 신민식, "보통주의 체계적 위험과 거시경제변수간의 관계", 재무관리연구, 제7권 제2호(1990), pp. 115-152.

Koo, B. Y., "An Empirical Study on the Consumption-Based CAPM", *Korean Journal of Financial Management*, Vol. 9, No. 1(1992), pp. 1-22(in Korean).
구본열, "소비에 근거한 CAPM의 실증적 연구", 재무관리연구, 제9권 제1호(1992), pp. 1-22.

Koo, B. Y., "An Empirical Study on the Production-Based CAPM", *Korean*

Journal of Financial Management, Vol. 10, No. 2(1993), pp. 117-136(in Korean).

구본열, "자산가격결정의 생산기저모형에 대한 실증적 검증", 재무관리연구, 제10권 제2호(1993), pp. 117-136.

Koo, B. Y., "Multivariate Tests of the Efficiency of Market Portfolio Proxies", *Korean Journal of Financial Management*, Vol. 12, No. 2(1995), pp. 43-71(in Korean).

구본열, "대용시장포트폴리오의 효율성에 대한 다변량 검증-무위험자산이 존재하지 않을 경우", 재무관리연구, 제12권 제2호(1995), pp. 43-71.

Koo, B. Y., "Multivariate Tests of the Efficiency of Market Portfolio Proxies in the Korean Stock Markets by Using the GMM method", *Korean Journal of Financial Management*, Vol. 15, No. 1(1998), pp. 1-30(in Korean).

구본열, "한국증권시장에서 대용시장포트폴리오 효율성의 GMM에 의한 다변량 검증", 재무관리연구, 제15권 제1호(1998), pp. 1-30.

Koo, B. Y., "Empirical Tests of the CAPM and the APT in Korea by Using Multivariate Tests", *Korean Journal of Financial Studies*, Vol. 5, No. 1(1999), pp. 135-164(in Korean).

구본열, "한국증권시장에서 다변량검증에 근거한 CAPM과 APM의 실증적 검증", 재무관리논총, 제5권 제1호(1999), pp. 135-164.

Kook, C. P. and S. I. Han, "The Cross-Sectional Explanation of the Variation in Expected Stock Returns Using Conditional CAPM", *Korean Journal of Finance*, Vol. 12, No. 1(1999), pp. 147-180(in Korean).

국찬표, 한상일, "조건부 CAPM을 이용한 주식수익률변화의 횡단면적 설명력", 재무연구, 제12권 제1호(1999), pp. 147-180.

Kwon, T. H. and J. W. Park, "A Study on the Liquidity Premium in Korean Stock Market", *Korean Journal of Finance*, Vol. 13(1997), pp. 223-259 (in Korean).

권택호, 박종원, "한국주식시장의 유동성 프리미엄에 관한 연구", 재무연구,

제13호(1997), pp. 223-259.

Kwon, T. H. and J. W. Park, "Relationship Between Foreign Exchange Risk Premiums and Firm Characteristics in the Korean Stock Market", *Korean Journal of Financial Management*, Vol. 16, No. 1(1999), pp. 245-260(in Korean).

권택호, 박종원, "한국주식시장에서의 환위험 프리미엄과 기업특성", 재무관리연구, 제16권 제1호(1999), pp. 245-260.

Lamont, O., "Economic tracking portfolios", *Journal of Econometrics*, Vol. 105(2001), pp. 161-184.

Lee, D. H., J. I. Park, B. W. Yu, T. I. Lim, K. C. Shin, H. Y. Lee, K. H. Kim, and K. S. Kho, "Usefulness of Fundamental Betas", *Korean Journal of Finance*, Vol. 5, No. 1(1992), pp. 155-180(in Korean).

이덕희, 박정인, 유병욱, 임태일, 신계철, 이희용, 김경휘, 고광수, "펀더멘탈 베타의 유용성 연구", 재무연구, 제5권 제1호(1992), pp. 155-180.

Lee, H. J. and Y. B. Kim, "Market Returns and Determinants of Expected Returns: An Empirical Analysis of the Korean Stock Market", *Journal of Industrial Economics and Business*, Vol. 19, No. 5(2006), pp. 2051-2069 (in Korean).

이한재, 김영빈, "시장수익률과 기대수익률의 결정요인 : 한국주식시장에서의 실증분석", 산업경제연구, 제19권 제5호(2006), pp. 2051-2069.

Lee, J. D. and M. S. Shin, "The Effect of Macroeconomics Variables on the Systematic Risk of Common Stocks", *Asia-Pacific Journal of Financial Studies*, Vol. 13, No. 1(1991), pp. 289-325(in Korean).

이정도, 신민식, "거시경제변수가 보통주의 체계적 위험에 미치는 효과", 증권학회지, 제13권 제1호(1991), pp. 289-325.

Lee, J. H. and J. H. Nam, "Estimating Asset Pricing Models by Using the GMM Method", *Korean Journal of Financial Management*, Vol. 9, No. 2(1992), pp. 57-75(in Korean).

이주희, 남주하, "GMM을 이용한 자본자산가격결정모형의 추정", 재무관리연구, 제9권 제2호(1992), pp. 57-75.

Lee, J. K., R. S. Park, and J. H. Cho, "An Empirical Analysis of the C-CAPM by Using A New Consumption Beta", *Journal of Finance and Banking*, Vol. 4, No. 2(1998), pp. 105-128(in Korean).
이준구, 박래수, 조재호, "새로운 소비베타를 이용한 CCAPM의 실증분석", 증권금융연구, 제4권 제2호(1998), pp. 105-128.

Lee, J. R., "Horizon-based Test of Simple Continuous Time CAPM", *Asia-Pacific Journal of Financial Studies*, Vol. 36, No. 5(2007), pp. 807-836(in Korean).
이종룡, "자료시차를 반영한 Continuous Time CAPM의 실증에 관한 연구", 증권학회지, 제36권 제5호(2007), pp. 807-836.

Lee, P. S., C. Jee, G. S. Yoon, J. C. Jang, G. H. Lee, and C. B. Park, "An Empirical Analysis and A Theoretical Examination of the Arbitrage Pricing Theory", *Asia-Pacific Journal of Financial Studies*, Vol. 6, No. 1(1984), pp. 1-30(in Korean).
이필상, 지청, 심상면, 윤계섭, 장재철, 이건희, 박창배, "재정가격 결정모형의 이론적고찰과 실증적 분석", 증권학회지, 제6권 제1호(1984), pp. 1-30.

Lee, Y. H., "A Empirical Study on the Economic Implications of Stock Return Determinants", *Korean Journal of Financial Management*, Vol. 11, No. 1(1994), pp. 97-122(in Korean).
이용호, "주식가격결정요인의 경제적 의미에 대한 실증적 연구", 재무관리연구, 제11권 제1호(1994), pp. 97-122.

Levhari, D. and H. Levy, "The Capital Asset Pricing Model and the Investment Horizon", *Review of Economics and Statistics*, Vol. 59(1977), pp. 92-104.

Lintner, J., "The Valuation of Risk Assets and the Selection of Risky Investments in Stock Portfolios and Capital Budgets", *Review of Economics and Statistics*, Vol. 47(1965), pp. 13-37.

Litzenberger, R. H. and K. Ramaswamy, "The Effect of Personal Taxes and Dividends on Capital Asset Prices: Theory and Empirical Evidence",

Journal of Financial Economics, Vol. 7(1979), pp. 163-195.

Lucas, R., "Asset Prices in An Exchange Economy", *Econometrica*, Vol. 46(1978), pp. 1429-1445.

Merton, R. C., "An Intertemporal Capital Asset Pricing Model", *Econometrica*, Vol. 41(1973), pp. 867-887.

Miller, M. and M. Scholes, "Rates of Return in Relation to Risk: A Re-Examination of Some Recent Findings", *Studies in the Theory of Capital Markets*, M. C. Jensen(ed.), New York: Praeger Publishers, Inc., 1972.

Nam, J. H., H. G. Choi, and J. K. Kim, "A Theoretical Extension and Empirical Studies of Tim-Inseparable Production-Based Capital Asset Pricing Models", *Journal of Money and Finance*, Vol. 8, No. 1(2003), pp. 27-60(in Korean).
남주하, 최희갑, 김종권, "시간비분리 생산준거 자산가격결정모형의 이론적 확장과 실증분석", 금융학회지, 제8권 제1호(2003), pp. 27-60.

Nam, J. H. and J. H. Lee, "Tests of the Time-Varying Behavior of Conditional Covariances and the Risk-Return Trade-Offin Asset Pricing Models", *Korean Journal of Finance*, Vol. 9(1995), pp. 67-91(in Korean).
남주하, 이주희, "자본자산가격결정모형의 조건부공분산과 위험에 대한 보상비율의 시간에 대한 가변성 여부 검증", 재무연구, 제9호(1995), pp. 67-91.

Nam, J. H. and C. W. Lee, "Empirical Studies on Production-Based Capital Asset Pricing Models", *Journal of Money and Finance*, Vol. 9, No. 1(1995), pp. 65-102(in Korean).
남주하, 이창욱, "투자수익률과 생산준거 자본자산가격결정모형의 실증분석", 금융연구, 제9권 제1호(1995), pp. 65-102.

Nam, S. K., J. H. Park, and K. S. Eom, "Is the Liquidity Common Factor a Priced Risk in the Korean Stock Markets?", *Korean Journal of Finance*, Vol. 18, No. 2(2005), pp. 289-319(in Korean).
남상구, 박종호, 엄경식, "한국주식시장에서 유동성 공통요인은 주가에 반영되는 위험의 원천인가?", 재무연구, 제18권 제2호(2005), pp. 289-319.

Oh, S. K., "A New Methodology to Test Market Efficiency", *Asia-Pacific Journal of Financial Studies,* Vol. 14, No. 1(1992), pp. 93-144(in Korean).
오세경, "새로운 검증방법론을 이용한 효율적 시장가설의 검증", 증권학회지, 제14권 제1호(1992), pp. 93-144.

Oh, S. K., "An Analysis for Price Per Earnings Ratio, Firm Size, and Stock Returns", *Journal of Money and Finance*, Vol. 8, No. 1(1994), pp. 1-29 (in Korean).
오세경, "주가수익비율, 기업규모 및 주가의 주가수익률에 대한 경향 분석", 금융연구, 제8권 제1호(1994), pp. 1-29.

Oh, S. K., "An Empirical Study of the Determinants of Stock Return Volatility", *Korean Journal of Finance*, Vol. 9(1995), pp. 93-117(in Korean).
오세경, "주가변동결정요인에 대한 실증적 분석", 재무연구, 제9호(1995), pp. 93-117.

Paek, W., "Reconciliation Between Book-to-Market Equity and Earnings-Price Ration Through Return on Equity", *Asia-Pacific Journal of Financial Studies*, Vol. 26, No. 1(2000), pp. 119-411(in Korean).
백원선, "자기자본이익률을 통한 장부가치-주가비율과 수익-주가비율의 조화", 증권학회지, 제26권 제1호(2000), pp. 119-141.

Park, J. H. and K. S. Eom, "The Usefulness of PIN As a Measurement for Private-Information Risk in Korean Stock Markets", *Asia-Pacific Journal of Financial Studies,* Vol.37, No. 3(2008), pp. 501-536(in Korean).
박종호, 엄경식, "한국주식시장에서 사적 정보위험 PIN의 유용성 분석 : 주식수익률에 미치는 영향을 중심으로", 증권학회지, 제37권 제3호(2008), pp. 501-536.

Park, J. S. and K. S. Eom, "The Characteristics of the Illiquidity Premium, Measured via Spread", *Korean Journal of Finance*, Vol. 21, No. 2(2008), pp. 77-114(in Korean).

박재성, 엄경식, "스프레드율을 통해 관찰된 비유동성 프리미엄 특성", 재무연구, 제21권 제2호(2008), pp. 77-114.

Park, S. S., "A Study on the Predictability of a Systematic Risk Forecasting Model", *Asia-Pacific Journal of Financial Studies*, Vol. 15, No. 1(1993), pp. 139-178(in Korean).
박순식, "체계적위험 예측모형의 예측능력에 관한 연구", 증권학회지, 제15집 제1호(1993), pp. 139-178.

Park, S. S., "Accounting Risk Variables Beta Prediction Model and Forecasting Error analysis by Risk Levels", *Korean Journal of Financial Management*, Vol. 16, No. 2(1999), pp. 215-241(in Korean).
박순식, "회계위험변수 베타예측모형과 위험수준별 예측오차분석", 재무관리연구, 제16권 제2호(1999), pp. 215-241.

Reinganum, M. C., "Misspecification of Capital Asset Pricing: Empirical Anomalies Based on Earnings Yield and Market Value", *Journal of Financial Economics*, Vol. 9(1981), pp. 19-46.

Richard, S. F., "A Generalized Capital Asset Pricing Model", *Portfolio Theory, 25 Years After*, E. J. Elton and M. J. Gruber(ed.), Amsterdam: North-Holland Publishing Company, 1979.

Roll, R., "A Critique of the Asset Pricing Theory's Tests; Part I. On Past and Potential Testability of the Theory", *Journal of Financial Economics*, Vol. 4(1977), pp. 129-176.

Roll, R., "A Simple Implicit Measure of the Effective Bid-Ask Spread in an Efficient Market", *Journal of Finance*, Vol. 39(1984), pp. 1127-1139.

Roll, R. and S. A. Ross, "An Empirical Investigation of the Arbitrage Pricing Theory", *Journal of Finance*, Vol. 35(1980), pp. 1073-1103.

Rosenberg, B., K. Reid, and R. Lanstein, "Persuasive Evidence of Market Inefficiency", *Journal of Portfolio Management*, Vol. 11(1985), pp. 9-17.

Ross, S. A., "The Arbitrage Theory of Capital Asset Pricing", *Journal of Economic Theory*, Vol. 13(1976), pp. 341-360.

Rubinstein, M., "The valuation of uncertain income streams and the pricing of options", *Bell Journal of Economics and Management Science*, Vol. 7(1976), pp. 407-425.

Ryu, D. J. and C. J. Lee, "A test of Learning CAPM with Kalman Filter", *Asian Review of Financial Research*, Vol. 22, No. 4(2009), pp. 63-92 (in Korean).

류두진, 이창준, "칼만 필터를 이용한 학습 자본자산 가격결정모형의 검증", 재무연구, 제22권 제4호(2009), pp. 63-92.

Shanken, J., "Multivariate Tests of the Zero-Beta CAPM", *Journal of Financial Economics*, Vol. 14(1985), pp. 327-348.

Shanken, J., "On the Estimation of Beta-Pricing Models", *Review of Financial Studies*, Vol. 5(1992), pp. 1-33.

Sharpe, W. F., "Capital Asset Prices: A Theory of Market Equilibrium under Conditions of Risk", *Journal of Finance*, Vol. 19(1964), pp. 425-442.

Sim, B. G., Y. C. Song, S. Y. Seo, B. Y. Park, Y. K. Song, and H. B. Park, "Nonstationarity of Betas and Optimal Length of Beta Estimation Periods", *Asia-Pacific Journal of Financial Studies*, Vol. 11(1989), pp. 313-337(in Korean).

심병구, 송영출, 서상용, 박병렬, 송영균, 박헌봉, "베타위험의 불안정성과 최적추정기간에 관한 실증연구", 증권학회지, 제11권(1989), pp. 313-337.

Son, S. H., T. H. Kim, and B. H. Yoon, "Testing the Linear Asset Pricing Models in the Korean Stock Market", *Korean Journal of Financial Studies*, Vol. 38, No. 4(2009), pp. 547-568(in Korean).

손삼호, 김태혁, 윤보현, "한국 주식시장에서의 선형 자산가격결정모형 검증", 한국증권학회지, 제38권 제4호(2009), pp. 547-568.

Song, Y. C., "The Effects of Size and Book-to-Market Ratio on the Cross Sectional Returns", *Asia-Pacific Journal of Financial Studies*, Vol. 24, No. 1(1999), pp. 83-103(in Korean).

송영출, "규모와 가치비율의 수익률차이 설명력에 대한 연구", 증권학회지,

제24권 제1호(1999), pp. 83-103.

Song, Y. C. and J. K. Lee, "Empirical Analyses for the Estimation of Cost of Equity Capital by Considering Firm Size and Book-to-Market", *Korean Journal of Financial Management*, Vol. 141, No. 3(1997), pp. 157-181(in Korean).

송영출, 이진근, "자기자본비용의 추정에 관한 연구-규모와 장부가/시장가 요인을 고려한 실증분석", 재무관리연구, 제14권 제3호(1997), pp. 157-181.

Stambaugh, R. F., "On the Exclusion of Assets from Tests of the Two-Parameter Model: A Sensitivity Analysis", *Journal of Financial Economics*, Vol. 10(1982), pp. 237-268.

Stattman, D., "Book Values and Stock Returns", *The Chicago MBA: A Journal of Selected Papers*, Vol. 4(1980), pp. 25-45.

Sunwoo, S. H., Y. S. Yun, H. S. Kang, S. W. Kim, W. H. Lee, and S. K. Oh, "Overreaction and Firm Specific Anomalies in the Korean Stock Market", *Asia-Pacific Journal of Financial Studies*, Vol. 17, No. 1(1994), pp. 167-218(in Korean).

선우석호, 윤영섭, 강효석, 김선웅, 이원흠, 오세경, "한국주식시장에서의 과잉반응과 기업특성적 이례현상에 관한 연구", 증권학회지, 제17집 제1호 (1994), pp. 167-218.

Vassalou, M., "News Related to Future GDP Growth as a Risk Factor in Equity Returns", *Journal of Financial Economics*, Vol. 68(2003), pp. 47-73.

Yu, I. S., "Measuring Foreign Currency Risk Exposure and Its Risk Premium", *Korean Journal of Financial Management*, Vol. 17, No. 2(2000), pp. 229-256(in Korean).

유일성, "한국주식시장에서 환율위험노출과 환율위험 프리미엄 측정", 재무관리연구, 제17권 제2호(2000), pp. 229-256.

Yu, I. S., "Conditional Foreign Exchange Risk Premium in Korean Stock

Market", *Korean Journal of Financial Management*, Vol. 19, No. 1(2002), pp. 107-131(in Korean).

유일성, "한국주식시장에서 조건부 환위험프리미엄", 재무관리연구, 제19 권 제1호(2002), pp. 107-131.

Yun, S. Y., B. I. Ku, Y. H. Eom, and J. H. Hahn, "The Cross-section of Stock Returns in Korea: An Empirical Investigation", *Asian Review of Financial Research*, Vol. 22, No. 1(2009), pp. 1-43(in Korean).

윤상용, 구본일, 엄영호, 한재훈, "한국 주식시장에서 유동성 요인을 포함한 3요인 모형의 설명력에 관한 연구", 재무연구, 제22권 제1호(2009), pp. 1-43.

Yun, Y. S., S. H. Sunwoo, S. W. Kim, H. S. Jang, and H. S. Choi, "Characteristics of Stock Price Movements and Seasonal Anomalies in Korean Stock Market", *Asia-Pacific Journal of Financial Studies*, Vol. 17, No. 1(1994), pp. 121-166(in Korean).

윤영섭, 선우석호, 김선웅, 장하성, 최흥식, "한국주식시장에서의 주가변동 특성과 계절적 이례현상에 관한 연구", 증권학회지, 제17권 제1호(1994), pp. 121-166.

Any citation of this article must refer to the following: Kho, Bong-Chan, "The Impact and Role of Foreign Investors in Korea", Asian Review of Financial Research, Vol. 24 (2011), No. 1, pp. 231-273.

Chapter 2

The Impact and Role of Foreign Investors in Korea

Bong-Chan Kho*   Professor, Business School, Seoul National University

Abstract

This paper reviews major studies accumulated over the last two decades in finance literature on the impacts and roles of foreign portfolio investors in emerging markets, and more specifically, reviews the studies on Korea in detail. The Korean economy successfully overcame two financial crises in 1997 and 2008, and stands out as the 15th largest economy in the world based on GDP in 2009, with foreign equity ownership composing about 40% of total market capitalization. Such growth of the Korean economy could be partly due to the benefits of capital market liberalization policies conducted since 1992. In fact, the literature provides generally positive evidence of the benefits gained after liberalization through a reduction in the cost of capital, increased economic growth, and better corporate governance; however, it provides very little consensus on the destabilizing effect of foreign capital flows.

In reality, Korea experienced a severe credit crunch until early 2009 due to massive capital outflows during the global financial crisis, despite the Korean economy's sound corporate performance and ample foreign currency reserves. Hot money flowing into the Korean bond and stock markets reached 40 trillion won by the end of 2010, which require Korea to take steps to control a potential sudden outflow of these funds and further capital in flows. This aspect of foreign capital flows is potentially damaging for emerging markets and may substantially weaken the benefits of opening capital markets.

Regarding the issue of the information advantage between domestic vs. foreign investors, the empirical evidence in the literature is mixed and varies across studies, depending on the specific markets or countries examined and the specific methods or horizons employed for the comparison of investment performances across different types of investors. More comprehensive analysis in this area would be desirable.

Keywords   Foreign Investor, Liberalization, Integration, Destabilization, Emerging Markets, Korea

---

* **Address:** Seoul National University, Gwanak-ro, Gwanak-gu, Seoul 151-916, Korea; **E-mail:** bkho@snu.ac.kr; **Tel:** 82-2-880-8798.

This survey paper is prepared as a part of the knowledge database project by the Korean Finance Association. Helpful comments were received from Hee-Joon Ahn (editor), Kwangsoo Ko, and an anonymous referee. Research support from the Korean Finance Association and the Institute of Management Research at Seoul National University is greatly appreciated.

I. Introduction

Since the early 1990s, financial markets throughout the world have become more open to international investors. Many explicit and implicit barriers have disappeared and cross-border capital flows have been increasing steadily. However, the globalization process is still underway, and the degree of integration to world capital markets differs across emerging countries.[1] An important issue of this globalization process is to assess the potential impact and role of foreign investors in emerging markets, which has drawn considerable attention from academicians, practitioners and policymakers since the Mexican crisis in 1994 and the Asian crisis in 1997.

The increase in foreign investment flows to emerging markets is often considered beneficial as they provide more capital and lower the cost of capital for the emerging markets. The corresponding foreign investment subjects firms and countries to the discipline of capital markets, which leads to the economic growth of the emerging market.[2] Conversely, many argue that foreign portfolio flows, unlike foreign direct investment widely regarded as beneficial, are potentially damaging for emerging markets as they can easily pull out of the market at times of financial crisis. As a result, it has been argued that emerging markets are more vulnerable to vacillations in foreign portfolio flows (Stiglitz, 1998) and that the benefits from opening capital markets to foreign investors are substantially weakened or reversed.

It is therefore crucially important to understand whether this is the case. In fact, there has been a slow but steady change over the last decade in the attitude toward controls on excessive capital flows which can counter the po-

---

1) For a review on this, see Karolyi and Stulz (2003) and Stulz (2005). For the empirical evidence on the varying degrees of integration across countries, see Bekaert and Harvey (1995), Bekaert, Harvey, and Lumsdaine (2002), Carrieri, Errunza, and Hogan (2007), and Bekaert, Harvey, Lundblad, and Siegel (2010).
2) For the empirical evidence on these benefits of liberalization, see for instance, Bekaert and Harvey (1997, 2000), Henry (2000), Kim and Singal (2000), etc.

tential negative effects of such flows. In this regard, this survey paper reviews the most important papers in the literature on the various impacts and roles of foreign portfolio investors in emerging markets, and links them with those for Korean markets to see both what has already been done and what still needs to be done for Korea. The literature reviewed in this paper starts from the early 1990s when most emerging markets started their liberalization processes and comprehensive international stock market databases became available.

Korea is one of the emerging markets and it experienced large foreign capital outflows twice during both the Asian crisis in 1997 and the global financial crisis in 2008. Nonetheless, the Korean economy stands out as the 15th largest economy in the world based on the GDP in 2009. The Korean stock market started the liberalization process in early 1992 and lifted most foreign ownership restrictions in May 1998. Since then, the Korean economy successfully overcame the 1997 Asian crisis and restructured the country's economy. In this regard, the Korean market provides a good example to evaluate the impacts and roles of foreign investors in emerging markets. In this survey paper, we will review the existing studies on the impacts and roles of foreign investors in emerging countries as well as in Korea, and will discuss the benefits and costs of foreign capital flows with suggestions for future research topics that have not yet been examined.

This paper is organized as follows. Section II describes the recent evolution of foreign equity flows and liberalizations in Korea, and section III reviews the benefits and costs of capital market liberalizations documented in the literature. Specifically, studies on measuring the degree of capital market integration are reviewed, and studies on the impacts of the liberalizations on the cost of equity capital, volatility, and correlations are also examined. Finally, the review on foreign portfolio flows and potential destabilization effects is provided. Section IV reviews the recent evidence on financial globalization, governance, and home bias. Section V reviews studies on investment performance and information asymmetries between foreign vs. domestic investors. Section VI summarizes and concludes the paper.

II. The Recent Evolution of Foreign Equity Flows in Korea

Since the Korean stock market liberalization started in January 1992, the Korea Exchange (KRX) has grown continuously with the active participation of foreign investors.[3] KRX was ranked as the 10th largest exchange in the world in 2009 in terms of trading value (1.56 US$ tril.), 17th in terms of market capitalization (0.83 US$ tril.), and 9th in terms of the number of listed companies (1,788 firms), whereas it was ranked as the 4th in terms of market size among Asian markets.[4] At the end of 2009, about 28,000 foreign investors participated in the Korean market, including investors from the U.S. (35.3%), Japan (9.5%), the U.K. (6.7%), Canada (5.7%), Taiwan (3.0%), and others (39.8%).[5] The proportion of Korean market capitalization held by foreign investors as a group amounts to 30.4%, whereas that held by domestic institutions, individuals, and others are 12.0%, 34.6%, and 23.0%, respectively. Therefore, foreign investors are the largest investor group that has led the growth of the Korean stock market since its liberalization. It has been alleged that both the scale and quality of the Korean stock market and its listed companies have been improved with the increasing participation of foreign investors, including the introduction of advanced investment techniques and

---

3) The Korea Exchange (KRX) was established in January 2005, after merging the previous three separate exchanges: the Korea Stock Exchange (KSE), the Korea Futures Exchange (KFE) and the KOSDAQ markets.
4) These statistics are obtained from the website of the World Federation of Exchanges.
5) See Korea Exchange Fact Book (2010) for details.

the improvement of corporate governance systems.

<Figure 1> Month-end foreign ownership, KOSPI index, and Won/U$ exchange
rate from 1992/1 to 2010/10

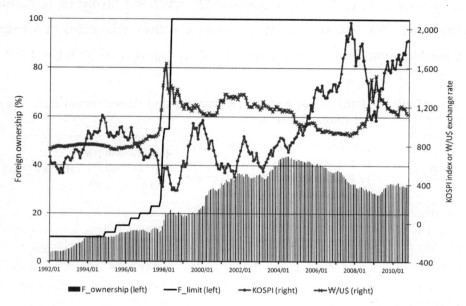

<Figure 1> shows the time-series plots of month-end foreign ownership, the KOSPI index, and the Won/U$ exchange rate (base rate) for the period from January 1992 to October 2010, obtained from KRX and the Bank of Korea's ECOS system. The solid stepped line depicts the foreign owner- ship limits imposed until May 25, 1998. For example, foreign investors as a group could not own more than 20% of a firm's shares just before May 2, 1997, when the limit increased to 23%. This limit then increased to 26% on November 3, to 50% on December 11, to 55% on December 30, 1997, and finally to 100% on May 25, 1998.[6] In addition, although not depicted

---

6) There were some exceptions to this complete lifting of the foreign ownership limit as some sectors and public corporations still had restrictions as in other countries shown in <Table 2> later, e.g., telecommunications (33%), airlines (50%), media (49%), and electricity (30%). Nonetheless, to avoid these foreign ownership limits, foreigners can access the Korean market by investing in country funds and ADRs launched in the U.S. At the end of 2010, Korea had 17 U.S. dollar denominated country funds and 17 non-U.S. dollar country funds, many

in the figure, there was another dimension of the foreign ownership limit applied to each individual foreign investor, which was 5% of a firm's shares just before May 2, 1997 when it increased to 6%. It then increased to 7% on November 3, to 50% on December 11, 1997, and finally to 100% on October 1, 1998. The stock market responses to these relaxations of foreign ownership limits were positive in general as reported in <Table 1>.

<Table 1> Foreign ownership limit changes and market responses in Korea (Data: KRX)

Dates	Limits to foreigner as a group (Limits to each individual foreigners)	KOSPI index (return) on the announcement date	Return over 1 week	Return over 1 month	Market phase
1992.01.03(Open)	10%(3%)	624.23(+2.2%)	-0.76%	10.76%	Correction
1994.12.01	12%(3%)	1,066.21(-0.8%)	-1.20%	-4.90%	Down trend
1995.07.01	15%(3%)	909.59(+1.7%)	4.11%	3.85%	Parallel
1996.04.01	18%(4%)	878.47(+0.5%)	-0.16%	9.45%	Parallel
1996.10.01	20%(5%)	789.47(-0.03%)	1.03%	-2.74%	Down trend
1997.05.02	23%(6%)	706.10(+0.4%)	-2.62%	7.41%	Parallel
1997.11.03	26%(7%)	511.66(+2.9%)	2.67%	-25.87%	Plunge
1997.12.11	50%(50%)	377.37(-5.6%)	5.21%	20.89%	Bottom
1997.12.30	55%(50%)	385.49(+2.4%)	14.34%	42.73%	Bottom
1998.05.25	Abolished	331.90(-6.8%)	1.45%	-9.44%	Correction

The foreign ownership depicted in <Figure 1> is measured as a ratio of the total value of foreign holdings to the total market value of all firms listed in KRX.[7] It shows that at the beginning of January 1997, foreign investors owned 12.5% of Korean stock market capitalization, which steadily increased over the next seven years, reaching the highest point of 43.8%

---

of which have a long history, originating in 1981.

7) The foreign ownership includes both foreign direct and portfolio investments, although the ratio of the foreign direct investment to the overall foreign ownership is very small, ranging from 4~5% over the sample period. Therefore, we will focus on the behavior and roles of foreign portfolio investments in this paper.

<Table 2> Restrictions on foreign equity investments in major Asian developing countries as of October 2010

Country	Restrictions on foreign equity investments
Korea	• Fully allowed after lifting its 55% limit in 1998 • Some sectors still have limits, e.g., telecommunications (33%), airlines (50%), media (49%), electricity (30%), etc.
China	• Only allowed to invest in B shares (denominated in U$ in Shanghai; HK$ in Shenzhen), except for the "Qualified Foreign Institutional Investors" (QFII) • Most sectors have stringent limits of 50%, e.g., service industries.
India	• Only allowed for "Foreign Institutional Investors (FIIs)", "Non-Resident Indians (NRIs)", and "Persons of Indian Origin (PIOs)", whose limits are 24%, 10%, and 10%, respectively • Most sectors have stringent limits, e.g., transportation, agriculture (0%), telecommunications (75%), and financial services (26~87%).
Indonesia	• Fully allowed after lifting its 49% limit in 1997~1998 • Many sectors still have stringent limits, e.g., publishing (0%), telecommunications, and transportation (50%).
Israel	• Fully allowed after lifting its 20% limit in 2003 • Some sectors have stringent limits, e.g., defense industry (15%).
Malaysia	• Fully allowed, but most sectors have limits, e.g., telecommunications (30%), infrastructure (30%), service providers (49%) including Malaysian stockbrokers
Philippines	• Fully allowed, but most sectors have limits of 40%, e.g., primary and service sectors
Saudi Arabia	• First opened to foreign capital in 2008, but only indirectly through funds • Many industries like mining, oil and gas, transportation, publishing, and media are closed by a "negative list" produced by the government. Financial services are allowed up to 60%.
Taiwan	• Fully allowed after lifting the QFII program in 1996, which was first introduced in 1990 • Some sectors still have limits, e.g., telecommunications (60%), electricity (50%), and high-speed railway (49%).
Thailand	• Fully allowed, but most sectors are subject to a 50% limit

in July 2004. This trend then shifted to a gradual decline over the next five years, reaching a low of 28.0% in March 2009. The steady increase in foreign ownership over the first seven years in the figure depicts the growing inflows of foreign portfolio investments in response to the successful recovery of the Korean economy under the IMF bailout program after the dramatic plunge of the KOSPI index and Korean won value during the late 1997 Asian crisis period. However, the increasing trend in foreign ownership ended in July 2004 and began a gradual decline through the outbreak of the global financial crisis in 2008. It is interesting to see that during this time period, the KOSPI index almost tripled from 735 in July 2004 to 2,064 in October 2007, when foreign investors pulled out by more than 10% of the Korean stock market capitalization.[8] Probably, the investment capital withdrawn from Korea during this time period could have been used for other investment vehicles in other markets, such as the mortgage-related products in the U.S., which eventually led to bubbles in real estate markets and the global financial crisis in late 2008.

Ⅲ. The Benefits and Costs of Capital Market Liberalizations

1. The Measure and Degree of Capital Market Integration

In an efficient and globally integrated equity market, assets of identical risk should command the same expected return, regardless of where they are traded. Although the liberalization process of financial markets around the world in recent decades has increased the level of global integration, implicit barriers such as political risk, information asymmetry, investor protection, and market regulation can still segment markets (Bekaert, Harvey, Lundblad and Siegel, 2010). In fact, the integration process is grad-

---

8) The rapid increase of the KOSPI index during this three-year period from 2004 to 2007 was largely due to the nation-wide popularity of mutual fund investments in Korea, which resulted in a larger fraction of institutional holdings in Korea than before.

ual and takes many years with occasional reversals. It usually involves major reforms and developments in the economy as well as the financial sector, such as the relaxation of legal barriers, launching of country funds and ADRs, improvements in governance and information environment, and so on. Since the transition from a segmented market to an integrated market should affect expected returns, volatilities, and correlations with world markets, the question of identifying the degree of integration and measuring its impact is central to international finance literature.

To model such a gradual change in the market integration process, Bekaert and Harvey (1995) provide a return-based methodology for 12 emerging markets from 1976 to 1992. Their econometric model nests the polar cases of complete separation and complete integration in a regime-switching framework, and allows a conditionally expected excess return on a market i, $E_{t-1}[r_{i,t}]$ to depend on both its variance and covariance with the world market excess return, $r_{w,t}$. That is,

$$E_{t-1}[r_{i,t}] = \phi_{i,t-1}\lambda_{t-1}Cov_{t-1}[r_{i,t}, r_{w,t}]$$
$$+ (1 - \phi_{i,t-1})\lambda_{i,t-1}Var_{t-1}[r_{i,t}]$$

(1)

where the parameter $\phi_{i,t-1}$ is the conditional probability of being in a regime of complete integration, and thus is regarded as an integration measure. In a completely segmented market (i.e., $\phi_{i,t-1} = 0$), the variance of the market itself is the only relevant measure of the expected return, whereas in a completely integrated market (i.e., $\phi_{i,t-1} = 1$), only the covariance counts. Therefore, the integration measure, $\phi_{i,t-1}$, will increase as the covariance becomes a more important determinant of the expected return. Although this model does not necessarily reflect equilibrium expected returns, it provides a reasonable approximation to expected returns. Bekaert and Harvey (1995) estimate the model using a multivariate GARCH regime-switching method on a country-by-country basis, and show that only four of the 12 emerging markets have fairly high degrees of integration in the early 1990s, and that the Korean market is one of those with a high integration measure, ranging from 0.85 to 1.00 over the entire sample period. This seems strange from the viewpoint of foreign ownership limits prohibiting direct access to the Korean market until January 1992. However, it makes sense when we consider that there were alternative ways for foreigners to access the Korean market through country funds and ADRs launched in the U.S. market in 1984 and 1990, respectively, long before the start of the official liberalization in January 1992. Therefore, it may be a mistake to conclude that a market is segmented based on statutory investment restrictions or legal barriers.

In contrast to Bekaert and Harvey's (1995) focus on a return-based measure of market integration, Bekaert, Harvey and Lumsdaine (2002) use broader sets of financial and macroeconomic variables that are likely related to the integration process for 20 emerging markets from 1980 to 1996, and identify structural break points in those multiple time-series. Their results are based on a VAR model with a Wald-type test to identify unknown structural breaks in the data, and show that the estimated break dates usually occur later than the official liberalization dates, highlighting the important distinction between the official liberalization and market integration. For example, Korea is estimated to have roughly four breaks which correspond to economic events: 1) September 1980: there was liberalization of foreign investment rules in Korea, which opened the market to foreign direct investment 2) August 1984: the Korea Fund was launched, which gave foreign investors their first chance to make portfolio investments in Korea 3) September 1988: sweeping liberalization plans were announced, but were not implemented until later and 4) January 1992: the official liberalization program began, allowing foreigners to own up to 10% of the capitalization of a company.[9] Taken together, regulatory changes or liberalization plans will have little impact on the degree of integration if they fail to attract foreign portfolio inflows.

Over a decade of liberalization in the 1990s, the integration process stalled in some emerging markets and even reversed after the Mexican crisis in 1994, the Asian crisis in 1997, and the Russian default in 1998.[10] Since then, foreign investors' access to emerging equity markets has begun again actively, and Carrieri, Errunza and Hogan (2007) revisited the issue of time-varying market integration for eight emerging markets over the period from 1977 to 2000 (Argentina, Brazil, Chile, India, Korea, Mexico, Taiwan, and Thailand). Their approach is based on the theoretical international asset pricing model (IAPM) of Errunza and Losq (1985), allowing for a partial segmentation in which both local and foreign components can impact expected returns.[11] The model states that,

$$E[R_i] = R_f = R_f + AMCov[R_i, R_w] + (A_u - A)M_I Cov[R_i, R_I | \underline{R_e}] \qquad (2)$$

where $E[R_i]$ is the expected return on the ith security in the Ith market that is accessible only to its nationals, R_f is the risk-free rate, $A(A_u)$ is the aggregate risk aversion coefficient for all (Ith) market investors, $R_W(R_I)$ is the return on the world (Ith) market portfolio, $M(M_I)$ is the market value of the global (Ith) market portfolio, and $\underline{R_e}$ is the vector of returns on all securities that can be bought by all investors irrespective of their nationality. Thus, the expected return on the ith security in a partially segmented market com-

---

9) A number of companies were already marked by more than 10% foreign ownership at that time, and thus, the government had to raise the foreign ownership limit to 25% for those 45 firms soon after the official liberalization.

10) For example, Malaysia defied a recovery package prescribed by the IMF, and imposed capital controls in 1998 to block foreign speculators from betting against the Malaysian Ringgit. Taiwan also announced in 1998 that it was reconsidering its plan for a full liberalization of capital flows in light of the Asian crisis.

11) Alternatively, one can use factor models with factor mimicking portfolios built on firm characteristics. See for example, Griffin (2002) and Hou, Karolyi and Kho (2010), who extend the domestic version of Fama and French's (1993) three-factor model to an international context.

mands a global risk premium and a super risk premium that is proportional to the conditional market risk. In sum, the model incorporates the intermediate case depending on the barriers to investments, and reduces to one of the two polar cases of a full integration or a complete segmentation.

The above model can be expressed in terms of the ineligible security market index R_I (i.e., ineligible for holdings by foreign investors) by aggregating the ineligible set of securities as follows:

$$E[R_I - R_f] = AMCov[R_i, R_w] + (A_u - A)M_I Var[R_I | \underline{R_e}] \qquad (3)$$

The above theoretical model suggests that the degree of integration depends critically on the availability of substitute assets that allow investors to duplicate returns on unavailable emerging markets' assets (R_I) through homemade diversification, thereby effectively integrating the emerging markets even if explicit barriers to portfolio flows may be in place. Following this model prediction, an "integration index" (Π) can be constructed as follows,

$$\Pi = 1 - Var[R_I | \underline{R_e}] / Var[R_I] \qquad (4)$$

By definition, this index lies within the range (0, 1) with a value of 1 for complete integration (i.e., $Var[R_I | \underline{R_e}] = 0$) and 0 for complete segmentation (i.e., $Var[R_I | \underline{R_e}] = Var[R_I]$). This measure is empirically similar to the R^2 of a regression of R_I on $\underline{R_e}$, which is the ratio of the unspanned variance to the total variance of the country index.

Using a GARCH-in-mean methodology to estimate the variation of market integration over time, Carrieri, Errunza and Hogan (2007) show that mild segmentation has been a reasonable characteristic for the eight emerging markets. Based on the integration index Π, none of the countries appears to be com-

<Figure 2> Integration index for Korea[12]

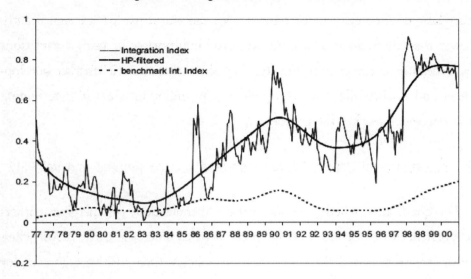

<Figure 2> Integration index for Korea[12]

pletely segmented: Mexico is the most integrated with $\Pi = 0.605$ throughout the sample period and India is the most segmented with $\Pi = 0.249$. The time-series plots of the index Π and its filtered series uncover the evolution toward more integration for all eight countries. For example, <Figure 2> shows that the Korean market has become more integrated in recent years. It appears mildly segmented throughout the sample period with an average index of 0.359, remaining at low levels until the mid-1980s and reaching an average index of 0.529 since 1992. This result is consistent with the availability of country funds since the mid-1980s and ADRs since the mid-1990s, as well as the gradual lifting of foreign ownership restrictions since early 1992. However, it is somewhat different from that of Bekaert and Harvey (1995), which suggests that Korea is fully integrated throughout the sample period. Interestingly, the benchmark Π (estimated without considering country funds and ADRs) in <Figure 2> is always lower than the Π, indicating that country funds and ADRs are very

---

12) This figure is reproduced from <Figure 1> of Carrieri, Errunza and Hogan (2007), with permission, 2009 © Cambridge Journals.

important in measuring the integration index. In addition, they show that the correlations of country index returns with the world market are significantly lower than the estimated Π s, implying the impropriety of using correlations as a measure of integration. Finally, they show that financial market development and financial liberalization policies play important roles in determining the degree of market integration.

2. The Impacts of Capital Market Liberalizations on Returns and Volatility

The question of whether capital market liberalizations of emerging markets are beneficial or not has been intensely debated since the early 1990s, when most countries started their liberalization policies. One positive argument for liberalization is that liberalization attracts foreign capital to finance the economic growth of emerging markets. The corresponding foreign capital flows can achieve a better opportunity to diversify globally, and the improved risk sharing through global diversification leads to a lower cost of equity capital for emerging markets. Such a liberalization process would also increase correlations with the world market returns, which would then shrink both diversification benefits and the magnitude of the reduction in the cost of equity capital.

Conversely, the argument against liberalization is that foreign capital flows, especially so-called hot money, are allegedly highly speculative and sensitive to fluctuations in the interest rates, exchange rates and economic growth of emerging markets. These speculative flows can result in a volatile fluctuation in foreign capital flows in response to even a small shock to the emerging market. The resulting excess volatility in stock prices would make investors demand a higher risk premium and lead to a higher cost of equity capital. Indeed, foreign investors have often been blamed for excessive volatility after liberalization, particularly during the Mexican crisis of 1994 and the Asian crisis of 1997. Therefore, understanding the effect of capital market liberalization on returns and volatility is of critical importance in judging the costs and benefits of liberalization policies.

The empirical evidence for the reduction in the cost of equity capital after liberalization has been largely positive in the literature. For example, Bekaert and Harvey (1997) examine the volatility in 20 emerging markets before and after liberalization, because volatility is a key input for the cost of equity capital calculation for a partially or completely segmented market based on models described by eq. (1) or (3) in subsection 3.1. They use an extended ARCH-type conditional model that explicitly accounts for leptokurtosis and skewness and allows world and local information to change over time in both expected returns and conditional variance processes. Using the IFC equity indices from 1976 to 1992, they show that the average conditional variance two years after major liberalization dates decreases significantly by more than 6% compared to the conditional variance two years before the dates. They also conclude that a decrease in volatility of this magnitude can have an important effect on the cost of equity capital in an emerging market.

Later, Bekaert, and Harvey (2000) focus on directly measuring the change in the cost of equity capital for the same 20 emerging markets with a more careful choice of liberalization dates. They build on a present value model to motivate the use of dividend yields as a measure of the cost of equity capital. They first identify the date of effective integration using three different definitions for liberalization: the actual lifting of investment restrictions, the introduction of ADRs/country funds, and the structural break of U.S. equity capital flows into a specific emerging market. For example, Korea's official liberalization began in January 1992, but the first country fund and ADR were launched in 1984 and 1990, respectively, and the structural break in cumulative net U.S. equity capital flows to Korea was estimated to be in March 1993. Across these three definitions of liberalization, their estimates show that the cost of equity capital decreases only by 5 to 75 basis points after liberalization across countries, which is somewhat less than we expected. A missing factor in this analysis would be the potential effect on economic growth, which can further decrease the cost of equity capital in the longer-term.[13]

Regarding correlations with the world market return after liberalization, Bekaert and Harvey (2000) find a small increase in the correlation, whose magnitude is unlikely to deter foreign investors from seeking diversification and affect the magnitude of the reduction in the cost of equity capital. Therefore, the small decrease in the cost of equity capital after liberalization is puzzling, because one would expect a greater decrease in the risk premium with higher weight given to the covariance component after the liberalization of emerging markets that are generally characterized by high return volatility and low covariance. This puzzling finding is also closely related to the major source of the home bias puzzle. That is, the dramatic change from local to global pricing after liberalization would take place only if foreign investors as a mean-variance optimizer begin to hold stocks of the liberalizing country in proportion to their weight in the world market portfolio. In reality, however, we continue to observe investors overweight domestic securities in their portfolios, which deters them from obtaining the full benefits of global pricing after liberalization.[14]

Other studies also provide evidence for the reduction in the cost of equity capital after liberalization. Henry (2000) estimates the abnormal return of 12 emerging equity market indices during the liberalization period, and finds that stock prices appreciate over the eight months prior to the market opening. Kim and Singal (2000) also examine 20 emerging markets from 1976

---

13) For example, Bekaert, Harvey, and Lundblad (2005) show that equity market liberalizations lead to a 1% increase in annual real economic growth on average, even after controlling for other variables related to economic growth.

14) This incomplete diversification could remain because the gains from global diversification may not be large enough to make foreign asset holdings worthwhile. We will review some other reasons for the home bias documented in the literature in section IV.

to 1996, and find that stock returns increase immediately after the market opening but fall subsequently once adjusted to new information on the market opening, supporting the evidence for a lower cost of equity capital.

Concerning the impact on volatility upon liberalization, the empirical evidence has been mixed. For example, Choe, Kho, and Stulz (1999) and Karolyi (2002) find that foreign investors pursue positive feedback and herding strategies in Korea and Japan, respectively, but they do not find that foreign investors have a destabilizing impact on stock prices. Kim and Singal (2000) find no increase in the volatility of stock returns after the opening of 20 emerging markets. They also provide evidence that the volatilities of inflation and exchange rates in emerging markets have dropped since stock market liberalization, suggesting that a market opening has generally favorable effects on emerging economies and market efficiencies. Chen and Lu (2007) also find an overall improvement in the quality of Chinese A- and B-share markets after their liberalization policies between 2001 and 2002. Bekaert and Harvey (1997) find that volatility decreases significantly in most emerging markets after liberalization, even after controlling for all of the potential impacts on volatility, which can in turn have an important effect on the cost of equity capital in emerging markets.

Conversely, an earlier paper by Kim and Singal (1994) find a volatility increase after liberalization, when based on average volatilities. Bekaert and Harvey (2000) also find a small but mostly insignificant increase in volatility following liberalizations. Bae, Chan, and Ng (2004) also find that the returns on stocks more open to foreign ownership (investible stocks) are more volatile for the period from 1989 to 2000 across 33 emerging markets, even after controlling for country, industry, firm size, and turnover. They also show that a highly investible portfolio is subject to a larger world market exposure than a non-investible portfolio. We will review some more studies

on the impact of foreign portfolio flows on volatility, contagion, destabilization, and the liquidity of emerging markets in the next section.

3. Foreign Portfolio Flows and Destabilization

It has been often believed that the increase in foreign portfolio flows
to emerging markets after capital market liberalizations is beneficial as these
flows provide more capital and lower the cost of capital. This increase
in foreign portfolio flows facilitates the flow of capital to firms with the
best investment opportunities regardless of their location, and leads to a
lower cost of capital and higher economic growth in emerging markets.
Empirical evidence for this positive effect of foreign portfolio flows has
been provided in the literature as reviewed in the previous subsection.
However, following the Mexican crisis of 1994 and the Asian crisis of 1997,
considerable attention has been drawn to the negative role of foreign portfolio investors as their large capital outflows during crisis periods can destabilize the emerging markets. Some policymakers have attributed the financial
crises to foreign speculators, and have advocated strong controls on capital
flows. Therefore, it is important to properly assess the potential destabilization effects of foreign portfolio flows before we conclude whether the benefits of foreign portfolio flows are substantially weakened or not.

With a free flow of capital across borders, markets are more connected than
they used to be, and the risk premium is determined more globally so that
changes in the risk premium in a market affect the risk premium in other
markets, which is consistent with an efficient incorporation of information
on the changes in common factors. This global pricing naturally induces some
extents of comovements in stock prices as well as volatility spillovers across
markets. Therefore, comovements or volatility spillovers could arise from either a rational incorporation of information or the irrational behavior of invest-

ors such as contagion or overreaction to news in one market.[15] To distinguish between the information effect and the contagion effect, one must undo the natural changes in comovements estimated from an asset pricing model before drawing conclusions about contagion[16] (Bekaert, Harvey, and Ng, 2005).

In addition, it is often argued that the trades of foreign investors show a strong tendency for herding and positive feedback trading, which are known by theoretical models such as DeLong et al. (1990) to have a destabilizing impact on prices as positive feedback traders can push prices away from fundamentals when they form a herd. However, positive feedback trading and herding are not necessarily destabilizing, if, for example, investors trading on fundamentals are sufficiently powerful in the market to prevent prices from moving away from fundamental values, or if positive feedback traders are trading in response to information about fundamentals. Therefore, in order to assess whether positive feedback trading and herding are destabilizing or not, one must examine reversals following positive feedback trading and herding, and see how much permanent impact remains afterwards. This is because as long as information does not change, the demand for stocks remains perfectly elastic at a given price in an efficient market, and positive feedback trading and herding would have a negligible impact on stock prices if they are formed purely for liquidity reasons, rather than for information motives.

The empirical question on the destabilization effect of foreign equity flows was examined by Choe, Kho, and Stulz (1999), who used a unique order and trade data in Korea at the stock level with the identification of investor types for each trade from December 1996 to December 1997. The results show strong evidence of positive feedback trading and herding by foreign investors in Korea before the Korean economic crisis period. However, the

---

15) Contagion is usually defined as the correlation between markets in excess of what is implied by economic fundamentals. However, there is considerable disagreement regarding the definition of contagion.

16) Another possibility is that many of the comovements and volatility spillovers could be spurious, having to do with infrequent trading.

positive feedback effect weakens and herding falls during the three months of the Korean economic crisis. As the positive feedback effect dissipates, trades by foreign investors are less likely to be destabilizing the Korean stock market over the sample period. Further, they test whether large block purchases and sales by foreign investors have a permanent impact on prices, and obtain the result that the effects of these trades are incorporated into prices within 10 minutes with no subsequent lasting impact. This implies that the market adjusted quickly and efficiently to large sales by foreign investors, and these sales were not followed by negative permanent impacts.

Unlike the work of Choe et al. (1999) for Korea, Karolyi (2002) documents a significant structural break in flows and returns in Japan during the Asian crisis, but, surprisingly, he finds that positive feedback trading intensifies with no clear evidence of destabilization. Kim, and Wei (2002) also investigate the positive feedback trading of foreign investors in Korea using monthly flow data from December 1996 to June 1998, and find strong positive feedback trading behavior during the crisis months. They attribute the differences between their results and those of Choe et al. to the fact that their dataset contains holdings (but not trades) of investors and to the fact that their sample period is longer by 6 months. However, because their crisis period until June 1998 is too long, it would be difficult to draw conclusions about the importance of feedback trading in the development of the crisis. It is possible that most of their feedback trading occurred in 1998 when the market started recovering from the crisis.

Concerning the well-known asymmetric volatility puzzle observed in Korea and other countries as well, Khil, Kim and Lee (2009) test an interesting hypothesis whether the asymmetric volatility arises more often from stock trades that are submitted by more risk averse investors, and confirm empirical evidence for this hypothesis using daily trade data for all stocks at KRX from 2000 to 2007. That is, as we expected, stocks with higher proportions of individual trading tend to show higher asymmetric volatility, while stocks with higher proportions of institutional investors and foreign investors tend to show lower asymmetric volatility. The results remain robust even after we control for firm size and leverage.

Kim and Singal (2000) examine many aspects of the changes in 20 emerging economies around market openings, i.e., changes in the level and volatility of stock prices, exchange rates, and inflation rates. They find that stock returns increase immediately after market openings but fall subsequently once adjusted to new information on market opening. There is neither an increase in the volatility of stock returns, nor an increase in inflation or an appreciation of exchange rates. Rather, inflation seems to decrease after market openings as do the volatilities of inflation and exchange rates. Also, stock markets become more efficient as determined by testing the random walk hypothesis. Taken together, their results suggest that market openings have generally favorable effects on emerging economies.

Concerning the relationship between foreign equity flows and liquidity, Agudelo (2010) studies seven emerging markets (India, Indonesia, Korea, Philippines, South Africa, Taiwan, and Thailand) and finds that foreign trade has a negative but transitory impact on the overall liquidity of an emerging market on a daily basis, implying that foreign investors demand liquidity more aggressively and incorporate market-wide information more actively. In contrast, foreign ownership in the market is positively related to im-proved liquidity. Therefore, foreign investors demand liquidity aggressively in the very short term, but have a lasting positive effect on the liquidity of emerging markets. Vagias and van Dijk (2010) also find supportive evi-dence for foreign investors providing liquidity on local markets in 46 coun-tries from 1995 to 2008, and do not support the view that foreign investors destabilize local markets through an adverse impact on liquidity.

Although most of the academic research mentioned above finds little clear evidence of the destabilization effect of foreign capital flows, many policy-makers and practitioners in emerging markets still face various uncertainties associated with foreign capital flows. In fact, there has been a slow but steady change in the attitude toward controls on excessive capital flows since the Asian crisis of 1997 when capital controls were perceived as taboo. A recent IMF study recognizes capital controls as part of the policy options available to the governments of emerging economies to counter the potential negative effects of sudden foreign capital inflows (See Ostry et al., 2010). This change in the perception of capital controls is similar at the World Bank, which recently states that Asian countries may need capital controls as the quantitative easing by the U.S. from November 2010 would create asset bubbles in the region.[17] Korea already experienced massive capital out-flows during the global financial crisis in 2008, which led to a severe credit crunch until early 2009, despite the Korean economy remaining in good shape (unlike in 1997) with sound corporate performance and ample foreign currency reserves. It is alleged that hot money flowing into Korean bond and stock markets had already reached 40 trillion won by the end of 2010[18], and that the Korean government needs to take steps to control a potential sudden outflow of these funds and further capital inflows.

4. The Effects of Foreign Investment Restrictions on Stock Prices

Another line of research related to market integration is the examination of the effect of foreign investment restrictions (explicit barrier) on stock prices in a partially segmented market. This has been done for Thailand by Bailey

17) Sri Mulyani Indrawati, a World Bank managing director, mentioned as such in a recent interview. Porter (2010) contains the details of it.
18) See Financial Supervisory Service of Korea (2011) for details.

and Jagtiani (1994), for China by Bailey (1994) and Chen, Lee and Rui (2001), for Mexico by Domowitz, Glen and Madhavan (1997), for Finland by Hietala (1989), and for Switzerland by Stulz and Wasserfallen (1995).

Bailey and Jagtiani (1994), for example, study the case of Thailand from 1988 to 1992, where shares that have reached foreign ownership limits are traded on two separate boards: the Main board for resident Thais and the Alien board for nonresident foreigners. If foreign ownership drops below legal limits, foreign class shares revert to local class shares which can be bought by both locals and foreigners. The results show significantly positive Alien board price premiums of 19 percent on average, which is consistent with other studies for other markets, e.g., Singapore, Malaysia, Philippines, Indonesia, Mexico, Finland, and Switzerland, where foreign class shares tend to command higher prices than local class shares.[19] Why do we observe such premiums for the foreign class shares? Four alternative hypotheses can be considered to answer this question.

H1: The differential risk loadings and risk premiums for local and foreign investors result in cross-sectional differences in the Alien Board price premiums.

H2: The downward-sloping demand curve for foreigners is due to greater deadweight costs such as political risk, information acquisition costs, withholding taxes, or transaction costs, implying that stocks with relatively tight foreign ownership limits will be in high demand and will exhibit large Alien Board price premiums.

H3: The liquidity argument of Amihud and Mendelson (1986) suggests

---

19) An exception to this is China, where a large price discount of 52~66% for B shares (foreign shares) relative to A shares (domestic shares) are observed from 1992 to 1997. Bailey (1994) and Chen, Lee and Rui (2001) attribute such price discounts in B shares primarily to illiquid B-share markets as B shares are available only to foreigners even when the foreign ownership limits are not binding. Korea does not have such separate forms of foreign and local class shares.

that relatively illiquid stocks have a higher expected return and are priced lower to compensate for the increased trading costs. This predicts that foreign investors will offer relatively high prices for relatively liquid Alien Board stocks.

H4: There is firm-specific information available to foreign investors who prefer assets with more information, suggesting that large, well-known firms with sufficient information will exhibit high Alien Board price premiums.

Bailey and Jagtiani (1994) find supporting evidence for hypotheses H2, H3, and H4 above, that the Alien board price premiums in Thailand are positively correlated with proxies for the severity of foreign ownership limits, liquidity, and information availability. This result suggests that high trading activity, good information flow, and the privatization of large, well-known companies will attract more foreign investors, and that it would be beneficial for emerging markets to include local and foreign class shares designed to accommodate such interests. Stulz and Wasserfallen (1995) also provide an event study regarding the removal of barriers, showing that the price of Nestle's restricted shares increased sharply when these shares became available to all investors.[20] This evidence suggests that the presence of differential demands for domestic shares by domestic and foreign investors creates incentives for firms to restrict their supply of shares available to foreign investors to increase the price of these shares. Domowitz, Glen and Madhavan (1997) also investigate the pricing of restricted and unrestricted shares in Mexico and find supporting evidence for the hypothesis that the demand curve for the Mexican shares by foreign investors is downward sloping.

---

20) Nestle's unrestricted shares are bearer shares that can be held by all investors irrespective of their residence or nationality, whereas restricted shares are registered shares that can only be held by resident investors until November 17, 1988, when all investors are allowed to hold registered shares.

IV. Financial Globalization, Governance, and Home Bias

The home bias puzzle refers to the phenomenon that investors overweight domestic securities in their portfolio. This directly contradicts the prediction of traditional portfolio theory that if investors are mean-variance optimizers in a world of perfect financial markets, they should hold the world market portfolio and there should be no home bias. Many authors have attempted to explain the home bias puzzle as reviewed in Karolyi and Stulz (2003). Explanations proposed in the literature include explicit barriers to international investment, information asymmetries, different inflation risks, hedging of human capital or non-traded assets, and behavioral bias toward local stocks. Stulz (2005) proposes a new theory in which the home bias persists even in the absence of the above barriers because rulers of sovereign states and corporate insiders pursue their own interests at the expense of outside investors (twin agency problems). When these twin agency problems are significant, concentrated ownership becomes optimal, which limits economic growth, risk-sharing, financial development, and the benefits of financial globalization. However, the empirical evidence in this vast literature has not yet succeeded in explaining the home bias completely.

From a corporate finance view, Dahlquist et al. (2003) point out the importance of float adjustment for the world market portfolio (the world float portfolio) in explaining the home bias. That is, foreign portfolio investors can only hold shares not held by insiders, which constitutes the upper bound for foreign ownership. Across the 51 countries they examine, 32% of the shares on average are held by controlling shareholders, and thus, are not available for trading by foreign investors. Taking this into account, they show that the home bias becomes significantly smaller for the U.S. and other countries. Using Swedish firm-level data, they confirm that foreign investors as a whole are close to holding the Swedish float portfolio.

Kho, Stulz, and Warnock (2009) further look at the role of controlling shareholders and monitoring shareholders in determining the float shares available for foreign investors, and find two main effects of governance on the home bias. The first is the "direct effect" of governance on the home bias: poorer governance leads to a higher level of insider ownership, which limits portfolio holdings by foreign investors. The second is the "indirect effect" of governance on the home bias: poorer governance also implies higher ownership by domestic monitoring shareholders due to their comparative advantage in monitoring controlling shareholders and, as the ownership of these investors increases, less float shares are available for foreign portfolio investors.[21] Using the U.S. Treasury data on the holdings of U.S. investors in foreign countries from 1994 to 2004, they find that the home bias decreases in countries where the stake of insiders falls, which supports the direct effect of governance. Further, using Korean firm-level ownership data, they find that the foreign ownership of Korean firms grows in firms where insider ownership falls and in firms where holdings by domestic monitoring share-holders fall, which confirms both direct and indirect effects of governance.

Concerning the question of whether foreign portfolio investments increase firm value through better corporate governance in emerging markets, Kim, Kim, and Kwon (2009) study domestic and foreign blockholders in Korea who switch their investment purpose from passive to active in 2005 but are not likely to engage in control-related activities, and show that the positive valuation effect around the time of the switch disclosure is greater for foreign blockholders who can conduct better monitoring activities. They also find evidence of significant increases in dividend payout ratios by 7.3%

---

21) Choi and Seo (2008) provide evidence of monitoring activities by domestic institutions in Korea, whose monitoring is far stronger than that by foreign investors.

for switched firms with high free cash flow, though not significant for those firms targeted by foreign switchers. Kim, Sung, and Wei (2010) further provide evidence for the positive valuation effect associated with better corporate governance brought by foreign investors, using the universe of foreign blockholding announcement data in Korea from 1998 to 2006. They find that the stock prices of Korean companies tend to increase (decrease) subsequent to buy (sell) announcements by foreign blockholders crossing the 5% threshold. Further, the positive (negative) valuation effect of a buy (sell) announcement by foreign blockholders only occurs when the buy (sell) is conducted by foreign investors from countries with good corporate governance. They also find that the tunneling tendency of family-controlled conglomerates (chaebols) tends to decline after the increased foreign blockholdings, which is consistent with the positive valuation effect due to better corporate governance brought by foreign investors.

V. Information Asymmetries and Investment Performances

1. Evidence for the Information Disadvantage of Foreign Investors

Foreign investors are often said to be disadvantaged in trading local stocks because of their inferior information, time zone differences, distances, etc. This view of information asymmetry in favor of domestic investors has been one of the leading explanations for the home bias puzzle in the previous section. However, there is a controversy on this view as there are competing arguments that support both sides of the view. One argument is that domestic investors have an advantage because local information is naturally more accessible to local investors. Conversely, the opposite argument is that foreign investors have an information advantage because they possess a superior investment expertise and experience. Empirical evidence for this issue differs vastly across studies, depending on the specific markets or countries examined and on the specific methods or horizons employed for the comparison of investment performances across different types of investors.

Choe, Kho, and Stulz (2005) find evidence supportive of foreign disadvantages, using a measure based on the volume-weighted average price, the so called "vwap", of all trades on a day for each stock. This measure has an advantage in that it relies less on the models of expected returns and there is no need to take risk into account. Their results, based on the transaction data for Korea from 1997 to 1998, show that foreign money managers buy at higher prices than domestic investors and sell at lower prices for medium and large trades, incurring greater transaction costs of 37 basis points on a round trip trade compared to domestic money managers. This magnitude can have a substantial adverse impact on the performance of a foreign money manager, and is not explained by firm and stock characteristics. Alternatively, three potential explanations for the disadvantage of foreign investors are investigated: 1) Foreign investors are not at a disadvantage but are simply more impatient such that they pay more to liquidity providers. In this case, their trades should have more of a temporary impact on prices than a long-term impact; 2) Foreign investors are better informed, so that their trades have a larger permanent impact on prices; 3) Foreign investors make their trades after prices have already moved against them. Among these three possibilities, they find support for the third explanation of the return-chasing behavior of foreign investors.

In a different perspective, Choe, Chung, and Lee (2008) find that large domestic individual investors play the most important role in moving stock prices, and thus, are better informed. They use a measure called the weighted price contribution (WPC) of trades of Barclay and Hendershott (2003) with four years of transactions data (1997~2000) for the largest 100 stocks traded on KRX. The WPC for an investor type is basically the weighted average of the price contribution of the investor's trades for a given time period across stocks, where the weight for each stock's price contribution is the ratio of the absolute value of the cumulative return over the time period. However, this measure does not determine how much of the price impact will be permanent or temporary. If the price impacts for large domestic individual investors turn out to consist of mostly temporary reversals, then their inference on the information advantage can be also reversed or weakened.

Other studies supportive of foreign disadvantages in KRX include the following: Kho and Kim (2005) implement the vwap measure for the KOSPI 200 index futures data from 1996 to 1999, and confirm that foreign investors are at a disadvantage in the index futures market as well. Park, Bae, and Cho (2006), using daily transaction data for all stocks on the KRX from 1995 to 2002, find that domestic individual investors perform better than foreign or domestic institutional investors, in terms of the implicit transaction costs and the performance measure on both short- and long-term horizons. They emphasize the importance of taking investment horizons into account when comparing investment performance across different investor types, and show that the poor performance of foreign investors lessens as the investment horizons lengthen.

Kang, Lee, Lee, and Park (2010) propose another potential reason for the return-chasing behavior of foreign investors in the KRX. They analytically show that investors paying less attention to a temporary component-driven price change will have a more extrapolative expectation for the future price of a domestic stock. This hypothesis can be regarded as a rational response of informationally disadvantaged investors who pay less attention to a temporary component-driven price change and respond more in line with the price change. Their empirical results, based on the KOSPI 200 index futures quote data from 2005 to 2006 as a measure of the expected future spot price, confirm that foreign investors extrapolate more than domestic individuals and institutions because they pay the least attention to a temporary component-driven price change (possibly due to their longer investment horizons). However, their results about the hypothesis that more extrapolative behavior arises from informational disadvantages are inconclusive.

For Indonesia, Dvorak (2005) uses transaction data for the 30 most liquid stocks from 1998 to 2001, and shows that domestic investors earn higher profits than foreign investors. In addition, he finds that global brokerages have better expertise in picking long-term winners, and suggests that the combination of local information and global expertise can lead to a higher profit. For the Korean Treasury Bond (KTB) futures market, Oh and Hahn (2006) find results similar to those of Dvorak (2005) and show that domestic institutions such as futures companies and banks have a short-lived informational advantage and that foreign investors are better at long-term position trading in the KTB futures market. Hau (2001) investigates the data on German equity trading profits of 756 professional traders located in 23 different cities and eight European countries (over four months from September 1998 to December 1998), and finds that foreign traders in non-German-speaking cities have inferior proprietary trading profits. Further analysis shows that local proximity to the corporate headquarters of the traded stock provides an information advantage for high-frequency (intraday) trading. This result supports the presence of international information barriers in equity trading, which has been regarded as a leading explanation for the home bias puzzle.

Similar results are also found by Shukla and van Inwegen (1995), who show that U.K. fund managers investing in the U.S. equity market under-perform relative to their U.S. colleagues even after controlling for differential tax and fund expenses. Kang and Stulz (1997) also find evidence that foreign investors in Japan hold more stocks of large firms for which the information asymmetry is presumably smaller, which is consistent with the information disadvantage of foreign investors. They also provide evidence that foreign investors' performance is not distinguished from that of domestic investors, using monthly data for 18 years. However, it has to be noted that their return measurement interval is monthly, which differs from the reality of the investment positions changing daily or even hourly.

2. Evidence for the Information Advantage of Foreign Investors

Although the studies detailed in the previous subsection provide evidence in support of the information disadvantage of foreign investors, the following studies are supportive of foreign advantages. For example, Grinblatt and Keloharju (2000) and Seasholes (2000) argue that foreign investors perform better than domestic investors due to their better expertise and talent. Specifically, Grinblatt and Keloharju (2000) calculate profit measures based on daily positions for the 16 largest Finnish stocks from 1995 to 1996, and find that foreign investors pursue momentum strategies and achieve superior performance by buying more stocks that perform well over the next 6 months than domestic individual investors. In contrast, domestic investors are found to pursue contrarian strategies and exhibit inferior performance. However, their sample period is too short for them to conduct a sensitivity analysis for various holding period returns. Seasholes (2000), in his study of Taiwan, finds that foreign investors tend to buy prior to positive and sell prior to negative earnings surprises while domestic investors do the opposite. He also interprets the VAR-based predictive power of foreign net inflows as an information advantage of foreign investors. However, foreign equity flows could appear to predict returns due to the price pressures resulting from foreign trades. Karolyi (2002) also finds that foreign investors in Japanese equity markets outperformed Japanese individuals and institutions during the Asian financial crisis period.

Regarding the earnings-related information in Korea, Eom, Hahn, and Sohn (2010) find results similar to those of Seasholes (2000) in that foreign investors' trades prior to earnings announcements predict earnings surprises over the sample period from 2000 to 2005 whereas those of domestic institutions do not. Hong and Shin (2007) also provide supporting evidence that net stock purchases by foreign investors tend to precede upward revisions of earnings forecasts whereas domestic individuals' trading flows exhibit the opposite pattern. For a subsample of stocks with large revisions in analysts' forecasts, net stock purchases by foreign investors also tend to predict a positive stock return, which confirms the earnings-related information advantage of foreign investors.

Oh and Hahn (2008) examine the cumulative returns over a long period of time for domestic and foreign investors, using the transaction data of the largest 100 stocks listed on the KRX from 2000 to 2005. They find that the cumulative return of foreign investors over the full 6-year period is significantly higher than that of domestic investors by about 61.3%. Further, their decomposition of the cumulative return shows that foreign investors outperform domestic investors in all three components (asset allocation, portfolio re-composition, and intra-day trading) over the full 6-year period, and the superior performance of foreign investors mainly comes from the informational advantage in their asset allocation strategies. However, it is worth noting that the cumulative return measure over the full 6 years would be potentially biased in favor of investors with a longer investment horizon. In fact, as the horizon becomes shorter, the performance of foreigners becomes lower than that of domestic investors, especially at the horizons of 1 and 2 years, indicating the importance of the difference in investment horizons across different investors when comparing their investment performance.

Ko and Kim (2004) also support the evidence for the information advantage of foreign investors in Korea by showing that the portfolio of foreign investors outperforms that of domestic investors over the period from 1993 to 2003, where portfolios are formed annually with 30 stocks that have the highest ownership proportion for each investor type. The results hold even after the risk is adjusted based on the Fama-French three-factor model. In addition, they show that foreign investors prefer low book-to-market growth stocks with large capitalization, high ROE, and low turnover ratios, whereas domestic individuals prefer value stocks with characteristics opposite to the preferences of foreign investors. Ko and Lee (2003) also find evidence that foreign investors' net buy ratios have short-term return predictability in both daily and weekly intervals from 1993 to 2001. The return predictability becomes stronger after the structural change due to the Asian crisis in 1997.

Concerning the question of the information advantage of foreign investors in options markets, Ahn, Kang, and Ryu (2008) use the KOSPI 200 index options trade data for the year 2002 and estimate the adverse-selection cost (as a proxy for the degree of informed trading) from the spread decomposition model developed by Madhavan, Richardson, and Roomans (1997). They first provide evidence for the presence of informed traders in the index options market by showing that the adverse-selection cost constitutes a significant portion of the option spread, and then examine which types of investors are better informed by comparing the magnitude of adverse-selection costs for trades initiated by three investor types: domestic individuals, domestic institutions, and foreign investors. The result shows that foreign investors are better informed compared to domestic investors, and among domestic investors, domestic institutions are better informed than domestic individuals.

In a subsequent paper, Ahn, Kang and Ryu (2010) further confirm that foreign investors have information advantages over domestic investors as they are more involved in information-motivated trading and incur the highest adverse-selection costs. However, this evidence for the information advantages of foreign investors in the index options market may not be directly applicable to stock markets. This is because in stock markets, both macroeconomic and firm-specific information are important, whereas in an index options market, it is mostly macroeconomic information that drives the prices. The physical and linguistic barriers of foreigners may render more difficulties in accessing the firm-specific information for stock markets. In contrast, foreign investors have an advantage in accessing macroeconomic information for index options markets as the yare generally institutional investors and have superior experience and expertise.

VI. Summary and Conclusions

This survey paper reviews major studies accumulated over the last two decades in finance literature on the various impacts and roles of foreign portfolio investors in emerging markets, and more specifically, reviews the studies done on Korea in detail. This survey work will contribute to the literature by organizing previous studies in Korea, making them verifiable and comparable to each other, and eventually narrowing the gap between the research performed in Korea and the research performed mostly in the U.S.

The literature reviewed in this paper began in the early 1990s, when most emerging markets started their liberalization processes and comprehensive international stock market databases became available. Korea is one of the emerging markets and it experienced large foreign capital outflows twice during the Asian crisis in 1997 and the global financial crisis in 2008. Nonetheless, the Korean economy successfully overcame the two crises and stands out as the 15th largest economy in the world based on the GDP in 2009. The foreign equity inflows to Korea have steadily increased toward a foreign equity ownership of about 40% of total market capitalization. It has been alleged that the increasing participation of foreign investors has improved both the scale and the quality of the Korean stock market and its listed companies by introducing advanced investment techniques and better corporate governance systems. In fact, such growth of the Korean economy could be partly due to the benefits of liberalization as Bekaert, Harvey, Lundblad, and Siegel (2010) note that the benefits are more attainable for countries with better institutions. The empirical evidence also has been largely positive regarding the questions on the reduction in the cost of equity capital, higher economic growth, and better corporate governance after liberalization, but provides little clear support for the destabilization effect of foreign capital flows.

However, after huge capital outflows during the Asian crisis in 1997, there has been a slow but steady change in the attitude toward controls on excessive capital flows which can counter the potential negative effects of such flows. Now, after experiencing the global financial crisis in 2008, both the IMF and the World Bank recognize capital controls as part of the policy options available to emerging economies. In fact, Korea experienced a severe credit crunch until early 2009 due to massive capital outflows during the global financial crisis. Moreover, hot money flowing into Korean bond and stock markets had already reached 40 trillion won by the end of 2010, which requires Korea to take steps to prepare for a potential sudden outflow of these funds and curb further capital inflows.

Regarding the question on the information advantage between domestic vs. foreign investors, there are two competing arguments that support both sides of the question, and the empirical evidence is also mixed and varies across studies, depending on the specific markets or countries examined and on the specific methods or horizons used for the comparison of investment performances across different types of investors. A typical approach in this analysis is that we classify investors into three or more groups of investors (e.g., domestic investors, domestic institutions, and foreign investors) and examine their average performance within each investor group. We probably cannot tell a priori whether a particular investor group will always show superior performance on average at any time in any market. We also cannot tell a priori whether a particular investor group will bring more outliers of superior performances that make the group appear to be informed traders on average. In this sense, the empirical results could naturally differ across studies and across markets and time. More comprehensive analysis would be desirable in this area.

References

Agudelo, D. A., "Friend or Foe? Foreign Investors and the Liquidity of Six Asian Markets", *Asia-Pacific Journal of Financial Studies*, Vol. 39, No. 3(2010), pp. 261-300.

Ahn, H.-J., J. Kang, and D. Ryu, "Informed Trading in the Index Option Market: The Case of KOSPI 200 Options", *Journal of Futures Markets*, Vol. 28, No. 12(2008), pp. 1118-1146.

Ahn, H.-J., J. Kang, and D. Ryu, "Information Effects of Trade Size and Trade Direction: Evidence from the KOSPI 200 Index Options Market", *Asia-Pacific Journal of Financial Studies*, Vol. 39, No. 3(2010), pp. 301-339.

Amihud, Y. and H. Mendelson, "Asset Pricing and the Bid-Asked Spread", *Journal of Financial Economics*, Vol. 17(1986), pp. 223-247.

Bae, K., K. Chan, and A. Ng, "Investibility and Return Volatility", *Journal of Financial Economics*, Vol. 71(2004), pp. 239-263.

Bailey, W., "Risk and Return on China's New Stock Markets: Some Preliminary Evidence", *Pacific-Basin Finance Journal*, Vol. 2(1994), pp. 243-260.

Bailey, W. and J. Jagtiani, "Foreign Ownership Restrictions and Stock Prices in the Thai Capital Market", *Journal of Financial Economics*, Vol. 36(1994), pp. 57-87.

Barclay, M. J. and T. Hendershott, "Price Discovery and Trading After Hours", *Review of Financial Studies*, Vol. 16(2003), pp. 1041-1073.

Bekaert, G. and C. Harvey, "Time-Varying World Market Integration", *Journal of Finance*, Vol. 50(1995), pp. 403-444.

Bekaert, G. and C. Harvey, "Emerging Equity Market Volatility", *Journal of Financial Economics*, Vol. 43(1997), pp. 29-78.

Bekaert, G. and C. Harvey, "Foreign Speculators and Emerging Equity

Markets", *Journal of Finance*, Vol. 55(2000), pp. 565-613.

Bekaert, G., C. Harvey, and R. Lumsdaine, "Dating the Integration of World Capital Markets", *Journal of Financial Economics*, Vol. 65(2002), pp. 203-247.

Bekaert, G., C. Harvey, and C. T. Lundblad, "Does financial liberalization spur growth?", *Journal of Financial Economics*, Vol. 77(2005), pp. 3-55.

Bekaert, G., C. Harvey, C. T. Lundblad, and S. Siegel, "What Segments Equity Markets?", *Working Paper*, Columbia University(2010).

Bekaert, G., C. Harvey, and A. Ng, "Market Integration and Contagion", *Journal of Business*, Vol. 78(2005), pp. 39-69.

Carrieri, F., V. Errunza, and K. Hogan, "Characterizing World Market Integration through Time", *Journal of Financial and Quantitative Analysis*, Vol. 42(2007), pp. 915-940.

Chen, G. M., B.-S. Lee, and O. Rui, "Foreign Ownership Restrictions and Market Segmentation in China's Stock Markets", *Journal of Financial Research*, Vol. 24(2001), pp. 133-155.

Chen, D.-H. and C.-Y. Lu, "The Effects of Market Liberalizations on Return, Risk, and Co-movement of China's A- and B-Share Stock Markets", *Asia-Pacific Journal of Financial Studies*, Vol. 36, No. 5(2007), pp. 695-730.

Choe, H., J. M. Chung, and W.-B. Lee, "Distribution of Private Information Across Investors: Evidence from the Korea Stock Exchange", *Asia-Pacific Journal of Financial Studies*, Vol. 37, No. 1(2008), pp. 101-137.

Choe, H., B.-C. Kho, and R. M. Stulz, "Do Foreign Investors Destabilize Stock Markets? The Korean Experience in 1997", *Journal of Financial Economics*, Vol. 54(1999), pp. 227-264.

Choe, H., B.-C. Kho, and R. M. Stulz, "Do Domestic Investors Have an Edge? The Trading Experience of Foreign Investors in Korea", *Review of Financial Studies*, Vol. 18, No. 3(2005), pp. 795-829.

Choi, S. K. and J. W. Seo, "Institutional Ownership and Accounting Transparency", *Asia-Pacific Journal of Financial Studies*, Vol. 37, No. 4(2008), pp. 627-673.

Dahlquist, M., L. Pinkowitz, R. M. Stulz, and R. Williamson, "Corporate Governance and the Home Bias", *Journal of Financial and Quantitative Analysis*, Vol. 38(2003), pp. 87-110.

DeLong, J. B., A. Shleifer, L. H. Summers, and R. J. Walmann, "Positive Feedback Investment Strategies and Destabilizing Rational Speculators", *Journal of Finance*, Vol. 45(1990), pp. 379-395.

Domowitz, I., J. Glen, and A. Madhavan, "Market Segmentation and Stock Prices: Evidence from an Emerging Market", *Journal of Finance*, Vol. 52(1997), pp. 1059-1085.

Dvorak, T., "Do Domestic Investors Have an Informational Advantage? Evidence from Indonesia", *Journal of Finance*, Vol. 60(2005), pp. 817-839.

Eom, Y., J. Hahn, and W. Sohn, "Post-Earnings-Announcement Drift and Foreign Investors' Trading Behavior in Korea", *Working Paper*, KDI School(2010).

Errunza, V. and E. Losq, "International Asset Pricing under Mild Segmentation: Theory and Test", *Journal of Finance*, Vol. 40(1985), pp. 105-124.

Fama, E. F. and K. R. French, "Common Risk Factors in the Returns on Stocks and Bonds", *Journal of Financial Economics*, Vol. 33(1993), pp. 3-56.

Financial Supervisory Service of Korea, *Report on Foreign Investors' Stock Ownership for December 2010*, Financial Supervisory Service of Korea, 2011.

Griffin, J. M., "Are the Fama and French Factors Global or Country Specific?", *Review of Financial Studies*, Vol. 15(2002), pp. 783-803.

Grinblatt, M. and M. Keloharju, "The Investment Behavior and Performance of Various Investor Types: A Study of Finland's Unique Data Set",

Journal of Financial Economics, Vol. 55(2000), pp. 43-67.

Hau, H., "Location Matters: An Examination of Trading Profits", *Journal of Finance*, Vol. 56(2001), pp. 1951-1983.

Henry, P. B., "Stock Market Liberalization, Economic Reform, and Emerging Market Equity Prices", *Journal of Finance*, Vol. 55(2000), pp. 529-564.

Hietala, P., "Asset Pricing in Partially Segmented Markets: Evidence from the Finnish Market", *Journal of Finance*, Vol. 44(1989), pp. 697-718.

Hong, K. and I. Shin, "Analysts' Earnings Forecasts and Trading Flows by Various Investor Types in the Korea Stock Exchange", *Asia-Pacific Journal of Financial Studies*, Vol. 36, No. 3(2007), pp. 321-349.

Hou, K., G. A. Karolyi, and B.-C. Kho, "What Factors Drive Global Stock Returns?", *Review of Financial Studies*, Vol. 24, No. 8(2010), pp. 2527-2574.

Kang, H. C., D. W. Lee, E. J. Lee, and K. S. Park, "Domestic vs. Foreign Investors: Who Extrapolate and Why?", *Working Paper*, Korea University (2010).

Kang, J. and R. M. Stulz, "Why is there a Home Bias? An Analysis of Foreign Portfolio Equity Ownership in Japan", *Journal of Financial Economics*, Vol. 46(1997), pp. 3-28.

Karolyi, G. A., "Did the Asian Financial Crisis Scare Foreign Investors out of Japan?", *Pacific Basin Finance Journal*, Vol. 10(2002), pp. 411-442.

Karolyi, A. and R. M. Stulz, "Are Assets Priced Locally or Globally?", in *The Handbook of the Economics of Finance*, edited by G. Constantinides, M. Harris, and R. M. Stulz, New York, North-Holland Publishers(2003), pp. 975-1020.

Khil, J., N. Y. Kim, and E. J. Lee, "Investors' Trading Behavior and Asymmetric Volatility", *Journal of Money and Finance*, Vol. 23, No. 3(2009), pp. 25-49(in Korean).

길재욱, 김나영, 이은정, "투자자별 거래행태와 비대칭 변동성", 금융연구,

제23권 제3호(2009), pp. 25-49.

Kho, B.-C. and J.-W. Kim, "Trading Performance of Domestic and Foreign Investors in KOSPI200 Index Futures Markets", *Korean Journal of Futures and Options*, Vol. 13, No. 1(2005), pp. 1-27(in Korean).
고봉찬, 김진우, "KOSPI 선물시장과 내외국인의 투자성과분석", 선물연구, 제13권 제1호(2005), pp. 1-27.

Kho, B.-C., R. M. Stulz, and F. Warnock, "Financial Globalization, Governance, and the Evolution of the Home bias", *Journal of Accounting Research*, Vol. 47, No. 2(2009), pp. 597-635.

Kim, E. H. and V. Singal, "Opening up of Stock Markets: Lessons from Emerging Economies", *Working Paper*, Virginia Polytechnic Institute (1994).

Kim, E. H. and V. Singal, "Stock Market Openings: Experience of Emerging Economies", *Journal of Business*, Vol. 73(2000), pp. 25-66.

Kim, W., W. Kim, and K.-S. Kwon, "Value of Outside Blockholder Activism: Evidence from the Switchers", *Journal of Corporate Finance*, Vol. 15(2009), pp. 505-522.

Kim, W., T. Sung, and S.-J. Wei, "When Does Foreign Portfolio Investment Increase Corporate Value in an Emerging Market Economy?", *Working Paper*, KDI School of Public Policy and Management(2010).

Kim, W. and S.-J. Wei, "Foreign Portfolio Investors Before and During a crisis", *Journal of International Economics*, Vol. 56(2002), pp. 77-96.

Ko, K. and K. Kim, "Portfolio Performance and Characteristics of Each Investor Type: Individuals, Institutions, and Foreigners", *Korean Securities Association Journal*, Vol. 33, No. 4(2004), pp. 35-62(in Korean).
고광수, 김근수, "투자 주체별 포트폴리오 특성과 성과 분석 : 개인, 기관, 외국인", 증권학회지, 제33권 제4호(2004), pp. 35-62.

Ko, K. and J. Lee, "Foreigner's Trading Information and Stock Market: Ten Year's Experience of Stock Market Liberalization", *Korean Journal of*

Finance, Vol. 16, No. 1(2003), pp. 159-192(in Korean).

고광수, 이준행, "외국인 거래 정보와 주식시장 : 개방 10년의 경험", 재무연구, 제16권 제1호(2003), pp. 159-192.

Korea Exchange, *KRX Fact Book 2009*, Korea Exchange, 2010.

Madhavan, A., M. Richardson, and M. Roomans, "Why Do Security Prices Change? A Transaction-level Analysis of NYSE Stocks", *Review of Financial Studies*, Vol. 10(1997), pp. 1035-1064.

Oh, S. H. and S. B. Hahn, "Trading Strategy and Performance by Investor Types in Korean Treasury Bond Futures Market", *Korean Journal of Finance*, Vol. 19, No. 2(2006), pp. 73-103(in Korean).

오승현, 한상범, "국채(KTB)선물시장의 투자자 유형별 투자성과 및 거래형태", 재무연구, 제19권 제2호(2006), pp. 73-103.

Oh, S. H. and S. B. Hahn, "Analyzing the Cumulative Returns on Investments of Domestic and Foreign Investors in Korean Stock Market", *Asia-Pacific Journal of Financial Studies*, Vol. 37, No. 3(2008), pp. 537-567(in Korean).

오승현, 한상범, "내국인과 외국인의 주식투자 누적손익 요인 분석", 증권학회지, 제37권, 제3호(2008), pp. 537-567.

Ostry, J., A. Ghosh, K. Habermeier, M. Chamon, M. Qureshi, and D. Reinhardt, "Capital Inflows: The Role of Controls", *IMF Staff Position Note*, IMF, 2010.

Park, K., K. Bae, and J. Cho, "Analyses on Performance by Different Types of Investors in Korean Stock Market", *Asia-Pacific Journal of Financial Studies*, Vol. 35, No. 3(2006), pp. 41-76(in Korean).

박경인, 배기홍, 조진완, "한국 증권시장의 투자자 유형에 따른 성과분석", 증권학회지, 제35권 제3호(2006), pp. 41-76.

Porter, B., "World Bank Says Asia May Need Capital Controls to Curb Bubbles", *Bloomberg*, No. 9(2010).

Seasholes, M. S., "Smart Foreign Traders in Emerging Markets", *Working*

Paper, University of California at Berkeley(2000).

Shukla, R. K. and G. B. van Inwegen, "Do Locals Perform Better Than Foreigners? An Analysis of UK and US Mutual Fund Managers", *Journal of Economics and Business*, Vol. 47(1995), pp. 241-254.

Stiglitz, J., "Boats, Planes and Capital Flows", *Financial Times*, March 25(1998).

Stulz, R. M., "The Limits of Financial Globalization", *Journal of Finance*, Vol. 60(2005), pp. 1595-1638.

Stulz, R. M. and W. Wasserfallen, "Foreign Equity Investment Restrictions, Capital Flight, and Shareholder Wealth Maximization: Theory and Evidence", *Review of Financial Studies*, Vol. 8(1995), pp. 1019-1057.

Vagias, D. and M. A. van Dijk, "International Capital Flows and Liquidity", *Working Paper*, Erasmus University(2010).

Any citation of this article must refer to the following: Eom, Kyong Shik, "Market Microstructure in the Korean Financial Markets: A Survey", Asian Review of Financial Research, Vol. 24 (2011), No. 2, pp.525-620.

Chapter 3

Market Microstructure in the Korean Financial Markets: A Survey

Kyong Shik Eom*   Associate Professor, College of Business Administration, University of Seoul

Abstract

We provide the first comprehensive review of the market microstructure literature on the Korean financial markets, published in the five leading Korean journals from 1990 to mid-2010. We also offer some perspective on the literature for investors, exchange officials, policy makers, and regulators and provide a roadmap for future research endeavors. This paper includes the following five main categories: (1) micro aspects of the microstructure world: orders and trades, basic market quality, price discovery, and trading mechanisms; (2) trading protocols: rules and regulations related to trading; (3) market transparency; (4) market macrostructure; (5) expansion of market microstructure to the fields of investments and corporate finance. We find that the current status of the Korean market microstructure research is as follows. The research in the Korean market microstructure has been disproportionately concentrated into the two categories of micro aspects and trading protocol. However, most of them were conducted during the 1990s, which has limited the perspectives on the academic and policy implications by periods, subjects, and trading protocols. The research on the categories of transparency and market macrostructure is very limited, even though these areas contain features of Korean markets that are unique among world markets. The research of market microstructure combined with investments has been fairly active, whereas that combined with corporate finance is at its inception.

Keywords   Market Microstructure, Market Macrostructure, Expansion to Investments and Corporate Finance, Korean Stock Markets

---

* **Address:** University of Seoul, 13 Siripdae-gil, Dongdaemun-gu, Seoul 130-743, Korea; **E-mail:** kseom@uos.ac.kr; **Tel:** 82-2-2210-5362.

It is an honor to write a survey for this field, which I have found endlessly fascinating throughout my career. I would like to express my deepest gratitude to Professors Robert Anderson and Jong-Ho Park, for their help on my understanding of the theoretical and empirical market microstructure. I am indebted to many research fellows, counterparties, and policy makers at KSRI, KRX, and financial watchdogs, who have sharpened my understanding of real-world market microstructure. I also would like to thank two anonymous referees and all the scholars who have made the great contributions to the market microstructure in the Korean financial markets surveyed here. This paper is prepared as part of the 2010 knowledge database project by the Korean Finance Association (KFA), and financially supported by the KFA. All errors are mine.

I. Introduction

Market microstructure is a branch of finance, defined as "the study of the process and outcomes of exchanging assets under a specific set of rules (O'Hara, 1995)." In contrast to the traditional equilibrium models for asset pricing, theoretical market microstructure models reflect not only the trading mechanisms of the real world, but also the informational asymmetries among market participants. Hence, market microstructure allows us to discuss the positive and normative aspects of price formation and discovery, transaction costs, informational disclosure, trading mechanisms, etc., all of which are very significant for policy makers and regulators mindful of market integrity and investor protection. For this reason, we have witnessed a tremendous growth in the academic research in this field throughout the major industrial countries, especially since the publication of two seminal papers by Glosten and Milgrom (1985) and Kyle (1985) on information-based models.[1] The availability of trade and quote (TAQ) data at much lower cost, due to the rapid advance of information-technology (IT), has contributed greatly to the rapid development of empirical work in market microstructure.

Korean financial scholars have developed a substantial body of market microstructure literature, primarily empirical in nature. Korea has benefited from a very well-designed TAQ data set since the mid-1990s, which has inspired empirical work, especially in relation to stock markets. This paper provides the first comprehensive review of the market microstructure literature on the Korean financial markets.[2] Our main objectives are first, to summarize

---

1) Prior to the information-based models, there were many influential studies such as Demsetz (1968), Garman (1976), and especially much research on inventory models such as Stoll (1978) and Amihud and Mendelson (1980).

2) There are some books and papers providing valuable summaries of market microstructure literature in contexts other than Korea. Among books, O'Hara (1995) offers an excellent and detailed survey of the theoretical literature in market microstructure, while Hasbrouck (2007) focuses on exemplifying the empirical literature and

all the papers related to Korean market microstructure issues published in the five leading Korean journals from 1990 to mid-2010; second, to offer some perspective on the literature for investors, exchange officials, policy makers, and regulators; and third, to provide a roadmap for future research endeavors.

Market microstructure literature addresses a wide range of issues. This breadth arises from three separate dimensions. The first dimension is the central idea in market microstructure, that asset prices need not equal the full-information expectations of value because of various frictions (Madhavan, 2000); this is closely related to the field of investments, which studies the equilibrium value of financial assets. The second dimension is the interaction of market microstructure with traditional corporate finance, because differences between the price and value of assets clearly affect financing and capital structure decisions. The third dimension is the application of market microstructure to a wide variety of financial markets, including stock markets, bond markets, derivatives markets, foreign exchange (FX) markets, and others; note that each of these markets has domestic and international components, and that all have differing trading operations, regulatory supervision, and so forth.

To reflect these multi-faceted aspects of market microstructure research, we organize all the academic research papers included in this survey into the following five main categories:

- **Micro Aspects of the Microstructure World: Orders and Trades, Basic**

Stoll (2003) relates both. Lyons (2001) examines foreign exchange (FX) markets using market microstructure approach. Harris (2003) focuses on practitioners' usage, not on academic literature, providing a general conceptual overview of trading and the organization of markets. De Jong and Rindi (2009) examine the recent developments in this area, reflecting more IT-related trading mechanisms such as electronic order book and various order types. Cohen, Maier, Schwartz, and Whitcomb (1986) offer a survey of the early literature in the area, especially based on inventory model. Among papers, Madhavan (2000) surveys the theoretical, empirical, and experimental literature on market microstructure relating to price formation, market structure and design, transparency, and applications to other areas of finance. Biais, Glosten, and Spatt (2005) survey market microstructure based on subjects, providing insights on adverse selection, inventory costs, market powers, degree of transparency, use of call auctions, pricing grid, and the regulation of competition between liquidity suppliers or exchanges. Goodhart and O'Hara (1997) survey the empirical literature focusing on FX markets.

Market Quality, Price Discovery, and Trading Mechanisms[3] — this topic relates orders and trades (including block trading, day-trading, and spoofing), basic market quality (including spread, volume, volatility, market impact cost, and asymmetric information risk), short-term (intraday) return predictability (including price discovery), and trading mechanisms.

- **Trading Protocols: Rules and Regulations Related to Trading** — this category covers the literature on trading rules and regulations designed to create a fair and orderly trading environment in Korea. Specifically, we include minimum tick size, liquidity providers, price-limit systems, sidecar systems (including program trading), and short sales (including stock lending and credit balance).

- **Market Transparency** — the papers in this category deal with how the revelation of information about the trading process affects the strategies of traders, and in turn market quality. We include the issues of pre-trade transparency and post-trade anonymity.

- **Market Macrostructure** — this area includes stock market design, especially the hierarchy of the Korean stock markets including the main board, the new (or growth) market, and the organized over-the-counter (OTC) market. We also include the issue of cross-listing between Korean and foreign stock markets.

- **Expansion of Market Microstructure to the Fields of Investments and Corporate Finance** — in this survey, the expansion to investments includes return behavior, the relationship between volume and volatility, the lead-lag effect of volume, and the roles of liquidity and private information risk in asset pricing. The expansion to corporate finance includes the relationship between ownership holdings by investor type

---

3) Market microstructure addresses the functional aspects of trading process: (1) price formation, (2) price discovery/trade execution, (3) clearing and settlement. However, since the Korean literature primarily addresses the second point, we have chosen the given, more narrow, description.

and informational asymmetry, and research combining corporate finance issues with asset pricing using the market microstructure variables.

Any survey will, by necessity, be selective and this is especially so for a field as large as market microstructure. Even though we try to include all the papers published in the five leading Korean journals since 1990, the related literature is so vast that we must necessarily omit some influential and important work. We must also inevitably limit the range of our survey since market microstructure research frequently crosses into other areas of finance. For example, we do not generally include literature associated with trading strategies, traders' types, and other financial markets, since this will be covered by the surveys of Behavioral Finance (Byun and Kim), Behavior of Foreign Investors (Kho), Derivatives (Kim), and Foreign Exchange (Park), planned by the Korea Finance Association simultaneously with this paper. If papers significantly focus on market microstructure such as day-trading and spoofing, however, we include them. The same principle is also applied to subjects related to returns and volatility, and specific information such as analysts' grades. We will make some brief comments on other financial markets in our concluding remarks. This paper presents an overview of the literature, attempting to synthesize all of the work within a common framework as much as possible, rather than just summarizing the contributions of individual papers in detail.

This paper proceeds as follows: Section II summarizes the literature on the basics of market microstructure including orders and trading, basic market quality, price discovery, and trading mechanisms. Section III surveys the literature related to trading protocols. Section IV deals with market transparency. Finally, Sections V and VI survey market macrostructure and the expansion of microstructure to the fields of investments and corporate finance, respectively. Section VII concludes this paper.

II. Micro Aspects of the Microstructure World: Orders and Trades, Basic Market Quality, Price Discovery, and Trading Mechanisms

The Korea Exchange (KRX) was formed in 2005 from the consolidation of the Korea Stock Exchange (KSE), a new (or growth) market (KOSDAQ), and the Korea Futures Exchange (KOFEX).[4] For clarity, we use KSE (or KOSPI), KOSDAQ, and KOFEX for papers published prior to 2005. Even after 2005, we continue to use these acronyms if we need to clarify the specific market within KRX.

1. Orders and Trades

KRX is an order-driven market in which buyers and sellers competitively place their orders through its Automated Trading System and the orders are automatically matched.[5] In contrast to the major international (especially European) stock markets that do not have market makers but allow many types of orders, KRX allows only the following order types: market order, limit order, limit to market-on-close order, immediately-executable limit order, and best limit order. KRX also allows to member firms or customers IOC (immediate or cancel) or FOK (fill or kill) execution conditions to market orders, limit orders, and immediately-executable limit orders. Since December 7, 1998, KRX has not opened the market on Saturday (previously, it was open 9:30~11:30) and since May 22, 2000, it has operated continuously from open to close (previously, it closed for

---

4) It also *legally* owns an IT company (Koscom) and the Korea Securities Depository (KSD) as affiliates. Due to the peculiar circumstances in the Korean financial markets and regulations, however, those two companies do exert their own management decisions as if they were independent companies.

5) KRX adopted the liquidity provider (LP) system for ELW in December 1, 2005 and for illiquid stocks in January 2, 2006. LP is a market maker with fewer privileges and responsibilities than market makers. Hence, KRX is not a pure order-driven market any longer.

lunch from 12:00 to 13:00). Trading hours in regular sessions are 09:00 ∼ 15:00 (quotation receiving hours are 08:00 ∼ 15:00), whereas off-hours sessions run from 7:30 to 8:30 and 15:10 to 18:00 (quotation receiving hours are 15:00 ∼ 18:00). The principle of price, time, and trade-size priority is applied.

1.1 Orders

An order is a trader's firm commitment to trade a security under specific conditions which may include price, size, and clearing and settlement arrangements. In general, an order is classified into a type by the combination of a basic order with three execution (or validity) conditions. The basic order usually consists of a market order, limit order, market-to-limit order or iceberg order. The three execution conditions are the execution condition for continuous trading (e.g., IOC; FOK), validity constraints (e.g., good-for-day; good-till-date; good-till-cancelled), and trading restrictions (e.g., opening auction only; closing auction only). Of course, there are many other additional order types such as hidden order, peg order, and stop order, among others.

As we can see from the definition, an order plays a significant role as the essential means through which a trader carries out his/her trading strategy. Notwithstanding that, there are only a limited number of papers concerning orders in the Korean stock markets, and they focus on issues of market- and limit-order dynamics. This mainly comes from the fact that only a very few order types are allowed in practice in the Korean stock markets.

Park, Lee, and Jang (2003a) report that 72.7% of all orders submitted to KSE are limit orders and the others are mostly market orders. Investors prefer limit orders to market orders especially when the volatility of stock prices is high; or the time-to-market-close is long. In addition, the proportion of informational volatility out of the total volatility is the main driving force that ultimately makes investors choose limit orders, which contrasts with Handa and Schwartz (1996) and Bae, Jang, and Park (2003) who argue that traders place more limit orders relative to market orders when they expect high transitory price volatility in the U.S. market. Park et al. (2003a) also find that the effect of time-to-market-close becomes stronger in case of buy orders than sell orders.

The findings by Kho (1999) complement Park et al. (2003a). According to him, the order type that is most popularly taken by traders in KSE is to place a limit sell (buy) order at the best quote as the price goes down (up). This suggests that the limit order play a role of liquidity supplier in an order-driven market. Measuring and testing pre-and post-performance by using the Harris and Hasbrouck (1996) method, he reports that limit orders perform better than do market orders.

In the U.S. since the early 2000s, automation and lower trading costs have allowed traders to economically slice orders into much smaller slices through what is known as *algorithm trading* (or *algo*). Specifically, equity trading in the U.S. tripled since 2001, whereas average trade size on the NYSE (New York Stock Exchange) dwindled from about 800 shares in 2004 to about 300 shares in 2009 (Angel, Harris, and Spatt, 2010). Based on Kyle (1985), some early observers on trading-related IT evolution such as Barclay and Warner (1993) and Chakravarty (2001) pay attention to the investors' submission of split orders by positing that the informed traders would split their orders to conceal their private information. Barclay and Warner (1993) find that mid-sized orders are found to have the highest contribution on the price movements of stocks. They claim that this is due to the incentive of informed traders, who would split their orders into mid-sized orders to conceal their private information (also called "stealth trading hypothesis"). Additionally, Chakravarty (2001) argues that the price contributions of the mid-sized orders mainly arise from the institutional investors.[6] Taking the method by Barclay and Warner (1993), Choe, Chung, and Lee (2003) confirm the stealth trading hypothesis for KSE. However, these studies do not directly test the impact of split orders since they do not have the data that would allow them to identify whether an order is a split part of a larger order or is originally a mid-sized order.

Addressing this problem, Lee (2008) makes an important contribution to the existing literature. She uses the complete transaction data of the KSE that includes the account number of investors, so that she can directly identify whether an order is part of a larger order and analyze whether it has a differential price impact over time. In addition, she tests not only whether split orders arise from stealth trading by informed traders, but she also analyzes whether market impact costs are another motivation for investors to split their orders ("market impact costs hypothesis"). Analyzing the measures of price contribution, she finds that investors strategically split their orders mainly to conceal their private information, which is consistent with the stealth trading hypothesis, and that the market impact costs are not a major concern for investors in splitting their orders. Among investor types, institutional investors show the largest price contribution in their split orders, while those of individual investors show relatively small price contribution.

1.2 Trades

The details of various phenomena from general trading will be discussed in most of the later sections. Hence, this subsection focuses on uncommon types of trading such as block trading, day-trading, and spoofing.

Block Trading: Currently, KRX has four sessions of block trading: Block

6) Anand and Chakravarty (2007) find that the stealth trading hypothesis holds for the individual stock options market.

Trading (volume requirement: over 50,000 shares or over 1 billion won) and Basket Trading (volume requirement: at least five different stocks and over 1 billion won) during the regular session, and Block Trading and Basket Trading during the after-hours trading session. KRX executes the block order with the K-Block system to which a coupled block order bilaterally negotiated and matched at OTC is sent. As of 2009, most of the block trading is crossing trading (83%), taking place during the after-hours trading session (87%) with half of block trading being done by foreign securities firms (52%). However, the percentage of block trading out of the total volume is only a meager (1.45%) in 2009. Since the current K-Block system does not guarantee traders' anonymity and price impact, KRX is slated for the introduction of a primitive type of *dark pool* for block trading in November 2010. The literature concerning block trading in Korea is very limited and tells only about the system prior to the adoption of the K-Block system.

Khil, Park, Shin, and Lee (2005) test the information hypothesis of block trading by investigating the impacts of block trading during after-hour trading sessions on stock price, volume, and volatility, and for the underlying motivation of block trading.[7] Decomposing price effects into temporary and permanent effects taken by a variation of the Keim and Madhavan (1996) method, they find that the information hypothesis is confirmed when the opening price of the block trading day is used as the previous equilibrium price, but not when the closing price of the block trading day is used as the previous equilibrium price. In addition, both volume and volatility increase after block trading occurs. They argue that these results suggest that the closing price reflects private information to which block traders have access about an impending block trade, confirming the alleged

---

7) More specifically, if traders initiate block trading to make profit from their access to private information on certain stocks, then block trading would send out a signal to the market on the intrinsic value of the corresponding stocks. However, if block trading is conducted for liquidity reasons such as portfolio rebalancing, then it would not have any impacts on the stock price, trading volume or volatility.

information hypothesis. Returns from block trading, involvement of foreign traders, and the beta of the stock determine especially the temporary price effect of block trading. For undervalued stocks, market capitalization and the block trading mechanism impact the price effect as well.

Examining block trading from August 1989 to July 1990, Jang (1993a) reports that the buyer-initiated (seller-initiated) block trading shows negative (positive) returns, but positive (negative) returns after the block trading execution. He points out that, while this phenomenon of block trading returns looks contrary to the direction of the returns that the order type forms, it comes from the existence of different price effects at each time when an order is initiated by a buyer or a seller and when the corresponding matching order is placed. He argues that this is evidence that the insiders take advantage of inside information concerning the block trading of a firm.

Day-trading: In general, day-trading is defined as the purchase and sale of the same stock by the same investor on the same day (see Barber, Lee, Liu, and Odean, 2008). In Korean stock markets, nearly 30% of trading is day-trading, and day-traders prefer lower-priced, more liquid, and more volatile stocks (Song, 2003; Chung, Choe, and Kho, 2009).

Regarding the profitability of day-trading, Lee, Park, and Jang (2007) report that the daily average return is a negative 0.39% for the four-month sample period of February 3 to May 30, 2003. Inclusion of trading fees worsens their profitability to a negative 0.81%, and the average abnormal return adjusted by the market index return and brokerage fee is also negative at -0.66%. These results are consistent with those of Barber et al. (2008) for the Taiwan Stock Exchange (TWSE). However, Lee et al. (2007) also find that 42.9% of the day-traders realize positive abnormal returns during the period, but they are silent as to whether there are any day-traders who have persistently earned positive abnormal returns over a certain period such as a year.[8] The profitability of day-trading is negatively correlated with trading size, length of trading time, and trading frequency. By contrast, firms with higher return volatility, smaller trading volume, lower proportion of day-trading show higher profitability for day-traders. The negative correlation between the profitability and trading size or trading frequency suggests that day-traders are not informed traders on a longer-term horizon at least. On the other hand, the positive abnormal returns for some day-traders suggest that they might have some information about short-term stock price movements and know how to utilize it.

The controversial policy issue associated with day-trading first raised in the Korean stock markets concerned whether day-trading causes unnecessary volatility, resulting in a negative effect on the market. Using daily data and multivariate Granger causality tests of the individual firm level from August 2000 to August 2001, Song (2003) argues that volatility Granger-causes day-trading, but day-trading does not Granger-cause volatility, suggesting that day-trading provides rather a positive effect on the market, not an alleged negative effect. By estimating various bivariate vector autoregression (VAR) models using minute-by-minute data from January 1999 to December 2000, however, Chung et al. (2009) find that greater day-trading activity leads to greater return volatility and that the impact of a day-trading shock dissipates gradually within an hour. They also report that past return volatility positively affects future day-trading activity, past day-trading activity negatively affects bid-ask spreads, and past bid-ask spreads negatively affect future day-trading activity. These results lead them to conclude that the day-traders take short-term contrarian strategies; the day-traders buy at the bottom and sell at the peak of the short-term price cycles.

---

8) Using customized transaction data including individual accounts for two years (2002~2003), Park and Cho (2010) report that *some* individual day-traders persistently have achieved superior performance. For example, Park and Cho (2010) identify 5,827 (0.18%) accounts out of 3,244,855 total accounts as day-traders and they find that 72 (0.019%) accounts are among the top 10% performances for six successive quarters.

To help resolve the controversy over the direction of causality between day-trading with volatility (with opposite results using daily and intraday data), Lee and Chae (2008) empirically test the hypothesis that day-traders in KSE provide liquidity. During the sample period from April 2003 to June 2003, day-traders submit more best bid/ask orders compared with other traders. Moreover, for stocks with less trading, day-trading decreases bid-ask spread and increases depth more than regular trading does. Arguing that these results suggest that day-traders behave more like liquidity providers, Lee and Chae (2008) additionally look into the spread, depth, and market impact cost in the next period following day-trading, and find that day-trading in a period actually improves the market quality. However, the effect is limited for less liquid stocks for which liquidity provision is most needed.

Spoofing: Eom, Lee, and Park (2008) define a spoofing order "as an order submitted to a stock exchange, without the intention of execution, in order to mislead other investors by injecting misleading information regarding the demand or supply of a stock. A spoofing trader later submits his/her real order, taking advantage of the price change resulting from his/her earlier spoofing order." This microstructure-based manipulation is a new-breed of manipulation, differing from previously studied forms of manipulation based on information (e.g., Chakraborty and Yilmaz, 2004) or transactions (e.g., Allen and Gale, 1992) in finance.

Until the end of 2001, KRX disclosed the total quantity on each side of the order book without fully disclosing the prices at which the orders were placed. This type of transparency unintentionally led to proliferate spoofing in KRX at that time. According to Park, Lee, and Jang (2004), the shares covered by the spoofing-buy orders represented 1.17% of the total shares covered by all buy orders, and almost all of the spoofing orders were placed by individual investors. Eom et al. (2008) report that spoofers are more frequently observed in stocks with lower price levels, lower market capitalization, higher return volatility, and lower managerial transparency, although trading volume is not a significant targeting determinant for spoofers. They also report that the average spoofing-buy order is 5.6 times larger than a typical buy order, and almost 90% of spoofing orders are priced more than 10 ticks away from the current best bid price, rendering the probability of execution extremely low.

Using the complete intraday order and trade data of KRX in a custom data set identifying individual accounts from November 2001 to February 2002, Eom et al. (2008) find that investors strategically placed spoofing orders which, given the KRX's order-disclosure rule at the time, created the impression of a substantial order book imbalance, with the intent to manipulate subsequent prices. Roughly half of the spoofing orders were placed in conjunction with day-trading. They also find that spoofing traders achieved substantial extra profits of 67 to 83 basis points in slightly less than 45 minutes. The frequency of spoofing orders decreased drastically after KRX altered its order-disclosure rule in January 2002.

2. Market Quality-Spread, Trading Volume, Volatility, Market Impact Cost, and Private-Information Risk

Market quality has many different aspects. Spread, trading volume and volatility, market impact cost, and private-information risk have been the market statistics most used to measure market quality in Korea. This subsection discusses the results from the studies of these statistics. As far as spread, volatility and volume are concerned, we only focus in this section on the intraday behaviors and patterns; studies of other aspects of these statistics will be discussed in subsection VI. 1. 2.

2.1 Spread

The NYSE and Nasdaq, quote-driven markets, have market makers so that a trade can be executed within the quoted best bid-ask prices. In contrast, KRX, an order-driven market, does not have a market maker for regular trading so that a trade should be executed at or below (above) the quoted best bid (ask) prices. Hence, effective spread, i.e., a trade cost that traders actually pay, is generally smaller than the quoted spread in the U.S. markets, whereas effective spread is *larger* than the quoted spread in KRX (Nam and Park, 2000).[9]

Notwithstanding these different features of the trading mechanisms and spreads, the pattern and determinants of the intraday spread in KSE by Jang and Ok (1996) are very similar to those in the U.S. markets by McInish and Wood (1992). Using twelve 20-minute intervals over the trading day for six months during 1993~1994, Jang and Ok (1996) report that the spread in KSE exhibits the inverse *J*-shaped diurnal pattern; the spread is higher early in the morning, then gradually decreases, and increases a little bit at the end of the day. They also find that the intraday spread is positively related to price and volatility and is negatively related to volume and trade size.

2.2 Return Volatility and Trading Volume

Diurnal Patterns: As in other fields in finance, early microstructure studies on the U.S. stock markets were concentrated on finding the patterns of the related variables. This is similar to the Korean stock markets as well. Hence, the research in this area was done using the data from the late 1980s to early 1990s, when KSE adopted market closure during the lunch break (12:00~13:00). This rule was repealed on May 2, 2002.

---

9) Using the method of Amihud and Mendelson (1987), Ku (1997b) reports that the average effective spreads for 168 stocks listed on KSE during two months in 1994 was 32 won (KRW). However, since the method is appropriate for markets with a market maker, rather than for a market like KSE, this may be a significant underestimate.

Jang (1992) examines the diurnal patterns of returns, volume, and number of trades on KSE from August 1989 to July 1990 and finds that returns exhibit an inverse *J*-shape with a disconnection from 12:00 to 13:00 whereas volume and number of trades show a *W*-shape. He also finds that return and volume at market-close were the highest in a trading day, and that return on Monday was the lowest in a week. Using a sub-sample of Jang (1992), Jang (1993b) investigates the diurnal patterns of volatility and reports that the patterns of volatility are somewhat different from those of return and volume. He measures the volatility by high-low price ratio and reports that the diurnal pattern of volatility is a *V*-shape with a disconnection from 12:00 to 13:00 during the lunch break. The decreasing slope of the *V*-shape in the morning session is less steep than its increasing slope in the afternoon session. Monday has the lowest volatility among the weekdays. According to Jang (1993b), volatility in KSE is positively related to number of trades, trading volume, and trade size, whereas it is negatively related to price level.

In contrast to the study of individual stocks by Jang (1992, 1993b), Nam (1991) examines the hourly KOSPI index. He shows that return is higher in the early morning session, slowly decreases to the middle of the afternoon session, and then increases a little bit for the rest of day. Volume exhibits a similar pattern to that of return, but it drastically increases at market-close and lags an hour to return.[10]

Sources of Volatility: There are two lines of research on the sources of volatility in the Korean stock markets. One is to study the effect of trading mechanisms on volatility; the other is to study the information effect (or

---

10) Utilizing the *U*-shaped diurnal patterns of volatility and volume and the *V*-shaped diurnal pattern of public news (the number of headline news), Khil and Chung (2005) show that public news can explain volatility in five out of twelve time periods and volume in eight out of twelve time periods. This result is very different from that of the U.S. market, where the public news does not play any significant role in explaining volatility and volume (Mitchell and Mulherin, 1994; Berry and Howe, 1994).

trading-period effect). Using seven major indices in KSE from June 1987 to February 1992, Lee and Ko (1993) examine both lines. They first test whether the change in trading mechanism for market-close from continuous trading to call-auction trading causes price volatility or not. Their results show that the variance of the opening price return in the morning session is not statistically significantly different from the variance of the closing price return in the afternoon session (note that KSE had the market closure during the lunch break), which contrasts greatly with the international evidence. They also find that the variance of the closing price return in the afternoon session decreases after the change in the trading mechanism into call-auction trading. Next, they test whether volatility is higher during trading periods than during non-trading periods and confirm that the trading-period effect holds in KSE.

Chang and Song (1997, 1999) and Park and Kim (2003) examine the sources of volatility focusing on the information effect. Park and Kim (2003) analyze the ratios of variances of trading period (open-to-close) returns relative to non-trading period (close-to-open) returns.

The design of their sample period, January 1998 to August 2000, is quite novel that it covers a few significant rule changes such as the termination of the Saturday trading session (December 1998) and the repeal of the lunch break (May 2000). They find that the variance of stock returns is much higher when the market is open, implying that the trading-period effect on stock return volatility exists in KSE. In addition, they find that private information is a main determinant for stock return volatility and that pricing error is partly a determinant as well. This evidence found in the Korean stock markets supports the explanation on the sources of volatility proposed by French and Roll (1986). Utilizing the George, Kaul, and Nimalendran (1991) method, Chang and Song (1997, 1999) also corroborate the trading-period effect in KSE. In contrast to Park and Kim (2003), they show that pricing error is a main determinant for stock return volatility in KSE.

2.3 Market Impact Cost

Market impact represents the price change caused by a specific trade or order. In general, it has an adverse affect, for example, by helping drive prices up (down) when a trader is trying to buy (sell). The exact market impact cost is the difference between the actual price chart and the hypothetical one that would have occurred if the order had not been created. Hence, it is very difficult to measure and estimate the market impact accurately.

Lee and Choe (1997) measure the market impact cost by summation of a half of bid-ask spread and the cost that should additionally pay in the case when the order size exceeds the depths at best bid and ask prices. Using three month TAQ data for 200 constituent stocks of KOSPI 200 index in 1995, they find that an investor must pay about 0.4~0.7% of the stock price in order to trade 100 shares immediately and that the market impact cost increases to 1.1~1.8% in order to trade 5,000 shares. They additionally show the following findings: the diurnal pattern of market impact cost is inverse *J*-shaped, which is similar to that found for bid-ask spread in KSE. As trade size increases, the market impact cost increases whereas the increasing rate gradually decreases. Both the magnitude of the market impact cost and the marginal market impact cost decrease as the competition among investors (measured as the thickness of the order book) increases. Market impact cost is greater for stocks with a greater return variance.

2.4 Information Asymmetry

Since Easley, O'Hara and co-authors[11] defined in a series of structural models, their PIN (probability of information-based trading) has been used as a proxy for private-information risk (or extent of information asymmetry)

---

11) The papers are Easley, Kiefer, and O'Hara (1996, 1997a, 1997b), Easley, Kiefer, O'Hara, and Paperman (1996), Easley, O'Hara, and Paperman (1998).

on individual stocks for various fields of financial studies in the U.S. Recently, however, Duarte and Young (2009) criticize that the Easley-O'Hara original PIN model cannot match the pervasive positive correlation between buyer- and seller-initiated order flow or the variances of buyer- and seller-initiated order flow. Modifying the Easley-O'Hara original PIN model to accommodate the positive correlation between buys and sells and generating variances closer to those observed in the data, these authors develop the adjusted PIN (AdjPIN) and show that "the PIN component related to asymmetric information is not priced, while the PIN component related to illiquidity is priced." In this subsection, we focus on the PIN and AdjPIN measures in KRX. The cross-sectional relationship between stock returns and private-information risk, or roles of PIN and AdjPIN as a factor for asset pricing in the Korean stock markets will be discussed in subsection VI. 1. 4.

To understand the extent of information asymmetry in the Korean stock markets, Choe and Yang (2006) choose the four measures derived from the structural models that are widely used in market microstructure literature: the Huang and Stoll model (1997, HS), the Madhavan, Richardson, and Roomans model (1997, MRR), the Hasbrouck (1991), Foster and Viswanathan (1993) model (HFV), and Easley, Hvidkjaer, and O'Hara's (2002) PIN measure. Using 416 common stocks listed on KSE during January 2002 to March 2002, Choe and Yang (2006) estimate and compare the four measures. Their correlation results show that "the HS, MRR, and HFV measures are highly correlated with each other (0.706~0.895 in Spearman correlation), but these three measures are weakly correlated with PIN (0.186~0.309 in Spearman correlation)." However, the correlation tests connote shortcomings arising from the joint hypothesis test; the hypothesis that both permanent (informational) component of spread and PIN estimate the same phenomenon of asymmetry information and the hypothesis that the structural models for these four measures are correct.

Utilizing Duarte and Young's (2009) intuition, Park and Eom (2008a) try to find whether PIN, as a measure of asymmetric information, is consistent with the empirical stylized fact in KRX. They estimate PIN using the Easley-O'Hara original model and find that the *implied* Pearson's correlation between buys and sells of each stock on KRX exhibits negative for all firms and all percentiles over the sample period from January 1997 to December 2005. In contrast, the *actual* correlation (median: 0.78) in KRX is positive for all firms and all percentiles.[12] The implied correlation using Duarte and Young's (2009) AdjPIN also shows positive for all firms and all percentiles. The results of Park and Eom (2008a) indicate that the Easley-O'Hara original PIN is not successful in representing the real-world phenomenon in the Korean stock markets, but the Duarte and Young's (2009) AdjPIN is.

3. Short-Term (Intraday) Return Predictability and Price Discovery

3.1 Short-Term (Intraday) Return Predictability

A limit order book in a pure order-driven market contains a considerable amount of information. When part of this information is publicly disclosed, it allows investors to draw inferences on market conditions and transaction costs. Hence, it is meaningful to examine whether the limit order book can predict the direction of short-term (intraday) price changes, indicating a failure of short-term market efficiency. Broadly, there are two lines of research on this issue. The one is to test the short-term (intraday) return predictability, the other is to test the information effect of quoted prices below the best bid and ask prices.

Jee, Jang, and Ok (1998) exemplify the first line of research. They provide an empirical model for a pure order-driven market which is a variant of

---

12) This empirical stylized fact in KRX is consistent with the facts in NYSE and AMEX studied by Duarte and Young (2009).

Huang and Stoll (1994), but consider the costs from asymmetric information and market frictions, and they test ten-minute return predictability. Using TAQ data of the 37 most liquid stocks listed on KSE from July 1994 to December 1995, they find that their variables (information-, market-depth-, and market-friction-related variables) to predict the ten-minute returns have similar magnitudes and statistical significances to those of Huang and Stoll (1994) and Harris and Panchapagesan (2005) who examine a quote-driven market. However, they also find that the order placed at the best price for immediate transaction does not make any contribution to ten-minute return prediction. This arises from investors' consideration of high intraday volatility when they submit the order, so that cumulative market depth plays a role as a barrier to trading. Meanwhile, there is a positive contemporaneous relationship between an order and a trade. The order predicts the trade more than the trade does the order.

In the second line of research, Lee and Choe (2007) find that informational content of limit order book does not proportionally increase and that additional explanatory power is dependent on a specific distance away from the best bid and ask prices. Using the intraday (five-minute and ten-minute) returns and associated data for 339 common stocks on KSE from January 2002 to December 2003, they run the Cao, Hansch, and Wang (2009) predictive regressions of two asymmetry variables of limit order book (asymmetry of limit price and asymmetry of cumulative depth) at the best quotes (step 1) and all displayed quotes from the second best (step 2) quotes to the tenth best (step 10) quotes on future returns. They find that the most dominant predictability comes from step 1, but that the imbalance between demand and supply from step 2 to step 10 also provides significant explanatory power in explaining future short-term (five-minute) returns after controlling for the effect of post-trade information. However, the explanatory power of step

6 to step 10 marginally increases. As the intraday return interval lengthens to 10 minutes, the coefficient of asymmetry variables in step 1 still remains significant, while the return predictability beyond step 1 disappears, which implies that short- term return predictability is only briefly effective.

3.2 Intraday Price Discovery

Lee and Choe (2006a) examine whether the intraday pattern of liquidity in the limit order book explains the intraday price discovery process of limit order trading. For intraday liquidity formation, they utilize the Kavajecz and Odders-White (2004) method. For intraday price discovery, they use the Cao et al. (2009) method which utilizes the Hasbrouck's (1995) method of "information share" into quotes.

Using the same data that Choe and Lee (2007) analyze, they find that the information share of best quotes (step 1) is concentrated at the opening of trading and then declines, which resembles an inverse *J*-shaped pattern. In contrast, the contributions of the higher-step quotes (step 2 to step 10) to the price discovery process increase slowly and then are stabilized in the afternoon. They also find that the contribution of step 1 to the price discovery process is positively related to spread but negatively related to cumulative depth. They argue that the intraday price discovery process is strongly related to the intraday liquidity formation process.

4. Trading Mechanisms and Related Issues

The trading sessions in the Korean stock markets are made up of a pre-opening session, regular trading session, and after-hours session. The transactions during pre-opening and after-hours sessions are executed by the previous closing price and the closing price of the day, respectively. That is, they are not allowed to have a price discovery function. The regular trading session has three distinct features: KSE opens the market at prices determined by the call auction, then sets up prices by the continuous auction, and finally closes the market at prices determined again by the call auction. Most papers in this survey study the price behavior during the continuous auction. In this subsection only, we focus on the literature on trading mechanisms outside the regular trading session.

4.1 Pre-Opening Session and Opening Call Auction

Park, Lee, and Jang (2003b) analyze investors' trading behaviors and price discovery during the pre-opening session in KSE for the period of November 2001 to March 2002.[13] They test two competing hypotheses: the noise hypothesis vs. learning hypothesis. The former claims that the prices decided during the pre-opening period can be very noisy since traders may want to simply mislead other investors by tendering false orders. On the other hand, the latter argues that despite the strategic behavior of investors, the indicative prices during the pre-opening session could reflect the information on the value of stocks through their learning process. To test those hypotheses, Park et al. (2003b) have to define the fictitious indicative prices and spoofing orders, since KSE did not provide any indicative information during their test period. They use the weighted average of the quotes, or the best ask or best bid quotes as proxies for the indicative prices. They also define the spoofing order, which is defined as a buy (or sell) order with prices 10% below (or above) the closing price of the previous day.

Park et al. (2003b) find that cancellation ratios are much higher and execution ratios of buy orders are much lower in comparison to those of sell orders.

---

13) KSE adopted the opening call auction on November 25, 1996. However, during the pre-opening session, it did not disclose any information. On September 30, 2002, KSE started to disclose indicative prices and volumes, and indicative best quotes and associated volumes. As of April 2011, the pre-opening session in KSE is from 7:30 to 8:30 for transactions only at the closing price on the previous day, and from 8:00 to 9:00 only for the opening call auction.

They interpret that this result comes from the incentive for investors to mislead the market by false buy orders that are eventually cancelled and replaced by sell orders since KSE disclosed then only the total number of orders for the opening call auction. However, they also report the evidence that such efforts on the part of spoofers generally fail and, instead, face increasing sell orders by other investors. Finally, they run the "unbiased regression" as suggested by Biais, Hillion, and Spatt (1999) and report that, despite the strategic behavior of investors, the indicative prices during the pre-opening session tend to reflect the intrinsic value of stocks, which supports the learning hypothesis.

Using TAQ data from July 1994 to December 1995, Jee and Ok (1997) insist that the call-auction system in KSE at that time does not have any mechanism reflecting order imbalances at the market-open. Hence, the opening price is not a proper equilibrium price having a negative effect on the price discovery during the continuous-trading session.

4.2 Closing Call Auction

Chung (2004) examines the information efficiency of closing prices in KSE over the entire year of 1999 and the second half of 2000 by using a sample of 422 common stocks. He finds that the price and volume contributions at the closing call-auction session, measured by the Barclay and Warner (1993) method, are 7.02% and 6.14% respectively, which are quite significant when compared to the time period of 2.2% that the closing auction has in daily trading session. In addition, the order imbalances at the closing call-auction session have a significant impact on the closing price, but they are not fully incorporated into the closing prices. Even though there is weak evidence of price reversal after the closing call auction, the price pressure is relatively strong for stocks with low volatility and low liquidity whereas the market under-reacts to order imbalances for stocks with high volatility and high liquidity. Overall, he maintains that the closing prices of KSE are highly efficient, but some measures to assess order imbalances will be helpful to enhance the price discovery of the current call-auction mechanism for stocks which experience problems with either excessive price pressure or market under-reaction.

As of December 8, 1989, KSE changed the pricing mechanism at the market-close from the continuous trading to the call auction. Ko, Lee, and Chung (1995) investigate this event and find that the pricing error of closing prices dropped drastically after the event.

Associated with the closing call-auction mechanism, Ko (2004) studies a very interesting issue. He notices that Chambers, Edelen, and Kadlec (2001) report that since the U.S. stock markets do not use the call-auction mechanism at the market-close, investors can make a profit under the current "forwarding pricing method" that calculates the net asset value (NAV) for a mutual fund. Ko (2004) tests whether the same situation occurs in the Korean stock markets. He argues that the current forwarding pricing method in the Korean stock markets gives no profit opportunity for equity funds since the closing prices in KSE are determined by the call auction, interpreting that the nonsynchronous trading problem at the market-close occurred in the U.S. stock markets is resolved by using the call-auction mechanism. However, he does not consider the possibility of partial price adjustment for the closing price which consists of a large portion of staleness in daily stock returns in the Korean stock markets (see Park and Eom, 2005a).

Ⅲ. Trading Protocols-Rules and Regulations Related to Trading

In all aspects, the stock markets in Korea are not yet on an equal footing with its world economic status. This is also reflected in the KRX trading protocols, which lack sophistication and international conformity. The underdevelopment of infrastructure related to orders and trades is the main source of this discrepancy: the current KRX trading system does not need to allow traders to carry out sophisticated trading such as algo, HFT (high-frequency trading), DMA (direct market access), etc. When the revision of *the Financial Investment Services and Capital Markets Act*, which is currently being undertaken, is finally complete, the KRX trading infrastructure and protocols will rapidly increase the status of the KRX to that of Korea's international economic status. Eventually, research in this area of the Korean market microstructure will become more valuable.

1. Minimum Tick Size

A minimum tick size (hereafter "tick size") is the smallest increment (tick) by which the price of stocks, futures contracts or other exchange-traded instruments can move. Hence, the tick size plays a minimum limit on the bid-ask spread and its change affects the traders' order behaviors, so that the tick size is an important basic element that determines liquidity or/and market quality in cross-section and time-series. The tick size of KRX is a step function of the stock price; six different quotation price units are used depending on the price of shares.[14] In contrast, the tick size of the U.S. stock exchanges is one cent regardless of the stock price.

There are three lines of research regarding tick size in finance. The three lines include (1) examination of the cross-sectional effect of tick size on market liquidity (see Harris, 1994; Chung, Kang, and Kim, 2010; among many others); (2) examination of the time-series effect of tick size on market quality,

---

14) They are as follows. Each set of parentheses shows the price range and tick size: [1 won to 5,000 won; 5 won), [5,000 won to 10,000 won; 10 won), [10,000 won to 50,000 won; 50 won), [100,000 won to 500,000 won; 500 won), [500,000 won +; 1,000 won).

which can be classified further into two sub-lines; (a) the study of the market-wide event of the change in minimum tick size, which most of the second line of research belong to, and (b) the analysis of the endogenous event in which tick size changes as price moves although this research is rare (see Bessembinder, 2003; Chung and Shin, 2005; Kang, Park, and Eom, 2009).

Chung et al. (2010) examine the effects of tick size and market structure on trading costs using TAQ data from KSE and NYSE over the sample period from April 2003 to June 2003. Utilizing the discrete spread model of Harris (1994) and the Easley-O'Hara PIN measure, they find that the large tick sizes imposed on high-price stocks on KSE are significant binding constraints on bid-ask spreads. As the tick size increases, the PIN increases, suggesting that informed traders on KSE are not discouraged by the additional trading costs imposed on high-price stocks through larger tick sizes. They also find that, except for their larger tick size group, the average spread of KSE stocks is smaller than that of the matched sample of NYSE stocks. They argue that this suggests the KSE's electronic limit-order market generally provides cheaper executions than the NYSE's specialist system.

To determine the appropriate tick size for KRX, Kang et al. (2009) analyze the effect of tick-size change on, first, the liquidity, measured by relative spread, market depth, and volume and, secondly, on the overall market quality. Using both TAQ and daily data of all 689 common stocks listed on KRX during the sample period from January 3 to June 30 in 2005, they test seven null hypotheses. Unlike previous studies, their analyses focus on the effect of changing the tick size on market depth among liquidity variables, by, among others, addressing the endogeneity problem among the variables. More specifically, they study the effect of changing the tick size by comparing stocks with prices just above and just below the level at which the tick size changes by utilizing the fact that KRX has a step function system for tick size.

Their findings illustrate an ambiguous effect of changing the tick size on market quality: reducing tick size has a favorable effect on relative spread and volume, but an unfavorable effect on market depth. A decrease in order size and an increase in the ratio of cancellation and correction orders are, at least, principal causes for decreasing market depth as tick size reduces. They also find that the price range hovering around 10,000 won is the only exception out of five price ranges at which market depth decreases with statistical significance as the tick size decreases. This phenomenon is closely related to the large change in the relative tick size (from 0.1% to 0.5%) at this price range (i.e., 10,000 won), which is a very abrupt change compared to that at other price ranges (from 0.1% to 0.2%, in particular for 5,000 won and 50,000 won price ranges). They conclude that KRX can reduce the relative tick size 0.2% without having significant adverse effects on market depth.

Chung and Shin (2005) also attempt to shed light on the effect of tick size on market quality in KSE using the same data period as Chung et al. (2010). Among their findings, the result on market depth by intraday event-study needs careful attention because market depth increases as the tick size decreases, which is opposite to those shown in previous studies. Based on this, they argue that "step-increasing tick sizes are detrimental to market quality, although the adverse effect of binding tick sizes can be somewhat mitigated by lower negotiation costs." This contrasts with the conclusions by Chung et al. (2010).

2. Liquidity Providers

As in the literal sense of the word, a liquidity provider (LP) provides liquidity for illiquid stocks and has limited obligations and privileges compared to a market maker. KRX adopted the LP system for equity-liked warrants (ELW) on December 1, 2005 and for stocks on January 2, 2006. Upon adopting the LP system, KRX started to trade ELW and currently KRX ranks second in the world for the ELW trading volume after the Hong Kong Exchange.

From the opening date of the Korean ELW market to May 10, 2007, Choe and Woo (2010) analyze minute-by-minute data to understand whether there are differences in the capability of liquidity provision among the LPs in the KRX ELW market, after controlling for potential factors which might affect liquidity. They show the results that there exist statistically significant differences in the capability of providing liquidity among LPs. The level of operational competencies or (unknown) intention of the LPs causes the difference in their capabilities of liquidity provision. They insist that the optimal liquidity provision might not be achieved only through market competition such as among LPs or among similar ELWs or among LPs and limit-order investors. However, they also argue that it is necessary for the financial regulators to develop periodic and systematic evaluation and feedback systems.

3. Price-Limit System

Price limits on *individual stocks* are daily upper and lower boundaries outside of which trading is prohibited.[15] Most Asian exchanges, including Korea (KRX), Shanghai (SSE), Taiwan (TWSE), and Tokyo (TSE), use explicit price-limit systems for individual stocks. These exchanges justify price-limit systems on individual stocks to provide cooling-off periods, lower idiosyncratic volatility, and allow more effective price discovery on days of abnormal volatility. Internationally, however, there is little evidence to support the claim that price limits on individual stocks provide the claimed benefits. On

---

15) Major European exchanges have a *volatility-interruption* system which implicitly and dynamically provides the benefits attributed to a price-limit system, even though they have a trading mechanism similar to Asian stock exchanges (see Eom, Kang, and Lee (2007)). In contrast, the U.S. stock exchanges, which have market makers, did not use a price-limit system on individual stocks until recently. In fact, since the May 6th Flash Crash, NYSE and Nasdaq started to have stock-by-stock circuit breakers, which are the U.S. version of the volatility interruption system.

the contrary, many papers (e.g., Kim and Rhee, 1997) conclude that the harm caused by price limits (delaying price discovery, producing volatility spillover, delaying trading, and the magnet effect (e.g., Cho, Russell, Tiao, and Tsay, 2003; Kim and Yang, 2008)) substantially outweighs the benefits.

Price limits on individual stocks on KRX are currently 15%. These limits were relaxed from 6% to 8% on November 25, 1996, from 8% to 12% on March 2, 1998, and from 12% to 15% on December 7, 1998. The price-limits have been studied by many scholars. However, all of them but Eom, Kang, and Kim (2010) examine how the events of expanding price limits prior to 1998 affect price volatility, so that they have a limitation for properly extracting their economic meanings under the context of recent developments in the Korean stock markets. Moreover, the effects of price limits and their changes on volatility are not even uniform within the research on the Korean stock markets.[16]

Nam and Ahn (1995) and Sonu (1997) argue that price limits do not affect price volatility, while Lee and Kim (1993) and Lee and Kim (1995) insist that price limits decrease price volatility. On the other hand, Jang and Park (1995) report that price limits restrain the short-term volatility, but do not restrain the long-term (around five days) volatility. Berkman and Lee (2002) also show that the price limits increase long-term volatility and reduce trading volume, supporting the results of Jang and Park (1995).

Eom et al. (2010), the most recent study on this field, examine the effects of price limits on the idiosyncratic volatility of individual stocks. When estimating idiosyncratic volatility, these authors adopt the Gibbs-sampling method by Chou (1997) to resolve the problem of censored returns caused

---

16) Very different from other areas in finance in Korea, there are some papers on the theory of the price-limits system. Using a Bayesian game, Park (1990) theoretically shows the existence of the magnet effect. Yoo (2001) provides a theoretical model to estimate true volatility from observed volatility when price-limits exist. However, he does not test it empirically. Kang and Khil (1999) analyze the market depth which is not executed for the day due to the hits on price limits, and argue that the market depth does not come from the magnet effect, but is a reflection of information.

by price limits. Results show that idiosyncratic volatility is significantly higher than would appear from OLS estimates using the observed censored return data. Tight price limits reduce idiosyncratic volatility, at significant cost; sufficiently loose price limits have no effect on idiosyncratic volatility. They argue that regulators should substitute volatility-interruption systems in place of price-limit systems for individual stocks.

4. Sidecar

Sidecar is a price stabilization mechanism which temporarily halts all program trade orders in order to restrain the risks in cash markets generated from the abrupt and extreme price volatility in futures markets. KRX has employed sidecar since November 25, 1996. In the early days of adoption, sidecar was triggered frequently, mainly due to the sharp increase of price volatility in the aftermath of the Asian financial crisis of 1997. However, the frequency of sidecar triggers has significantly decreased after twice modifying the rule that raises the threshold and limits the number of triggers to once a day.[17] Since May 11, 2001, sidecar has been triggered when the price in the futures market moves more than +/-5% with a movement which lasts more than a minute.

Program trading, which is subject to a sidecar trigger, is the sophisticated trading of a large portfolio of securities in combination with an offsetting position in a futures contract. The ability to pursue this strategy for earning a risk-free return depends on integrating computer programs with trades involving one of the many new products in the securities markets—stock index futures.

Examining the effect of the sidecar on the extent of information asymmetry, Park, Lee, and Kwon (2009) analyze the changes in spread and price impact

---

17) In the U.S., sidecar was abolished on February 16, 1999.

before and after the sidecar event using the intraday data of KSE from January 1999 to December 2004.[18] They find that quote spread and effective spread in the post-halt period decrease significantly following the halt period. This effect is more prominent in down markets than in up markets and in the morning session than in the afternoon session. Price impact in the post-halt period decreases dramatically after the sidecar event. In addition, they find that sidecar effectively reduces information asymmetry in not only the index-arbitrage sample but also the non-index arbitrage sample. Their findings suggest that the sidecar mechanism has a positive role in reducing information asymmetry and mitigating the adverse effect of program trading in KSE.

Non-arbitrage program trading occurs based on the fundamental value on a stock, so that it seems more close to information-based trading than arbitrage program trading. Conducting an intraday event study for relatively extreme events at the individual stock level, Choe and Yoon (2007) show the empirical result that there exists a strong liquidity effect (i.e., liquidity problem) in large arbitrage program trading whereas there exists an information effect in large excess non-arbitrage program trading. This result is contrary to Harris, Sofianos, and Shapiro (1994).

5. Short Sales Including Stock Lending and Credit Balance

A short sale (or short selling) is the sale of a stock you do not own. Investors who sell short believe that the price of the stock will fall. If the

---

18) The empirical results on program trading in KSE are not uniformly confirmed among papers. Park, Eom, and Chang (2009) find similar results to Park et al. (2009). However, contrary to Park et al. (2009), Park, Eom, and Chang (2007a) insist that since July 1998, sidecar delays the normal price discovery process and undermines the market liquidity. Examining the data from 1997 to 2004, Park, Eom, and Chang (2007b) analyze return, volatility, and liquidity dynamics and illustrate that there are no distinct differences for index arbitrage group and non-arbitrage group surrounding the sidecar events. Hahn and Oh (2007) present evidence that both program trading and non-program trading have no impact on the long-run component of volatility, but increase the short-run component of volatility. In case of short-run component, program trading has three times larger impact than non-program trading. Kang and Ohk (2006) find that a buy-program trading activity has the strongest impact on stock return volatility among all types of trading activities.

price drops, you can buy the stock at the lower price and make a profit. If the price of the stock rises and you buy it back later at the higher price, you will incur a loss. Most of theoretical research on short sales conclude that a short-selling restriction stunts market efficiency and delays price discovery (e.g., Miller, 1977; Diamond and Verrecchia, 1987). Empirical research generally confirms these theoretical conclusions; the short-selling restriction delays the incorporation of negative information into stock price, overvalues the stock price, and deteriorates market quality (e.g., Asquith, Pathak, and Ritter, 2005; Boehmer, Jones, and Zhang, 2008).

Before the worldwide short-selling restrictions in 2008 when most of the major industrial countries prohibited short-selling for financial stocks in an effort to stabilize their stock markets, Korea had already adopted relatively more strict standards than other major countries. Currently, Korea does not allow investors to employ naked short-selling. KRX also has the uptick rule where short-selling must be either at a price above the last traded price of the stock, or at the last traded price if that price was higher than the price in the previous trade. Short sales in Korea were around 1% of total volume of sells before 2007. Since then, short sales have increased rapidly, reaching a peak 7.3% in mid-2007 and currently ranging 4~5%. Almost 90% of short sales have been executed by foreign investors in Korea (Yi, Binh, and Jang, 2010).

Research on short sales in Korea has been very limited and has not acknowledged the various economic issues associated with short sales because it was virtually prohibited to obtain the short sale data. Yi et al. (2010) are the first researchers using the real (not proxy variable) short sales data in KRX.[19] With the short sales data of individual firms from January 2006

---

19) Prior to Yi et al. (2010), there are a few papers using stock lending (Kim, 2000; Song, 2006) and credit balance (Nam and Park (1996)) as proxy variables for short sales in KSE. Nam and Park (1996) show that credit balance does not provide any information for stock return predictability. Kim (2000) presents that stock returns react more negatively to stock lendings executed at market-order prices than to those executed at limit-order

to September 2008, Yi et al. (2010) analyze the causality between short sales and stock price drops through three methods: VAR, panel VAR, and IV (instrumental variables) regression. They find that a short sale does not induce a stock price drop at neither the entire market nor the individual firm levels, while a stock price drop leads to an increase of a short sale. Especially, they observe that the stock price drop resulting from bad news on individual firms plays a significant role in contemporaneous causation with respect to a short sale. In addition, they report that the firms for which a short sale causes a stock price drop have larger size, higher liquidity, higher proportion of foreign investors, higher market beta, and lower unsystematic risk than the firms for which a stock price drop causes a short sale.

IV. Market Transparency

Transparency represents the amount of market information that is available before and after a trade has occurred. *Pre-trade (post-trade)* transparency in stock markets is generally defined as a measure of the public release of information concerning participants' buy and sell orders before (after) these orders are executed.

KRX enjoys legally-sponsored monopolistic status, so that the Korean stock markets does not have a problem of market fragmentation as other major stock markets face. Hence, in Korea, post-trade transparency is not a big issue and research in pre-trade transparency has been actively conducted.

Pre-trade transparency: In addition to the bid and ask prices, KRX publicly

---

prices. Examining the daily stock lending data from 2000 to 2002 in KSE, Song (2006) finds that the proportion of stock lending is higher for stocks with large capitalization, high price, high liquidity and volatility. He also reports that a negative relationship between stock lending and stock returns is very weak, and that stock lending is done mostly for hedging and arbitrage purposes, but very few for speculative purpose.

discloses a certain number of next best buy and sell offer prices and the number of shares desired or offered at those prices. The number of publicly disclosed prices was increased from 3 to 5 (on each side of the market, including the bid or ask) on March 6, 2000 and from 5 to 10 on January 2, 2002.[20] Using the standard event-study for these two events, Park and Eom (2005b) analyze the effect of pre-trade transparency on market quality.[21] They find that the relationship between pre-trade transparency and market quality is nonlinear; the first increase in transparency, starting from a low level, clearly resulted in an increase in market quality, while the second increase in transparency, starting from a higher level, on balance, resulted in a decrease in market quality. Based on the mixed nature of the evidence in the 2002 event and the fact that their most reliable test shows a decline in market quality, they conclude that it appears that the optimal number of publicly disclosed prices in KRX probably lies somewhere between 5 and 10.

Using the same event as Park and Eom (2005b) do and the Hasbrouck's (1995) method that measures information share, Lee and Choe (2006b) show the empirical finding that the information share increases statistically significantly from the second best quotes to the seventh best quotes, but there are no statistically significant increases in information share for the quote below the eighth best quotes. The latter argues that, under consideration of expected costs and benefits, the optimal level of disclosure in KRX might exist between the fifth best and the tenth best quotes, confirming the implication suggested by Park and Eom (2005b).

However, Eom, Ok, and Park (2007) point out that the standard event-study

---

20) Prior to March 6, 2000, there were two other events (June 15, 1992 and April 1, 1995) which expanded publicly available quote disclosure. Chang and Song (1996, 1998) investigate these two events and report that market quality is improving in pre-trade transparency in both events.

21) There have been relatively few real-world events in which disclosure policy changed, so that there have been relatively few studies of the effects of pre-trade transparency on market quality. In these few studies, there is no consensus on whether an increase in pre-trade transparency results in an improvement or deterioration in market quality (e.g., Madhavan, Porter, and Weaver, 2005; Boehmer, Saar, and Yu, 2005).

by Park and Eom (2005b) does not consider the endogeneity problem; market quality is affected by some relevant variables, notably volume and price, whereas volume and price are determined endogenously as well. Eom et al. (2007) rerun Park and Eom's (2005b) analyses of the two events, controlling for volume and price using a panel-data design and computing the standard errors in the clustered standard errors method (Rogers (1993)), clustering by time. They find that market quality is increasing and concave in pre-trade transparency, with significantly diminishing returns above a certain point. They argue that previous event studies of the effect of transparency have been econometrically flawed, and propose a procedure to correct this flaw, and show that this procedure can reverse the result of an event study.

Anonymity: Anonymity is an aspect of market transparency. A decrease (increase) in anonymity implies an increase (decrease) in market transparency. More specifically, if information about the order submitters is publicly disclosed before (after) the trade occurs, then pre-trade (post-trade) anonymity decreases. In general, pure electronic order-driven markets provide a higher level of anonymity than the hybrid market with the specialist or the dealers such as NYSE and Nasdaq. In the specialist or dealer mechanisms, the identity of the specialist or dealers providing the buy and sell quotes is known; in addition, the specialist can see who is placing each of the orders. By contrast, in an electronic market, generally only the buy and sell quotes, and not the identity of the individuals, are public information. Although KRX is an entirely electronic order-driven market, it differs significantly from other such markets in that it discloses the five largest cumulative sellers and buyers in real time which provides far less anonymity (i.e., more transparency) than most electronic order-driven markets.

Anonymity has a significant effect on market quality, specifically on liquidity, on the informational efficiency of prices, and on wealth transfers among traders. As mentioned above, KRX provides a running public disclosure of the largest five cumulative sellers and buyers, which gives such a good reference point for researchers to examine the roles of anonymity in the stock markets. Seon, Eom, and Hahn (2006) utilize this rule to analyze the effect of post-trade anonymity on market quality in KRX. Their study goes a step further than the currently available literature (e.g., Grammig, Schiereck and Theissen, 2001) that had focused only on comparisons of multiple markets or mechanisms with different levels of anonymity because they analyze a single market in which foreign traders are, in a sense, less anonymous than domestic traders.

In their study, Seon et al. (2006) consider an event whenever a foreign securities firm is added to the list of a running public disclosure of the largest five cumulative sellers and buyers. The authors examine approximately 8,000 events, roughly equally divided between selling or buying transactions, in the trade of the stocks of 28 sample firms listed on KRX during 2003. Seon et al. (2006) find that after the event, the volume increases and the duration between trades decreases, and that the informational efficiency of the prices improves.[22]

V. Market Macrostructure

Advanced major industrial countries have a hierarchy of stock markets based on their own capital market policies which facilitate funding capitals for established firms and newly-founded firms, protect investors, and maintain market integrity. The way to build up the hierarchy of stock markets

---

22) Seon et al. (2006) conclude that their results indicate that foreign investors have superior information.

is generally referred to as market macrostructure. The macrostructure of the Korean stock markets consists of the KOSPI market (main board) for established firms, the KOSDAQ market (new market) for IT or growth-oriented and newly-founded firms, and the FreeBoard (organized OTC stock market) for unlisted firms. In this subsection, we will discuss the comparisons between the KOSPI and the KOSDAQ markets and the comparisons between the KOSDAQ market and FreeBoard. We also discuss cross-listing between domestic and overseas markets. However, we will not deal with price comovement or integration of the Korean stock markets and foreign stock markets.

1. Comparisons among Markets in the Korean Stock Market Hierarchy

Main Board vs. New (or Growth) Market: When stock markets are classified from a market macrostructure perspective, a new market is generally defined as a capital market for firms that are relatively small, newly incorporated, rapidly growing, or IT-related, whereas a main board is generally defined as a capital market for firms that are larger and belong to traditional industries (Eom, Seon, and Chang, 2010). KRX has two securities markets: a main board (KOSPI or KSE before the 2005 consolidation) and a new market (KOSDAQ), both of which have the same trading mechanism, i.e. electronic limit-order book. KOSDAQ was established in July 1997 originally as the OTC stock market and was consolidated as a division of KRX in 2005. Since its inauguration, KOSDAQ has achieved remarkable growth owing to the boom in initial public offerings sponsored by venture capital firms. KOSDAQ has become another regulated securities market whose market activities are comparable with KOSPI on many measures; for example, even though the market capitalization of KOSDAQ was only approximately 10% of that of KOSPI in 2007, the number of shares outstanding and the turnover ratio were 69% and 244% of those of KOSPI, respectively (Eom et al., 2010). KOSDAQ is considered one of the very few successful new markets in the world; KOSDAQ ranked third out of 41 new markets in the world by market capitalization as of 2006 (Thornton, 2008).

First of all, Park, Nam, and Eom's (2007) study is unique, even internationally, in that they attempt to evaluate the market efficiency in KOSDAQ not only by considering its economic status in the Korean stock markets, but also by comparing KOSDAQ to Nasdaq and AIM. These later three markets are the most successful new markets in the world and have similar economic status in the stock markets of their respective countries. From a market macrostructure perspective, the authors apply the Engle and Lee (1999) component model to the *indices* representing the main board and new market of Korea along with the U.S. and the U.K. stock markets, where the component model decomposes volatility into a permanent and a transitory component. More specifically, they use the permanent component for the extent reflecting the arrival of new information and the transitory component for the extent reflecting market inefficiency.

Using various series of intraday and daily data from 1990 to 2005 and the test statistics that they develop, Park et al. (2007) find that the market efficiency in KOSDAQ was not inferior to that in KOSPI over their whole sample period. On the other hand, they claim that KOSDAQ was less efficient than KOSPI in their last subperiod (2001 to 2005). They also find that given the market efficiency of the main board in Korea, U.S. and U.K. stock markets, the relative efficiency of KOSDAQ is as great as that of Nasdaq, but it is greater than the relative efficiency of AIM.

However, the Engle and Lee (1999) component model is a time-series model so that it is difficult to clearly interpret permanent and transitory components into steady inflow of market-wide information and market friction, respectively (see Park et al., 2007, <Table 1>). In order to overcome this problem, Eom et al. (2010) directly estimate the efficiency of price discovery in *individual stocks* and examine the relative efficiency of price discovery between KOSPI and KOSDAQ in the Korean stock markets, focusing on the comparisons of each market's efficiency of price discovery in three aspects: speed, degree, and accuracy.

Eom et al. (2010) cover 200 KOSPI firms and 200 KOSDAQ firms which, for each market, have the 200 highest daily average volumes for all of 2007. They find that, for their entire firm sample, price discovery on KOSDAQ is less efficient than on KOSPI. However, the price discovery of the most liquid group (top 40 stocks) on KOSDAQ turns out to be as efficient as the forty lowest ranked among the top 200 liquid stocks on KOSPI. These two quintiles are comparable in terms of their firm characteristics, so it appears that the greater overall efficiency of price discovery on KOSPI is due to the characteristics of its listed firms, rather than any inherent difference between a main board and a new market. The authors also report evidence that the speed of price discovery is mainly determined by turnover, whereas the accuracy of price discovery is mainly determined by turnover and intraday volatility. All together, their results provide some policy implications not only for developing but also even for developed countries eager to establish a viable new market as follows: price discovery in a successful or viable new market in an emerging economy behaves as predicted in the market microstructure literature, even though that literature is based primarily on main boards in advanced stock markets. In addition, price discovery in the most liquid group in a new market is more accurate, though slower, than in the lowest group among the liquid stocks on a main board. On balance, the main board and new markets are comparable.

On the other hand, Lee and Seo's (2007) study is worth looking at even though it is not based on a market macrostructure perspective. Using the daily data of individual stocks listed on KOSPI from 1987 to 2005 and on KOSDAQ from 1996 to 2005, Lee and Seo (2007) decompose the (aggregate) volatility into the market volatility and idiosyncratic volatility components suggested by the Goyal and Santa-Clara's (2003) indirect method. They find that the idiosyncratic volatility consists of a primary portion of the (aggregate) volatility in both KOSPI and KOSDAQ markets; KOSPI (KOSDAQ) shows 60% (77%).[23] They also find that the aggregate and the idiosyncratic volatility measures predict statistically significantly the excess returns in KOSPI, whereas all the volatility measures including the aggregate, market and idiosyncratic volatility predict statistically significantly the excess returns in KOSDAQ. However, their empirical results show that there is no meaningful difference in information efficiency between KOSPI and KOSDAQ, which confirms the conclusions of Park et al. (2007) from a different perspective.[24]

Role of an Organized OTC Market. The first organized OTC stock market in Korea was the Third Market,[25] which was created in March 2000, specifically for the purpose of providing liquidity for stocks which could not meet the listing requirements for the regulated markets (the KOSPI and the KOSDAQ markets), particularly venture-related growth stocks; or which had been delisted from the regulated markets. Except for the first couple of years, however, the Third Market suffered from illiquidity arising mainly from regulatory inadequacy and the aftermath of the IT-bubble burst. Hence, the

---

23) In contrast, Goyal and Santa-Clara (2003) report that 75% of the (aggregate) volatility in the U.S. stock market comes from idiosyncratic volatility from July of 1962 to December of 1999.

24) During the first two years right after the inauguration of KOSDAQ, KOSPI had a special rule by which the firms transferred from KOSDAQ to KOSPI were exempted from the listing requirement for minimum distribution of a firm's shares. Yon (1998) examines 43 KOSDAQ firms associated with this rule over the period of July 1996 to December 1997. He shows empirical results that trading on KOSDAQ before the listing transfer to KOSPI is not helpful to reduce the information asymmetry about the firms. However, we cannot generalize Yon's (1998) result to the KOSDAQ's current situation because his sample comes from data before the time KOSDAQ can be considered an established market.

25) As aforementioned, KOSDAQ was originally founded as the OTC stock market in July 1997. Since it promptly became the new market in Korea, however, we do not categorize even the early phase of KOSDAQ as the OTC market.

Third Market did not fulfill the goals for which it was created. The Korean government decided to revamp the Third Market under its "Plan to Support Finance and Tax for Developing the Venture Industry." As a result, in July 2005, the Third Market was replaced by FreeBoard, market rules were strengthened, and some tax benefits were added. However, the tax benefits fell short of the tax benefits provided to the regulated markets and FreeBoard retained an archaic trading mechanism in which orders are usually matched only if they are identical in both price and quantity.

Eom, Park, and Yoon (2009) examine how effectively FreeBoard (including the Third Market, the predecessor of FreeBoard) has served three particular roles as the organized OTC stock market in Korea. The roles examined are as follows: providing liquidity and market quality, providing financing, and bridging the OTC and regulated markets.[26]

Using intraday transaction data for all stocks registered on both the Third Market and FreeBoard from March 2000 to December 2007, Eom et al. (2009) find the following results. First, market statistics of the firms registered on FreeBoard are qualitatively very low and its market quality measured by Bandi and Russell's (2006) FITC (full-information transaction cost) or Hasbrouck's (1991) pricing errors is much lower than those of KOSDAQ. Hence, FreeBoard does not provide adequate liquidity or market quality, and thus does not provide an attractive new investment opportunity for investors. Second, few public offerings have been made since its inauguration, so FreeBoard has not significantly facilitated financing for unlisted and unregulated firms. Third, for stocks moving from regulated markets down to FreeBoard, liquidity has dried up and volatility has increased substantially. In contrast, for stock trans-

---

26) Eom et al. (2009) study is the first paper that uses the intraday data to test FreeBoard's functional efficiency and economic significance. Major international papers have conducted analyses for the *one-way* bridging function from NYSE and Nasdaq down to OTCBB and Pink Sheets (e.g., Bollen and Christie, 2005; Macey, O'Hara, and Pompilio, 2005; Harris et al., 2008). Eom et al. (2009) conduct a complete comparative analysis of the OTC market's *two-way* bridging function, both from the regulated markets down to OTC, and from OTC up to the regulated markets, in order to investigate the significance of the OTC market's macrostructure.

ferring from FreeBoard up to KOSDAQ, both liquidity and volatility have improved tremendously. In the latter case, perhaps surprisingly, the stock prices have declined slightly, which the authors interpret as the prices were too high on FreeBoard since the greater liquidity suggests that pricing on KOSDAQ should be more efficient than it is on FreeBoard. Hence, Eom et al. (2009) conclude that these results, taken together, imply that FreeBoard's market efficiency is very low and that the functional gap between FreeBoard and KOSDAQ is huge, thereby exacerbating the inefficiency in the macro-structure of the Korean stock markets. In addition, they argue that FreeBoard's archaic trading mechanism has been the essential cause of inefficiency on FreeBoard and should be improved immediately.

2. Cross-Listing between Domestic and Foreign Stock Markets

In 1990, the Korean government allowed Korean firms to list their deposi-tary receipts (DRs) on foreign exchanges. Since then, most major Korean firms have listed their stocks or DRs on NYSE, Nasdaq, LSE, DB, and Luxemburg Stock Exchange. According to the extant literature, there are two main motiva-tions for cross-listing in the literature: the market segmentation hypothesis and the bonding hypothesis.[27] These two hypotheses have seemed to be ap-propriate to explain the reasons that Korean firms had cross-listed their DRs on both KRX and foreign exchange(s) until Eom, Binh, and Lee (2007) show that neither seems to apply to the POSCO's cross-listing on TSE.

POSCO, the Korean steel corporation, is the world's fourth-largest steel producer. POSCO cross-listed the American depositary receipts (ADRs) of its stock, traded in Japanese yen, on TSE on November 22, 2005; this was the first cross-listing, whether actual stock or ADRs, for any Korean com-

---

27) For details on the recent academic developments concerning cross-listing, see Karolyi (2006) and King and Segal (2009).

pany on TSE. For the cross-listing, POSCO retired 3.5 million shares listed on KRX and cross-listed the corresponding ADRs on TSE, so the transaction neither changed the effective number of outstanding POSCO shares nor raised capital for POSCO. It is also noteworthy that both exchanges have exactly the same trading hours, i.e., 9:00 a.m. to 3:00 p.m. (except for TSE which has a lunch break) and are in the same time zone.

Eom et al. (2007) examine the location of price discovery of POSCO stock cross-listed on KRX and TSE. They analyze the information share which is defined as the relative contribution to the discovery of one price by the other price in a cointegrated time-series system of prices which share common stochastic trends. They estimate the information share using a vector error correction model (VECM) and the long-run impact matrix obtained in a vector moving average (VMA) representation of the VECM, as developed by Grammig, Melvin, and Schlag (2005). Using minute-by-minute data during the regular trading hours for stock prices and exchange rates (April 20, 2006 to June 8, 2006), they find that price discovery of POSCO stock occurs mostly in the home market, KRX, and that the Korean won/Japanese yen exchange rate is exogenous with respect to POSCO stock prices on KRX and TSE.[28] They also report that this result is robust regardless of the ordering of the prices in the Cholesky factorization. They propose a new hypothesis concerning the motivation for cross-listing beyond the market segmentation hypothesis and bonding hypothesis, which would/should focus on the firm's business strategy pursuing the round-the-clock trading of this stock and the globalization strategy of the exchange.

On the other hand, Park (2009) utilizes global trading of cross-listed Korean stocks to explain an empirical stylized fact that open-to-open return variance

---

28) This result might be affected by the data which covers too early and brief a period of POSCO's cross-listing on TSE. Using a longer and later time span over 85 trading days from March 9, 2007 to July 10, 2007, however, Binh, Chong, and Eom (2010) prove that the result is very robust.

is greater than close-to-close returns variance in KRX. Using the largest 13 cross-listed firms and 87 non-cross-listed firms which make up the KOSPI 200 index, he finds that the variance ratio of open-to-open relative to close-to-close returns reduces significantly for the sample of 13 cross-listed stocks. He claims that this result in KRX supports the explanation by Amihud and Mendelson (1989, 1991) that the overnight non-trading period causes greater volatility at the market opening. Park's (2009) study is an interesting attempt to combine a macrostructure issue with a microstructure issue, showing a worthwhile direction for future research on Korean market microstructure.

VI. Expansion of Market Microstructure to the Fields of Investments and Corporate Finance

1. Expansion to Investments

As the definition implies, market microstructure overlaps a subfield of investments, especially focusing on price formation. The market microstructure model is an equilibrium model with asymmetric information. In this subsection, we discuss some issues related to empirical asset pricing: return behavior, the relationship between volume and volatility, the lead-lag effect of trading volume, and the roles of liquidity and private-information risk in price formation. For this discussion, we only include papers which discuss these issues from a market microstructure viewpoint. We do not include literature on issues such as momentum, contrarian and similar strategies.

1.1 Return Behavior

Since Fisher (1966), the short-term autocorrelation of portfolio returns has received much attention from academic researchers and securities traders. For U.S. stock markets, daily individual stock returns exhibit either positive or negative autocorrelation, but the average autocorrelation over all individual stocks is typically not statistically significant. By contrast, daily (and longer-term) portfolio returns exhibit positive autocorrelation. The coefficient of positive first-order autocorrelation is large and statistically very significant for portfolios of small and medium firms, while the findings on statistical significance are somewhat mixed for portfolios of large firms (e.g., Campbell, Lo, and MacKinlay, 1997, pp. 66-68).

There are three main possible explanations of these stylized facts: market microstructure biases including nonsynchronous trading effect and bid-ask bounce effect, time-varying risk premia, and partial price adjustment. Since time-varying risk premia are not significant for daily return autocorrelation over a short period of time (Anderson, 2011), market microstructure biases and partial price adjustment are the main focuses for research. Thus far, however, Anderson, Eom, Hahn, and Park (2008) are the only study for the U.S. stock markets which tests those hypotheses directly. Their tests "are *direct*, using disjoint time intervals, separated by a trade, to eliminate the nonsynchronous trading effect and minimize bid-ask bounce." They find "compelling evidence that stock return autocorrelation is not spurious; partial price adjustment is an important source, and in some cases the main source, of the autocorrelation."

For Korean stock markets, most of all the related papers (Kim and Bae, 1994; Khil, 1997; Lee and Ahn, 1997; Chang and Kim, 2002; Chung and Kim, 2002) prior to Park and Eom (2005a) examine only the existence of (positive) autocorrelation of daily (or weekly) portfolio returns and those papers have generally found that daily returns on the KOSPI exhibit positive first-order autocorrelation.[29]

---

29) Ku (1992) is an exception who tests 180 individual firms over the period of 1990 to 1991. His variance ratio

To understand the sources of autocorrelations in Korean individual stock and portfolio returns, Park and Eom (2005a) examine the relative contributions of the nonsynchronous trading effect and partial price adjustment to the autocorrelation in Korean stock returns. For this, the authors directly test whether or not the positive autocorrelation in portfolio returns results entirely from the nonsynchronous trading effect by using the method of covariance decomposition of Anderson et al. (2008).

With the various daily and transaction data of individual stocks and major stock indices on KSE (January 4, 1980 to April 3, 2003 and January 4, 1998 to December 28, 2001), Park and Eom (2005a) find that the partial price adjustment hypothesis is strongly supported. More specifically, they find the following results: first, the hypothesis that partial price adjustment plays a significant part in the autocorrelation was strongly supported, regardless of the test method. Second, this finding staunchly holds up in three additional robustness tests (separating periods of bull and bear markets, calculating returns from opening price (which on KSE is set by a call auction) to the next opening price, rather than from closing price to closing price, and comparing the first-order autocorrelation coefficients of the opening and the closing price returns). Third, daily portfolio returns show positive autocorrelation for each of their five portfolios, whereas the weekly and monthly portfolio returns show positive autocorrelation only for an equally-weighted market index and a small-firm index. Daily individual stock returns predominantly show statistically significant positive autocorrelation, in contrast with the U.S. stock markets, where individual stock returns show positive or negative autocorrelation.

On the other hand, Ko (2008) examines the effects of infrequent trading

---

tests show that the less frequently stocks are traded on a daily basis, the more the daily autocorrelation of stock returns is positive or negative. Choi and Na (1998) find the positive cross-autocorrelation between small stocks' concurrent returns and lagged response to the large stocks' returns. They report that nonsynchronous trading fails to explain this directional asymmetry in KSE.

or overnight non-trading on the behavior of daily, overnight, and daytime returns. Developing a simple theoretical model and empirically analyzing the individual stock and portfolio returns, Ko (2008) finds that the covariance of the observed close-to-open and open-to-close returns of the same day is negative, while that of the observed open-to-close return on day t-1 and close-to-open return on day t is indeterminate. These relationships are consistent with the empirical evidence by Stoll and Whaley (1990) and George and Hwang (1995).

1.2 The Relationship between Volume and Return Volatility

There is extensive literature in finance on the relationship between volume and return volatility.[30] Clark's (1973) mixture-of-distributions hypothesis (MDH) provides a theoretical foundation for most empirical research on this topic. According to MDH, volume and return volatility are positively correlated because they are driven by the same underlying latent news arrival or information flow.

There are two empirical research lines on the contemporaneous relationship between volume and volatility and on the asymmetric effect of volatility. Tauchen and Pitts (1983) exemplify one research line of MDH that focuses on estimating the parameters and the latent variable(s) of the model, and subsequently evaluates the adequacy of the model based on how well the data fit and explain the behaviors of volume and volatility. Lamoureux and Lastrapes (1990) exemplify the other research line of MDH that includes trading volume in the conditional variance equation of the generalized autoregressive conditional heteroskedasticity (GARCH) model.

---

30) Generally, we define the volume of a stock as the total number of shares of the stock traded in a day. "Trade size" usually means the number of shares traded in a single transaction. However, some authors whose papers we reference use "trade size" to mean "volume" as defined here. A useful summary of the empirically stylized relationship between volume and stock returns is found in Karpoff (1987), Goodhart and O'Hara (1997), and Lo and Wang (2000).

This line of studies does not specifically estimate the model, but it tests MDH by comparing the theoretical implications of MDH for the volume-volatility dynamics with the actual empirical dynamics.

In this subsection, we discuss the empirical studies within the context of MDH only. Theoretical market microstructure models also provide a different approach, predicting positive correlation between volume and return volatility which basically arises from asymmetric information among market participants (e.g., O'Hara, 1995). The research from this approach will be discussed in subsection VI. 1. 3.

The Contemporaneous Relationship and the Asymmetric Effect of Return Volatility: Internationally, it is well-established empirically that the volatility of financial returns is conditionally time-varying, clustering, and persistent in weekly, daily, or intraday data (Engle, 1982; Bollerslev, 1986). The persistence of conditional volatility tends to increase with the sampling frequency. However, there is little consensus on the sources of these ARCH/GARCH effects. One possible theoretical explanation is the role of new information in the financial markets.

In Korea, most studies on the contemporaneous or dynamic relationships between volume and return volatility have been conducted either with or without considering ARCH/GARCH effects. Even when the effects are considered, the researchers have tested this topic mostly using ARCH/GARCH models as suggested by, for example, Lamoureux and Lastrapes (1990) and Gallant, Rossi, and Tauchen (1992, 1993). In contrast, only limited numbers of studies utilize the other research line, which estimates the parameters and latent variable(s) of the MDH model, which attempts to theoretically reflect the sources of the ARCH/GARCH effects.

Volume and return volatility in the Korean stock markets is contemporaneously positively related and the conditional volatility is persistent. This empirical evidence is unanimously confirmed by all the papers on this topic (see Gong, 1997; Kho, 1997; Jeong, 2001; Kang and Yoon, 2007); it is robust irrespective of the sample periods, the types of GARCH models, and the sample firms or the indices used for the tests.[31]

However, the empirical evidence on the existence of an asymmetric effect in return volatility is mixed in the Korean stock markets. According to an international empirical-stylized fact, return volatility tends to be higher in a falling market than in a rising market. Ohk (1997) and Ku (2000) support this asymmetric effect of daily return volatility; Ohk (1997) examines the daily KOSPI data from 1991 to 1996 by using the Glosten, Jagannathan, and Runkle (1993) method, whereas Ku (2000) examines the daily data of 355 stocks from 1990 to 1998 by using the Hentschel (1995) method. In contrast, Kho (1997) reports that the asymmetric effect of return volatility is not supported over the sample period of 1980 to 1995 by estimating a semi-nonparametric model suggested by Gallant et al. (1992, 1993) for the daily KOSPI data.

Internationally, leverage effect, volatility feedback effect, and information inefficiency are referred to as three possible sources for the asymmetric effect of daily return volatility. Using the daily KOSPI return data from 1993 to 2000 and estimating the Glosten et al. (1993) method, Byun, Jo, and Cheong (2003) find that leverage effect and information inefficiency are determinants of the asymmetric effect in the Korean stock markets. However, they find little evidence in support of the volatility feedback effect. On the other hand, Gong (1997) finds that there is no statistically

---

31) Instead of using trading volume as a proxy for information arrival, Khil and Chung (2005) directly use the number of E-Daily news headlines, i.e. public information, during an intraday time interval (30 minutes, 1 hour, 3 hours, and a day). Then, they examine the relationship between the number of E-Daily news headlines and the market volatility in KSE by employing the GARCH model in a similar way that Kalev, Liu, Pham, and Jarnecic (2004) do for the Australian Securities Exchange. For return volatility, Khil and Chung (2005) use one-minute KOSPI data for the period of 2001 to 2003. They find that there is a positive contemporaneous relationship between the arrival of public information and return volatility. As the intraday time interval is expanded to 3 hours or a day, the relative impact of public information on market return volatility decreases. In addition, the relative impact of international news is larger than that of domestic news.

significant relationship between the coefficient of volume in the EGARCH variance equation and debt to equity ratio or fixed-asset to total-asset ratio, arguing that leverage effect is not supported.

The Short-Term Predictability of the Level and Volatility of Trading Volume: Most papers which examine the contemporaneous relationship between volume and return volatility using GARCH models also test the short-term predictability of trading volume on return or return volatility. In general, there is a consensus that the previous (*t*-1) daily return has a positive impact on the current (*t*) daily volume (see Gong, 1997; Kho, 1997; Ku and Choi, 1998).

However, there are mixed results on the impact of the previous (*t*-1) daily volume on the current (*t*) daily stock return.[32] Gong (1997) and Kho (1997) report that the current stock price decreases when the previous volume is (relatively) high, but the statistical significance is very weak. In order to explain this statistical insignificance, Ku and Choi (1998) pay attention to the method of calculating the daily stock returns. They insist that the previous day's volume affects the current day's stock return when the open-to-close return is used, instead of the close-to-close return. On the other hand, Chang (1997) emphasizes the importance of detrending seasonality and the long-term trend of volume or volume volatility in order to understand the short-term prediction of volume or volume volatility on stock return. Using the daily KOSPI data from 1987 to 1996, he finds that the volume and volume volatility of the previous days (*t*-1 to *t*-4) are not helpful for predicting the current day's stock return. Once the seasonality and long-term trend are detrended, however, the volume and volume volatility of the previous days (*t*-2 to *t*-4) are helpful for predicting the current day's stock return with statistical significance. Chang's (1997) emphasis on considering the seasonality of the level and volatility of

---

32) Note that we have discussed another type of short-term predictability in section II. 3, where we examine whether the limit order book can predict the direction of short-term price changes.

volume is consistent with the Jeong's (2001) finding that there exists a seasonal pattern in the conditional heteroskedasticity in daily excess returns of KOSPI and three firm-size-based indices from 1982 to 1999.

Thus far, we have discussed the short-term predictability of the level and volatility of daily volume by using the GARCH models. Now, we turn to the papers investigating the same issue by different methods. Campbell, Grossman, and Wang (1993) argue that if an uninformed trader sells for exogenous reasons and the smart money takes it, then the stock price falls on that day but the fall tends to be reversed on subsequent days. Hence, an increase in the trading volume decreases the autocorrelation of stock returns. Using daily return and volume data of all individual stocks listed on KSE from 1980 to 2000, Kook and Jeong (2001) test the theoretical prediction of Campbell et al. (1993) in the Korean stock markets by using non-parametric analyses. They find that the daily stock return reversal occurs more frequently if trading volume has increased in the previous trading day.

The Lead-Lag Effect of Trading Volume: Park and Chang (2003) test whether the lead-lag effect on stock returns is related to trading volume by using all individual firms listed on KSE from 1980 to 2000. They annually form portfolios based on the trading volume at the end of the year and then conduct the cross-autocorrelation and the VAR analyses of the portfolio returns. The cross-autocorrelation test shows that the correlation between lagged high-trading-volume portfolio returns and current low-trading-volume portfolio returns is always larger than the correlation between lagged low-trading-volume portfolio returns and current high-trading-volume portfolio returns. This lead-lag effect of trading volume is stronger in a bullish market than in a bearish market.[33]

---

33) Choi and Na (1998) analyze the lead-lag effect of portfolio returns according to firm size. Comparing common

1.3 The Roles of Liquidity in Asset Pricing

Harris (2003) defines liquidity as the ability to trade a large quantity of stock quickly, at low [implicit and explicit] cost and at will. Liquidity is the most important characteristic of well-functioning markets. As the definition indicates, trading volume is a liquidity measure, in fact, which has been very popularly used from the early days of market microstructure research.

In the financial world, there is an adage, "it takes volume to move prices," which succinctly summarizes the informational role of trading volume in the stock price adjustment process. This adage is modeled in the noisy rational expectations equilibrium (NREE) model. According to the NREE model, a stock price is determined from the results of a game occurred among three types of market participants: informed traders, uninformed traders, and market makers. All of these market participants have asymmetric information on the intrinsic value of the stock. The stock price determined in the game reflects *partially*, not fully, the information possessed by these various participants. The remaining part of information will be reflected in market statistics such as trading volume, number of trades, order flow, or even past prices (see Appendix in Eom and Yoon, 2001).

In this subsection, we start our discussion from the papers on appropriate measures of liquidity, and then talk about the liquidity commonality, liquidity factor, and, finally, liquidity risk. Similarly, we can also search for other sources which reveal the remaining part of information within the NREE framework. Asymmetric information is one, the details of which we will discuss in the next subsection.

---

stocks in KSE for the period of 1985 to 1996, they find that asymmetric cross-autocorrelation exists; the current return of the small firm portfolio has a positive relationship with the previous return of the large firm portfolio, but not vice versa.

Practical Measures of Liquidity: Ku (1994) recognizes, first in Korea, the possibility that the differences of the level of liquidity among stocks will affect investors' trading decisions and, in turn, will be reflected in the price movements. He attempts to find practically usable measures for the level of liquidity. He defines "a 'phenomenal variable' as a measurable pattern in the price and trading volume which is attributable to the liquidity differential," whereas he also defines "a 'characteristic variable' as the variable that explains the difference of phenomenal variables." Then, he analyzes the correlations between these two variables by using intraday price and volume data from June 29 to October 2 in 1992 for 580 stocks listed on KSE. He finds that, among the characteristic variables such as the instantaneous rate of price change, the implicit bid-ask spread, and the number of price changes, trading volume is the most prominent variable in explaining the differences among stocks.

Since Ku's (1994) prescient work, no papers have followed up on the effective measure of liquidity. In this regards, Yang (2010) is one of the few. Using the intraday data of relative spread in KSE from April 1993 to December 2004, he constructs the daily market liquidity by the Chordia, Roll, and Subrahmanyam (2001) method and finds some interesting characteristics of it as follows. First, the daily percentage change of market liquidity in KSE is 7% to 9%, which is a substantially large variation compared to the 2% of NYSE found in Chordia et al. (2001). It is strongly negatively autocorrelated, which is similar to the U.S. market. Second, the increase in the short interest rate and default spread affects the considerable decrease in market liquidity. Market return (KOSPI return) is statistically significantly related to market liquidity, which responds asymmetrically to contemporaneous market movement; market liquidity decreases much more in down markets than it increases in up markets. Third, in the day-of-the-week effect, market liquidity is the highest on Monday and then decreases gradually.

Liquidity Commonality and Liquidity Factor: There are three approaches in the literature to analyzing the relationship between liquidity and stock returns. The first approach tests whether liquidity is a characteristic variable to explain stock returns (e.g., Amihud and Mendelson, 1986). The second approach tests whether liquidity commonality exists and tries to determine its causes (e.g., Chordia, Roll, and Subrahmanyam, 2000; Hasbrouck and Seppi, 2001). The third approach analyzes the effect of liquidity commonality as an undiversifiable risk factor on the equilibrium pricing of securities. For the U.S. stock markets, Pastor and Stambaugh (2003) and Acharya and Pedersen (2005) argue that the liquidity might be a risk reflected in the stock price.

Seon, Eom, and Hahn (2005) examine the existence, causes, and characteristics of liquidity commonality in KSE. Liquidity commonality is a phenomenon in which the liquidity of individual stocks comoves with the market-wide liquidity. Using intraday data on 244 firms listed on KSE from 1999 to 2000 and the same methodology as Chordia et al. (2000), Seon et al. (2005) find that the liquidity commonality in KSE (an electronic order-driven market) is greater than that in NYSE (a market with specialists). Analyzing the liquidity commonality in three portfolios by firm size, they find different patterns from those found in previous studies on NYSE. For example, Chordia et al. (2000) find that the liquidities of large NYSE firms are more responsive than those of small firms to changes in the market-wide liquidity. In contrast, Seon et al. (2005) find the opposite in KSE, which is consistent with theoretical market microstructure models.[34] Second, liquidity commonality has a J-shaped intraday pattern, in contrast to the inverse J-shaped pattern exhibited by individual

---

34) Seon et al. (2005) explain the different results between KSE and NYSE in the following way. On exchanges with market makers, the market maker incurs inventory costs, and these play a significant role in liquidity (the inverse of trading costs). However, on an exchange without market makers, inventory costs are very small and the bulk of trading costs arise from asymmetric information. However, because the individuals providing the liquidity (limit order traders) have much less information than would a specialist, these asymmetric information costs may be significantly higher, leading to lower liquidity.

stock and market-wide liquidity. They claim that this suggests that there are additional sources, such as program trading, for liquidity commonality in KSE.

Choe and Yang (2010) also confirm that there exists liquidity commonality in KSE during 2003 to 2004. In addition to information asymmetry and program trading that Seon et al. (2005) report as determinants of liquidity commonality, Choe and Yang (2010) find that order imbalance and investor sentiment are associated with higher liquidity commonality.[35] However, volume and stock returns are not significantly related to liquidity commonality.

Liquidity commonality generally suggests that there exists an undiversifiable common factor underlying the liquidities of individual stocks, just as there is an undiversifiable common factor underlying the prices of individual stocks. Nam, Park, and Eom (2005) examine whether the common factor exists in liquidity in KSE and if so, how many common factors exist. Using intraday data on the 30 largest firms on KSE and the one-minute transaction data of the KOSPI 200 stock index futures for the calendar year 2001, they do three analyses suggested by Hasbrouck and Seppi (2001), specifically, principal components analysis, canonical correlation analysis, and time-varying regression analysis. Nam et al. (2005) find that only a single common factor exists in all of their liquidity variables. The canonical correlation between the liquidity common factor and the common factor in stock returns is very low (0.14) and the explanatory power of the liquidity common factor for the common factor in stock returns is virtually zero. Moreover, the effect of the liquidity common factor on the informational component of price impact is much smaller than the effect of own-firm liquidity. Taken together, they insist that their results indicate that the liquidity common factor exists, but it is not a source of priced risk in the Korean stock markets.

---

35) On the other hand, Ku (1997a) shows that trading volume and intraday price movements explain the stock returns statistically significantly by using the Engle, Lilien, and Robins (1987) ARCH-M model during the six months sample period (1995~1996).

Liquidity Risk: The studies above confirm the existence of liquidity commonality and liquidity factor(s) in KSE. Given these favorable preconditions, the tests on the liquidity risk by Park and Eom (2008b) and Yun, Ku, Eom, and Hahn (2009) provide some support that liquidity plays a risk in determining stock returns in the Korean stock markets.

Park and Eom (2008b) examine how the illiquidity premium affects the portfolio returns for all the stocks listed on the KOSPI and KOSDAQ markets by using 10 years (1996 to 2006) of daily data. Their Fama and MacBeth (1973) cross-sectional regression results show that the relative spread is a significant and robust characteristic variable in explaining the expected excess return for each portfolio.[36] In contrast, their Fama and French (1993) time-series regression results show that the economic significance of a liquidity risk factor (IMV) is limited; the single-factor model that used IMV as its sole factor explains the expected portfolio excess return. However, no other meaningful model specification is found when combining or using other explanatory factors such as the market risk factor (MKT), the size factor (SMB) or the B/M factor (HML). This is in a contrast to the case of U.S. markets for which SMB and HML reportedly have their own economic significances when added to a single-factor model that uses MKT. Park and Eom (2008b) also find that the statistical significance of relative spread in the KOSPI market is very strong, while that in the KOSDAQ market is weak.

Using monthly return data over the period from 1991 to 2007, Yun et al. (2009) find no evidence for book-to-market or momentum effect, but find for turnover effect in KRX by using the Fama-MacBeth regression framework. Based on this result, they construct a three-factor model which replaces the

---

36) Kwon and Park (1997) report similar results to those of Park and Eom's (2008b) cross-sectional regression analysis. Instead of relative spread, Kwon and Park (1997) estimate the implicit liquidity cost developed by George et al. (1991) for the analysis. Choe and Yang's (2009) cross-sectional analysis supports this result by estimating the Amihud (2002) illiquidity measure from TAQ data for the period of 1993 to 2004, but their time-series regression result supports it very marginally.

book-to-market factor (HML) with the liquidity factor (NMP) in the Fama-French three-factor model. Yun et al. (2009) find that NMP shows significant explanatory power for the cross-section of stock returns. Comparing their alternative three-factor model to the Fama-French three-factor model, they argue that their alternative three-factor model which incorporates a liquidity factor may be more useful and relevant for understanding the systematic variation of stock returns in Korea than the Fama-French three-factor model.

1.4 The Private-Information Risk in Asset Pricing

After theoretically providing explicit estimates of the extent of private information (PIN) by a series of papers,[37] Easley and O'Hara, with a co-author Hvidkjaer, have finally demonstrated that these information probabilities affect cross-sectional asset returns by incorporating their PIN estimates into a Fama and French (1992) asset pricing framework for NYSE (Easley et al., 2002). Using adjusted PIN (AdjPIN), however, Duarte and Young (2009) claim that the liquidity effect unrelated to information asymmetry is the key element driving the relation between PIN and the cross-section of expected returns.

Research on the role of private-information risk in asset pricing in the Korean stock markets also confirms that PIN is a biased measure explaining the cross-sectional relation of stock returns. For this examination, Choe and Yang (2007) conduct three different asset pricing tests: Fama and French (1992) cross-section analysis, Fama and French (1993) time-series analysis, and Brennan and Subrahmanyam (1996) pooling regression analysis. Choe and Yang (2007) find that the measures of information risk by the Glosten and Harris (1988, GH) model and the Hasbrouck (1991), Foster and Viswanathan (1993, HFV) model support the positive relation with excess return, while PIN does not support it using any of the three approaches.

---

37) See subsection II. 2. 4 about the details on the measure of PIN and on Duarte and Young's (2009) critics on PIN.

Using intraday transaction data on individual stocks in KRX from January 1997 to December 2005, Park and Eom (2008a) estimate both PIN and AdjPIN and conduct the cross-sectional regression analyses for comparing these measures. They find that the cross-sectional relationship between PIN and portfolio excess returns is economically insignificant when they analyze the relationship using PIN estimated from the previous year's data and the firm size measured by market capitalization at the end of the previous year. Reducing the estimation interval for PIN to a quarter does not increase the statistical significance of the relationship between PIN and portfolio excess returns. Only when they analyze the relationship between PIN in the current period and current portfolio returns, then do they observe the relationship to be positive and statistically significant. This generally indicates that the PIN does not explain portfolio returns, but it is only useful for detecting the private-information risk that occurs during an extremely short period of time in the Korean stock markets. In contrast, Park and Eom (2008a) find that AdjPIN generally has an economically significant relationship with portfolio excess returns. The KRX data also reflects positive correlations between buyer-initiated trade and seller-initiated trade. The measure of AdjPIN shows the same positive correlations as the real-world results from using KRX data, whereas the measure of PIN reflects negative ones. This suggests that PIN should be revised in order to explain the empirically stylized facts found in KRX, an order-driven market, as Duarte and Young (2009) insist that it should be in the U.S. quote-driven market.

2 Expansion to Corporate Finance

We have no papers, save Ahn (2006) and Park (2011), concerning corporate finance combined with market microstructure framework. Therefore, this might well be a promising area for further research in market micro-structure in Korea.

Ahn (2006) investigates how the degree of informed trading is related to the percentage of ownership held by the four investor types: insiders, individual investors, institutional investors, and foreign investors. For the measure for the degree of informed trading, he utilizes the Madhavan, Richardson, and Roomans (1997) model which has been commonly used in market microstructure literature to decompose the adverse-selection cost component out of the spread. Using a sample of 437 common stocks on KSE and sample periods of the three first quarters of 1997, 1999, and 2001, he employs the 2SLS (two-stage least squares) regression analysis. The higher insider ownership (retail individual ownership) is, the higher (lower) adverse-selection costs are. Ahn (2006) claims that higher insider ownership results in poorer corporate governance as well as a reduction in the transparency of information available for investors. He further claims that small individual investors are uninformed traders. Institutional investors' ownership is not related to adverse-selection costs. The relation between foreign ownership and adverse-selection costs becomes significantly positive only after the 1997 Asian financial crisis. This contrasts to the finding that the relationships among other equity ownerships and adverse-selection costs are invariant across different sample periods. The author interprets the results to suggest that institutional investors are either information-based or uninformed liquidity traders, and that foreign investors begin to have a significant influence on the price information in the Korean stock markets after the post-crisis period.

Park (2011) examines whether the impact of the liquidity on the expected stock return varies according to the payout policy. He uses the daily relative spread as the proxy of illiquidity and treats it with linear spline functions to measure the change of its impact on the expected return in each sub-range specified by those functions during the sample period from 1999 to 2008. Using the 2SLS regression with instrumental variables (IV), he finds that convexity exists for the stock repurchasing portfolios in the sub-range, while only concavity exists for the cash-dividend portfolios. This result supports the proposition that the relation between the relative spread and the expected return is convex for the repurchasing firms. This is due to the tax effect as proposed by Gottesman and Jacoby (2006) who modify the Amihud and Meldelson (1986) proposition that the relation between them is concave piecewise-linear. Park's (2011) finding is unique in that it is internationally the first confirmation of Gottesman and Jacoby (2006). Park (2011) also shows that his results are generally robust by employing the Heckman's (1976) two-step estimation and the probit regression analysis.

VII. Concluding Remarks

Market microstructure studies the process by which investors' latent demands are ultimately translated into prices and volumes under a specific set of rules. This paper provides the first comprehensive review of the empirical market microstructure literature on the Korean financial markets, published in the five leading Korean journals from 1990 to mid-2010. It includes the following five main categories: (1) micro aspects of the microstructure world: orders and trades, basic market quality, price discovery, and trading mechanisms; (2) trading protocols: rules and regulations related to trading; (3) market transparency; (4) market macrostructure; and (5) expansion of market microstructure to the fields of investments and corporate finance.

This survey addresses the current status and future perspectives on market microstructure in the Korean financial markets as follows:

- **Micro Aspects of the Microstructure World and Trading Protocol** — we address not only general features of the electronic limit-order book mechanism, but also many empirical phenomena specific to the Korean financial markets. The research in the Korean market microstructure has been disproportionately concentrated into these two categories of micro aspects and trading protocol. Although there have been many papers, most of them were conducted during the 1990s, which has not permitted good perspectives on the academic and policy implications by periods, subjects, and trading protocols. Traditionally, this area has been a core of market microstructure. Moreover, the rapid advance in trading-associated IT (e.g., algo, HFT, DMA, etc.) and the wide spread globalization of trading, and the continuing emphasis of regulators on investor protection and market integrity ensure that this area of research will continue to grow and evolve.

- **Transparency and Market Macrostructure** — to date, the research on this area is very limited. Even today, Korea is categorized as an emerging market, albeit an advanced emerging market. The efficiency of price discovery may be approaching that of advanced markets, but it has yet to attain that status. Given this stage of capital market development, it is essential to establish the appropriate market macrostructure (including a consideration of transparency for the relevant hierarchical level of each market) that reflects well the uniqueness of the Korean financial markets. Thus, this area could result in international publications. In addition, the urgent but long delayed introduction of multilateral trading facilities (MTFs) has left a vacuum in the Korean research. Research in this area should be greatly expanded.

- **Expansion to the Fields of Investments, Corporate Finance, and Other Markets** — it is very important to apply the issues and framework of market microstructure to financial markets other than stocks. So far, the research of market microstructure combined with investments has been fairly active, whereas that combined with corporate finance is at its inception. For financial markets other than stocks, we need to make a concerted effort to encourage research beyond the current nascent stages. For derivatives markets, the market microstructure framework has been mostly used to examine the relationship between futures and options markets and the spot market(e.g., Kho and Kim, 2002; Bae and Jang, 2003; Bae, Kwon, and Park, 2004; Kang, 2009). (For example, the effects of futures or options markets on volume and/or volatility on the spot market; the effect of the introduction of derivatives markets on the spot market.) In contrast, the pure market microstructure research, which investigates the futures or options market independently, is very rare (e.g., Eom, Oh, and Hahn, 2006; Moon and Hong, 2007; Kang and Park, 2008; Ahn, Kang, and Ryu, 2008, 2010) and is limited mostly to subjects such as the maturity effect (e.g., Eom and Hahn, 2005; Chay and Ryu, 2006; Choe and Eom, 2007). There are almost no studies in the category of trading protocol. There is only a single microstructure paper for bond markets (Park, Shin, and Rhee, 2007). The situation for FX market microstructure research is not much different (e.g., Seon and Eom, 2006, 2010, 2011; Chung, 2008).

References[38)]

Acharya, V. V. and L. H. Pedersen, "Asset Pricing with Liquidity Risk", *Journal of Financial Economics*, Vol. 77(2005), pp. 375-419.

Ahn, H., "Ownership Holdings by Investor Type and Information Asymmetry", *Asian-Pacific Journal of Financial Studies*, Vol. 35, No. 2(2006), pp. 35-73(in Korean).
안희준, "투자자별 소유지분과 정보비대칭", 증권학회지, 제35권 제2호 (2006), pp. 35-73.

Ahn, H., J. Kang, and D. Ryu, "Informed Trading in the Index Option Market: The Case of KOSPI 200 Options", *Journal of Futures Markets*, Vol. 28(2008), pp. 1-29.

Ahn, H., J. Kang, and D. Ryu, "Information Effects of Trade Size and Trade Direction: Evidence from the KOSPI 200 Index Options Market", *Asia-Pacific Journal of Financial Studies*, Vol. 39, No. 3(2010), pp. 301-339.

Allen, F. and D. Gale, "Stock Price Manipulation", *Review of Financial Studies*, Vol. 5(1992), pp. 503-529.

Amihud, Y., "Illiquidity and Stock Returns: Cross-Section and Time-Series Effects", *Journal of Financial Markets*, Vol. 5(2002), pp. 31-56.

Amihud, Y. and H. Mendelson, "Dealership Market: Market Making with Inventory", *Journal of Financial Economics*, Vol. 8(1980), pp. 31-53.

Amihud, Y. and H. Mendelson, "Asset Pricing and the Bid-Ask Spread", *Journal of Financial Economics*, Vol. 17(1986), pp. 223-249.

Amihud, Y. and H. Mendelson, "Trading Mechanisms and Stock Returns: An Empirical Investigation", *Journal of Finance*, Vol. 42(1987), pp. 533-553.

Amihud, Y. and H. Mendelson, "Market Microstructure and Price Discovery in the Tokyo Stock Exchange", *Japan and the World Economy*, Vol.

---

38) * denotes an article with a Korean title of a work published in Korean; the title here is our English translation.

1(1987), pp. 341-370.

Amihud, Y. and H. Mendelson, "Volatility, Efficiency, and Trading: Evidence from Japanese Market", *Journal of Finance*, Vol. 46(1991), pp. 1765-1789.

Anand, A. and S. Chakravarty, "Stealth Trading in Options Markets", *Journal of Financial and Quantitative Analysis*, Vol. 42(2007), pp. 167-188.

Anderson, R. M., "Time-Varying Risk Premia", *Journal of Mathematical Economics*, forthcoming(2011).

Anderson, R. M., K. S. Eom, S. B. Hahn, and J.-H. Park, "Stock Return Autocorrelation is Not Ppurious", *Working paper*, UC Berkeley(2008).

Angel, J., L. Harris, and C. Spatt, "Equity Trading in the 21st Century", *Quarterly Review of Finance*, forthcoming(2010).

Asquith, P., A. P. Pathak, and R. J. Ritter, "Short Interest, Institutional Ownership, and Stock Returns", *Journal of Financial Economics*, Vol. 78(2005), pp. 243-276.

Bae, K.-H. and S. Jang, "A Comparative Analysis of Informational Efficiency of KOSDAQ50 and KOSPI200 Index Futures", *Korean Journal of Futures and Options*, Vol. 11, No. 2(2003), pp. 27-49(in Korean).
배기홍, 장수재, "KOSDAQ50 지수선물시장과 KOSPI200 지수선물시장의 정보효율성 비교분석", 선물연구, 제11권 제2호(2003), pp. 27-49.

Bae, K., H. Jang, and K. S. Park, "Trader's Choice between Limit and Market Orders: Evidence from NYSE Stocks", *Journal of Financial Markets*, Vol. 6(2003), pp. 517-538.

Bae, S. C., T. H. Kwon, and J. W. Park, "Futures Trading, Spot Market Volatility, and Market Efficiency: The Case of the Korean Index Futures Markets", *Journal of Futures Markets*, Vol. 24(2004), pp. 1195-1228.

Bandi, F. M. and J. R. Russell, "Full-Information Transaction Costs", *Working paper*, University of Chicago(2006).

Barber, B., Y.-T. Lee, Y. J. Liu, and T. Odean, "Day Trading in Equilibrium",

Working paper, UC Berkeley(2008).

Barclay, M. J. and J. B. Warner, "Stealth and Volatility: Which Trades Move Prices?", *Journal of Financial Economics*, Vol. 34(1993), pp. 281-306.

Berkman, H. and J. B. T. Lee, "The Effectiveness of Price Limits in an Emerging Market: Evidence from the Korean Stock Exchange", *Pacific-Basin Finance Journal*, Vol. 10(2002), pp. 517-530.

Berry, T. D. and K. M. Howe, "Public Information Arrival", *Journal of Finance*, Vol. 49(1994), pp. 1331-1346.

Bessembinder, H., "Trade Execution Costs and Market Quality after Decimalization", *Journal of Financial and Quantitative Analysis*, Vol. 38(2003), pp. 747-777.

Biais, B., L. Glosten, and C. Spatt, "Market Microstructure: A Survey of Microfoundations, Empirical Results, and Policy Implications", *Journal of Financial Markets*, Vol. 8(2005), pp. 217-264.

Biais, B., P. Hillion, and C., Spatt, "Price Discovery and Learning during the Pre-Opening in the Paris Bourse", *Journal of Political Economy*, Vol. 107(1999), pp. 1218-1248.

Binh, K. B., B.-U. Chong, and K. S. Eom, "Cross-Border Price Discovery and a New Motivation for Cross-Listing", *International Research Journal of Finance and Economics*, Vol. 42(2010), pp. 89-95.

Boehmer, E., M. C. Jones, and X. Zhang, "Which Shorts are Informed?", *Journal of Finance*, Vol. 63(2008), pp. 491-527.

Boehmer, E., G. Saar, and L. Yu, "Lifting the Veil: An Analysis of Pre-Trade Transparency at the NYSE", *Journal of Finance*, Vol. 60(2005), pp. 783-815.

Bollen, N. P. B. and W. G. Christie, "Microstructure of the Pink Sheets Market", *Working paper*, Vanderbilt University(2005).

Bollerslev, T., "Generalized Autoregressive Conditional Heteroskedasticity", *Journal of Econometrics*, Vol. 31(1986), pp. 307-327.

Brennan, M. J. and A. Subrahmanyam, "Market Microstructure and Asset Pricing: On the Compensation for Illiquidity in Stock Returns", *Journal of Financial Economics*, Vol. 41(1996), pp. 441-464.

Byun, J.-C., J.-I. Jo, and K.-W. Cheong, "Study on Determinants of the Asymmetric Volatility in Stock Return", *Korean Journal of Finance*, Vol. 16, No. 2(2003), pp. 31-65(in Korean).
변종국, 조정일, 정기웅, "주식수익률의 비대칭적 변동성의 결정요인에 관한 연구", 재무연구, 제16권 제2호(2003), pp. 31-65.

Campbell, J. Y., S. J. Grossman, and J. Wang, "Trading Volume and Serial Correlation in Stock Returns", *Quarterly Journal of Economics*, Vol. 108(1993), pp. 905-940.

Campbell, J. Y., A. W. Lo, and C. A. MacKinlay, *The Econometrics of Financial Markets*, Princeton University Press, Princeton, NJ, 1997.

Cao, C., O. Hansch, and X. Wang, "The Informational Content of an Open Limit Order Book", *Journal of Futures Markets*, Vol. 29(2009), pp. 16-41.

Chakravarty, S., "Stealth-Trading: Which Traders' Trades Move Stock Prices?", *Journal of Financial Economics*, Vol. 61(2001), pp. 289-307.

Chakraborty, A. and B. Yilmaz, "Informed Manipulation", *Journal of Economic Theory*, Vol. 114(2004), pp. 132-152.

Chambers, J., R. Edelen, and G. Kadlec, "On the Perils of Security Pricing by Financial Intermediaries: The Wildcard Option in Transacting Mutual-Fund Shares", *Journal of Finance*, Vol. 56(2001), pp. 2209-2236.

Chang, K. H., "Trading Volume, Volume Volatility and Stock Return Predictability", *Korean Journal of Finance*, Vol. 10, No. 2(1997), pp. 1-27(in Korean).
장국현, "주식거래량과 거래량 변동성의 주가예측력에 관한 연구", 재무연구, 제10권 제2호(1997), pp. 1-27.

Chang, K.-C. and H.-S. Kim, "An Empirical Study on the Chaotic Characteristics of Stock Returns", *Journal of Korean Securities Association*, Vol.

30, No. 1(2002), pp. 99-130(in Korean).

장경천, 김현석, "주식 수익률의 카오스적 특성에 관한 실증연구", 증권학회지, 제30권 제1호(2002), pp. 99-130.

Chang, Y. K. and C. S. Song, "A Study of the Effects of Publicly Disclosing Order Information on Price Volatility",* *Korean Journal of Finance*, Vol. 9, No. 1(1996), pp. 171-214(in Korean).

장영광, 송치승, "주문호가정보의 공개가 주가 변동성에 미치는 영향에 관한 연구", 재무연구, 제9권 제1호(1996), pp. 171-214.

Chang, Y. K. and C. S. Song, "An Empirical Study on the Korean Stock Market Microstructure and the Source of Stock Volatility", *Journal of Korean Securities Association*, Vol. 20, No. 1(1997), pp. 233-271(in Korean).

장영광, 송치승, "한국증권시장의 미시구조와 주가변동성의 원천에 관한 연구", 증권학회지, 제20권 제1호(1997), pp. 233-271.

Chang, Y. K. and C. S. Song, "The Changes of Trading Mechanism and Operation Efficiency on the Stock Market", *Journal of Korean Securities Association*, Vol. 22, No. 1(1998), pp. 33-73(in Korean).

장영광, 송치승, "매매거래제도의 변경과 증권시장의 운영효율성", 증권학회지, 제22권 제1호(1998), pp. 33-73.

Chang, Y. K. and C. S. Song, "The Relative Measurement of Components in the Short Horizon Individual Stock Returns: Bid-Ask Spreads, Time Varying Expected Returns, and Pricing Errors", *Korean Journal of Finance*, Vol. 12, No. 2(1999), pp. 199-227(in Korean).

장영광, 송치승, "단기간 증권수익률 구성요소의 상대적 비중 측정 : 매도-매수 호가스프레드, 기대수익률, 가격설정오차", 재무연구, 제12권 제2호(1999), pp. 199-227.

Chay, J.-B. and H.-S. Ryu, "Expiration-Day Effects of the KOSPI 200 Futures and Options", *Asia-Pacific Journal of Financial Studies*, Vol. 35, No.

1(2006), pp. 69-101(in Korean).

최종범, 류혁선, "KOSPI 200 선물 및 옵션의 만기일 효과", 증권학회지, 제35권 제1호(2006), pp. 69-101.

Cho, D. D., J. Russell, G. C. Tiao, and R. Tsay, "The Magnet Effect of Price Limits: Evidence from High-Frequency Data on Taiwan Stock Exchange", *Journal of Empirical Finance*, Vol. 10(2003), pp. 133-168.

Choe, H., J. M. Chung, and W.-B. Lee, "Stealth Trading on the Korea Stock Market", *Korean Journal of Finance*, Vol. 16, No. 2(2003), pp. 1-29(in Korean).

최 혁, 정재만, 이우백, "한국주식시장의 은닉거래", 재무연구, 제16권 제2호(2003), pp. 1-29.

Choe, H. and Y. Eom, "Expiration-Day Effects: The Korean Evidence", *Korean Journal of Financial Management*, Vol. 24, No. 2(2007), pp. 41-79(in Korean).

최 혁, 엄윤성, "주가지수 선물과 옵션의 만기일이 주식시장에 미치는 영향 : 개별 종목 분석을 중심으로", 재무관리연구, 제24권 제2호(2007), pp. 41-79.

Choe, H. and M.-C. Woo, "Difference in Capability of Liquidity Provision among Liquidity Providers in Korean ELW Market", *Korean Journal of Financial Studies*, Vol. 39, No. 2(2010), pp. 161-190(in Korean).

최 혁, 우민철, "ELW 시장에서의 유동성공급자 간 차이", 한국증권학회지, 제39권 제2호(2010), pp. 161-190.

Choe, H. and C.-W. Yang, "Comparisons of Information Asymmetry Measures in the Korean Stock Market", *Asia-Pacific Journal of Financial Studies*, Vol. 35, No. 5(2006), pp. 1-44(in Korean).

최 혁, 양철원, "한국주식시장에서의 정보비대칭 측정치 비교", 증권학회지, 제35권 제5호(2006), pp. 1-44..

Choe, H. and C.-W. Yang, "Information Risk and Asset Returns in the Korean Stock Market", *Asia-Pacific Journal of Financial Studies*, Vol.

36, No. 4(2007), pp. 567-620(in Korean).

최 혁, 양철원, "한국주식시장에서 정보위험과 수익률과의 관계", 증권학회지, 제36권 제4호(2007), pp. 567-620.

Choe, H. and C.-W. Yang, "Liquidity Risk and Asset Returns: The Case of the Korean Stock Market", *Korean Journal of Financial Management*, Vol. 26, No. 4(2009), pp. 103-139.

Choe, H. and C.-W. Yang, "Liquidity Commonality and Its Causes: Evidence from the Korean Market", *Asia-Pacific Journal of Financial Studies*, Vol. 39, No. 5(2010), pp. 626-658.

Choe, H. and S. H. Yoon, "The Impact of Program Trading on Stock Returns", *Asia-Pacific Journal of Financial Studies*, Vol. 36, No. 2(2007), pp. 281-320(in Korean).

최 혁, 윤선흠, "프로그램매매가 주식가격에 미치는 영향", 증권학회지, 제36권 제2호(2007), pp. 281-320.

Choi, J. Y. and I. C. Na, "Cross-Autocorrelation of Portfolio Returns in Korea: Delayed Reaction Depending on Firm Size and Good/Bad News", *Journal of Korean Securities Association*, Vol. 23, No. 1(1998), pp. 89-119(in Korean).

최종연, 나인철, "한국 주식시장에서의 선도/지연 효과에 관한 실증연구 : 기업규모 및 정보의 호/악재에 따른 교차상관관계를 중심으로", 증권학회지, 제23권 제1호(1998), pp. 89-118.

Chordia, T., R. Roll, and A. Subrahmanyam, "Commonality in Liquidity", *Journal of Financial Economics*, Vol. 56(2000), pp. 501-530.

Chordia, T., R. Roll, and A. Subrahmanyam, "Market Liquidity and Trading Activity", *Journal of Finance*, Vol. 56(2001), pp. 501-530.

Chou, P. H., "A Gibbs Sampling Approach to the Estimation of Linear Regression Models under Daily Price Limits", *Pacific-Basin Finance Journal*, Vol. 5(1997), pp. 39-62.

Chung, C.-S., "The Role of Information in the Seoul Foreign Exchange

Market", *Journal of Money and Finance*, Vol. 22, No. 4(2008), pp. 159-184(in Korean).

정재식, "외환거래량을 이용한 정보모형의 비교분석 : 서울외환시장을 중심으로", 금융연구, 제22권 제4호(2008), pp. 159-184.

Chung, J. M., "The Information Efficiency of Closing Price on the Korea Stock Exchange", *Asian-Pacific Journal of Financial Studies*, Vol. 33, No 2(2004), pp. 107-153(in Korean).

정재만, "한국증권거래소 종가의 정보효율성", 증권학회지, 제33권 제2호 (2004), pp. 107-153.

Chung, J. M., H. Choe, and B.-C. Kho, "The Impact of Day-Trading on Volatility and Liquidity", *Asian-Pacific Journal of Financial Studies*, Vol. 38(2009), pp. 237-275.

Chung, K. H., J. K. Kang, and J. S. Kim, "Tick Size, Market Structure, and Market Quality", *Review of Quantitative Finance and Accounting*, forthcoming(2010).

Chung, C. H. and D. H. Kim, "Performance Analyses of Investment Strategies Based on the Past Stock Prices",* *Korean Journal of Financial Management*, Vol. 19, No. 2(2002), pp. 49-75(in Korean).

정정현, 김동회, "과거의 주가에 근거한 투자전략의 성과분석", 재무관리연구, 제19권 제2호(2002), pp. 49-75.

Chung, K. H. and J. S. Shin, "Tick Size and Trading Costs on the Korea Stock Exchange", *Asian-Pacific Journal of Financial Studies*, Vol. 34(2005), pp. 165-193.

Clark, P. K., "A Subordinated Stochastic Process Model with Finite Variance for Speculative Prices", *Econometrica*, Vol. 41(1973), pp. 135-155.

Cohen, K., S. Maier, R. Schwartz, and D. Whitcomb, *The Microstructure of Securities Markets*, Prentice-Hall, Englewood Cliffs, 1986.

De Jong, F. and B. Rindi, *The Microstructure of Financial Markets*, Cambridge

University Press, Cambridge, 2009.

Demsetz, H., "The Cost of Transacting", *Quarterly Journal of Economics*, Vol. 82(1968), pp. 33-53.

Diamond, W. D. and E. R. Verrecchia, "Constraints on Short-Selling and Asset Price Adjustment to Private Information", *Journal of Financial Economics*, Vol. 18(1987), pp. 277-311.

Duarte, J. and L. Young, "Why is PIN Priced?", *Journal of Financial Economics*, Vol. 91(2009), pp. 119-138.

Easley, D., S. Hvidkjaer, and M. O'Hara, "Is Information Risk a Determinant of Asset Returns?", *Journal of Finance*, Vol. 57(2002), pp. 2185-2221.

Easley, D., N. M. Kiefer, and M. O'Hara, "Cream-Skimming or Profit Sharing? The Curious Role of Purchased Order Flow", *Journal of Finance*, Vol. 51(1996), pp. 811-833.

Easley, D., N. M. Kiefer, and M. O'Hara, "The Information Content of the Trading Process", *Journal of Empirical Finance*, Vol. 4(1997a), pp. 159-186.

Easley, D., N. M. Kiefer, and M. O'Hara, "One Day in the Life of a Very Common Stock", *Review of Financial Studies*, Vol. 10(1997b), pp. 805-835.

Easley, D., N. M. Kiefer, M. O'Hara, and J. Paperman, "Liquidity, Information, and Less-Frequently Traded Stocks", *Journal of Finance*, Vol. 51(1996), pp. 1405-1436.

Easley, D., M. O'Hara, and J. Paperman, "Financial Analysts and Information-Based Trade", *Journal of Financial Markets*, Vol. 1(1998), pp. 175-201.

Engle, R. F., "Autoregressive Conditional Heteroscedasticity with Estimates of the Variance of United Kingdom Inflation", *Econometrica*, Vol. 50(1982), pp. 987-1007.

Engle, R. F. and G. G. J. Lee, "A Permanent and Transitory Component Model of Stock Return Volatility", In Engle, R. F. and H. White, eds:

Cointegration and Forecasting, *A Festschrift in Honor of Clive, W. J. Granger*, Oxford University Press, Oxford, 1999.

Engle, R. F., D. Lilien, and R. Robins, "Estimating Time Varying Risk Premia in the Term Structure: The ARCH-M Model", *Econometrica*, Vol. 55(1987), pp. 391-407.

Eom, K. S., K. B. Binh, and H. J. Lee, "Price Discovery in Cross-Listed Stock across the Border: The Case of POSCO Stock Cross-Listed on the KRX and the TSE", *Korean Journal of Money and Finance*, Vol. 12, No. 4(2007), pp. 257-295(in Korean).
엄경식, 빈기범, 이현진, "양국간 동일 거래시간대 교차상장시 가격발견효과 : POSCO 주식의 KRX, TSE 교차상장 사례", 금융학회지, 제12권 제4호 (2007), pp. 257-295.

Eom, K. S. and S. B. Hahn, "Traders' Strategic Behavior in an Index Options Market", *Journal of Futures Markets*, Vol. 25(2005), pp. 105-133.

Eom, K. S., H. C. Kang, and J.-S. Kim, "Idiosyncratic Volatility under a Price-Limit System Using Gibbs-Sampling", *Global Journal of Finance and Management*, Vol. 2(2010), pp. 95-102.

Eom, K. S., H. C. Kang, and Y. J. Lee, *An Alternative to the Price-Limit System on the Korea Exchange*, Research report 08-01, Korea Capital Market Institute(2007)(in Korean).
엄경식, 강형철, 이윤재, KRX 가격제한폭제도의 유효성에 관한 연구, 한국 증권연구원 연구보고서 08-01, 2008.

Eom, K. S., E. Lee, and K. S. Park, "Microstructure-Based Manipulation: Strategic Behavior and Performance of Spoofing Traders", *Working paper*, University of Seoul(2008), http://ssrn.com/abstract=1328899.

Eom, K. S., S. H. Oh, and S. B. Hahn, "Effect of Traders' Strategic Behavior on ATM and OTM Options of the KOSPI 200 Stock Index", *Korean Journal of Money and Finance*, Vol. 10, No. 2(2006), pp. 33-67(in Korean).

엄경식, 오승현, 한상범, "KOSPI 200 주가지수 ATM과 OTM 옵션에 대한 전략적 투자행동의 영향", 금융학회지, 제10권 제2호(2006), pp. 33-67.

Eom, K. S., J. Ok, and J.-H. Park, "Pre-Trade Transparency and Market Quality", *Journal of Financial Markets*, Vol. 10(2007), pp. 319-341.

Eom, K. S., J.-H. Park, and J.-A. Yoon, "The Korean OTC Stock Market: Micro and Macrostructure Analysis", *Asian Review of Financial Research*, Vol. 22, No. 4(2009), pp. 33-62(in Korean).
엄경식, 박종호, 윤지아, "한국의 장외주식시장 '프리보드'의 미시구조 및 거시구조 분석", 재무연구, 제22권 제4호(2009), pp. 33-62.

Eom, K. S., J. Seon, and K.-H. Chang, "Relative Efficiency of Price Discovery on an Established New Market and the Main Board: Evidence from Korea", *Asia-Pacific Journal of Financial Studies*, Vol. 39, No. 4(2010), pp. 459-494.

Eom, K. S. and J.-A. Yoon, *Stock Trading After-Hours: Scholarly Research and Lessons for Korea*, Research report 01-04, Korea Capital Market Institute, 2001(in Korean).
엄경식, 윤지아, "시간외 주식 거래 : 주요국의 거래 메커니즘별 역할 및 교훈", 한국증권연구원 연구보고서 01-04, 2001.

Fama, E. F. and K. R. French, "The Cross Section of Expected Stock Returns", *Journal of Finance*, Vol. 47(1992), pp. 427-465.

Fama, E. F. and K. R. French, "Common Risk Factors in Returns on Stocks and Bonds", *Journal of Financial Economics*, Vol. 33(1993), pp. 3-56.

Fama, E. F. and J. MacBeth, "Risk, Return, and Equilibrium: Empirical Tests", *Journal of Political Economy*, Vol. 71(1973), pp. 607-636.

Fisher, L., "Some New Stock Market Indexes", *Journal of Business*, Vol. 39(1966), pp. 191-225.

Foster, F. D. and S. Viswanathan, "Variation in Trading Volume, Return Volatility, and Trading Costs: Evidence on Recent Price Formation

Models", *Journal of Finance*, Vol. 48(1993), pp. 187-211.

French, K. R. and R. Roll, "Stock Return Variances: The Arrival of Information and the Reaction of Traders", *Journal of Financial Economics*, Vol. 17(1986), pp. 99-117.

Gallant, A. R., P. E. Rossi, and G. Tauchen, "Stock Prices and Volume", *Review of Financial Studies*, Vol. 5(1992), pp. 199-242.

Gallant, A. R., P. E. Rossi, and G. Tauchen, "Nonlinear Dynamic Structures", *Econometrica*, Vol. 61(1993), pp. 871-907.

Garman, M., "Market Microstructure", *Journal of Financial Economics*, Vol. 3(1976), pp. 257-275.

George, T. J., G. Kaul, and M. Nimalendran, "Estimation of the Bid-Ask Spread and Its Components: A New Approach", *Review of Financial Studies*, Vol. 4(1991), pp. 623-656.

George, T. J. and C.-Y. Hwang, "Transition Price Changes and Price-Limit Rules: Evidence from the Tokyo Stock Exchange", *Journal of Financial and Quantitative Analysis*, Vol. 30(1995), pp. 313-327.

Glosten, L., R. Jagannathan, and D. E. Runkle, "On the Relation between the Expected Value and the Volatility of the Nominal Excess Return on Stocks", *Journal of Finance*, Vol. 48(1993), pp. 1779-1801.

Glosten, L. and L. Harris, "Estimating the Components of the Bid/Ask Spreads", *Journal of Financial Economics*, Vol. 21(1988), pp. 123-142.

Glosten, L. and P. Milgrom, "Bid-Ask and Transaction Prices in a Specialist Market with Heterogeneously Informed Traders", *Journal of Financial Economics*, Vol. 14(1985), pp. 71-100.

Gong, J. S., "Information Effects of Trading Volume in the Korean Stock Market",* *Korean Journal of Finance*, Vol. 10, No. 1(1997), pp. 37-68(in Korean).
공재식, "한국주식시장에서의 거래량 정보효과에 관한 연구", 재무연구, 제10권 제1호(1997), pp. 37-68.

Goodhart, C. A. E. and M. O'Hara, "High Frequency Data in Financial Markets: Issues and Applications", *Journal of Empirical Finance*, Vol. 4(1997), pp. 73-114.

Gottesman, A. A. and G. Jacoby, "Payout Policy, Taxes, and the Relation between Returns and the Bid-Ask Spread", *Journal of Banking and Finance*, Vol. 30(2006), pp. 37-58.

Grammig, J., M. Melvin, and C. Schlag, "Internationally Cross-Listed Stock Prices during Overlapping Trading Hours: Price Discovery and Exchange Rate Effects", *Journal of Empirical Finance*, Vol. 12(2005), pp. 139-164.

Grammig, J., D. D. Schiereck, and E. Theissen, "Knowing Me, Knowing You: Trader Anonymity and Informed Trading in Parallel Markets", *Journal of Financial Markets*, Vol. 4(2001), pp. 385-412.

Goyal, A. and P. Santa-Clara, "Idiosyncratic Risk Matters!", *Journal of Finance*, Vol. 58(2003), pp. 975-1008.

Hahn, S. B. and S. H. Oh, "The Impact of Program Trading on the Short-Run and Long-Run Volatility of Korean Stock Market", *Korean Journal of Futures and Options*, Vol. 15, No. 1(2007), pp. 101-133(in Korean). 한상범, 오승현, "프로그램거래가 주식시장의 변동성에 미치는 장단기 효과", 선물연구, 제15권 제1호(2007), pp. 101-133.

Handa, P. and R. Schwartz, "Limit Order Trading", *Journal of Finance*, Vol. 51(1996), pp. 1835-1861.

Harris, L., "Minimum Price Variations, Discrete Bid-Ask Spreads, and Quotation Sizes", *Review of Financial Studies*, Vol. 7(1994), pp. 149-178.

Harris, L., *Trading and Exchanges, Market Microstructure for Practitioners*, Oxford Press, Oxford, 2003.

Harris, L. and J. Hasbrouck, "Market vs. Limit Orders: The SuperDOT Evidence on Order Submission Strategy", *Journal of Financial and Quantitative Analysis*, Vol. 31(1996), pp. 213-231.

Harris, J. H. and V. Panchapagesan, "The Information Content of the Limit Order Book: Evidence from NYSE Specialist Trading Decisions", *Journal of Financial Markets*, Vol. 8(2005), pp. 25-67.

Harris, J. H., V. Panchapagesan, and I. M. Werner, "Off but not Gone: A Study of Nasdaq Delistings", *Working paper*, Ohio State University (2008).

Harris, L., G. Sofianos, and J. E. Shapiro, "Program Trading and Intraday Volatility", *Review of Financial Studies*, Vol. 7(1994), pp. 653-685.

Hasbrouck, J., "Measuring the Information Content of Stock Trades", *Journal of Finance*, Vol. 46(1991), pp. 179-207.

Hasbrouck, J., "One Security, Many Markets: Determining the Contributions to Price Discovery", *Journal of Finance*, Vol. 50(1995), pp. 1175-1199.

Hasbrouck, J., *Empirical Market Microstructure*, Oxford Press, Oxford, 2007.

Hasbrouck, J. and D. J. Seppi, "Common Factors in Prices, Order Flows, and Liquidity", *Journal of Financial Economics*, Vol. 59(2001), pp. 383-411.

Heckman, J. J., "The Common Structure of Statistical Models of Truncation, Sample Selection, and Limited Dependent Variables and a Simple Estimator for Such Models", *Annals of Economic and Social Measurement*, Vol. 5(1976), pp. 475-492.

Hentschel, L., "All in the Family: Nesting Symmetric and Asymmetric GARCH Models", *Journal of Financial Economics*, Vol. 39(1995), pp. 71-104.

Huang, R. and H. Stoll, "Market Microstructure and Stock Return Predictions", *Review of Financial Studies*, Vol. 7(1994), pp. 179-213.

Huang, R. and H. Stoll, "The Components of the Bid-Ask Spread: A General Approach", *Review of Financial Studies*, Vol. 10(1997), pp. 995-1034.

Jang, H., "Technical Analysis on Intraday Returns and Trading in the Korean

Stock Market",* *Korean Journal of Finance*, Vol. 5, No. 1(1992), pp. 1-47(in Korean).

장하성, "한국증권시장에서의 하루 중 수익률과 거래량에 관한 기술적 분석", 재무연구, 제5권 제1호(1992), pp. 1-47.

Jang, H., "The Price Effect of Block Trading: Empirical Analysis in the Korean Stock Market",* *Korean Journal of Finance*, Vol. 6, No. 1 (1993a), pp. 1-31(in Korean).

장하성, "대량거래의 가격효과 : 한국주식시장에서의 실증분석", 재무연구, 제6권 제1호(1993a), pp. 1-31.

Jang, H., "Intraday Price Volatility: Empirical Investigation on Korean Stock Market", *Journal of Korean Securities Association*, Vol. 15, No. 1(1993b), pp. 395-435(in Korean).

장하성, "한국증권시장에서의 하루중 주가변동성에 관한 실증연구", 증권학회지, 제15권 제1호(1993b), pp. 395-435.

Jang, H. and J. Ok, "A Study on Spread in the Korean Stock Market: Empirical Analysis for Determinants and Intraday-Patterns",* *Korean Journal of Finance*, Vol. 9, No. 1(1996), pp. 21-63(in Korean).

장하성, 옥진호, "한국증권시장에서의 스프레드에 관한 연구 : 결정요인과 하루 중의 행태에 관한 실증분석", 재무연구, 제9권 제1호(1996), pp. 21-63.

Jang, H. S. and J. B. Park, "A Study on the Effects of Price-Limit System on Delaying Price Discovery and Restraining Price Volatility",* *Korean Journal of Finance*, Vol. 8, No. 1(1995), pp. 147-197(in Korean).

장하성, 박주범, "가격제한폭제도의 가격발견 지연효과와 가격변동성 억제 효과에 관한 연구", 재무연구, 제8권 제1호(1995), pp. 147-197.

Jee, C., H. Jang, and J. Ok, "Intraday Return Predictability in an Order-Driven Market: The Korea Stock Exchange",* *Korean Journal of Finance*, Vol. 11, No. 2(1998), pp. 119-157(in Korean).

지 청, 장하성, 옥진호, "주문 주도시장에서의 단기수익률 예측", 재무연구,

제11권 제2호(1998), pp. 119-157.

Jee, C. and J. Ok, "The Price Effect of Order Imbalances at Openings in Korea Stock Market", *Korean Journal of Finance*, Vol. 10, No. 2(1997), pp. 29-57(in Korean).

지 청, 옥진호, "한국주식시장에서의 개장주문불균형의 가격효과", 재무연구, 제10권 제2호(1997), pp. 29-57.

Jeong, J. Y., "The Seasonality in Stock Returns Volatility", *Journal of Korean Securities Association*, Vol. 29, No. 1(2001), pp. 345-372(in Korean).

정재엽, "주식수익률 변동성의 계절성", 증권학회지, 제29권 제1호(2001), pp. 345-372.

Kalev, P. S., W.-M. Liu, P. K. Pham, and E. Jarnecic, "Public Information Arrival and Volatility of Intraday Stock Returns", *Journal of Banking and Finance*, Vol. 28(2004), pp. 1441-1467.

Kang, S.-K., "A Study on the Price Discovery in Korea Stock Index Markets: KODEX200, KOSPI200, and KOSPI200 Futures", *Korean Journal of Options and Futures*, Vol. 17, No. 3(2009), pp. 67-97(in Korean).

강석규, "한국주가지수시장의 가격발견에 관한 연구 : KODEX200, KOSPI 200과 KOSPI200 선물", 선물연구, 제17권 제3호(2009), pp. 67-97.

Kang, B. H. and J. Khil, "The Informational Role of Remaining Volume due to Price Limits", *Journal of Korean Securities Association*, Vol. 20, No. 1(1997), pp. 395-420(in Korean).

강병호, 길재욱, "가격제한에 의한 잔량의 정보효과에 관한 연구", 증권학회지, 제20권 제1호(1997), pp. 395-420.

Kang, B. H. and K. Y. Ohk, "Types of Investors' Trading Activities and Stock Market Volatility", *Asia-Pacific Journal of Financial Studies*, Vol. 35, No. 5(2006), pp. 137-174(in Korean).

강병호, 옥기율, "투자자 거래활동 유형별 주식시장 변동성에 미치는 영향에 관한 비교연구", 증권학회지, 제35권 제5호(2006), pp. 137-174.

Kang, J. and H.-J. Park, "The Information Content of Net Buying Pressure: Evidence from the KOSPI 200 Index Option Market", *Journal of Financial Markets*, Vol. 11(2008), pp. 36-56.

Kang, H. C., J.-H. Park, and K. S. Eom, "The Role of Market Depth in Determining Appropriate Tick Size in the Korea Exchange", *Asian Review of Financial Research*, Vol. 22, No. 2(2009), pp. 71-102(in Korean).

강형철, 박종호, 엄경식, "한국주식시장에서 호가단위의 적절성 : 시장깊이를 중심으로", 재무연구, 제22권 제2호(2009), pp. 71-102.

Kang, S. H. and S.-M. Yoon, "Can Trading Volume Explain Persistence and Asymmetry of Return Volatility?", *Korea Journal of Finance*, Vol. 20(2007), pp. 35-56.

Karolyi, A., "The World of Cross-Listings and Cross-Listings of the World: Challenging Conventional Wisdom", *Review of Finance*, Vol. 9(2006), pp. 2-54.

Karpoff, J., "The Relation between Price Changes and Trading Volume: A Survey", *Journal of Financial and Quantitative Analysis*, Vol. 22(1987), pp. 109-126.

Kavajecz, K. A. and E. R. Odders-White, "Technical Analysis and Liquidity Provision", *Review of Financial Studies*, Vol. 17(2004), pp. 1043-1071.

Keim, D. B. and A. Madhavan, "The Upstairs Market for Large Block Transactions: Analysis and Measurement of Price Effect", *Review of Financial Studies*, Vol. 9(1996), pp. 1-36.

Khil, J., "A Study on the Patterns of Time-Series of Short-Term Portfolio Returns in Korea",* *Korean Journal of Finance*, Vol. 10, No. 1(1997), pp. 197-222(in Korean).

길재욱, "한국 주식 수익률의 시계열 행태에 관한 소고 : 단기 수익률을 중심으로", 재무연구, 제10권 제1호(1997), pp. 197-222.

Khil, J. and K. Chung, "The Arrival of Public Information and the Intraday

Market Volatility", *Korean Journal of Finance*, Vol. 18, No. 1(2005), pp. 93-120(in Korean).

길재욱, 정귀자, "시장정보 도착과 일중 변동성의 상호 관계", 재무연구, 제18권 제1호(2005), pp. 93-120.

Khil, J. and K. Chung, "The Impact of Public News on the Korean Stock Market", *Asian-Pacific Journal of Financial Studies*, Vol. 34, No. 1(2005), pp. 1-33(in Korean).

길재욱, 정귀자, "시장정보가 과연 일중 주가 변동성과 거래량에 반영되는 가?", 증권학회지, 제34권 제1호(2005), pp. 1-33.

Khil, J., Y. S. Park, J. Shin, and J. Lee, "Studies on the Impact of Block Trading and Information Leakage on Market Performance", *Asian-Pacific Journal of Financial Studies*, Vol. 34, No. 3(2005), pp. 139-182(in Korean).

길재욱, 박영석, 신진영, 이재현, "시간외대량매매 정보의 시장반응과 정보 유출에 관한 연구", 증권학회지, 제34권 제3호(2005), pp. 139-182.

Kho, B.-C., "Stock Prices and Volume: A Semi-Nonparametric Approach",* *Korean Journal of Finance*, Vol. 10, No. 1(1997), pp. 1-35(in Korean).

고봉찬, "주가와 거래량 : 반비모수적 접근방법", 재무연구, 제10권 제1호 (1997), pp. 1-35.

Kho, B.-C., "Execution Performance of Market vs. Limit Orders in the Korean Stock Markets", *Korean Journal of Finance*, Vol. 12, No. 2(1999), pp. 165-197(in Korean).

고봉찬, "시장가 및 지정가주문의 거래체결성과에 관한 실증연구", 재무연 구, 제12권 제2호(1999), pp. 165-197.

Kho, B.-C. and J.-W. Kim, "Intraday Price Change and Trading Volume in the KTB Futures and Futures Option Markets", *Korean Journal of Futures and Options*, Vol. 10, No. 2(2002), pp. 57-94(in Korean).

고봉찬, 김진우, "국채선물 및 옵션시장의 일중 가격변화와 거래량", 선물연구, 제10권 제2호(2002), pp. 57-94.

Kim, J.-O., "An Empirical Investigation of Short Sales: Evidence from the Korea Stock Exchange", *Journal of Korean Securities Association*, Vol. 26, No. 1(2000), pp. 343-398(in Korean).

김종오, "한국 증권시장에서 공매의 정보효과에 관한 연구", 증권학회지, 제26권 제1호(2000), pp. 343-398.

Kim, Y. K. and J. B. Bae, "A Study on Time-Series Dependence of Stock Returns in Korea",* *Korean Journal of Finance*, Vol. 7, No. 2(1994), pp. 1-29.

김영규, 배재봉, "한국 주식 수익률의 시계열적 종속성에 관한 연구", 재무연구, 제7권 제2호(1994), pp. 1-29.

Kim, K. A. and S. G. Rhee, "Price Limit Performance: Evidence from Tokyo Stock Exchange", *Journal of Finance*, Vol. 52(1997), pp. 885-901.

Kim, Y. H. and J. J. Yang, "The Effect of Price Limits on Intraday Volatility and Information Asymmetry", *Pacific-Basin Finance Journal*, Vol. 16(2008), pp. 522-638.

King, M. R. and D. Segal, "The Long-Term Effects of Cross-Listing, Investor Recognition, and Ownership Structure on Valuation", *Review of Financial Studies*, Vol. 22(2009), pp. 2393-2421.

Ko, K., "Market Microstructure and Unfair Trading Profit of Equity Funds", *Korean Journal of Finance*, Vol. 17, No. 2(2004), pp. 77-101(in Korean).

고광수, "시장미시구조와 주식형 펀드의 부당 이익", 재무연구, 제17권 제2호(2004), pp. 77-101.

Ko, K., "The Effects of Infrequent Trading and Overnight Trading Halts on the Returns Behavior", *Korea Journal of Finance*, Vol. 21(2008), pp. 41-68.

Ko, K., S. Lee, and J. Chung, "Volatility, Efficiency, and Trading: Further Evidence", *Journal of International Financial Management and Accoun-*

ting, Vol. 6(1995), pp. 26-42.

Kook, C. P. and W. H. Jeong, "An Empirical Study on Information Effect of Increase or Decrease in Stock Trading Volume", *Journal of Korean Securities Association*, Vol. 29, No. 1(2001), pp. 87-115(in Korean).
국찬표, 정완호, "주식거래량 증감의 정보효과에 관한 실증연구 : 단기 수익률의 역전현상분석을 중심으로", 증권학회지, 제29권 제1호(2001), pp. 87-115.

Ku, B. I., "A Study on the Behavior of Stock Price and Liquidity",* *Korean Journal of Finance*, Vol. 5, No. 1(1992), pp. 103-128(in Korean).
구본일, "주식의 유동성과 주가행태에 관한 연구", 재무연구, 제5권 제1호(1992), pp. 103-128.

Ku. B. I., "Searching an Operational Measure for the Comparison of the Level of Stock's Liquidity", *Journal of Korean Securities Association*, Vol. 16, No. 1(1994), pp. 51-80(in Korean).
구본일, "주식간 유동성차이에 영향을 주는 주식속성변수의 탐색", 증권학회지, 제16권 제1호(1994), pp. 51-80.

Ku, B. I., "An Empirical Investigation on the Dynamic Risk Factors", *Journal of Korean Securities Association*, Vol. 21, No. 1(1997a), pp. 75-105(in Korean).
구본일, "동태적 수익률 결정요인에 관한 실증연구", 증권학회지, 제21권 제1호(1997a), pp. 75-105.

Ku, B. I., "A Testing of the Random Walk of Price and an Estimation of Effective Spread Using Trade Data",* *Korean Journal of Finance*, Vol. 10, No. 2(1997b), pp. 237-262(in Korean).
구본일, "체결주가데이터를 이용한 주가의 랜덤워크 검증과 내재 호가스프레드 추정", 재무연구, 제10권 제2호(1997b), pp. 237-262.

Ku, B. I., "Asymmetric Volatility of the Stock Prices in Korean Stock Market", *Korean Journal of Finance*, Vol. 13, No. 1(2000), pp. 129-159(in

Korean).

구본일, "한국 주식시장에서의 주가변동성의 비대칭성에 관한 연구", 재무
연구, 제13권 제1호(2000), pp. 129-159.

Ku, B. I. and W. S. Choi, "Stock Prices and Trading Volume: Opening Prices versus Closing Prices",* *Korean Journal of Finance*, Vol. 11, No. 2(1998), pp. 163-183(in Korean).

구본일, 최완수, "주가와 거래량 : 시가대 종가", 재무연구, 제11권 제2호
(1998), pp. 163-183.

Kwon, T. H. and J. W. Park, "A Study on the Liquidity Premium in Korean Stock Market", *Korean Journal of Finance*, Vol. 10, No. 1(1997), pp. 223-259(in Korean).

권택호, 박종원, "한국주식시장의 유동성 프리미엄에 관한 연구", 재무연구,
제10권 제1호(1997), pp. 223-259.

Kyle, A. S., "Continuous Auctions and Insider Trading", *Econometrica*, Vol. 53(1985), pp. 1315-1335.

Lamoureux, C. and W. Lastrapes, "Heteroskedasticity in Stock Return Data: Volume versus GARCH Effects", *Journal of Finance*, Vol. 45(1990), pp. 221-229.

Lee, E., "Why Stock Investors Split Their Orders? An Analysis of Strategic Trading Behaviors in the Korea Stock Exchange", *Asia-Pacific Journal of Financial Studies*, Vol. 37, No. 3(2008), pp. 391-424(in Korean).

이은정, "주식시장의 투자자는 왜 분할주문을 하는가? 한국주식시장에서의
분할주문거래에 관한 연구", 증권학회지, 제37권 제3호(2008), pp. 391-424.

Lee, J.-D. and Y.-G. Ahn, "The Study on the Serial Correlation and the Conditional Heteroscedasticity of the Stock Return in Korea Stock Market", *Journal of Korean Securities Association*, Vol. 20, No. 1(1997), pp. 105-138(in Korean).

이정도, 안영규, "한국주식시장에서 주식수익률의 시계열상관과 조건부 분
산", 증권학회지, 제20권 제1호(1997), pp. 105-138.

Lee, E. and J. Chae, "Liquidity Provision by Day-Traders", *Korean Journal of Finance*, Vol. 21, No. 2(2008), pp. 115-147(in Korean).

이은정, 채 준, "데이트레이더는 유동성을 공급하는가?", 재무연구, 제21권 제2호(2008), pp. 115-147.

Lee, J. H. and H. Choe, "Market Impact Costs on the Korea Stock Exchange", *Journal of Korean Securities Association*, Vol. 20, No. 1(1997), pp. 205-232(in Korean).

이준행, 최 혁, "KOSPI200 종목의 시장충격비용 측정과 그 결정요인 분석", 증권학회지, 제20권 제1호(1997), pp. 205-232.

Lee, W.-B. and H. Choe, "Liquidity Formation and Price Discovery", *Korean Journal of Finance*, Vol. 19, No. 2(2006a), pp. 1-38(in Korean).

이우백, 최 혁, "하루 중 유동성 형성 과정과 가격발견", 재무연구, 제19권 제2호(2006a), pp. 1-38.

Lee, W.-B. and H. Choe, "Pre-Trade Information and Price Discovery", *Asia-Pacific Journal of Financial Studies*, Vol. 35, No. 4(2006b), pp. 143-190 (in Korean).

이우백, 최 혁, "거래 전 정보공개와 가격발견", 증권학회지, 제35권 제4호 (2006b), pp. 145-190.

Lee, W.-B. and H. Choe, "Short-Term Return Predictability of Information in the Open Limit Order Book", *Asia-Pacific Journal of Financial Studies*, Vol. 36, No. 6(2007), pp. 963-1007(in Korean).

이우백, 최 혁, "공개주문원장 정보의 단기수익률 예측력 분석", 증권학회지, 제36권 제6호(2007), pp. 963-1007.

Lee, S. B. and K. J. Kim, "An Empirical Study on the Effects of Price-Limit System on Stock Return Volatility in the Korean Stock Market",* *Korean Journal of Financial Management*, Vol. 10, No. 1(1993), pp. 231-248(in Korean).

이상빈, 김광정, "한국주식시장에서의 가격제한폭제도가 주가변동성에 미치는 효과에 관한 실증적 연구", 재무관리연구, 제10권 제1호(1993), pp. 231-248.

Lee, S.-B. and K.-J. Kim, "The Effect of Price Limits on Stock Price Volatility: Empirical Evidence in Korea", *Journal of Business Finance and Accounting*, Vol. 22(1995), pp. 257-267.

Lee, S. B. and K. Ko, "Market Microstructure and Price Volatility: A Study on Major Indices in Korea",* *Journal of Korean Securities Association*, Vol. 15, No. 1(1993), pp. 327-352(in Korean).
이상빈, 고광수, "증권시장 미시구조와 주가변동성 : 주요 지수별 연구", 증권학회지, 제15권 제1호(1993), pp. 327-352.

Lee, E., K. S. Park, and H. Jang, "How Profitable is Day-Trading? A Study on Day-Trading in Korean Stock Market", *Asia-Pacific Journal of Financial Studies*, Vol. 36, No. 3(2007), pp. 351-386(in Korean).
이은정, 박경서, 장하성, "한국주식시장에서 데이트레이딩의 수익성에 관한 연구", 증권학회지, 제36권 제3호(2007), pp. 351-386.

Lee, S. B. and J. H. Seo, "Study on the Dynamic Relationship between the Excess Returns of the Stock Market and Idiosyncratic Volatility and the Information Efficiency", *Asia-Pacific Journal of Financial Studies*, Vol. 36, No. 3(2007), pp. 387-423(in Korean).
이상빈, 서정훈, "주식시장의 초과수익률과 고유변동성의 동적 관계 및 정보효율성에 관한 연구", 증권학회지, 제36권 제3호(2007), pp. 387-423.

Lo, A. and J. Wang, "Trading Volume: Definitions, Data Analysis, and Implications of Portfolio Theory", *Review of Financial Studies*, Vol. 13(2000), pp. 257-300.

Lyons, R. K., *The Microstructure Approach to Exchange Rates*, MIT Press, Cambridge(2001).

Macey, J. R., M. O'Hara, and D. Pompilio, "Down and Out in the Stock Market: The Law and Economics of the Delisting Process", *Working paper*, Cornell University(2005).

Madhavan, A., "Market Microstructure: A Survey", *Journal of Financial Markets*, Vol. 3(2000), pp. 205-258.

Madhavan, A., D. C. Porter, and D. G. Weaver, "Should Securities Markets Be Transparent?", *Journal of Financial Markets*, Vol. 8(2005), pp. 265-287.

Madhavan, A., M. Richardson, and M. Roomans, "Why Do Security Prices Change? A Transaction-Level Analysis of NYSE Stocks", *Review of Financial Studies*, Vol. 10(1997), pp. 1035-1064.

McInish, T. and R. A. Wood, "An Analysis of Intraday Patterns in Bid/Ask Spreads for NYSE Stocks", *Journal of Finance*, Vol. 47(1992), pp. 753-764.

Miller, E., "Risk, Uncertainty, and Divergence of Opinion", *Journal of Finance*, Vol. 32(1977), pp. 1151-1168.

Mitchell, M. I. and J. H. Mulherin, "The Impact of Public Information on the Stock Market", *Journal of Finance*, Vol. 49(1994), pp. 923-950.

Moon, G.-H. and C.-H. Hong, "The Relationship among Returns, Volatilities, Trading Volume and Open Interests of KOSPI 200 Futures Markets" *Korean Journal of Financial Management*, Vol. 24, No. 4(2007), pp. 107-134(in Korean).
문규현, 홍정효, "코스피 200 선물시장의 수익률, 변동성, 거래량 및 미결제 약정간의 관련성", 재무관리연구, 제24권 제4호(2007), pp. 107-134.

Nam, M. S., "An Empirical Study on the Relationship between Hourly Returns and Volume",* *Journal of Korean Securities Association*, Vol. 13, No. 1(1991), pp. 39-65(in Korean).
남명수, "시간대별 거래량과 수익률의 형태와의 관계에 관한 실증적 연구", 증권학회지, 제13권 제1호(1991), pp. 39-65.

Nam, M. S., C. M. Ahn, "Daily Price Limits and Stock Price Volatility", *Journal of Korean Securities Association*, Vol. 18, No. 1(1995), pp. 419-

439(in Korean).

남명수, 안창모, "상한가제도와 주가변동성", 증권학회지, 제18권 제1호
(1995), pp. 419-439.

Nam, S.-K. and J.-H. Park, "Is the Credit Balance in Margin Account a
Predictor of the Stock Price Index?", *Journal of Korean Securities
Association*, Vol. 19, No.1(1996), pp. 27-51(in Korean).

남상구, 박종호, "신용 잔고가 주가지수의 예측치인가", 증권학회지, 제19권
제1호(1996), pp. 27-51.

Nam, S.-K. and J.-H. Park, "The Composition of Effective Spread in the
Korean Stock Markets",* *Korean Journal of Financial Management*, Vol.
18, No. 2(2000), pp. 215-244(in Korean).

남상구, 박종호, "한국증권시장에서 실효 스프레드의 구성", 재무관리연구,
제18권 제2호(2000), pp. 215-244.

Nam, S.-K., J.-H. Park, and K. S. Eom, "Is the Liquidity Common Factor
a Priced Risk in the Korean Stock Markets?", *Korean Journal of Finance*,
Vol. 18, No. 2(2005), pp. 289-319(in Korean).

남상구, 박종호, 엄경식, "한국주식시장에서 유동성 공통요인은 주가에 반
영되는 위험의 원천인가?", 재무연구, 제18권 제2호(2005), pp. 289-319.

Nelson, D., "Conditional Heteroskedasticity in Asset Returns: A New
Approach", *Econometrica*, Vol. 59(1991), pp. 347-370.

O'Hara, M., *Market Microstructure Theory*, Blackwell, Oxford(1995).

Ohk, K. Y., "An Empirical Study on the Asymmetric Effect of News on
Volatility", *Journal of Korean Securities Association*, Vol. 21, No.
1(1997), pp. 295-324(in Korean).

옥기율, "주가변동성의 비대칭적 반응에 관한 실증적 연구", 증권학회지,
제21권 제1호(1997), pp. 295-324.

Park, J., "The Impact of Global Trading of Stocks on Return Volatility:
Evidence from the Korean Stock Market", *Asian Review of Financial*

Research, Vol. 22(2009), pp. 45-62.

Park, J.-H., "A Study of How Investors' Behaviors Are Affected by Price-Limits System",* *Korean Journal of Finance*, Vol. 3, No. 1(1990), pp. 135-155(in Korean).

박종호, "가격제한폭 제도에 의한 투자자의 투자행태에 관한 연구", 재무연구, 제3권 제1호(1990), pp. 135-155.

Park, J. J., "Stock Repurchase vs. Cash Dividends: Choosing between the Two and the Illiquidity Premium", *Asian Review of Financial Research*, Vol. 24, No. 1(2011), pp. 1-40(in Korean).

박재성, "자사주매입, 현금배당의 선택과 비유동성 프리미엄", 재무연구, 제24권 제1호(2011), pp. 1-40.

Park, Y.-K. and S.-Y. Chang, "Trading Volume and Lead-Lag Effect in Korean Stock Market", *Asia-Pacific Journal of Financial Studies*, Vol. 32, No. 2(2003), pp. 105-139(in Korean).

박영규, 장순영, "한국주식시장에서의 거래량에 의한 선도-지연효과 연구", 증권학회지, 제32권 제2호(2003), pp. 105-139.

Park, K. S. and Y.-H., Cho, "Day Traders' Performance Persistence and Market Quality", *Korean Journal of Financial Studies*, Vol. 39, No 3(2010), pp. 367-395(in Korean).

박경서, 조영현, "데이트레이더의 성과지속성과 시장효율성", 한국증권학회지, 제39권 제3호(2010), p. 367-395.

Park, J.-H. and K. S. Eom, "Positive Autocorrelation of Portfolio Returns in the Korean Stock Markets: Nonsynchronous Trading Effect vs. Partial Price Adjustment", *Asian-Pacific Journal of Financial Studies*, Vol. 34, No. 2(2005a), pp. 33-77(in Korean).

박종호, 엄경식, "한국주식시장에서 포트폴리오 수익률의 양의 1차 자기상관 : 비동시성 거래효과 vs. 부분가격조정가설", 증권학회지, 제34권 제2호 (2005a), pp. 33-77.

Park. J.-H. and K. S. Eom, "The Effect of Expanding Publicly Available

Quote Disclosure on Korean Stock Markets", *Korean Journal of Finance*, Vol. 18, No. 1(2005b), pp. 157-198(in Korean).

박종호, 엄경식, "한국주식시장에서 투명성과 질적 수준과의 관계 : 호가공개범위 확대를 중심으로", 재무연구, 제18권 제1호(2005b), pp. 157-198.

Park, J.-H. and K. S. Eom, "The Usefulness of PIN as a Measurement for Private-information Risk in Korean Stock Markets", *Asia-Pacific Journal of Financial Studies*, Vol. 37, No. 3(2008a), pp. 501-536(in Korean).

박종호, 엄경식, "한국주식시장에서 사적 정보위험 PIN의 유용성 분석 : 주식수익률에 미치는 영향을 중심으로", 증권학회지, 제37권 제3호(2008), pp. 501-536.

Park, J. J. and K. S. Eom, "The Characteristics of the Illiquidity Premium, Measured via Spread", *Korean Journal of Finance*, Vol. 21, No. 2(2008b), pp. 77-114(in Korean).

박재성, 엄경식, "스프레드율을 통해 관찰된 비유동성 프리미엄 특성", 재무연구, 제21권 제2호(2008), pp. 77-114.

Park, J. W., Y. Eom, and U. Chang, "Sidecar Performance: Evidence from the Korean Stock Market", *Korean Journal of Futures and Options*, Vol. 15, No. 1(2007a), pp. 1-40(in Korean).

박종원, 엄윤성, 장 욱, "사이드카가 프로그램매매종목의 가격·변동성·유동성에 미치는 영향", 선물연구, 제15권 제1호(2007a), pp. 1-40.

Park, J. W., Y. Eom, and U. Chang, "The Effects of Sidecar on Index Arbitrage Trading and Non-Index Arbitrage Trading: Evidence from the Korean Stock Market", *Korean Journal of Financial Management*, Vol. 24, No. 3(2007b), pp. 91-131(in Korean).

박종원, 엄윤성, 장 욱, "한국주식시장에서 사이드카의 역할과 재설계 : 차익거래와 비차익거래에 미치는 효과를 중심으로", 재무관리연구, 제24권 제3호(2007b), pp. 91-131.

Park, J. W., Y. Eom, and U. Chang, "Effects of Program Trading Halts on Information Asymmetry: Program Trading Stocks, Index Arbitrage Stocks, and Non-Index Arbitrage Stocks", *Korean Journal of Financial Management*, Vol. 26, No. 3(2009), pp. 65-101(in Korean).

박종원, 엄윤성, 장 욱, "프로그램매매 중단장치가 차익거래종목과 비차익거래종목의 정보비대칭에 미치는 영향", 재무관리연구, 제26권 제3호(2009), pp. 65-101.

Park, J. and M. Kim, "Information and Volatility: Evidence Found in the Korean Stock Market", *Asia-Pacific Journal of Financial Studies*, Vol. 32, No. 2(2003), pp. 141-163(in Korean).

박진우, 김민혁, "정보와 주가변동성 : 한국증권시장에 대한 실증연구", 증권학회지, 제32권 제2호(2003), pp. 141-163.

Park, K. S., E. Lee, and H. Jang, "Investor's Choice between Limit and Market Orders in Korean Stock Market", *Korean Journal of Finance*, Vol. 16, No. 1(2003a), pp. 115-158(in Korean).

박경서, 이은정, 장하성, "한국주식시장에서 투자자의 주문유형 선택에 관한 연구", 재무연구, 제16권 제1호(2003a), pp. 115-158.

Park, K. S., E. Lee, and H. Jang, "Manipulative Order Behavior and Price Discovery in the Pre-Opening Market of the Korea Stock Exchange", *Asia-Pacific Journal of Financial Studies*, Vol. 32, No. 2(2003b), pp. 209-244(in Korean).

박경서, 이은정, 장하성, "한국주식시장에서 동시호가 기간 중 주문행태와 가격발견기능에 관한 연구", 증권학회지, 제32권 제2호(2003b), pp. 209-244.

Park, K. S., E. Lee, and H. Jang, "Manipulative Orders in Korea Stock Exchange", *Korean Journal of Finance*, Vol. 17, No. 1(2004), pp. 105-142 (in Korean).

박경서, 이은정, 장하성, "한국주식시장의 허수주문에 관한 연구", 재무연구, 제17권 제1호(2004), pp. 105-142.

Park, J. W., W.-B. Lee, and T.-H. Kwon, "Program Trading Halts and

Information Asymmetry: Evidence from the Korean Securities Market", *Korean Journal of Financial Studies*, Vol. 38, No. 3(2009), pp. 325-369(in Korean).

박종원, 이우백, 권택호, "프로그램매매 중단장치가 주식시장의 정보비대칭에 미치는 영향", 한국증권학회지, 제38권 제3호(2009), pp. 325-369.

Park, J.-H., S.-K. Nam, and K. S. Eom, "Market Efficiency in KOSDAQ: A Volatility Comparison between Main Boards and New Markets Using a Permanent and Transitory Component Model", *Asia-Pacific Journal of Financial Studies*, Vol. 36, No. 4(2007), pp. 533-566(in Korean).

박종호, 남상구, 엄경식, "KOSDAQ의 시장 효율성 : 영구적 요소와 일시적 요소의 분해를 통한 주시장과 신시장의 변동성 비교분석", 증권학회지, 제36권 제4호(2007), pp. 533-566.

Park, D., S. H. Shin, and C. Rhee, "Evaluating of the Introduction of the Electronic Trading Platform in the Government Bond Market", *Korean Journal of Money and Finance*, Vol. 12, No. 1(2007), pp. 1-28(in Korean).

박대근, 신성환, 이창용, "국채 전자거래 시스템 도입의 성과 : 미시자료를 이용한 평가", 금융학회지, 제12권 제1호(2007), pp. 1-28.

Pastor, L. and R. Stambaugh, "Liquidity Risk and Expected Stock Return", *Journal of Political Economy*, Vol. 111(2003), pp. 642-685.

Rogers, W., "Regression Standard Errors in Clustered Samples", *Stata Technical Bulletin*, Vol. 13(1993), pp. 19-23.

Seon, J. and K. S. Eom, "Trading Intensity and Informational Effect of Trades in the Won/Dollar FX Market: Event Uncertainty Hypothesis vs. Hot Potato Hypothesis", *Asia-Pacific Journal of Financial Studies*, Vol. 35, No. 6(2006), pp. 77-102(in Korean).

선정훈, 엄경식, "원/달러 외환시장에서 거래집중도와 거래정보효과와의 관계 : 사건 불확실성 가설과 뜨거운 감자 가설을 중심으로", 증권학회지, 제35권 제6호(2006), pp. 77-102.

Seon, J. and K. S. Eom, "The Efficiency of Intraday Price Discovery in the Seoul Won/Dollar FX Market", *Asian Review of Financial Research*, Vol. 23, No. 1(2010), pp. 1-26(in Korean).

선정훈, 엄경식, "원/달러 외환시장의 일중 가격발견 효율성", 재무연구, 제23권 제1호(2010), pp. 1-26.

Seon, J. and K. S. Eom, "Microstructure Approach to Private Information in the Won/Dollar FX Market: The Influence of Domestic and Foreign Dealers' Order Flows", *Quarterly Economic Analysis*, Vol. 16, No. 4(2011), pp. 116-149(in Korean).

선정훈, 엄경식, "원/달러 외환시장 사적정보에 대한 미시구조 접근 : 국내 딜러와 외국딜러의 주문흐름 영향력을 중심으로", 경제분석, 제16권 제4호 (2011), pp. 116-149.

Seon, J., K. S. Eom, and S. B. Hahn, "Liquidity Commonality on the Korea Stock Exchange", *Asian-Pacific Journal of Financial Studies*, Vol. 34, No. 1(2005), pp. 129-163(in Korean).

선정훈, 엄경식, 한상범, "한국주식시장의 유동성 동행화", 증권학회지, 제34권 제1호(2005), pp. 129-163.

Seon, J., K. S. Eom, and S. B. Hahn, "Traders' Anonymity and Market Quality on the Korea Exchange", *Korean Journal of Money and Finance*, Vol. 11, No. 2(2006), pp. 1-34(in Korean).

선정훈, 엄경식, 한상범, "투자자 익명성과 주식시장의 질적 수준 : 외국계 증권사 대량매매 정보의 실시간 공개를 중심으로", 금융학회지, 제11권 제2호(2006), pp. 1-34.

Song, C.-S., "Day Trading and Price Volatility: Observation of the Korea Stock Exchange", *Asia-Pacific Journal of Financial Studies*, Vol. 32, No. 3(2003), pp. 45-84(in Korean).

송치승, "Day Trading과 주가변동성", 증권학회지, 제32권 제3호(2003), pp. 45-84.

Song, C.-S, "Motives for Short Selling from Securities Lending and Stock Returns", *Asia-Pacific Journal of Financial Studies*, Vol. 35, No. 6(2006), pp. 1-37(in Korean).

송치승, "주식대차에 의한 공매 동기와 수익률", 증권학회지, 제35권 제6호 (2006), pp. 1-37.

Sonu, S., "Impact of the Price Limit Change upon Stock Market Volatility in Korea", *Journal of Korean Securities Association*, Vol. 20, No. 1(1997), pp. 369-393(in Korean).

선우석호, "주가제한폭 확대와 변동성", 증권학회지, 제20권 제1호(1997), pp. 369-393.

Stoll, H., "The Supply of Dealer Services in Securities Markets", *Journal of Finance*, Vol. 33(1978), pp. 1133-1151.

Stoll, H., "Market Microstructure", In Constantinides, G. M., M. Harris, and R. M. Stulz(eds.), *Handbook of the Economics of Finance*, Elsevier, Amsterdam(2003).

Stoll, H. and R. Whaley, "Stock Market Structure and Volatility", *Review of Financial Studies*, Vol. 3(1990), pp. 37-71.

Tauchen, G. E. and M. Pitts, "The Price Variability-Volume Relationship in Speculative Markets", *Econometrica*, Vol. 51(1983), pp. 485-505.

Thornton, G., "Global Growth Markets Guide: Overview"(2008), Accessed June 2010. Available from: http://www.git.org/Publications/2007-Global-growth-markets-guide.asp.

Yi, J., K. B. Binh, and G. Jang, "The Causal Relationship between Stock Price and Short Sales: Evidence from the Korean Stock Market", *Korean Journal of Financial Studies*, Vol. 39, No. 3(2010), pp. 449-489(in Korean).

이준서, 빈기범, 장광익, "주가와 공매도간 인과 관계에 관한 실증 연구", 한국증권학회지, 제39권 제3호(2010), pp. 449-489.

Yang, C.-W., "A Study on Determinants of Market Liquidity in the Korean Stock Market", *Korean Journal of Financial Studies*, Vol. 39, No. 1(2010), pp. 103-132(in Korean).

양철원, "한국주식시장에서 시장유동성의 결정요인", 한국증권학회지, 제39권 제1호(2010), pp. 103-132.

Yon, K. H., "An Empirical Investigation of KOSDAQ Market Efficiency Through Stock Exchange Listing", *Journal of Korean Securities Association*, Vol. 23, No. 1(1998), pp. 289-323(in Korean).

연강흠, "장외종목의 기업공개를 통한 코스닥(KOSDAQ)시장의 효율성 분석", 증권학회지, 제23권 제1호(1998), pp. 289-323.

Yoo, J., "Daily Price Limits and Estimation of True Volatility", *Journal of Korean Securities Association*, Vol. 28, No. 1(2001), pp. 543-577(in Korean).

유 진, "1일 주가수익률 제한과 진실한 변동성의 추정", 증권학회지, 제28권 제1호(2001), pp. 543-577.

Yun, S. Y., B. Ku, Y. Eom, and J. Hahn, "The Cross-Section of Stock Returns in Korea: An Empirical Investigation", *Asian Review of Financial Research*, Vol. 22, No. 1(2009), pp. 1-44(in Korean).

윤상용, 구본일, 엄영호, 한재훈, "한국 주식시장에서 유동성요인을 포함한 3요인 모형의 설명력에 관한 연구", 재무연구, 제22권 제1호(2009), pp. 1-44.

Any citation of this article must refer to the following: Kim, Keunsoo and Byun, Jinho, "Studies on Korean Capital Markets from the Perspective of Behavioral Finance", Asian Review of Financial Research, Vol. 24 (2011), No. 3, pp. 953-1020.

Chapter 4

Studies on Korean Capital Markets from the Perspective of Behavioral Finance

Keunsoo Kim   Associate Professor, Graduate School of Pan-Pacific International Studies, Kyung Hee University

Jinho Byun*   Associate Professor, Ewha School of Business, Ewha Womans University

Abstract   Behavioral finance encompasses research that gives up the traditional assumptions of expected utility maximization with rational investors in an efficient market. It is defined as the application of psychology to financial decision making and financial markets. Based on this definition, our review essay summarizes recent work of behavioral studies in Korean capital markets along with some pioneering papers in the behavioral finance literature.

In Korea, behavioral studies are in their early stages of development. First, we start with discussion of the limits of arbitrage as a foundation of behavioral finance. We discuss the limits of arbitrage to explain why Friedman's (1953) paradigm of arbitrage may not eliminate pricing errors in capital markets. Second, the prospect theory of Kahneman and Tversky (1979) and its related empirical results are reviewed. Third, empirical results related to overreaction and underreaction are addressed. Fourth, investors' trading behaviors and return patterns as influenced by psychological biases are discussed.

In conclusion, we address several areas to explore as promising research fields. First, experimental investigation with psychologists is warranted. Second, regional anomalies need be explored from behavioral perspectives. Investors' behavior across cultures is also an interesting topic in behavioral finance. Third, collaborative work with other business areas is needed. Finally, corporate behavioral finance has much room for further investigation.

Keywords   Behavioral Finance, Limits of Arbitrage, Psychological Bias, Long-term Performance, Irrational Investors, Korean Capital Markets

---

* Corresponding Author. Address: Ewha Womans University, 52 Ewhayeodae-gil, Seadaemun-gu, Seoul 120-750, Korea; E-mail: jbyun@ewha.ac.kr; Tel: 82-2-3277-3971.

This survey paper was accomplished as a part of the 2010 knowledge database project by the Korean Finance Association and was financially supported by the KFA. The authors thank two referees, Yunsung Eom and one anonymous referee, and the Editor, Hee-Joon Ahn, for their helpful comments. The authors also thank Seong-Soon Cho for her excellent assistantship.

I. Introduction

Over the past several decades, traditional finance has developed a successful paradigm based on the notions that investors and managers are generally rational and the prices of securities are generally "efficient." In recent years, however, anecdotal evidence as well as theoretical and empirical research has shown that this paradigm may be insufficient to describe various features of actual financial markets. Several financial economists (Thaler, 1999; Shefrin, 2005, 2010; Shiller, 2002) claim that behavioral finance is an alternative finance to account for the decision making of investors and anomalies of financial markets.

Behavioral papers are now routinely presented in every major academic finance journal. In 1999, best paper recognition for those published in the *Journal of Finance* was given to Daniel, Hirshleifer and Subrahmanyam (1998). Additionally, Shefrin and Statman's (2000) paper appearing in the *Journal of Financial and Quantitative Analysis* was also selected as the best paper. The *Review of Financial Studies* (2002), the *Financial Analysts Journal* (1999) and the *Journal of Empirical Finance* (2004) have devoted entire issues to behavioral finance. On October 18, 2004, Eugene Fama, one of the pillars of the efficient market school, expressed his concession in the *Wall Street Journal* and admitted that the stock prices could become "somewhat irrational." The growing popularity of behavioral finance is observed in other areas of business academia. Among them, *Management Science* is planning a fall 2011 issue dedicated to "behavioral economics and finance."

Where is behavioral finance heading? Thaler (1999) suggests that the end point is for behavioral elements to become a part of regular finance, instead of a special finance. He calls this state of affairs as the end of behavioral finance, implying that finance could mean behavioral finance someday.

Although we have not seen the end of behavioral finance yet, financial economists have obviously become more interested in behavioral finance and examine individual investor and capital markets behavior from the perspective of behavioral finance, this being particularly true after the observed IT bubble collapse of the early 2000s.

We, however, observe that the current academic climate in Korea tends to be reluctant to reflect the psychological biases of practitioners in investment management or corporate finance. Virtually no financial journal in Korea admits experimental tests or surveys as academic methodologies, although these are generally accepted in overseas psychology or finance journals. As such, studies on Korean capital markets from the perspective of behavioral finance are limited to a few topics, and it is not easy to find studies focused on the psychological biases of investors.

Furthermore, academic studies of Korean capital markets usually address comprehensive literature reviews on overseas studies but frequently miss existing studies on the same topic in Korean capital markets. As a result, knowledge of the empirical results has not been accumulated. For example, although new empirical results in Korean capital markets sometimes appear to be opposing those of earlier papers, there are no further analyses or debates on why their results are different from each other or whose finding is more accurate. For academic development and a better understanding of Korean capital markets, it is essential to examine comprehensive literature reviews about Korean capital markets as well. The purpose of this paper is to provide a comprehensive review of behavioral finance studies on Korean capital markets.

Shefrin (2010) defines behavioral finance as the application of psychology to financial decision making and financial markets. Based on his definition, our review essay summarizes recent work of behavioral studies in Korea.[1]

---

1) This essay is intended to focus on behavioral finance as related to Korean capital markets. Hence, the citations

Anomalies in financial markets that are not strongly claimed to be related to psychological biases are not included in our survey.

This review is divided into six main chapters. Chapter II discusses the limit of arbitrage to explain why Friedman's (1953) paradigm of arbitrage may not eliminate price errors in capital markets. Chapter III explains the prospect theory and its related empirical studies. In chapter IV, empirical studies related to the overreaction and underreaction hypotheses are discussed. Chapter V addresses investor trading behavior or return behavior related to psychological biases such as overconfidence and weather related moods. In the same chapter, we also address research in corporate finance. Finally, we conclude our survey of behavioral finance in Korea and suggest of some promising future directions in behavioral finance.

II. Foundation of Behavioral Finance

1. Beginning of Behavioral Finance

Behavioral finance is a relatively new subject. The first formal paper in behavioral finance was Slovic's (1972) "Psychological study of human judgment: Implication for investment decision making" published in the *Journal of Finance* (Shefrin, 2010). This paper did not attract the interest of most financial economists. More and more financial economists, however, began to take interest in behavioral approaches as many empirical studies in the financial literature helped find substantial evidence about anomalies such

---

are not necessarily complete. For a more comprehensive review of this field, see earlier survey papers. Shleifer (2000) provides a detailed discussion of theoretical and empirical work on limits of arbitrage. Hirshleifer (2001) and Barberis and Thaler (2003) present a good summary of behavioral finance literature, although they devote less space to corporate finance and more to individual investors. Baker, Ruback and Wurgler (2007) evaluate behavioral issues on corporate finance. Shefrin (2010) provides a recent survey including a survey of earlier surveys.

as the size effect, book-to-market effect, anomalies related to past returns, first day abnormal return on IPO, closed-end fund discount puzzle, equity premium puzzle, several calendar related anomalies, and others.

While financial economists attempt to find the sources of these anomalies, some of them claim that these anomalies are due to the behavioral biases of investors. DeBondt and Thaler's (1985) paper is one of the pioneering papers that claim that the anomaly of long-term price reversal is due to the overreaction bias of investors. On the other hand, Shefrin and Statman's (1985) paper, another pioneering paper, employs a different approach. They find new irrational behavior of investors based on the prospect theory of Kahneman and Tversky (1979) that explains investors' irrational decision making under uncertainty. After these two papers were published, the approach of behavioral finance has collided with that of traditional finance in several issues, and controversial debates sometimes went near an emotional level.[2]

2. Limits of Arbitrage

The main arguments of behavioral finance may be summarized as 1) agents are semi-irrational or subject to psychological biases, and 2) the price errors of securities caused by the agents can be persistent. Traditional finance hardly accepts these two arguments. Particularly, the solid objection to the second argument of behavioral finance is based on Friedman's (1953) paradigm that rational traders will quickly purse arbitrage profits from any price error of a security, moving the security price toward its fundamental value. For example, arbitragers who recognize an undervalued security will buy it at the

2) A few of papers about the closed-end fund puzzle were published in the *Journal of Finance*. Their papers debate each other about whether discounts of closed-end funds' trading prices are a sentiment index. Chopra, Lee, Shleifer and Thaler (1993) mention in their first sentence, "Chen, Kan and Miller (1993, best pronounced CheK'M) provide a detailed critique of our earlier paper (Lee, Shleifer, and Thaler, 1991). CKM accuse Lee et al. of trying to kill two birds - the closed-end fund puzzle and the small firm effect - with one stone and missing both. Their approach is to throw at Lee et al. every stone they can, presumably hoping that one will hit. This reply shows that none does."

bargain price and hedge their long position by shorting a substitute security. The buying pressure on the undervalued security will increase its price, eliminating any pricing error. As far as rational arbitragers exist, the financial market will be efficient since they will drive irrational investors out.

Behavioral finance, however, provides several reasons why arbitrage is limited. First, Barberis and Thaler (2003) suggest that the fundamental risk that arbitragers face in fact limits the arbitrager's activity. Suppose that Ford's fundamental value is $20 per share but its stock price has been pushed down to $15. If arbitragers buy the stock at $15, the fundamental risk that the arbitragers face is the possibility that a piece of bad news about Ford's fundamental value may happen. The arbitrage should take the risk that Ford's fundamental value may go down below $15. In order to hedge the risk, arbitragers may short a substitute stock such as GM, but GM is not a perfect substitute. Although shorting GM protects the arbitragers somewhat from adverse news about the car industry as a whole, it still leaves them vulnerable to news that is specific to Ford.

Second, DeLong, Shleifer, Summers, and Waldman (1990a) and Shleifer and Vishny (1993) argue that noise trading may not be predictable particularly in the short run and thus limit arbitrage. Uncertainty of noise trading is the risk that mispricing can be worsened in the short run. Arbitrage is conducted in practice by a relatively small number of highly specialized professional investors. Most of them manage funds from outside investors such as wealthy individuals, banks, endowments, and other investors who evaluate the capability of a professional investor based on her investment performance. Since outside investors with only limited financial knowledge do not know or understand what the professional manager is doing, they will evaluate her investment performance simply based on whether she loses or earns money over a certain period. Under such a situation, noise trader risk can force an arbitrageur to liquidate her position early and may bring her losses. As a result, prices can deviate substantially from fundamental value even if the fundamental risk does not exist.

Third, DeLong, Shleifer, Summers, and Waldman (1990b) suggest that when rational investors can predict the behavior of irrational investors, the former may destabilize security prices instead of stabilizing them. For example, rational investors will buy overpriced stocks when they predict that momentum traders will chase the buying trend of these stocks. In this situation, the rational investors begin to sell the stocks before the momentum traders stop chasing. DeLong et al. (1990b) shows that rational investors can obtain more profit by destabilizing security prices.

Fourth, implementation costs also limit arbitrage. Transaction costs such as commission fees, bid-ask spreads, and price impact can make it less attractive to exploit price errors. Short-sale constraints are also an important source of persistent price errors.

If arbitrage activities are limited in practice, as we mentioned above, it is essential to understand the behaviors of noise traders because their behaviors may deviate securities' prices from their fundamental values over a certain period. Further, understanding their behaviors may enable us to predict price errors in capital markets. As such, the behavioral approach naturally pays attention to the psychological biases of human beings that may determine trading behaviors of investors. Such cognitive biases include heuristics, overconfidence, mental accounting, representativeness, conservatism, and the disposition effect. For example, heuristics is a bias of making a selection easier which can mislead investors to make a sub-optimal choice. If investors face N investment choices that they can take, many of them tend to allocate their money by using $1/N$ rule. Benartzi and Thaler (2001) have documented that many people follow the $1/N$ rule. The other biases will be discussed in detail in the following chapters.

III. Prospect Theory and Empirical Results

1. Prospect Theory

The majority of asset pricing models in traditional finance assume that investors evaluate gambles based on the expected utility framework suggested by Von Neumann and Morgenstern (1947). They show that preferences can be represented by the expectation of a utility function. Suppose a prospect $(x_1, p_1; \cdots; x_n, p_n)$ is a contract that yields outcome x_i with probability p_i where $p_1 + p_2 + p_3 \cdots + p_n = 1$. Application of the expected utility theory to overall utility of this prospect can be expressed as $U(x_1, p_1; \cdots; x_n, p_n) = U(x_1)p_1 + U(x_2)p_2 \cdots + U(x_n)p_n$.

This expected utility theory plays an underpinning role in developing the portfolio theory and capital asset pricing model (CAPM). The expected utility theory provides the two important features of wealth integration and risk aversion. First, wealth integration indicates that when a rational person makes a decision about the acceptance of a prospect, she integrates the prospect with her original own wealth. For example, when a person has assets w and makes a decision about the prospect, it is acceptable only if $U(w + x_1, p_1; \cdots; w + x_n, p_n) > u(w)$. Second, the expected utility theory assumes that a utility function is concave, indicating $U'' < 0$. The concave utility function suggests that a person is risk averse.

Although the expected utility theory provides a normative model of how a rational person should make a decision about alternative courses of actions, it does not successfully explain how people actually make a decision under uncertainty. Particularly, experimental survey results demonstrated by Kahneman and Tversky (1979) appear to violate wealth integration and risk aversion.

The following questions show how people make selections under uncertainty and how their selections violate wealth integration and risk aversion.

A = ($2,000, 0.5)

B = ($1,000, 1)

Gamble A gives a 50% chance to win $2,000 and 50% chance for nothing. *B* provides a sure gain of $1,000. *B* is more popular, indicating people are risk averse over gains.

On the other hand, people's reaction to a negative prospect is different. Suppose that people have been given $2,000 and then asked to choose between the followings:

C = (- $2,000, 0.5)

D = (- $1,000, 1)

Gamble C is preferred to *D*, which is against the prediction of the expected utility theory. In case of a negative prospect, people hate to realize losses and the uncertain choice holds out the hope that losses can be avoided. Such a loss aversion indicates risk seeking behavior. People are risk seeking in a domain of losses, a tendency that is not consistent with the traditional assumption of risk aversion. The prospect theory suggests an S-shape utility function which is concave in a domain of gains and convex in a domain of losses.

Preference of *C* over *D* is not consistent with the rule of wealth integration as well. Since people receive $2,000 before choosing either *C* or *D*, the outcome of selecting *C* (*D*) is identical to that of *A* (*B*). If people prefer *B* to *A*, they should prefer *D* to *C*. According to the prospect theory, such a contradicting choice results from people's mental framing when making a decision about different types of gambles. Instead of integrating $2,000 with *C* or *D*, people tend to separate $2,000 from making a choice of *C* or *D*. Thaler (1985) names such a tendency as mental accounting. He argues that decision makers tend to segregate the different types of gambles into separate accounts. They apply their decision rules to each account without integrating their accounts, which is against the wealth integration implied by the expected utility theory.

The final piece of prospect theory is about the overweighing of small probabilities. For example, a gamble of ($5000, 0.001) is preferred to sure gain of ($5, 1), while sure loss of (- $5, 1) is preferred to a gamble of (- $5,000, 0.001). Kahneman and Tversky attribute these preference patterns to the tendency of people to overweight small probabilities. An overweight of small probabilities explains the preferences for insurance and for buying lotteries at the same time.

Shefrin and Statman (1985) apply the prospect theory to an individual investor's decision making for stock investment. Consider an investor who purchased 100 shares of *stock G* at $100 and 200 shares of *stock L* at $50 in the previous period. He finds out that *stock G* is selling at $110 and *stock L* is selling at $45. Although his net wealth from stock investment does not change, he opened two mental accounts for *stock G* and *L* when he purchased both stocks. The natural reference points for *stock G* and *L* are their purchase prices. In his mental account for *stock G (L)*, he currently has $1,000 of paper gains (losses). Suppose that *stock G (L)* has an equal chance to increase or decrease by $10 ($5) in the next period. According to the prospect theory, our investor should make a selection between the following choices about *stock G* in this period.

G1: Hold *stock G* for one more period. Given $100 of reference point, his money can be defined as a positive prospect of ($2,000, 0.5)

G2: Sell *stock G* to lock in sure gain of $1,000.

Since *G1 (G2)* is exactly the same as Gamble *A (B)*, our investor is more likely to sell the winner whose price has increased. Likewise, our investor has a selection to make between the following choices about *stock L*.

L1: Hold *stock L* for one more period. Given $50 as a reference point, his money can be defined as a negative prospect of (- $2,000, 0.5)

   L2 : Sell *stock L* to lock in sure loss of $1,000.

Since *L1 (L2)* is exactly the same as Gamble *C (D)*, our investor is more likely to hold the loser whose price has decreased. As such, the important implication of the prospect theory is that investors are more likely to sell winners than losers. Shefrin and Statman (1985) name this phenomenon as the disposition effect.

2. Psychological Bias of Gamblers

Kim and Seog (2007) examine whether rules of thumb for black jack players in Kangwon Land are consistent with the prospect theory.[3] In principle, every player can make his or her own decision about hitting or standing a card in the black jack game. However, each player's decision can change the outcome of black jack games. For example, consider the situation in which if a play decided to stand, a dealer would go bust. In this situation, other players may complain about the player's decision on hitting, particularly when hitting is believed to have a lower probability of winning the game than standing. In the early period after Kangwon Land opened, there were many quarrels about the hitting or standing decisions among players in Kangwon Land. To prevent quarrels, some rules among players began to appear and have been developed as the rules of thumb. As such, these rules of thumb are players' consensus that may reflect psychological biases. Kim and Seog compare these rules to the basic strategy that gives the best choice based on each situation.

They show that the main bias shown in the rules of thumb is that a player tends to stand when he or she has to hit or take an action such as a split to obtain a higher chance to win. This is consistent with regret aversion. Regret occurs when people would have been better off if they

---

3) The Kangwon Land is a unique casino in Korea which allows Korean citizen to play.

had made a different decision in the past. Particularly, people tend to regret more when they take active decisions rather than passive decisions. As such, a player tends to be passive by standing to avoid a highly regrettable situation that may occur if he or she takes active action such as hitting or splitting. Further, standing suggests that a player tends to overvalue the probability that a dealer will be bust, which is consistent with the prospect theory.

3. Disposition Effect

3.1 Basic Finding

Choi, Lee, and Jeong (2004) test the disposition effect by randomly collecting 1,400 active cyber accounts from a Korean securities company between March 1999 and February 2003 which are required to be at least one year old. They use Odean's (1998) PGR (proportion of gains realized) and PLR (proportion of losses realized) to examine whether individual investors tend to sell winners rather than losers.

PGR and PLR are defined as following. $PGR = \dfrac{\text{Realized Gains}}{\text{Realized Gains} + \text{Paper Gains}}$, $PLR = \dfrac{\text{Realized Losses}}{\text{Realized Losses} + \text{Paper Losses}}$. Every day when a stock's sale takes place in an account, this stock is considered to be a realized gain or loss. When the selling price of the stock in a portfolio is higher (lower) than its average purchase price, the stock is counted as a realized gain (loss) on that day. Each stock which is in the portfolio at the beginning of a day but is not sold is a paper gain (loss) on that day when both high and low daily prices of that stock are higher (lower) than its average purchase price. When its average purchase price lies between the high and the low, neither paper gain or loss is counted. On days when no sales take place in an account, gains or losses are not counted.

The data used by Choi et al. (2004) has two types of accounts: managerial accounts and non-managerial accounts. Since trading through a managerial account can be influenced by a broker of the securities company, the result of the non-managerial account may describe an individual investor's behavior better than that of the managerial account. From March of 1999 to February of 2003, the difference between proportion of losses realized and proportion of gain realized (PLR-PGR) for managerial accounts and for non-managerial accounts was -0.023 (t = -2.45) and -0.031 (t = -2.12), respectively, indicating that individual investors are more willing to sell winners than losers. They find the disposition effect in Korea.

Even though many of studies find evidence about the disposition effect, there is little evidence in the futures market. Coval and Shumway (2005) and Locke and Mann (2005) show the existence of the disposition effect in the futures market. However, their analysis is restricted to market makers or professional traders. Using Korean index futures market data, Choe and Eom (2009) examine whether if the disposition effect exists in Korea and find evidence for it. They find individual investors are more susceptible to the disposition effect than institutional and foreign investors and also find a negative relationship between the disposition effect and investment performance. Choe and Eom (2010) analyze the disposition effect in Korean options markets. They suggest that the changes in volatility can be explained by changes in the disposition effect.

The disposition effect, however, appears to be weak in Korea, compared to that in the U.S. For example, Odean (1998) finds that PLR-PGR is -0.050 from 1987 to 1993 and its *t*-value is -35, which indicates that the disposition effect is stronger and more reliable in U.S. than in Korea. Furthermore, his sub-period analysis consistently shows a strong disposition effect. However, sub-analysis by Choi et al. (2004) shows that PLR-PGR of non-managerial accounts is statistically significant only from March 1999 to January 2000, while that of managerial accounts is statistically significant only from February 2000 to January 2001.

It remains questionable in Korea whether the disposition effect can be explained by other possible hypotheses. For example, Odean (1998) suggests three alternative hypotheses for the disposition effect. First, the disposition effect may be motivated by investors' belief that today's losers will soon outperform today's winners. He does not provide any evidence to differentiate the prospect theory from investors' belief in mean reversion. However, he finds that average excess returns for winners over the following year are 3.4 percent higher than those for losers that are not sold, which is consistent with Jegadeesh and Titman's (1993) finding of price momentum. Odean's finding suggests that the disposition effect actually harms the wealth of individual investors and investors' mean reversion belief may not be rational if such a belief is a motivation of the disposition effect. Since there is no convincing evidence on price momentum in Korean stock markets, it is interesting to examine whether the disposition effect is really harmful to Korean individual investors. Second, investors may have an incentive to rebalance their portfolios for diversification by selling the winners. Since the weights of winners become higher, investors may reduce their weights by selling those winners for diversification. Third, since the price of losers tends to be lower than that of winners, the transaction costs of winners may be lower than those of losers given the inverse relation between trading costs and stock prices. When investors want to sell stocks for liquidity, selling winners may be better so that they can reduce transaction costs. Odean shows that the second and third hypotheses are not supported by their additional results.

Choi and Jeong (2004) provide similar but more reliable results by combining non-managerial accounts and managerial accounts during the same period as Choi et al. (2004). They examine whether the disposition effect can result from investors' motivation to rebalance. If investors are motivated to rebalance their portfolios, they will buy other stocks for diversification soon after they sell winners. They test the disposition effect by excluding all accounts where new purchases occur within one week after they sell stocks. After excluding those accounts, they find the disposition effect again at a 1% significance level, which indicates the disposition effect does not result from portfolio rebalancing.

In addition, Choi and Jung (2004) compare market adjusted abnormal returns to stocks that investors sell with those to stocks that investors buy for 88 and 256 trading days after their trading. They find that stocks that they sell have higher abnormal returns than those they buy during the period from March 1999 to February 2000. This empirical result is consistent with Odean's (1999). They attribute this result to the overconfidence of investors. Investors are more likely to sell stocks when their expected returns are lower than those of stocks that investors purchase. The empirical result suggests that the expectation of the investors in Korea is wrong like in the U.S. However, we need more robust empirical testing since the result of Choi and Jung (2004) is valid only for the period from March 1999 to February 2000. Given that price momentum is not found in Korean stock markets, it is questionable why stocks that individual investors sell outperform those that they buy in Korea.

3.2 Price Momentum

Grinblatt and Han (2005) suggest the possibility that the disposition effect of investors may influence the valuation of stocks. They consider a model of equilibrium prices in which a group of investors is subject to behaviors implied by the prospect theory and mental accounting. Their demand functions distort equilibrium prices relative to those predicted by the standard utility theory. The disposition effect results from the selling pressure of a stock with more prior good news than adverse information. If demand for a stock by rational investors is not perfectly elastic, the distorted demand caused by the disposition behavior tends to generate underreaction to public information. As such, past winners tend to be undervalued and past losers overvalued, resulting in price momentum for the following period. They claim that the disposition effect may be an important factor in generating intermediate price momentum.

Park and Ahn (2007) examines whether the disposition behavior influences the expected returns in Korean stock markets by using Grinblatt and Han's (2005) model. Their regression model is basically the same with Grinblatt and Han's. If the disposition behavior of investors influences the valuation of stocks, aggregate capital gains with reference prices are positively related to subsequent expected returns. Their cross-sectional regression includes four, twenty six, and fifty two weeks of past returns (Jegadeesh and Titman, 1993; DeBondt and Thaler, 1985), one year's average turnover ratio (Lee and Swami-nathan, 2000), and size and capital gains-related proxy. The unrealized capital gain proxy is defined as $\frac{P^i_{t-2} - R^i_{t-1}}{P^i_{t-2}}$ where t is the week and a return of stock i is measured as the dependent variable. In order to avoid the confounding market microstructure effects such as bid-ask spread, one week is lagged. The reference price is defined as follows. $R_{t-1} = \left(\frac{1}{k}\right) \sum_{n=1}^{T} (V_{t-1-n} \Pi_{\tau=1}^{n-1}[1 - V_{t-1-n-\tau}]) P_{t-1-n}$. where V_{t-1} is week $t-1$' turnover ratio in the stock. The term in parenthesis multiplying P_{t-1-n} is a weight, and k makes all the weights on past prices sum to one. As such, the reference price is the weighted average of serial market prices from $t-2$ to $t-1-T$. The weight on P_{t-1-n} can be interpreted as the probability that a share was last purchased at date $t - n - 1$ and has not been traded since then. In other words, this probability is the probability that P_{t-1-n} is a reference price to investors who purchase the stock at date $t - 1 - n$ but do not trade since then.

Park and Ahn (2007) find a positive relation between a firm's size and its expected return from 2000 to 2005, and also between a proxy for aggregate unrealized capital gain and its expected return with a sample excluding January. However, their empirical results do not present that the disposition effect reliably influences the valuation of stocks with the total sample including January. As such, it is difficult to argue that the disposition behavior of investors influences stock prices in Korea. Given the fact that there is no price momentum in Korean stock markets, it is questionable as to why the disposition effect does not cause price momentum in Korea if the disposition effect is a main source of price momentum as Grinblatt and Han (2005) claim.

Choe and Eom (2008) examine the disposition effect on futures market prices through a transactions dataset of the Korean index futures. Using high frequency transaction data, they examine the disposition effect at the market-level on market volatility and short-term return to test the hypothesis that irrational traders can influence futures prices. They find that the increased disposition effect in the long (short) position has a tendency to decrease (increase) prices over a short-term period. Their findings suggest that the disposition effect has an impact on short-term prices in the futures market. Whether the disposition effect, however, causes price momentum of several weeks or not would require more examinations.

3.3 Past Investment Experience

Jeong and Park (2008) examine how the past investment experiences of investors affect their decisions to buy stocks by using samples from randomly collected 5,000 cyber and 5,000 non-cyber active accounts from

February 1999 to December 2005. Their major findings are as follows. First, individual investors tend to repurchase stocks they realized gains from selling rather than stocks they realized losses from selling in the past. Jung and Park argue that investors want to repeat the good experience of realizing investment gains by repurchasing stocks which gave gains to them.

Second, individual investors tend to repurchase stocks whose prices have fallen after being sold rather than stocks whose prices have risen. They ascribe this finding to the anchoring effect of Tversky and Kahneman (1974). The anchoring effect is a cognitive bias that describes the common human tendency to rely too heavily, or "anchor", on one trait or initial piece of information when making decisions. The price at which investors sell may function as an anchor. If a stock price is higher (lower) than the anchoring price, the stock price looks expensive (cheap) to investors. As such, they want to repurchase those stocks whose prices have decreased after being sold. Another possible explanation is that people tend to avoid regret. Individual investors do not have any reason to regret when they repurchase stocks whose prices decrease after selling them. On the other hand, if individual investors repurchase stocks whose prices have increased after selling them, they should accept the fact that they would not have missed out on capital gains if they had held these stocks without selling them. In order to avoid explicit regret, individual investors do not want to repurchase stocks the prices of which have increased after being sold.

Third, individual investors tend to repurchase losers, the prices of which have recently decreased, rather than winners among stocks they hold. These findings are also explained by the anchoring effect. There is another possible explanation. If investors initially purchase stocks because of good, private information, they may believe that this information is reflected in winners but not in losers. Then, they may want to keep buying losers.

IV. Over-reaction and Under-reaction

1. Over-reaction and Under-reaction Models

DeBondt and Thaler (1985) initially document evidence of the profitability of the original contrarian strategy; that is, buying long-term losers and selling long-term winners. They argue that investors tend to overreact to good news associated with past winners and bad news associated with past losers. As such, stocks exhibiting the former (latter) become overvalued (undervalued), and thus contrarian profits are obtained because the prices of both types of stocks eventually return to equilibrium values. This phenomenon is referred to as long-term reversal. On the other hand, Jegadeesh and Titman (1993) document that short-term winners, based on three to twelve-month past returns, continue to outperform short-term losers over the next three to twelve months, referred to as intermediate price momentum.

A few behavioral models attempt to explain both anomalies. Barberis, Shleifer, and Vishny (1998; henceforth BSV) develop a model based on two established psychological biases: representativeness (Kahneman, Slovic, and Tversky, 1982) and conservatism (Edwards, 1986). The representative bias is the tendency of people to view individual events as typical or representative of some specific class and to ignore the laws of probability in the process.

Suppose that news arriving in each period will be either good or bad, following a random walk. When a series of good news happens to arrive, investors who are subject to the representative bias tend to believe that the trend of good news will continue. As such, investors predict that the next signal is more likely to be good news, resulting in overreaction to a series of good news. On the other hand, conservatism is a mental process in which people cling to their prior views of forecasts at the expense of acknowledging new information. If a series of past signal or news does not show any trend, conservatism relatively strongly influences investors' predictions. When a bad signal follows a good signal, investors are more likely to underreact to the bad signal because of their conservatism. In short, BSV suggest that long-term reversal results from the representativeness bias and intermediate momentum from the conservative bias.

In the model of Daniel, Hirshleifer, and Subrahmanyam (1998; henceforth DHS), the market includes both informed and uninformed investors. The uninformed are not subject to judgment biases. However, informed investors, who are subject to judgment biases, set stock prices. Especially, informed investors exhibit overconfidence and biased self-attribution.[4] Overconfidence leads them to exaggerate the precision of their private information about a firm's value, causing overreaction. Bias self-attribution of informed investors accelerates overreaction in the early stage and thereafter delays correction of overreaction. Under their model, price momentum occurs in the process of overreaction, and the delayed correction of overreaction causes long-term price reversal. As such, intermediate price momentum as well as long-term price reversal results from overreaction.

Hong and Stein's (1999) model includes momentum traders. Thus, their over-reaction style is similar to that of the DHS model. Their model may be classi-fied as the extended overreaction model. However, Hong and Stein's model is different from the other two models in that the market initially underreacts to information because of slow diffusion of information across investors.

2. Profitability of Contrarian Strategy in Korea

2.1 Basic Finding

Kim, Nam, Cho, Lee, Bae, Park, and Yoon (1988) examines the possibility

---

4) Self-attribution bias occurs when people attribute successful outcomes to their own skill but blame un-successful outcomes on bad luck.

of stock price overreaction in Korean stock market. They suggest that stocks with extreme price movements in the past may be influenced by investors' optimism or pessimism biases. In order to test the overreaction phenomena, they form up-portfolios constituted of stocks whose daily prices closed as upper-limit prices in July 1981 (May 1984) and down-portfolios with stocks whose daily prices closed as bottom limit prices for the same sample periods. They find that cumulative abnormal returns of up-portfolios tend to decrease over time, while those of down-portfolios tend to increase.[5] However, since their finding about price reversal is based on one day's upper- or down-limit price, it is different from the long-term price reversal documented by DeBondt and Thaler (1985).

Chang (1993) examines whether the loser portfolio outperforms the winner portfolio in the Korea stock market for the period from January 1986 to December 1992. He calculates market adjusted returns for individual stocks every month and sorts them into 7 portfolios in ascending order accroding to market adjusted returns. A winner portfolio is constituted of 41 or 42 stocks with the highest market adjusted returns in a month, a loser portfolio is constituted of those with the lowest returns. He tests whether the winner (loser) portfolio has negative (positive) abnormal returns in the following month. His empirical results show that the loser portfolio tends to have positive abnormal returns but the winner portfolio does not. He concludes that the overreaction phenomenon is not found in the Korean stock market. However, since his sorting period and holding period is assumed to be one month, it is fair to say that he does not find price reversal within a one-month sorting period and a one-month holding period.

Sonu et al. (1994) follow the method of DeBondt and Thaler (1985) from the sample period from 1980 to 1992. Their sorting period and holding

---

5) They use market adjusted daily returns to calculate cumulative abnormal returns.

period are 36 months, respectively, with no overlapping period. For example, the first sorting period is from 1980 to 1982 and the last sorting period is from 1987 to 1989, while the first testing period is from 1983 to 1985 and the last testing period is from 1990 to1992. They show that the average cumulative abnormal return of the winner portfolio is -7.99 percent over 36 months, while that of the loser portfolio is 47.25 percent. Their difference is 55.24 percent, which is 2.24 times higher than the contrarian profits shown in DeBondt and Thaler (1985).

2.2 Various Sorting and Testing Periods, and Survivorship Bias

Hwang (1994) examines 12-, 24-, 36-, and 48-month sorting and testing periods. He shows that reliable reversal is found in all except the 12-month sorting period and the reversal becomes more apparent in the late testing period. Consistent with Seon et al.'s result, his results also suggest that the average cumulative abnormal return of the contrarian strategy that buys a loser portfolio and sells a winner portfolio is much higher in Korea than in the U.S. While contrarian profits in the U.S. are typically concentrated in January, those in Korea are observed not only in January but also in the months of February through April. When risk is adjusted by market model, return reversal still exists.

Shin (1997) argues that long-term reversal found by earlier studies may be heavily influenced by survivorship bias because return data may include only surviving stocks. Shin's data includes returns on delisted bankrupt stocks from the beginning of 1994, although they were also subject to survivorship bias before 1994. They select 30 extreme losers and 30 winners based on three years' past return performance. Among the 30 losers that exhibited the worst performance from 1991 to 1993, 24 stocks went bankrupt during the period from 1994 to 1996. When these stocks are included in the loser portfolio, its three-year returns are -38.89 percent from 1993 to 1995 and -77 percent from 1994 to 1996 when bankrupt stocks are included. His empirical result shows the second order stochastic dominance of the winner portfolio/KOSPI over the loser portfolio when delisted bankrupt stocks are included. This result indicates that a risk averse investor prefers the KOSPI and the winner portfolio to the loser portfolio. As such, his result casts doubt on the reliability of long-term reversal in Korea.

2.3 Time Varying Risk and Three Factor Model

Ball and Kothari (1989) and Chan (1988) argue that price reversals are primarily due to systematic changes in equilibrium required returns after the ranking period. Extreme losers have dramatic increases in financial leverage through which equity betas also increase. Woo and Kwak (2000) examine this possibility for 16 years from 1982 to 1996. Betas are estimated through a sorting period of three years and a testing period of three years. They find that the beta of a loser portfolio increases from the sorting period to the testing period, while that of a winner portfolio decreases. As a result, the contrarian strategy's beta increases during the testing period. After controlling for a time varying beta, the contrarian monthly abnormal return decreases from 1.32 percent (t = 10.452) to 0.87 percent (t = 3.153), when the abnormal return is estimated by using the market model. As such, the time varying risk is one of the importance sources for contrarian profits.

Kim and Jeong (2008) provide more comprehensive results covering the period from 1987 to 2002 by using a number of pricing models. Particularly, they find positive abnormal returns of contrarian strategy by using the Fama-French three factor model. When they select the winner portfolio and loser portfolio based on either 24- or 36-month sorting period, the contrarian strategy of buying the loser portfolio and selling the winner portfolio provides a significantly positive Jensen alpha even after controlling for Fama-French's three risk factors. Unlike in the U.S., this result suggests that long-term reversal in Korea is not a simple outcome caused by three risk factors. This result is consistent with the evidence of Lee and Ahn (2002) that long-term reversal is found even after controlling the size and the book to market ratio (book value of equity divided by market value of equity). When Kim and Jung classify the sorting period into up-market and down-market periods based on plus or minus signs of monthly average return, contrarian profits are stronger in the down-market period. In the down-market period when the monthly average return is negative, buy-and-hold abnormal return on the loser portfolio is 56 percent for 12 months. However, it is only 6 percent in the up-market period. They argue that long-term reversal can be partially accounted for by their negative coskewness that is a risk factor but may be mainly due to overreaction. Long-term reversal in Korea is found even after minimizing the survivorship bias.

2.4 Trading Volume and KOSDAQ

Ahn and Lee (2004) examine the profitability of a strategy based on past returns and trading volume like Lee and Swaminathan (2000). They sort stocks into quintiles based on 3-, 6-, 9-, and 12-month past returns and sort them again into tertiles based on trading volume. They find that a portfolio with low trading volume tends to outperform a portfolio with high trading volume over 3 to 12 months, which is consistent with that of Datar, Naik, and Radcliffe (1998). According to the liquidity premium hypothesis, a low liquid stock tends to have a higher required return than that of a high liquid stock since investors ask liquidity premium to hold the low liquid stock. Contrarian strategies among high trading volume are more profitable than others. Contrary to evidence in the U.S., these results are mainly driven by winner portfolios with high trading volume.

Lee, Guahk, and Wi (2006) investigate robustness of long-term reversal by examining whether long-term reversal exists in KOSDAQ. They use market adjusted abnormal returns and risk adjusted abnormal returns by using market model.[6] They construct winner and loser portfolios by using a two-years sorting period for the sample period of 2000 to 2004. They find that contrarian profit becomes significant from a 14-month testing period and on when the market adjusted abnormal return is used. However, abnormal return on the winner portfolio does not show poor performance for the 24-month testing period. On the other hand, contrarian profits become much stronger in case of the risk adjusted abnormal returns. As such, they conclude that price reversal is found in KOSDAQ as well.

2.5 Decomposition of Contrarian Profitability

Chung and Kim (2002) also provide evidence that price reversal exists in Korea. They follow Lo and MacKinlay's (1990) method to construct contrarian and momentum strategies. The portfolio with N number of stocks has a weight for stock i as follows. $w_{it} = -\dfrac{1}{N}(R_{it-1} - \overline{R}_{t-1})$. For $t-1$ period, if stock i has lower returns than equally weighted average return for N stocks, the weight of this stock in the portfolio is positive and proportional to the difference between the return on this stock and the equally weighted average return. If stock i has higher returns, the weight of stock i is negative. As such, $\pi_t = w_{it}R_{it}$ can be regarded as a zero-cost contrarian strategy, while $-\pi_t$ is a momentum strategy. They find that contrarian strategies provide significant positive returns based on sorting periods of one week, one, two, and three months. Jung and Kim show that cross autoco-

---

6) Market adjusted abnormal return is defined as $R_{jt} - R_{mt}$ where R_{jt} is a return on stock j at time t and R_{mt} is a market return at time t. Risk adjusted abnormal return is defined as $R_{jt} - (\hat{\alpha} + \hat{\beta}R_{mt})$ where $\hat{\alpha}$ and $\hat{\beta}$ are estimated.

variances consistently show significant positive magnitudes, but the signs of own-autocovariances are not consistent. As such, their result implies that the main source of contrarian profits may be due to non-synchronous trading or lead-lag effect. Positive abnormal returns of these contrarian strategies are significant although their magnitudes become smaller after the risk is controlled by Fama and French three factor model.

<Table 1> Long-term Price Reversal

Paper	Major Findings	Note	Period
Seon et al. (1994)	The contrarian strategy yields 2.24 times higher returns in Korean than in the U.S.	36-month sorting and holding periods	1980~1992
Hwang (1994)	Reliable long-term reversal except in the 12-month sorting period.	12, 24, 36, and 48-month sorting and holding periods	1980~1992
Shin (1997)	Survivorship bias explains long-term price reversal.	30 extreme losers and winners based on 36-month sorting period	1980~1996
Woo and Kwak (2000)	A contrarian strategy has still positive abnormal returns after considering time varying beta.	Sorting and testing periods are 36 months.	1982~1996
Lee and Ahn (2002)	A contrarian strategy earns positive abnormal returns even after controlling for size and book-to-market effect.	The research includes delisted stocks to reduce survivorship biases.	1992~1996
Kim and Jung (2008)	A contrarian strategy still has positive abnormal returns after controlling risk by Fama and French three factor model.	24 or 36-month sorting period	1987~2002
Ahn and Lee (2004)	Contrarian strategies with high trading volume have higher abnormal returns	Sorting based on 3, 6, 9, and 12- month past returns and based on trading volume.	1994~2001
Lee, Guahk, and Wi (2006)	Contrarian profits become statistically significant in the holding period that is as long as 14 months.	Two years' sorting period in KOSDAQ market	2000~2004
Jung and Kim (2002)	Positive cross-autocovariances of contrarian portfolios	Lo and MacKinlay (1990)'s methodology,	1998~2002

<Table 1> summarizes long-term price reversal in regards to various sorting and testing periods, time varying risk, survivorship bias, and trading volume. In general, Korean stock markets exhibit strong long-term price reversal even after the Fama and French three-factor model controls risk. Long-term reversal is also strongly related to trading volume.

3. Profitability of Momentum Strategy in Korea

3.1 Basic Finding

Kho (1997) examines whether intermediate price momentum exists in the Korea stock exchange by following the methodology of Jegadeesh and Titman (1993). He compares the result in Korea for the sample period of 1980~1995 to that of the U.S. for the sample period of 1963 to 1989. He uses four different sorting periods (J = 3, 6, 9, and 12 months) and four different holding periods (K = 3, 6, 9, and 12 months). A momentum strategy of buying winners and losers does not provide any profit at all but exhibits negative returns in Korea, while any momentum strategy provides positive returns with most of them being statistically significant in the U.S. He concludes that there is no price momentum in Korea.

Kim and Eom (1997) examine the effectiveness of momentum and contrarian strategies from 1980 to 1995 at various sorting and testing periods. They measure market adjusted buy-and-hold returns (BHAR) for 1 through 48- month sorting periods and BHARs for 6 through 48-month holding periods. They find a significant positive relation between a sorting period's returns and a holding period's returns in only two cases, specifically the 1-month sorting period with 6-month holding period and with 48-month holding period. Except these two cases, they find a negative relation between them. They claim that a contrarian strategy is the more effective strategy if there are any price errors in Korea. The best contrarian strategy is to form loser and winner portfolios based on the 42-month sorting period's returns and hold it for 24 months. This strategy provides 2.53 percent monthly abnormal returns.

From the sample period from 1980 to 2005, Chae and Eom (2009) analyze the source of negative momentum profits by modifying Lo and MacKinlay's methodology.[7] They confirm that there is no price momentum but price reversal in Korea at the sorting and holding period of 1 through 6 months where price momentum is found in the U.S. They divide decomposition of Lo and MacKinlay (1990) into winners' and losers' auto- and cross-serial covariances. They suggest that the negative auto-covariance of losers and the positive cross-serial covariance between lagged winners and current losers contribute to the negative momentum profit in the Korea stock market. The negative auto-covariance of the losers indicates that the market over-reacts to the firm-specific information of the losers, while the positive cross-serial covariance implies that the market underreacts to reflect market-wide information on losers' prices. If so, it is an interesting research question to ask why the market tends to overreact to the firm specific information of the losers but underreact to the market-wide information.

3.2 Industry Price Momentum and KOSDAQ

Lee and Ahn (2002) present that individual industries exhibit price momentum, although individual stocks do not. Their sample period is 1992 to 1996 and the sample data include only stocks that have been listed for the entire sample period and industries the market value of which accounts for at least 1% of total industry market value and which have at least 20 stocks listed on the Korea stock exchange. When they sort 10 individual industries based on 24 months of value weighted average returns, the winner

---

7) Instead of momentum profit, negative momentum profit is found in Korea (Kho, 1997; Chae and Eom, 2009). Since the sorting and holding periods are 3 to 6 months, Chae and Eom call the negative profit of a momentum strategy as negative momentum profit rather than as contrarian profit.

industry portfolio whose return performance is best among the 10 industries consistently outperforms the loser industry portfolio whose return performance is the worst. The momentum strategy of buying the winner industry portfolio and selling the loser industry portfolio provides a 2.86 percent return over one month and 1.93 percent over three months. Price momentum in industry tends to be stronger with increases in a sorting period.

Kim (2000) examines price momentum and reversal in KOSDAQ from April of 1999 to December of 1999. He finds price momentum with one week's sorting period and one week or 4 weeks of holding period. Such a price momentum is stronger for large stocks. However, since his sample period matches with the extreme bull market and is too short, it may be difficult to generalize his results as robust evidence for price momentum in Korea.

3.3 Bond Market

Kho (2006) examines the existence of price momentum in bond and stock markets for the sample period of 2001 to 2004. He collects bonds that are at least investment grade (BBB) and are not underlying assets for call or put options. In order to analyze bond and stock price behaviors at the same time, bonds are excluded from his sample when stock trading records are not available for the same issuing companies. Finally, 1,596 bonds with 217 companies are examined. He confirms that stock price momentum does not exist in Korea based on 1-through 24-week sorting periods and holding periods. He, however, finds bond price momentum based on the same sorting and holding periods. The momentum strategy of buying a winner portfolio and selling a loser portfolio provides about 0.06%~0.10% of returns for a one-week holding period. As the holding period increases from 1 week to 24 weeks, average weekly return tends to be smaller but still statistically significant. After controlling credit grades and remaining maturity of bonds, bond price momentum tends to be smaller but still statistically significant.

<Table 2> summarizes empirical results about price momentum in Korea. In general, reliable price momentum is not found in Korean stock markets at all. Instead, a momentum strategy tends to generate negative abnormal returns. Industry price momentum in Korean stock markets and bond price momentum, however, are found in Korea.

<Table 2> Profitability of Momentum Strategy

Paper	Major Findings	Note	Period
Kho (1997)	A momentum strategy provides negative abnormal returns.	Sorting periods of 3 to 12 months and holding period of 3 to 12 months	1980~1995
Kim and Eom (1997)	Onlya momentum strategy with one month sorting period provides positive abnormal returns for 6 and 48-month holding periods.	Diverse sorting and holding periods from one month to 48 months	1980~1995
Lee and Ahn (2002)	Individual industry exhibits price momentum although individual stocks don't.	24-month sorting period based on value weighted average returns.	1992~1996
Kim (2000)	Price momentum is found and stronger for large stocks.	1 week's sorting period with 1 week's or 4 weeks' holding period	April of 1999~December of 1999
Kho (2006)	Bond price momentum is found in 1 through 24-week sorting and holding periods.	Bonds with at least investment grade	2001~2004
Chae and Eom (2009)	The negative auto-covariance of loser portfolios and positive cross-serial covariance contribute to negative momentum profits.	Decomposition of Lo and MacKinlay (1990)'s method.	1980~2005

4. Other Anomalies Related to Over-reaction or Under-reaction

4.1 Event Studies and Long-term Performance

A number of studies have examined stock returns following important corporate announcements, a type of analysis known as event study. Event studies, introduced by Fama, Fisher, Jensen and Roll (1969), produce useful evidence on how stock prices respond to information. According to traditional finance theory, the stock price instantaneously adjusts to and fully reflects new information. Thus, there is no tendency for subsequent increases and decreases in the long run. However, many studies on long-term performance after corporate events indicate that the initial market response may be over-reaction or underreaction to corporate events. For example, Loughran and Ritter (1995) study firms that undertook IPOs and SEOs between 1970 and 1990 in the U.S. They find that the average return of shares over five years after the issuance is below the average return of non-issuing firms.

Using Korean data, Kim and Byun (1998) find that the long-run performance of SEO firms is significantly low relative to non-issuing firms, a result that is consistent with that of Loughran and Ritter. The size-adjusted and the market-adjusted cumulative abnormal returns for 36 months after SEO are -18.10% and -6.31%, respectively. Kim and Byun (2003) also analyze equity carve-outs (ECO). For homo-industry ECOs, the 12-month CAR of subsidiary firms is 26.52% and significantly positive, while the BHAR is 22.19%. For hetero-industry ECOs, the subsidiary 12-month CAR and BHAR are 35.14% and 39.64%, respectively. Studies on long-term performance of IPOs in Korea make long lists.[8] Among them, recently, Kim and Jung (2010) explore if the higher initial returns and the poorer long-run performance observed in the IPOs markets are associated with the firm's IPO into hot markets, and then empirically examine the effect of optimistic investors' sentiment on this phenomenon using 432 IPO firms from 2001 to 2005. They find that initial returns and long-run underperformance of IPOs in the hot market are significantly higher than those of IPOs in the cold market.

---

8) Kim and Kim (2000); Ihm (1997); Lim and Lee (1995); Choi and Heo (2000).

They provide evidence that the optimistic investors' sentiment has a positive effect on the initial return and a negative effect on the long-run performance.

Long-term performance reversal is also found in other corporate events in Korea. Kang and Kim (2009) investigate the post merger performance of acquiring firms in Korea. They find long-run stock performance on average is not significantly different from zero in the two years following the acquisition. However, the acquirer's long-run operating performance significantly outperforms the benchmark. They also show that the long-run stock performance tends to move inversely to announcement returns, which may imply a manifestation of 'long-term return reversals' in the merger and acquisition market.

Ikenberry, Lakonishok and Vermaelen (1995) find that on average, the shares of repurchase firms outperform those of a control group matched in size and book-to-market over four years following the event. In Korea, Shin, Kim and Lee (2002) find the significant positive long-term performance of repurchasing stocks using the Fama-French three factor model. Jung and Lee (2003) examine the long-term performance of 470 stock repurchases in Korea from 1994 to 1998. Positive long-term performance is found using holding-period abnormal returns and CAR. With the calendar-time approach, however, positive long-term performance is found only for firms that have frequently repurchased their shares during the sample period. Their findings suggest that model specification affects long-run performance.

Desai and Jain (1997) and Ikenberry, Rankine and Stice (1996) find that stock splits are followed by 7% abnormal returns in the year after the split. Abnormal returns are calculated relative to benchmarks that control for size, book-to-market, and price momentum in Desai and Jain. Byun and Rozeff (2003) retest stock splits with a longer sample period using various methodologies to avoid the misspecification model problem. They could not find significant one-year abnormal returns of stock splits and suggest that the stock market is efficient with respect to stock splits. In Korea, Byun and Jo (2007) find interesting results on stock splits. The long-term abnormal returns of stock splits for three years after the announcements of stock splits are significantly negative. The negative long-term abnormal returns are confirmed by the calendar-time portfolio approach. The results suggest that the positive short-term abnormal return followed by a negative long-term return seems to be the result of the market's overreaction to the stock split announcement. The difference in the two countries with the same corporate event would be a puzzle for further research.

On the other hand, Fama (1998) reviews behavioral studies related to post-event returns from the view point of the efficient market hypothesis. He argues that these anomalies are chance results and long-term return anomalies are fragile because they tend to disappear with reasonable changes in measures.

4.2 Accrual Anomaly

Sloan (1996) studies the stock market responses on the operating accruals produced largely by managers' discretion and finds the strong tendency of firms with high operating accruals to earn lower stock returns on average than those with low operating accruals. Since then, many studies have reported evidence that such an accrual anomaly is a common phenomenon in stock markets. Accruals are commonly measured by the difference between accounting earnings and operating cash flows, and have been considered the most important accounting variable for measuring the degree of earnings management and earnings quality in the literature. There are two explanations for the possible sources of the accrual anomaly. The first one is a risk factor hypothesis based on market efficiency, which predicts that the accrual anomaly arises from the compensation for a potential risk factor that is not included in the existing asset pricing models. In contrast, the second explanation is a mispricing hypothesis based on behavioral finance, which says that the accrual anomaly arises from investors' overreaction. In other words, investors are too optimistic about firms with high accruals and too pessimistic about firms with low accruals.

Kho and Kim (2007) examine whether the accrual anomaly exists in the Korean stock markets as in the US, and test whether the accrual anomaly is associated with a potential risk factor that can be included in a rational asset pricing model. Empirical results of Kho and Kim (2007) confirm the presence of the accrual anomaly in Korea over the period from 1987 to 2005, irrespective of the alternative accrual measures used. They find that stocks for firms with low accruals significantly outperform those with high accruals. They conclude that all of the test results consistently indicate that the accrual anomaly is more likely to arise from a mispricing of accruals of individual firms rather than from a potential risk factor, which is consistent with the behavioral explanation.

V. Trading and Return Behavior with Psychological Bias

1. Investor Trading Behavior

1.1 Overconfidence and Demographic Factors

Barber and Odean (2000) examine the trading activity from 1991 to 1996 in a large sample of accounts at a national discount brokerage firm. They find that after taking trading costs into account, the average return of retail investors is well below the return of standard benchmarks. The underperformance in the sample is largely due to transaction costs. Their results show that investors trade too frequently although such frequent trading is costly, and thus harmful to their portfolios and overall wealth. Using similar data, Goetzmann and Kumar (2007) show that the equity portfolios of individual investors are much less diversified than could be normally predicted by portfolio theory.

The most prominent behavioral explanation of such excessive trading is over-confidence; People believe that they have enough reliable information to justify trading, whereas in fact the information is too weak to warrant any action. This hypothesis immediately predicts that more overconfident people will trade more frequently and, because of transaction costs, earn lower returns. Consistently with this hypothesis, Barber and Odean (2000) show that the most frequent trader in their sample earned by far the lowest average returns.[9]

Using Korean data, Byun, Kim, and Choi (2007) investigate the effects of individual investors' personalities on trading behavior and investor perfor-mance. Based on the sample of individual trading data collected from an internet investment game company, they survey sample participants to measure confidence level, personality traits, and demographics. Although it was the first paper to collect personal data, the survey method inevitably shows possible bias from subjective responses. They find overconfident in-vestors tend to show excessive trading behavior. Their analysis is consistent with Barber and Odean (2000). In other words, overconfident individual investors, on average, exhibit excessive trading behavior, and excessive trad-ing is harmful to wealth. In addition, Barber and Odean (2001) provide evidence that men are more overconfident than women. Using the same

---

9) Working with the same data again, Barber and Odean (2002) study the sub-sample of individual investors who switch from phone-based trading to online trading. They argue that for a number of reasons, the switch should be accompanied by an increase in overconfidence. First, better access to information and a greater degree of control - both features of an online trading environment - have been shown to increase overconfidence. Moreover, the investors who switch have often earned high returns prior to switching, which may only increase their overconfidence further. If this is indeed the case, they should trade more actively after switching and per-form worse. Barber and Odean provide the evidence that confirm these predictions.

data as in their earlier study, Barber and Odean confirm that men trade more and earn, on average, lower returns. They attribute this to the notion that men tend to be more overconfident than women.

In Korea, Han and Kim (2007) indicate that there were gender differences in the factors of self-enhancement perception on individual investors' confidence. They investigate the factors of self-enhancement perception on investor confidence to find whether these psychological biases lead to irrational investment behaviors using 255 repliers to the questionnaire. Their sample is composed of 176 male and 79 female investors. Male investors were confident of their investment capability but female investors were confident of optimistic expectation of return. Male investors were more confident than female investors, a result that is consistent with Barber and Odean's (2001) conjecture. In addition, the result shows that the risky investment behaviors of individual investors were influenced by psychological factors. They suggest that further research needs to search for other variables which can mediate between psychological factors and the investment behaviors of individual investors. Investment behavior, however, is not real trading behavior like excessive trading. The data comes from a self-reporting questionnaire which depends on the memory of respondents and is supposed to be influenced by psychological biases.

Byun (2005), however, finds that women trade 30% more than men and thus incur greater return reduction using the balance record of 7,325 individual investors. This result is totally opposite to the result of Barber and Odean (2001). He also finds men perform substantially better than women, earning 8.1%p more annually. When investment size is controlled, however, it turns out that men trade more than women and return reduction is about the same between men and women. The difference in the result is caused by investors in the top investment size decile, where women trade 32% more and incur higher trading costs than men in the same size range.

Byun et al. (2007) propose hypotheses that gender and personalities play important roles in making investment decisions using trading data. They find that investor gender, marital status, and trading experience have no explanatory power to produce excessive trading or investment performance. More extroverted investors, among big-five personalities, tend to trade more frequently, a behavior that can lead to lower investment return than that experienced by other investors with lower extraversion trait.

Baek and Cha (1994) analyze stock investment attitudes by applying gambling theories using a questionnaire towards 503 investors. To analyze stock investment behavior, they create hypotheses based on factors influencing gambling attitudes such as differences in personality and social condition. The results say that internal/external control, risk attitude, win/loss ratio, occupation, religion, gender, and investment career may not have close correlations with investment behavior. However, factors such as desire for achievement, age, and investment scale have strong correlations with aggressive stock investment attitude using indebted and margin trading.

In summary, demographic factors do not provide any consistent or predictable relation with investor trading behavior or overconfidence and warrant more rigorous studies.

1.2 Motivation of Investment Selection Change

Choi, Ji, and Jung (2003) study what determines investors' intention to change stock investment selection from major large stocks to alternative stocks during a bull market which is defined as at least six-month increase in Korean Stock Price Index (KOSPI). They provide 312 samples from surveying investors who traded in May, 2002 and were customers of securities companies located in Seoul. Their survey questionnaire asked respondents about their investment experiences during the bull market from October 2001 to March 2002. Index-related large stocks are defined as the top 10 stocks that substantially influence the KOSPI such as Samsung Electronics, SK Telecom, KT, Kookmin Bank, and Korea Electric Power Corporation. Alternative stocks are defined as all the other stocks excluding these top 10 stocks. They define investors' intention to buy alternative stocks as their intention to buy alternative stocks after originally considering buying index-related stocks.

The attractiveness of alternative stocks, the degree of concern on an uncertain outcome from investing in alternative stocks, and the personalities of respondents are surveyed. As alternative stocks are more attractive, investors' intention to buy these stocks instead of index-related stocks is stronger. When they are more worried about uncertain outcomes from alternative stocks, they are less willing to buy alternative stocks. Investors with a higher endurance of risk and a higher searching desire for new information are more willing to change stock investment from index-related stocks to alternative stocks. They also find that technical analysis and financial statement analysis positively influence their intention to buy alternative stocks. However, their results show that companies' prospects for growth are negatively related to investors' intention to buy those stocks. Although companies' prospects for growth are the most important factor in determining the fundamental value of stocks, investors do not appear to invest in those stocks with promising growth prospects.

1.3 Herding

Herding is the trading behavior of a group of investors that follow each other by trading the same securities in the same direction over a certain short period. Such herding behavior can be rational or irrational.[10]

---

10) Hypothetical motivation of herding can be divided into five categories · informational cascades, investigative

Freidman (1984) and Dreman (1979) argue that herding may occur when investors rationally infer information from each other's trading. When the aggregate information inferred from trading of the crowd is so overwhelming, it may be rational for investors to follow the crowd's decision. On the other hand, Barberis and Shleifer (2001) argue that herding may result from irrational psychological factors and cause temporary price errors. Kindleberger and Aliber (2005) provide a top 10 list of 'era of crowds' events. These include historic famous bubble events: the Dutch tulip bulb bubble of 1936, the South Sea bubble of 1720, the 1929 stock market crash, and the dot.com bubble at the end of the 1990s. Each of these financial crises represents the herding behavior of crowds in history.

Herding is found in the trading behavior of institutional investors such as pension funds and mutual funds (Lakonishok, Shleifer, and Vishny, 1992; Wermers, 1999; Sias, 2004). However, the literature offers less clear conclusions regarding the impact of institutional herding on stock prices. For example, there is no return reversal over a short horizon after institutional herding (Sias, 2004) but there is return reversal over a long horizon after herding (Gutierrez and Kelly, 2009; Brown, Wei and Wermers, 2009).

In Korean stock markets, Hong and Yi (2006) investigate whether fund managers in Korea actually show herding behavior by using monthly stock ownership of stock funds from 2002 to 2005. They find that fund managers in Korea herd more substantially than those in other countries as reported in the previous literature and the degree of herding is stronger in buying stocks than in selling them. Seon and Kim (2010) examine the herding behavior of asset management companies by using 36-month data from January of 2007 to December of 2009. They argue that herding behavior of fund managers may be overstated in Korea since a single fund manager on average

---

herding, reputational herding, fads, and characteristic herding. See Graham (1999) and Sias (2004) in detail.

manages several funds. They find that there exists herding behavior for asset management companies and significant negative returns over 3 months after their herding to buy stocks. They suggest that the second finding may result from the irrational herding of asset management companies.

2. Corporate Behavioral Finance

Irrational investors and managers affect the financing and investment decisions of firms. In other words, behavioral finance also explains corporate financial decision behaviors. According to Baker, Ruback and Wurgler (2007), there are two main ways to research behavioral corporate finance. The first emphasizes that investors are less than fully rational. It views managerial financing and investment decisions as rational responses to the mispricing of securities market. The second approach emphasizes that managers are less than fully rational. It studies the effect of judgmental biases on managerial decisions. Following Baker et al. (2007), we summarize behavioral corporate finance studies into two approaches. The first approach emphasizes the effect of *investor* behavior that is irrational or semi-rational, and the second considers *managerial* behavior that is not fully rational.

In the irrational investor approach, irrational investors influence security prices and managers are smart in the sense of being able to distinguish between market price and fundamental value. Several lines of evidence suggest that overvaluation is a motive for equity issuance. For example, when a firm's stock price is too high, the rational manager should issue more shares so as to take advantage of investor exuberance. Conversely, when the price is too low, the manager repurchases shares. This view of security issuance is generally referred to as "market timing" view.

The market timing view comes from the survey evidence of Graham and Harvey (2001). They report that 67% of surveyed CFOs said that "the amount by which our stock is undervalued or overvalued" was an important consideration when issuing common stock. There is some evidence that irrational investor sentiment affects financing decisions. Under the market timing theory of Baker and Wurgler (2002), managers may issue more shares at the time to take advantage of possible overvaluation. The evidence shows that managers tend to issue equity before low returns, on average, and repurchase before higher returns. In US data, Jung, Kim, and Stulz (1996) and Hovakimian, Opler, and Titman (2001) find a strong relationship between stock prices and seasoned equity issuance. Of course, there are many non-behavioral reasons why equity issuance and market valuations should be positively correlated. More evidence for equity market timing comes from the subsequent pattern of low long-term returns following new issues. Other samples show similar market timing results (Ritter, 1991; Spiess and Affleck-Graves, 1995; Loughran and Ritter, 1995).

The market timing behaviors of managers in Korea are examined by Byun and Kim (2010). They examine the investor sentiment and market timing of stock repurchases using 835 samples of KRX (Korea Exchange) stock repurchase announcements between 1999 and 2007. By employing the framework of Baker and Wurgler (2006) to measure investor sentiment on stock market, they find that firms with higher sensitivity to sentiment tend to underreact to the repurchase announcements and argue that there exists market timing of repurchasing firms. They find that investor sentiment is an important factor for firms to decide stock repurchases, especially for firms with higher sensitivity to sentiment such as a younger operating age and higher volatility. The result is consistent with the market timing hypothesis. Byun (2010) also finds similar results using KOSDAQ repurchase data.

Kim and Jung (2010) examine both the pricing mechanism and the opportunistic behavior of IPO firms in Korea. They report that the results do not support 'the windows of opportunity hypothesis' that low quality firms take advantage of hot market condition for successful IPOs. To test the opportunistic behavior of managers, Byun (2004) examines the long-term performance of false signaling firms that announced open-market repurchases. The results are consistent with the notion that the false signaling of repurchase announcements bears very little effect in terms of a rise in the stock price in the long run. The managerial opportunism hypothesis is reexamined by Byun and Pyo (2006) for the stock repurchase announcement. By analyzing managerial trading behavior, they suggest that the managerial opportunistic behavior less likely exists in well monitored firms. Only in a relatively small scale corporation, the majority shareholder tends to sell the stock after the repurchase announcement, which may imply his or her opportunistic behavior.

On the other hand, the irrational manager's approach assumes that managers are vulnerable to psychological biases. They may have excessive optimism and get drawn into accepting negative NPV investments. For example, Roll (1986) suggests the optimism and overconfidence approach to corporate finance with his "hubris" theory of acquisitions. He suggests that successful acquirers may be optimistic and overconfident in their own valuation of synergies, and fail to properly account for the winner's curse. Roll interprets the evidence on merger announcement effects as surveyed by Jensen and Ruback (1983) and Moeller, Schlingemann, and Stulz (2004), as well as the lack of evidence of fundamental value creation through mergers, as consistent with this theory. Much of empirical takeover literature reports statistically insignificant small losses to bidders and statistically significant large gains to target shareholders. But when weighted by market capitalization, there is little doubt that on average, takeovers destroy shareholder wealth.

Unlike in the U.S. sample, both bidders and targets show market gains from acquisitions in Korea (Joo and Song, 1997; Kang, Kim and Bae, 2001).

The positive gains of bidders are still unsolved questions in Korean takeover studies. Byun and Ahn (2007) find the size effect of M&A as found in Moeller et al. (2004). The announcement abnormal return for small acquirers averages 6.53% compared to 4.84% of large acquirers. The size effect is robust to firm, and it does not disappear even if there is control of the irrelativeness of acquisitions, past performance, free cash flows, or growth potentials. This suggests a possible explanation for the size puzzle of acquisition announcement, which managers of large firms might be more subject hubris.

In corporate finance, the most developed application of anchoring or reference-point bias[11] has been the abnormal first day return on IPO shares (Baker, Ruback and Wugler, 2007). Of course, there are many non-behavioral explanations for the underpricing of IPOs. Loughran and Ritter (2002) develop an explanation that combines reference-point bias and mental accounting. Unfortunately, however, we could not find many studies of IPOs focusing on behavioral explanations in Korea.

3. Investor Sentiment and Corporate Event

Many studies in the behavioral finance literature suggest a number of proxies to use as time-series conditioning variables and commonly argue that stocks tend to be overpriced (underpriced) during periods of high (low) sentiment, which leads to predictably low (high) subsequent returns. However, there are no definitive or uncontroversial measures. Baker and Wurgler (2006, 2007) form a composite index of sentiment based on a common variation in six underlying proxies of sentiment: the closed-end fund discount (Lee et al., 1991), NYSE share turnover (Baker and Stein, 2004), the number and average first-day returns on IPOs (Ritter, 1991; Derrien, 2005), the equi-

---

11) The concept of anchoring draws on the tendency to attach or "anchor" our thoughts to a reference point - even though it may have no logical relevance to the decision at hand.

ty share in new issues (Baker and Stein, 2004), and the dividend premium (Baker and Wurgler, 2004). Baker and Wurgler (2006) for the investor sentiment index, use the principal component analysis to isolate common component of investor sentiment. They find that when beginning-of-period proxies for sentiment are low, subsequent returns are relatively high for small stocks, young stocks, high volatility stocks, unprofitable stocks, non-dividend-paying stocks, extreme growth stocks, and distressed stocks.

Kim and Byun (2010) create a Korean version of the monthly investor sentiment index by using Baker and Wurgler's (2006, 2007) principal component analysis. Their empirical results show that investor sentiment in Korea has a strong negative relation with the subsequent six-month, buy-and-hold return. These results confirm Baker and Wurgler (2007)'s empirical result that the monthly sentiment index may have predictability of future stock returns. Kim and Byun also find a positive effect of investor sentiment on split announcement return. They report that the market response to a stock split is much more pronounced during the high sentiment period for small, young, highly volatile, and low profit stocks for the test period from 1999 to 2007. In fact, investor sentiment influences stock valuation mainly through these stocks. The initial effects of size, age, volatility, and profitability in times of high investor sentiment tend to be reversed over a twelve-month, post-split performance. These empirical results imply that the market tends to overreact to stock split announcements for small, young, high volatile, and low profitable firms in a high sentiment period but thereafter correct overvaluation of those firms over a twelve-month, post-split performance.

Byun and Kim (2010) examine how investor sentiment affects stock valuation in regarding to stock repurchase. According to market timing hypothesis, a company will repurchase stocks in order to maximize shareholders' wealth if its stock is undervalued and the market is expected to underreact to a stock repurchase announcement. Byun and Kim argue that under-reaction to a stock repurchase announcement is more likely to occur during low investor sentiment than during high investor sentiment.

4. Irrational Return Behavior

4.1 Weather and Stock Returns

Several studies of psychology have found that emotion and mood affects the judgment and behavior of investors. Individuals who are in good moods make more optimistic decisions. Several studies have reported that bad moods tend to stimulate people to engage in detailed analytical activity, whereas good moods are associated with less critical modes of information processing.

Weather has been shown to have significant effects on human behavior in psychological experiments. A few financial papers confirm the weather effect. Saunder (1993) finds that the weather in New York City has a significant correlation with major stock indices. Using cloud-cover measures, he shows that sunshine weather is positively related to stock returns. The effect also appears to be robust with respect to a variety of market anomalies, including January, the weekend, and small firm effects. This sunshine effect has been criticized by Trombley (1997) on the grounds that the results documented for New York weather in Saunders (1993) are not statistically significant in each month of the year and sub-period of the data.

Hirshleifer and Shumway (2003) examine the relationship between morning sunshine in the city of a country's leading stock exchange and daily market index returns across 28 countries from 1982 to 1997. They find sunshine is strongly positively correlated with stock daily returns. After controlling for sunshine, however, rain and snow are unrelated to stock returns. They show that these results strongly exist in Northern European countries where sunshine is relatively rare. Although the sunshine effect appears most weak in New York in the 1980s and strong during the 1990s, the results are consistent with a stable sunshine effect through the entire sample period.

Using Korean data, several studies were conducted. Following Saunders (1993), Kim (1996) examines the relationship between stock price and weather in for the Korean stock market from 1980 to 1994. He finds a positive relation between daily stock prices and sunny days. He arbitrarily divides the sample period into four sub-periods according to the market condition and finds positive results only in the ascending and recession periods.[12]

Shin and Park (2003) examine any statistically significant relation between weather measured by the sky cover of the Seoul area and the daily stock index returns of the Korean Stock Exchange from 1983 to 2002. Their sky cover variable is adjusted by the monthly sky cover to exclude the seasonal effect of weather. According to their study, the weather effect on stock returns has almost disappeared after the 1997 Korean financial crisis, when foreign investors started to establish a significant presence in Korean markets. They conjecture the weakening weather effect may result from the globalization of world financial markets. As found in Hirshleifer and Shumway (2003), however, the weather effect of New York in 1990s is stronger than that of 1980s.

Chang and Kim (2006) also examine the weather effect by using KOSDAQ data from 1997 to 2006. Their testing methodology is similar to Shin and Park (2003) adding a temperature variable. Chang and Kim try to reexamine the globalization hypothesis of Shin and Park (2003) using KOSDAQ data controlling on market conditions as in Kim (1996). At this time, they classify market conditions using 6-month market trends. Their results show that both sky cover and temperature do not have correlations with KOSPI which

---

12) Arbitrary sub-periods are from 1981 to 1985, from 1986 to 1989/April 1, from 1989/April 2 to 1992/August 21, and from 1992/August 22 to 1994.

is consistent with the result of Shin and Park (2003). With KOSDAQ, stock index returns during sunny days are consistently higher than stock index returns on cloudy days, although it is statistically insignificant. In sum, there seems to be no weather effect in Korean markets after the IMF financial crisis. However, the globalization of financial markets or the role of foreign investors does not seem to be a convincing reason for the non-existence of a weather effect in Korea after the 1997 financial crisis because the weather effect is found globally (Hirshleifer and Shumway, 2003).

4.2 Listing or Delisting Effect

The event of change in stock market index composition is one of the main subjects for the test of EMH. According to traditional finance, derived from frictionless economics with rational investors, index changes don't affect the stock's price and risk. However, behavioral finance theory, derived from friction economics with irrational investors, predicts that the changes may affect price and risk due to a change in noise traders' trading patterns. Barberis, Shleifer and Wurgler (2005) present models of comovement, and then assess empirically using data on stock inclusions into the S&P 500 index and deletions from the S&P 500 index. Index changes are noteworthy because they change a stock's category and investor clientele but do not change its fundamentals. They find that when a stock is added to the index, its beta and R-squares with respect to the index increase, while its beta with respect to stocks outside the index falls. The reversal happens when a stock is deleted. Their results are broadly supportive of the category and habitat views of comovement, but not of the fundamental view.

In Korea, Ahn and Park (2005) analyze the change in stock returns included and excluded from the KOSPI 200 list. Building on the Barberis et al. (2005) model, they use daily, weekly, monthly data from 1994 to 2000 and employ univariate regressions, bivariate regressions based on event-time approach and calendar-time approach. However, their results fail to confirm predictions of the model for changes in stock returns, cash flows, beta, R^2, and turnover. They conclude that inclusion and exclusion from the KOSPI are not significant events in the Korean market. Also, behavioral related explanations cannot shed light on them either. Park, Lee and Kim (2009) retested the index change event, expanding the sample period from 1996 to 2006. In the case of newly enlisted firms, they found evidence supporting the price pressure hypothesis on average.

Recently, Han, Yun and Hong (2010) show that a stock added to the index exhibits a significant positive CAR in the short run. The positive market reaction, however, is followed by an immediate price reversal and, furthermore, turns an insignificant positive CAR in the long run. On the other hand, delisted stocks exhibit a significant negative CAR in the short run but an insignificant one in the long run. They suggest that index change on the Korea Exchange provides a more powerful signal in the case of bad news about being delisted from the index than in the case of good news about being included in the index.

VI. Conclusion

Behavioral finance is defined as the application of psychology to financial decision making and financial markets. Based on this definition, our review essay summarizes recent work of behavioral studies in Korean capital markets. There are many common findings between overseas and domestic studies. For example, the Korean capital market has a disposition effect of individual investors that is consistent with the prospect theory and long-term price reversal that is consistent with the overreaction hypothesis. However, price momentum does not exist in the Korean stock market unlike in the U.S. and European markets. Lack of price momentum in Korea weakens Grinblatt and Han's (2005) argument that the disposition effect may cause price momentum. If then, why does the Korean stock market observe the disposition effect but not price momentum? We may have to cast doubt on the behavioral models of Barberis et al. (1998), Daniel et al. (1998), and Hong and Stein (1999) that simultaneously account for long-term reversal and intermediate momentum. As such, there are so many research questions about why the Korea capital market has different features from overseas markets.

Behavioral finance is a young field with its formal beginning in the 1980s. In Korea, behavioral studies are in their early stages of development. Thus, it is a promising area in the future for exploring new ideas. Much of the research in Korea we have discussed was completed in the past five years. In sum, behavioral finance literature has grown by leaps and bounds in recent years, however much work remains to be done in this field.

We address several areas to explore in the future. First, experimental investigation with a psychologist is warranted. Investors' decision-making process and their behavior is still a puzzling area. We have begun to understand how investors make their portfolio choices. Much of this work is investigated by psychologists who want to understand human behavior. We financial economists can collaborate with psychologists to analyze investors, both individual and professional, using surveys or experimental methodologies, since a model formed without enough knowledge about the behavior of the agents in the economy cannot be a general model.

Second, regional anomalies need be explored from behavioral perspectives. For example, there is room to study cross-country variation in biases and their implications for return predictability. Although efficient communication technology has encouraged globalization in recent years, some regional differences in markets are observed and unanswered. For example, we are not sure of why the short-term momentum phenomenon does not exist in Korea.[13] Our future research could focus on investigating regional differences and finding out an explanation behind these anomalies. Investors' behavior across cultures is another interesting topic in behavioral finance. As Statman (2008) discussed about the cultural importance in investment, the collective set of common experiences that people of the same culture share will influence their cognitive and emotional approach to investing.

Third, collaborative work with other business areas is needed. The current academic trend in business areas is moving toward integration, so called inter-disciplinary or cross-disciplinary studies. Future studies in finance will not be confined in the narrow area as those of traditional finance were. Broadly defined participants such as producers, customers, investors, fund managers, analysts, and corporate managers are playing in also broadly defined markets such as commodity, stock, fixed-income, retail, business to business, and virtual markets. Behavioral finance and its applications in related fields including marketing, operations management, and organizational behavior will be broadly appreciated.

Fourth, corporate finance has much room to explore. The field of behavioral corporate finance is a growing area. A basic question that arises from the literature is whether managers are dealing with an irrational market, or whether a rational market is dealing with irrational managers, or both. An interesting issue is whether we can predict corporate events such as M&A activity, stock splits, security offerings and so on, using CEO profiles

---

13) Chui, Titman, and Wei (2010) find a positive relation between the magnitude of price momentum and individualism across countries. They claim that individualism is related to overconfidence and self-attribution bias. Since East Asian countries have relatively less individualism, they are less likely to be subject to these biases that cause price momentum. The psychological biases, however, are also sources of long-term overreaction according to Daniel et al. (1998). Chui et al. (2010)'s argument does not successfully explain why the magnitude of long-term reversal in East Asia is as strong as in the U.S. and Europe if East Asians are not influenced by the biases.

or characteristics. In corporate finance, the behavioral approach has stimulated interest in the determinants and the quality of executive decision making, e.g., excessive risk aversion, optimism, hubris and so on.

References

Ahn, Y. G. and J. D. Lee, "Investment Strategy Based on Past Stock Returns and Trading Volume", *Journal of Korea Securities Association*, Vol. 33, No. 1(2004), pp. 105-137(in Korean).

안영규, 이정도, "주식수익률과 거래량을 이용한 투자전략의 성과분석", 경영학회지, 제33권 제1호(2004), pp. 105-137.

Ahn, Y. G. and S. S. Park, "The Comovement of Stock Returns Associated with Changes in the KOSPI 200 List", *Journal of Business Research*, Vol. 20, No. 1(2005), pp. 175-206(in Korean).

안영규, 박순식, "KOSPI 200 구성종목변경과 위험에 관한 연구", 경영연구, 제20권 제1호(2005), pp. 175-206.

Baek, Y. H. and M. J. Cha, "Applying Gambling Theories to Stock Investment Behavior", *Asia-Pacific Journal of Financial Studies*, Vol. 16(1994), pp. 395-435(in Korean).

백용호, 차명준, "도박심리를 이용한 주식투자 행태분석", 증권학회지, 제16권(1994), pp. 395-435.

Baker, M., R. S. Ruback, and J. Wurgler, "Behavioral Corporate Finance: A Survey", In *Handbook of Corporate Finance: Empirical Corporate Finance*, Edited by B. E. Eckbo. Amsterdam, Holland: Elsevier, 2007.

Baker, M. and J. C. Stein, "Market Liquidity as a Sentiment Indicator", *Journal of Financial Markets*, Vol. 7(2004), pp. 271-299.

Baker, M. and J. Wurgler, "Market Timing and Capital Structure", *Journal of Finance*, Vol. 57(2002), pp. 1-32.

Baker, M. and J. Wurgler, "A Catering Theory of Dividends", *Journal of Finance*, Vol. 59(2004), pp. 1125-1165.

Baker, M. and J. Wurgler, "Investor Sentiment and Cross-Section of Stock Returns", *Journal of Finance*, Vol. 61(2006), pp. 1645-1680.

Baker, M. and J. Wurgler, "Investor Sentiment in the Stock Market", *Journal of Economic Perspectives*, Vol. 21(2007), pp. 129-152.

Ball, R. and S. P. Kothari, "Non-stationary Expected Returns: Implications for Tests of Market Efficiency and Serial Correlation in Returns", *Journal of Financial Economics*, Vol. 25(1989), pp. 51-74.

Barber, B. M. and T. Odean, "Trading is Hazardous to Your Wealth: The Common Stock Investment Performance of Individual Investors", *Journal of Finance*, Vol. 55(2000), pp. 773-806.

Barber, B. M. and T. Odean, "Boys Will Be Boys: Gender, Overconfidence, and Common Stock Investment", *Quarterly Journal of Economics*, Vol. 116(2001), pp. 261-292.

Barber, B. M. and T. Odean, "Online Investors: Do the Slow Die First?", *Review of Financial Studies*, Vol. 15(2002), pp. 455-488.

Barberis, N., A. Shleifer, and R. Vishny, "A Model of Investor Sentiment", *Journal of Financial Economics*, Vol. 49(1998), pp. 307-345.

Barberis, N., A. Shleifer, and J. Wurgler, "Comovement", *Journal of Financial Economics*, Vol. 75(2005), pp. 283-317.

Barberis, N. and R. Thaler, "A Survey of Behavioral Finance", in George Constantinides, Milton Harris, Rene Stulz, eds., *Handbook of the Economics of Finance*, Amsterdam: North-Holland, 2003.

Benartzi, S. and R. Thaler, "Naïve diversification strategies in defined contribution savings plans", *American Economic Review*, Vol. 91(2001), pp. 79-98

Brown, N., K. Wei, and R. Wermers, "Analyst Recommendations, Mutual Fund Herding, and Overreaction in Stock Prices"(2009), http://ssrn.com/abstract = 1092744.

Byun, J. C. and J. I. Jo, "Long-Term Performance of Stock Splits", *Korean Journal of Financial Management*, Vol. 24, No. 1(2007), pp. 1-27(in Korean).

변종국, 조정일, "주식분할의 장기성과", 재무관리연구, 제24권 제1호(2007), pp. 1-27.

Byun, J. H., "Signaling Effects and the Long-Term Performance of False Signaling Firms: Evidence from the Undervaluation Stock Repurchases", *Journal of Korea Securities Association*, Vol. 33, No. 1(2004), pp. 207-248 (in Korean).
변진호, "저평가 자사주 매입 공시의 허위정보 신호효과와 장기성과", 증권학회지, 제33권 제1호(2004), pp. 207-248.

Byun, J. H., "Investor Sentiment and Stock Repurchase in KOSDAQ Market", (Korean) *Productivity Review*, Vol. 24, No. 2(2010), pp. 149-169(in Korean).
변진호, "투자자 감정과 코스닥시장 자사주매입에 관한 연구", 생산성논집, 제24권 제2호(2010), pp. 149-169.

Byun, J. H. and S. L. Ahn, "Acquirer's Firm Size and Stock Market Response to M&A Announcement", *Korean Journal of Finance*, Vol. 20, No. 2(2007), pp. 37-68(in Korean).
변진호, 안소림, "합병 인수기업의 규모효과에 관한 연구", 재무연구, 제20권 제2호(2007), pp. 37-68.

Byun, J. H. and K. S. Kim, "Investor Sentiment and Market Timing of Stock Repurchase", *Deahan Journal of Business*, Vol. 23, No. 4(2010), pp. 2271-2288(in Korean).
변진호, 김근수, "투자자의 감정이 자사주 매입에 미치는 영향", 대한경영학회지, 제23권 제4호(2010), pp. 2271-2288.

Byun, J. H., M. S. Kim, and I. C. Choi, "Individual Investors' Excessive Trading and Investment Performance", *Korean Management Review*, Vol. 36, No. 7(2007), pp. 1707-1730(in Korean).
변진호, 김민수, 최인철, "개인 투자자의 과도거래와 투자성과", 경영학연구, 제36권 제7호(2007), pp. 1707-1730.

Byun, J. H. and M. K. Pyo, "Majority Shareholders Selling Behavior after the Repurchasing Announcement: Signaling or Managerial Opportunism?" *Korean Management Review*, Vol. 35, No. 3(2006), pp. 695-716(in Korean).

변진호, 표민교, "자사주 매입 기회주의 가설과 대주주의 보유주식 매도 거래", 경영학연구, 제35권 제3호(2006), pp. 695-716.

Byun, J. H. and M. S. Rozeff, "Long-Run Performance after Stock Splits: 1927~1996", *Journal of Finance*, Vol. 58(2003), pp. 1063-1085.

Byun, Y. H., "An Analysis of the Effect of Investor Gender and Overconfidence on Trading Volume and Performance", *Korean Journal of Applied Economics*, Vol. 7, No. 3(2005), pp. 3-65(in Korean).

변영훈, "투자자 성별과 과잉확신이 거래량과 투자성과에 미치는 영향 분석", 응용경제, 제7권 제3호(2005), pp. 3-65.

Chae, J. and Y. S. Eom, "Negative Momentum Profit in Korea and its Sources", *Asia-Pacific Journal of Financial Studies*, Vol. 38, No. 2(2009), pp. 211-236.

Chan, K. C., "On the Contrarian Investment Strategy", *Journal of Business*, Vol. 61(1988), pp. 147-163.

Chang, K. C. and Y. G. Kim, "Does Weather and Temperature Affect Stock Returns?: Focusing on the KOSDAQ", *Korean Corporation Management*, Vol. 13(2006), pp. 239-252.

Chen, N., R. Kan, and M. Miller, "Are the Discounts on Closed-end Funds a Sentimental Index?", *Journal of Finance*, Vol. 48(1993), pp. 795-800.

Choe, H. and Y. S. Eom, "The Aggregate Price Impact of the Disposition Effect", 2008 EFA Conference at Athens.

Choe, H. and Y. S. Eom, "The Disposition Effect and Investment Performance in the Futures Market", *Journal of Futures Markets*, Vol. 29, No. 6(2009), pp. 496-522.

Choe, H. and Y. S. Eom, "The Disposition Effect in the KOSPI 200 Options

Market", 2010 APAD Conference in Busan.

Choi, M. S. and H. J. Heo, "The Long-Run Performance of Initial Public Offerings Revisited", *Korean Journal of Finance*, Vol. 13, No. 1(2000), pp. 99-122(in Korean).

최문수, 허형주, "신규공모주의 장기성과에 대한 재고찰", 재무연구, 제13권 제1호(2000), pp. 99-122.

Choi, W. Y. and S. H. Jeong, "An Empirical Study on the Cognitive Biases of the Korea Stock Market", (Korean) *Journal of Money and Finance*, Vol. 9, No. 1(2004), pp. 71-97(in Korean).

최운열, 정성훈, "투자자들의 인지적 편의에 관한 소고", 금융학회지, 제9권 제1호(2004), pp. 71-97.

Choi, W. Y., S. G. Ji, and S. H. Jeong, "Determents of Alternative Stock Switching Intent during the Equity Market Rally", *Korean Management Review*, Vol. 32, No. 6(2003), pp. 1571-1592(in Korean).

최운열, 지성구, 정성훈, "대세상승장에서 개인투자자의 대체주 전환의도 결정요인", 경영학연구, 제32권 제6호(2003), pp. 1571-1592.

Choi, W. Y., K. K. Lee, and S. H. Jeong, "An Empirical Study of the Disposition Effect in the Behavioral Finance", *Journal of Korea Securities Association*, Vol. 33, No. 2(2004), pp. 83-105(in Korean).

최운열, 이근경, 정성훈, "인지행위적 재무론에서 개인투자자들의 처분효과에 관한 연구", 증권학회지, 제33집 제2호(2004), pp. 83-105.

Chopra, N., C. Lee, A. Shleifer, and R. Thaler, "Yes, Discounts on Closed-end Funds are a Sentiment Index", *Journal of Finance*, Vol. 48(1993), pp. 801-808.

Chui, A. C. W., Sheridan Titman, and K. C. J. Wei, "Individualism and Momentum around the World", *Journal of Finance*, Vol. 65(2010), pp. 361-392.

Chung, C. H. and D. H. Kim, "Performance of Investment Strategies based on Past Stock Prices", *Korean Journal of Financial Management*, Vol. 9, No. 2(2002), pp. 49-75(in Korean).

정정현, 김동회, "과거의 주가에 근거한 투자전략의 성과분석", 재무관리연구, 제19권 제2호(2002), pp. 49-75.

Coval, J. D. and T. Shumway, "Do Behavioral Biases Affect Prices?", *Journal of Finance*, Vol. 60(2005), pp. 1-34.

Daniel, K., D. Hirshleifer, and A. Subrahmanyam, "Investor Psychology and Security Market Underand Over-Reactions", *Journal of Finance*, Vol. 53(1998), pp. 1839-1886.

Daniel, K., D. Hirshleifer, and A. Subrahmanyam, "Overconfidence, Arbitrage and Equilibrium Asset Pricing", *Journal of Finance*, Vol. 56(2001), pp. 921-965.

Datar, V. T., N. Naik, and R. Radcliffe, "Liquidity and Stock Returns: An Alternative Test", *Journal of Financial Markets*, Vol. 1(1998), pp. 203-219.

DeBondt, W. and R. Thaler, "Does the Stock Market Overreact?", *Journal of Finance*, Vol. 40(1985), pp. 793-808.

DeLong, J. B., Shleifer A., Summers L., and R. Waldmann, "Noise Trader Risk in Financial Markets", *Journal of Political Economy*, Vol. 98(1990a), pp. 703-738.

DeLong, J. B., Shleifer A., Summers L., and R. Waldmann, "Positive Feedback Investment Strategies and Destabilizing Rational Speculation", *Journal of Finance*, Vol. 45(1990b), pp. 375-395.

Derrien, F., "IPO Pricing in "Hot" Market Conditions: Who Leaves Money on the Table?", *Journal of Finance*, Vol. 60(2005), pp. 487-521.

Desai, H. and P. Jain, "Long-Run Common Stock Returns Following Splits and Reverse Splits", *Journal of Business*, Vol. 70(1997), pp. 409-433.

Dreman, D., *Contrarian Investment Strategy*, New York: Random House, 1979.

Edwards, W., "Conservatism in Human Information Processing", in B. Kleinmutz, ed., *Formal Representation of Human Judgment*, New York: John Wiley and Sons, 1986.

Fama, E., "Market Efficiency, Long-Term Returns and Behavioral Finance", *Journal of Financial Economics*, Vol. 49(1998), pp. 283-307.

Fama, E., Fisher, L., Jensen, M. and R. Roll, "The Adjustment of Stock Prices to New Information", *International Economic Review*, Vol. 10(1969), pp. 1-21.

Friedman, M., "The Case for Flexible Exchange Rates", *Essays in Positive Economics*, Chicago: University of Chicago Press, 1953.

Goetzmann, W. N. and A. Kumar, "Why Do Individual Investors Hold Underdiversified Portfolios?", *Working Paper*, Yale University(2007).

Graham, J. R. and C. R. Harvey, "The Theory and Practice of Corporate Finance: Evidence from the Field", *Journal of Financial Economics*, Vol. 60(2001), pp. 187-243.

Grinblatt, M. and B. Han, "Prospect Theory, Mental Accounting, and Momentum", *Journal of Financial Economics*, Vol. 78(2005), pp. 311-339.

Gutierrez, V. and E. Kelley, "Institutional Herding and Future Stock Returns"(2009), http://ssrn.com/abstract = 71107523.

Han, A. R., J. S. Yun, and C. H. Hong, "Index Effects of KOSPI 200 and Behavior of Individual Investors", *Korean Journal of Financial Management*, Vol. 27, No. 4(2010), pp. 207-234(in Korean).
한아름, 윤정선, 홍정훈, "KOSPI 200 지수편입 효과와 개인투자자의 투자행태", 재무관리연구, 제27권 제4호(2010), pp. 207-234.

Han, M. Y. and J. H. Kim, "The Effect of Self-Enhancement Perception and Confidence of Investment of Individual Investors on Risky Investment Behaviors", *Korean Journal of Psychological and Social Issues*, Vol. 13, No. 3(2007), pp. 89-109(in Korean).
한미영, 김재휘, "개인투자자의 자기고양적 지각과 투자확신이 위험투자행동에 미치는 영향", 한국심리학회지 : 사회문제, 제13권 제3호(2007), pp. 89-109.

Hirshleifer, D., "Investor Psychology and Asset Pricing", *Journal of Finance*, Vol. 56(2001), pp. 1533-1597.

Hirshleifer, D. and T. Shumway, "Good Day Sunshine: Stock Returns and the Weather", *Journal of Finance*, Vol. 58(2003), pp. 1009-1032.

Hong, G. H. and K. Y. Yi, "On the Herding Behavior of Fund Managers in the Korean Stock Market", *Journal of Korea Securities Association*, Vol. 35(2006), pp. 1-38(in Korean).
홍광헌, 이가연, "우리나라 주식시장에서의 펀드 매니저의 군집행동에 관한 연구", 증권학회지, 제35권 제4호(2006), pp. 1-38.

Hong, H. and J. C. Stein, "A Unified Theory of Underreaction, Momentum Trading and Overreaction in Asset Markets", *Journal of Finance*, Vol. 54 (1999), pp. 2143-2184.

Hwang, S. W., "Empirical Analysis on Overreaction Hypothesis in Korean Stock Market", *Korean Journal of Financial Management*, Vol. 12, No. 2(1994), pp. 131-159(in Korean).
황선웅, "한국주식시장에서의 주가과잉반응가설에 관한 종합적 실증분석", 재무관리연구, 제12권 제2호(1994), pp. 131-159.

Ihm, B. K., "Short-Term and Long-Term Performance of IPOs and Operating Performance", *Korean Journal of Financial Management*, Vol. 14, No. 2(1997), pp. 253-271(in Korean).
임병균, "IPO 주식의 장단기 성과와 영업성과", 재무관리연구, 제14권 제2호(1997), pp. 253-271.

Ikenberry, D., J. Lakonishok and T. Vermaelen, "Market Under-Reaction to Open Market Share Repurchases", *Journal of Financial Economics*, Vol. 39(1995), pp. 181-208.

Ikenberry, D., Rankine, G., and E. Stice, "What Do Stock Splits Really Signal?", *Journal of Financial and Quantitative Analysis*, Vol. 31(1996), pp. 357-377.

Jegadeesh, N. and S. Titman, "Returns to Buying Winners and Selling Losers: Implications for Stock Market Efficiency", *Journal of Finance*, Vol. 48 (1993), pp. 65-91.

Jensen, M. and R. S. Ruback, "The Market for Corporate Control: the Scientific Evidence", *Journal of Financial Economics*, Vol. 11(1983), pp. 5-50.

Jeong, S. H. and C. W. Park, "The Past Learning Effect of Individual Investor in the Korean Stock Market", *Korean Industrial Economic Research*, Vol. 21, No. 6(2008), pp. 2671-2695(in Korean).
정성훈, 박창욱, "한국 주식시장에서 개인투자자의 과거 학습효과 분석", 산업경제연구, 제21권 제6호(2008), pp. 2671-2695.

Joo, S. L. and Y. K. Song, "A Study on the Performance of the Merger in Korea: Cash Flow Analysis", *Journal of Korea Securities Association*, Vol. 20, No. 1(1997), pp. 71-103(in Korean).
주상용, 송영균, "한국에서의 기업합병의 성과에 관한 연구", 증권학회지, 제20권 제1호(1997), pp. 71-103.

Jung, K. Y., Y. C. Kim, and R. M. Stulz, "Timing, Investment Opportunities, Managerial Discretion, and the Security Issue Decision", *Journal of Financial Economics*, Vol. 42(1996), pp. 159-185.

Jung, S. C. and Y. G. Lee, "Long-Term Performance of Repurchased Stocks", *Korean Journal of Finance*, Vol. 16, No. 1(2003), pp. 129-162(in Korean).
정성창, 이용교, "자사주 취득 기업들의 장기성과에 관한 연구", 재무관리, 제16권 제2호(2003), pp. 129-162.

Kahneman, D., P. Slovic, and A. Tversky, *Judgment under Uncertainty: Heuristics and Biases*, New York: Cambridge University Press, 1982.

Kahneman, D. and A. Tversky, "Prospect Theory: An Analysis of Decision under Risk", *Econometrica*, Vol. 47(1979), pp. 13-32.

Kahneman, D. and A. Tversky, *Choices, Values, and Frames*, Russell Sage

Foundation, Cambridge University Press, UK, 2000.

Kang, H. S. and S. P. Kim, "Long-Run Performance of Mergers and Acquisitions in Korea", (Korean) *Journal of Money and Finance*, Vol. 23, No. 4(2009), pp. 63-101(in Korean).
강효석, 김성표, "기업인수 합병의 장기성과", 금융연구, 제23권 제4호 (2009), pp. 63-101.

Kang, J. K., J. M. Kim, and K. H. Bae, "Business Group and Agency Problem: The Comparison of Chaebol and Non-Chaebol Bidding Firms", *Korean Journal of Finance*, Vol. 14, No. 2(2001), pp. 49-89(in Korean).
강준구, 김진모, 배기홍, "기업집단과 대리인문제 : 재벌 및 비재벌 인수기업 의 합병성과 비교연구", 재무연구, 제14권 제2호(2001), pp. 49-89.

Kho, B. C., "Risk Premium and Investment Returns of Relative Strength Strategies", *Korean Journal of Financial Management*, Vol. 14, No. 1(1997), pp. 1-21(in Korean).
고봉찬, "위험 프리미엄과 상대적 세력 투자전략의 수익성", 제14권 제1호 (1997), pp. 1-21.

Kho, B. C., "Interaction of Momentum Returns in Stock and Bond Markets in Korea", *Asia- Pacific Journal of Financial Studies*, Vol. 35, No. 1(2006), pp. 103-133(in Korean).
고봉찬, "국내 채권시장 모멘텀과 주식시장과의 선행관계", 증권학회지, 제 35권 제1호(2006), pp. 103-133.

Kho, B. C. and J. W. Kim, "Does Accrual Anomaly Reflect a Risk Factor? The Case of the Korean Stock Market", *Asia-Pacific Journal of Financial Studies*, Vol. 36, No. 3(2007), pp. 425-461(in Korean).
고봉찬, 김진우, "발생액 이상 현상에 대한 위험평가", 증권학회지, 제36권 제3호(2007), pp. 425-461.

Kim, B. J. and H. J. Jeong, "A Study on the Long-term Reversal in the Korean Stock Market", *Korean Journal of Finance*, Vol. 21, No. 2(2008), pp. 1-48(in Korean).

김병준, 정호정, "한국 주식 수익률의 장기 반전현상에 관한 연구", 재무연구, 제21권 제2호(2008), pp. 1-48.

Kim, C. S., "On the Efficiency of the KOSDAQ Market", *Journal of Korea Securities Association*, Vol. 27(2000), pp. 331-361(in Korean).
김창수, "코스닥 시장의 효율성에 관한 연구", 증권학회지, 제27권(2000), pp. 331-361.

Kim, H. A. and S. C. Jung, "The Effect of Optimistic Investors' Sentiment on Anomalious Behaviors in the Hot Market IPOs", *Korean Journal of Financial Management*, Vol. 27, No. 2(2010), pp. 1-33(in Korean).
김현아, 정성창, "낙관적 투자자의 기대가 핫마켓상황 IPO 시장의 이상현상에 미치는 영향력 검증", 재무관리연구, 제27권 제2호(2010), pp. 1-33.

Kim, H. J., S. K. Nam, J. H. Cho, K. J. Lee, C. M. Bae, J. Park, and J. Y. Yoon, "Evidence on Stock Market Overreaction in Korea", *Journal of Korea Securities Association*, Vol. 10(1988), pp. 1-25(in Korean).
김희집, 남상구, 조지호, 이건중, 배창모, 박 준, 윤정용, "우리나라 증권시장에서의 주가의 과민반응에 관한 연구", 증권학회지, 제10권(1988), pp. 1-25.

Kim, K. S. and J. H. Byun, "Effect of Investor Sentiment on Market Response to Stock Split Announcement", *Asia-Pacific Journal of Financial Studies*, Vol. 39, No. 6(2010), pp. 687-719.

Kim, K. Y., "Stock Price and Weather", *Korean Journal of Financial Studies*, Vol. 3, No. 1(1996), pp. 69-83(in Korean).
김규영, "주가와 날씨", 재무관리논총, 제3권 제1호(1996), pp. 69-83.

Kim, S. C. and H. S. Byun, "The Long-Run Performance of Seasoned Equity Offerings of Korean Firms", *Korean Journal of Finance*, Vol. 16(1998), pp. 23-50(in Korean).
김석진, 변현수, "유상증자의 장기성과 연구", 재무연구, 제16호(1998), pp. 23-50.

Kim, S. C. and H. S. Byun, "Long-Run Performance from Korean Equity Carve-Outs: Additional Evidence", *Korean Journal of Financial Management*, Vol. 20, No. 1(2003), pp. 331-339(in Korean).

김석진, 변현수, "분리공모를 통한 구조조정의 성과", 재무관리연구, 제20권 제1호(2003), pp. 331-339.

Kim, S. K. and S. H. Seog, "Prospect Theoretic Approach to Blackjack Market", (Korean) *Journal of Money and Finance*, Vol. 12, No. 1(2007), pp. 141-180(in Korean).

김서경, 석승훈, "블랙잭시장에 대한 전망이론적 분석", 금융학회지, 제12권 제1호(2007), pp. 141-180.

Kim, T. H. and C. J. Eom, "Comparison of Contrarian Strategy and Momentum Strategy in Korean Stock Market", *Korean Journal of Financial Management*, Vol. 14, No. 3(1997), pp. 73-111(in Korean).

김태혁, 엄철준, "한국주식시장에 있어서 반전거래전략과 계속거래전략의 경제적 유용성에 관한 비교연구", 재무관리연구, 제14권 제3호(1997), pp. 73-111.

Kim, Y. K. and Y. H. Kim, "Long-Term Performance of IPO Firms and Earnings Management", *Korean Journal of Financial Management*, Vol. 17, No. 2(2000), pp. 71-98(in Korean).

김영규, 김영혜, "최초공모주의 장기성과와 이익관리", 재무관리연구, 제17권 제2호(2000), pp. 71-98.

Kindleberger, C. P. and R. Aliber, *Manias, Panics, and Crashes: A History of Financial Crises*, 5th ed., Wiley, 2005.

Lakonishok, J., A. Shleifer, and R. W. Vishny, "The Impact of Institutional Trading on Stock Prices", *Journal of Financial Economics*, Vol. 32(1992), pp. 23-43.

Lee, C., A. Shleifer, and R. Thaler, "Investor Sentiment and the Closed-end Puzzle", *Journal of Finance*, Vol. 46(1991), pp. 75-109.

Lee, C. M. C. and B. Swaminathan, "Price Momentum and Trading Volume",

Journal of Finance, Vol. 55(2000), pp. 2017-2070.

Lee, C. W., S. Y. Guahk, and H. J. Wi, "Over-reaction of Stock Prices in KOSDAQ Market", *Daehan Journal of Business*, Vol. 19, No. 1(2006), pp. 181-198(in Korean).

이채우, 곽세영, 위한종, "KOSDAQ 시장에서의 주가과민반응", 대한경영학회지, 제19권 제1호(2006), pp. 181-198.

Lee, J. D. and Y. G. Ahn, "Performance Analysis of Investment Strategy in the Korean Stock Market", *Journal of Korea Securities Association*, Vol. 30(2002), pp. 33-74(in Korean).

이정도, 안영규, "한국 주식시장에서 계속투자전략과 반대투자전략의 수익성분석", 증권학회지, 제30집(2002), pp. 33-74.

Lim, U. K. and S. K. Lee, "Long-Run Performance of IPOs in Korean Market", *Journal of Korea Securities Association*, Vol. 18(1995), pp. 333-369(in Korean).

임웅기, 이성규, "우리나라 최초공모주의 장기성과에 관한 연구", 증권학회지, 제18권(1995), pp. 333-369.

Lo, A. W. and A. C. Mackinlay, "When Are Contrarian Profits Due to Stock Market Overreaction?", *Review of Financial Studies*, Vol. 3(1990), pp. 175-205.

Locke, P. R. and S. C. Mann, "Professional Trader Discipline and Trade Disposition", *Journal of Financial Economics*, Vol. 76(2005), pp. 401-444.

Loughran, T. and J. Ritter, "The New Issues Puzzle", *Journal of Finance*, Vol. 50(1995), pp. 23-52.

Loughran, T. and J. Ritter, "Why Don't Issuers Get Upset about Leaving Money on the Table in IPOs?", *Review of Financial Studies*, Vol. 15(2002), pp. 413-443.

Moeller, S. B., F. P. Schlingemann, and R. Stulz, "Firm Size and the Gains from Acquisitions", *Journal of Financial Economics*, Vol. 73(2004), pp. 201-228.

Odean, T., "Are Investors Reluctant to Realize Their Losses?", *Journal of Finance*, Vol. 53(1998), pp. 1775-1798.

Odean, T., "Do Investors Trade Too Much?", *American Economic Review*, Vol. 89(1999), pp. 1279-1298.

Park, S. S. and Y. G. Ahn, "A Study on the Disposition Effect in Korea Stock Market", *International Business Review*, Vol. 11, No. 1(2007), pp. 91-114(in Korean).
박순식, 안영규, "한국 주식시장에서의 투자성향효과 분석", 국제경영리뷰, 제11권 제1호(2007), pp. 91-114.

Park, Y. S., J. H. Lee, and D. S. Kim, "The Market Effect of Additions or Deletions for KOSPI 200 Index: Comparison between Groups by Size and Market Condition", *Korean Journal of Financial Management*, Vol. 26, No. 1(2009), pp. 65-94(in Korean).
박영석, 이재현, 김대식, "KOSPI 200 지수종목의 변경에 따른 시장반응 : 규모와 시장규모에 따른 그룹간 비교분석", 재무관리연구, 제26권 제1호 (2009), pp. 65-94.

Pompain, M., *Behavioral Finance and Wealth Management*, Wiley and Sons, New Jersey, 2006.

Ritter, J. R., "The Long-Run Performance of Initial Public Offerings", *Journal of Finance*, Vol. 46(1991), pp. 3-27.

Roll, R., "The Hubris Hypothesis of Corporate Takeovers", *Journal of Business*, Vol. 59(1986), pp. 197-218.

Saunders, E. M. Jr., "Stock Prices and Wall Street Weather", *American Economic Review*, Vol. 83(1993), pp. 1337-1345.

Seon, J. H. and S. W. Kim, "Study on Herding Behavior of Asset Management Company", *Working Paper*, 2010 Joint Conference of Business Related Academic Associations(in Korean).
선정훈, 김수원, "국내 자산운용사들의 군집행동에 관한 연구", 2010년 경영학관련학회 통합학술대회.

Sonu, S. H., Y. S. Yoon, H. S. Kang, S. W. Kim, W. H. Lee, and S. K. Oh, "Overreaction and Firm Specific Anomalies in the Korean Stock Market", *Journal of Korea Securities Association*, Vol. 17(1994), pp. 167-218(in Korean).

선우석호, 윤영섭, 강효석, 김선웅, 이원흠, 오세경, "한국주식시장에서의 과잉반응과 기업특성적 이례현상에 관한 연구", 증권학회지, 제17집(1994), pp. 167-218.

Shefrin, H., *A Behavioral Approach to Asset Pricing*, Elsevier Academic Press, 2005.

Shefrin, H., *Behavioralizing Finance*, Now Publishers Inc., 2010.

Shefrin, H. and M. Statman, "The Disposition to Sell Winners Too Early and Ride Losers Too Long: Theory and Evidence", *Journal of Finance*, Vol. 40(1985), pp. 777-790.

Shefrin, H. and M. Statman, "Behavioral Portfolio Theory", *Journal of Financial and Quantitative Analysis*, Vol. 35(2000), pp. 127-151.

Shiller, A., *Inefficient Markets: An Introduction to Behavioral Finance*, Oxford Press, UK, 1999.

Shiller, R. J., "Bubbles, Human Judgment and Expert Opinion", *Financial Analyst Journal*, Vol. 58, No. 3(2002), pp. 18-26.

Shin, M. S., S. C. Kim, and S. Y. Lee, "Long-Term Performance of Repurchasing Firms", *Korean Journal of Financial Studies*, Vol. 8, No. 1(2002), pp. 117-156(in Korean).

신민식, 김석진, 이선윤, "자사주매입기업의 장기성과", 재무관리논총, 제8 권 제1호(2002), pp. 117-156.

Shin, S. H., "Economic Implications of Long-Horizon Stock Return Reversal: Are Loser-Portfolios Worth Investing?", *Korean Journal of Finance*, Vol. 14(1997), pp. 105-124(in Korean).

신성환, "우리나라 장기 주식수익률 역전현상이 갖는 경제적 의미? : 과연

패자포트폴리오에 투자하겠는가?", 재무연구, 제14권(1997), pp. 105-124.

Shin, J. Y. and S. H. Park, "Does Weather Effect Stock Returns?: Behavioral Finance Approach", *Korea Institute of Finance*, Vol. 17, No. 2(2003), pp. 105-128(in Korean).
신진영, 박승호, "날씨와 주가지수 수익률간의 상관관계", 금융연구, 제17권 제2호(2003), pp. 105-128.

Shleifer, A. and R. W. Vishny, "Corruption", *Quarterly Journal of Economics*, Vol. 108(1993), pp. 599-617.

Sias R., Institutional Herding, *Review of Financial Studies*, Vol. 17(2004), pp. 165-206.

Sloan, R. G., "Do Stock Prices Fully Reflect Information in Accruals and Cash Flows about Future Earnings?", *Accounting Review*, Vol. 71(1996), pp. 289-315.

Slovic, P., "Psychological Study of Human Judgment: Implications for Investment Decision Making", *Journal of Finance*, Vol. 27(1972), pp. 779-801.

Spiess, D. K. and J. Affleck-Graves, "Underperformance in Long-Run Stock Returns Following Seasoned Equity Offerings", *Journal of Financial Economics*, Vol. 38(1995), pp. 243-268.

Statman, M., "Countries and Culture in Behavioral Finance", *CFA Institute Conference Proceedings Quarterly*, September(2008), pp. 38-44

Subrahmanyam, A., "Behavioural Finance: A Review and Synthesis", *European Financial Management*, Vol. 14(2007), pp. 12-29.

Thaler, R. H., "Mental Accounting and Consumer Choice", *Marketing Science*, Vol. 4(1985), pp. 199-214.

Thaler, R. H., *Advances in Behavioral Finance*, Sage Press, New York, 1993.

Thaler, R. H., "The End of Behavioral Finance", *Financial Analysts Journal*, Vol. 55(1999), pp. 12-17.

Trombley, M. A., "Stock Prices and Wall Street Weather: Additional Evidence", *Quarterly Journal of Business and Economics*, Vol. 36(1997), pp. 11-21.

Tversky, A. and D. Kahneman, "Judgment under Uncertainty: Heuristics and Biases", *Science*, Vol. 185(1974), pp. 1124-1131.

Von Neumann, J. and O. Morgenstern, *Theory of Games and Economic Behavior*, Princeton: Princeton University Press, 1947.

Wermers, R., "Mutual Fund Herding and the Impact on Stock Prices", *Journal of Finance*, Vol. 54(1999), pp. 581-623.

Woo, C. S. and J. S. Kwak, "Empirical Analysis on Performance of Contrarian Strategy and Time-varying Systematic Risk", *Korean Journal of Financial Management*, Vol. 17, No. 1(2000), pp. 67-89(in Korean).
우춘식, 곽재석, "반전거래전략의 투자성과와 체계적 위험의 변화에 관한 실증연구", 재무관리연구, 제17권 제1호(2000), pp. 67-89.

Any citation of this article must refer to the following: Sonu, Sukho and Choi, Hyungsuk, "Capital Market Anomalies in Korea", Asian Review of Financial Research, Vol. 24 (2011), No. 4, pp. 1231-1284.

Chapter 5

Capital Market Anomalies in Korea

Sukho Sonu*   Professor, College of Business Administration, Hongik University

Hyungsuk Choi   Assistant Professor, College of Business Administration, Hongik University

Abstract

Empirical studies have identified a variety of capital market regularities that are commonly known as anomalies including the size effect, book-to-market effect, the January effect, the weekend effect, long-term reversal effect, net stock issues effect, the first-day underpricing and the long-term underperformance of Initial Price Offerings (IPOs) and the post-merger underperformance. For each anomaly, we discuss the existence and consequences of these well-known effects in the Korean stock market. The empirical evidence on the anomalies in Korea can be summarized as follows. The anomalous returns are significant in most of the cross-sectional regressions. The anomalous returns associated with net stock issues are positive in the short period around the issue date, a finding opposite to the evidence found in the U.S. markets. Momentum phenomenon in average returns exist on the industry level, but they are absent for individual stocks. Also, momentum anomalies are only found at the individual level when stock markets are less volatile. That is, Momentum anomalies are less robust in Korea than in the U.S. and European countries. Additionally, dividend yields and market interest rates have no ability to predict stock market returns in Korea contrary to U.S. findings, while earning price ratios have some predictability. The turn-of-the-year effect, the weekend effect and the long-term reversal effect are persistent in Korea.

Keywords   Market Anomalies in Korea, January Effect, Predictability of Stock Returns, Asset Pricing Models, Capital Market Efficiency

* **Corresponding Author. Address:** Hongik University, 94 Wawoosan-ro, Mapo-gu, Seoul 121-791, Korea; E-mail: sonu@hongik.ac.kr; **Tel:** 82-2-320-1717.

This survey paper was accomplished as a part of the 2010 knowledge database project by the Korean Finance Association and was financially supported by the KFA. The authors thank two anonymous referees for very helpful comments and suggestions. We also thank Catherine Heyjung Sonu for excellent proofreading to improve the English expression in the paper.

I. Introduction

This paper reviews empirical evidence on capital market anomalies in Korea. Capital market anomalies are cross-sectional and intertemporal regularities in security returns that are not predicted by asset pricing models. The finance literature is replete with empirical evidence of such anomalies. Three possible interpretations for those phenomena have emerged. The first interpretation is that those findings may simply be sample-specific artifacts. This could happen when data problems such as selection bias, noise, and data snooping are not properly controlled.

The other two interpretations are the inability of properly controlling for risk (i.e., the use of misspecified asset pricing model) and the inefficiency of the markets. In fact, tests for market efficiency should be a joint test of these two possibilities. In other words, since previously-found empirical evidence may be the result of the use of misspecified models, the results should not be directly interpreted as evidence of market inefficiency. This can happen when returns do not behave according to a pre-specified equilibrium model such as the capital asset pricing model (CAPM). Fama and French (1992) provide evidence showing that CAPM has little explanatory power for the risk-return tradeoff. Instead, they show that their three-factor model, including the market factor and the other two factors associated with size and book-to-market ratio, has better explanatory power than the CAPM. Since then, however, many studies report that the previously-found anomalies have still survived or even continued to grow in some cases, even when the three-factor model is used.

Well-specified asset pricing models should allow us to determine whether to reject the null hypothesis that security markets are informationally efficient. While we may conclude that the anomalies are due to market inefficiency, we are still left with a puzzling question of how the anomalous phenomena were able to endure for such long periods. The magnitude of the anomalies must dissipate as smart investors seek to profitably exploit the imperfect rationality. If the anomaly is a true one, then it should disappear quickly because of the arbitrage-seeking behavior of investors. This argument brings us back to the misspecification issue of asset pricing models. The regularities found in stock returns may be indicative of using misspecified asset pricing models. Alternatively, it may be possible that some unidentified risk factors explain such regularities. Identification of such risk factors may be an important task for future research. In a related stream of research, the behavioral approach has been considered as an explanation for the anomalies.

The first comprehensive study of capital market anomalies in Korea is Sonu et al. (1994). Using the Korea Investors Service (KIS) database for the period between 1980 and 1992, they test various types of regularities in stock returns including the long-term reversal effect, size effect, the January effect, weekend effect, with-in-month effect, negligible stock effect, and IPO underpricing. They show that most of the regularities are apparent in stock returns in the Korean market, consistent with the U.S. evidence. Afterwards, many financial empiricists report an increasing array of anomalies with respect to the existence and causes of the capital market regularities. The heightened interest in the area of anomalies is stimulated by a series of unexplained anomalous phenomena which have survived for a long period of time in the U.S. and the emergence of new pricing models such as the Fama and French three-factor model (1992).

This paper broadly classifies the findings as being cross-sectional or intertemporal. We compare test results found in Korea to those in the

U.S. markets. We provide explanation for the differences found between these two countries as well as for the unique characteristics of the Korean stock market and its environment. We contribute to the literature by enhancing understanding of the issues and debates involved with each anomaly in Korea and providing insight into the implications of market efficiency.

The remainder of this article is organized as follows. Section Ⅱ discusses the regularities found in the cross-section of stock returns. These are the size effect, the book-to-market effect (or the value premium effect), the turn-of-the-year effect (or the January effect), and the weekend effect. Section Ⅲ describes the regularities in the time-series of returns that include the persistent impact of short-term interest rate, dividend yield and earning-price ratio on equity returns. Section Ⅳ discusses abnormal returns found in different types of markets such as the IPO markets, SEO markets, and M&A markets. This section also compares the results in Korea to those from the corresponding U.S. markets. Section Ⅴ discusses the implications of the anomalies to capital market efficiency and corporate finance decision makings in Korea. Section Ⅵ concludes.

Ⅱ. Cross-sectional Empirical Regularities

1. Size and Book-to-Market Effect

The finance literature provides substantial empirical evidence that questions the validity of the CAPM. For instance, the size effect, also known as the small cap effect, is the tendency of small cap stocks to outperform large cap stocks. Banz (1981) finds that smaller firms earn higher risk-adjusted returns than do larger firms. He documents this size effect as evidence that the CAPM is misspecified because the effect has sustained for at least forty years. Reinganum (1981) also finds that size-sorted portfolios earn average returns systematically different from those predicted by the CAPM and that these abnormal returns persist for at least two years. Also, Stattman (1980) and Rosenberg, Reid, and Lanstein (1985) report that average returns in the US stock markets are positively related to the ratio of a firm's book value of common stock to its market value (BE/ME). This tendency of stocks with high book-to-market ratios to outperform the market in the long term is called the book-to-market or the value premium effect. Chan, Hamao and Lakonishok (1991) find a similar positive relation between BE/ME and average returns in the Japanese stock market.

Using the method devised by Fama and MacBeth (1973), Fama and French (1992) analyze the relation between average stock returns and three risk factors which are size (market capitalization), BE/ME, and market beta (β) over the period from 1963 to 1990. They find that the relationship between market beta and average return is unexpectedly negative and statistically insignificant, which is contradictory to the prediction by the CAPM. Rather, they find that firm specific characteristic variables such as size and BE/ME have reliable power in explaining the cross-section of average returns. Based on these findings, Fama and French (1992) suggest a three-factor model which includes the market factor and two other factors related to size and BE/ME. Fama and French (1993, 1995, 1996) and Davis, Fama, and French (1999) highlight the effectiveness of the three-factor model in explaining the size effect, the book-to-market effect, and other market anomalies found in the U.S. markets.

However, Kothari, Shanken, and Sloan (1995) document a strong positive relation between the beta and average returns and argue that the relation between average return and BE/ME is seriously exaggerated by survivorship bias. Daniel and Titman (1997) suggest that size and BE/ME have no power to explain stock returns, invalidating the claims by Fama and French regarding the three-factor model. They suggest that the book-to-market traces the value characteristic, not risk. Daniel and Titman (1999) corroborate this statement by showing that the three-factor model suggested by Fama and French is invalid in the Japanese stock market. In response to this objection, Davis, Fama, and French (2000) argue that the results of Daniel and Titman (1999) are specific to their short sample period and reaffirm the existence of a book-to-market effect for the period between 1929 and 1963. Schwert (2003) demonstrates that the financial market anomalies related to profit opportunities, including the size and book-to-market effects in the cross-section of average return, disappear or attenuate following the discovery of the anomalies.

A series of studies have been conducted to investigate the abnormal performance related to size and the book-to-market anomalies in the Korean stock market. Kim (1994) examines whether the size anomaly is prevalent in Korea over the period between 1981 and 1992. Based on 15 stock portfolios formed on the basis of size and beta, he implements the Fama and MacBeth (1973) approach to find a negative and statistically insignificant relation between returns and size. He finds no conclusive evidence of size effects in Korea.

Kam (1997) investigates whether variables such as BE/ME, earnings-to-price ratio (E/P), cash flows-to-price ratio (C/P), and leverage have any predicative power in explaining cross-section of stock returns. Using the cross-sectional regression of Fama and MacBeth (1973), he documents that average stock returns are significantly related to BE/ME and C/P, but not size. Interestingly, he finds the Fama and French three-factor model to be a useful predictor of common fluctuations and changes in the domestic stock market and interprets this result as evidence that the model holds in Korea.

In order to demonstrate whether the size and the BE/ME, not the stock beta, are useful in explaining the difference in returns in the Korean stock market, Song and Lee (1997) perform time-series analyses using 25 portfolios formed based on size and BE/ME over the period between 1980 and 1995. They employ a regression with the market premium (MKT), the size premium (SMB), and the value premium (HML) as independent variables and portfolio returns as the dependent variable. They document that SMB considerably explains the difference in returns that are not explained by the market risk while HML does not have any additional explanatory power.

Kim and Yun (1999) select a sample of non-financial firms listed on the Korean Stock Exchange from January 1980 to March 1997. They confirm that size and BE/ME are among the most significant financial variables which explain the cross-sectional difference in stock returns. While macroeconomic factors have reliable power to explain the difference in stock returns, they become insignificant with the inclusion of the size and book-to-market-ratio.

Kim and Kim (2000) examine whether the size effect and the book-to-market effect exist in the Korean stock market and analyze the usefulness of Fama-French three-factor model in explaining stock returns in Korea. Over the sample period between 1990 and 1997, they classify their sample into four groups to account for new listing bias and survivorship bias. Each group is then divided into a total of 25 portfolios based on size and BE/ME for cross-sectional and time series analysis of each portfolio return. Based on the cross-sectional analysis, they confirm that the size effect exists as the size coefficient is negative and significant; however, they further show that the size anomaly is subject to new listing bias but not to survivorship bias. They document that the BE/ME coefficient is significantly positive and robust to new listing bias and survivorship bias, suggesting the existence of a strong book-to-market effect. On the other hand, the regression coefficient of stock beta is insignificant and negative. Their time series analysis shows that the market premium (MKT), size premium (SMB) and value premium (HML) are statistically significant, implying that the Fama-French three-factor model is useful in explaining stock returns in Korea.

Within a sample of non-financial firms in the Korean Stock Exchange Market from 1980 to 2001, Chang and Kim (2003) find that value stocks with high value ratios such as BE/ME, E/P, C/P, and sales-to-price ratio (S/P) produce high buy-and-hold-abnormal returns (BHAR), which suggests that value premium exists in Korea. Notably, a high value premium exists when portfolios are organized based on BE/ME and C/P while portfolios formed based on E/P ratio show lower investment performance.

Yun, Ku, Eom, and Hahn (2009) is an example of research that attempts to understand which firm characteristics have explanatory power for variations in stock returns from 1991 to 2007 in Korea. They find no evidence of the book-to-market effect. Firm characteristics which show significant relations with the cross-section of stock returns in Korea are size measured by market capitalization and liquidity measured by turnover. Although the Fama-French three-factor model is widely used in research and practice for risk adjustment and performance evaluation in both the U.S. and Korea, they raise a question about the relevance of the value factor in the Fama-French three-factor model in understanding the determinants of stock returns due to the lack of clear empirical evidence of the book-to-market effect in Korea.

The general consensus in the U.S. literature until early 1990s was that the size effect and the book-to-market effect are strong empirical evidence against the validity of the CAPM. However, recent studies such as Schwert

(2003) report the disappearance of the tendency of stocks with small market capitalization or high book-to-market ratios to outperform the market in the recent period in the U.S. stock market. This may reflect the trading activities of practitioners who implement strategies to take advantage of abnormal profits by exploiting size and book-to-market related anomalies. Interestingly, financial studies in Korea still find evidence of a negative relation between the average return and the market capitalization and a positive relation between the average return and the book-to-market ratio in the recent periods including the late 1990s and early 2000s.

2. Turn-of-the-Year Effect (January Effect)

Keim (1983) provides empirical evidence that daily abnormal returns in January have large means relative to the remaining eleven months and that the negative relation between abnormal returns and size is more pronounced in January than in any other months. Reinganum (1983) also shows that small-cap stocks experience large returns in the first few trading days of January. The significantly higher abnormal returns for small firms in early January are known as the turn-of-the-year effect or the January effect. This anomaly is further investigated by Blume and Stambaugh (1983) and Roll (1983).

Roll (1983) hypothesizes that the higher volatility of small-cap stocks creates substantial short-term capital losses and that investors have an incentive to sell those stocks for income tax purposes before the end of the year. This selling pressure might reduce the prices of small-cap stocks in December, leading to a rebound in early January as investors repurchase these stocks to reestablish their investment positions. However, Reinganum (1983) argues that tax-loss selling cannot entirely explain the January seasonal effect by providing empirical evidence that small firms with relatively higher prior year returns also exhibit large average January returns.

Gultekin and Gultekin (1983) examine stock market seasonality in 17 major industrialized countries over the period between 1970 and 1979. They show that turn-of-the-year effects occur in most of the capital markets around the world. Lakonishok and Smidt (1988) examine 90 years of daily data on the Dow Jones Industrial Average to test for the existence of persistent seasonal patterns in stock returns. They find no evidence of high January return for large U.S. firms. The turn-of-the-year effect is a phenomenon in which small-cap stocks receive higher returns as indicated by Keim (1983), we cannot interpret the findings documented by Lakonishok and Smidt (1988) as evidence against the January effect because their sample is composed of large-cap blue-chip stocks.

Schwert (2003) examines the turn-of-the-year effect for the period between 1962 and 2001 and the period between 1962 and 1979 which corresponds to sample period used by Reinganum (1983), as well as the subsequent periods between 1980 and 1989 and between 1990 and 2001. To examine the impact of size on the January effect, he uses the difference in the daily returns to the CRSP NYSE small-cap portfolio (decile 1) and the return to the CRSP NYSE large-cap portfolio (decile 10) as the dependent variable and the indicator variable of whether daily return occurs during the first 15 calendar days of January as the independent variable. He finds that the turn-of-the-year anomaly has not completely disappeared since it was originally documented. The estimates of the turn-of-the-year coefficients are around 0.4% per day over the periods 1980 ~1989 and 1990~2001. Thus, while the January effect is less pronounced than that observed by Keim (1983) and Reinganum (1983), it is still reliably positive.

Longer sample periods are required to assure more reliable empirical results for the seasonal patterns of stock returns. In spite of the relatively short history of stock markets in Korea, a number of studies have examined the seasonal regularities in stock returns in the Korean stock market. Choi and Kim (1994) analyze the calendar month effect using the Korea Composite Stock Price Index (KOSPI) and the size portfolio index (small-cap, mid-cap, and large-cap) between 1980 and 1992. They examine the prevalence of seasonal effects using both raw return and risk-adjusted return derived from the CAPM in order to increase the reliability of their findings. Using raw returns, they find that the seasonal effect exists in mid-cap stock and small-cap stock and that the return in January is extraordinarily higher than that of other months. However, they show that size does not have any impact on the January effect as small-cap stock return is higher than that of large-cap stock return but lower than that of mid-cap stock return in January. In risk-adjusted returns, they not only find evidence of the turn-of-the-year effect but also that the effect is pronounced in small-cap stocks.

Yoon and Lee (2009) analyze whether the January effect exists in both KOSPI and Korean Securities Dealers Automated Quotations Index (KOSDAQ index) stocks. Their sample includes the KOSPI, the large-cap index, the mid-cap index, and the small-cap index from 1980 to 2002, the KOSPI 200 from 1990 to 2002, and the KOSDAQ index, the large-cap index, the mid-cap index, and the small-cap index from 2002 to 2006. They find that the average KOSPI return of 0.95% in January is the highest relative to that in the remaining eleven months, but it is not statistically significant. The average returns in January in the large-cap, mid-cap, and small-cap index are 1.85%, 1.46%, and 0.90%, respectively, and are higher than the average return in any other months, and only the small-cap index return is statistically significant. In case of the KOSPI 200 index, the average return of 0.87% in January is the highest of all months, but it is not statistically significant. Therefore, the size effect on the returns in January seems to exist in the KOSPI market. However, they failed to find any evidence of the January effect in the KOSDAQ market. Specifically, the return of 8.60% in November is the highest of all months in the KOSDAQ index. For large-cap stocks, the month of November shows the highest return of 8.39% while for mid-cap and small-cap stocks, the month of January shows the highest returns of 6.77% and 6.30%, respectively. However, the monthly returns in the KOSDAQ index are not statistically different across months or size. In summary, they provide mixed evidence on the existence of the January effect of which only some evidence is identified in the KOSPI market.

In both the U.S. and the Korean stock markets, the literature documents persistent abnormal positive stock returns in January even for the recent period including the early 2000s. This January effect is observed only in small-cap stocks. One of the possible reasons for this anomaly is tax-loss selling. Considering the different tax treatment for capital gains tax between the two countries, it is quite intriguing that this seasonal pattern of stock returns is observed in both countries. In addition, we conjecture that window dressing activities by institutional investors at the end of year may explain a major portion of the persistent phenomena, as this kind of activity become more regular.

3. Weekend Effect

Cross (1973) examines the distribution of price changes on Fridays and Mondays to test whether stock prices move randomly. He documents a significantly negative average stock return on Monday and a higher than average positive return on Friday. French (1980) investigates whether the stock return generation process operates continuously or only during active trading. He examines the process by comparing the returns for different days of the week: the returns reported for Monday represent a three-calendar-day investment, from the close of trading Friday to the close of trading Monday, while the returns for other days reflect a one-day investment. Interestingly, the average return for Monday was significantly negative while the average return for the other four days of the week was positive in his sample period. This anomaly is extensively examined by Gibbons and Hess (1981), Keim and Stambaugh (1984), Rogalski (1984), Jaffe and Westfield (1985), and Schwert (2003).

Jaffe and Westfield (1985) examine the daily stock market returns for four countries (the U.K., Japan, Canada, and Australia) to find the weekend effect in each country. Unlike the U.S. stock market, the lowest mean returns for both the Japanese and Australian stock markets occur on Tuesday. Schwert (2003) examines the weekend effect from 1885 to 2002, a period, not included in French's (1980) study. He documents a negative Monday return over the period between 1885 and 1977; however, he finds that the estimate of the weekend effect since 1978 is not significantly different from the other days of the week, suggesting that the weekend effect has diminished.

Similar to the empirical findings in the Japanese stock markets, the day of the week patterns in stock returns in Korea are different from those in the U.S. Yun, Sonu, Kim, Jang, and Choi (1994) analyze daily returns in the KOSPI market for a 13-year-period between 1980 and 1992. They find that the day of the week effect exists in the Korean stock market as the return on Monday is negative and the returns on the other days of the week are positive. They divide their sample into three subsample periods: stable (1980~1986), bullish (1987~1989), and bearish (1990~1992) periods. In a stable period, the mean returns are significantly different across five weekdays at the 1 percent level but in a bullish or a bearish period, the mean returns across weekdays are not significantly different.

They conclude that the day-of-the-week effect exists in the long run but the effects are not always present in the Korean stock market.

Kim and Chung (2004) examine whether the day-of-the-week effect exists in both stock return and volatility in the KOSPI market over the period between 1995 and 2002. The lowest mean return is reported on Monday and the highest mean return is reported on Wednesday in the KOSPI market. It is noted that the stock market volatility is the highest on Wednesday and the lowest on Tuesday and Saturday. These findings imply the strategy that sells stocks on Wednesday may not be beneficial to investors as the return as well as the volatility of the return are on average the highest on that day.

In sum, even though the weekend effect with relatively lower average stock returns on Monday and higher returns on Friday is documented by a voluminous literature in the U.S. stock market until the 1970s, this effect seems to have disappeared after 1980. However, in Korea, the academic literature shows that the day of the week effect for the average stock return still exits even in the recent period. It notes that the day of the week with the highest average stock return is Wednesday, not Friday in Korea. However, since Wednesday has the highest volatility in Korea, investors should consider not only the average stock return but also the level of risk shown on Wednesday.

III. Time-Series Empirical Regularities

1. Long-Term Reversal and Momentum Effect

Jegadeesh and Titman (1993, 1999) show that past winners (portfolios formed on the last year of past returns) continue to outperform past losers in the next period with an average excess return of about 1% per month. This is an empirically documented anomaly known as momentum, which finance theory struggles to explain because an increase in asset prices should not warrant further increase. Such increase is warranted only by changes in demand and supply or new information. In the related stream of research, DeBondt and Thaler (1985) document an anomaly whereby long-term past losers have higher average returns than long-term past winners, which is known as a "long-term reversal" effect.

DeBondt and Thaler (1985) investigate whether the investor's overreaction to new events will affect stock prices. If stock prices systematically overreact, then their reversal should be predictable from past return data alone. Using monthly return data for New York Stock Exchange (NYSE) common stocks over the period from January 1926 to December 1982, they form the winner portfolio (top decile) and the loser portfolio (bottom decile) based on the previous 36-month performance. They find that the loser portfolios outperform the market by, on average, 19.6%, three years after portfolio formation and that the winner portfolios underperform the market by 5.0%. The evidence of stock price reversals is consistent with the overreaction hypothesis. Utilizing the observed stock price reversal, the contrarian strategy of selling long-term past winners and buying long-term past losers generates an average return of 24.6% over the following three years.

However, Conrad and Kaul (1993) show that the returns to the long-term contrarian strategy implemented by DeBondt and Thaler (1985) are upwardly biased because they are calculated by cumulating single-period (monthly) returns over long intervals. Instead, they show that the measurement errors in observed prices due to bid-ask errors, non-synchronous trading, or price discreteness, lead to substantial spurious returns to the long-term zero-investment contrarian strategies. When they measure long-term performance of contrarian strategies using the buy-and-hold return rather than the cumulative abnormal return, the average holding period return for non-January months reveals that losers consistently underperform winners for the one-, two-, and three-year evaluation periods.

Jegadeesh and Titman (1993) suggest that strategies which buy past winner stocks and sell past loser stocks generate significant positive returns over the three- to 12-month holding periods. They find that the profitability of these strategies is not due to the systematic risk or delayed stock price reactions to common factors. The long-term performance of these past winners and losers reveals that half of their excess returns in the year following the portfolio formation date dissipate within the following two years. Based on their findings, they argue that interpreting return reversals as evidence of overreaction and return persistence as evidence of underreaction is probably overly simplistic.

Rouwenhorst (1998) finds that international equity markets exhibit medium-term return continuation. Between 1980 and 1995, an internationally diversified portfolio of past medium-term winners outperforms a portfolio of medium-term losers by more than one percent per month. This momentum in returns is not limited to a particular market, but is present in all 12 European markets in their sample. They provide evidence that European and U.S. momentum strategies have a common component, which suggests that exposure to a common factor may drive the profitability of momentum strategies.

Fama and French (1996) examine whether the three-factor model can explain the profitability of momentum strategies and contrarian strategies. The three-factor model captures the reversal of long-term returns documented by DeBondt and Thaler (1985). Past long-term loser stocks tend to have positive size-factor (SMB) loadings and value-factor (HML) loadings and higher future average returns. On the other hand, past long-term winner stocks tend to have strong negative value-factor (HML) loadings and low future returns. The three-factor model, however, cannot explain the continuation of short-term returns documented by Jegadeesh and Titman (1993). Like past long-term losers, stocks that have low short-term past returns tend to load positively on the value-factor (HML); like long-term winners, short-term past winners load negatively on the value-factor (HML). As it does for long-term returns, this pattern in the value-factor (HML) loadings predicts reversal rather than continuation for future returns. The continuation of short-term returns is thus left unexplained by the three-factor model.

Similarly, Schwert (2003) argues that the Fama-French three-factor model does not explain the momentum effect. When he runs the Fama and French three-factor model including the momentum factor (UMD), which is the difference in returns between portfolios with high and low prior return, the intercept remains statistically significant at the one percent level over the sample period between 1926 and 2001.

A number of studies have examined the continuation of short-term returns and the reversal of long-term returns in the Korean stock market. Sonu et al. (1994) document the existence of the contrarian premium using a three-year portfolio formation period and a three-year performance measurement period for stocks that are listed for at least six years. They estimate the cumulative abnormal returns over the portfolio formation period and classify the top quintile as the winner portfolio and the bottom quintile as the loser portfolio. The first formation period is between 1980 and 1982 and the last formation period is between 1987 and 1989. The first measurement period is between 1983 and 1985, and the last measurement period is between 1990 and 1992. They calculate the cumulative abnormal returns (CAR) of eight winner portfolios and loser portfolios for 36 months and calculate the average cumulative abnormal returns

(ACAR) for each portfolio. Following DeBondt and Thaler (1985), they use the market-adjusted excess return model. They find that the ACAR of the winner portfolios and the loser portfolios is -7.99% and 47.25%, respectively, in the subsequent 36 months after the portfolio formation, which gives the difference of 55.24% (t=3.298). The difference in return between the extreme portfolios from this contrarian strategy in the Korean stock market is 2.24 times higher than the difference (24.60%) observed by DeBondt and Thaler in the U.S.

Another study which examines the long-term reversal in the Korean stock market is Kim and Jeong (2008). Within a sample of Korean firms from 1987 to 2002, they document return reversals from the past performance of individual stocks using buy-and-hold abnormal returns. They find that cross-sectional contrarian premium over the one- to 36-month holding period is significantly positive. In the 12-month formation period, the contrarian premium can be explained by the systematic risk factors in the Fama-French three-factor model, but in the 24- and 36- month formation periods, the contrarian premium cannot be explained by such risk factors, but by investor overreaction.

Following Jegadeesh and Titman (1993), Lee and Ahn (2002) examine the performance of investment strategies that are based on the information contained in the past returns. They show that the contrarian strategy generally yields positive and statistically significant returns over long horizons for individual stocks and that stock beta or industry component is not the likely source of the performance. In addition, the momentum strategy yields positive and statistically significant returns at long horizons at the industry level and stock beta, firm size, BE/ME, and firm-specific components are the likely sources of the performance. Therefore, they conclude that the long-term reversal effect exists at the individual stock level and the momentum effect exists at the industry level in the Korean stock market.

Kho (1997) examines the profitability of the momentum strategies, buying long past short-run winner stocks and selling short past short-run loser stocks in both the Korean and the U.S. stock markets. He documents that the momentum strategy generates a monthly abnormal return of 1% which is statistically significant in the U.S. stock market over the period between 1963 and 1989. The profitability of the strategy remains statistically significant even after controlling the systematic risk or in the subsample analysis which uses the stock beta-sorted portfolios. In the Korean stock market, however, the strategy yields a monthly abnormal return of -0.34% which is statistically insignificant over the period between 1980 and 1989. Controlling for systematic risk or using stock beta-sorted portfolios does not affect the results. Thus, he concludes that the momentum effect does not exist in the Korean stock market.

Park and Jee (2006) examine whether the profitability of the momentum strategy and contrarian strategy is affected by the individual stock return volatility or the stock market volatility in Korea over the period between 1980 and 2003. They find that the momentum strategy yields significant returns only from 1980 to 1986 when the stock market volatility is the lowest during the sample period and that the contrarian strategy generates significant profit in other sub-periods. They examine the effect of the firm-level volatility on the performance of the momentum/contrarian strategy by forming portfolios based on the individual stock return volatility. The momentum strategy earns significant profits in the portfolio composed of firms with low volatility while the contrarian strategy is profitable when using portfolios composed of firms with high volatility. In summary, not only the past performance of stock return but also the stock return volatility must be considered in implementing such strategies to generate returns.

Yoon and Kim (2009) raise questions about the methodology employed in verifying the superiority of the momentum strategy and contrarian strategy. Specifically, their "Monte Carlo Reality Check" procedure adopted by White (2000) shows that the research method for testing the significance of momentum and contrarian strategy has significant levels of distortion. Therefore, it is very likely that the existing research would wrongfully conclude the superiority of such strategies based on the positive performance when the portfolio returns follow a random walk. They expand the formation and investment periods to a maximum of 36 months using monthly data between May 1985 and November 2007 for 230 individual stocks listed on the Korean Stock Exchange. They find that the superiority of the momentum and the contrarian strategy can be determined by whether the mean return outperforms the dollar cost average return of KOSPI. However, if the Sharpe ratio, which measures both the return and the risk of an investment strategy, is used, neither the momentum nor the contrarian strategy is superior to the dollar cost average return of KOSPI. They conclude that when considering risk, one cannot reject a weak-form efficient market hypothesis (EMH) on the grounds that the momentum strategy and the contrarian strategy are superior to investing in the stock market index in Korea.

In sum, most research except for Yoon and Kim (2009) find consistent evidence that the long-term reversal effect exists in the Korean stock market. And the momentum effect exists at the industry level, but not at the firm level as reported in Lee and Ahn (2002). As Park and Jee (2006) document, however, the momentum strategy would be profitable when the stock market volatility or the individual stock volatility in the portfolio is low.

2. Short-Term Interest Rate and Dividend Yield

If market returns vary because of underlying economic fundamentals which can be revealed through various indicators, such as yield spreads, dividend yields, and momentum, the time-series predictability of returns would not be an anomaly that would allow investors to trade to make abnormal profits. However, it is still questionable whether the time-series predictability of returns is evidence of market inefficiency, or simply evidence of time-varying equilibrium expected returns. Many papers have provided empirical evidence for a small degree of predictability in stock returns based on prior information (Fama and Schwert, 1977; Keim and Stambaugh, 1986; Campbell, 1987; French, Schwert, and Stambaugh, 1987; Fama and French, 1988; Kothari and Shanken, 1997; Baker and Wurgler, 2000).

Fama and Schwert (1977) provide the empirical evidence that excess returns to the CRSP value weighted portfolio of NYSE stocks are negatively related to the expected component of the inflation rate during the 1953~1971 period. Using CRSP data for the period between 1927 and 1986, Fama and French (1988) show that aggregate dividend yields predict subsequent stock returns. Many subsequent studies have extended this finding and several have questioned aspects of the statistical procedures used, including Schwert (2003). By using the Cowles (1939) data for 1872~1926 and additional CRSP data for 1987~2000, he shows that the incremental data both before and after the 1927~1986 period studied by Fama and French produces a much weaker relation between aggregate dividend yields and subsequent stock returns.

Torous, Valkanov, and Yan (2004) argue that statistical inference in predictive regressions depends on the order of integration for the explanatory variable. They investigate the effects of the uncertainty surrounding the commonly used explanatory variables' order of integration on inferences drawn in predictive regressions. When they use the traditional confidence intervals ignoring uncertainty surrounding the order of integration of the explanatory variables such as log dividend yield series or the book-to-market ratio, they find that those variables reliably forecast long horizon (12, 24, and 48 months) CRSP value weighted average returns both in the entire sample for 1926~1994 period and the subsamples. However, once they explicitly allow the uncertainty about the order of integration of the explanatory variables and rely on the Bonferroni statistics, this predictability is substantially reduced, leaving evidence only in the post-1952 sample and then only at relatively short horizons which are less than three months.

Lewellen (2004) show that dividend yield predicts market returns during the period from 1946 to 2000 and that book-to-market and the earnings-price ratio predict returns during the shorter sample period from 1963 to 2000. Campbell and Yogo (2006) provide the test that is robust to the persistence problem and they find that the earnings-price ratio reliably predicts returns at all frequencies (annual, quarterly, and monthly) in the sample period 1926~2002. The dividend/price ratio also predicts returns at annual frequency, but they fail to reject the null hypothesis at quarterly and monthly frequencies.

Unlike the U.S. studies which show empirical evidence for predictability of stock returns based on financial ratios, little predictable power of such prior information for stock returns is reported in Korea. Kim and Kim (2004) examine whether aggregate financial ratios and market interest rates predict stock returns in Korea. They employ both OLS regression model and Lewellen's approach with dividend yields and earnings-price ratios for the January 1984 to December 2003 sample period, and with market interest rates for the January 1987 to December 2003 sample period. No statistically significant relationship is found in either the OLS or Lewellen model between monthly stock market return and value weighted dividend yield. The prediction of the divided yield ratio exists at the 5% significance level in OLS model over the period between 1984 and 1996 but no significance is found in the bias adjusted regression analysis by Lewellen over the same period. For 1987~2003 period, no statistically significant relations between the stock market return and the market interest rate in both the OLS and Lewellen model. However, the prediction of the earnings-price ratio exists at the 5% significance level both in OLS model and in Lewellen's approach over the period between 1984 and 2003.

IV. Returns to Different Types of Markets

1. IPO Markets

There is a voluminous literature that has studied large returns available to investors who can purchase stocks in an initial public underwritten firm-commitment offering at the offering price. There are two persistent anomalies that characterize IPOs. One is the first-day underpricing and the other is the long-term underperformance of IPOs. Ritter and Welch (2002) report the first-day IPO price appreciation of close to 20%, on average, during 1980~2001, while Aggarwal and Rivoli (1990) report the long-term (over a year) performance of IPOs to be -13.73% on average during 1977~1987. To resolve both short- and long-term anomalies of IPOs, considerable research effort has enabled substantial analytical advances and provided empirical insights into this subject.

1.1 Explaining the Short-term IPO Anomalies

McDonald and Fisher (1972) test a number of hypotheses, based on the efficient market model, with data on 142 IPOs of common stock offered in the first quarter 1969. They find significantly large market adjusted returns for the initial subscribers in the first week following the offering. The mean excess return to initial purchasers in the first week after offering was 28.5%, which is statistically significant at the 5% level. However, one cannot reject the hypothesis that issues with high initial rates of return have rates of return for the remainder of the first year equivalent to that of the entire population of new issues. Thus, consistent with the efficient market notion of rapid adjustment of prices to available information, the early price behavior has no value in predicting later behavior in the IPO markets.

Ibbotson (1975) studies both the initial performance on the randomly selected 120 IPOs out of newly issued common stocks which were offered to the public during the period between 1960 and 1969. He confirms that average initial performance (measured by risk-adjusted returns) is positive (11.4 percent). This positive initial performance indicates that new issue offerings are underpriced. Ritter (1984) analyzes the hot issue market (January 1980~March 1981) during which the average initial return on unseasoned new issues of common stock was 48.4% and the cold issue market (the rest of the 1977~1982 period) during which the average initial return was merely 16.3%. He investigates an equilibrium explanation for this difference in average initial returns but that explanation is found to be insufficient.

Chalk and Peavy (1987) examine the daily returns for 649 firms that went public between 1975 and 1982. They report the mean return of 21.65% on the initial day and 0.97% on the second day, both of which are statistically significant at the one percent level. Also, the entire aftermarket period from the initial offering day through 190 days had a cumulative return of 17.99 %. Miller and Reilly (1987) examine daily returns for 510 initial public offerings during their first week of trading, and four weeks after the offering over the period between 1982 and 1983. They find that the market adjusts to any mispricing during the first day of trading, and that excess returns are not available to investors who trade in the after-market.

1.2 Explaining the Long-Term IPO Anomalies

Aggarwal and Rivoli (1990) conduct a comprehensive analysis of long-term aftermarket price behavior of 1,580 common stock IPOs. They find that IPOs are subject to overvaluation or fads in early aftermarket trading. The returns to investors purchasing in early aftermarket trading and holding for one year are -13.73%, which is significantly negative after adjusting for market movements. This pattern is evident in aggregate, over time, and in various cross-sectional groupings.

Ritter (1991) shows that the initial public offerings are overpriced in the long-run by examining 1,526 IPOs that went public in the U.S. in the 1975~1984 period. In the three years after going public these firms significantly underperformed a set of comparable firms matched by size and industry based on the three-year holding period returns and the three-year wealth relatives (WR) as a performance measure, defined as

$$WR = \frac{1 + average\ three\ year\ total\ return\ on\ IPOs}{1 + average\ three\ year\ total\ return\ on\ matching\ firms}$$

The mean IPO 3-year holding period return is only 34.47% compared to a mean of 61.86% for the matching firms and the wealth relative value is less than one. He provides the evidence that many firms go public near the peak of industry-specific fads when investors are irrationally over-optimistic about the future potential of the industry.

If firms choose to go public when investors are irrationally over-optimistic about the future potential of certain industries, then the significant returns in the early aftermarket may not necessarily be the result of intentional underpricing. Levis (1993) tests the robustness of Ritter's conclusions by examining 712 IPOs that are listed in the London Stock Exchange in 1980~1988 period. He shows that initial public offerings in the UK underperformed a number of relevant benchmarks in the 36 full months of public listing following their first day of trading. Thus, the long-run underperformance of initial public offerings is not a phenomenon unique to U.S. new issues.

Teoh, Welch, and Wong (1998) explore a possible source for this over-optimism for the possible source of the long-run IPO underperformance. They examine whether discretionary accruals predict the cross-sectional variation in post-IPO long-run stock return performance. Other things equal, the greater the earnings management at the time of the offering, the larger the ultimate price correction. They find that issuers with unusually high accruals in the IPO year experience poor stock return performance in the three years thereafter.

1.3 Explaining the Short- and Long-Term IPO Anomalies in the Korean Stock Market

Kang (1994) examines the short- and long-term performance of IPOs of common stock offered over the period between 1988 and 1991 in Korean stock market. He finds significantly large market adjusted returns of 90%, on average, for the initial subscribers in the first day of the offering. This extraordinary return cannot be consistent with the efficient market for the new issues. The mean excess return to initial purchasers in the first week after offering remains positive, which implies it takes longer time to find the equilibrium in the Korean stock market unlike the U.S. The average return on the strategy that buys the offered stock at the closing price of the offering day and sells it on the 6th trading day was 5%, on average, which brings a question to the efficiency of the IPO market. No significant trend of stock prices exists between a few days and one year after the offering. This shows that the abnormally underpriced IPO price finally finds it true value and remains stable in the aftermarket trading. He fails to find evidence to reject the hypothesis of an inefficient aftermarket, unlike Aggarwal and Rivoli (1990) and Ritter (1991) who find overvaluation in the aftermarket in U.S.

Lim and Lee (1995) examine the three year performance of stocks that were initially offering in the period between January 1980 and March 1990 to study the long-run aftermarket performance of IPOs in Korea. To control the effect of the regulation change June 1988 which allows the underwriter to determine the initial offering price, they examine the performance of the IPO aftermarket with two separate periods - before and after the regulation change. They find that since the seasoned offerings are considered positive signals to the market, whether the underwritten firm issues new shares after the IPO is the most influent factor for the long-run performance. They suggest that the effects of subsequent equity offerings should be controlled to measure the long-run performance of IPOs more properly. When they controlled the effect of subsequent seasoned equity offerings, the IPO stocks underperform the stock market in the long-run. The average cumulated return on the IPO stocks over the period between the third day of the offering and three years after the offering is -11.53%, -7.5%, and -15.28% over the whole sample period, and before and after the regulation change in 1988, respectively. This long-run underperformance of IPOs is consistent with Ritter (1991) albeit the magnitudes are rather small. However, Choi and Huh (2000) find the positive long-run performance of the IPOs if the performance measurement period start two months after the offering with the data examined in Lim and Lee (1995).

Ihm (1997) analyzes the short- and long-term performance of the IPO stock between 1988 and 1994. He considers the effect of the daily limit of the price change on the aftermarket performance of IPOs. He finds that when the limit of the daily return is considered IPO stock realizes an abnormal initial yield that is much higher than the abnormal return when the limit is not considered. This abnormal initial return tends to be higher in the bullish market. IPO stocks gain additional excess return after the offering, and it is mostly achieved around one month after the offering. In Korean IPO market, fads exist in the early period of the offering, but such overshooting phenomenon disappears after around one month, the range of downward adjustment is bigger in the bearish market. In the long-run, IPO stock does not outperform the stock market, on average.

Ihm and Choi (1998) study 399 firms that were initially offered to the public between 1988 and 1994. To calculate the excess return, they use not only the return on the Korea Composite Stock Price Index (KOSPI) but also the return on the comparable size portfolio. They find that Korean IPO stock realizes positive excess earning in the early period of the aftermarket. Relaxing price restricting effect of the price limit system, they find that the excess earning increases. To examine the long-term performance of the IPO stocks after the offering, they analyze the cumulative average residual pattern for 36 months and the wealth relatives used by Ritter (1991). They find that the long-term performance of IPO stocks in Korea is superior to the stock market index.

Choi and Huh (2000) study the long-term performance of IPO stocks between 1992 and 1996 with a number of holding periods. For the performance measure, they use the BHAR, the cumulative abnormal return (CAR), and the abnormal return from the return across time and securities (RATS) model, three-factor model and calendar-time abnormal returns (CTAR). They use KOSPI, total market portfolio, comparable size portfolio, and Fama-French size/book-to-market portfolio for matching samples used for estimating the expected return. The reason to use various long-term measurement sample and matching sample is to find the occurrence of bad model problems that Fama (1998) points out. With KOSPI as a benchmark, the long-term performance after 36 months is 36% (BHAR) and 58% (CAR). Since the bad model problems can occur, the credibility of the measurement result about the effect of domestic IPO market will be compromised. With matching portfolios that control the size effect or relative financial risk, BHAR and CAR show mostly negative values. Especially in case of the RATS model, three-factor model and CTAR, there is slight difference in statistical significance but show negative values in almost all holding periods. Similar to the foreign countries, therefore, they confirm that IPOs in Korean stock market also show poor long-term performance.

With the IPO stocks listed on the KOSDAQ market from July 1996 to December 1998, Kim and Moon (2002) examine the long-term performance by using the monthly stock price data for 36 months period. They use CAR, BHAR and relative return to benchmark portfolio represented by the relative wealth (WR) to measure the long-term performance. For matching samples, in addition to the market index (KOSDAQ) and the industry index, they use four size (MV) portfolios that are formed by all listed stocks excluding IPO stocks based on the market value at the end of the offering year for the IPO stocks to control all bad model problems and 16 book-to-market (BV/MV) portfolios. They find that

CARs relative to the KOSDAQ index return and the industry index return were as 256% and 190%, respectively. With the benchmark of the size portfolio and book-to-market portfolio, CARs are 16% and -5%, respectively. BHARs relative to the KOSDAQ index return and the industry index return are 107% and 51% and BHARs are -55% and -101% with the benchmark of the size portfolio and book-to-market portfolio. The wealth relatives with the market return and the industry index return are bigger than one to show high long-term performance. The wealth relatives with the size and book-to-market portfolio are smaller than one indicating poor long-term performance.

Joh, Koh, and Kwon (2003) select 62 sample firms out of the IPOs in Korean stock market between 1990 and 1997 to examine the long-term performance. They use CAR, BHAR and WR in order to measure the long-term performance of IPO stock and select a matching firm that is most similar to IPO firm. They find that the average CAR and the average BHAR are -30.98% (t-value = -2.21) and -59.77% (t-value = -9.41), respectively. Further, the wealth relative is 0.51 for 36 months after the offering, which confirms that IPO firms show poor long-term performance compared to the matching companies.

In sum, consistent with the findings in the U.S. literature, the IPO performance in the Korean stock market is highly positive on the offering day (in the short-run) and negative in the long-run. However, the magnitude of the effect is rather sensitive to the conditions of the capital market.

2. SEO Markets

2.1 Foreign Studies about the Short-Term Announcement Effect

Mikkelson and Partch (1986), Asquith and Mullins (1986), Kalay and Shimrat (1987) and Dierkens (1991) provide the evidence that the announcement of the seasoned equity offerings (SEOs) causes statistically significant negative excess return in the U.S. stock market where the seasoned equity offering is mostly conducted through a common public offering and issue at market price. But for cases that the method of paid-in capital increase is not a common public offering, such as the equity carve-outs by Schipper and Smith (1986), paid-in capital increase through private offering by Wruck (1989), paid-in capital increase through right offering to shareholders by Heinkel and Schwartz (1986), and paid-in capital increase through the private offering for small corporations by Hertzel and Smith (1993), the announcements of the paid-in capital increase are reported to cause positive excess return.

2.2 Foreign Studies about the Long-Term Price Effect

Loughran and Ritter (1995) study the long-term performance of 3,702 SEOs conducted between 1970 and 1990. The average holding period return for three years after the increase of capital is 15% in corporations with increase of capital but 48% in corporations with no increase of capital. In addition, the average holding period return for five years after capital increase is 33.4% in corporations with increase of capital but 92.8% in corporations with no increase of capital. This demonstrates that firms with paid-in capital increase show inferior performance in price earnings ratio compared to the firms with no paid-in capital increase. They confirm that such phenomenon still exists even after controlling the three Fama-French factors.

Spiess and Affleck-Graves (1995), Lee (1997) confirm that long-term poor performances exist in all firms with capital increase. Especially, Spiess and Affleck-Graves (1995) report that poor performance appears more clearly in small firms, new firms, firms with low book-to-market ratio, and firms listed on NASDAQ.

2.3 Explaining the Short- and Long-term SEO Performance in Korean Stock Market

Shin (1995) examines the stock price reaction at the time of disclosing the paid-in capital increase by selecting 548 samples out of 1,529 announcements of SEOs between 1985 and 1993, according to the standard method of sample selection. He estimates the abnormal return using the market model. He finds that the cumulative abnormal return for three days before and after the announcement is, on average, 1.02%, which is statistically significant. Such result is inconsistent with the previous studies showing that the announcement effect of paid-in capital increase has negative average abnormal return in the U.S. stock market.

Yoon (1996) examines the announcement effect of SEOs for 490 companies over the period between 1993 and 1995, excluding five companies that conducted allotment to the third party or commodity allotment and one company under court administration. He classifies methods of SEOs into the right offering and the rights with standby underwriting, and studies the excess return for two days after the announcement of SEOs. He also classifies the sample firms into three subgroups, manufacturing firms with no increase of capital stock without consideration, financial firms with no increase of capital stock without consideration, and firms with the announcement of capital increase. He finds that the average excess return of right offering method is 1.05% and the average excess return of the rights with standby underwriting is 0.67%. Both methods gain statistically significant positive values and there is no statistically significant difference between two methods. In both methods, the average excess returns of the manufacturing firms with no increase of capital stock without consideration are statistically significantly positive. For financial firms, however, the average excess returns are statistically insignificantly positive in both methods. The average excess returns of firms that conducted capital increase with and without consideration are statistically significantly positive in both methods, and it shows bigger positive reactions compared to the case of disclosing only paid-in capital increase.

Yoon (1999) examines the short-term excess return and long-term excess return on 213 issues of common stock opened to the pubic between 1990 and 1993. He calculates the excess return using the market model. The average excess return on the day of announcement is a statistically significantly positive in the t-test, but the results are insignificant in the Z-Sign test and the Wilcoxon signed-rank t-test. The ratio of excess return exceeding zero are 49~52%. It is difficult to conclude that such result corresponds to that of prior literature that the disclosure of paid-in capital increase provides positive information to stock prices. In addition, the long-term cumulative average return on the firms with paid-in capital increase during that period is about -15%, which is statistically significant.

Kim and Kong (2000) study the long-term performance of SEO firms between 1987 and 1997. They select the matching Non-SEO firms that have similar size, book-to-market ratio and profitability to compare the excess returns for 3 years after announcement. For excess return calculation model, they use both market model and market adjusted model. CARs for five days before and after announcement are statistically significant positive in the t-test regardless of the excess return calculation model. For three years after the announcement, firms with capital increase show statistically significant lower BHAR compared to firms with no capital increase. When the market average return is used instead of the return of the matching firms, a similar poor performance appeared in firms with capital increase. It is found that poor performance generally continued in firms with capital increase when the CARs are used for the long-term performance measure. These findings suggest that the long-

term price earnings ratio of firms with capital increase after the announcement is poor compared to the return of the matching firms and the average market return. In the United States, both short-term announcement
effect and long-term price effect of the seasoned offerings are negative.
In Korea, however, the announcement effect is positive and the price effect
is negative.

Jang, Lee, and Hwang (2010) examine the relationship between the announcement effect of the SEOs and the stock issue method for 10 days
before and after the announcement. For 251 SEOs (50 offerings to shareholders and 210 allotments to the third party) between 2000 and 2007,
they calculate the excess return using the market adjusted model. In case
of offerings to shareholders method, no significant reaction appeared from
the -10 day to the occurrence day, which is the day of submitting the
paid-in capital increase decision report. On the contrary, a significant negative excess return appears on +1 day and no significant change appears
after that. In case of the allotment to the third party method, the excess
returns are similar to the offering to shareholders method from the -10
day to -1 day. On the day of occurrence, a big positive excess return
appeared, but no significant reaction appears after the day of occurrence,
which is similar to the period before the day of occurrence. These findings
suggest that in Korean stock market, the investors consider the offering
to shareholders method a positive signal and the allotment to the third
party method a negative signal.

In sum, the performance of SEOs in the U.S. stock markets has been
reported to be poor in the short-run as well as in the long-run, especially
for small firms, new firms, firms with low book-to-market ratio, and firms
listed on NASDAQ. However, the announcement effect of SEOs in Korea
has yielded positive abnormal returns contrary to the U.S. evidence. In
the long-run, excess returns of SEO stocks in Korea are negative.

3. M&A Markets

3.1 Foreign Studies about the Post-Merger Performance

Several studies have investigated whether acquisitions create value, and they have noted that while the target shareholders generally fare pretty well, most acquisitions fail to create value for acquirers. One interpretation of this post-merger loss to the acquirer is that they overpay and that it takes the market some time to gradually learn about this mistake. Agrawal, Jaffe, and Mandelker (1992) examine the post-merger performance of acquiring firms, and they find that stockholders of acquiring firms suffer a statistically significant loss of about 10% over the five-year post-merger period. With a comprehensive sample of U.S. acquisitions in the period between 1966 and 1986, Loderer and Martin (1992) show that acquiring firms underperform a control portfolio only during the three years but not five years following the acquisition. Especially, the negative post-merger performance of the acquirer occurs mainly in the 1960s and 1970s and disappears in the 1980s.

Summarizing the findings of 21 studies, Bruner (2004) consistently finds evidence of significant target abnormal returns while acquirer firm shareholders essentially break-even earn their required rate of returns. He argues that M&A is at least a value-maintaining proposition. Hazelkorn, Zenner, and Shivdasani (2004) study 1,547 M&As announced between January 1990 and January 2002 by non-financial U.S. acquirers. They find that on average, the acquiring firm's stock loses around 0.5%~0.7% on a market-adjusted basis around the initial announcement date. Controlling for size and the form of payment, they find that the market reacts more positively to acquisitions of private companies than to acquisitions of whole public companies.

3.2 Studies about the Post-Merger Performance in Korea

Oh (1994) examines the stock price of target and acquiring firms for 60 months before and after the merger using the M&As announced in Korean stock market between 1984 and 1988. He finds that there was no change in the return on the target firm and argues that there is no medium and long-term effect of merger in Korea. However, this result cannot be generalized because only six firms are examined in his sample.

Jung and Park (1999) study 120 M&As announced between 1980 and 1994. They calculate the excess return of the acquiring firm's stock for three years after the day of merger. In the whole sample, the cumulative abnormal return (CAR) and the buy and hold abnormal return (BHAR) of the acquirer showed negative values for three years after the day of merger, albeit no statistical significance is reached. Also, they find that the long-term performance of the acquirer is significantly negative for transactions that acquired the firms under the same affiliation or the privately held firms. In the regression model, the underperformance of the acquirer gets worsens when the target firms are under the same affiliation and privately held before the merger. These results suggest that M&As between firms under the same affiliation have been used not for value creation but for delaying the bankruptcy of weak subsidiaries in Korea.

Following Fama and French (1992), Seo and Sin (2003) form benchmark portfolios with similar size and book-to-market ratios to calculate the relative long-term performance of the acquiring firms after the merger. They find that for three years following the mergers, acquiring firms show a negative performance compared to the benchmark portfolios. Also, the acquiring firm produces far larger negative accumulated excess yield ratios when it merged a growth firm than a value firm. Acquiring firms with a sizable cash reserve ratio at the time of merger consistently underperform the benchmark portfolios over the long term. Firms acquiring a non-affiliate outperform the ones acquiring an affiliate.

Kang and Kim (2009) examine 396 acquisitions announced and completed by non-financial companies listed in the Korea Exchange (KRX) from January 2000 to June 2008. They find that acquiring shareholders consistently earn positive abnormal returns for as long as ten days prior to the announcement date, but they seldom gain abnormal returns after the announcement date. The CARs (-5, 1) around the announcement date, on average, amounts to 5.9%, statistically significant at the 1% level. Unlike the previous studies, acquirers of diversifying acquisitions significantly outperform in shareholders' abnormal returns relative to acquirers of non-diversifying acquisitions. They argue that the stock market highly values developing new business areas for future growth through diversifying acquisitions. Consistent with Seo and Sin (2003), they find that acquirers of non-affiliated mergers significantly outperform in shareholders' abnormal returns relative to those of affiliated mergers. They also find that announcement returns are inversely related to the acquirers' firm size. This size effect is significant and robust in all the variations of regression models. Although the foreign literature documents significant relations between the form of acquisition payment and announcement returns, they find no evidence in Korea that the method of payment conveys information about the acquirer's intrinsic value.

In sum, U.S. literature has found that the performance of the acquiring firms after the M&As is negative in the long-run but that this underperformance depends on the sample period or the characteristics of the M&As, not on market inefficiency. In Korea, however, the long-term underperformance of acquirer is persistent and statistically significant. Especially, the greater the announcement effect of M&As, the more the acquiring firm's stock suffers. Therefore, we may conclude that Korean stock markets seem to overreact more to good news in the short-term compared to the U.S.

V. Implications for Market Efficiency and Corporate Finance

Persistent patterns in security returns and existence of market regularities do not necessarily indicate that capital markets are inefficient since the patterns and regularities may be manifestations of sample-specific artifacts caused by data problems and/or by using imperfect asset pricing models. Empirical evidence, after controlling for data problems, shows that cross-sectional and time-series anomalies have survived for a long period of time even with the existence of investors' trading activities which exploit arbitrage opportunities. The incompleteness of pricing models theory is more reliable than the inefficiency argument in explaining the cause of the anomalous phenomena. But the anomalous findings on IPO, M&A, and SEO markets show mostly short-term positive returns and long-term negative returns, which indicates that the market seems to overreact more to good news in the short-term but ultimately makes a reversion to the stationary state. This suggests that the general trend of hot and slow reactions to the true price levels reveals a fair amount of market inefficiency.

Though the empirical findings on the market anomalies do not clearly suggest that the financial market is efficient, they have important implications for corporate finance. First, to financial managers, it is difficult to make financial decisions under the assumption that the market-determined asset price may not correct itself in the sense that it reflects all available corporate information. Therefore, corporate managers must enforce investor relations (IR) activities to narrow the information gap. Second, when financial managers are involved in corporate activities such as project selection, capital structure, dividend, IPO, M&A, or SEO, they should consider each relevant anomalous phenomenon in connection with maximization of firm value. Since the momentum related anomaly, the predictability of dividend yields and short-term interest rates are relatively weak in Korea, their effects on future stock prices may not be considered substantially in the financial decision making process. Instead, financial managers may take into account the implications of contrarian strategies which generate positive abnormal returns in Korea and new issue markets in Korea. These two phenomena, respectively, imply the mean reverting behavior of stock prices and a high level of information asymmetry in the relevant markets. Thus, financial managers should be more concerned with the market timing of finance-related decisions such as capital budgeting, capital structure restructuring and new issue of stocks and bonds.

Finally, SEO announcement which generates a positive return to corporations in Korea, gives the opposite signal to financial managers compared to other countries such as the U.S. This might be interpreted as stock market placing more weight on SEO's reduction effect of financial distress cost than its dilution effect, since Korean companies have long suffered from high financial risk. Therefore, corporate financial policy should be designed to place more emphasis on the reduction of bankruptcy possibility rather than the dilution effect as far as investors are more sensitive to the financial distress in making SEO decisions.

VI. Conclusions

This paper reviews the Korean and foreign literature on capital market anomalies, which do not conform to the prediction by the asset pricing model. Many researchers have initially uncovered most of the anomalies in the U.S. stock market. In order to rule out the possibility that these anomalies are simply the outcome of an elaborate data snooping process, it is required to test the anomalies on an independent sample such as the international stock market data or data from different time periods. In a similar vein, voluminous Korean literature has examined whether the abnormal return patterns exist in the Korean stock market as well.

Most of the anomalies mentioned in the Korean literature show similar patterns to those reported in the literature abroad. The size effect, the book-to-market effect, and the January effect are evident in the Korean stock market. The long-term reversal effect is also evident, albeit the momentum effect has been reported to exist only on the industry level. Although many of the well-known anomalies have disappeared or at least weakened after the papers that highlighted them were published, some of the anomalies remain robust even in the recent period in Korea. Persistent evidence of these abnormal patterns in Korean stock returns may reflect that the level of market efficiency is slightly weaker compared to that in the U.S. market. We conjecture that the persistence of the anomalous patterns is partly caused by the practitioners' inactive exploitation of anomaly related profit opportunities as documented by prior literature.

There is an interesting difference in the empirical findings on the performance of SEO issuers between Korea and the U.S. While the U.S. literature provides evidence of the underperformance of SEO issuers, literature on this phenomenon in the Korean stock market has reported that the SEO issuers have gained abnormal positive returns upon announcement. It is more plausible to expect better performance of SEO issuers as they lower leverage by issuing more stocks to decrease their financial risk. To the best of our knowledge, the bankruptcy risk of relevant firms has not been properly controlled in the Korean literature. Thus, we suggest that researchers control for this risk to obtain reliable empirical result from SEO-related anomaly tests for future studies.

References

Agarwal, R. and P. Rivoli, "Fads in the Initial Public Offering Market?", *Financial Management*, Vol. 19(1990), pp. 45-57.

Agrawal, A., Jaffe, J., and Mandelker, G., "The Post-Merger Performance of Acquiring Firms: A Re-examination of an Anomaly", *Journal of Finance*, Vol. 47(1992), pp. 1605-1621.

Asquith, P. and D. W. Mullins, Jr., "Equity Issue and Offering Dilution", *Journal of Financial Economics*, Vol. 15(1986), pp. 61-89.

Baker, M. and J. Wurgler, "The Equity Share in New Issues and Aggregate Stock Returns", *Journal of Finance*, Vol. 55(2000), pp. 2219-2257.

Banz, R., "The Relationship between Return and Market Value of Common Stock", *Journal of Financial Economics*, Vol. 9(1981), pp. 3-18.

Blume, Marshall and Robert Stambaugh, "Biases in Computed Returns: An Application to the Size Effect", *Journal of Financial Economics,* Vol. 12(1983), pp. 387-404.

Bruner, R., "Where M&A Pays and Where it Strays: A Survey of the Research", *Journal of Applied Corporate Finance*, Vol. 16(2004).

Campbell, John Y., "Stock Returns and the Term Structure", *Journal of Financial Economics*, Vol. 18(1987), pp. 373-399.

Campbell, J. Y. and M. Yogo, "Efficient Tests of Stock Return Predictability", *Journal of Financial Economics*, Vol. 81(2006), pp. 27-60.

Chalk, A. and J. Peavy, "Initial Public Offerings: Daily Returns, Offering Types and the Price Effect", *Financial Analysts Journal*, (Sep/Oct. 1987), pp. 65-69.

Chang, Y. K. and C. T. Kim, "A Value Investment Strategy: Its Performance and Source", *Asia-Pacific Journal of Financial Studies*, Vol. 32(2003), pp. 165-208(in Korean).

장영광, 김종택, "한국 주식시장에서 가치투자전략의 투자성과와 그 원천",

증권학회지, 제32권 제2호(2003), pp. 165-208.

Choi, H. S. and S. H. Kim, "Regularities in Monthly Stock Returns in Korea", Books written by S. H. Sonu, Y. S. Yun et al., "Stock Price Volatility and Anomaly", Hakhyunsa, Seoul, Korea(1994), pp. 33-51 (in Korean).

최홍식, 김상환, "월별효과", 선우석호, 윤영섭외 공저, 주가변동과 이례현상, 학현사(1994), pp. 33-51.

Choi, M. S. and H. J. Huh, "Reconsidering Long-Run performance of IPOs", *Korean Journal of Finance*, Vol. 13(2000), pp. 99-122(in Korean).

최문수, 허형주, "신규공모주의 장기성과에 대한 재고찰", 재무연구, 제13권 제1호(2000), pp. 99-122.

Conrad, J. and G. Kaul, "Long-term Market Overreaction or Biases in Computed Returns?", *Journal of Finance*, Vol. 48(1993).

Cowles, A. III and Associates, *Common-Stock Indexes 2nd ed.*, Cowles Commission Monograph, Bloomington, Indiana, Principia Press Inc., Vol. 3(1939).

Cross, F., "The Behavior of Stock Price on Fridays and Mondays", *Financial Analysts Journal*, Vol. 29(1973), pp. 67-69.

Daniel, K. and S. Titman, "Evidence on the Characteristics of Cross-sectional Variation in Stock Returns", *Journal of Finance*, Vol. 52(1997), pp. 1-33.

Davis, J. L., E. F. Fama, and K. R. French, "Characteristics, Covariances and Average Returns", *Journal of Finance*, Vol. 55(2000), pp. 389-406.

DeBondt, W. F. M. and R. Thaler, "Does the Stock Market Overreact?", *Journal of Finance*, Vol. 40(1985), pp. 793-805.

Dierkens, N., "Information Asymmetry and Equity Issues", *Journal of Financial and Quantitative Analysis*, Vol. 26(1991), pp. 181-199.

Fama, E. F., "Market Efficiency, Long-term Returns, and Behavioral Finance", *Journal of Financial Economics*, Vol. 49(1998), pp. 283-306.

Fama, E. F. and K. R. French, "Dividend Yields and Expected Stock

Returns", *Journal of Financial Economics*, Vol. 22(1988), pp. 3-25.

Fama, E. F. and K. R. French, "The Cross-section of Expected Returns", *Journal of Finance*, Vol. 47(1992), pp. 427-465.

Fama, E. F. and K. R. French, "Common Risk Factors in the Returns on Stocks and Bonds", *Journal of Financial Economics*, Vol. 33(1993), pp. 3-56.

Fama, E. F. and K. R. French, "Multifactor Explanations of Asset Pricing Anomalies", *Journal of Finance*, Vol. 51(1996), pp. 55-84.

Fama, E. F. and G. W. Schwert, "Asset Returns and Inflation", *Journal of Financial Economics*, Vol. 5(1977), pp. 115-146.

French, K. R., "Stock Returns and the Weekend Effect", *Journal of Financial Economics,* Vol. 8(1980), pp. 55-70.

French, K. R., G. W. Schwert, and R. F. Stambaugh, "Expected Stock Returns and Volatility", *Journal of Financial Economics*, Vol. 19(1987), pp. 3-29.

Gibbons, M. R. and P. Hess, "Day of the Week Effects and Asset Returns", *Journal of Business*, Vol. 54(1981), pp. 579-596.

Gultekin, M. N. and N. B. Gultekin, "Stock Market Seasonality and the Turn of the Tax-Year Effect: Information Evidence", *Journal of Financial Economics*, Vol. 12(1983), pp. 469-481.

Hazelkorn, T., M. Zenner, and A. Shivdasani, "Creating Value with Mergers and Acquisitions", *Journal of Applied Corporate Finance*, Vol. 16(2004).

Heinkel, R. and E. Schwartz, "Rights versus Underwritten Offerings: An Asymmetric Information Approach", *Journal of Finance*, Vol. 41(1986), pp. 1-18.

Hertzel, M. and R. L. Smith, "Market Discounts and Shareholder Gains for Placing Equity Privately", *Journal of Finance*, Vol. 48(1993), pp. 459-485.

Ibbotson. R. G., "Price Performance of Common Stock New Issues", *Journal Financial Economics*, Vol. 2(1975), pp. 235-272.

Ihm, B. K., "The Long-and Short-Run Performance of IPOs and Operating Performance", *Korean Journal of Financial Management*, Vol. 14(1997), pp. 253-271(in Korean).

임병균, "IPO 주식의 장단기 성과와 영업성과", 재무관리연구, 제14권 제2호(1997), pp. 253-271.

Ihm, B. K. and H. S. Choi, "The Long-and Short-Run Performance of IPOs and Operating Performance of IPO Firms before and after Listing", *DAEHAN Journal of Business*, Vol. 18(1998), pp. 235-268(in Korean).

임병균, 최해술, "IPO 주식의 장, 단기 성과와 IPO 기업의 상장 전후 영업성과", 대한경영학회지, 제18권(1998), pp. 235-268.

Jang, J. Y., H. J. Lee, and S. H. Hwang, "The Effect of Seasoned Equity Offering Methods on Firm Characteristics and Stock Market Reaction Shareholder Priority Public Offering and Allotment to the Third Party", *Business Education Research*, Vol. 59(2010), pp. 83-105(in Korean).

장지영, 이혜진, 황성현, "주주배정 유상증자와 제 3자 배정 유상증자 방식에 따른 기업특성과 자본시장의 반응", 경영교육연구, 제59권(2010), pp. 83-105.

Jaffe, J. and R. Westerfield, "The Weekend Effect in Common Stock Returns: The International Evidence", *Journal of Finance*, Vol. 40(1985), pp. 433-454.

Jaffe, J. and R. Westerfield, "Patterns in Japanese Common Stock Returns: Day of the Week Effects and Turn of the Year Effects", *Journal of Financial and Quantitative Analysis*, Vol. 20(1985), pp. 261-272.

Jegadeesh, N. and S. Titman, "Returns to Buying Winners and Selling Loser: Implications for Stock Market Efficiency", *Journal of Finance*, Vol. 48(1993), pp. 65-91.

Joh, K. S., G. S. Koh and S. T. Kwon "A Study on the Long-run Performance of IPO", *Business Education Research*, Vol. 32(2003), pp. 267-286(in Korean).

조경식, 고강석, 권숙태, "최초공모주의 장기성과에 관한 연구", 경영교육연구, 제32권(2003), pp. 267-286.

Jung, H. C. and K. H. Park, "Postmerger Share-Price Performance of Acquiring Firms in the Korean Stock Market", *Korean Journal of Financial Management*, Vol. 16(1999), pp. 83-114(in Korean).
정형찬, 박경희, "합병일 이후 합병기업 주가의 장기성과", 재무관리연구, 제16권 제1호(1999), pp. 83-114.

Kalay, A. and A. Shimrat, "Firm Value and Seasoned Equity Issues: Price Pressure, Wealth Redistribution, or Negative Information", *Journal of Financial Economics*, Vol. 19(1987), pp. 109-126.

Kam, H. K., "An Empirical Study of Relationship between Fundamental Variables and Korean Stock Market", *Korean Journal of Financial Management*, Vol. 14(1997), pp. 21-55(in Korean).
감형규, "기본적 변수와 주식수익률의 관계에 관한 실증적 연구", 재무관리연구, 제14권 제2호(1997), pp. 21-55.

Kang, H. S., "IPO underpricing in Korean Stock Market Returns", Books written by S. H. Sonu and Y. S. Yun et al., "Stock Price Volatility and Anomaly", Hakhyunsa, Seoul, Korea(1994), pp. 213-228(in Korean).
강효석, "IPO 효과", 선우석호, 윤영섭외 공저, 주가변동과 이례현상, 학현사(1994), pp. 213-228.

Kang, H. S. and S. P. Kim, "Long-Run Performance of Mergers and Acquisitions in Korea", *Journal of Money and Finance*, Vol. 23(2009), pp. 63-101(in Korean).
강효석, 김성표, "기업 인수합병의 장기성과", 금융연구, 제23권 제4호(2009), pp. 63-101.

Keim, D. B., "Size-Related Anomalies and Stock Market Seasonality: Further Empirical Evidence", *Journal of Financial Economics*, Vol. 12(1983), pp. 13-32.

Keim, D. B. and R. F. Stambaugh, "A Further Investigation of the Weekend Effect in Stock Returns", *Journal of Finance*, Vol. 39(1984), pp. 819-834.

Kho, B. C., "Risk Premium and Profitability of Contrarian Strategy", *Korean Journal of Financial Management*, Vol. 14(1997), pp. 1-21(in Korean).

고봉찬, "위험 프레미엄과 상대적세력 투자전략의 수익성", 재무관리연구, 제14권 제1호(1997), pp. 1-21.

Kim, B. G. and M. J. Kong, "Long-Run Abnormal Stock Returns and Operating Performance Following Seasoned Equity Offerings", *Korean Journal of Financial Management*, Vol. 17(2000), pp. 13-44(in Korean).

김명기, 공명재, "유상증자 후의 장기 주식수익률 및 영업성과", 재무관리연구, 제17권 제1호(2000), pp. 13-44.

Kim, B. J. and H. J. Jeong, "A Study on the Long-term Reversal in the Korean Stock Market", *Korean Journal of Finance*, Vol. 21(2008), pp. 29-76(in Korean).

김병준, 정호정, "한국 주식 수익률의 장기 반전현상에 관한 연구", 재무연구, 제21권 제2호(2008), pp. 29-76.

Kim, D. H. and C. H. Chung, "The Day of the Week Effect on Stock Market Volatility: Evidence from the Korean Stock Market", *Journal of Financial Engineering*, Vol. 3(2003), pp. 43-60(in Korean).

김동회, 정정현, "한국증권시장의 변동성과 요일효과", 금융공학연구, 제3권 제1호(2004), pp. 43-60.

Kim, K. Y. and Y. B. Kim, "Testing the Predictability of Stock Return in the Korean Stock Market", *Journal of Industrial Economic*, Vol. 17(2004), pp. 1255-1271(in Korean).

김규영, 김영빈, "한국 주식시장에서 수익률의 예측에 관한 연구", 산업경제연구, 제17권 제4호(2004), pp. 1255-1271.

Kim, S. C. and J. Y. Kim, "Firm Size and Book-to-Market Factors in Korean Stock Returns", *Korean Journal of Finance*, Vol. 13(2000), pp. 21-47(in Korean).

김석진, 김지영, "기업규모와 장부가/시가 비율과 주식수익률의 관계", 재무연구, 제13권 제2호(2000), pp. 21-47.

Kim, S. M. and S. J. Moon, "Long-Run Performance in KOSDAQ Market", *Korean Securities Association Symposium*(2002)(in Korean).
김성민, 문승주, "코스닥 등록기업 주식의 장기성과", 한국증권학회 학술발표회(2002).

Kim, S. P. and Y. S. Yun, "Fundamental Variables, Macroeconomic Factors, Risk Characteristics and Equity Returns", *Korean Journal of Financial Management*, Vol. 16(1999), pp. 179-213(in Korean).
김성표, 윤영섭, "기본적 변수, 거시경제요인, 기업특성적 위험과 주식수익률", 재무관리연구, 제16권 제2호(1999), pp. 179-213.

Kim, S. U., "Analysis of Size Effect in Korean Stock Market Returns", Books written by Sukho Sonu and YS Yun et al., "Stock Price Volatility and Anomaly", Hakhyunsa, Seoul, Korea(1994), pp. 131-140(in Korean).
김선웅, "기업규모 효과", 선우석호, 윤영섭외 공저, 주가변동과 이례현상, 학현사(1994), pp. 131-140.

Kothari, S. P. and J. Shanken, "Book-To-Market, Dividend Yield, and Expected Market Returns: A Time-Series Analysis", *Journal of Financial Economics*, Vol. 44(1997), pp. 169-203.

Lakonishok, J. and S. Smidt, "Are Seasonal Anomalies Real? A Ninety-Year Perspective", *Review of Financial Studies*, Vol. 1(1988), pp. 403-425.

Lee, I., "Do Firms Knowingly Sell Overvalued Equity", *Journal of Finance*, Vol. 52(1997), pp. 1439-1466.

Lee, J. D. and Y. G. Ahn, "Performance Analysis of Investment Strategy in the Korean Stock Market", *Asia-Pacific Journal of Financial Studies*, Vol. 30(2002), pp. 33-71(in Korean).
이정도, 안영규, "한국 주식시장에서 계속투자전략과 반대투자전략의 수익성분석", 증권학회지, 제30권(2002), pp. 33-71.

Levis, M., "The Long-run Performance of Initial Public Offerings: The UK

Experience 1980~1988", *Financial Management*, Vol. 22(1993), pp. 28-41.

Lewellen, J., "Predicting Returns with Financial Ratios", *Journal of Financial Economics*, Vol. 74(2004), pp. 209-235.

Lim, U. K. and S. K. Lee "The Long-run Performance of IPOs in Korean Market", *Journal of Korean Securities Association*, Vol. 18(1995), pp. 333-369(in Korean).

임웅기, 이성규, "우리나라 최초공모주의 장기성과에 관한 연구", 증권학회지, 제18권(1995), pp. 333-369.

Loderer, C. and K. Martin, "Post-Acquisition Performance of Acquiring Firms", *Financial Management*, Vol. 19(1992), pp. 69-79.

Loughran, T. and J. R. Ritter, "The New Issues Puzzle", *Journal of Finance*, Vol. 50(1995), pp. 23-51.

McDonald, J. and A. K. Fisher, "New Issue Stock Price Behavior", *Journal of Finance*, Vol. 27(1972), pp. 97-102.

Mikkelson, W. H. and M. M. Partch, "Valuation Effect of Security Offerings and the Issuance Process", *Journal of Financial Economics*, Vol. 15(1986), pp. 31-60.

Miller, R. and F. Reilly, "An Examination of Mispricing, Returns, and Uncertainty of Initial Public Offerings", *Financial Management*, Vol. 16(1987), pp. 33-38.

Oh, H. T., "Acquiring Firms Return Behavior and Long-term Effect", *Korean Journal of Financial Management*, Vol. 11(1994), pp. 171-189(in Korean).

오현탁, "합병기업의 수익률행태와 장기적 효과", 재무관리연구, 제11권 제1호(1994), pp. 171-189.

Park, K. I. and C. Jee, "Contrarian Strategy Based on Past Stock Return and Volatility", *Korean Journal of Financial Management*, Vol. 23(2006), pp. 1-25(in Korean).

박경인, 지청, "변동성을 이용한 반대투자전략에 대한 실증분석", 재무관리연구, 제23권 제2호(2006), pp. 1-25.

Reinganum, M. R., "Misspecification of Capital Asset Pricing: Empirical Anomalies Based on Earning's Yield and Market Values", *Journal of Financial Economics*, Vol. 9(1981), pp. 19-46.

Reinganum, M. R., "The Anomalous Stock Market Behavior of Small Firms in January: Empirical Tests for Tax-loss selling Effect", *Journal of Financial Economics*, Vol. 12(1983), pp. 89-104.

Ritter, J., "The 'Hot Issue' Market of 1980", *Journal of Business*, Vol. 57(1984), pp. 215-240.

Ritter, J., "The Long-run Performance of Initial Public Offerings", *Journal of Finance*, Vol. 46(1991), pp. 3-27.

Ritter, J. R. and I. Welch, "A Review of IPO Activity, Pricing, and Allocations", *Journal of Finance*, Vol. 57(2002), pp. 1795-1828.

Rogalski, R. J., "New Findings Regarding Day-of-the-Week Returns over Trading and Non-Trading Periods: A note", *Journal of Finance*, Vol. 39(1984), pp. 1603-1614.

Roll, R., "On computing mean returns and the small firm premium", *Journal of Financial Economics*, Vol. 12(1983), pp. 371-386.

Rosenberg, B., K. Reid, and R. Lanstein, "Persuasive Evidence of Market Inefficiency", *Journal of Portfolio Management*, Vol. 11(1985), pp. 9-17.

Rouwenhorst, K. G., "International Momentum Strategies", *Journal of Finance*, Vol. 53(1998), pp. 267-284.

Schipper, K. and A. Smith, "A Comparison of Equity Carve-Outs and Seasoned Equity Offerings: Share Price Effects and Corporate Restructuring", *Journal of Financial Economics*, Vol. 15(1986), pp. 153-186.

Schwert, G. W., "Anomalies and Market Efficiency", in G. M. Constantinides, M. Harris, and R. Stulz, eds, *Handbook of the Economics of Finance*(2003), pp. 939-974.

Seo, B. D. and D. S. Sin, "An Empirical study on the Long-term Post-Merger

Performance of Acquiring Firms", *Journal of Accounting and Finance*, Vol. 21(2003), pp. 101-133(in Korean).

서병덕, 신달순, "합병기업의 합병 후 장기성과에 관한 실증연구", 회계정보연구, 제21권(2003), pp. 101-133.

Shin, Y. K., "Announcement Effects of Seasoned Equity offerings", *Korean Journal of Financial Management*, Vol. 12(1995), pp. 75-92(in Korean).

신용균, "유상증자의 공시효과", 재무관리연구, 제12권 제1호(1995), pp. 75-92.

Song, Y. C. and J. K. Lee, "A Study for Estimation of Cost of Equity", *Korean Journal of Financial Management*, Vol. 14(1997), pp. 157-181(in Korean).

송영출, 이진근, "자기자본 비용의 추정에 관한 연구", 재무관리연구, 제14권 제3호(1997), pp. 157-181.

Sonu, S. H., Y. S. Yun, H. S. Kang, W. H. Lee, S. W. Kim, and S. K. Oh, "Overreaction and Firm Specific Anomalies in the Korean Stock Market", *Journal of Korean Securities association*, Vol. 17(1994), pp. 167-218(in Korean).

선우석호, 윤영섭, 강효석, 이원흠, 김선웅, 오세경, "한국 주식시장에서의 과잉반응과 기업특성적 이례현상에 관한 연구", 증권학회지, 제17권(1994), pp. 167-218.

Sonu, S. H., Y. S. Yun, S. W. Kim, H. S. Kang, W. H. Lee, S. K. Oh, H. S. Choi, and H. S. Jang, *Stock Price Volatility and Anomaly*, Hakhyunsa, Seoul, Korea, 1994(in Korean).

선우석호, 윤영섭, 김선웅, 강효석, 이원흠, 오세경, 최홍식, 장하성, 주가변동과 이례현상, 학현사, 1994.

Spiess, D. K. and J. Affleck-Graves, "Underperformance in Long-run Stock Returns Following Seasoned Equity Offering", *Journal of Financial Economics*, Vol. 38(1995), pp. 243-267.

Stattman, D., "Book Values and Stock Returns", *The Chicago MBA: A Journal of Selected Papers*, Vol. 4(1980), pp. 25-45.

Teoh, S. H., I. Welch, and T. J. Wong, "Earnings Management and the Long-run Performance of Initial Public Offerings", *Journal of Finance*, Vol. 53(1998), pp. 1935-1974.

Torous, W., R. Valkanov, and S. Yan, "On Predicting Stock Returns with Nearly Integrated Explanatory Variables", *Journal of Business,* Vol. 77(2004), pp. 937-966.

White, H., "A Reality Check for Data Snooping", *Econometrica*, Vol. 68(2000), pp. 1097-1126.

Wruck, K. H., "Equity Ownership Concentration and Firm Value: Evidence from Private Equity Financings", *Journal of Financial Economics*, Vol. 23(1989), pp. 3-28.

Yoon, H. G. and Y. H. Lee, "An Revisit on the Monthly Effect in Korean Stock Market", *Korean Association of Logos Management Symposium* (2009), pp. 271-294(in Korean).
윤홍근, 이용환, "유가증권시장과 코스닥시장에서의 월별효과에 관한 재검증", 한국로고스경영학회 춘계학술발표대회논문집(2009), pp. 271-294.

Yoon, J. I. and S. S. Kim, "Reality Check Test on the Momentum and Contrarian Strategy", *Korean Journal of Financial Management*, Vol. 25(2009), pp. 189-220(in Korean).
윤종인, 김성수, "모멘텀전략과 반대전략에 대한 사실성 체크검정", 재무관리연구, 제26권 제1호(2009), pp. 189-220.

Yoon, P. S., "Short-term and Long-term Effect of Seasoned Equity Offerings", *Journal of Korean Securities Association,* Vol. 25(1999), pp. 71-105 (in Korean).
윤평식, "유상증자의 장단기 효과", 증권학회지, 제25권(1999), pp. 71-105.

Yoon, Y. K., "The Decision on Seasoned Equity Offerings by Korean Management", *Korean Journal of Finance*, Vol. 12(1996), pp. 77-105(in Korean).

윤영걸, "우리나라 경영자의 유상증자에 관한 의사결정", 재무연구, 제12권 (1996), pp. 77-105.

Yun, S. Y., B. I. Ku, Y. H. Eom, and J. H. Hahn, "The Cross-section of Stock Returns in Korea: An Empirical Investigation", *Korean Journal of Finance*, Vol. 22(2009), pp. 1-44(in Korean).
윤상용, 구본일, 엄영호, 한재훈, "한국 주식시장에서 유동성 요인을 포함한 3요인 모형의 설명력에 관한 연구", 재무연구, 제22권 제1호(2009), pp. 1-44.

Yun, Y. S., S. H. Sonu, S. W. Kim, H. S. Jang, and H. S. Choi, "Characteristics of Stock Price Movements and Seasonal Anomalies in Korean Stock Market", *Journal of Korean Securities Association*, Vol. 17(1994), pp. 121-166(in Korean).
윤영섭, 선우석호, 김선웅, 장하성, 최흥식, "한국 주식시장에서의 주가변동 특성과 계절적 이례현상에 관한 연구", 증권학회지, 제17권(1994), pp. 121-166.

Any citation of this article must refer to the following: Ko, Kwangsoo, "A Survey of Mutual Fund Studies: Implications for Korean Markets", Asian Review of Financial Research, Vol. 24 (2011), No. 1, pp. 275-365.

Chapter 6

A Survey of Mutual Fund Studies: Implications for Korean Markets

Kwangsoo Ko*   Associate Professor, College of Business Administration, Pusan National University

Abstract

This study surveys research into mutual funds, with special emphasis placed on the implications for Korean markets. Mutual fund studies, here in this study, are divided into three important categories: The economics of mutual funds, agency problems, and other issues. The category of the economics of mutual funds is again divided into 7 sub-categories, the category of agency problem sinto 5 sub-categories, and the category of other issues into 8 sub-categories. For each category, we review the overall trend of overseas mutual fund studies from the 1960s through 2010. After that, the period spanning 1991 through 2010 is focused primarily on Korea. The number of mutual fund articles in academic journals has increased at a surprising rate since the 1990s. In this review, we propose possible directions for future studies with special emphasis on both the protection of investors and the investment behavior of investors. We are confident that careful studies will prove quite helpful in resolving a variety of agency problems in Korean fund markets, and should also help provide investors with efficient investment opportunities in a fair manner. We also hope that mutual fund studies will ultimately bridge the gap between academia and the practical society of mutual funds.

Keywords   Mutual Fund, Economics of Mutual Funds, Agency Problems, Investors Protection, Behavioral Finance

* **Address:** Pusan National University, 30 Jangjeon-dong, Geumjeong-gu, Busan 609-735, Korea; E-mail: kks1201@pnu.edu; **Tel:** 82-51-510-3730.

This survey paper is prepared as a part of the 2010 knowledge database project by the Korean Finance Association (KFA) and financially supported by the KFA. I am very grateful for the assistance of Yeonjeong Ha, Miyoun Paek, Yaping Wang, and Sunghoon Choi in selecting and summarizing a huge amount of mutual fund articles. Special thanks go to Hyuk Choe, Sooyoung Song, and Kwangwoo Park at the Fall Korean Finance Association meeting in November 2010, and to the editor(Hee-Joon Ahn) of this journal and two referees(Young K. Park and Junesuh Yi) for helpful comments. The full lists of references (Excel and Word files) and abstracts (Word files) are available upon request to the author.

I. Introduction

Although 'mutual funds' have been popular in the U.S. since the 1980s, the concept proved very awkward to academicians and investors, as well as regulators, in Korea. Prior to the 21st century, only a few studies addressed mutual funds using the data of traditional investment trusts, which are very similar economically to mutual funds.[1] After the American-style mutual funds system became allowed in 1999, interests began to build in fund investments, with special emphasis on Korean stock markets. Since 2000, academicians also have come to realize the importance of mutual funds in Korean capital markets and the broad Korean economy. In the 2000s, a variety of studies have been published in Korean academic journals.

The principal objective of this study is to review overseas and Korean mutual fund studies and determine some of the relevant implications for Korean markets and academicians. In the U.S., a great number of papers have been, and will continue to be published in academic and trade journals. This trend will be followed closely by Korean academics, because the sizes of mutual fund markets and industries will flourish with both the growing complexity of capital markets and the rapid increase in pension assets resulting from the activity of the baby boomer generation. In this regard, we would like to point out two important issues in the mutual funds markets and industry. The first issue is the protection of fund investors, and the second involves understanding their investment behavior. We anticipate that these two issues will be the principal concerns of academic society in Korea in the future.

Although a handful of studies have developed and propounded theories regarding both performance evaluation techniques of mutual funds and the

---

[1] This study considers investment trusts as mutual funds.

relationship between fund returns and fund flows, the majority of mutual fund studies focus on empirical analysis. For this reason, we review mutual fund studies in an empirical sense, but do not exclude theoretical studies from this analysis. For the purpose of reviewing mutual fund studies, they are classified into three categories herein: the economics of mutual funds, agency problems, and other issues. The category of the economics of mutual funds addresses economic issues related to the mutual funds themselves, and their role and function in capital markets. Although agency problems of mutual funds also are a component of the category of the economics of mutual funds, they are allocated into another category because of their importance and their essential features for investor protection. The other important remaining studies are classified into the category of other issues. The category of the economics of mutual funds is again divided into 7 sub-categories, the category of agency problems into 5 sub-categories, and the category of other issues into 8 sub-categories.

From our review, we propose some possible directions for future studies, with special emphasis placed on the protection of investors and on their investment behavior. We are confident that careful studies should prove very helpful in resolving a number of agency problems in Korean fund markets, and should also provide investors with efficient investment opportunities in a fair manner. We also hope that mutual fund studies will ultimately fill the gap between academia and the practices of fund markets.

This study is organized as follows: The second section provides an overview of the U.S. and Korean mutual fund markets and industries. Overseas mutual fund studies are reviewed in the third section. Section IV provides a review of Korean mutual fund studies. The final section provides some implications from the overall review, and concludes the paper.

II. Review of Mutual Fund Markets and Industry

1. A Brief History of the U.S. Mutual Fund Markets and Industry

People often assert that the concept of 'mutual fund' originates from the British East India Company, an early English joint-stock company. The first mutual fund, however, was established in 1924 in Boston, and was named the 'Massachusetts Investors Trust'. As previously asserted by Gremillion (2005), mutual funds are a purely American invention. Pozen (2002) is an excellent book in a legal and academic sense, and Gremillion (2005), in a practical sense. In the 1920s and 1930s, the U.S. fund market and industry had been very chaotic, owing to the absence of both a well-organized system of mutual funds and investor protection. Financial rogues had engaged in a lot of cheatings and unfair practices. For these reasons, the mutual fund system has been repeatedly developed and modified. To better protect investors, the U.S. Congress passed legislation regulating securities markets and trading: the Securities Act of 1933 and the Securities Exchange Act of 1934. A special study ('A Study of Mutual Fund') undertaken in 1935 by the Securities and Exchange Commission (henceforth the SEC) led to the passage of the Investment Company Act of 1940 and the Investment Advisory Act of 1940. Both acts provide leeway for a well-organized mutual fund system.

Since the end of the Great Depression, the U.S. mutual fund industry experienced a small growth spurt during the late 1950s and 1960s due to the strong economy and stock market. At that time, most mutual funds were equity-type, and broker-dealers charged front-end sales charge (or loads) of 8.5% of the initial investment for fund sales. In the early 1970s, however, the U.S. stock market declined steadily. As a consequence, it became very difficult to sell equity mutual funds. Instead, the interests of investors turned to short-term or income-oriented investments. In 1972, the SEC allowed the mutual fund industry to create money market funds (henceforth MMFs) which became the savior of the industry during the late 1970s and early 1980s. The success of MMFs was attributed to the high interest rates in the U.S. While commercial banks were legally prevented from paying more than a specified rate of 4% or 5%, the returns of MMFs were substantially higher than the banks' interests, without any restrictions. This regulation arbitrage caused MMFs to account for a larger percentage of industry assets than either equity or bond funds. Despite the growth of MMFs in the 1970s, practitioners believe that MMFs are inappropriate for the concept of mutual funds because they are not perfectly appropriate for the concept of money management.

Over the past 20 years, the mutual fund market and industry have grown at a surprisingly rapid pace in the U.S. The total net assets (henceforth TNAs) of mutual funds amounted to less than $1 trillion in 1989 and climbed to more than $11 trillion at the end of 2009, a compound annual growth rate of 13%. The figure reached its record high of $12 trillion at the end of 2007. As of August 2010, the TNAs of U.S. mutual funds are $10.8 trillion, of which equity funds comprise of 43.74%, and MMFs, 26.24%. Many believe that the following factors resulted in the rapid growth of the mutual fund industry: a bull market in U.S. stocks, the growth of retirement assets, the creation of attractive new fund products, new enhanced investor services, a broad variety of distribution channels, and pricing structures. A host of studies have assessed these and other interesting issues in a scientific fashion.

On the other hand, many practitioners and academicians are somewhat confused regarding the proper definition of the term 'mutual fund'. According to the Investment Company Act of 1940, there are three kinds of investment companies: Face-amount certificates, unit-investment trusts, and management companies. There are two types of management companies: open-end management companies and closed-end management companies. An open-end management company is called a 'mutual fund' by practitioners on Wall Street; however, this is not a formal or legal appellation. Closed-end management companies, conversely, are colloquially referred to as 'closed funds.' Hence, closed funds are not included as part of the definition of a mutual fund. In the 1980s and 1990s, the TNAs of closed-end funds were approximately 5% of mutual funds, and we have seen a large number of closed-end fund studies. At this stage, however, the proportion of closed-end funds is less than 2%, and few studies have addressed the issue of closed-end funds.

2. The History of the Korean Mutual Fund Markets and Industry[2]

In Korea, fund investment began in 1974. At the outset, the Korean fund market system copied that of Japanese investment trusts that were similar to UK unit trusts.[3] Until the introduction of the U.S. mutual fund system in 1999, fund investment had long been considered simply an alternative saving instrument which yielded more interest than bank savings accounts. Despite the introduction of the U.S. mutual fund system, it is currently not popular in Korea because of both relatively high set-up and maintenance costs and unfamiliarity to Korean practitioners. The majority of funds were legally established on the basis of traditional systems of investment trusts, which were contract-type funds. Hence, most funds are not U.S.-style mutual funds at this stage.

Prior to 1988, the mutual fund industry consisted of three large investment trust companies, the so-called "Big Three", i.e., investment advisors in the

---

2) A part of this sub-section is cited from Ko and Ha (2010c).

3) Each country has its own legal system for publicly available 'mutual funds', but each country's mutual fund plays the same role in an economic sense. Hence, the following funds could be referred to as mutual funds: U.S. open-end management company, U.K. unit trusts and OEICs under the UCITS, Japan's investment trust, Korea's investment trust and securities investment company.

sense of US markets.[4] Their businesses included both fund sales and fund management. They functioned as market stabilizers and played a pivotal role in the markets, because the Korean stock and bond markets were relatively small. Korean capital markets developed quickly in the 1980s. In an effort to meet the needs of both investors and the market, five regional investment trust companies were additionally licensed in 1988. After the very rapidly growing Korean stock market achieved record highs in 1989, it declined to significantly below investors'expectations. To sustain the stock market and to protect investors from market decline, the Korean government injected three trillion Korean won into the stock market through the Big Three.[5] That is, the Bank of Korea loaned three trillion Korean won to the Big Three, with which they then bought stocks through their own accounts. The Korean stock market, unfortunately, confronted a long-run downhill trend, and the injection program failed. Eventually, the Big Three incurred enormous losses, which ultimately proved fatal, causing their bankruptcy in just 10 years.

During the long-run decline of the stock market, Korean firms experienced a variety of obstacles to financing their required capital, as they generally perceived stock prices as too low and interest rates as too high. As a means of boosting capital markets and of establishing investors' demand base, the government licensed a host of financial firms to conduct investment management business in the mid-1990s. Despite the efforts of the Korean government, unfortunately, the Korean economy experienced a serious financial crisis in 1997. Due to the financial crisis, many commercial banks went bankrupt, and a large portion of bank savings was moved into bond funds. Consequently, the total assets under management (henceforth AUMs) increased markedly, up to 300 trillion Korean won until July 1999, when the Korean Chaebol, Daewoo, went bankrupt, and its defaulted bonds

4) They were called "three whales in a small pond (Korean stock market)".
5) At that time, three trillion Korean won seemed a sufficiently large sum to boost the Korean stock market.

became a fatal cause of the collapse of the Korean fund markets.

At that time, the fund industry used the book value method to calculate the daily net asset values (henceforth NAVs) of bond funds. With the bankruptcy of Daewoo, the book value method exacerbated the soundness and credibility of the fund industry. In 1999, in an effort to resolve this issue, the Financial Supervisory Commission (henceforth referred to as the FSC) enforced the market value method when calculating the daily NAVs of bond funds.[6] Additionally, another problem faced by the fund industry was the 'backward pricing' of equity funds. In 2000, the FSC abolished backward pricing and enforced a 'forward pricing' protocol for equity and bond funds. Since that time, the Korean fund industry has been re-structured as a sufficiently sound and credible financial sector to induce a flow of investor money. All of these efforts rendered the mutual fund industry a strong competitor for the banking and insurance industries in the 21st century.

Since 2000, investors have recognized the risk-and-return trade-off of equity mutual funds, and have been capable of differentiating them from bond funds and bank savings. To attract money from new investors, newly established investment management companies attempted to promote their funds aggressively via public advertising. Due to governmental efforts to develop the fund industry, aggressive advertisements, and the temporary good performance of equity funds, the AUMs of equity funds began to grow. Simultaneously, new regulations of banks' trust accounts kicked the money out to mutual funds.[7] The changing climate of financial markets allowed commercial banks to conduct fund sales businesses with their abundant retail networks, so as not to lose their profits. The fund sales businesses of com-

---

6) Currently, the FSC is called the 'Financial Services Commission'.

7) The FSC ordered that bank trust divisions should be independent of the main business of commercial banks (i.e., fire wall between them), and trust accounts should follow the regulations of mutual funds at the same level. This caused commercial banks to gradually abandon their trust account businesses. These regulations appeared to mimic those of the US Gramm-Leach-Bliley Act of 1999.

mercial banks accelerated the growth of both equity funds and bond funds.

With the changing structure of financial sectors, public investors demanded fresh investment tools capable of replacing regular bank savings. In an effort to fulfill investors' demands, a few aggressive new investment management companies attempted to promote their equity funds and to strongly advertise dollar cost averaging investment techniques for mutual fund investments. Finally, they succeeded in launching new equity funds that were designed specifically as dollar cost averaging investments. The other investment management companies mimicked their behavior in an effort to induce huge quantities of money seeking novel financial instruments. At the end of 2004, consequently, the demand base of equity funds strengthened and became more widespread, and their AUMs due to preponderant dollar cost averaging investments began to grow rapidly, which elicited structural changes in the Korean fund market and industry.

Since 2000, the amounts of total AUMs have steadily increased, except in 2003 and 2009. The AUMs began at 138 trillion won at the end of 2000, to 332 trillion won at the end of 2009. The structural changes in the mutual fund market and industry after 2004, however, altered the investment propensities of fund investors. That is, investors began to prefer equity funds to bond funds more than previously, and to understand the risk-and-return concept inherent to equity fund investments. As a consequence, at the end of 2009, the AUMs of equity funds (126 trillion won) were much larger than those of bond funds (46 trillion won) and MMFs (72 trillion won). The rapid growth of equity fund size was attributable to dollar cost averaging investments. While dollar cost averaging investments had proven unpopular by 2004, associated promotion and advertisements rendered it prevalent among individual investors after 2004. Ko and Ha (2010a, b, c) explain the causes and consequences of the structural changes of the Korean fund industry in detail.

On the other hand, as of November 2010, to our understanding, there are three possible sources of mutual funds data: Zeroin, FnGuide, and Morningstar Korea. All the data sources acquire their mutual funds data from the same source of the Korea Financial Investment Association. The data contains a great deal of mutual fund information including daily NAVs, TNAs, monthly portfolio holdings, fees and loads, and associated information. Due to the lack of fees and loads data, however, fee-related studies are not feasible. Additionally, not all of the portfolio holdings data have been reported, which may be misleading, ultimately leading to incorrect analyses. As an academician, we hope that the industry provides the academic society of finance and economics with more complete mutual fund information to enhance the quality and credibility of the mutual fund markets and industry in Korea.

III. Overseas Mutual Fund Studies

In this section, we will review overseas mutual fund studies. For the purpose of reviewing overseas mutual fund studies, the following 16 academic journals are selected on the basis of their academic impact and importance: Journal of Finance (JF), Journal of Financial Economics (JFE), Review of Financial Studies (RFS), Journal of Financial and Quantitative Analysis (JFQA), Journal of Business (JB), Journal of Banking and Finance (JBF), Financial Analysts Journal (FAJ), Journal of Business Finance and Accounting (JBFA), Financial Management (FM), Journal of Financial Intermediation (JFI), Journal of Financial Markets (JFM), Journal of Empirical Finance (JEF), Pacific-Basin Finance Journal (PBFJ), American Economic Review (AER), Quarterly Journal of Economics (QJE), and the Journal of Political Economy (JPE). The statistics of the overseas mutual fund studies are computed from the 16 journals listed above, even though not all of the mutual fund articles published in the above journals are cited in this study.

<Table 1> shows the time trend of the number of mutual fund studies published in each academic journal. Among the above 16 journals, mutual fund studies are most frequently published in the Journal of Finance, with aproportion of 18.39%. The second is the Financial Analysts Journal. The three top-tier economic journals (AER, QJE, and JPE) published only 15 articles in total. Most of the relevant studies deal with analyses of the U.S. markets; however, some articles in the Journal of Business Finance and Accounting and the Journal of Banking and Finance address the other markets, including Europe and Australia. Mutual fund studies have been published since 1963. By 1990, in our personal judgment, mutual funds were not an interesting and main issue in finance. With the rapid growth of mutual fund markets and the industry since 1990, academicians have become increasingly interested in the economic behavior of mutual funds. As can be observed in <Table 1>, the number of mutual fund articles in academic journals has increased profoundly since 1991. At this stage, we believe that as of 2010, mutual funds must be included as a component of mainstream finance.

The taxonomy of mutual fund studies is shown in <Table 2>. Panel A provides cross-sectional taxonomy spanning 1961 through 2010. As expected, the category of the economics of mutual funds produces almost half of all published papers. Among all of these papers, 28.24% deal with performance evaluation. The fewest number of papers are published in the category of agency problems. In the category of other issues, closed-end funds are the most highlighted area. In Panel B of the time-series taxonomy, with the increase in the total number of mutual fund studies, the number of performance evaluation studies is also increasing. However, there is clear evidence that, since 1996, some issues other than performance evaluation

<Table 1> The Number of Mutual Fund Studies in Each Journal

Journal	~1985	1986~1990	1991~1995	1996~2000	2001~2005	2006~2010	Total
JF	11	4	5	16	19	16	71 (17.11%)
JFE	1	0	2	9	12	22	46 (11.08%)
RFS	0	1	2	5	6	16	30 (7.23%)
JFQA	7	1	1	6	9	10	34 (8.19%)
JB (by 2006)	7	4	3	3	9	2	28 (6.75%)
JBF	0	0	3	2	9	31	45 (10.84%)
FAJ	2	7	8	19	13	6	55 (13.25%)
JBFA	2	1	6	7	6	11	33 (7.95%)
FM/JFI/JFM/JEF/PBFJ	0	1	2	9	12	34	58 (13.98%)
AER/QJE/JPE/	0	1	1	5	5	3	15 (3.61%)
Total	30	20	33	81	100	151	415 (100%)
	[7.23%]	[4.82%]	[7.95%]	[19.52%]	[24.10%]	[36.39%]	

\<Table 2\> Taxonomy of Mutual Fund Studies

Panel A: Cross-sectional taxonomy of mutual fund studies from 1961 through 2010

	JF	JFE	RFS	JFQA	JB	JBF	FAJ	JBFA	FM/JFI/JFM /JEF/PBFJ	AER/QJE/ JPE	Total
Economics of mutual funds	*42*	*23*	*10*	*19*	*17*	*17*	*19*	*21*	*33*	*5*	*206 (49.64%)*
Performance evaluation	24	8	6	11	14	9	13	17	17	2	121 (29.16%)
Costs, fees, and expenses	4	3	1	1	1	2	1	0	2	0	15 (3.61%)
Fund flows	8	7	0	3	0	4	0	4	7	1	34 (8.19%)
Growth, set-up, and termination	3	1	1	0	1	1	0	0	0	0	7 (1.69%)
Risk and return	3	1	1	3	0	1	1	0	2	0	12 (2.89 %)
Style analysis	0	1	1	0	0	0	3	0	1	0	6 (1.45%)
Fund size, information, and tax	0	2	0	1	1	0	1	0	4	2	11 (2.65%)
Agency problems	*10*	*10*	*11*	*5*	*0*	*7*	*7*	*3*	*8*	*4*	*65 (15.66%)*
Governance	3	5	2	1	0	1	0	0	1	0	13 (3.13%)
Managerial incentive	3	2	7	2	0	4	3	0	6	2	29 (6.99%)
Mutual fund scandal	2	1	0	1	0	2	2	2	0	1	11 (2.65%)
Tournaments	1	1	1	1	0	0	0	1	1	1	7 (1.69%)
Relationship with broker	1	1	1	0	0	0	2	0	0	0	5 (1.20%)
The other issues	*19*	*13*	*9*	*10*	*11*	*21*	*29*	*9*	*17*	*6*	*144 (34.70%)*
Pension issues	0	0	0	1	0	0	1	0	1	0	3 (.72%)
Data and survivorship bias	1	0	3	0	0	0	0	0	2	0	6 (1.45%)
Index funds	1	0	1	1	1	1	3	0	1	1	10 (2.41%)
Closed-end funds	6	5	3	1	4	5	3	6	6	2	41 (9.88%)
Behavioral finance	4	2	1	2	2	0	1	0	2	1	15 (3.61%)
The other funds	2	1	1	0	3	5	3	1	1	1	18 (4.34%)
Fund rating	0	0	0	2	0	0	4	1	1	0	8 (1.93%)
The others	5	5	0	3	1	10	14	1	3	1	43 (10.36%)
Total	71	46	30	34	28	45	55	33	58	15	415 (100%)
	(17.11%)	(11.08%)	(7.23%)	(8.19%)	(6.75%)	(10.84%)	(13.25%)	(7.95%)	(13.98%)	(3.61%)	

Panel B: Time-series taxonomy of mutual fund studies from 1961 through 2010

	~1985	1986~1990	1991~1995	1996~2000	2001~2005	2006~2010	Total
Economics of mutual funds	*20*	*11*	*16*	*41*	*49*	*69*	*206 (49.64%)*
Performance evaluation	15	9	13	22	25	37	121 (29.16%)
Costs, fees, and expenses	1	1	0	4	3	6	15 (3.61%)
Fund flows	0	0	2	4	10	18	34 (8.19%)
Growth, set-up, and termination	0	0	0	3	3	1	7 (1.69%)
Risk and return	4	0	0	2	3	3	12 (2.89%)
Style analysis	0	0	0	3	3	0	6 (1.45%)
Fund size, information, and tax	0	1	1	3	2	4	11 (2.65%)
Agency problems	*0*	*2*	*7*	*12*	*18*	*32*	*65 (15.66%)*
Governance	0	0	0	2	2	9	13 (3.13%)
Managerial incentive	0	2	1	6	5	15	29 (6.99%)
Mutual fund scandal	0	0	0	1	8	2	11 (2.65%)
Tournaments	0	0	0	2	2	3	7 (1.69%)
Relationship with broker	0	0	0	1	1	3	5 (1.20%)
The other issues	*10*	*7*	*16*	*28*	*33*	*50*	*144 (34.70%)*
Pension issues	0	0	0	0	1	2	3 (.72%)
Data and survivorship bias	0	0	1	2	3	0	6 (1.45%)
Index funds	1	1	0	1	3	4	10 (2.41%)
Closed-end funds	2	3	6	11	9	10	41 (9.88%)
Behavioral finance	0	0	3	5	2	5	15 (3.61%)
The other funds	1	0	2	2	4	9	18 (4.34%)
Fund rating	0	0	0	3	2	3	8 (1.93%)
The others	6	3	4	4	9	17	43 (10.36%)
Total	30 [7.23%]	20 [4.82%]	33 [7.95%]	81 [19.52%]	100 [24.10%]	151 [36.39%]	415 [100%]

are studied more frequently than they were previously. Agency problems had not been studied prior to 1995, with the exception of just three papers. The rapid development of mutual fund markets and the industry demanded such studies on agency problems since 1996. In the category of other issues, closed-end fund studies have dominated. Interestingly, the area of behavioral finance has been a subject of intensive study since 1991. Nowadays, fund rating is also a good issue for an academic study.

1. The Economics of Mutual Funds

1.1 Performance Evaluation

Not surprisingly, one can readily find numerous mutual fund studies concerning performance evaluations from the 1960s. In the 1970s and 1980s, mutual fund studies employed traditional techniques to evaluate mutual fund portfolios. Nowadays, performance evaluation studies can be divided into the following four parts: pure performance evaluation, performance persistence, performance evaluation techniques, and performance-enhancing factors.

To the best of our knowledge, performance evaluation studies began with the work of Sharpe (1966) and Jensen (1968), although Brown and Vickers (1963) briefly study mutual fund performance and its impact on the market. Sharpe (1966) and Jensen (1968) fail to find outperformance of mutual funds over randomly selected portfolios. Horowitz (1966)refutes Sharpe (1966) in the sense that performance differences are explained by management skill and past performance. Cohen and Pogue (1968) make some comments on mutual fund versus random portfolio performance. Regarding this issue, academicians have had different views and research results from the outset. At the end of the 1970s, Kon and Jen (1979) find a changing risk level of mutual funds and significantly different stock selectivity performance, and conclude that the selectivity performance persistent to the efficient market hypothesis is mixed. Kon (1983) finds that there is, at the individual fund level, evidence of significant superior timing ability and performance. However, fund managers as a group have no special information regarding the formation of expectations on market portfolio returns.

Treynor and Mazuy (1966) and Henriksson and Merton (1981) provide the basic empirical models of performance evaluation. Their models are able to differentiate the market timing ability from the selection ability. Many studies, in a fundamental sense, are based on their empirical models. Henriksson (1984) does not support the hypothesis that mutual fund managers are capable of following an investment strategy that successfully times market portfolio returns. Chang and Lewellen (1984) also find that few fund managers display much market-timing skill, and that fund managers are collectively incapable of outperforming a passive investment strategy. Cumby and Glen (1990) and Malkiel (1995) also find no superior performance of mutual funds. Elton, Gruber, and Blake (1996a) assert that a combination of index funds is likely to outperform an active fund of similar risk. They explain why investors select an actively managed fund in the following way: An investor could rationally select an actively managed fund if he or she had the ability to select a fund that outperforms the average fund by a sufficient amount to beat a passive portfolio.

Ippolito (1984) finds that risk-adjusted returns in the mutual fund industry, the net of fees and expenses, are comparable to returns available in index funds, and portfolio turnover and management fees are unrelated to fund performance. Jagannathan and Korajczyk (1986) demonstrate theoretically and empirically that it is possible to construct portfolios that show artificial timing ability when no true timing ability exists. Lee and Rahman (1990) demonstrate theoretically and empirically how to create a portfolio that would exhibit positive timing performance and negative security se-lection when no true timing or selectivity exists. Kothari and Warner (2001) study standard performance measures, using simulated funds whose character-istics mimic actual funds. They find that the performance measures used in previous mutual fund research have minimal ability to detect economically large magnitudes of abnormal fund performance, particularly if a fund's style characteristics differ from those of the value-weighted market portfolio.

On the contrary, Grinblatt and Titman (1989) find that the risk-adjusted gross returns of some funds are significantly positive. Bollen and Busse (2001) sug-gest that mutual funds may possess more timing ability on a daily basis than documented previously. Kosowski, Timmermann, Wermers, and White (2006) find that a sizable minority of managers pick stocks well enough to more than cover their costs. Moreover, the superior alphas of these managers persist.

The empirical results for other countries are also not unanimous. McDonald (1973) finds superior performance of French mutual funds in a unique French context. Kim (1978), however, fails to find outperformance of equity mutual funds. Almost 10 years later, Cai, Chan, and Yamada (1997) demonstrate that, regardless of the performance measures and benchmarks employed, most of the Japanese mutual funds underperform the benchmarks by between 3.6% and 10.8% per annum. Dahlquist, Engstrom, and Soderlind (2000) study the relationship between fund performance and fund attributes in the Swedish market. They show that good performance occurs among small equity funds, low fee funds, funds whose trading activity is high and, in some cases, funds with good past performance. Cesari and Panetta (2002) find that the funds' performance in Italy does not differ significantly from zero. However, Pinnuck (2003) demonstrates that fund managers have the ability to select stocks in Australia.

Beyond static performance evaluation, many studies investigate the performance persistence of mutual funds. Grinblatt and Titman (1992) show evidence that differences in performance between funds persist over time and that this persistence is consistent with the ability of fund managers to generate abnormal returns. Hendricks, Patel, and Zeckhauser (1993) find that portfolios of recent poor performers perform significantly less well than standard benchmarks; those of recent top performers perform better, though not significantly so. Brown and Goetzmann (1995) assert that performance persistence is mostly due to funds that lag the S&P 500 while the relative risk-adjusted performance of mutual funds persists. However, Carhart (1997) demonstrates that Hendricks, Patel and Zeckhauser's (1993) 'hot hands'result is driven principally by the one-year momentum effect, but individual funds do not earn higher returns from following the momentum strategy in stocks. More recently, Bollen and Busse (2005) demonstrate that superior performance is a short-lived phenomenon, which can be observed only when funds are evaluated several times a year.

A great number of studies are concerned with performance evaluation techniques and methods rather than performance evaluations *per se*. Joy and Porter (1974) and Meyer (1977) apply stochastic dominance theory in performance evaluation. Some studies focus on the statistical properties of performance measurement: Miller and Gressis (1980), Breen, Jagannathan, and Ofer (1986), Grinblatt and Titman (1994), Baks, Metrick, and Wachter (2001), Farnsworth, Ferson, Jackson, and Todd (2002), Pastor and Stambaugh (2002b), Jones and Shanken (2005), Busse and Irvine (2006), Mamaysky, Spiegel, and Zhang (2008), Moreno and Rodriguez (2009). Lehmann and Modest (1987) investigate the role of benchmarks in performance evaluation. On the other hand, the availability of portfolio holdings data makes it possible for researchers to study mutual fund performance by assessing the individual stocks included in each mutual fund: Grinblatt and Titman (1993), Daniel, Grinblatt, Wermers, and

Titman (1997), Chen, Jegadeesh, and Wermers (2000), Cohen, Coval, and Pastor (2005), Jiang, Yao, and Yu (2007). Grinblatt and Titman (1993) develop a method to evaluate performance without benchmarks. Daniel, Grinblatt, Titman, Wermers (1997) extend Grinblatt and Titman (1993) to evaluate performance with characteristic-based benchmarks. Their models now constitute the basic form of portfolio-based performance evaluation. Wermers (2000) decompose mutual fund performance into various components. Goetzmann, Ingersoll, and Ivkovik (2000) invent a method to evaluate daily timing ability via monthly measurement. Cremers and Petajisto (2009) introduce a new measure of active portfolio management, 'Active Share', which represents the share of portfolio holdings that differ from the benchmark index holdings. Very recently, Barras, Scaillet, and Wermers (2010) and Fama and French (2010) identify the role of luck in mutual fund performance.

Meanwhile, many studies are interested in specific characteristics or strategies that enhance the performance of mutual funds. Ferson and Schadt (1996) measure fund strategy and performance in changing economic conditions. Chevalier and Ellison (1999a) find that managers who attended higher-SAT undergraduate institutions have systematically higher risk-adjusted excess returns. Gottesman and Morey (2006) extend Chevalier and Ellison (1999a) and find that the mean GMAT score of the MBA program is positively and significantly related to fund performance. Gottesman and Morey (2006) extend Chevalier and Ellison (1999a), and find that the mean GMAT score of the MBA program is positively and significantly related to fund performance. Keim (1999) shows that both the investment rules and the trading strategy components of the fund's design contribute significantly to differences in returns. Subsequent studies analyze the effects of top management turnover, historical returns and passive index, family strategy, fund size, predictability, fund closure, public information, liquidity, and city size on mutual fund returns, that is Khorana (2001), Pastor and Stambaugh (2002a), Massa (2003), Chen, Hong, Huang, and Kubik (2004), Avramov and Wermers (2006), Bris, Gulen, Kadiyala, and Rau (2007), Kacperczyk and Seru (2007), Yan (2008), Christoffersen and Sarkissian (2009), respectively. More interestingly, Kacperczyk, Sialm, and Zheng (2005) indicate that, on average, more concentrated funds perform better after controlling for risk and style differences using a variety of performance measures. Their findings imply that investment ability is more apparent among managers who hold portfolios concentrated in a few industries. From the perspective of fund cash flow, Alexander, Cici, and Gibson (2007) find that managers making purely valuation-motivated purchases beat the market by a substantial margin, but are incapable of so doing when compelled to invest excess cash from investor inflows.

1.2 Costs, Fees, and Expenses

The first paper on mutual fund fee is Herman (1963) which is based on the report to the SEC: 'A Study of Mutual Funds'.[8] He reviews the report and stresses the significance of mutual fund fee. More than 20 years later, Rule 12b-1, which was approved by the SEC in 1980 leads Chance and Ferris (1987) to investigate the role of 12b-1 fees. They conclude that since a 12b-1 plan would not be expected to affect the management of the fund, the only impact it could have would be on the expense ratio. Their findings would provide important implications regarding the current issue of the validity of the 12b-1 fee in the U.S. mutual fund industry.

Chordia (1996) shows that aggressive funds are sensitive to cash flows and likely to rely on fees to dissuade redemptions. In a theoretical sense, Nanda, Narayanan, and Warther (2000) develop a model of the mutual

---

8) Herman (1963) is merely a summary of the material presented by him and his three colleagues at the Wharton School to the SEC which was submitted to Congress as a Report of the Committee on Interstate and Foreign Commerce (House Rept. No. 2274 [87th Cong., 2d sess. (Washington, 1962)]).

fund industry in which the management fees and loads charged by the mutual fund and average fund returns are determined endogenously in a competitive market setting. Elton, Gruber, and Blake (2003) identify incentive fees as useful marketing tools. Barber, Odean, and Zheng (2005) find that investors are more sensitive to salient in-your-face fees such as front-end loads and commissions, than to operating expenses. Their findings imply that investors are uninterested in the existence of 12b-1 fees. Gil-Bazo and Ruiz-Verdu (2009) demonstrate the fact that funds with worse before-fee performance charge higher fees. Recently, Khorana, Servaes and Tufano (2009) study the fees charged by 46,580 mutual fund classes offered for sale in 18 countries. They find that larger funds and fund families charge lower fees while fees are higher for funds distributed in more countries and funds domiciled in so-called offshore locations.

A few studies investigate the trading costs of mutual funds. Edelen (1999) documents the statistically significant indirect cost of liquidity-motivated trading in the form of negative relationship between a fund's abnormal return and investor flows. Bollen and Busse (2006) show that the move to decimal pricing preceded increased trading costs for some actively managed mutual funds. These costs are ultimately borne by individual fund shareholders.

1.3 Fund Flows

At the aggregate market level, Warther (1995) is the first to investigate the relationship between fund flows and market returns. Edelen and Warner (2001) extend Warther (1995) on the basis of daily frequency. They find that aggregate flow follows market returns with a one-day lag.

At the individual fund level, many studies investigate the relationship between fund flows and fund returns. Sirri and Tufano (1998) find the interesting phenomenon that investors base their fund purchase decisions on prior performance information, but do so asymmetrically, investing disproportionately more in funds that performed very well in the prior period. They report the same findings as Chevalier and Ellison (1997). Lynch and Musto (2003) show the asymmetric relation to be consistent with fund incentives, as funds discard exactly those strategies that under perform.

Zheng (1999) finds evidence that funds receiving more money subsequently perform significantly better than those losing money, the so-called 'smart money' effect. Sapp and Tiwari (2004) show that the smart money effect can be explained by the stock return momentum phenomenon. In the U.K., however, Keswani and Stolin (2008) find a robust smart money effect.

In regard to advertisement, Jain and Wu (2000) show that the pre-advertisement performance of mutual funds is significantly higher than those of the benchmarks; however, no superior performance is detected in the post-advertisement period. Bergstresser and Poterba (2002) present evidence suggesting that after-tax returns have more explanatory power than pretax returns in explaining inflows.

Berk and Green (2004) quantitatively model the flow-performance relationship, which is consistent with high average levels of skills and considerable heterogeneity across managers. Huang, Wei, and Yan (2007), by incorporating participation costs into a model, show that mutual funds with lower participation costs have a higher flow sensitivity to medium performance and a lower flow sensitivity to high performance than their higher-cost peers.

From an economic viewpoint, Cha and Lee (2001) find that equity fund flows appear to be affected by the performance of the stock market, and that investors attempt to forecast the fundamentals of firms and accordingly adjust their demand for stocks. Overall, these findings are consistent with a horizontal market demand curve for equities. Cooper, Gulen, and Rau (2005) find that the year after a fund changes its name to reflect a current hot style, the fund experiences an average cumulative abnormal flow of

28% without any improvements in performance; this suggests that investors are irrationally influenced by cosmetic effects.

Many studies are interested in the effects of some fund characteristics on the relationship between fund flows and returns. Bollen (2007) demonstrates that fund flows for socially responsible funds exhibit substantially lower volatility than do flows for conventional funds. He concludes that socially responsible funds attract loyal investors. Coval and Stafford (2007) show that investors who trade against constrained mutual funds earn significant returns for providing liquidity. Boyer and Zheng (2009) document a significant and positive contemporaneous relationship between stock market returns and flows of mutual funds. Their analysis is somewhat different from others in the sense that they use net purchase of equity by mutual funds, not cash flows from mutual fund investors. Ivkovic and Weisbenner (2009) study the relationship between individuals' mutual fund flows and various fund characteristics. Interestingly, Sensoy (2009) provides evidence that performance relative to the specified benchmark is a significant determinant of a fund's subsequent cash inflows, even controlling for performance measures that better capture the fund's style. Chen, Goldstein, and Jiang (2010) find that, consistent with a theoretical model, funds with illiquid assets exhibit stronger sensitivity of outflows to bad past performance than funds with liquid assets. Recently, Rakowski (2010) documents a significant negative relationship between the volatility of daily fund flows and cross-sectional differences in risk-adjusted performance.

1.4 Growth, Set-up, and Termination

Gruber (1996) and Khorana, Servaes, and Tufano (2005) are interested in why investors buy mutual funds and what drives the growth of the mutual fund industry, respectively. Khorana, Servaes, and Tufano (2005) find that laws and regulations, supply-side and demand-side factors simultaneously affect the size of the fund industry.

Regarding the determinants of mutual fund starts, Khorana and Servaes (1999) find that fund initiations arerelated positively to the level of assets invested in and the capital gains embedded in other funds with the same objective, the fund family's prior performance, the fraction of funds in the family in the low range of fees, and the decision by large families to open similar funds in the prior year.

Rozeff (1998) finds evidence that mutual fund splits bring per account shareholdings back up to normal levels, and argues that signaling, liquidity, and tick size theories do not apply to mutual fund splits. In the case of mutual fund merger, however, Jayaraman, Khorana, and Nelling (2002) find significant improvements in post-merger performance and a reduction in expense ratios for target fund shareholders. They point out the pros of mutual fund mergers. The SEC cited their findings to amend the SEC rule 17a-8 regarding mutual fund mergers in July 2002. However, their findings are not sufficiently clear for use in policy decision-making. On the other hand, Zhao (2005) assesses the similarities and differences in the determinants of the three mutual fund exit forms: liquidation, within-family merger, and across-family merger. He finds that all defunct mutual fund portfolios are smaller in size and have lower inflows.

1.5 Risk and Return

Many studies focus on the investment risk of mutual funds in regard to performance. Koch (1975) tests the basic hypothesis that the management objectives of a particular mutual fund, to a large extent, determine the risk and return structure of the fund's portfolio. The relationship between time-varying systematic risk and performance for mutual fund portfolios are analyzed by Kon and Jen (1978). Fabozzi and Francis (1979) also empirically study mutual fund systematic risk for bull and bear markets. Non-stationary or time varying systematic risk is further analyzed, both theoretically and empirically, by Alexander, Benson, and Eger (1982). Twenty years later, Karceski (2002) develops an agency model in which returns-chasing behavior by mutual fund investors induces systematic risk, i.e., beta, not to be priced to the degree predicted by the standard CAPM.

Under the agency framework, Golec and Starks (2004) find that a group of mutual funds changes their portfolio risk levels after being forced to change their performance fee schedule. In the context of the fund family, a matter of recent concern in the industry, Elton, Gruber, and Green (2007) find that restricting investment to one fund family leads to a greater total portfolio risk than diversifying across fund families, because mutual fund returns are correlated more closely within than between fund families.

Busse (1999) proposes a very interesting issue of volatility timing, i.e., a fund's ability to time market volatility. People believe it to be very difficult to predict market returns, but not market volatility. Additionally, in a practical or empirical sense (but not in a theoretical sense), market volatility evidences a contemporaneous negative relation with market return. His idea is simple and intuitive, in that a fund would outperform other funds, if its fund manager were able to predict market volatility. He shows volatility timing to be an important factor in the returns of mutual funds, and also that it leads to higher risk-adjusted returns.

1.6 Style Analysis

Brown and Goetzmann (1997) are the first to classify manager 'style'. They contend that their classifications are superior to common industry classifications in terms of predicting cross-sectional future performance, as well as past performance. In a subsequent study, Chan, Chen, and Lakonishok (2002) provide evidence that growth managers on average outperform value managers after adjusting for style.

1.7 Economies of scale, information, and tax

Dermine and Roller (1992) evaluate economies of scale and scope in the French mutual funds (SICAV) industry. They suggest economies of scale and scope for small institutions and diseconomies for larger firms. An appropriate size for a diversified company is in the range of FF 2.9 billion. Collins and Mack (1997) show the optimal asset size for a multiproduct fund complex in the U.S. to be between $20 billion and $40 billion, and also that the average fund complex could realize some efficiency gains by increasing its asset size. The optimal size of the U.S. is far larger than that of France. However, we fail to find any study sufficiently powerful to draw any conclusions regarding the optimal size of fund family.

Coval and Moskowitz (2001) find that fund managers earn substantial abnormal returns in nearby investments. Their results indicate that investors trade local securities at an informational advantage and point toward a link between such trading and asset prices. From the perspective of social networks, Cohen, Frazzini, and Malloy (2008) try to identify information transfer in security markets by focusing on connections between mutual fund managers and corporate board members via shared education networks. They find that portfolio managers place larger bets on connected firms and perform significantly better onthese holdings relative to their non-connected holdings. This implies that social networks may be important mechanisms for information flow into asset prices. From a financial conglomerate perspective, Massa and Rehman (2008) analyze the relationship between mutual funds and banks belonging to the same financial group. They find that financial conglomerates exploit privileged inside information that is unavailable to other market participants. Their results points to information flows within conglomerates through informal channels, such as personal acquaintances.

Regarding the effect of taxes, Barclay, Pearson, and Weisbach (1998) present a theoretical model to explain why most open-end mutual funds regularly realize and distribute a large portion of their gains despite the advantage of deferred tax payments. They show that, in equilibrium, managers seeking to attract new investors pass through taxable capital gains to reduce the overhang of unrealized gains. In the U.S., Gibson, Safieddine and Titman (2000) show that the tax-motivated trading of mutual funds mitigate potential price pressures by applying the foresight to spread tax-motivated sales over relatively long time horizons. On the other hand, Brown, Goetzmann, Hiraki, Otsuki and Shiraishi (2001) find that Japanese tax-dilution effects differ across manager styles and that these differences constitute a significant component of measured managerial inefficiency. They assert that the Japanese experience provides a framework for policy makers around the world who are considering the potential consequences of simplifying their tax code. Recently, Bae and Yi (2008) also find that the timing performance of mutual fund managers improves significantly afterrepeal of a tax regulation, which is the short-short rule. They argue that the perverse timing ability documented in the previous literature is partly due to the tax regulation imposed on mutual funds.

2. Agency Problems

2.1 Governance

People believe mutual fund governance to be related to performance. Directors' ownership is a matter of mutual fund governance. Chen, Goldstein, and Jiang (2008) and Cremers, Driessen, and Maenhout (2009) find that directors' ownership is related strongly with directors' monitoring and fund performance. Khorana (1996) conducts a study on boards of directors. He finds an inverse relationship between managerial replacement and prior fund performance, which is consistent with the presence of well-functioning internal and external market mechanisms for mutual fund managers. Dangl,

Wu, and Zechner (2008) develop a continuous-time model in which a portfolio manager is hired by a management company. With regard to board characteristics, Adams, Mansi, and Nishikawa (2010) find an inverse relationship between board size and fund performance.

Then, the next question is the effect of governance on mutual fund fees and compensation rates. Tufano and Sevick (1997) find that shareholder fees are lower when fund boards are smaller, have a greater fraction of independent directors, and are composed of directors who sit on a large fraction of the fund sponsor's other boards. Regarding compensation rate, Deli (2002) shows that advisors of funds with greater turnover and close-end funds receive higher marginal compensation, and marginal compensation is lower for advisors of large funds and large fund families. Further, Warner and Wu (2011) find that rate increases are associated with superior past market-adjusted performance, whereas rate decreases reflect economies of scale associated with growth, and are not associated with extremely poor performance.

Almazan, Brown, and Carlson (2004) examine the economic rationale for various mutual fund investment restrictions. Restrictions are related more closely with more experienced managers, single management, and small mutual fund families.

Davis and Kim (2007) study voting behavior of mutual funds. They find that aggregate votes at the fund family level indicate a positive relation between business ties and the propensity to vote with management.

The final important issue of governance is the effect of board structure on mergers. Khorana, Tufano, and Wedge (2007) are the first to find that across-family mergers are more likely when funds underperform and their boards have a larger percentage of independent trustees. This finding implies that more-independent boards tolerate less underperformance before initiating across-family mergers.

2.2 Managerial Incentives

Managerial incentives include a host of agency problems which may include mutual fund scandals, tournaments, and relationships with brokers, as discussed immediately below. Starks (1987) is the first to study the impact of compensation contracts on investment decisions in a restricted mean-variance world. She finds that the symmetric contract dominates the bonus contract in aligning the manager's interests with the investor's interests. Lemmon, Schallheim, and Zender (2000) examine the effect of financial incentives on real behavior. They model the behavior that an expected compensation-maximizing agent would exhibit when faced with such contracts, and derive several testable implications. Das and Sundaram (2002), from a theoretical perspective, show that the fee structure used to compensate investment advisors is central to the study of fund design and affects investor welfare. Their surprising finding is that the incentive fee is often more attractive than fulcrum fee from the standpoint of investor welfare, which is not consistent with Starks (1987). From an empirical standpoint, Dass, Massa, and Patgiri (2008) show that the incentives contained within the mutual funds' advisory contracts induce managers to overcome their tendency to herd, thereby reducing their holding of bubble stocks. Massa and Patgiri (2009) empirically support Das and Sundaram (2002). They find that high-incentive contracts induce managers to take more risk and reduce the funds' probability of survival, but that funds with high-incentive contracts deliver higher risk-adjusted returns and their superior performance remains persistent.

Chevalier and Ellison (1999b) investigate mutual fund managers from the standpoint of the labor market. They find that termination is more performance-sensitive for younger managers, and identify possible implicit incentives created by the termination-performance relationship. The termination-performance relationship may give younger managers an incentive to avoid unsystematic risk and to herd into popular sectors. Chen and Pennacchi (2009) model a manager's portfolio choice for the compensation rules of a concave, linear, or convex function of the fund's performance relative to that of a benchmark. They find a tendency for mutual funds to increase the standard deviation of tracking errors, but not the standard deviation of returns, as their performance declines. They conclude that this risk-shifting behavior appears more common for funds whose managers have longer tenures.

Gervais, Lynch, and Musto (2005) find that a fund family that learns what the manager learns can ameliorate this inefficiency cost, given a family of sufficient size. They note that the family's incentive is to retain any given manager regardless of his/her skill but, when the family has enough managers, it adds value by boosting the credibility of its retentions through the firing of others.

Khorana, Servaes, and Wedge (2007) find that future risk-adjusted performance is positively related to managerial ownership. Their findings support the notion that managerial ownership has desirable incentive alignment attributes for mutual fund investors, and indicate that the disclosure of this information is useful in making portfolio allocation decisions-making.

Evans (2010) addresses the very interesting issue of mutual fund incubation. He finds that funds in incubation outperform non-incubated funds, and when they are opened to the public they attract higher flows. Interestingly, this outperformance disappears in the post-incubation period.

Very recently, Wahal and Wang (2011) examine the impact of the entry of new mutual funds on incumbents using the overlap in their portfolio holdings as a measure of competitive intensity. They find that incumbents having high overlap with entrants subsequently engage in price competition by reducing management fees.

Cici, Gibson, and Moussawi (2010) examine the performance of mutual funds managed by firms that simultaneously manage hedge funds. Proponents of this practice assert that it is essential to hire and retain star fund managers, particularly for small advisory companies. The other side, however, argues that the temptation for abuse in this circumstance is high, and the practice should be banned. Cici, Gibson, and Moussawi (2010) find that the reported returns of mutual funds in these side-by-side associations with hedge funds significantly underperformed those of mutual funds that share similar fund and family characteristics, but differ in that they are unaffiliated with hedge funds. Contrary to Cici, Gibson, and Moussawi (2010), Nohel, Wang, and Zheng (2010) show that side-by-side mutual fund managers significantly out-perform peer funds, consistent with this privilege being granted primarily to star performers. They find no evidence of welfare loss for mutual fund investors, due to the exploitation of conflicts of interests.

Some recent studies concerned themselves with family matters. Nanda, Wang, and Zheng (2004) document that star performance results in greater cash flows to both the fund and other funds in its family. They argue that spillovers may induce less able families to pursue star-creating strategies. Such strategy may cause subsidization to a very limited number of funds in a family. Gaspar, Massa, and Matos (2006) investigate whether mutual fund families strategically transfer performance across member funds to favor those more likely to increase family profits. They find that high-value funds over-perform at the expense of low-value funds. Their findings imply that the family organization may generate distortions in delegated asset management.

In an attempt to elucidate the issue of incomplete disclosure, Kacperczyk, Sialm, and Zheng (2008) estimate the impact of unobserved actions on fund returns using the return gap between the reported return and the return on a portfolio that invests in the previously disclosed fund holdings. They document that the unobserved actions of some funds persistently create value, while such actions of other funds destroy value.

Carhart, Kaniel, Musto, and Reel (2002) assess the fascinating issue of portfolio pumping in mutual funds. They present evidence that fund managers inflate quarter-end portfolio prices with last-minute purchases of stocks already held. Gallagher, Gardner, and Swan (2009) support Carhart, Kaniel, Musto, and Reel (2002).

2.3 Mutual Fund Scandals

Generally, mutual funds calculate net asset value (henceforth NAV) at the end of each trading day. Investors buy and sell (or redeem) mutual funds at this NAV. NAV is determined at 4:00 PM, i.e., the close of New York Stock Exchange. Orders arriving prior to 4:00 PM should be executed at that NAV after the close of market. This is referred to as 'forward pricing'. 'Backward pricing' is its opposite concept that is illegal. Against the legal practice of forward pricing, mutual fund scandal occurred in 2003. The first principal issue in the scandal was 'late trading' which refers to the practice of both accepting buy and sell orders after NAV is determined at the market close, and executing the orders at the pre-determined NAV. Late trading is a violation of the Investment Company Act of 1940. Some clear evidence of late trading is found by Chalmers, Edelen, and Kadlec (2001), Greene and Hodges (2002), Johnson (2004), and Zitzewitz (2006). Empirical findings led the SEC to amend the related SEC rules.

The second issue is called 'market timing' which is not illegal; however, this practice also exploits stale prices deriving from differences in time zones. Bhargava, Bose, and Dubofsky (1998) show this unfair international fund investors' behavior, i.e., hedge funds' trades, at the early stage. Their sample size and period are, however, quite limited, and this was not a popular academic issue at that time. A few years later, Bhargava and Dubofsky (2001) and Goetzmann, Ivkovic, and Rouwenhorst (2001) show that international mutual funds are exposed to speculative traders. Nobody has yet provided, however, any clear or satisfactory answer to this issue, despite many interesting findings.

2.4 Tournaments

Brown, Harlow, and Starks (1996) first attempt to investigate the risk adjustment behavior of fund managers using monthly mutual fund returns. They find that mid-year losers tend to increase fund volatility in the second part of an annual assessment to a greater extent than do mid-year winners. Chevalier and Ellison (1997) show that the shape of the flow-performance relationship creates incentives for fund managers to increase or decrease the riskiness of the fund that are dependent on the fund's year-to-date return. They support Brown, Harlow, and Starks (1996).

Busse (2001) re-tests the tournament behavior using daily returns of mutual funds, and concludes that the results of Brown, Harlow, and Starks (1996) are more likely an artifact of inefficient monthly volatility estimates. In the context of a fund family, Kempf and Ruenzi (2008) attempt to test tournaments as an extension of Brown, Harlow, and Starks (1996) using monthly returns of equity mutual funds. They find that fund managers adjust the risk they take depending on their relative position within their fund family, and conclude that the direction of risk adjustment depends on the competitive situation pertaining to that family. They stress the role of the family in the tournament behavior of fund managers, which is referred to as the family tournament. Kempf and Ruenzi, and Thiele (2009) also investigate the effects of managerial risk-taking incentives due to either employment risk or compensation. They show that when employment risk is low, compensation incentives become more relevant and poor mid-year performers increase risk to catch up with the mid-year winners.

2.5 Relationship with Brokers

The agency problems between mutual fund investors and brokers are more recent issues, despite their importance to investors' interests. Initial public offerings are a useful tool to unfairly benefit both mutual fund families and brokers. Reuter (2006) finds a positive correlation between commissions paid to lead underwriters and the reported holdings of the IPOs they underwrite. Ritter and Zhang (2007) further investigate how investment banks employ initial public offerings (IPOs) in relation to their affiliated funds. They find little evidence to support the dumping ground hypothesis, although there is some support for the nepotism hypothesis during the internet bubble period of 1999~2000. This means that the lead underwriter does not allocate more cold IPOs to its affiliated funds.

On the other hand, Bergstresser, Chalmers, and Tufano (2009) attempt to compare broker-sold and direct-sold funds; they fail to find that brokers deliver substantial tangible benefits. This finding implies that broker-sold funds do not exhibit any superior skill to direct-sold funds. This finding raises the question as to why investors buy mutual funds through brokers.

3. Other Issues

3.1 Pension Issues

Since 1990s, undoubtedly, the U.S. mutual fund markets have grown very quickly with the increase in baby boomers' pension assets. At this stage, huge amounts of U.S. pension assets are invested in mutual funds as well as capital instruments such as stocks and bonds. Total U.S. retirement assets, as of June 20, 2010, are $15.7 trillion. Interestingly, retirement savings account for 36% of all household financial assets in the U.S. Individual retirement accounts (henceforth IRAs) account for a total of $4.2 trillion, of which 45% assets are invested in mutual funds. Americans hold $4.0 trillion in all employer-based defined contribution (henceforth DC) plans, $2.7 trillion of which is held in 401(k) plans. Mutual funds manage $2.0 trillion of assets in all DC plans. When combined with IRA assets, a total of $3.89 trillion is managed by mutual funds. This close relationship between pension assets and mutual funds makes pension issues an important field of inquiry.

Not many scholars have studied this area. Del Guercio and Tkac (2002) compare the relations between asset flow and performance in retail mutual funds and pension funds. They find a striking difference in the shape of the flow-performance relation between mutual funds and pension funds. Generally, pension clients punish poorly performing managers by withdrawing assets under management, and do not herd to recent winners to a disproportionate degree. They conclude that pension fund managers have little incentive to engage in risk-shifting behavior such as tournaments. Meanwhile, Elton, Gruber, and Blake (2007) are the first to investigate both the efficacy with which plan administrators select funds for 401(k) plans, and the manner in which participants react to plan administrators' decisions. They find that 401(k) plan administrators select funds that outperform randomly selected funds of the same type although they do not outperform index funds of the same type, and participant allocations in the aggregate perform no better than naive allocation rules. Bodie and Treussard (2007) also present the issues with self-directed investment choices in retirement plans, and examine target-date funds as a proposed solution.

3.2 Survivorship Bias

Survivorship bias may lead mutual fund researchers in wrong directions. Brown, Goetzmann, Ibbotson, and Ross (1992) show that the evidence of mutual fund return predictability derives from the spurious relationship between volatility and returns attributable to survivorship bias. Elton, Gruber, and Blake (1996b) estimate the size of the survivorship bias to evaluate its effect on performance. Elton, Gruber, and Blake (2001) further scrutinize the CRSP and Mornigstar mutual fund database, and conclude that the CRSP database also has an omission bias that exerts the same effects as survivorship bias. Carhart, Carpenter, Lynch, and Musto (2002) demonstrate theoretically that when survivor depends on multi-period performance, the survivorship bias in average performance typically increases with the sample length. They find that survivor conditioning weakens the evidence of performance persistence. With regard to survivorship bias, no other issues have been studied ever since. Ter Horst, Nijman, and Verbeek (2001) provide a correction method for look-ahead bias using weights based on probit regressions. Their bias-corrected results imply no evidence for performance persistence on a risk-adjusted basis.

3.3 Index Funds

Burgess and O'Dell (1978) are the first to study the efficiency of index funds. Their empirical results imply that the performance of an index fund or a pension fund based on the DJIA or the S&P 500 would be superior to individual stocks and mean-variance efficient portfolios as well as to mutual funds. In contrast to Burgess and O'Dell (1978), Elton, Gruber, and Busse (2004) show that the selection of funds based on low expenses or high past returns outperforms the portfolio of index funds selected by investors. Their results exemplify the fact that dominated products can prosper in a market without any arbitrage.

Goetzmann and Massa (2003) find a strong contemporaneous correlation between inflows and returns, with no evidence for positive feedback trading. Their two measures of the dispersion of expert opinion, i.e., open interest in S&P 500 futures and the dispersion of investor newsletter recommendations, correlate to outflows from funds. They suggest that the analysis of the relationship between expert opinion and small investor beliefs may prove fruitful.

Some studies have interested themselves in the role of non-portfolio fund differentiation and search frictions in the existence of a large number of funds and the sizable dispersion in fund fees. In a case study, Hortacsu and Syverson (2004) find that despite the financial homogeneity of S&P 500 index funds, this sector exhibits the fund proliferation and fee dispersion noted in the broader industry. Choi, Laibson, and Madrian (2010) attempt to determine why individuals invest in high-fee index funds. They reject the hypothesis that investors buy high-fee index funds because of bundled non-portfolio services. They also find that search costs for fees matter; however, fees are not minimized even when eliminating these costs. Choi, Laibson, and Madrian (2010) conclude that fees decrease with financial literacy, and interestingly, investors who choose high-fee funds sense that they are making a mistake.

3.4 Closed-end Funds

While closed-end fund studies have been conducted in many ways, early approaches have focused on the discounts and premia of close-end fund prices. Generally, when closed-end funds go public, they trade at a premium, however, in the near future, they trade at a discount. Boudreaux (1973) is the first to analyze discounts and premia on closed-end funds. Brauer (1988) asserts that the precise nature of information contained in a discount of closed-end fund is not clear. Peavy (1990) studies the price behavior of closed-end fund IPO returns. He finds that the mean initial day's return is not significantly different from zero in contrast to previous findings for non-fund IPOs, and that after-market returns are significantly negative unlike other new issues; this implies closed-end fund discounts. Brickley, Manaster, and Schallheim (1991) show that the discounts are positively cross-sectionally correlated with the average variance of the constituent assets in the fund, and that, in the time series, the value of discount vanes counter-cyclically. On the other hand, Pontiff (1995) investigates closed-end fund premium. He finds fund premium to be correlated negatively with future returns, and also that motivated explanations do not account economically for this effect. Swaminathan (1996) describes the relation between closed-end fund discounts and time-varying expected excess returns on small firms, which provides significant support for a rational explanation of the time-series relationship between discounts and expected returns on small firms. Chay and Trzcinka (1999) find that the discounts and premia of closed-end funds reflect the market's assessments of anticipated managerial performance.

As pointed out by Lee, Shleifer, and Thaler (1991), closed-end fund discounts might be used as a proxy for investor sentiment. Regarding arbitrage using closed-end funds, Pontiff (1996) finds that arbitrage costs lead to large deviations of prices from fundamentals. That is, cost factors are related to the magnitude of the price deviation from NAV. Gemmill and Thomas (2002) show that noise-trader sentiment, as proxied by retail-investor flows, leads to fluctuations in the discount. Johnson, Lin, and Song (2006) describe an interesting relationship between dividend policy and discounts on closed-end funds. They contend that the minimum dividend policy of close-end funds exerts a signaling effect on discounts, such that this policy represents deliberate attempts to reduce share price undervaluation relative to NAV. Recently, Berk and Stanton (2007) show that the existence of managerial ability, coupled with the labor contract prevalent in the industry, implies that the closed-end fund discount should exhibit many of the primary features documented in the relevant literature. To our knowledge, however, no satisfactory explanation has yet been advanced with regard to closed-end fund premia and discounts.

In addition to the closed-end fund discounts, Pontiff (1997) investigates the variance of close-end fund returns. If investors are rational, the variance should equal that of underlying securities. He finds, however, that the average closed-end fund monthly return is 64 percent more volatile than its assets.

Information reflection is also analyzed in this area. Klibanoff, Lamont, and Wizman (1998) find that closed-end country fund prices under-react to news in a typical week, however, react much more in weeks with news appearing on the front page of the New York Times. Repurchase could be an important piece of information which has asignaling effect. Porter, Roenfeldt, and Sicherman (1999) show that repurchases increase share price even when there is no asymmetric information regarding the value of the underlying assets, and the percentage discount remains unchanged after the repurchase.

A number of studies investigate various issues of closed-end funds. Fund advisory compensation is analyzed by Coles, Suay, and Woodbury (2000), agency conflicts by Khorana, Wahal, and Zenner (2002), governance by Guercio, Dann, and Partch (2003). Cherkes, Sagi, and Stanton (2009) develop a rational liquidity-based model of closed-end funds which provides an economic motivation for the existence of this organizational form. Their empirical investigation provides more support for a liquidity-based model than for an alternative sentiment-based explanation.

Recently, two studies on closed-end country funds are available. Patro (2005) investigates the effects of financial market liberalization on emerging market country fund premium, share prices, and net asset values. He shows that the listing of new country funds resulted in 8.8% decrease in the premia on the old funds during the 4 months beginning with the announcement of the new funds. Approaching this from a different perspective, Nishiotis (2006) studies the long-run relationship between country fund premia and international capital flows.

The final issue relevant to closed-end funds is open-ending attempts. After the 1992 proxy reform which reduces the costs of communication among shareholders, activist arbitrageurs have frequently attempted to open-end discounted closed-end funds. Bradley, Brav, Goldstein, and Jiang (2010) find that open-ending attempts significantly affect discounts, reducing them, on average, to half their original level. That is, the size of the discount is a major determinant of whether or not a fund is attacked.

3.5 Behavioral Finance

From the viewpoint of behavioral finance, market or investor sentiments are very important issues in fund markets. Lee, Shleifer, and Thaler (1991) are the first to examine the proposition that fluctuations in discounts of closed-end funds are driven by changes in individual investor sentiment. They find that both closed-end funds and small stocks tend to be held by individual investors, andthat the discounts on closed-end fundsnarrow when small stocks perform well. In a subsequent study, Bodurtha, Kim, and Lee (1995) investigate closed-end country funds in relation to U.S. market sentiment. They show that country fund premium movements reflect a U.S.-specific risk, which may be interpreted as U.S. market sentiment. However, Elton, Gruber, and Busse (1998) dispute the market sentiment view of closed-end fund discounts. They fail to find any evidence that small investor sentiment (i.e., discount on closed-end funds) is an important factor in the return generating process.

Neal and Wheatley (1998) examine the forecast power of three popular measures of individual investor sentiment: the level of discounts on closed-end funds, the ratio of odd-lot sales to purchases, and net mutual fund redemptions. They find that only funddiscounts and net redemptions predict the size premium. Furthermore, Frazzini and Lamont (2008) employ mutual fund flows as a measure of individual investor sentiment for different stocks, and find that high sentiment predicts low future returns. Ben-Rephael, Kandel, and Wohl (2011) focus on contemporaneous relation between investor sentiment and market returns. They employ aggregate exchanges of equity funds as a sentiment proxy. In their study, this measure is positively and contemporaneously correlated with aggregate stock market excess returns, which supports the notion that 'noise' in aggregate market prices is induced by investor sentiment.

The second issue in behavioral finance is the herd behavior of mutual funds and momentum. Grinblatt, Titman, and Wermers (1995) note that 77% of mutual funds are momentum investors, buying stocks that are past winners, but most do not systematically sell past losers; this results in the observed herd behavior of mutual funds. They also find that mutual funds that exploit momentum strategies tend to realize significantly better performance than other funds on average. They conclude that relatively weak evidence exists to suggest the existence of mutual fund herd behavior. Falkenstein (1996) finds that mutual funds have a significant preference towards stocks with high visibility and low transaction costs, and are averse to stocks with low idiosyncratic volatility. His findings arerelevant to theories concerning investor recognition, a potential agency problem in mutual funds, tests of trend-following and herd behavior by mutual funds, and corporate finance. Wermers (1999) finds little herding by mutual funds in average stocks, butmuch higher levels of herding in trades of small stocks and in trading by growth-oriented funds. He concludes that the observed results are consistent with mutual fund herding speeding the price-adjustment process. Goetzmann and Massa (2002) identify classes of momentum and contrarian investors to build up behavioral factors based on contrarian and momentum flows, and show that they are relevant to pricing. By way of contrast with the U.S. results, Wylie (2005) shows that U.K. mutual fund managers tend to herd out of large stocks after high excess returns.

Using data regarding mutual fund holdings, Frazzini (2006) tests the disposition effect of mutual funds, i.e., the tendency of investors to ride losses and realize gains. He finds a disposition effect of mutual funds, which induces under-reactions to news, thereby resulting in return predictability.

3.6 Fund Rating

Most studies on fund ratings consider the effects of the Monrnigstar star rating on future fund performance. Sharpe (1998) show that neither Morningstar's measure nor the excess-return Sharpe ratio is an efficient tool for choosing mutual funds within peer groups for a multi-fund portfolio. Blake and Morey (2000) also examine the Morningstar rating system as a predictor of mutual fund performance for U.S. domestic equity funds. They find that low-rated funds indicate relatively poor future performance, but highest-rated funds do not outperform the next-to-highest and median-rated funds. They conclude that Morningstar ratings, at best, perform only slightly better than alternative predictors in terms of forecasting future fund performance.

Then, the next question involves the degree of sensitivity of mutual fund flows to Monningstar ratings. Morey (2002) analyzes the age bias in the Morningstar rating that the average overall star ratings of seasoned funds are consistently higher than the average overall star ratings of younger funds. He warns against Morningstar ratings stating that if star ratings affect fund flows, then the age bias in the Morningstar ratings is of significance to the mutual fund industry and to investors. According to Morey (2002), Morningstar adjusted their rating system. Adkisson and Fraser (2003) show that a potential age bias still exists in the new star ratings. Del Guercio and Tkac (2008) study the effect of Morningstar ratings on mutual fund flows in a scientific way. They find economically and statistically abnormal flow in the expected direction. In other words, there exist abnormally positive fund flows for rating upgrades, and abnormally negative fund flows for rating downgrades. They conclude that Morningstar ratings have unique power to affect asset flows. Faff, Parwada, and Poh (2007) also find very similar evidence in Australia that investors flock to newly upgraded funds while they penalize those that have been downgraded by withdrawing funds.

3.7 Various funds

Academicians are also interested in a variety of funds aside from equity mutual funds. Rosen and Katz (1983) show that the deregulation caused the astounding growth of money market funds in the late 1970s and early

1980s. Christoffersen (2001) discovers why more than half of money fund managers voluntarily waive their fees.

On the other hand, Blake, Elton, and Gruber (1993) investigate bond funds and their underperformance relative to benchmark indices. Very recently, Chen, Ferson, and Peters (2010) also find that, adjusting for nonlinearity, the performance of many bond funds is significantly negative on an after-cost basis.

Comer (2006) examines the stock market timing ability of two samples of hybrid mutual funds, and finds that the timing ability exists for the period of 1992~2000, but not for the 1981~1991 period. Recently, Comer, Larrymore, and Rodriguez (2009) stress the role of controlling for fixed-income exposure in portfolio evaluation.

Elton, Gruber, Comer, and Li (2002) study a specific type of ETFs, i.e., Spider (ETF for S&P 500), and find that Spider underperform the S&P index by 28 basis points and low-cost index funds by 18 points owing to the lost income caused by holding dividends received on the underlying shares in cash. Poterba and Shoven (2002) compare the pre-tax and after-tax returns of Spider.

3.8 The Others

At an early stage, Simonson (1972) and Lee and Lerro (1973) study the speculative behavior of mutual funds and optimal portfolio selection. Fabozzi, Francis, and Lee (1980) present the implications of the generalized return-generating model in estimating the variables of the model for mutual funds. Gatto, Geske, Litzenberger, and Sosin (1980) examine the valuation and demand for the mutual fund insurance sold in the U.S. by the Harleysville and Prudential Insurance Companies.[9]

Koski and Pontiff (1999) examine the use of derivatives and show that mutual funds use derivatives to reduce the cost of maintaining a certain risk exposure, rather than to manipulate fund risk opportunistically. Deli

---

9) Mutual fund insurance is just insurance against investment loss.

and Varma (2002) extend Koski and Pontiff (1999) by showing that the option to invest in derivatives is retained only by those funds where the potential gains from reduced transaction costs are large.

Meanwhile, home bias is investigated by Chan, Covrig, and Ng (2005). They find robust evidence that their world-wide sample funds allocate a disproportionately larger fraction of investment to domestic funds. Hau and Rey (2008) study international equity mutual fund trading practices, and describe the manner in which international investment behavior and patterns of heterogeneity can constitute a useful rubric for determining the causal factors of home bias. In a domestic sense, Parwada (2008) traces the employment and geographic heritage of 358 entrepreneurial fund managers and analyzes the determinants of where they locate their firms and stock selections. He finds that the propensity to invest closer to home is strongly correlated with the presence of sub-advisory opportunities from institutional investors in the vicinity.

Wilcox (2003) examines investors' choice of mutual funds within a given class of funds. He finds that investors pay a great deal of attention to past performance, and vastly overweight loads relatively to expense ratios, which is consistent with Barber, Odean, and Zheng (2005).

The relation between fund size and diversification is analyzed by Pollet and Wilson (2008). They find that large funds and small-cap funds diversify their portfolios in response to growth, and that greater diversification, especially for small-cap funds, is associated with better performance.

Mola and Guidolin (2009) document that sell-side analysts are likely to assign frequent and favorable ratings to a stock after the analysts' affiliated mutual funds invest in that stock.

Massa, Reuter, and Zitzewitz (2010) study the choice between named and anonymous mutual fund managers. They argue that fund families weigh the benefits of naming managers against the costs associated with their increased future bargaining power.

Matvos and Ostrovsky (2010) study voting in corporate director elections and find that heterogeneity and peer effects are as important in shaping voting outcomes as firm and director characteristics.

Firth, Lin, and Zou (2010) investigate the role of state and mutual fund ownership in the split-share structure reform in China. Their evidence is consistent with their predictions that state shareholders have incentives to complete the split-share structure reform quickly and exert political pressure on mutual funds to accept the terms without a fight.

IV. Mutual Fund Studies in Korea

For the purpose of reviewing Korean mutual fund studies, we select the following 7 Korean academic journals: Asia-Pacific Journal of Financial Studies (AJFS), Korean Journal of Financial Studies (KJFS, formerly Journal of Korea Securities Association), Asian Review of Financial Research (ARFR, formerly Korean Journal of Finance), (Korean) Journal of Business Research (KJBR), Daehan Journal of Business (DJB), Korean Journal of Financial Management (KJFM), and Journal of Insurance and Finance (JIF). Because equity funds are pertinent to the concept of money management, most studies focus on them. Hence, we also review mutual fund studies with an emphasis on equity mutual funds.

<Table 3> shows the time trend of the number of mutual fund studies published in each Koran academic journal. Among the 7 selected journals, mutual fund studies are most frequently published in both the Korean/ Asia-Pacific Journal of Financial Studies and Daehan Journal of Business,

comprising a proportion of 28.89% each. Very few articles on mutual funds are published in Korean economics journals. We include only mutual fund studies that focus on Korean markets. Mutual fund studies have been appearing since as early as 1992. With the rapid growth of the mutual fund markets and industry since 2001, academicians have become increasingly interested in the economic behavior of mutual funds. As can be seen in <Table 1>, the number of mutual fund articles in academic journals has increased at a surprising rate since 2001. At this stage, as of 2010, the area of mutual funds can be considered a component of mainstream finance in Korea.

<Table 3> The Number of Mutual Fund Studies in Each Koran Journal

ARFR (Asian Review of Financial Research, 재무연구, formerly Korean Journal of Finance (KJF)), KJFS/APJFS (Korean Journal of Financial Studies/Asia–Pacific Journal of Financial Studies, 국문 증권학회지/영문 증권학회지, formerly Journal of Korea Securities Association (JKSA)), KJFM (Korean Journal of Financial Management, 재무관리연구), DJB (Daehan Journal of Business, 대한 경영학회지), KJBR ((Korean) Journal of Business Research, 경영연구), JIF (Journal of Insurance and Finance, 보험금융연구). Because the KJFS and AJFS are originated from the JKSA very recently, we treat them as the same journal.

Journal	1991~1995	1996~2000	2001~2005	2006~2010	Total
ARFR (KJF)	0	0	4	3	7 (15.56%)
KJFS/APJFS (JKSA)	1	2	5	4	13 (28.89%)
KJFM	1	2	0	6	9 (20.00%)
DJB	0	0	1	12	13 (28.89%)
KJBR	0	0	0	1	1 (2.22%)
JIF	0	0	0	2	2 (4.44%)
Total	2 (4.44%)	4 (8.89%)	10 (22.22%)	29 (64.44%)	45 (100%)

The taxonomy of mutual fund studies is provided in <Table 4>. Panel A shows cross-sectional taxonomy from 1991 through 2010. As in the U.S., the category of economics of mutual funds is responsible for more than half of all published papers. Among all the papers, 28.89% deal with performance evaluation. The fewest papers are published in the category of

\<Table 4\> Taxonomy of Mutual Fund Studies in Korea

Panel A: Cross-sectional taxonomy of mutual fund studies from 1991 through 2010

	ARFR (KJF)	KJFS/APJFS (JKSA)	KJFM	DJB	KJBR	JIF	Total
Economics of mutual funds	*3*	*7*	*7*	*6*	*1*	*0*	*24 (53.33%)*
Performance evaluation	0	3	5	4	1	0	13 (28.89%)
Costs, fees, and expenses	0	0	1	0	0	0	1 (2.22%)
Fund flows	3	2	1	0	0	0	6 (13.33%)
Growth, set-up, and termination	0	0	0	0	0	0	0 (.00%)
Risk and return	0	0	0	1	0	0	1 (2.22%)
Style analysis	0	2	0	0	0	0	2 (4.44%)
Fund size, information, and tax	0	0	0	1	0	0	1 (2.22%)
Agency problems	*1*	*0*	*0*	*1*	*0*	*1*	*3 (6.67%)*
Governance	0	0	0	0	0	0	0 (.00%)
Managerial incentive	0	0	0	0	0	0	0 (.00%)
Mutual fund scandal	1	0	0	0	0	0	1 (2.22%)
Tournaments	0	0	0	1	0	1	2 (4.44%)
Relationship with broker	0	0	0	0	0	0	0 (.00%)
The other issues	*3*	*6*	*2*	*6*	*0*	*1*	*18 (40.00%)*
Pension issues	0	0	0	0	0	0	0 (.00%)
Data and survivorship bias	0	0	0	0	0	0	0 (.00%)
Index funds	0	0	0	2	0	0	2 (4.44%)
Closed-end funds	1	1	2	1	0	0	5 (11.11%)
Behavioral finance	0	2	0	1	0	0	3 (6.67%)
The other funds	1	1	0	1	0	0	3 (6.67%)
Fund rating	0	0	0	0	0	0	0 (.00%)
The others	1	2	0	1	0	1	5 (11.11%)
Total	7 (15.56%)	13 (28.89%)	9 (20.00%)	13 (28.89%)	1 (2.22%)	2 (4.44%)	45 (100%)

Panel B: Time-series taxonomy of mutual fund studies from 1991 through 2010

	1991~1995	1996~2000	2001~2005	2006~2010	Total
Economics of mutual funds	*2*	*2*	*4*	*16*	*24 (53.33%)*
Performance evaluation	2	1	2	9	13 (28.89%)
Costs, fees, and expenses	0	0	0	1	1 (2.22%)
Fund flows	0	0	2	4	6 (13.33%)
Growth, set-up, and termination	0	0	0	0	0 (.00%)
Risk and return	0	0	0	1	1 (2.22%)
Style analysis	0	1	0	1	2 (4.44%)
Fund size, information, and tax	0	0	0	1	1 (2.22%)
Agency problems	*0*	*0*	*1*	*2*	*3 (6.67%)*
Governance	0	0	0	0	0 (.00%)
Managerial incentive	0	0	0	0	0 (.00%)
Mutual fund scandal	0	0	1	0	1 (2.22%)
Tournaments	0	0	0	2	2 (4.44%)
Relationship with broker	0	0	0	0	0 (.00%)
The other issues	*0*	*2*	*5*	*11*	*18 (40.00%)*
Pension issues	0	0	0	0	0 (.00%)
Data and survivorship bias	0	0	0	0	0 (.00%)
Index funds	0	0	0	2	2 (4.44%)
Closed-end funds	0	2	2	1	5 (11.11%)
Behavioral finance	0	0	0	3	3 (6.67%)
The other funds	0	0	2	1	3 (6.67%)
Fund rating	0	0	0	0	0 (.00%)
The others	0	0	1	4	5 (11.11%)
Total	2	4	10	29	45 (100%)
	(4.44%)	(8.89%)	(22.22%)	(64.44%)	

agency problems. In the category of other issues, closed-end funds are the most highlighted area. In Panel B of the time-series taxonomy, with the increase in the total number of mutual fund studies, the number of performance evaluation studies is also increasing. There exists clear evidence that academicians have seldom studied agency problems in Korea, although the rapid growth of mutual fund markets and investors has necessitated studies into that issue. In the category of other issues, a relatively large proportion of studies are closed-end fund studies. Recently, the area of behavioral finance has been the subject of a large proportion of studies. Unfortunately, the effect of fund ratings has not been studied yet in Korea.

1. The Economics of Mutual Funds

1.1 Performance Evaluation

As in the U.S., the most popular area of mutual fund study in Korea is performance evaluation. Song and Jinn (1992) and Cho (1994) attempt to evaluate the performance of equity funds via traditional performance measures, and find that fund managers do not have market timing and stock selection abilities; this is quite similar to the empirical results found in the U.S. Lim and Woo (1997) use the fund holdings data to evaluate fund performance, but fail to find out performance of equity funds to benchmarks. Park and Chang (2001) make another attempt to evaluate fund performance using traditional measures and the pseudo-DGTW method which does not employ portfolio holdings. Their findings are also consistent with those of previous Korean studies. Han and Lim (2006) analyze the long-term performance of equity funds via direct and reverse regression, and detect neither the outperformance of equity funds nor return dependence. Kim and Park (2009) focus on the timing ability of equity funds. They find market timing and volatility timing of fund managers in a few funds, but draw no conclusions as to whether such ability derives from luck or skill. In a recent study, Kim and Cho (2010) the evaluate performance of equity mutual funds via stochastic factor model, and find that while approximately one-third of the analyzed funds generate positive excess returns, most of their magnitudes are not statistically significant. They conclude that domestic funds do not outperform the passive strategy using reference assets. According to the empirical results above, it's difficult to say whether or not equity fund managers possess market timing and stock selection abilities.

Some studies attempt to test the performance persistence of equity funds. Min (2007) investigates the performance persistence of equity funds, and provides some ambiguous evidence to suggest that this depends on the fund style or sample period. Ko, Wang, Ha, and Paek (2010) find short-term performance persistence of equity funds which is consistent with Bollen and Busse (2005). Kho and Kim (2010) also find the performance persistence of equity funds and the price pressure effects of fund trading due to fund flows, but do not address the smart money effect.

Kim (2001) develops a practical model of measuring mutual fund performance. He examines various ways to measure investment performance of mutual funds, and investigates the effect of foreign exchange rate on mutual fund performance.

Park (2007) investigates the determinants of mutual fund returns. He concludes that the growth character of fund is positively related to its performance, and that lagged fund cash flow has no effect on current fund return. Kim (2010) evaluates the relationship between changes in analysts' recommendations and fund performance, and demonstrates that down-graded recommendation is more reliable than up-graded recommendation.

1.2 Costs, Fees, and Expenses

Won (2009) investigates the function of fund distributors and the appropriateness of sales, and finds a negative relationship between sales fees and fund performance. Until now, the relation between management fees and fund performance has not been studied.

1.3 Fund Flows

A few studies have addressed fund flows. Ko (2002) is the first to investigate the relationship between fund flows and performance at an aggregate level, and find that fund flows are not detrimental to the stock market. He reports the positive feedback trading from market returns to fund flows, but does not report the existence of a flow effect on market returns. Recently, Kim and Kim (2010) re-test the above relation using a nonlinear model, i.e., smooth transition autoregressive (STAR) model. Their results are somewhat different from those of Ko (2002) in the sense that there exists mutual Granger causality between market returns and fund flows. We believe that Kim and Kim (2010) leave this issue for future research in the realm of financial research methodology.

At the individual fund level, Park (2005) investigates the relationship between fund flows and certain characteristics. He shows that fund flows are affected by fund size, age, beta, and sector and family performance, in addition to the fund's own performance. One important finding isthe irrelevance of fund flows to future fund performance, which is not consistent with the smart money effect. Yoo and Hwang (2010b) also fail to find the smart money effect. Recently, Ko and Ha (2010a) investigate the asymmetric relationship between fund flows and returns with an emphasis on structural changes and start-up and survivorship biases, which reflect the unique features of the Korean fund market. They find an asymmetric relationship between the fund flows and returns reported in the U.S. studies and a profound effect of market structural changes on the relation, but fail to show start-up bias and survivorship biases.

From a different perspective, Chung and Park (2010) study the effects of fund flows on market risk. They find somewhat positive relationship between equity fund flows and market risk, but conclude the absence of fund-run possibility because of weak evidence of results.

1.4 Risk and Return

Yi and Park (2008) investigate the effects of derivatives use on fund performance and risk. They show that derivatives use exerts a positive effect on performance and a null effect on risk changes.

1.5 Style Analysis

The relationship between equity style and performance is analyzed first by Lee, Lee, and Park (2000) which finds, using the performance evaluation technique developed by Daniel, Grinblatt, Titman, and Wermers (1997), that the 46% of equity fund returns derives from fund style, whereas stock selection and market timing result in 30% and 24% of returns, respectively. Recently, Kang and Lee (2010) investigate the investment styles and performance persistence of equity funds via Sharpe's style analysis methodology. They document that, relative to the market capitalization of stocks in each style portfolio, equity funds in Korea have a high degree of exposure to small and value stocks, although the absolute exposure of large and growth stocks is higher than that of small and value stocks. Additionally, they show time-varying patterns of equity fund styles.

1.6 Economies of Scale, Information, and Tax

Suh, Hong, and Lee (2008) investigate the relationship between fund size and performance, and find a second-order concave relationship. They conclude that there exists an optimal fund size, and that diseconomies of scale may arise if the fund size exceeds a given level from a perspective of performance.

2. Agency Problems

2.1 Mutual Fund Scandals

Ko (2004) studies the agency problem of wealth transfer from the backward pricing of equity funds. His analysis illustrates the drawback of the old backward pricing in Korea and the advantage of call auction at the close of the day for the current forward pricing of equity funds. Finally he questions the possibility of wealth transfer due to late trading of equity funds after 3:00 pm.

2.2 Tournaments

Ko and Ha (2008) test the tournament behavior of equity fund managers which is well documented in the U.S. Tournament behavior is also observed in the daily, weekly, and monthly frequency data. Such behavior is more salient in start-up and liquidated funds than middle-aged and seasoned funds. The absence of tournament behavior in privately placed equity funds and balanced funds also confirms their findings of tournaments. Yi (2009) re-tests the tournament behavior of equity fund managers, and finds the existence of tournaments, which is consistent with those of Ko and Ha (2008).

3. Other Issues

3.1 Index Funds

There currently exist two recent studies regarding index funds. Min and Cha (2008) compare the performance between index funds and actively managed funds, and show that the index funds outperform the actively managed funds. They attribute the out performance of index funds to the fact that Korean index funds are actually created as enhanced-index funds.

Approaching from a different perspective, Min (2009) investigates the effects of fund fees and tracking errors on the performance of index funds. He finds negative relations both between fund fees and performance and between tracking errors and performance (or information ratio).

3.2 Closed-end Funds

As in the U.S., there exist relatively many studies on closed-end funds in Korea. The first Korean study is Kim (1996) which investigates the determinants of discounts on closed-end funds. He finds an unequal magnitude of discounts for different types of funds and strong evidence of a tax-timing option effect. Yoon and Khil (2000) further investigate the relation between the closed-end fund premium and performance for growth funds. They find that the closed-end fund premium has a negative or null relation with future performance and a statistically insignificant positive relation with past performance. Oh, Kim, and Yang (2002) present a competitive rational expectations equilibrium model to explain the closed-end fund puzzle. They show that the closed-end fund puzzle can be explained as an equilibrium phenomenon arising from an institutional feature of the fund when the fund manager possesses private information. Yoo and Park (2002), however, show that closed-end funds trade at a discount which is statistically insignificant. Park (2006) tests a few theories to study the closed-end fund puzzle, but fails to explain it via any theory.

3.3 Behavioral Finance

Hong and Yi (2006) investigate the herd behavior of fund managers in Korea. They find that fund managers in Korea herd to a more substantial extent than those in other countries, as reported in previous relevant literature. The concurrent relation between the degree of herding and stock returns is positive for buy trades and negative for sell trades. Finally, they show that the trading behavior of fund managers is not associated with future returns, which suggests that the impact of herd behavior does not significantly predict future price movements, and is not detrimental to market stability.

Meanwhile, Yoo and Hwang (2010a) first study the disposition effects of fund investors and fund managers in Korea, but fail to show the existence of both disposition effects. Ko and Ha (2010b), however, find the disposition effect of fund investors using a within-fund rank measure and the effect of start-up funds on the disposition effect.

3.4 Various Funds

Park and Joo (2004) find the performance persistence of bond funds. A more recent study conducted by Kim (2008) supports Park and Joo (2004) with regard to short-term persistence. He finds short-term persistence in low-return bond funds, but not in high-return bond funds.

Lee and Hong (2004) study the arbitrage trading strategy via ETF. They show that ETF-creation and cancellation arbitrage opportunities persist for 1-2 and 3-5 minutes on average, and that ETF under-pricing occurs to a marked degree following the ex-dividend date. They conclude that the Korean ETF markets have gradually become more efficient despite a clear tendency for continuous under-pricing over time.

3.5 The Others

Shin (2003) studies outsourcing investment using equity and bond funds. His finding is consistent with the performance persistence of both equity and bond funds, but not against outsourcing investment.

Lee and Yi (2007) investigate the asset allocation effect on fund performance, and find that the asset allocation effect of equity growth funds is 59.3%.

Joo (2009) studies the dollar-cost-averaging and lump-sum investment behavior of households from demographic, socioeconomic, and psychological perspectives. She finds that dollar-cost averaging investment is popular in the low-age group, women, and low-asset group.

Park and Lee (2010) compare the differences in performance between dollar-cost averaging and lump-sum investments. They find that, in the short run, lumps-sum investments outperform dollar-cost averaging investments, but, in the long run, the reverse is true in Korean equity fund markets. Recently, Choe and Ban (2010) give analytic calculation and scientific evidence on this issue. They conclude that dollar-cost averaging investment is not advantageous as is advertized by financial institutions, and regulators should be cautious not to follow misleading comments and opinions of market practitioners.

V. Concluding Remarks

This study broadly reviews overseas and Korean mutual fund studies since the 1960s, which are published in 16 overseas and 8 Korean academic journals. For the purpose of a succinct review, all of the mutual fund studies are divided into three categories: The economics of mutual funds, agency problems, and other issues. Almost half of all the studies concentrate on the category of the economics of mutual funds. We believe this is because, at an early stage, academicians were fundamentally interested in the economic roles and functions of mutual funds. The Korean financial academic society followed an identical trend. When we refer to the overseas mutual fund studies, we can anticipate that a broad variety of useful Korean studies will favorably affect both Korean mutual fund markets and the Korean economy in general.

For the purpose of studying mutual funds, two fundamental principles mustbe taken into consideration: protecting investors and understanding irrational investor behavior. It is well known that the principal objective of the U.S. Investment Company Act of 1940 is to protect investors. As a fundamental duty of the academic society, it will prove very desirable for mutual fund studies to be employed as appropriate evidence in the policy-making process for investor protection. On the other hand, contrary to traditional views in the finance and economics fields, mutual fund investors are, in many ways, not rational. Sometimes they may be over-sensitive to misleading news and advertisements, and herding into the wrong investments. Hence, understanding the irrational behavior of investors is the first step in guiding investors to efficient and appropriate investments. Particularly, with increasing pension assets, it is crucial to possess knowledge on how to invest in risky assets for after-retirement income security.

Regarding investors protection, managerial incentives should be studied from the viewpoint of agency problems. Numerous agency problems are likely to be uncovered in the mutual fund industry: misleading advertisements, window dressing, subsidization between same family funds, side-by-side management of public and privately-placed funds, inappropriate relationship between management and brokerage companies, fund incubation, the star phenomenon, and tournament behavior. In this regard, costs, fees, and expenses are also very important issues to be studied in Korea. Although investors are really interested in this issue, few studies have investigated it perhaps due to the lack of data. For example, surprisingly, the relationship between management fees and fund performance has not yet been studied. Another example of this could be the relation between brokerage expenses or turnover ratio and fund performance. Fund ratings may also constitute an appropriate research topic that has yet to be clearly elucidated in Korea.

Behavioral finance is another new area of mainstream finance,as pointed out by Barberis and Thaler (2003). According to their classification, behavioral finance might be divided into two building blocks--limits to arbitrage and psychology. To understand the behavior of Korean investors, the issues of the above two building blocks should be investigated in the context of

Korean capital markets, but not in the context of U.S. capital markets. Currently, many studies are replicating the U.S. research using Korean data. In a sense, this approach may also provide us witha greater understanding of Korean investors. If we incorporate many unique features of the Korean mutual fund markets and industry, however, we can understand Korean investors more accurately. For example, when we ignore start-up bias in a mutual fundstudy using the most recent 10 years of data, the empirical results could be misleading. And, if we do not consider the micro-structure of Korean mutual funds, we will be unable to achieve clear-cut results. As demonstrated by Chui, Titman, and Wei (2010), cross-country cultural differences in individualism clearly exist. Consequently, they fail to find the momentum factor in Japan, Korea, Taiwan, and Turkey. We believe that many countries must have detected behavioral phenomena different from those in the U.S. Such different behavior provides us with greater insight into Korean mutual fund markets and industry than was previously the case.

The final point we would like to propose is the issue of pension finance. Korea began to be classified as an aging society in 2000, in which the population aged above 64 years comprises over 7.0% of the entire Korean population. As anticipated by the U.N. and OECD, Korean society is aging most rapidly among the OECD countries. We are expecting Korea to become an aged society (more than 14%) in 2018 and a super-aged society (more than 20%) in 2026. The early baby boomer generation is currently retiring. However, financial studies on this issue are not, at this stage, popular. As we mentioned earlier in this paper, mutual funds play a very important role in the U.S. retirement savings. We anticipate an identical phenomenon in Korea, because this trend is world-wide, and not specific to the U.S. Hence, more Korean studies are expected to focus on this issue, and these studies should both enhance the protection of investors and guide them to appropriate investments.

References

Adams, J. C., S. A. Mansi, and T. Nishikawa, "Internal Governance echanisms and Operational Performance: Evidence from Index Mutual Funds", *Review of Financial Studies*, Vol. 23, No. 3(2010), pp. 1261-1286.

Adkisson, J. A. and D. R. Fraser, "Reading the Stars: Age Bias in Morningstar Ratings", *Financial Analysts Journal*, Vol. 59, No. 5(2003), pp. 24-27.

Alexander, G. J., P. G. Benson, and C. E. Eger, "Timing Decisions and the Behavior of Mutual Fund Systematic Risk", *Journal of Financial and Quantitative Analysis*, Vol. 17, No. 4(1982), pp. 579-602.

Alexander, G. J., G. Cici, and S. Gibson, "Does Motivation Matter When Assessing Trade Performance? An Analysis of Mutual Funds", *Review of Financial Studies*, Vol. 20, No. 1(2007), pp. 125-150.

Almazan, A., K. C. Brown, and M. Carlson, "Why Constrain Your Mutual Fund Manager?", *Journal of Financial Economics*, Vol. 73, No. 2(2004), pp. 289-321.

Avramov, D. and R. Wermers, "Investing in Mutual Funds When Returns Are Predictable", *Journal of Financial Economics*, Vol. 81, No. 2(2006), pp. 339-377.

Bae, K. and J. Yi, "The impact of the short-short rule repeal on the timing ability of mutual funds", *Journal of Business Finance and Accounting*, Vol. 35, No. 7(2008), pp. 969-997.

Baks, K. P., A. Metrick, and J. Wachter, "Should Investors Avoid All Actively Managed Mutual Funds? A Study in Bayesian Performance Evaluation", *Journal of Finance*, Vol. 56, No. 1(2001), pp. 45-85.

Barber, B. M., T. Odean, and L. Zheng, "Out of Sight, Out of Mind: The Effects of Expenses on Mutual Fund Flows", *Journal of Business*, Vol. 78, No. 6(2005), pp. 2095-2119.

Barberis, N. and R. Thaler, "A Survey of Behavioral Finance", *Handbook of the Economics of Finance*, Edited by G.M. Constantinides, M. Harris, and R. Stultz(2003), Elsevier Science B.V.

Barclay, M. J., N. D. Pearson, and M. S. Weisbach, "Open-End Mutual Funds and Capital-Gains Taxes", *Journal of Financial Economics*, Vol. 49, No. 1(1998), pp. 3-43.

Barras, L., O. Scaillet, and R. Wermers, "False Discoveries in Mutual Fund Performance: Measuring Luck in Estimated Alphas", *Journal of Finance*, Vol. 65, No. 1(2010), pp. 179-216.

Ben-Rephael, A., S. Kandel, and A. Wohl, "Measuring Investor Sentiment with Mutual Fund Flows", *Journal of Financial Economics*, forthcoming (2011).

Bergstresser, D., J. M. R. Chalmers, and P. Tufano, "Assessing the Costs and Benefits of Brokers in the Mutual Fund Industry", *Review of Financial Studies*, Vol. 22, No. 10(2009), pp. 4129-4156.

Bergstresser, D. and J. Poterba, "Do After-Tax Returns Affect Mutual Fund Inflows?", *Journal of Financial Economics*, Vol. 63, No. 3(2002), pp. 381-414.

Berk, J. B. and R. C. Green, "Mutual Fund Flows and Performance in Rational Markets", *Journal of Political Economy*, Vol. 112, No. 6(2004), pp. 1269-1295.

Berk, J. B. and R. Stanton, "Managerial Ability, Compensation, and the Closed-End Fund Discount", *Journal of Finance*, Vol. 62, No. 2(2007), pp. 529-556.

Bhargava, R., A. Bose, and D. A. Dubofsky, "Exploiting International Stock Market Correlations with Open-End International Mutual Funds", *Journal of Business Finance and Accounting*, Vol. 25, No. 5-6(1998), pp. 765-773.

Bhargava, R. and D. A. Dubofsky, "A Note on Fair Value Pricing of Mutual Funds", *Journal of Banking and Finance*, Vol. 25, No. 2(2001), pp.

339-354.

Blake, C. R., E. J. Elton, and M. J. Gruber, "The Performance of Bond Mutual Funds", *Journal of Business*, Vol. 66, No. 3(1993), pp. 371-403.

Blake, C. R. and M. R. Morey, "Morningstar Ratings and Mutual Fund Performance", *Journal of Financial and Quantitative Analysis*, Vol. 35, No. 3(2000), pp. 451-483.

Bodie, Z. and J. Treussard, "Making Investment Choices as Simple as Possible, but Not Simpler", *Financial Analysts Journal*, Vol. 63, No. 3(2007), pp. 42-47.

Bodurtha, J. N., D. S. Kim, and C. M. C. Lee, "Closed-End Country Funds and U.S. Market Sentiment", *Review of Financial Studies*, Vol. 8, No. 3(1995), pp. 879-918.

Bollen, N. P. B., "Mutual Fund Attributes and Investor Behavior", *Journal of Financial and Quantitative Analysis*, Vol. 42, No. 3(2007), pp. 683-708.

Bollen, N. P. B. and J. A. Busse, "On the Timing Ability of Mutual Funds Managers", *Journal of Finance*, Vol. 56, No. 3(2001), pp. 1075-1094.

Bollen, N. P. B. and J. A. Busse, "Short-Term Persistence in Mutual Fund Performance", *Review of Financial Studies*, Vol. 18, No. 2(2005), pp. 569-597.

Bollen, N. P. B. and J. A. Busse, "Tick Size and Institutional Trading Costs: Evidence from Mutual Funds", *Journal of Financial and Quantitative Analysis*, Vol. 41, No. 4(2006), pp. 915-937.

Boudreaux, K. J., "Discounts and Premiums on Closed-End Mutual Funds: A Study in Valuation", *Journal of Finance*, Vol. 28, No. 2(1973), pp. 515-522.

Boyer, B. and L. Zheng, "Investor Flows and Stock Market Returns", *Journal of Empirical Finance*, Vol. 16, No. 1(2009), pp. 87-100.

Bradley, M., A. Brav, I. Goldstein, and W. Jiang, "Activist Arbitrage: A Study of Open-Ending Attempts of Closed-End Funds", *Journal of Financial*

Economics, Vol. 95, No. 1(2010), pp. 1-19.

Brauer, G. A., "Closed-End Fund Shares' Abnormal Returns and the Information Content of Discounts and Premiums", *Journal of Finance*, Vol. 43, No. 1(1988), pp. 113-127.

Breen, W., R. Jagannathan, and A. R. Ofer, "Correcting for Heteroscedasticity in Tests for Market Timing Ability", *Journal of Business*, Vol. 59, No. 4(1986), pp. 585-598.

Brickley, J., S. Manaster, and J. Schallheim, "The Tax-Timing Option and the Discounts on Closed-End Investment Companies", *Journal of Business*, Vol. 64, No. 3(1991), pp. 287-312.

Bris, A., H. Gulen, P. Kadiyala, and P. R. Rau, "Good Stewards, Cheap Talkers, or Family Men? The Impact of Mutual Fund Closures on Fund Managers, Flows, Fees, and Performance", *Review of Financial Studies*, Vol. 20, No. 3(2007), pp. 953-982.

Brown, S. J. and W. N. Goetzmann, "Performance Persistence", *Journal of Finance*, Vol. 50, No. 2(1995), pp. 679-698.

Brown, S. J. and W. N. Goetzmann, "Mutual Fund Styles", *Journal of Financial Economics*, Vol. 43, No. 3(1997), pp. 373-399.

Brown, S. J., W. N. Goetzmann, T. Hiraki, T. Otsuki, and N. Shiraishi, "The Japanese Open-End Fund Puzzle", *Journal of Business*, Vol. 74, No. 1(2001), pp. 59-77.

Brown, S. J., W. Goetzmann, R. G. Ibbotson, and S. A. Ross, "Survivorship Bias in Performance Studies", *Review of Financial Studies*, Vol. 5, No. 4(1992), pp. 553-580.

Brown, K. C., W. V. Harlow, and L. T. Starks, "Of Tournaments and Temptations: An Analysis of Managerial Incentives in the Mutual Fund Industry", *Journal of Finance*, Vol. 51, No. 1(1996), pp. 85-110.

Brown, F. E. and D. Vickers, "Mutual Fund Portfolio Activity, Performance, and Market Impact", *Journal of Finance*, Vol. 18, No. 2(1963), pp.

377-391.

Burgess, R. C. and B. T. O'Dell, "An Empirical Examination of Index Efficiency: Implications for Index Funds", *Journal of Financial and Quantitative Analysis*, Vol. 13, No. 1(1978), pp. 93-100.

Busse, J. A., "Volatility Timing in Mutual Funds: Evidence from Daily Returns", *Review of Financial Studies*, Vol. 12, No. 5(1999), pp. 1009-1041.

Busse, J. A., "Another Look at Mutual Fund Tournaments", *Journal of Financial and Quantitative Analysis*, Vol. 36, No. 1(2001), pp. 53-73.

Busse, J. A. and P. J. Irvine, "Bayesian Alphas and Mutual Fund Persistence", *Journal of Finance*, Vol. 61, No. 5(2006), pp. 2251-2288.

Cai, J., M. C. Chan, and T. Yamada, "The Performance of Japanese Mutual Funds", *Review of Financial Studies*, Vol. 10, No. 2(1997), pp. 237-274.

Carhart, M. M., "On Persistence in Mutual Fund Performance", *Journal of Finance*, Vol. 52, No. 1(1997), pp. 57-82.

Carhart, M. M., J. N. Carpenter, A. W. Lynch, and D. K. Musto, "Mutual Fund Survivorship", *Review of Financial Studies*, Vol. 15, No. 5(2002), pp. 1439-1463.

Carhart, M. M., R. Kaniel, D. K. Musto, and A. V. Reed, "Leaning for the Tape: Evidence of Gaming Behavior in Equity Mutual Funds", *Journal of Finance*, Vol. 57, No. 2(2002), pp. 661-693.

Cesari, R. and F. Panetta, "The Performance of Italian Equity Funds", *Journal of Banking and Finance*, Vol. 26, No. 1(2002), pp. 99-126.

Cha, H. J. and B. S. Lee, "The Market Demand Curve for Common Stocks: Evidence from Equity Mutual Fund Flows", *Journal of Financial and Quantitative Analysis*, Vol. 36, No. 2(2001), pp. 195-220.

Chalmers, J. M. R., R. M. Edelen, and G. B. Kadlec, "On the Perils of Financial Intermediaries Setting Security Prices: *The Mutual Fund Wild Card Option*", *Journal of Finance*, Vol. 56, No. 6(2001), pp. 2209-2236.

Chan, K., V. Covrig, and L. Ng, "What Determines the Domestic Bias and Foreign Bias? Evidence from Mutual Fund Equity Allocations Worldwide", *Journal of Finance*, Vol. 60, No. 3(2005), pp. 1495-1534.

Chan, L. K. C., H. L. Chen, and J. Lakonishok, "On Mutual Fund Investment Styles", *Review of Financial Studies*, Vol. 15, No. 5(2002), pp. 1407-1437.

Chance, D. M. and S. P. Ferris, "The Effect of 12b-1 Plans on Mutual Fund Expense Ratios: A Note", *Journal of Finance*, Vol. 42, No. 4(1987), pp. 1077-1090.

Chang, E. C. and W. G. Lewellen, "Market Timing and Mutual Fund Investment Performance", *Journal of Business*, Vol. 57, No. 1(1984), pp. 57-72.

Chay, J. B. and C. A. Trzcinka, "Managerial Performance and the Cross-Sectional Pricing of Closed-End Funds", *Journal of Financial Economics*, Vol. 52, No. 3(1999), pp. 379-408.

Chen, H. L., N. Jegadeesh, and R. Wermers, "The Value of Active Mutual Fund Management: An Examination of the Stockholdings and Trades of Fund Managers", *Journal of Financial and Quantitative Analysis*, Vol. 35, No. 3(2000), pp. 343-368.

Chen, H. L. and G. G. Pennacchi, "Does Prior Performance Affect a Mutual Fund's Choice of Risk? Theory and Further Empirical Evidence", *Journal of Financial and Quantitative Analysis*, Vol. 44, No. 4(2009), pp. 745-775.

Chen, J., H. Hong, M. Huang, and J. D. Kubik, "Does Fund Size Erode Mutual Fund Performance? The Role of Liquidity and Organization", *American Economic Review*, Vol. 94, No. 5(2004), pp. 1276-1302.

Chen, Q., I. Goldstein, and W. Jiang, "Directors' Ownership in the U.S. Mutual Fund Industry", *Journal of Finance*, Vol. 63, No. 6(2008), pp. 2629-2677.

Chen, Q., I. Goldstein, and W. Jiang, "Payoff Complementarities and Financial Fragility: Evidence from Mutual Fund Outflows", *Journal of*

Financial Economics, Vol. 97, No. 2(2010), pp. 239-262.

Chen, Y., W. Ferson, and H. Peters, "Measuring the Timing Ability and Performance of Bond Mutual Funds", *Journal of Financial Economics*, Vol. 98, No. 1(2010), pp. 72-89.

Cherkes, M., J. Sagi, and R. Stanton, "A Liquidity-Based Theory of Closed-End Funds", *Review of Financial Studies*, Vol. 22, No. 1(2009), pp. 257-297.

Chevalier, J. and G. Ellison, "Risk Taking by Mutual Funds as a Response to Incentives", *Journal of Political Economy*, Vol. 105, No. 6(1997), pp. 1167-1200.

Chevalier, J. and G. Ellison, "Are Some Mutual Fund Managers Better Than Others? Cross-Sectional Patterns in Behavior and Performance", *Journal of Finance*, Vol. 54, No. 3(1999a), pp. 875-899.

Chevalier, J. and G. Ellison, "Career Concerns of Mutual Fund Managers", *Quarterly Journal of Economics*, Vol. 114, No. 2(1999b), pp. 389-432.

Cho, D., "Empirical Analysis of Investment Performance of Korean Equity Funds", *Korean Journal of Financial Management*, Vol. 11, No. 2(1994), pp. 109-130(in Korean).
조담, "우리나라 주식형 펀드의 투자성과에 관한 실증적 연구", 재무관리연구, 제11권 제2호(1994), pp. 109-130.

Choe, H. and J. I. Ban, "Does Dollar Cost Averaging Strategy Improve Investment Performance? Evidence from the Korean Fund Mareket", *Korean Journal of Financial Studies*, Vol. 39, No. 4(2010), pp. 573-609(in Korean).
최혁, 반주일, "적립식 투자전략이 투자성과를 개선하는가?", 증권학회지, 제39권 제4호(2010), pp. 573-609.

Choi, J. J., D. Laibson, and B. C. Madrian, "Why Does the Law of One Price Fail? An Experiment on Index Mutual Funds", *Review of Financial Studies*, Vol. 23, No. 4(2010), pp. 1405-1432.

Chordia, T., "The Structure of Mutual Fund Charges", *Journal of Financial Economics*, Vol. 41, No. 1(1996), pp. 3-39.

Christoffersen, S. E. K., "Why Do Money Fund Managers Voluntarily Waive Their Fees?", *Journal of Finance*, Vol. 56, No. 3(2001), pp. 1117-1140.

Christoffersen, S. E. K. and S. Sarkissian, "City Size and Fund Performance", *Journal of Financial Economics*, Vol. 92, No. 2(2009), pp. 252-275.

Chui, A., S. Titman, and K. Wei, "Individualism and Momentum around the World", *Journal of Finance*, Vol. 70, No. 1(2010), pp. 361-392.

Chung, H. Y. and J. W. Park, "Fund Flow and Market Risk", *Korean Journal of Financial Management*, Vol. 27, No. 2(2010), pp. 169-204(in Korean).
정효윤, 박종원, "펀드플로우와 시장위험", 재무관리연구, 제27권 제2호 (2010), pp. 169-204.

Cici, G., S. Gibson, and R. Moussawi, "Mutual Fund Performance When Parent Firms Simultaneously Manage Hedge Funds", *Journal of Financial Intermediation*, Vol. 19, No. 2(2010), pp. 169-187.

Cohen, L., A. Frazzini, and C. Malloy, "The Small World of Investing: Board Connections and Mutual Fund Returns", *Journal of Political Economy*, Vol. 116, No. 5(2008), pp. 951-979.

Cohen, R. B., J. D. Coval, and L. Pastor, "Judging Fund Managers by the Company They Keep", *Journal of Finance*, Vol. 60, No. 3(2005), pp. 1057-1096.

Cohen, K. J. and J. A. Pogue, "Some Comments Concerning Mutual Fund versus Random Portfolio Performance", *Journal of Business*, Vol. 41, No. 2(1968), pp. 180-190.

Coles, J. L., J. Suay, and D. Woodbury, "Fund Advisor Compensation in Closed-End Funds", *Journal of Finance*, Vol. 55, No. 3(2000), pp. 1385-1414.

Collins, S. and P. Mack, "The Optimal Amount of Assets under Management in the Mutual Fund Industry", *Financial Analysts Journal*, Vol. 53, No.

5(1997), pp. 67-73.

Comer, G., "Hybrid Mutual Funds and Market Timing Performance", *Journal of Business*, Vol. 79, No. 2(2006), pp. 771-797.

Comer, G., N. Larrymore, and J. Rodriguez, "Controlling for Fixed-Income Exposure in Portfolio Evaluation: Evidence from Hybrid Mutual Funds", *Review of Financial Studies*, Vol. 22, No. 2(2009), pp. 481-507.

Cooper, M. J., H. Gulen, and P. R. Rau, "Changing Names with Style: Mutual Fund Name Changes and Their Effects on Fund Flows", *Journal of Finance*, Vol. 60, No. 6(2005), pp. 2825-2858.

Coval, J. and T. J. Moskowitz, "The Geography of Investment: Informed Trading and Asset Prices", *Journal of Political Economy*, Vol. 109, No. 4(2001), pp. 811-841.

Coval, J. and E. Stafford, "Asset Fire Sales (and Purchases) in Equity Markets", *Journal of Financial Economics*, Vol. 86, No. 2(2007), pp. 479-512.

Cremers, M., J. Driessen, and P. Maenhout, "Does Skin in the Game Matter? Director Incentives and Governance in the Mutual Fund Industry", *Journal of Financial and Quantitative Analysis*, Vol. 44, No. 6(2009), pp. 1345-1373.

Cremers, M. and A. Petajisto, "How Active Is Your Fund Manager? A New Measure That Predicts Performance", *Review of Financial Studies*, Vol. 22, No. 9(2009), pp. 3329-3365.

Cumby, R. E. and J. D. Glen, "Evaluating the Performance of International Mutual Funds", *Journal of Finance*, Vol. 45, No. 2(1990), pp. 497-521.

Dahlquist, M., S. Engstrom, and P. Soderlind, "Performance and Characteristics of Swedish Mutual Funds", *Journal of Financial and Quantitative Analysis*, Vol. 35, No. 3(2000), pp. 409-423.

Dangl, T., Y. Wu, and J. Zechner, "Market Discipline and Internal Governance in the Mutual Fund Industry", *Review of Financial Studies*, Vol. 21, No. 5(2008), pp. 2307-2343.

Daniel, K., M. Grinblatt, S. Titman, and R. Wermers, "Measuring Mutual Fund Performance with Characteristic-Based Benchmarks", *Journal of Finance*, Vol. 52, No. 3(1997), pp. 1035-1058.

Das, S. R. and R. K. Sundaram, "Fee Speech: Signaling, Risk-Sharing, and the Impact of Fee Structures on Investor Welfare", *Review of Financial Studies*, Vol. 15, No. 5(2002), pp. 1465-1497.

Dass, N., M. Massa, and R. Patgiri, "Mutual Funds and Bubbles: The Surprising Role of Contractual Incentives", *Review of Financial Studies*, Vol. 21, No. 1(2008), pp. 51-99.

Davis, G. F. and E. H. Kim, "Business Ties and Proxy Voting by Mutual Funds", *Journal of Financial Economics*, Vol. 85, No. 2(2007), pp. 552-570.

Del Guercio, D. and P. A. Tkac, "The Determinants of the Flow of Funds of Managed Portfolios: Mutual Funds vs. Pension Funds", *Journal of Financial and Quantitative Analysis*, Vol. 37, No. 4(2002), pp. 523-557.

Del Guercio, D. and P. A. Tkac, "Star Power: The Effect of Morningstar Ratings on Mutual Fund Flow", *Journal of Financial and Quantitative Analysis*, Vol. 43, No. 4(2008), pp. 907-936.

Deli, D. N., "Mutual Fund Advisory Contracts: An Empirical Investigation", *Journal of Finance*, Vol. 57, No. 1(2002), pp. 109-133.

Deli, D. N. and R. Varma, "Contracting in the Investment Management Industry: Evidence from Mutual Funds", *Journal of Financial Economics*, Vol. 63, No. 1(2002), pp. 79-98.

Dermine, J. and L. H. Roller, "Economies of Scale and Scope in French Mutual Funds", *Journal of Financial Intermediation*, Vol. 2, No. 1(1992), pp. 83-93.

Edelen, R. M., "Investor Flows and the Assessed Performance of Open-End Mutual Funds", *Journal of Financial Economics*, Vol. 53, No. 3(1999), pp. 439-466.

Edelen, R. M. and J. B. Warner, "Aggregate Price Effects of Institutional

Trading: A Study of Mutual Fund Flow and Market Returns", *Journal of Financial Economics*, Vol. 59, No. 2(2001), pp. 195-220.

Elton, E. J., M. J. Gruber, and C. R. Blake, "The Persistence of Risk-Adjusted Mutual Fund Performance", *Journal of Business*, Vol. 69, No. 2(1996a), pp. 133-157.

Elton, E. J., M. J. Gruber, and C. R. Blake, "Survivor Bias and Mutual Fund Performance", *Review of Financial Studies*, Vol. 9, No. 4(1996b), pp. 1097-1120.

Elton, E. J., M. J. Gruber, and C. R. Blake, "A First Look at the Accuracy of the CRSP Mutual Fund Database and a Comparison of the CRSP and Morningstar Mutual Fund Databases", *Journal of Finance*, Vol. 56, No. 6(2001), pp. 2415-2430.

Elton, E. J., M. J. Gruber, and C. R. Blake, "Incentive Fees and Mutual Funds", *Journal of Finance*, Vol. 58, No. 2(2003), pp. 779-804.

Elton, E. J., M. J. Gruber, and C. R. Blake, "Participant Reaction and the Performance of Funds Offered by 401(k) Plans", *Journal of Financial Intermediation*, Vol. 16, No. 2(2007), pp. 249-271.

Elton, E. J., M. J. Gruber, and J. A. Busse, "Do Investors Care about Sentiment?", *Journal of Business*, Vol. 71, No. 4(1998), pp. 477-500.

Elton, E. J., M. J. Gruber, and J. A. Busse, "Are Investors Rational? Choices among Index Funds", *Journal of Finance*, Vol. 59, No. 1(2004), pp. 261-288.

Elton, E. J., M. J. Gruber, G. Comer, and K. Li, "Spiders: Where Are the Bugs?", *Journal of Business*, Vol. 75, No. 3(2002), pp. 453-472.

Elton, E. J., M. J. Gruber, and T. C. Green, "The Impact of Mutual Fund Family Membership on Investor Risk", *Journal of Financial and Quantitative Analysis*, Vol. 42, No. 2(2007), pp. 257-277.

Evans, R. B., "Mutual Fund Incubation", *Journal of Finance*, Vol. 65, No. 4(2010), pp. 1581-1611.

Fabozzi, F. J. and J. C. Francis, "Mutual Fund Systematic Risk for Bull and Bear Markets: An Empirical Examination", *Journal of Finance*, Vol. 34, No. 5(1979), pp. 1243-1250.

Fabozzi, F. J., J. C. Francis, and C. F. Lee, "Generalized Functional Form for Mutual Fund Returns", *Journal of Financial and Quantitative Analysis*, Vol. 15, No. 5(1980), pp. 1107-1120.

Faff, R. W., J. T. Parwada, and H. L. Poh, "The Information Content of Australian Managed Fund Ratings", *Journal of Business Finance and Accounting*, Vol. 34, No. 9-10(2007), pp. 1528-1547.

Falkenstein, E. G., "Preferences for Stock Characteristics as Revealed by Mutual Fund Portfolio Holdings", *Journal of Finance*, Vol. 51, No. 1(1996), pp. 111-135.

Fama, E. F. and K. R. French, "Luck versus Skill in the Cross Section of Mutual Fund Returns", *Journal of Finance*, Vol. 65, No. 5(2010), pp. 1915-1947.

Farnsworth, H., W. Ferson, D. Jackson, and S. Todd, "Performance Evaluation with Stochastic Discount Factors", *Journal of Business*, Vol. 75, No. 3 (2002), pp. 473-503.

Ferson, W. E. and R. W. Schadt, "Measuring Fund Strategy and Performance in Changing Economic Conditions", *Journal of Finance*, Vol. 51, No. 2(1996), pp. 425-461.

Firth, M., C. Lin, and H. Zou, "Friend or Foe? The Role of State and Mutual Fund Ownership in the Split Share Structure Reform in China", *Journal of Financial and Quantitative Analysis*, Vol. 45, No. 3(2010), pp. 685-706.

Frazzini, A., "The Disposition Effect and Underreaction to News", *Journal of Finance*, Vol. 61, No. 4(2006), pp. 2017-2046.

Frazzini, A. and O. A. Lamont, "Dumb Money: Mutual Fund Flows and the Cross-Section of Stock Returns", *Journal of Financial Economics*, Vol. 88, No. 2(2008), pp. 299-322.

Gallagher, D. R., P. Gardner, and P. L. Swan, "Portfolio Pumping: An Examination of Investment Manager Quarter-End Trading and Impact on Performance", *Pacific-Basin Finance Journal*, Vol. 17, No. 1(2009), pp. 1-27.

Gaspar, J. M., M. Massa, and P. Matos, "Favoritism in Mutual Fund Families? Evidence on Strategic Cross-Fund Subsidization", *Journal of Finance*, Vol. 61, No. 1(2006), pp. 73-104.

Gatto, M. A., R. Geske, R. Litzenberger, and H. Sosin, "Mutual Fund Insurance", *Journal of Financial Economics*, Vol. 8, No. 3(1980), pp. 283-317.

Gemmill, G. and D. C. Thomas, "Noise Trading, Costly Arbitrage, and Asset Prices: Evidence from Closed-end Funds", *Journal of Finance*, Vol. 57, No. 6(2002), pp. 2571-2594.

Gervais, S., A. W. Lynch, and D. K. Musto, "Fund Families as Delegated Monitors of Money Managers", *Review of Financial Studies*, Vol. 18, No. 4(2005), pp. 1139-1169.

Gibson, S., A. Safieddine, and S. Titman, "Tax-motivated trading and price pressure: An analysis of mutual fund holdings", Vol. 35, No. 3(2000), pp. 369-386.

Gil-Bazo, J. and P. Ruiz-Verdu, "The Relation between Price and Performance in the Mutual Fund Industry", *Journal of Finance*, Vol. 64, No. 5(2009), pp. 2153-2183.

Goetzmann, W. N., J. Ingersoll, and Z. Ivkovic, "Monthly Measurement of Daily Timers", *Journal of Financial and Quantitative Analysis*, Vol. 35, No. 3(2000), pp. 257-290.

Goetzmann, W. N., Z. Ivkovic, and K. G. Rouwenhorst, "Day Trading International Mutual Funds: Evidence and Policy Solutions", *Journal of Financial and Quantitative Analysis*, Vol. 36, No. 3(2001), pp. 287-309.

Goetzmann, W. N. and M. Massa, "Daily Momentum and Contrarian Behavior of Index Fund Investors", *Journal of Financial and Quantitative*

Analysis, Vol. 37, No. 3(2002), pp. 375-389.

Goetzmann, W. N. and M. Massa, "Index Funds and Stock Market Growth", *Journal of Business*, Vol. 76, No. 1(2003), pp. 1-28.

Golec, J. and L. Starks, "Performance Fee Contract Change and Mutual Fund Risk", *Journal of Financial Economics*, Vol. 73, No. 1(2004), pp. 93-118.

Gottesman, A. A. and M. R. Morey, "Manager Education and Mutual Fund Performance", *Journal of Empirical Finance*, Vol. 13, No. 2(2006), pp. 145-182.

Greene, J. T. and C. W. Hodges, "The Dilution Impact of Daily Fund Flows on Open-End Mutual Funds", *Journal of Financial Economics*, Vol. 65, No. 1(2002), pp. 131-158.

Gremillion, L., *Mutual Fund Industry Handbook*, Wiley, 2005.

Grinblatt, M. and S. Titman, "Mutual Fund Performance: An Analysis of Quarterly Portfolio Holdings", *Journal of Business*, Vol. 62, No. 3(1989), pp. 393-416.

Grinblatt, M. and S. Titman, "The Persistence of Mutual Fund Performance", *Journal of Finance*, Vol. 47, No. 5(1992), pp. 1977-1984.

Grinblatt, M. and S. Titman, "Performance Measurement without Benchmarks: An Examination of Mutual Fund Returns", *Journal of Business*, Vol. 66, No. 1(1993), pp. 47-68.

Grinblatt, M. and S. Titman, "A Study of Monthly Mutual Fund Returns and Performance Evaluation Techniques", *Journal of Financial and Quantitative Analysis*, Vol. 29, No. 3(1994), pp. 419-444.

Grinblatt, M., S. Titman, and R. Wermers, "Momentum Investment Strategies, Portfolio Performance, and Herding: A Study of Mutual Fund Behavior", *American Economic Review*, Vol. 85, No. 5(1995), pp. 1088-1105.

Gruber, M. J., "Another Puzzle: The Growth in Actively Managed Mutual Funds", *Journal of Finance*, Vol. 51, No. 3(1996), pp. 783-810.

Guercio, D. D., L. Y. Dann, and M. M. Partch, "Governance and Boards of Directors in Closed-End Investment Companies", *Journal of Financial Economics*, Vol. 69, No. 1(2003), pp. 111-152.

Han, D. and K. W. Lim, "A Long-Term Performance Analysis on Domestic Equity-Type Funds through Direct and Reverse Regression", *Daehan Journal of Business*, Vol. 19, No. 6(2006), pp. 2185-2213(in Korean).
한동, 임경원, "직접-역회귀분석을 이용한 국내 주식형펀드의 장기성과분석", 대한경영학회지, 제19권 제6호(2006), pp. 2185-2213.

Hau, H. and H. Rey, "Home Bias at the Fund Level", *American Economic Review*, Vol. 98, No. 2(2008), pp. 333-338.

Hendricks, D., J. Patel, and R. Zeckhauser, "Hot Hands in Mutual Fund: Short-Run Persistence of Relative Performance, 1974~1988", *Journal of Finance*, Vol. 48, No. 1(1993), pp. 93-130.

Henriksson, R. D., "Market Timing and Mutual Fund Performance: An Empirical Investigation", *Journal of Business*, Vol. 57, No. 1(1984), pp. 73-96.

Herman, E. S., "Growth and Impact of Mutual Funds: Some Analytical and Public Policy Issues: Mutual Fund Management Fee Rates", *Journal of Finance*, Vol. 18, No. 2(1963), pp. 360-376.

Hong, G. H. and K. Y. Yi, "On the Herding Behavior of Fund Managers in the Korean Stock Market", *Korean Journal of Financial Studies*, Vol. 35, No. 4(2006), pp. 1-38(in Korean).
홍광헌, 이가연, "우리나라 주식시장에서의 펀드 매니저의 군집행동에 관한 연구", 증권학회지, 제35권 제4호(2006), pp. 1-38.

Horowitz, I., "The 'Reward-to-Variability' Ratio and Mutual Fund Performance", *Journal of Business*, Vol. 39, No. 4(1966), pp. 485-488.

Hortacsu, A. and C. Syverson, "Product Differentiation, Search Costs, and Competition in the Mutual Fund Industry: A Case Study of S&P500 Index Funds", *Quarterly Journal of Economics*, Vol. 119, No. 2(2004), pp. 403-456.

Huang, J., K. D. Wei, and H. Yan, "Participation Costs and the Sensitivity of Fund Flows to Past Performance", *Journal of Finance*, Vol. 62, No. 3(2007), pp. 1273-1311.

Ippolito, R. A., "Efficiency with Costly Information: A Study of Mutual Fund Performance, 1965~1984", *Quarterly Journal of Economics*, Vol. 104, No. 1 (1989), pp. 1-23.

Ivkovic, Z. and S. Weisbenner, "Individual Investor Mutual Fund Flows", *Journal of Financial Economics*, Vol. 92, No. 2(2009), pp. 223-237.

Jain, P. C. and J. S. Wu, "Truth in Mutual Fund Advertising: Evidence on Future Performance and Fund Flows", *Journal of Finance*, Vol. 55, No. 2(2000), pp. 937-958.

Jayaraman, N., A. Khorana, and E. Nelling, "An Analysis of the Determinants and Shareholder Wealth Effects of Mutual Fund Mergers", *Journal of Finance*, Vol. 57, No. 3(2002), pp. 1521-1551.

Jagannathan, R. and R. A. Korajczyk, "Assessing the Market Timing Performance of Managed Portfolios", *Journal of Business*, Vol. 59, No. 2(1986), pp. 217-235.

Jensen, M. C., "The Performance of Mutual Funds in the Period 1945~1964", *Journal of Finance*, Vol. 23, No. 2(1968), pp. 389-416.

Jiang, G. J., T. Yao, and T. Yu, "Do Mutual Funds Time the Market? Evidence from Portfolio Holdings", *Journal of Financial Economics*, Vol. 86, No. 3(2007), pp. 724-758.

Johnson, S. A., J. C. Lin, and K. Roy Song, "Dividend Policy, Signaling and Discounts on Closed-End Funds", *Journal of Financial Economics*, Vol. 81, No. 3(2006), pp. 539-562.

Johnson, W. T., "Predictable Investment Horizons and Wealth Transfers among Mutual Fund Shareholders", *Journal of Finance*, Vol. 59, No. 5(2004), pp. 1979-2012.

Jones, C. S. and J. Shanken, "Mutual Fund Performance with Learning Across

Funds", *Journal of Financial Economics*, Vol. 78, No. 3(2005), pp. 507-552.

Joo, S. H., "Dollar Cost Averaging and Lump Sum Investment in Mutual Funds by Households", *Journal of Insurance and Finance*, Vol. 20, No. 3 (2009), pp. 247-281(in Korean).
주소현, "가계의 적립식펀드와 거치식펀드 투자 행동", 보험금융연구, 제20권 제3호(2009), pp. 247-281.

Joy, O. M. and R. B. Porter, "Stochastic Dominance and Mutual Fund Performance", *Journal of Financial and Quantitative Analysis*, Vol. 9, No. 1(1974), pp. 25-31.

Kacperczyk, M. and A. Seru, "Fund Manager Use of Public Information: New Evidence on Managerial Skills", *Journal of Finance*, Vol. 62, No. 2(2007), pp. 485-528.

Kacperczyk, M., C. Sialm, and L. Zheng, "On the Industry Concentration of Actively Managed Equity Mutual Funds", *Journal of Finance*, Vol. 60, No. 4(2005), pp. 1983-2011.

Kacperczyk, M., C. Sialm, and L. Zheng, "Unobserved Actions of Mutual Funds", *Review of Financial Studies*, Vol. 21, No. 6(2008), pp. 2379-2416.

Kang, J. K. and C. J. Lee, "Investment Styles and Performance Persistence of Equity Funds in Korea Using Sharpe's Style Analysis", *Korean Journal of Financial Studies*, Vol. 39, No. 2(2010), pp. 307-339(in Korean).
강장구, 이창준, "Sharpe의 방법론을 이용한 한국 주식형펀드의 운용스타일 및 성과분석", 증권학회지, 제39권 제2호(2010), pp. 307-339.

Karceski, J., "Returns-Chasing Behavior, Mutual Funds, and Beta's Death", *Journal of Financial and Quantitative Analysis*, Vol. 37, No. 4(2002), pp. 559-594.

Keim, D. B., "An Analysis of Mutual Fund Design: The Case of Investing in Small-Cap Stocks", *Journal of Financial Economics*, Vol. 51, No. 2(1999), pp. 173-194.

Kempf, A. and S. Ruenzi, "Tournaments in Mutual-Fund Families", *Review of Financial Studies*, Vol. 21, No. 2(2008), pp. 1013-1036.

Kempf, A., S. Ruenzi, and T. Thiele, "Employment Risk, Compensation Incentives, and Managerial Risk Taking: Evidence from the Mutual Fund Industry", *Journal of Financial Economics*, Vol. 92, No. 1(2009), pp. 92-108.

Keswani, A. and D. Stolin, "Which Money Is Smart? Mutual Fund Buys and Sells of Individual and Institutional Investors", *Journal of Finance*, Vol. 63, No. 1(2008), pp. 85-118.

Kho, B. C. and J. W. Kim, "Mutual Funds Trading and Its Impact on Stock Prices", *Korean Journal of Financial Management*, Vol. 27, No. 2(2010), pp. 35-62(in Korean).
고봉찬, 김진우, "뮤추얼펀드의 자금흐름과 주식거래가 주가에 미치는 효과", 재무관리연구, 제27권 제2호(2010), pp. 35-62.

Khorana, A., "Top Management Turnover: An Empirical Investigation of Mutual Fund Managers", *Journal of Financial Economics*, Vol. 40, No. 3(1996), pp. 403-427.

Khorana, A., "Performance Changes Following Top Management Turnover: Evidence from Open-End Mutual Funds", *Journal of Financial and Quantitative Analysis*, Vol. 36, No. 3(2001), pp. 371-393.

Khorana, A. and H. Servaes, "The Determinants of Mutual Fund Starts", *Review of Financial Studies*, Vol. 12, No. 5(1999), pp. 1043-1074.

Khorana, A., H. Servaes, and P. Tufano, "Explaining the Size of the Mutual Fund Industry Around the World", *Journal of Financial Economics*, Vol. 78, No. 1(2005), pp. 145-185.

Khorana, A., H. Servaes, and P. Tufano, "Mutual Fund Fees Around the World", *Review of Financial Studies*, Vol. 22, No. 3(2009), pp. 1279-1310.

Khorana, A., H. Servaes, and L. Wedge, "Portfolio Manager Ownership and Fund Performance", *Journal of Financial Economics*, Vol. 85, No.

1(2007), pp. 179-204.

Khorana, A., P. Tufano, and L. Wedge, "Board Structure, Mergers, and Shareholder Wealth: A Study of the Mutual Fund Industry", *Journal of Financial Economics*, Vol. 85, No. 2(2007), pp. 571-598.

Khorana, A., S. Wahal, and M. Zenner, "Agency Conflicts in Closed-End Funds: The Case of Rights Offerings", *Journal of Financial and Quantitative Analysis*, Vol. 37, No. 2(2002), pp. 177-200.

Klibanoff, P., O. Lamont, and T. A. Wizman, "Investor Reaction to Salient News in Closed-End Country Funds", *Journal of Finance*, Vol. 53, No. 2(1998), pp. 673-699.

Kim, B. J. and J. H. Cho, "A Performance Evaluation of Stock Mutual Funds Using the Stochastic Discount Factor and the Artificial Fund", *Korean Journal of Financial Management*, Vol. 27, No. 3(2010), pp. 183-228(in Korean).
김봉준, 조재호, "확률할인요소 및 가상펀드를 이용한 주식형 펀드의 성과평가", 재무관리연구, 제27권 제3호(2010), pp. 183-228.

Kim, C. S., "Empirical Evidence on Closed-End Mutual Fund Discounts", *Korean Journal of Financial Management*, Vol. 13, No. 1(1996), pp. 311-340.

Kim, H. B., "Performance Persistence of fixed income funds", *Daehan Journal of Business*, Vol. 21, No. 2(2008), pp. 567-585(in Korean).
김홍배, "채권형 펀드의 성과 지속성", 대한경영학회지, 제21권 제2호(2008), pp. 567-585.

Kim, S. B. and J. G. Park, "Is There Timing Ability in Korean Equity Funds?", *Korean Journal of Financial Management*, Vol. 26, No. 2(2009), pp. 93-112(in Korean).
김상배, 박종구, "국내 주식형 펀드의 타이밍 능력은 존재하는가?", 재무관리연구, 제26권 제2호(2009), pp. 93-112.

Kim, S. S., "Analyst Recommendation Change and Fund Performance in

Korea Fund Stock Market", *Daehan Journal of Business*, Vol. 23, No. 3(2010), pp. 1351-1370(in Korean).

김성신, "애널리스트의 투자의견 변경에 의한 펀드의 운용성과 연구", 대한경영학회지, 제23권 제3호(2010), pp. 1351-1370.

Kim, S. W. and Y. M. Kim, "Nonlinear Dynamic Relations Between Equity Return and Equity Fund Flow: Korean Market Empirical Evidence", *Asia-Pacific Journal of Financial Studies*, Vol. 39, No. 2(2010), pp. 361-392.

Kim, T., "An Assessment of the Performance of Mutual Fund Management: 1969~1975", *Journal of Financial and Quantitative Analysis*, Vol. 13, No. 3(1978), pp. 385-406.

Kim, Y. M., "A New Approach to Measuring Performance of Mutual Funds", *Daehan Journal of Business*, Vol. 27, No. 1(2001), pp. 237-261(in Korean).

김유만, "뮤추얼펀드의 성과 측정을 위한 모형의 개발", 대한경영학회지, 제27권 제1호(2001), pp. 237-261.

Ko, K., "Equity Funds' Cash Flow and Stock Market", *Korean Journal of Financial Studies*, Vol. 31, No. 1(2002), pp. 71-107(in Korean).

고광수, "주식형 펀드의 현금흐름과 주식시장", 증권학회지, 제31권 제1호 (2002), pp. 71-107.

Ko, K., "Market Microstructure and Unfair Trading Equity Funds", *Korean Journal of Finance*, Vol. 17, No. 2(2004), pp. 77-101(in Korean).

고광수, "시장 미시구조와 주식형 펀드의 부당 이익", 재무연구, 제17권 제2호(2004), pp. 77-101.

Ko, K. and Y. Ha, "Mutual Fund Tournaments and Structural Changes in an Emerging Fund Markets: The Case of Korea", *Seoul Journal of Business*, Vol. 17, No. 1(2011), pp. 37-64.

Ko, K. and Y. J. Ha, "Mutual Fund Tournaments in Korea", *Journal of Insurance and Finance*, Vol. 19, No. 3(2008), pp. 209-228(in Korean).

고광수, 하연정, "우리나라 펀드 시장의 토너먼트 현상 연구", 보험금융연구,

제19권 제3호(2008), pp. 209-228.

Ko, K. and Y. J. Ha, "Equity Fund Performance and Cash Flows: Structural Changes, and Start-up and Survivorship Biases", *Asian Review of Financial Research*, Vol. 23, No. 4(2010a), pp. 437-468(in Korea).
고광수, 하연정, "주식형 펀드의 성과와 현금흐름 : 구조적 변화와 신설 및 생존 편의 효과", 재무연구, 제23권 제4호(2010a) pp. 437-468.

Ko, K. and Y. J. Ha, "Disposition Effect in Korean Equity Funds", *Korean Journal of Financial Studies*, Vol. 39, No. 4(2010b), pp. 517-453(in Korean).
고광수, 하연정, "주식형 펀드 투자의 디스포지션 효과", 증권학회지, 제39권 제4호(2010b) pp. 517-453.

Ko, K., Y. P. Wang, Y. J. Ha, and M. Y. Paek, "Performance Persistence of Korean Equity Funds: Stock Selection and Market Timing Abilities", *(Korean) Journal of Business Research*, Vol. 25, No. 1(2010), pp. 227-246(in Korean).
고광수, 왕아평, 하연정, 백미연, "주식형 펀드의 성과 지속성에 관한 연구", 경영연구, 제25권 제1호(2010), pp. 227-246.

Koch, E. B., "The Validity of Composite Risk-Return Measures Within Mutual Fund Subgroups", *Journal of Finance*, Vol. 30, No. 4(1975), pp. 1153-1154.

Kon, S. J., "The Market-Timing Performance of Mutual Fund Managers", *Journal of Business*, Vol. 56, No. 3(1983), pp. 323-347.

Kon, S. J. and F. C. Jen, "Estimation of Time-Varying Systematic Risk and Performance for Mutual Fund Portfolios: An Application of Switching Regression", *Journal of Finance*, Vol. 33, No. 2(1978), pp. 457-475.

Kon, S. J. and F. C. Jen, "The Investment Performance of Mutual Funds: An Empirical Investigation of Timing, Selectivity, and Market Efficiency", *Journal of Business*, Vol. 52, No. 2(1979), pp. 263-289.

Koski, J. L. and J. Pontiff, "How Are Derivatives Used? Evidence from the Mutual Fund Industry", *Journal of Finance*, Vol. 54, No. 2(1999), pp.

791-816.

Kosowski, R., A. Timmermann, R. Wermers, and H. White, "Can Mutual Fund 'Stars' Really Pick Stocks? New Evidence from a Bootstrap Analysis", *Journal of Finance*, Vol. 61, No. 6(2006), pp. 2551-2595.

Kothari, S. P. and J. B. Warner, "Evaluating Mutual Fund Performance", *Journal of Finance*, Vol. 56, No. 5(2001), pp. 1985-2010.

Lee, C. and S. Rahman, "Market Timing, Selectivity, and Mutual Fund Performance: An Empirical Investigation", *Journal of Business*, Vol. 63, No. 2(1990), pp. 261-278.

Lee, C. M. C., A. Shleifer, and R. H. Thaler, "Investor Sentiment and the Closed-End Fund Puzzle", *Journal of Finance*, Vol. 46, No. 1(1991), pp. 75-109.

Lee, J. H. and J. P. Hong, "Arbitrage in the Korean ETF Markets: ETF versus NAV", *Korean Journal of Financial Studies*, Vol. 33, No. 3(2004), pp. 49-93(in Korean).
이재하, 홍장표, "상장지수펀드(ETF) 차익거래전략", 증권학회지, 제33권 제3호(2004), pp. 49-93.

Lee, S. M. and A. J. Lerro, "Optimizing the Portfolio Selection for Mutual Funds", *Journal of Finance*, Vol. 28, No. 5(1973), pp. 1087-1101.

Lee, W. H., H. D. Lee, and S. S. Park, "Fund Style Analysis and Benchmark-Free Ability Tests of Korea Stock Funds", *Korean Journal of Financial Studies*, Vol. 26, No. 1(2000), pp. 65-90(in Korean).
이원흠, 이한득, 박상수, "주식형 펀드의 스타일 분석과 운용능력 분석", 증권학회지, 제26권 제1호(2000), pp. 65-90.

Lee, Y. G. and K. Y. Yi, "An Empirical Study on the Asset Allocation Effect to Fund Performance in Korea Fund Market", *Daehan Journal of Business*, Vol. 20, No. 4(2007), pp. 1977-1999(in Korean).
이윤구, 이가연, "한국 펀드시장에서 자산배분효과에 대한 실증분석", 대한경영학회지, 제20권 제4호(2007), pp. 1977-1999.

Lehmann, B. N. and D. M. Modest, "Mutual Fund Performance Evaluation: A Comparison of Benchmarks and Benchmark Comparisons", *Journal of Finance*, Vol. 42, No. 2(1987), pp. 233-265.

Lemmon, M. L., J. S. Schallheim, and J. F. Zender, "Do Incentives Matter? Managerial Contracts for Dual-Purpose Funds", *Journal of Political Economy*, Vol. 108, No. 2(2000), pp. 273-299.

Lim, U. K. and J. R. Woo, "A Study on the Performance Evaluation of Stock Investment Trusts: Using Fund's Asset Holding Data", *Korean Journal of Financial Studies*, Vol. 20, No. 1(1997), pp. 139-180(in Korean).
임웅기, 우재룡, "투자신탁 주식형 펀드의 주식보유자료를 이용한 투자성과 평가", 증권학회지, 제20권 제1호(1997), pp. 139-180.

Lynch, A. W. and D. K. Musto, "How Investors Interpret Past Fund Returns", *Journal of Finance*, Vol. 58, No. 5(2003), pp. 2033-2058.

Malkiel, B. G., "Returns from Investing in Equity Mutual Funds 1971 to 1991", *Journal of Finance*, Vol. 50, No. 2(1995), pp. 549-572.

Mamaysky, H., M. Spiegel, and H. Zhang, "Estimating the Dynamics of Mutual Fund Alphas and Betas", *Review of Financial Studies*, Vol. 21, No. 1(2008), pp. 233-264.

Massa, M., "How Do Family Strategies Affect Fund Performance? When Performance-Maximization is Not the Only Game in Town", *Journal of Financial Economics*, Vol. 67, No. 2(2003), pp. 249-304.

Massa, M. and R. Patgiri, "Incentives and Mutual Fund Performance: Higher Performance or Just Higher Risk Taking?", *Review of Financial Studies*, Vol. 22, No. 5(2009), pp. 1777-1815.

Massa, M. and Z. Rehman, "Information Flows within Financial Conglomerates: Evidence from the Banks-Mutual Funds Relation", *Journal of Financial Economics*, Vol. 89, No. 2(2008), pp. 288-306.

Massa, M., J. Reuter, and E. Zitzewitz, "When Should Firms Share Credit with Employees? Evidence from Anonymously Managed Mutual Funds",

Journal of Financial Economics, Vol. 95, No. 3(2010), pp. 400-424.

Matvos, G. and M. Ostrovsky, "Heterogeneity and Peer Effects in Mutual Fund Proxy Voting", *Journal of Financial Economics*, Vol. 98, No. 1(2010), pp. 90-112.

McDonald, J. G., "French Mutual Fund Performance: Evaluation of Internationally-Diversified Portfolios", *Journal of Finance*, Vol. 28, No. 5(1973), pp. 1161-1180.

Meyer, J., "Further Applications of Stochastic Dominance to Mutual Fund Performance", *Journal of Financial and Quantitative Analysis*, Vol. 12, No. 2(1977), pp. 235-242.

Miller, T. W. and N. Gressis, "Nonstationarity and Evaluation of Mutual Fund Performance", *Journal of Financial and Quantitative Analysis*, Vol. 15, No. 3(1980), pp. 639-654.

Min, S. K., "The Performance Persistence of Mutual Funds in Korea", *Daehan Journal of Business*, Vol. 20, No. 3(2007), pp. 1413-1431(in Korean).
민성기, "공모펀드들의 유형별 성과 지속성", 대한경영학회지, 제20권 제3호(2007), pp. 1413-1431.

Min, S. K., "The Effects of Fund Expenses and the Tracking Error on the Performance of Index Funds", *Daehan Journal of Business*, Vol. 22, No. 2(2009), pp. 931-947(in Korean).
민성기, "펀드보수와 추적오차가 인덱스펀드의 성과에 미치는 영향", 대한경영학회지, 제22권 제2호(2009), pp. 931-947.

Min, S. K. and M. H. Cha, "Empirical Analysis on the Active Funds and the Index Funds in Korea", *Daehan Journal of Business*, Vol. 21, No. 2(2008), pp. 527-543(in Korean).
민성기, 차문현, "우리나라 액티브펀드와 인덱스펀드의 실증분석", 대한경영학회지, 제21권 제2호(2008), pp. 527-543.

Mola, S. and M. Guidolin, "Affiliated Mutual Funds and Analyst Optimism", *Journal of Financial Economics*, Vol. 93, No. 1(2009), pp. 108-137.

Moreno, D. and R. Rodriguez, "The Value of Coskewness in Mutual Fund Performance Evaluation", *Journal of Banking and Finance*, Vol. 33, No. 9(2009), pp. 1664-1676.

Morey, M. R., "Mutual Fund Age and Morningstar Ratings", *Financial Analysts Journal*, Vol. 58, No. 2(2002), pp. 56-63.

Nanda, V., M. P. Narayanan, and V. A. Warther, "Liquidity, Investment Ability, and Mutual Fund Structure", *Journal of Financial Economics*, Vol. 57, No. 3(2000), pp. 417-443.

Nanda, V., Z. J. Wang, and L. Zheng, "Family Values and the Star Phenomenon: Strategies of Mutual Fund Families", *Review of Financial Studies*, Vol. 17, No. 3(2004), pp. 667-698.

Neal, R. and S. M. Wheatley, "Do Measures of Investor Sentiment Predict Returns?", *Journal of Financial and Quantitative Analysis*, Vol. 33, No. 4(1998), pp. 523-547.

Nishiotis, G. P., "Further Evidence on Closed-End Country Fund Prices and International Capital Flows", *Journal of Business*, Vol. 79, No. 4(2006), pp. 1727-1754.

Nohel, T., Z. J. Wang, and L. Zheng, "Side-by-Side Management of Hedge Funds and Mutual Funds", *Review of Financial Studies*, Vol. 23, No. 6(2010), pp. 2342-2373.

Oh, G. T., K. H. Kim, and C. Y. Yang, "Asymmetric Information and the Closed-End Fund Puzzle", *Korean Journal of Finance*, Vol. 15, No. 1(2002), pp. 251-272(in Korean).
오규택, 김규형, 양채열, "비대칭정보와 폐쇄형펀드 수수께끼", 재무연구, 제15권 제1호(2002), pp. 251-272.

Park, B. J., "The Determination Factors of Mutual Fund Return", *Korean Journal of Financial Management*, Vol. 24, No. 1(2007), pp. 85-107(in Korean).
박범진, "한국주식시장에서 주식형 펀드의 성과결정요인에 관한 연구", 재무관리연구, 제24권 제1호(2007), pp. 85-107.

Park, S. B., "An Empirical Research on Characteristics of the Closed End Fund in Korea", *Daehan Journal of Business*, Vol. 19, No. 6(2006), pp. 2167-2183(in Korean).

박상범, "한국형 폐쇄형 뮤추얼펀드의 특성에 관한 실증연구", 대한경영학회지, 제19권 제6호(2006), pp. 2167-2183.

Park, Y. K., "A Study on the Behavior of Fund Investors and Fund Managers", *Korean Journal of Finance*, Vol. 18, No. 1(2005), pp. 31-67(in Korean).

박영규, "펀드 투자자와 펀드 매니저의 투자행태에 관한 연구", 재무연구, 제18권 제1호(2005), pp. 31-67.

Park, Y. K. and U. Chang, "The Performance Measurement and Attribute Analysis on Equity Style Funds", *Korean Journal of Financial Studies*, Vol. 29, No. 1(2001), pp. 117-143(in Korean).

박영규, 장욱, "국내 주식형 펀드시장에 대한 성과평가연구", 증권학회지, 제29권 제1호(2001), pp. 117-143.

Park, Y. K. and H. K. Joo, "Measuring Performance and Persistence of Performance for the Fixed Income Funds in Korea", *Korean Journal of Finance*, Vol. 17, No. 1(2004), pp. 143-174(in Korean).

박영규, 주효근, "채권형 펀드의 성과평가 및 성과지속성 연구", 재무연구, 제17권 제1호(2004), pp. 143-174.

Park, Y. K. and S. Y. Lee, "Does Dollar-Cost-Averaging Strategy Really Outperform Lump-Sum Strategy in the Fund Investment?", *Asian Review of Financial Research*, Vol. 23, No. 1(2010), pp. 55-88(in Korean).

박영규, 이상엽, "적립식투자전략과 거치식투자전략의 펀드투자 성과비교", 재무연구, 제23권 제1호(2010), pp. 55-88.

Parwada, J. T., "The Genesis of Home Bias? The Location and Portfolio Choices of Investment Company Start-Ups", *Journal of Financial and Quantitative Analysis*, Vol. 43, No. 1(2008), pp. 245-266.

Pastor, L. and R. F. Stambaugh, "Investing in Equity Mutual Funds", *Journal of Financial Economics*, Vol. 63, No. 3(2002a), pp. 351-380.

Pastor, L. and R. F. Stambaugh, "Mutual Fund Performance and Seemingly Unrelated Assets", *Journal of Financial Economics*, Vol. 63, No. 3(2002b), pp. 315-349.

Patro, D. K., "Stock Market Liberalization and Emerging Market Country Fund Premiums", *Journal of Business*, Vol. 78, No. 1(2005), pp. 135-168.

Peavy, J. W., "Returns on Initial Public Offerings of Closed-End Funds", *Review of Financial Studies*, Vol. 3, No. 4(1990), pp. 695-708.

Pinnuck, M., "An Examination of the Performance of the Trades and Stock Holdings of Fund Managers: Further Evidence", *Journal of Financial and Quantitative Analysis*, Vol. 38, No. 4(2003), pp. 811-828.

Pollet, J. M. and M. Wilson, "How Does Size Affect Mutual Fund Behavior?", *Journal of Finance*, Vol. 63, No. 6(2008), pp. 2941-2969.

Pontiff, J., "Closed-End Fund Premia and Returns Implications for Financial Market Equilibrium", *Journal of Financial Economics*, Vol. 37, No. 3(1995), pp. 341-370.

Pontiff, J., "Costly Arbitrage: Evidence from Closed-End Funds", *Quarterly Journal of Economics*, Vol. 111, No. 4(1996), pp. 1135-1151.

Pontiff, J., "Excess Volatility and Closed-End Funds", *American Economic Review*, Vol. 87, No. 1(1997), pp. 155-169.

Porter, G. E., R. L. Roenfeldt, and N. W. Sicherman, "The Value of Open Market Repurchases of Closed-End Fund Shares", *Journal of Business*, Vol. 72, No. 2(1999), pp. 257-276.

Poterba, J. M. and J. B. Shoven, "Exchange-Traded Funds: A New Investment Option for Taxable Investors", *American Economic Review*, Vol. 92, No. 2(2002), pp. 422-427.

Pozen, R. C., The mutual Fund Business, 2nd ed., Houghton Mifflin, 2002.

Rakowski, D., "Fund Flow Volatility and Performance", *Journal of Financial and Quantitative Analysis*, Vol. 45, No. 1(2010), pp. 223-237.

Reuter, J., "Are IPO Allocations for Sale? Evidence from Mutual Funds", *Journal of Finance*, Vol. 61, No. 5(2006), pp. 2289-2324.

Ritter, J. R. and D. Zhang, "Affiliated Mutual Funds and the Allocation of Initial Public Offerings", *Journal of Financial Economics*, Vol. 86, No. 2(2007), pp. 337-368.

Rosen, K. T. and L. Katz, "Money Market Mutual Funds: An Experiment in Ad Hoc Deregulation: A Note", *Journal of Finance*, Vol. 38, No. 3(1983), pp. 1011-1017.

Rozeff, M. S., "Stock Splits: Evidence from Mutual Funds", *Journal of Finance*, Vol. 53, No. 1(1998), pp. 335-349.

Sapp, T. and A. Tiwari, "Does Stock Return Momentum Explain the 'Smart Money' Effect?", *Journal of Finance*, Vol. 59, No. 6(2004), pp. 2605-2622.

Sensoy, B. A., "Performance Evaluation and Self-Designated Benchmark Indexes in the Mutual Fund Industry", *Journal of Financial Economics*, Vol. 92, No. 1(2009), pp. 25-39.

Sharpe, W. F., "Mutual Fund Performance", *Journal of Business*, Vol. 39, No. 1(1966), pp. 119-138.

Sharpe, W. F., "Morningstar's Risk-Adjusted Ratings", *Financial Analysts Journal*, Vol. 54, No. 4(1998), pp. 21-33.

Shin, S. H., "A Study on Outsourcing in Korean Stock and Bond Fund Markets", *Korean Journal of Financial Studies*, Vol. 32, No. 3(2003), pp. 165-190(in Korean).
신성환, "국내 주식 및 채권 펀드를 통한 위탁투자에 관한 연구", 증권학회지, 제32권 제3호(2003), pp. 165-190.

Simonson, D. G., "The Speculative Behavior of Mutual Funds", *Journal of Finance*, Vol. 27, No. 2(1972), pp. 381-391.

Sirri, E. R. and P. Tufano, "Costly Search and Mutual Fund Flows", *Journal of Finance*, Vol. 53, No. 5(1998), pp. 1589-1622.

Song, Y. C. and T. H. Jinn, "A Study on the Performance Evaluation of Fund Managers", *Korean Journal of Financial Studies*, Vol. 14, No. 1(1992), pp. 425-452(in Korean).

송영출, 진태홍, "펀드매니저의 성과평가에 관한 연구", 증권학회지, 제14권 제1호(1992), pp. 425-452.

Starks, L. T., "Performance Incentive Fees: An Agency Theoretic Approach", *Journal of Financial and Quantitative Analysis*, Vol. 22, No. 1(1987), pp. 17-32.

Suh, B. D., D. H. Hong, and M. Y. Lee, "A Study on the relationship of Fund Size and Performance: Does There Exist an Optimal Funds Size?", *Daehan Journal of Business*, Vol. 21, No. 1(2008), pp. 323-345(in Korean).

서병덕, 홍동현, 이미영, "펀드의 성과와 규모에 관한 연구 펀드의 최적규모는 존재하는가?", 대한경영학회지, 제21권 제1호(2008), pp. 323-345.

Swaminathan, B., "Time-Varying Expected Small Firm Returns and Closed-End Fund Discounts", *Review of Financial Studies*, Vol. 9, No. 3(1996), pp. 845-887.

Ter Horst, J. R., T. E. Nijman, and M. Verbeek, "Eliminating Look-Ahead Bias in Evaluating Persistence in Mutual Fund Performance", *Journal of Empirical Finance*, Vol. 8, No. 4(2001), pp. 345-373.

Tufano, P. and M. Sevick, "Board Structure and Fee-Setting in the U.S. Mutual Fund Industry", *Journal of Financial Economics*, Vol. 46, No. 3(1997), pp. 321-355.

Wahal, S. and A. Y. Wang, "Competition among Mutual Funds", *Journal of Financial Economics*, Vol. 99, No. 1(2011), pp. 40-59.

Warner, J. B. and J. S. Wu, "Why Do Mutual Fund Advisory Contracts Change? Performance, Growth, and Spillover Effects", *Journal of Finance*, Vol. 66, No. 1(2011), pp. 271-306.

Warther, V. A., "Aggregate Mutual Fund Flows and Security Returns", *Journal of Financial Economics*, Vol. 39, No. 2-3(1995), pp. 209-235.

Wermers, R., "Mutual Fund Herding and the Impact on Stock Prices", *Journal of Finance*, Vol. 54, No. 2(1999), pp. 581-622.

Wermers, R., "Mutual Fund Performance: An Empirical Decomposition into Stock-Picking Talent, Style, Transactions Costs, and Expenses", *Journal of Finance*, Vol. 55, No. 4(2000), pp. 1655-1695.

Wilcox, R. T., "Bargain Hunting or Star Gazing? Investors' Preferences for Stock Mutual Funds", *Journal of Business*, Vol. 76, No. 4(2003), pp. 645-663.

Won, S. Y., "Function of Fund Distributor and Appropriateness of Sales Fees in Funds", *Korean Journal of Financial Management*, Vol. 26, No. 1(2009), pp. 31-64(in Korean).
원승연, "펀드 판매사의 역할과 판매 보수의 적정성 : 한국의 주식형 펀드를 대상으로", 재무관리연구, 제26권 제1호(2009), pp. 31-64.

Wylie, S., "Fund Manager Herding: A Test of the Accuracy of Empirical Results Using U.K. Data", *Journal of Business*, Vol. 78, No. 1(2005), pp. 381-403.

Yan, X., "Liquidity, Investment Style, and the Relation between Fund Size and Fund Performance", *Journal of Financial and Quantitative Analysis*, Vol. 43, No. 3(2008), pp. 741-767.

Yi, K. Y., "Risk-Taking Behavior in Korean Fund Industry", *Daehan Journal of Business*, Vol. 22, No. 6(2009), pp. 3851-3872(in Korean).
이가연, "한국 주식형 펀드의 과거성과와 위험변화간 연관성 연구", 대한경영학회지, 제22권 제6호(2009), pp. 3851-3872.

Yi, K. Y. and K. I. Park, "The Effect of the Derivatives Using to Fund Risk in Korean Fund Market", *Daehan Journal of Business*, Vol. 21, No. 2(2008), pp. 615-638(in Korean).
이가연, 박경인, "한국펀드시장에서 파생상품사용여부가 펀드위험증대에 미치는 영향", 대한경영학회지, 제21권 제2호(2008), pp. 615-638.

Yoo, K. R. and H. Y. Park, "Are Closed-End Funds Traded at a Discount?",

Korean Journal of Financial Studies, Vol. 30, No. 1(2002), pp. 435-456(in Korean).

유극열, 박혜연, "우리나라 뮤추얼펀드는 주식시장에서 할인되어 거래되나?", 증권학회지, 제30권 제1호(2002), pp. 435-456.

Yoo, S. Y. and S. K. Hwang, "The Disposition Effect to Fund Flow and Performance in the Korean Mutual Fund Marketplace", *Daehan Journal of Business*, Vol. 23, No. 2(2010a), pp. 853-872(in Korean).

유시용, 황승규, "국내 펀드투자자의 펀드자금흐름과 처분효과에 관한 연구", 대한경영학회지, 제23권 제2호(2010a), pp. 853-872.

Yoo, S. Y. and S. K. Hwang, "Is Money Smart in the Korean Mutual Fund Market?", *Asian Review of Financial Research*, Vol. 23, No. 3(2010b), pp. 287-325(in Korean).

유시용, 황승규, "국내 펀드투자자의 펀드선정능력에 관한 연구", 재무연구, 제23권 제3호(2010b), pp. 287-325.

Yoon, Y. C. and J. Khil, "Premium and the Future Net Asset Value Returns in the Korean Fund Market", *Korean Journal of Financial Management*, Vol. 17, No. 2(2000), pp. 99-124(in Korean).

윤영철, 길재욱, "폐쇄형 뮤추얼펀드의 프리미엄과 기대 운용성과에 관한 실증연구", 재무관리연구, 제17권 제2호(2000), pp. 99-124.

Zhao, X., "Exit Decisions in the U.S. Mutual Fund Industry", *Journal of Business*, Vol. 78, No. 4(2005), pp. 1365-1401.

Zheng, L., "Is Money Smart? A Study of Mutual Fund Investors' Fund Selection Ability", *Journal of Finance*, Vol. 54, No. 3(1999), pp. 901-933.

Zitzewitz, E., "How Widespread Was Late Trading in Mutual Funds?", *American Economic Review*, Vol. 96, No. 2(2006), pp. 284-289.

Any citation of this article must refer to the following: Choi, Mun-Soo, "Review of Empirical Studies on IPO Acitivity and Pricing Behavior in Korea", Asian Review of Financial Research, Vol. 24 (2011), No. 2, pp.621-663.

Chapter 7

Review of Empirical Studies on IPO Activity and Pricing Behavior in Korea

Mun-Soo Choi*   Professor, School of Business, Soongsil University

Abstract

This paper reviews the hypotheses and empirical evidence that have been proposed to explain IPO activities and pricing behavior in Korea. The paper particularly reviews empirical evidence and explanations related to the three patterns associated with Korean IPOs: underpricing, hot issue markets, and long-run underperformance. Explanations for underpricing can be grouped under two broad categories: deliberate underpricing and behavioral approaches. The first category can be divided into two subcategories: asymmetric information and price stabilization. While the first subcategory attempts to explain underpricing in the efficient market framework and consider it as a part of the costs associated with IPOs, the last subcategory turns to one of the services that underwriters use to provide price stabilization. While the hypotheses based on asymmetric information are well established and supported by the literature, the significant variation in the degree of underpricing over time together with the poor long-term performance makes many researchers doubtful whether information-based theories could be enough to explain the large initial returns. Some researchers thus turn to behavioral explanations which put more emphasis on the effect of investors' irrational behavior or sentiment on stock prices. Evidence suggests that no hypothesis can dominantly explain large initial returns. Thus the hypotheses reviewed here are not mutually exclusive and a given hypothesis can be more relevant to some IPOs than to others.

Keywords   IPO Pricing, Underpricing, Price Stabilization, Hot Issue Markets, Long-Run Performance

* **Address:** Soongsil University, 511 Sangdo-dong, Dongjak-gu, Seoul 156-743, Korea; **E-mail:** mschoi@ssu.ac.kr; Tel: 82-2-820-0586.

The paper was accomplished as a part of the knowledge database project by the Korean Finance Association and was supported by the Korean Finance Association and Soongsil University. The author thanks two anonymous referees, and the Editor, Hee-Joon Ahn, for their helpful comments.

I. Introduction

Initial public offering of shares (IPO) provides access for a privately held firm to raise equity capital in a public market and may lower the cost of capital needed for the firm's operations and investments. It also provides an opportunity for current shareholders to realize their capital gains and diversify their investments. But IPOs can be quite risky to each of the three major parties involved: issuers, investment bankers, and investors. The big risk stems from the pricing of IPO shares which is complicated by the fact that the valuation of shares is based on relatively incomplete and imperfect information since issuers tend to be young, private firms.

If the price is set too high, then the investor will earn an inferior return and consequently might avoid the IPO market. If it is priced too low, the issuer does not gain the full advantage of its ability to raise capital and will be unwilling to participate in the IPO market.

The empirical evidence on the pricing of IPOs provides a puzzle to those who otherwise believe in efficient markets. Many empirical studies have shown that when firms go public, their shares tend to be significantly underpriced, for which the market price jumps substantially on the initial day of trading. That is, the initial returns, estimated as the percentage difference between the offer price and the initial market price, are positive. Numerous studies document that this phenomenon exists in every nation with a stock market, although the extent of initial returns varies from country to country. The Korean IPO market is no exception to the phenomenon. The average initial return of IPOs is 57.6% over the period 2000~2007 (Lee and Kim 2009). It is markedly larger than the extent of initial returns in the U.S., which averages 25.68% over the period 2000~2007.[1]

---

1) The average initial return is calculated by using IPO data available from the homepage of Jay R. Ritter, a professor of University of Florida.

Given the level of competition and information efficiency in financial markets, this is a surprising result and is considered anomalous to the efficient market hypothesis. A number of hypotheses have been offered to explain this phenomenon in the Korean IPO market, focusing on various aspects of the relations among underwriters, issuers, and investors. In general, these hypotheses can be grouped under two broad categories: deliberate underpricing and behavioral approaches. The first category can be further divided into two subcategories: asymmetric information and price stabilization. While the first subcategory attempts to explain underpricing in the framework of the efficient market and consider it as a part of the necessary costs associated with initial public offerings, the last subcategory turns to one of services that underwriters provide in connection with IPOs-the price support practice which is designed to reduce price drops in the aftermarket. Behavioral approaches regard initial returns as fads or bubbles caused by irrational investors who bid up the price of IPO shares beyond true value.

Empirical evidence documented in the literature suggests that each of the hypotheses alone cannot fully account for the large initial returns observed in the Korean IPO market. The hypotheses reviewed in this paper thus are not mutually exclusive and a given hypothesis can be more relevant to some IPOs than to others.

The purpose of this paper is to review the hypotheses and empirical evidence that have been proposed to explain IPO activities and pricing behavior in the Korean market. The paper particularly reviews the three patterns associated with IPOs: large initial returns, hot issue markets, and long-run underperformance. The IPO literature in Korea is now fairly mature and has accumulated a large body of evidence, which is enough to cast light on the Korean IPO market. Because of limited space, however, this paper sets its main focus on papers presented in academic finance journals such as the Asia-Pacific Journal of Financial Studies, The Korean Journal of Finance (Asian Review of Financial Research), The Korean Journal of Financial Management, and The Korean Journal of Financial Studies.

The remainder of this paper is organized as follows. First, evidence regarding IPO underpricing is presented. Second, the principal hypotheses proposed to explain IPO underpricing are discussed under the two subcategories mentioned above: information asymmetry and price stabilization. Third, the cyclical pattern of IPO activities (i.e., hot and cold issue markets) and the aftermarket performance of IPOs in the long run are presented and discussed in conjunction with behavioral explanations. Finally, concluding remarks are provided.

II. Evidence of IPO Underpricing in the Korean IPO Market

The well-known phenomenon associated with going public is one of large initial returns accruing to investors in the secondary market. These initial returns are considered evidence of the underpricing of IPOs. <Table 1> summarizes the evidence of underpricing in the Korean IPO markets documented by empirical studies since Kang (1990). As shown in <Table 1>, there have been in general two measures used to show the extent of underpricing: initial returns and market-adjusted initial returns. Initial returns are estimated as the percentage difference between the offer price and the market price on the first day of trading. Market-adjusted abnormal returns are initial returns adjusted by market returns which are the percentage difference between the market index on the offer day and the market index on the first trading day. The difference between the two measures appears to be minimal according to several studies including Kang (1990), Jung (1992), Joo (1995), Choi (1999), Choi and Huh (2000), Choi (2000),

\<Table 1\> Evidence of Underpricing in the Korean IPO market

Evidence is collected from the academic finance journals such as the Asia–Pacific Journal of Financial Studies, The Korean Journal of Finance (Asian Review of Financial Research), The Korean Journal of Financial Management, and The Korean Journal of Financial Studies.

Average under-pricing	Underpricing measures[1]	Sample size	Sample firms	Sample period	Authors
80.84%	Market adjusted abnormal returns	126	KSE firms	1988~1989	Kang (1991)
99.80%	Initial returns	153	KSE firms	1988~1989	Kang (1990)
97.20%	Market adjusted abnormal returns	153	KSE firms	1988~1989	Kang (1990)
70.00%	Initial returns	361	KSE firms	1980.09~1991.04	Jung (1992)
68.70%	Market adjusted abnormal returns	361	KSE firms	1980.09~1991.04	Jung (1992)
54.21%	Initial returns	108	KSE firms	1989~1994	Joo (1995)
54.56%	Market adjusted abnormal returns	108	KSE firms	1989~1994	Joo (1995)
30.62%	Initial returns	61	KSE firms	1990~1992	Jang and Woo (1997)
75.45%	Market adjusted abnormal returns	342	KSE firms	1988~1994	Ihm (1997)
77.96%	Initial returns	62	KSE firms	1994.01~1996.09	Choi (1999)
78.70%	Market adjusted abnormal returns	62	KSE firms	1994.01~1996.09	Choi (1999)
69.55%	Initial returns	107	KSE firms	1992.01~1996.10	Choi and Huh (2000)
70.21%	Market adjusted abnormal returns	107	KSE firms	1992.01~1996.10	Choi and Huh (2000)
62.74%	Initial returns	141	KSE firms	1992~1998	Choi (2000)
64.11%	Market adjusted abnormal returns	141	KSE firms	1992~1998	Choi (2000)
19.01%	Market adjusted abnormal returns	130	KOSDAQ firms	1999.01~2000.12	Huh, Yoon and Lee (2002)
58.29%	Initial returns	125	KSE firms	1992~1998	Choi (2003)
14.98%	Market adjusted abnormal returns	161	KOSDAQ firms	1997~2000	Lee and Yi (2003)
56.66%	Market adjusted abnormal returns	39	KSE firms	1997~2000	Lee and Yi (2003)
31.69%	Market adjusted abnormal returns	360	KOSDAQ firms	2000.09~2003.12	Choi (2005)

<Table 1> Continued

Average under-pricing	Underpricing measures[1]	Sample size	Sample firms	Sample period	Authors
57.00%	Initial returns	453	KOSDAQ firms	2000.07~2005.05	Choi and Jun (2006)
74.90%[2]	Market adjusted cumulative abnormal returns	256	KOSDAQ firms	1999.11~2001.01	Kim and Lee (2006)
61.00%	Market adjusted abnormal returns	343	KOSDAQ firms	2001.01~2003.09	Park, Lim, and Sung (2006)
61.10%	Market adjusted abnormal returns	363	KOSDAQ firms	2001.01~2003.12	Park, Kim, and Sung (2007)
45.50%	Market adjusted abnormal returns	174	KSE (20), KOSDAQ (154)	2003.09~2006.06	Lee andJoh (2007)
45.60%	Initial returns	174	KSE (20), KOSDAQ (154)	2003.09~2006.06	Lee andJoh (2007)
34.70%	Market adjusted abnormal returns	50	KSE firms	1999.01~2006.12	Park and Shin (2007)
46.20%	Market adjusted abnormal returns	819	KOSDAQ firms	1999.01~2006.12	Park and Shin (2007)
45.79%	Initial returns	33	KSE firms	2000.02~2007.07	Lee and Kim (2009)
58.29%	Initial returns	569	KOSDAQ firms	2000.02~2007.07	Lee and Kim (2009)
10.24%	Market adjusted abnormal returns	91	KOSDAQ venture firms	2004.01~2007.12	Lee, Lee, and Yoon (2010)
55.53%	Market adjusted abnormal returns	432	KOSDAQ firms	2001.01~2005.12	Kim and Jung (2010)

Note: [1] Initial returns are estimated as the percentage difference between the offer price and the market price on the first day of trading, and market-adjusted abnormal returns are initial returns adjusted by market returns which are the percentage difference between the market index on the offer day and the market index on the first trading day.
[2] The cumulative abnormal return for 20 days.

and Lee and Joh (2007). For instance, Kang (1990) reports an initial return of 99.8% and a market-adjusted abnormalreturn of 97.2%. Academics in the U.S. and other countries use the terms underpricing and initial returns (not market-adjusted abnormal returns) interchangeably.

Some studies also calculate initial returns using the market prices after several days of initial trading, although they are not reported here. In Korea, the stock market has a 'daily price limit' of 15% restricting price fluctuations.[2]

Thus, aftermarket prices may take several days before they reach the equilibrium price. In such a case, it makes sense to measure initial returns over a longer window.[3)]

As <Table 1> shows, the distribution of initial returns is highly skewed, with a large positive mean. There is also substantial variation in IPO under-pricing over time. In the 1980s, the average initial return is 70% for 361 KSE firms, according to Jung (1992). Over the period of 1992~1996, Choi and Huh (2000) reports 69.55% for 107 KSE firms. Lee and Yi (2003) report 56.66% for 39 KSE firms over the period of 1997~2000. In the period 2000 to 2007, there were only 33 KSE firms that went public and their initial returns averaged 45.79%, according to Lee and Kim (2009), which is appro-ximately two thirds of the average returns for the 1980s and 1990s. In con-trast, over the period of 2000~2007, 569 firms reportedly went public on the KOSDAQ market with an average initial return of 58.29% accruing to investors, again Lee and Kim (2009). This drastic decrease in the number of IPOs in the KSE market inspired a large body of empirical literature in the 2000s focusing more on the IPOs occurring on the KOSDAQ market.

The degree of IPO underpricing in Korea is still large compared to other developed countries, but as <Table 1> shows, there is a substantial decrease in underpricing over time. This decreasing trend can be attributed to a learning process for each of the major parties involved: issuers, underwriters, and investors. But it is more likely that this trend is strongly associated with changes in regulations covering the mechanics and the valuation process of IPOs.[4)]

---

2) The daily price limit was 12% prior to December 1998. Furthermore, as described in Appendix 2, there exists a change in the opening price of initial trading. Prior to June 2000, the opening price of initial trading was the offer pricebut now is the first asking price. These changes in the daily price limit and the opening price of initial trad-ing could have an impact on initial returns when the aftermarket price of some IPO shares has run up to the limit.

3) Most studies presented in <Table 1> present the initial return results measured by using a variety of longer windows. Thus some studies contain many different measures for the initial return. Because of limited space, this paper presents only the initial return on the first trading day of each study.

4) Regulatory changes in the Korean IPO process, including the bookbuilding process, the allocation mechanics, and the valuation methods, are presented in Appendix 1 and 2.

Such regulatory changes could have influenced the size of initial returns. The most critical regulatory change in the pricing of IPO shares is the implementation of the bookbuilding process. Prior to bookbuilding, every IPO in Korea had to use the intrinsic pricing method to estimate the initial price of IPO shares. This practice normally sets the offer price relatively low and enables investors who successfully received an allocation to reap significant profits (see e.g., Lim (1991), Kang and Cho (2000)). Despite its significant impact of initial returns, most empirical studies have not controlled for the effect of regulatory changes on initial returns. This could lead to an invalidation of their hypotheses testing based on initial returns.

III. Asymmetric Information Hypotheses

Among the IPO underpricing hypotheses reviewed, the hypotheses based on asymmetric information are well established and have accumulated a large body of evidence. Asymmetric information models assume that one of the major parties, such as investors, issuers, and investment bankers, knows more than the others and that such informational frictions give rise to underpricing.

1. Winner's Curse

Rock (1986) assumes that investors are differentially informed such that some investors are actually better informed regarding the true value of IPO shares. Informed investors are more likely to buy underpriced shares, but other investors buy shares without distinction. Thus, other investors will be allocated more of the least desirable IPO shares, resulting in a winner's curse. Faced with this problem, the uninformed investors will purchase shares only if IPOs are underpriced sufficiently to compensate them for the bias in the allocation of IPO shares. This requires that all IPOs should be underpriced in expectation so that the uninformed earns a non-negative expected return even after adjusted for rationing. The earliest empirical study on the winner's curse model is Kang's (1990) analysis for IPOs in the KSE market, where oversubscribed IPO shares are allocated on a pro-rata basis. Kang (1990) examines the underpricing behavior of 247 KSE firms which went public over the period of 1988~1989 and finds that the extent of underpricing is negatively related to the subscription rate which measures the likelihood of receiving oversubscribed IPOs. He also shows that average expected returns decrease significantly, from 99.8% to 2%, when adjusted for pro-rated allocations.

Since Kang's (1990) study, there has been no attempt to test the winner's curse model. But Kang's analysis on IPOs can be replicated using subscription rates reported by the literature. The unconditional expected returns reported by Choi (1999), Choi and Huh (2000), Choi (2000), Kim and Lee (2006), Lee and Joh (2007), and Lee and Kim (2009) are well above 45% during the sample period, but they decline to less than 1.1% when adjusted for subscription rates reported in their papers. Although the competition for IPO shares among investors and the subsequent rationing sharply reduces the expected returns, they never decline to less than zero. Rock's model suggests that when properly adjusted for rationing, uninformed investors earn zero expected returns and informed investors earn returns which are just enough to cover their costs of becoming informed. Since it is difficult to identify whether investors are informed or uninformed, non-zero expected returns for every investor who receives an allocation can be regarded as evidence supporting the winner's curse hypothesis.

2. Ex Ante Uncertainty

In line with Rock's winner's curse, Beatty and Ritter (1986) propose a hypothesis that the greater is the ex ante uncertainty about the value of IPO shares, the larger is the extent of underpricing. The intuition behind this hypothesis is that being informed in the IPO market is similar to implicitly investing in a call option on an IPO.[5] An increase in ex ante uncertainty will make the call option more valuable and thus induce more investors to become informed. This will further worsen the winner's curse and force issuing parties to raise the degree of underpricing to attract more uninformed investors. This explanation has a relatively simple testable implication-a positive relation between the ex ante valuation uncertainty and the degree of IPO underpricing.

All theories of underpricing based on asymmetric information share the prediction that underpricing is positively related to ex ante uncertainty, which supposedly contributes to the degree of asymmetric information. Thus, any empirical test on hypotheses based on asymmetric information must control for ex ante uncertainty. Indeed, this hypothesis has been tested by various empirical studies, but the testing has been conducted only as one of the controlling variables i.e., there has been no attempt to directly test the hypothesis.

<Table 2> summarizes the proxies for the ex ante uncertainty used in the literature, including their estimation results. As shown in <Table 2>, there is a wide range of proxies for ex ante uncertainty and their estimation results differ across studies.

<Table 2> shows that variables representing the size of IPO firms, such as total assets, sales, and gross proceeds, are the most commonly used proxies for ex ante uncertainty. However, their estimated results are not consistent across studies. It is well known that the size variables can proxy anything. A potentially more promising approach might be to identify potential uses of IPO proceeds as disclosed in the prospectus (Ljungqvist and Wilhelm, 2003) or the number of risk factors listed in the prospectus (Beatty and Welch,

---

5) This option is exercised if the true value of IPO shares exceeds the offer price.

\<Table 2\> Survey of Proxies for Ex Ante Uncertainty

Evidence is collected from the academic finance journals, such as the Asia–Pacific Journal of Financial Studies, The Korean Journal of Finance (Asian Review of Financial Research), The Korean Journal of Financial Management, and The Korean Journal of Financial Studies.

Authors	Proxy variables	Predicted sign	Results (sign)
Lee et al. (2010)	Age	+/ –	Significant (+)
	Venture dummy	+/ –	Significant (+)
	Log total assets	+/ –	Insignificant (+)
Kim and Jung (2010)	Age	+/ –	Insignificant (+)
	Gross proceeds	+/ –	Significant (-)
	Log total assets	+/ –	Insignificant (-)
Lee and Kim (2009)	Log age	+/ –	Insignificant (+/-)
	Log gross proceeds	–	Insignificant (-)
Lee and Joh (2007)	Gross Proceeds	+	Significant (+)
	Age	+	Insignificant (+)
Park and Shin (2007)	Age	–	Significant (-)
	Total assets	–	Significant (-)
	Gross Proceds	–	Significant (-)
Kim and Lee (2006)	Gross Proceds	–	Significant (-)
	Age	–	Significant (-)
Park et al. (2006)	Age	–	Insignificant (-)
	Gross proceeds	–	Significant (-)
	Leverage	+/ –	Significant (-)
	Venture dummy	+/ –	Insignificant (-)
Choi (2005)	Total Assets (per share)	+	Significant (+)
	Gross Proceeds	–	Significant (-)
Yoon (2003)	Age	–	Significant (-)
	Log total assets	–	Significant (-)
Lee and Yi (2003)	Age	–	Significant (-)
	Log capital	–	Insignificant (+)
Huh et al. (2002)	Age	+/ –	Significant or insignificant (-)
	Log total assets	+/ –	Significant (-)
Kang (2001)	Log total assets	–	Significant (-)
	Age	–	Insignificant (-)
Jang and Khil (2000)	Venture dummy	+/ –	Insignificant (+)
	Gross proceeds	+/ –	Insignificant (+)
	Age	+/ –	Insignificant (+)
Choi (1999)	Age	–	Insignificant (-)
	Log Sales	–	Significant (-)
	Standard deviation of net income	+	Significant (+)
Lee, Lim, and Yon (1995)	1/gross proceeds	+	Significant (+)
Joo (1995)	Total assets	–	Significant (-)
	Total equity	+	Insignificant (+)
	Gross Proceeds	+	Insignificant (+)

1996).[6] These variables could provide more interesting insights on the issue.

3. Partial Adjustment (Information Extraction)

Bookbuilding methods give underwriters wide discretion over allocations, allowing them to elicit private information from investors which can be used in setting the offer price. In so doing, investment bankers must compensate investors through underpricing. In this framework, the ex ante measure of firm-specific uncertainty is directly related to the marginal value of investors' (positive) private information. If the firm-specific uncertainty about the value of IPO shares is great, any information that reduces such uncertainty will be valuable to an issuer, who is then expected to collect such information as much as possible via the bookbuilding process (Benveniste and Spindt, 1989), Benveniste and Wilhelm, 1990). However, when the issuer is faced with the truth-telling constraint, information gathering becomes costly in the form of underpricing as uncertainty increases. This leads to a prediction that there will be a partial adjustment of the offer price from that specified in the preliminary prospectus. More precisely, from the positive information revealed, the issuer and underwriter factor in their expectations about what the full-information price of shares will be and raise the offer price from that set prior to the bookbuilding period but set the final offer price less than the full-information price. This leads to a positive relation between the price revision over the process of bookbuilding and underpricing.

Testing this hypothesis is relatively new to the Korean IPO literature. This is because it has been just 10 years since the bookbuilding process was introduced to the Korean market. Choi (2005) has directly tested this partial-adjustment hypothesis using 390 KOSDAQ firms. His study documents the

---

6) Ljungqvist and Wilhelm (2003) argue that firms intending to use their IPO proceeds to fund operating activities rather than investing activities or debt repayment are potentially more risky.

supporting evidence that underpricing is positively related to revisions in the offer price made during the bookbuilding period.[7] This evidence, however, is applicable only to the sample IPO firms which adopt the comparative pricing method, such as price multiples, for the initial valuation of IPO shares. The other method commonly used for the initial pricing of IPO shares is the intrinsic pricing method based on the book value of net assets, the future profitability predicted over 2 years following the IPO year, and the market value of competing firms in the same industry. Prior to the deregulation of the pricing practice of the IPO, every IPO in Korea must adopt the intrinsic pricing method to estimate the initial price of IPO shares. This practice is known according to the literature (see e.g., Lim, 1991), Kang and Cho, 2000) that the offer price tends to be set too low and investors who successfully received allocation can reap significant gains. If the initial price of IPO shares is set too low prior to the bookbuilding process and investors who participate in the bookbuilding know it, then there will be no motivation for investors who participate in bookbuilding to reveal their private information in the partial-adjustment framework. That is, these investors can potentially benefit by not revealing positive information about new issues. For this reason, Choi (2005) argues, the partial-adjustment hypothesis is not supported when the sample IPOs use the intrinsic pricing practice.[8]

On the other hand, the average initial price based on the comparative pricing practice is reportedly far less than that based on the intrinsic pricing method.[9]

---

7) Although there has been a strict restriction on how underwriters in Korea allocate IPO shares to their clients until recently, underwriters in Korea had discretion of the allocation of IPO shares to those who participate in the bookbuilding process (high-yield funds or institutional investors). The allotment to high-yield funds and institutional investors at that time was 30% to 55% and 15% to 30%, respectively. IPO shares were allocated to high-yield funds and institutional investors participating in the bookbuilding process according to their weights deter mined by their credit ratings and the proximity of their bidding price to the potential offer price. Thus, the bookbuilding system at that time allowed underwriters to have discretion on the allocation to investors and provided some inducements for informed investors (high-yield funds and institutional investors participating in the bookbuilding) to reveal their information.

8) More detailed information on the current rule regarding how to set offer prices is explained in Appendix 2.

9) For instance, the average initial prices based on the comparative pricing practice and the intrinsic pricing practice are ₩8,777 and ₩10,195, respectively, according to the results presented by Choi (2005).

This would mean additional pressure on underwriters for aggressive road show activities in order to secure more (positive) information from investors. Since investors are assured of positive returns as a compensation for revealing their private information, this implies that there will be a positive relation between the price revision and underpricing for the sample IPO firms with the comparative pricing method. The author finds the evidence consistent with this prediction.

4. Information Spillover

In conjunction with the partial-adjustment hypothesis, there may exist the effect of information spillover in the IPO market. If underwriters and invest- ors deal with each other repeatedly in the IPO market, the cost of information acquisition can be reduced. Investment banks that are more active in the IPO market have a natural advantage in pricing IPOs i.e., their larger IPO deals allow them to obtain investors' cooperation more cheaply than less active underwriters can. Thus, repeated interaction creates information spillover from the primary market to the secondary market and results in less underpricing. This information spillover effect can be intensified by bundling offerings across time.[10] Obtaining information from other offerings allows investors to evaluate other offerings more cheaply. Such economies of scale could result in much less underpricing. In contrast, the first firm going public (i.e., pioneering IPO firm) should compensate investors for their whole in- formation production effort, thereby resulting in larger underpricing.

Choi and Jun (2006) have examined the effects of information spillover, bundling, and pioneering IPOs on underpricing in the Korean market. Their results indicate that the information spillover from bundling indeed decreases the marketing and information production expenditures through higher offer prices and lower underpricing. Their study also finds that pio-

---

10) Refer to Ljungqvist (2006) for further detail on the information spillover hypothesis.

neering IPO firms tend to have lower offer prices and larger underpricing than their followers do.

5. Certification Effect

The repeated interaction between investment bankers and investors as mentioned above can also create a certification effect on IPO underpricing. If an underwriter and investor interact repeatedly in the IPO market, the investor could become afraid of being excluded from all the current and future IPO deals being managed by that underwriter. This enables underwriters who are more active in the IPO market to have a natural advantage in collecting information from investors and pricing IPOs. Then, hiring underwriters who are more active and more prestigious can certify the quality of IPOs and reduce underpricing. This is because investment bankers who accumulate valuable reputation capital through repeated interactions will restrain themselves from underwriting low-quality issuers (Booth and Smith, 1986; Carter and Manaster, 1990; Michaely and Shaw, 1994).

The earliest empirical study on this issue is done by Kang (1991), who has examined the role of an underwriter's reputation on the underpricing of a Korean IPO. He first identifies prestigious and non-prestigious underwriters based on the equity size of underwriters and the size and number of IPOs undertaken by them during the period of 1988~1989. His study shows that average initial returns for prestigious and non-prestigious banks are 76.01% and 84.24%, respectively, and their difference is not significant according to t-test. He argues that one of the reasons for this weak result is the short history of the Korean IPO market.

This certification effect has been extended to examine the role of venture capitalists in the IPO market by several empirical studies (e.g., Lee, Ihm and Choi, 1998; Jang and Khil, 2000; Huh et al., 2002; Yoon, 2003). The authors suggest that because venture capitalists repeatedly bring firms to the public market, they can credibly stake their reputation that the firms they bring to market are not overvalued. They test the idea using samples of venture (capital)-backed IPOs and non-venture (capital)-backed IPOs. Their empirical results, however, are mixed. It appears that the results are quite sensitive to the market and period examined. Lee et al. (1998), report that there has been no significant relation between the reputation of venture capitalists and underpricing, after examining a matched set of 25 venture-backed and non-venture-backed KSE IPOs between 1987 and 1996.

Jang and Khil (2000) also confirm their finding that the underpricing of venture-backed IPOs is not significantly less than that of non-venture-backed IPOs, after examining a matched set of 34 KOSDAQ IPOs between 1996 and 1999.

Huh, Yoon, and Lee (2002) have examined the difference of underpricing between IPOs backed by a prestigious venture capitalist (KTB) and IPOs backed by other (non-KTB) venture capitalists. They report that the prestigious venture capitalist (KTB) is associated with lower underpricing than other venture capitalists, after examining a matched set of 65 venture-backed and non-venture-backed KOSDAQ IPOs between 1999 and 2000. They argue that KTB-backed IPOs are less underpriced because the prestigious venture capitalist (KTB) has monitored the quality of the offering.

Yoon (2003), however, finds mixed evidence for the certification effect of the prestigious venture capitalists which include KTB. He has compared underpricing of IPOs backed by the prestigious venture capitalists including KTB with that of IPOs backed by other venture capitalists using both average abnormal returns of the initial trading day and average abnormal returns of the trading day at which successive daily price limits end. His results show that there is no significant difference in abnormal returns for the initial trading day between the two groups. But when KTB is excluded from the prestigious group, the result becomes significant at the 10% level. When the abnormal returns of the trading at which successive daily price limits end are used, IPOs backed by the prestigious group including KTB are less underpriced. But when KTB is excluded from the prestigious group, there is no difference between the two groups.

Park et al. (2006), investigate, using a sample of 343 IPO firms over the period of 2001~2003, whether an IPO firm's relationship with a merchant bank has a certification effect on underpricing. They document no supporting evidence for the certification effect of merchant banks.

The results on this issue are in general mixed. This suggests that they are sensitive not only to the sample firms and period examined, but also to the methodologies used. For instance, some studies that examined venture capitalists for KOSDAQ IPOs do not clearly explain how their prestigious venture capitalists are defined. They simply classify prestigious and non-prestigious groups based on the government regulations that guide how venture capitalists are formed. But it would be more plausible to use a proxy for the reputation capital of venture capitalists, such as the market share of the venture capital industry.

There may be an endogeneity bias on the certification effect on underpricing. An issuer doesn't select an underwriter randomly, nor does an investment bank randomly agree on which firms are to go public (Habib and Ljungqvist, 2001). The choices we actually observe are presumably made by agents. But issuers also likely base their choices on the underpricing they expect to suffer. This leads to an endogeneity bias when initial returns are regressed for underwriter choice.

The certification effect may also be impeded by a conflict of interest arising from the relationship between the underwriting business and the asset management business which coexist in a security firm. Park and Shin (2007) examine IPOs from 1999 through 2006 and find that the extent of underpricing is larger when IPOs are underwritten by securities firms that have asset management businesses. They also find that the degree of underpricing is positively associated with the market share of the asset management business. Their findings imply that securities firms may have favored customers of their asset management business at the expense of those of the underwriting business because they can get more profit from the former which is growing much faster than the latter.[11]

This does not mean that security firms make the underwriting business a scapegoat for the growth of asset management business. On the contrary, security firms expand their underwriting businesses to continuously favor customers of their asset management businesses. In so doing, they must make their underwriting business attractive and prestigious enough to attract more IPO customers, but at the same time they must deeply underprice IPO shares to satisfy the greed of their asset management customers. This conflict of interest potentially reduces the certification effect arising from the good reputation and prestige of underwriters.

IV. Price Stabilization

Several studies turn to the practice of price stabilization for explaining IPO underpricing. One of the services that underwriters provide in connection with an IPO is price support. This service is intended to reduce price drops in the aftermarket for a few weeks or months and used to be

---

11) However, it is not evident that the conflict of interest occurs in the market. To be evident, we need the allocation data to examine whether the asset management business benefits from the allocation of IPO shares. Furthermore, their approach ignores the endogeneity bias mentioned above. That is, issuers also likely base their choices of underwriters on the underpricing they expect to suffer.

legally mandatory in the Korean IPO market. Ruud (1993) argues that the positive initial returns observed are not the result of deliberate underpricing, but the result of the price stabilization practice of IPOs whose prices threaten to fall below the offer price. The price support of underwriters reduces IPOs with negative initial returns that would be observed in the aftermarket. This censoring of the negative tail of the distribution produces positive mean initial returns even if IPOs are priced at their intrinsic value. Accordingly, Ruud hypothesizes that if there is no deliberate underpricing, then the initial return distribution of unsupported offerings should have a mean zero. This hypothesis is developed under the efficient market hypothesis.

Unlike the U.S. market where direct evidence of price support is limited because price support activities are not generally public information, under-writers in Korea must make a public announcement with regard to which IPOs are initially supported, how the intensity of stabilization varies over-time, and at what time support is withdrawn. This makes it possible to test directly the price support hypothesis in Korea.[12]

Jang and Woo (1997) examine the price stabilization hypothesis proposed by Ruud. To investigate whether the observed initial returns are the by-product of price stabilization, as Ruud proposes, or deliberate underpricing, Jang and Woo estimate average initial returns for the two hypothesized distributions of supported and unsupported IPOs. If Ruud is correct in saying that there is no deliberate underpricing, then the initial return distribution of unsupported offerings should have a mean zero. This, however, is not what they find. They find that the distribution of unsupported IPOs has

---

12) The price stabilization hypothesis proposed by Ruud is different from the price stabilization hypothesis pro-posed and tested by other studies appearing in this paper such as Shin et al. (2004), Kim and Lee (2006), Lee and Kim (2009), and Lee and Joh (2007). Ruud has to investigate the price support hypothesis through the examination of the skewness of initial returns. In Korea, however, any activities supporting the aftermarket price is public information and this makes it possible to test directly the price support of underwriters. Thus, the hypothesis and results presented by those studies (except Jang and Woo, 1997) are not directly com-parable to those of Ruud (1993).

a mean first-day return of 35.54%, while the distribution of supported IPOs has a mean first-day return of 18.86%. They argue that the mean of first-day return for unsupported IPOs is too large to justify the price stabilization hypothesis proposed by Ruud and suggest that underpricing in the Korean IPO market is caused by factors other than price support.

Kim and Lee (2006) also confirm the finding that the distribution of IPOs without the aftermarket intervention has an average 20-day cumulative abnormal return of 86.4%, while the distribution of IPOs with the aftermarket intervention has a mean 20-day cumulative abnormal return of 6%. This result also rejects the price stabilization hypothesis proposed by Ruud.[13]

Shin, Chang, and Chung (2004) take a different approach to examine the effect of the aftermarket price support on underpricing. In the Korean IPO markets, price stabilization was legally mandatory until May 1999 and was abolished briefly over the period from May 1999 to February 2000. The practice, however, was reinstated from March 2000 as a recommended system rather than an obligatory system. This unique regulatory environment provides an opportunity to test their hypothesis that without the mandatory price support system, the extent of underpricing would be less because of decreased uncertainty faced by underwriters with regard to aftermarket price stabilization. They find no difference in underpricing between the two periods and argue that the reintroduction of the aftermarket price support system does not affect the magnitude of underpricing.

Their hypothesis is also examined by Kim and Lee (2006). They report that average 20-day cumulative returns are 91% before the reinstatement and 65.4% after the reinstatement and their difference is statistically significant. Their regression analysis also confirms the significant difference between them even after controlling other factors that presumably influence

---

13) Although Kim and Lee (2006) do not directly examine Ruud's hypothesis, they have shown the result consistent with that of Jang and Woo.

underpricing. Their evidence thus does not support the hypothesis proposed by Shin et al. (2004), and indicates that the existence of the price support system decreases, rather than increases, the extent of underpricing.

Lee and Kim (2009), however, provide evidence that supports the price stabilization hypothesis. They analyze the data of 602 IPO stocks listed on the Korea Exchange (KRX) along with KSE and KOSDAQ from February 2000 to July 2007 and find that average initial returns are 62.26% for the period with price support and 49.17% for the period without support. Their finding is consistent with the hypothesis that the existence of price stabilization increases the extent of IPO underpricing because of the aftermarket uncertainty faced by underwriters. They also report that the effect of the non-trading period, which is defined as the period from the first day of offering to the first day of trading, is one of the important factors which determine IPO underpricing. Using the option pricing approach, they find that the option value for the non-trading period is on average 11.98% of the offering price.[14] They also report that the degree of IPO underpricing increases as the option value of the IPO stock increases, and thus the loss of the option value that investors may suffer during the non-trading period is another important factor in IPO underpricing in the Korean market.[15]

Price stabilization can be thought of as a put option written by underwriters and held by IPO investors, in the sense that the price support activities put a floor under initial aftermarket prices and thus act as insurance against price falls. In fact, security-issuance regulation in Korea allows investors to have the right to sell their stocks back to underwriters within the first month

---

14) They first define the non-trading period effect as the expected losses that can occur during the non-trading period and then measure an option value of the non-trading period effect with an option pricing model and analyze the effect of the option values on the IPO underpricing.

15) But, the value of an option increases as the time to expiration increases. Thus, their result may be due to the characteristics of the option pricing model. That is, the longer the non-trading period is, the larger the value of the option is. The length of the non-trading period may depend on the timing of the initial trading. Underwriters of 'cold offerings' may wait for the 'hot issue market' or the time to bundle cold offerings with hot offerings for the initial trading.

of trading at 90% of the offer price.[16] With such put-back options, investors investing in IPO shares are protected against price falls below 90% of the offer price, while underwriters are exposed to the risk arising from the sale of a put option. Thus the value of a put-back option reflects the risk faced by underwriters, which is similar to the risk of price stabilization.

Lee and Joh (2007) have examined the relationship between underpricing and the ex ante value of put-back options, using a sample of 174 KSE and KOSDAQ IPO firms over the period of 2003~2006. They argue that the larger the ex ante risk of the aftermarket price falling below the offer price is, the larger the ex ante value of the put-back option is. Underwriters as market makers then deliberately lower the initial offer price of an IPO to reduce the ex ante risk of the price falling below the 90% threshold. They hypothesize that the initial return and the ex ante value of a put-back option are negatively correlated and find the evidence of negative correlation between them.

However, lowering the offer price means a larger initial return(larger underpricing), rather than a smaller initial return. Contrary to their own hypothesis, this leads to a positive relation between the ex ante value of put-back option and the initial return.[17] That is why they use the volatility of the industry index to which an IPO firm belongs (instead of the volatility of the market price of the IPO firm) to estimate the value of the put-back option.

This view of the origin of underpricing together with such mixed results leaves a critical question regarding the pricing mechanism of IPOs. Under the efficient market hypothesis, the market price of IPO shares reflects the true value so that positive initial returns indicate underpricing. Then any activity of the aftermarket price stabilization may implicitly indicate

16) The put-back option system existed over the period from September, 2003 to July, 2007.
17) Of course, there should be a negative relation between initial returns and the ex-post (not ex ante)value of put-back option. But what Lee and Joh (2007) attempt to find is a relation between underpricing (initial returns) and the ex ante (not ex-post) value of put-back option.

a failure of the IPO pricing mechanism. That is, the offer price is overvalued or the market price reflects bubbles or fads, instead of the true value, and thus would burst quickly leaving the market price to fall below the offer price. This suggests that a different approach may be needed to examine the relation between price stabilization and underpricing.

A possible approach is to measure underpricing using the premarket information. Kim and Lee (2006) adopt this approach and measure the extent of premarket underpricing using the ratio of the offer price to the 'intrinsic value' specified in the preliminary prospectus. This allows them to eliminate a possible introduction of fads or bubbles in measuring underpricing (Choi, 1999). Their regression result indicates that their premarket underpricing measure (the average ratio of the offer price to the 'intrinsic value') after the reinstatement is significantly larger than that before the reinstatement even after controlling other factors. This evidence is consistent with the price stabilization hypothesis: the existence of price stabilization increases the aftermarket uncertainty faced by underwriters, thereby lowering the offer price further.

V. Hot Issue Markets

Some researchers attempt to find an explanation for underpricing from the phenomenon known as hot issue markets(e.g., Ibbotson and Jaffe, 1975; Ritter, 1984). They note that cycles exist in both the volume and average initial returns of IPOs; high initial returns tend to be followed by rising IPO volume.[18] The periods of high average initial returns with rising IPO volume are referred to as 'hot issue' markets. This empirical regularity is often observed in Korea and other countries and can be hardly accounted for in the frame-

---

18) One of referees points out that underpricing can exist in even cold markets.

work of the market efficiency. For this reason, the empirical literature turns to a behavioral explanation for the hot issue markets phenomenon.

Kim and Jung (2010) have examined 432 IPOs over the period of 2001~ 2005. They first identify sample IPOs based on the return of the industry index to which an IPO belongs over the 3 months preceding the closing of the order book. This market conditions variable is then split into terciles, and each IPO is assigned to one of the terciles. They find that initial returns and long-run underperformance of IPOs in the upper tercile (hot market samples) are larger than those in the lower tercile (cold market samples) and their differences are significant. Their analysis further shows that the proxies for the optimistic investors' sentiment have positive effects on initial returns and negative effects on long-term performance. Therefore, the observed initial returns of IPOs, they argue, are more likely to reflect bubbles or fads that would eventually burst rather than deliberate underpricing the favorable market conditions that prevail at the time of an offering generate over-optimism from some investors about the prospects of the offering.[19]

Although Kim and Jung turn to a behavioral explanation for the phenomenon, their results provide interesting aspects to be explored further from the perspective of information acquisition. Kim and Jung's distinction of hot issue markets does not accord with the cyclical nature of hot issue markets in the literature, where they are characterized by not only high levels of initial return but also high IPO volumes (see e.g., Ibbotson and Jaffe, 1975; Ritter, 1984). This is because Kim and Jung classify the sample IPOs based on the industry-index returns rather than on the cyclical nature of IPO activities. Although their approach seems appropriate, it could ignore the effect arising from IPO volumes on underpricing. This effect is closely related to the information spillover effect from bundling IPOs in

---

19) One of referees points out that this could result from investors' overexcitement over a certain industry at a time, as experienced during the internet bubble period.

the same industry. Benveniste et al. (2002), offer an alternative explanation to the hot issue markets phenomenon. They develop a model in which underwriters bundle IPOs in the same industry in order to share the costs of information production (i.e., underpricing). The central idea is that obtaining information about the industry component allows investors to evaluate other offerings from that industry more cheaply. Such economies of scale could lead to many firms in the same industry going public at the same time. This is consistent with Kim and Jung's empirical observation that companies tend to go public in industry-specific waves.[20]

Kim and Jung's results also imply that initial returns can be predicted using market conditions, which are measured by industry-index returns in the 3-month period prior to the offerings, prevailing prior to the offering that is, there is a positive relation between the pre-market condition and initial returns. This contradicts the information extraction theory proposed by Benveniste and Spindt (1989), since the industry-index returns are public information which is freely available, so there is no need to compensate investors for it by leaving money on the table.

VI. Long-Run Performance

Another unique pattern associated with IPOs is the poor aftermarket performance of IPOs in the long run. Measured from the aftermarket prices over the various time frames, <Table 3> summarizes the evidence on the long-term performance of the Korean IPOs documented by empirical studies since Lim and Lee (1995).

As shown in <Table 3>, there are in general three measures used to

20) Booth and Chua (1996) also argue that when there is a sequence of many offerings in the market, the marginal cost of information production is less, thereby reducing underpricing.

show the long-term performance: cumulative abnormal returns (CARs), buy and hold abnormal returns (BHARs), and relative wealth (WR). Results presented in <Table 3> show a declining tendency of long-term performance of IPOs over a period of 36 months and these measures appear to be different across studies.[21] This suggests that they are sensitive to the methods and benchmarks used. Thus, research on this area has been subject to more rigorous empirical testing. Fama (1970) particularly emphasizes that all models for expected returns are incomplete descriptions of the systematic patterns in average returns during any sample period. As a result, tests of performance are always contaminated by a bad-model problem. The bad-model problem is less serious in performance studies that focus on short return windows (a few days), although the problem grows with the return horizon.

To mitigate the problem, Choi and Huh (2000) have used various benchmarks that are carefully constructed to avoid known biases. They have also adopted a monthly calendar-time portfolio approach for measuring long-term abnormal performance. By forming monthly calendar-time portfolios, all cross-correlations of event-firm abnormal returns are automatically accounted for in the portfolio variance. Any methodology that ignores cross-sectional dependence of event-firm abnormal returns that are overlapping in calendar-time is likely to produce overstated test statistics (Mitchell and Stafford, 1998). Their results show that long-term abnormal returns based on a calendar-time portfolio approach are 0.31% for 12 months, 0.48% for 24 months, and 0.54% for 36 months, confirming the poor long-term performance of IPOs.[22]

21) The result of Kim and Kim (2000) presented in <Table 3> is the only one that shows positive long-term performance over a 36-month period. Their long-term returns are adjusted only by the return of control firms comparable to IPO firms. Their tests of the long-term performance could be contaminated by a bad-model problem as suggested by Fama (1998). One way to mitigate the problem is to adjust returns of IPO shares by various benchmarks which are carefully constructed to avoid known biases, as suggested by Choi and Huh (2000).

22) Returns are estimated by the Fama-French three factor model. The three factors are zero-investment portfolios representing the excess return of the market; the difference between a portfolio of small stocks and big stocks, SMB; and the difference between a portfolio of high BE/ME stocks and low BE/ME stocks, HML. BE/ME is the ratio of the book value of equity to the market value of equity.

\<Table 3\> Survey of Long-Term Performance of Korean IPOs

*BHAR*s are calculated as the difference between the average monthly returns for the event firms and the benchmark portfolios. *CAR*s are calculated by summing the average monthly abnormal returns. The wealth relative (*WR*) is the average gross return of the sample firms divided by the average gross return of the benchmark.

Author(s)	Sample period	Sample size	Under pricing (%)	Market	Period (months)	Performance measure		
						CAR (%)	BHAR (%)	WR
Lim and Lee[1] (1995)	1980~1990	331	46.77	KSE	6	2.38	-	-
					12	1.33	-	-
					24	-4.96	-	-
					36	-11.53	-	-
Ihm (1997)	1988~1994	342	75.45	KSE	12	-	-	0.99
					24	-	-	0.96
					36	-	-	0.95
Choi and Huh[5] (2000)	1992~1996	107	70.21	KSE	12	-0.31	-	0.99
					24	-0.48	-	0.98
					36	-0.54	-	0.93
Kim and Kim[3] (2000)	1988~1994	267			6	4.47	2.31	-
					12	5.47	1.04	1.14
					24	10.46	-0.12	1.01
					36	18.87	-3.76	-
Choi (2000)[2]	1992~1998	141	114.37	KSE	36	7.71	2.94	-
Lee and Yi[1] (2003)	1997~2000	39	56.66	KSE	6	9.27	-	1.63
					12	-6.6	-	1.56
					24	10.02	-	1.93
					36	-21.31	-	1.80
		131	14.98	KOSDAQ	6	25.58	-	1.53
					12	31.9	-	1.30
					24	14.01	-	1.35
					36	-7.83	-	1.08
Kim and Jung[4] (2010)	2001~2005	432	55.53	KOSDAQ	6	-5.25	-13.71	-
					12	-11.34	-23.31	-
					24	-25.72	-50.53	-
					36	-30.81	-90.67	-

Note : [1] Returns (CAR) are adjusted to control for the market risk premium.

[2] Returns (CAR & BHAR) are adjusted to control for the benchmark return based on size portfolios.

[3] Returns (CAR & BHAR) are adjusted to control for the return of control firms.

[4] Returns (CAR & BHAR) are adjusted to control for the return of Fama-French portfolios.

[5] Returns are estimated by the Fama-French three factor model. The three factors are zero-investment portfolios representing the excess return of the market; the difference between a portfolio of small stocks and big stocks, SMB; and the difference between a portfolio of high BE/ME stocks and low BE/ME stocks, HML. BE/ME is the ratio of the book value of equity to the market value of equity.

The large initial returns together with the poor long-term performance, as shown in <Table 3>, cast doubt on the explanations based on information asymmetry and price stabilization. Some researchers, thus, turn their attention to behavioral explanations for IPO underpricing. Behavioral theories assume that the favorable market conditions that prevail at the time of an offering generate over-optimism from some investors about the prospects of IPO firms. Such investors bid up the price of IPO shares beyond true value and the aftermarket share price eventually falls below the IPO price in the months following the offering. There are several empirical studies that build on this explanation.

Choi (2000) has examined the effect of optimistic investors' sentiment on the large initial returns and the poor aftermarket performance. He uses the subscription rate at the time of offering as a proxy for investors' demand for IPOs at the time of trading and reports its positive relation with the initial return but negative relation with long-term performance.[23]

Kim and Jung (2010) also examine the relation between investors' sentiment and the underpricing phenomenon. They report that the proxies for the optimistic investors' sentiment, as measured by the volatility of initial returns, have positive effects on initial returns and negative effects on long-term performance. The result of these studies suggests that the observed initial returns of IPOs are more likely to reflect bubbles or fads rather than deliberate underpricing.

Several studies attempt to relate long-term underperformance to poor operating performance occurring since the offering. If managers attempt to window-dress their accounting numbers prior to going public, this will lead to pre-IPO performance being overstated and post-IPO performance being understated. Managers of IPO firms also tend to offer their issues to co-

---

23) Benveniste and Spindt's (1989) model also suggests that underpricing should be concentrated among the IPOs drawing the highest level of pre-market interest.

incide with periods of unusually good performance levels, which cannot be sustained in the future.

Ihm (1997) find that firms going public exhibit a substantial decline in ROA, ROE, and total assets turnover ratio over the 4 years from the offering. Kim and Kim (2000) also confirm Lim's result that post-issue sales growth, account receivables turnover ratio, and ROS decline significantly over the 3 years after the IPO, as compared to those ratios in the IPO year.

Choi and Kim (2008) examine underwriters' opportunistic earnings forecast behavior and its relation with the long-term performance of IPO firms. They find that the earnings forecast errors of IPO firms, which are estimated by using earnings forecasts made at the time of filing the registration statements, are positive and significantly large, suggesting that their future earnings have been too optimistic. They also report that such forecast errors have positive effects on initial returns and negative effects on long-term performance.

Overall, these studies report that the performance of IPO firms declines significantly relative to their pre-IPO levels, based on several performance measures. Further, they present evidence to support the contention that high pre-IPO operating performance levels may lead investors to develop optimistic assessments of earnings growth for the IPO firms.

The natural question that arises is whether the long-run decline in operating performance subsequent to the IPO is anticipated by the market. In the efficient market framework, the market is not fooled by this behavior and correctly anticipates and accounts for it in its valuation of the firm. If the market is able to account for window dressing, the long-term stock price performance of IPOs should be normal. As we have seen in the literature, however, the decline in operating performance is not anticipated and investors are constantly surprised by the poor operating performance of IPO firms, resulting in the long-term underperformance of IPO shares. Therefore, the results in the literature suggest that potential investors initially have high expectations of future earnings growth, which are not subsequently fulfilled, and bid up the aftermarket price of IPO shares beyond true value at the time of initial trading. This is also consistent with behavioral explanations.

VII. Concluding Remarks

This paper reviews the hypotheses and empirical evidence that have been proposed to explain IPO activities and pricing behavior in the Korean market. In particular, the paper reviews empirical evidence and explanations related to the three patterns associated with IPOs: underpricing(positive initial returns), hot issue markets, and long-run underperformance.

A number of hypotheses have been offered to explain large initial returns in the Korean IPO market, focusing on various aspects of the relations between underwriters, issuers, and investors. In general, these hypotheses can be grouped under two broad categories: deliberate underpricing and behavioral approaches. The first category can be further divided into two subcategories: asymmetric information and price stabilization. While the first subcategory attempts to explain underpricing in the framework of the efficient market and consider it as a part of necessary costs associated with initial public offerings, the last subcategory turns to one of services that underwriters provide in connection with IPOs - the price stabilization practice which is intended to reduce price drops in the aftermarket. Behavioral approaches regard initial returns as fads or bubbles caused by irrational investors who bid up the price of IPO shares beyond true value.

Among the hypotheses of IPO underpricing reviewed, the hypotheses based on asymmetric information are well established and supported by the empirical literature. However, the significant variation in the degree of underpricing over time (e.g., hot and cold issue markets) and the poor long-term performance make many researchers doubtful whether information-based theories could be enough to explain large initial returns. For this reason, some researchers turn their attention to behavioral explanations which put more emphasis on the effect of investors' irrational behavior or sentiment on stock prices.

The hot issue market phenomenon and the long-term underperformance of IPOs suggest that if the market conditions prevailing at the time of an offering are favorable, optimistic assessments can be generated from investors about the prospects of the offering, thereby resulting in abnormalities in the aftermarket price. This evidence is not consistent with the efficient market and calls into question the explanatory power of the information-based hypotheses. Abnormalities in the market price can also shed some light on the mixed evidence presented by the empirical studies reviewed in this paper, particularly studies related to the price stabilization and the certification effect. A different approach may be needed to examine the relation between the information-based hypotheses and underpricing. One of potentially promising approaches is to measure underpricing using the premarket information. This will allow us to eliminate a possible introduction of abnormalities, such as fads or bubbles, in measuring underpricing.

Behavioral approaches to IPO underpricing are still in the early stage of development and one of the potentially promising research areas. There have been several studies that examine the effect of investors' irrational behavior or sentiment on the aftermarket price of IPOs but no studies on the effect of the behavioral biases of issuers and underwriters on underpricing.

Evidence documented in the literature suggests that there is no dominant explanation for the large initial returns observed in the Korean IPO market. Thus, the hypotheses reviewed here are not mutually exclusive and a given hypothesis can be more relevant to some IPOs than to others.

References

Beatty, R. P. and J. R. Ritter, "Investment Banking, Reputation, and the Underpricing of Initial Public Offerings", *Journal of Financial Economics*, Vol. 15(1986), pp. 213-232.

Beatty, R. P. and I. Welch, "Issuer Expenses and Legal Liability in Initial Public Offerings", *Journal of Law and Economics*, Vol. 39(1996), pp. 545-602.

Benveniste, L. M., W. Y. Busaba, and W. J. Wilhelm, Jr., "Price Stabilization as a Bonding Mechanism in New Equity Issues", *Journal of Financial Economics*, Vol. 42(1996), pp. 223-255.

Benveniste, L. M., W. Y. Busaba, and W. J. Wilhelm, Jr., "Information Externalities and the Role of Underwriters in Primary Equity Markets", *Journal of Financial Intermediation*, Vol. 11(2002), pp. 61-86.

Benveniste, L. M. and P. A. Spindt, "How Investment Bankers Determine the Offer Price and Allocation of New Issues", *Journal of Financial Economics*, Vol. 24(1989), pp. 343-361.

Benveniste, L. M. and W. J. Wilhelm, Jr., "A Comparative Analysis of IPO Proceeds under Alternative Regulatory Environments", *Journal of Financial Economics*, Vol. 28(1990), pp. 173-207.

Booth, J. R. and L. Chua, "Ownership Dispersion, Costly Information and IPO Underpricing", *Journal of Financial Economics*, Vol. 41(1996), pp. 291-310.

Booth, J. R. and R. Smith, "Capital Raising, Underwriting and the Certification Hypothesis", *Journal of Financial Economics*, Vol. 15(1986), pp. 261-281.

Carter, R. B. and S. Manaster, "Initial Public Offerings and Underwriter Reputation", *Journal of Finance*, Vol. 45(1990), pp. 1045-1067.

Choi, M.-S., "A Study on Initial Returns and Underpricing of IPOs", *The*

Korean Journal of Finance, Vol. 12, No. 1(1999), pp. 197-226(in Korean).

최문수, "신규공모주의 공모가격 할인과 초기성과에 대한 연구", 재무연구, 제12권 제1호(1999) pp. 197-226.

Choi, M.-S., "An Empirical Study on the Initial Performance of Korean IPOs Before and After the Liberalization of Issue Price Setting", *The Korean Journal of Financial Studies*, Vol. 27, No. 1(2000), pp. 139-181(in Korean).

최문수, "발행가격 자율화 이전과 이후의 IPO 초기성과에 대한 연구", 증권학회지, 제27집 제1호(2000), pp. 139-181.

Choi, M.-S., "The Role of Intangible Assets on the Valuation of IPO Shares", *The Korean Journal of Financial Management*, Vol. 20, No. 1(2003), pp. 1-27(in Korean).

최문수, "신규공모주의 가치평가와 무형자산의 역할", 재무관리연구, 제20권 제1호(2003), pp. 1-27.

Choi, M.-S., "Pre-Issue Information Gathering Activities of the Bookbuilding Process and the Partial Adjustment Hypothesis in the Korean IPO Market", *The Korean Journal of Financial Studies*, Vol. 34, No. 3(2005), pp. 1-35(in Korean).

최문수, "수요예측을 통한 신규공모주의 공모가격 결정과 부분조정 가설 (Partial-Adjustment Hypothesis)에 관한 연구," 증권학회지, 제34권 제3호 (2005), pp. 1-35.

Choi, M.-S. and H.-J. Huh, "The Long-Run Performance of IPOs Revisited", *The Korean Journal of Finance*, Vol. 13, No. 1(2000), pp. 99-127(in Korean).

최문수, 허형주, "신규공모주의 장기성과에 대한 재 고찰", 재무연구, 제13권 제1호(2000), pp. 99-127.

Choi, M.-S. and S.-Y. Jun, "An Empirical Study on the Effect of Bundling and Information Spillover from the KOSDAQ Primary and Secondary Markets", *The Korean Journal of Finance*, Vol. 19, No. 2(2006), pp.

1-34(in Korean).

최문수, 전수영, "코스닥 발행주식시장 및 유통시장의 정보전이 효과와 동시상장 효과에 대한 실증 연구", 재무연구, 제19권 제2호(2006), pp. 1-34.

Choi, M.-S. and W.-K. Kim, "A Study on Underwriters' Opportunistic Behavior of Earnings Forecast and Long-Term Performance of IPO firms", *The Korean Journal of Business Administration*, Vol. 21, No. 3(2008), pp. 931-960(in Korean).

최문수, 김웅겸, "코스닥 신규공개기업(IPO)에 대한 주관회사의 미래이익 예측행태와 장기성과에 관한 연구", 대한경영학회지, 제21권 제3호(2008), pp. 931-960.

Fama, E. F., "Efficient Capital Markets: A Review of Theory and Empirical Work", *Journal of Finance*, Vol. 25(1970), pp. 383-417.

Fama, E. F., "Market Efficiency, Long-Term Returns, and Behavioral Finance," *Journal of Financial Economics*, Vol. 49(1998), pp. 283-306.

Habib, M. A. and A. Ljungqvist, "Underpricing and Entrepreneurial Wealth Losses in IPOs: Theory and Evidence", *Review of Financial Studies*, Vol. 14(2001), pp. 433-458.

Huh, N.-S., B.-S. Yoon, and K.-H. Lee, "An Analysis on the IPO of Venture Firms and the Role of Venture Capitalists", *The Korean Journal of Financial Management*, Vol. 19, No. 1(2002), pp. 153-181(in Korean).

허남수, 윤병섭, 이기환, "벤처기업공개와 벤처캐피탈리스트의 역할 분석", 재무관리연구, 제19권 제1호(2002), pp. 153-181.

Ibbotson, R. G. and J. F. Jaffe, "Hot Issue" Markets", *Journal of Finance*, Vol. 30(1975), pp. 1027-1042.

Ihm, B.-K., "The Long- and Short-Term Performance of IPOs and their Operating Performance", *The Korean Journal of Financial Management*, Vol. 14, No. 2(1997), pp. 253-271(in Korean).

임병균, "IPO 주식의 장단기 성과와 영업성과", 재무관리연구, 제14권 제2호(1997), pp. 253-271.

Jang, B.-S. and Y.-H. Woo, "A Simple Test of Underwriter Price Support Hypothesis in Korean Stock Market", *The Korean Journal of Financial Studies*, Vol. 20(1997), pp. 329-367(in Korean).

장범식, 우영호, "간사회사의 시장조성 활동이 신규공모주식의 가격형성에 미치는 영향에 관한 연구", 증권학회지, 제20권(1997), pp. 329-367.

Jang, S.-S. and J. Khil, "A Study on the Role of Certification of Venture Capitalists and Initial Public Offering of KOSDAQ Venture Firms", *The Korean Journal of Financial Management*, Vol. 17, No. 1(2000), pp. 111-136(in Korean).

장상수, 길재욱, 벤처기업의 장외등록과 벤처캐피탈의 보증 역할에 관한 연구", 재무관리연구, 제17권 제1호(2000), pp. 111-136.

Joo, S.-L., "The Study of Factors Which Affect Underpricing in Korean IPO Market-Insider Ownership and Net Asset Value Per Share", *The Korean Journal of Financial Studies*, Vol. 18(1995), pp. 233-255(in Korean).

주상용, "기업공개시 저평가에 영향을 미치는 요인에 관한 연구", 증권학회지, 제18권(1995), pp. 233-255.

Jung, S.-C., "Pricing Behavior of IPO Shares", *The Korean Journal of Finance*, Vol. 5(1992), pp. 181-206(in Korean).

정성창, "기업공개와 주가행태 : 공개 전 유·무상증자의 영향을 중심으로", 재무연구, 제5호(1992), pp. 181-206.

Kang, H. S., "A Study on IPO Pricing", *The Korean Journal of Finance*, Vol. 3(December 1990), pp. 157-176(in Korean).

강효석, "기업공개시 공모주 가격결정에 관한 연구", 재무연구, 제3권(1990), pp. 157-176.

Kang, H. S., "An Empirical Study on the Effect of the Activities of Investment banks on IPO Pricing", *The Korean Journal of Financial Management*, Vol. 8, No. 2(1991), pp. 31-45(in Korean).

강효석, "투자은행이 IPO의 가격형성에 미치는 영향에 관한 실증분석", 재무관리연구, 제8권 제2호(1991), pp. 31-45.

Kang, H. S., "The Effect of R&D Expenditures of Venture Firms on Returns of IPOs: Evidence from KOSDAQ Firms", *The Korean Journal of Finance*, Vol. 14, No. 2(2001), pp. 251-279(in Korean).

강효석, "벤처기업의 R&D 투자비가 IPO수익률에 미치는 영향 : 코스닥등록기업을 중심으로", 재무연구, 제14권 제2호(2001), pp. 251-279.

Kang, H. S. and J. Y. Cho, "The Valuation of IPOs Using Franchise-Factor Model", *The Korean Journal of Financial Studies*, Vol. 26, No. 1(2000), pp. 91-118(in Korean).

강효석, 조장연, "상대가치에 의한 신규공모주의 가치평가 : 성장기회가치모형을 중심으로", 증권학회지, 제26권 제1호(2000), pp. 91-118.

Kim, S. and S. Lee, "Underpricing of IPOs and Underwriters' Market Making Activities", *The Korean Journal of Financial Studies*, Vol. 35, No. 3(2006), pp. 141-173(in Korean).

김성민, 이상혁, "IPO 주식의 시장조성제도 부활 이후 주간사회사의 공모가 산정행태", 증권학회지, 제35권 제3호(2006), pp. 141-173.

Kim, Y.-K. and Y.-H. Kim, "The Long-Term Performance of IPOs and Earnings Management", *The Korean Journal of Financial Management*, Vol. 17, No. 2(2000), pp. 71-98(in Korean).

김영규, 김영혜, "최초공모주의 장기성과와 이익관리", 재무관리연구, 제17권 제2호(2000), pp. 71-98.

Kim, H.-A. and S.-C. Jung, "The Effect of Optimistic Investors' Sentiment on Anomalious Behaviors in the Hot Market IPOs", *The Korean Journal of Financial Management*, Vol. 27, No. 2(2010), pp. 1-33(in Korean).

김현아, 정성창, "낙관적 투자자의 기대가 핫마켓 상황 IPO 시장의 이상현상에 미치는 영향력 검증", 재무관리연구, 제27권 제2호(2010), pp. 1-33.

Lee, J.-R. and S. W. Joh, "Initial Returns of IPO Firms and Options", *Asia-Pacific Journal of Financial Studies*, Vol. 36, No. 4(2007), pp. 657-694(in Korean).

이종룡, 조성욱, "풋백옵션 규제이후 신규공모주의 초기 저평가와 시장조성

가설에 관한 연구", 증권학회지, 제36권 제4호(2007), pp. 657-694.

Lee, J.-R. and J.-W. Kim, "The Effect of Non-Trading Period on IPO Underpricing in Korean Stock Market", *Asian Review of Financial Research*, Vol. 22, No. 3(2009), pp. 1-34(in Korean).
이종룡, 김진욱, "거래지연이 신규공모주 저평가에 미치는 효과", 재무연구, 제22권 제3호(2009), pp. 1-34.

Lee, K.-H., G.-S. Lee, and B.-S. Yoon, "Ownership Disperses When a Venture Firms Its Initial Public Offerings", *The Korean Journal of Financial Management*, Vol. 27, No. 1(2010), pp. 63-87(in Korean).
이기환, 이길수, 윤병섭, "신규공모주의 저가발행과 벤처기업의 소유분산", 재무관리연구, 제27권 제1호(2010), pp. 63-87.

Lee, K.-H., B.-K. Ihm, and Hae-Sul Choi, "The Long- and Short-Term Performance of Venture IPOs and the Role of Venture Capitalists", *The Korean Journal of Finance and Banking*, Vol. 4, No. 1(1998), pp 49-80(in Korean).
이기환, 임병균, 최해술, "벤처기업의 장단기 성과와 벤처캐피탈리스트의 역할", 증권금융연구, 제4권 제1호(1998), pp. 49-80.

Lee, K.-H. and M. C. Yi, "Underpricing of IPOs on KOSDAQ Versus KSE", *The Korean Journal of Financial Management*, Vol. 20, No. 1(2003), pp. 233-260(in Korean).
이기환, 이명철, "코스닥시장과 거래소시장의 최초공모주 저가발행 비교", 재무관리연구, 제20권 제1호(2003), pp. 233-260.

Lee, S.-K., W.-K. Lim, and K. H. Yon, "IPO Underpricing Phenomenon and Pricing Behavior of Underwriters", *The Korean Journal of Finance*, Vol. 9(1995), pp. 119-145(in Korean).
이성규, 임웅기, 연강흠, "주간사회사의 공모가격결정행태와 최초공모주의 저가발행현상", 재무연구, 제9호(1995), pp. 119-145.

Lim, U.-K., "A Study on the Pricing Mechanism of IPOs in the Korean

Market", *The Korean Journal of Financial Studies*, Vol. 13(1991), pp. 103-137(in Korean).

임웅기, "우리나라 최초공모주시장의 가격기능에 관한 연구 : 발행가결정 자율화 조치를 중심으로", 증권학회지, 제13권(1991), pp. 103-137.

Lim, U.-K. and S.-K. Lee, "The Long-Term Performance of IPOs in Korean Market", *The Korean Journal of Financial Studies*, Vol. 18(1995), pp. 333- 369(in Korean).

임웅기, 이성규, "우리나라 최초공모주의 장기성과에 관한 연구", 증권학회 지, 제18권(1995), pp. 333-369.

Ljungqvist, A., "IPO Underpricing", *Handbook of Corporate Finance: Empirical Corporate Finance*, Elsevier/North-Holland, 2006.

Ljungqvist, A. and W. J. Wilhelm, "IPO Pricing in the Dot-Com Bubble", *Journal of Finance*, Vol. 58(2003), pp. 723-752.

Michaely, R. and W. H. Shaw, "The Pricing of Initial Public Offerings: Tests of Adverse-Selection and Signaling Theories", *Review of Financial Studies*, Vol. 7(1994), pp. 279-319.

Mitchell, M. L. and E. Stafford, "Managerial Decisions and Long-Term Stock Price Performance", *Working Paper*, University of Chicago(1998).

Park, K., J.-I. Kim, and S.-Y. Sung, "Trade Credit and IPO Underpricing", *Asia-Pacific Journal of Financial Studies*, Vol. 36, No. 1(2007), pp. 77-109 (in Korean).

박광우, 김종일, 성상용, "기업간 신용거래와 최초공모주의 초기성과", 증권 학회지, 제36권 제1호(2007), pp. 77-109.

Park, K., S. J. Lim, and S.-Y. Sung, "The Effect of Banking Relationships on IPO Underpricing: Evidence from Korea", *The Korean Journal of Financial Management*, Vol. 23, No. 1(2006), pp. 135-163(in Korean).

박광우, 임성준, 성상용, "은행과의 관계가 최초공모주 가격결정에 미치는 영향에 관한 연구", 재무관리연구, 제23권 제1호(2006), pp. 135-163.

Park, R. S. and B. S. Shin, "Conflicts of Interest Among Securities Firms Running Asset Management Businesses", *The Korean Journal of Finance*, Vol. 20, No. 3(2007), pp. 127-153(in Korean).

박래수, 신보성, "증권회사의 자산운용업 겸업에 따른 이해상충에 관한 연구 : IPO 저가 발행을 중심으로", 재무연구, 제20권 제2호(2007), pp. 127-153.

Ritter, J. R., "The Hot Issue Market of 1980", *Journal of Business*, Vol. 57(1984), pp. 215-240.

Ritter, J. R. and I. Welch, "A Review of IPO Activity, Pricing, and Allocations", *Journal of Finance*, Vol. 57(2002), pp. 1795-1828.

Rock, K., "Why New Issues Are Underpriced", *Journal of Financial Economics*, Vol. 15(1986), pp. 187-212.

Ruud, J. S., "Underwriter Price Support and the IPO Underpricing Puzzle", *Journal of Financial Economics*, Vol. 34(1993), pp. 135-151.

Shin, H.-H., J. Chang, and J.-W. Chung, "IPO Underpricing and Market Stabilization", *The Korean Journal of Financial Studies*, Vol. 33, No. 2(2004), pp. 155-190(in Korean).

신현한, 장진호, 정지웅, "신규공모주의 저평가 발행과 시장조성제도", 증권학회지, 제33권 제2호(2004), pp. 155-190.

Yoon, B.-S., "The Certification Role by the Types of Venture Capitalists in KOSDAQ", *The Korean Journal of Financial Management*, Vol. 20, No. 1(2003), pp. 29-60(in Korean).

윤병섭, "벤처캐피탈회사의 유형과 보증역할에 대한 연구", 재무관리연구, 제20권 제1호(2003), pp. 29-60.

<Appendix 1> Regulatory Changes inthe Bookbuilding and Allocation Process of Korean IPOs

Year and Month	Bookbuilding process and allocation of IPO Shares
1997. 8	• Implement the bookbuilding system.
2000. 2	• The standardized bookbuilding process is proposed.
2000. 6	• A band of the desired offer price should be proposed to investors who participate in the bookbuilding.
2000. 12	• Abolish the standardized bookbuilding process. • Underwriting rules are enacted by Korea Financial Investment Association. • Allocate IPO shares propotionately to ESOP (20% for KSE, 0~20% for KOSDAQ), regular investors (20% for KSE, 15~35% for KOSDAQ), institutional investors (15% for KSE, 10% for KOSDAQ), and high-yield funds (45% for KSE, 55% for KOSDAQ). • Allocate IPO shares to institutional investors who submit a bidding pricewithin the range from top 15% to bottom 15% of the bidding prices. • Allocate IPO shares to institutional investors participating in the bookbuilding according to their weight determined by their credit ratings and the proximity of their bidding price to the offer price.
2002. 7 (8)	• The method and process of the bookbuilding are liberalized and autonomously determined by underwriters and issuers. • Implement the over-allotment option or Green Shoe option which allows underwriters to borrow outstanding shares (up to 15% of IPO shares) at the offer price from large shareholders and allocate them to investors on the pro-rata basis.
2003. 9	• The allocation of IPO shares to high-yield funds is gradually reduced by Sept. 2004 from 45% (KSE) and 55% (KOSDAQ) to 30% (KSE and KOSDAQ). Remaining shares are allocated to institutional investors. • Revise the over-allotment option to allow underwriters to borrow shares at the 95% of the offer price from large shareholders.
2005. 4 (7)	• Remove the mandatory 30% allocation to high-yield funds. Allocation to institutional investors becomes 60% of IPO shares. • Revise the over-allotment option to borrow shares at the 90% of the offer price.
2007. 7	• A proposal to advance the underwriting process of IPOs is proposed. • Reduce a period between the bookbuilding and the initial trading from two weeks to one week. • IPOs in the KSE market can be offered with existing shares as well as new issues. For the KOSDAQ IPOs, only new issues are allowed. • Revise the over-allotment option to borrow shares at the 100% of the offer price from large shareholders and allocate them autonomously to investors.

\<Appendix 2\> Regulatory Changes in the Price Support and the Pricing Methods of Korean IPOs

Year and Month	Price support	Pricing methods
1991. 6		• Determine the offer price within the arithmetic mean of the 'intrinsic value' and the 'relative value' of comparable firms. • The opening price of initial trading is the offer price.
1996. 8		• Determine the offer price through an agreement between underwriters and issuing firms based on the intrinsic and relative values, and market situation, etc.
1997. 8	• Abolish the mandatory price support system	
1998. 11	• The mandatory price support is reinstated to protect IPO investors against price falls below 90% of the offer price for one month after the initial trading.	
1999. 5		• Determine the offer price based on the weighted average price established through the bookbuilding process.
2000. 2	• Maintain the aftermarket price above the 80% of the offer price for (at least) 1 month after the initial trading. • At least 50% of IPO shares should be supported.	
2000. 6	• Maintain the aftermarket price above the 80% of the offer price for 2 months after the initial trading. • 100% of IPO shares should be supported.	• Determine the offer price within ±10% of the weighted average price established through the bookbuilding. • The opening price of initial trading is the first asking price.
2000. 12	• The aftermarket price is supported for a period over 1-6 months after the initial trading.	• Determine the offer price within ±30% of the weighted average price established through the bookbuilding.

Year and Month	Price support	Pricing methods
2002. 7 (8)	• Maintain the aftermarket price above the 90% of the offer price for (at least) 1 month after the initial trading. • 100% of IPO shares should be supported.	• The offer price is autonomously determined by underwriters and issuers based on the bookbuilding. • Remove from the underwriting regulation the details of the pricing of IPO shares such as the method of intrinsic and relative valuation. • Determine the offer price within ±10% of the weighted average price established through the bookbuilding process.
2003. 9	• Abolish the mandatory price support system. • Introduce the put-back option system that provides investors with a right to sell IPO shares back to underwriters at more than 90% of the offer price.	
2007. 7	• Abolish the put-back option system.	• The top tier price offered in the bookbuilding process can be considered in determining the final offer price.

Any citation of this article must refer to the following: Kim, Sungmin, "Payout Policy in Korea: A Review of Empirical Evidence", Asian Review of Financial Research, Vol. 24 (2011), No. 2, pp. 665-723.

Chapter 8

Payout Policy in Korea: A Review of Empirical Evidence

Sungmin Kim*   Professor, College of Business and Economics, Hanyang University

Abstract   There have been fundamental changes in corporate dividend policy over the last several decades. Firms decide whether to pay out the corporations' earnings to shareholders as dividends and share repurchases or to keep the profits as retained earnings for future investments. Corporate payout policy is a complicated financial decision-making process that considers future growth opportunities and corporate governance, as well as financing conditions in markets. Determining the payout amount is crucial for corporate finance managers since it is directly related to firm value.

Korean corporations' payout policy has changed dramatically since the Asian financial crisis in 1997.Until the Asian financial crisis, the Korean stock market had not experienced the appropriate conditions to test the various hypotheses based on dividend theory because firms did not have an optimal dividend policy based on their needs and capabilities to maximize firm value. However, after 1997, the paradigm shift in the business environment brought about shareholder-value maximization management, transparency enhancement in corporate governance, and investor-favorable regulation changes, making the Korean stock market more qualified for sophisticated empirical tests of payout policy.

This paper reviews the empirical evidence on dividends and stock repurchases over the last three decades in Korea that consider market imperfections such as tax, information asymmetry, and agency costs. Also this paper covers the major survey results on dividend policy.

Keywords   Dividends, Dividend Policy, Share Repurchases, Payout Policy, Korean Stock Markets

---

* **Address:** Hanyang University, 55 Hanyangdaehak-ro, Sangnok-gu, Ansan-si, Kyeonggi-do 426-791, Korea; **E-mail:** sminkim@hanyang.ac.kr; **Tel:** 82-31-400-5643.

The paper was accomplished as a part of the knowledge database project by the Korean Finance Association and was financially supported by the Korean Finance Association. The author thanks two anonymous referees, and the Editor, Hee-Joon Ahn, for their helpful comments. The author also thanks Yong-Won Jang, Mu-Jeong Park, and Sang-Jeon Han for their excellent contribution in selecting, discussing, and summarizing a huge amount of papers and empirical data at the special seminar course on dividend policy during the fall semester, 2010, Hanyang University.

I. Introduction

There have been fundamental changes in corporate dividend policy over the last several decades (Fama and French, 2001; DeAngelo, DeAngelo, and Skinner, 2000; Brav, Graham, Harvey, and Michaely, 2005 Choi and Kim, 2005). The purpose of this paper is to review the empirical evidence on payout policy in Korea.[1] Firms decide whether to pay out the corporations' earnings to shareholders as dividends or to keep the profits as retained earnings for future investments. Retained earnings are a source of internal financing that is needed for a corporation's further growth, while dividends are a direct compensation to shareholders. Dividend policy is an execution process providing decision making standards for managements to determine dividend amounts. This includes the size, type and payout timing of dividends. Corporate dividend policy is a complicated financial decision-making process that considers future growth opportunities and corporate governance, as well as financing conditions in the markets, for example, whether to issue new shares, corporate bonds, or use loans. Determining the dividend payment amount is crucial for corporate finance managers since it is directly related to maximizing the firm's value.

Lintner (1956), as well as Brav, et al. (2005) asked financial managers why they pay dividends in an attempt to infer why investors want dividends. Lintner (1956) found evidence that firms have long-run target dividend payout ratios that lead to a smoothing of dividend payments over time. Thus, changes in dividends only partially adjust to changes in earnings. Managers are also very reluctant to cut dividends unless adverse circumstances are likely to persist. Nearly 50 years after Lintner (1956), Brav et al. (2005) summarize survey responses from 384 financial executives. Their findings indicated that maintaining the dividend level is on par with investment decisions, while

---

1) Here, payout policy includes both dividend and share repurchase policy.

repurchases are made out of the residual cash flow after investment spending. Perceived stability of future earnings still affects dividend policy, as in Lintner (1956). Brav et al. (2005) found that the link between dividends and earnings had weakened. Many managers now favor share repurchases because they are viewed as being more flexible than dividends and can be used in an attempt to time the equity market or to increase earnings per share.

Understanding payout policy is important because firms pay significant amounts of capital to shareholders in the form of dividends and share repurchases. <Table 1> shows summary statistics on the payout policies of Korean companies via dividend payments and share repurchases for each year from 1981 to 2008. The Asian financial crisis in 1997 was an important turning point for Korean corporations' dividend policies. The 10-year dividend payout ratio from 1987 to 1996, before the Asian financial crisis in 1997, ranged between 25% and 43%, and dividend yield ranged between 1.55% and 2.9%. The low level of dividends during this period was mostly due to the par value dividend policy which had determined dividend amounts based on the face value of a stock, not on its market price, and lack of manager interest in shareholder value maximization.

According to survey evidences from Woo (1988) and Oh and Choi (1992), dividend policy was determined not by a firm's internal factors such as maintaining the optimal capital structure, increasing the firm's value and signaling the future prospect of firms, but rather it was determined by external factors such as the previous dividend level, competitors' dividend amounts, and the regulatory interest rate. Therefore, until the Asian financial crisis in 1997, the optimal dividend policy to maximize firm value was not effectively embedded in Korea.

Comparing the 10 years before and after the Asian financial crisis in 1997, dividend yields increased from an average of 1.78% to 2.86%. There have

⟨Table 1⟩ Corporate Payout Trends over the Three Decades

Year	Number of firms	Number of dividend firms	Net income (billion)	Cash dividend (billion)	Share repurchase (billion)	Payout ratio [%]			Payout yield [%]			Repurchase as % of total payout
						Total	Cash dividend	Share repurchase	Total	Cash dividend	Share repurchase	
1981	134	98	93	75		80.24	80.24		0.83	0.83		
1982	133	109	207	71		34.21	34.21		0.63	0.63		
1983	134	119	357	74		20.82	20.82		0.56	0.56		
1984	139	118	319	133		41.63	41.63		0.52	0.52		
1985	145	128	206	156		75.45	75.45		0.54	0.54		
1986	146	131	361	186		51.65	51.65		0.52	0.52		
1987	166	147	598	255		42.74	42.74		2.19	2.19		
1988	211	194	1,162	436		37.52	37.52		1.98	1.98		
1989	263	237	1,953	635		32.51	32.51		1.72	1.72		
1990	279	257	1,927	701		36.39	36.39		2.30	2.30		
1991	289	262	2,209	639	79	32.52	28.95	3.57	2.76	2.49	0.27	11%
1992	290	247	1,996	668	44	35.68	33.48	2.19	1.73	1.57	0.16	6%
1993	294	242	1,901	708	401	58.31	37.23	21.07	1.84	1.25	0.58	36%
1994	311	270	3,951	828	512	33.92	20.96	12.97	1.55	1.05	0.51	38%
1995	329	275	6,526	1,114	529	25.17	17.07	8.10	2.22	1.51	0.71	32%
1996	357	291	2,494	1,071	575	66.01	42.96	23.05	2.90	1.77	1.13	35%
From 1987 to 1996	279	242	2,472	706	356	40.08	32.98	11.83	2.12	1.78	0.56	26%

〈Table 1〉 Continued

Year	Number of firms	Number of dividend firms	Net income (billion)	Cash dividend (billion)	Share repurchase (billion)	Payout ratio [%]			Payout yield [%]			Repurchase as % of total payout
						Total	Cash dividend	Share repurchase	Total	Cash dividend	Share repurchase	
1997	363	243	1,080	800	225	94.84	74.00	20.84	3.49	2.56	0.93	22%
1998	366	242	-2,443	1,278	1,873	-	-	-	3.68	1.72	1.97	59%
1999	388	278	12,889	2,595	2,650	40.69	20.13	20.56	4.40	2.95	1.44	51%
2000	395	264	9,294	2,807	2,854	60.91	30.21	30.71	4.68	3.46	1.22	50%
2001	404	258	5,414	2,706	2,301	92.49	49.98	42.51	3.64	2.53	1.11	46%
2002	423	298	24,105	4,454	3,943	34.84	18.48	16.36	4.53	3.21	1.32	47%
2003	437	314	26,165	5,915	5,219	42.55	22.61	19.95	4.29	3.81	0.84	47%
2004	451	342	45,921	7,220	4,789	26.15	15.72	10.43	4.67	3.73	1.54	40%
2005	464	354	41,160	7,197	5,770	31.50	17.49	14.02	2.8	2.17	1.08	44%
2006	482	370	37,725	7,033	5,493	33.20	18.64	14.56	2.55	2.22	0.55	44%
2007	497	380	43,610	9,048	2,795	27.16	20.75	6.41	2.14	1.82	0.62	24%
2008	517	358	26,068	6,804	722	28.87	26.10	2.77	2.70	2.65	0.54	10%
From 1999 to 2008	446	321	27,235	5,578	3,654	41.84	24.01	17.83	3.64	2.86	1.03	40%
Total Mean	315	244	10,616	2,343	2,265	38.89	31.99	10.75	2.44	1.94	0.92	36%
Median	320	258	2,103	814	2,087	36.03	31.36	14.29	2.26	1.90	0.89	39%
Maximum	517	380	45,921	9,048	5,770	94.84	80.24	42.51	4.68	3.81	1.97	59%
Minimum	133	98	-2,443	71	44	20.82	15.72	2.19	0.52	0.52	0.16	6%

Note: The table results from analyzing the manufacturing companies with December fiscal year using Database of Korea Listed Company Association, excluding delisted company, administered company and fiscal year changing company.
Payout ratio = (Dividend + Stock repurchase) ÷ Net income, Dividend ratio = Dividend ÷ Net income, Share repurchase ratio = Share repurchase ÷ Net income, Payout yield = (Dividend + Share repurchase) ÷ Market value of equity, Dividend yield = Dividend ÷ Market value of equity, Share repurchase yield = Share repurchase ÷ Market value of equity.

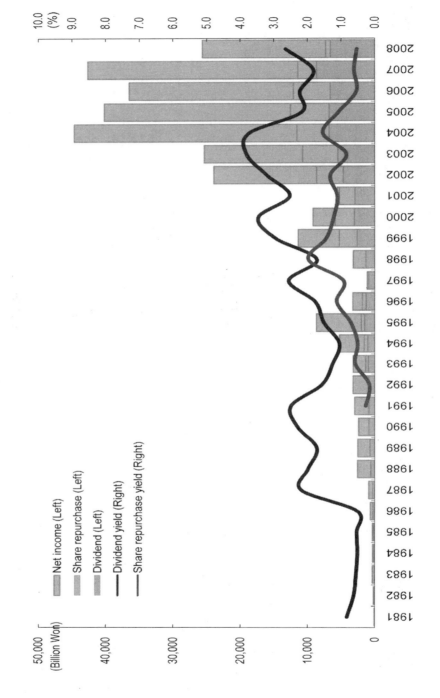

〈Figure 1〉 Corporate Payout Trends over the Three Decades

Net income (Left)
Share repurchase (Left)
Dividend (Left)
Dividend yield (Right)
Share repurchase yield (Right)

Note: In 1998, it could not be indicated on graph due to net loss.

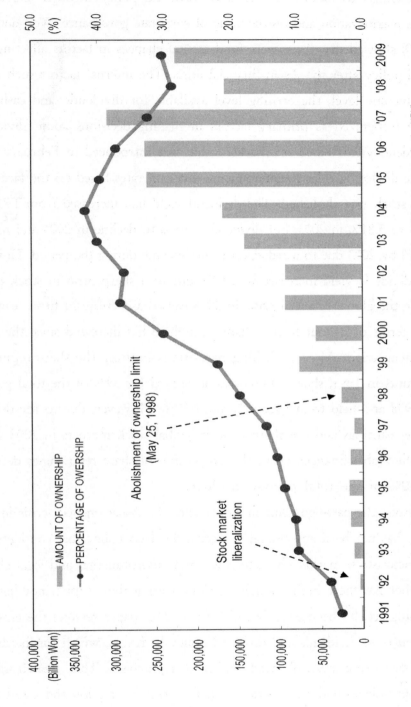

〈Figure 2〉 Foreign Investors Ownership Trend for the Korean Exchange Market

Note: Jan. 3, 1992 : Stock market liberalization (Ownership limit of 10% for foreign investors as a whole, and 3% for individual investors for the KRX)
May 25, 1998 : Abolishment of ownership limit for foreign investors and individual investors for the KRX listed firms.

been efforts to modify the domestic dividend policy through shareholder value maximization and restructuring of corporate governance. Won and Kim (1999) showed that there were fundamental changes in factors affecting dividend policy after the Asian financial crisis. The internal factors such as the net income level, the earning level available for dividends, and cash flow were recognized as primary factors in making decisions about dividends. Dividend yields based on market value was introduced in February 2003, while disclosing rules for announcing dividend rates based on the face value of a stock was abolished. The dividend yield had increased from 1.72% in 1998 to 3.81% in 2003, but dividends started to decline in 2004 and reached 1.82% by 2007 due to a reduction in net income during the period. However, the dividend yield increased to 2.65% due to a sharp drop in stock prices, while the global financial crisis in 2008 caused a decrease in firms' earnings.

In terms of payout forms, share repurchase has increased since the Asian financial crisis. After abolishing regulations limiting the share repurchase amounts in 1998, share repurchases accounted for 59% of the total payouts in 1998 and held to at least 40% until 2006. However, due to the decrease in net earnings and the sharp drop in global stock markets in 2008 caused by the global financial crisis, the proportion of share repurchases decreased to 10% of the total payouts in 2008.

Despite the paradigm shift in Korea since the Asian financial crisis in 1997, there has not been an optimal corporate dividend policy that considers firm characteristics, market characteristics, and environmental and legal change. Neither has there been enough articles covering these topics, nor have the existing articles been entirely satisfactory. This paper reviews the empirical evidence on dividends and dividend policy in Korea, which can be divided into two major areas, dividends and stock repurchases. This research includes payout policies under the perfect capital market assumption and a real world

⟨Table 2⟩ Number of Research Papers on Dividends and Share Repurchases in Korea, published in Major Journals*

Year	Dividends					Share repurchases	Total
	Empirical analysis		Theoretical analysis	Survey	Sub-total		
	Using domestic sample	Using overseas sample					
1987	1				1		1
1988		2	1	1	4		4
1989	3		2		5		5
1990	1	2			3		3
1991	1				1		1
1992			1	1	2		2
1993	2	1	1		4		4
1994	1	1			2		2
1995		1			1		1
1996	3				3	1	4
1997	3		1		4	2	6
1998	1				1	1	2
1999				1	1		1
2000	2			1	3	1	4
2001							0
2002						2	2
2003	1				1	2	3
2004	5				5	5	10
2005	2	1			3	3	6
2006	2				2	1	3
2007	5	1			6	2	8
2008	1				1	6	7
2009	6				6	1	7
Sum	40	9	6	4	59	27	86

Note: *Korean Journal of Financial Studies, Asia Pacific Journal of Financial Studies, Korean Journal of Financial Studies, Korean Journal of Financial Managements and Asian Review of Financial Research.

⟨Table 3⟩ Number of Research Papers on Dividends and Share Repurchases in Korea, classified by Main Subjects

Year	Dividend						Share repurchase			
	Ex-dividend	Agency	Signaling	Others*	Survey	Total	Agency	Signaling	Others**	Total
1987			1			1				
1988					1	1				
1989		1	2			3				
1990				1		1				
1991			1			1				
1992					1	1				
1993	1	1				2				
1994		1				1				
1995										
1996		1	2			3		1		1
1997	1			2		3		2		2
1998	1					1		1		1
1999					1	1				
2000			1	1	1	3		1		1
2001										
2002								2		2
2003	1					1		2		2
2004	1	1	2	1		5	1	3	1	5
2005		1		1		2	2	1		3
2006		2				2		1		1
2007	1	2	1	1		5	1	1		2
2008		1				1	1	4	2	7
2009	1	3	1	1		6				
Sum	7	14	11	8	4	44	5	19	3	27

Note: * Unequal Dividend (3) Dividend initiation (1), Capital structure (4).
    ** Substitute hypothesis(2), Takeover deterrence hypothesis (1)

imperfect capital market that considers tax, information asymmetry, and agency costs. Also this paper covers major survey results on dividend policy. <Table 2> and <Table 3> describe the distributions of those papers categorized by major subjects.[2]

Empirical evidence from domestic studies on dividend policy will be reviewed in Section 2, and Section 3 covers the information on stock repurchase. A summary and concluding remarks will follow in Section 4.

II. Dividends: Empirical Evidences

1. Dividend IrrelevanceTheory

The Nobel Prize winners, Miller and Modigliani (1961), hereafter called M&M, first posed this dividend puzzle in their classic paper. They provide a compelling and widely accepted argument for dividend irrelevance in the context of a perfect capital market with rational investors. Their premise is that valuation depends only upon the productivity of the firm's assets, not on the form of payout. The irrelevance argument implies that no matter how much care managers take in choosing a dividend policy for their firm, the chosen policy has no beneficial impact on shareholder wealth. Thus, all dividend policies are equivalent.

On the other hand, most arguments against dividend irrelevance focus on market imperfections as M&M (1961) assumed a perfect capital market. Some authors, such as Lease, John, Kalay, Loewenstein, and Sarig (2000) and Baker, Powell, and Veit (2002) sort market imperfections into two groups: the major topics and the minor topics. The former are taxes, information asymmetry,

---

2) This research is based on the existing empirical papers using domestic data and mostly published by the majoracademic journals of corporate finance.

and agency costs, whereas the latter are transaction costs, flotation expenses, and behavioral considerations. We categorize the empirical papers on dividends and dividend policy in Korea based on the above major topics.

2. The Impact of Market Imperfections on Dividend

2.1 Tax and Ex-dividend

One of the earliest explanations for paying dividends is based on a tax-preference argument where investors who receive favorable tax treatment on capital gains (lower capital gains tax rate and deferral of capital gains tax) may prefer stocks with low dividend payouts. Thus, different dividend policies may result from tax-induced clientele effects. Brennan (1970) developed a version of the capital asset pricing model with an additional premium based on dividend yield. The empirical results of Brennan's model, however, are mixed. Black and Scholes (1974) and Kalay and Michaely (2000) found no evidence of such a tax effect. On the other hand, Litzenberger and Ramaswamy (1979) found evidence that pretax returns are related to dividend yield.

Another way to test the tax-preference hypothesis is to examine the stock price drop on the ex-dividend day. The theoretical analysis of stock price behavior around the ex-dividend day compares the expected stock price drop to the dividend amount per share. In a perfect capital market, assuming complete certainty, the stock price drop should be equal to the dividend amount per share. The existing empirical evidence documents a stock price drop that is significantly smaller than the dividend per share (Campbell and Beranek, 1955; Elton and Gruber, 1970; Kalay, 1982; Lakonishock and Vermaelen, 1983; Eades, Hess, and Kim, 1984). Although theory does not predict a specific relationship between the relative ex-dividend day stock price drop and the preferential long-term capital gains tax rate, the empirical evidence is consistent with the hypothesis that a dollar of capital gains is worth more than a dollar of dividends. However, further investigations of the stock price behavior on the ex-dividend day cast serious doubt on this explanation. Eades et al. (1984) find positive excess returns both before and on the ex-dividend day and abnormally negative returns following it.

Previous literature in Korea empirically tested whether the stock price drop on the ex-dividend day was adjusted efficiently because there was a unique situation in the Korea Exchange market (hereafter, KRX). Before 1998 the KRX authorities artificially took the ex-dividend procedure in which the ex-dividend price was calculated from subtracting the cum-dividend price by the former period dividend amount. In this case, however, if the upcoming current-period dividend amount is not the same as the former period dividend amount, there would be a mispricing of the ex-dividend. With this idea, Kim (1997) investigated the efficiency of the Korean stock market by analyzing the stock price behavior of December-fiscal-year firms around the ex-dividend day. He conjectured that investors with perfect foresight for the future expected the current-period dividend amount would eliminate this mispricing on the ex-dividend day by exploiting possible arbitrage profits. He empirically tested the relationship between the amount of mispricing and the stock return around the ex-dividend day. The empirical results showed that stock price was not fully adjusted to the sign and the magnitude of the mispricing, implying that the Korean stock market was inefficient and/or that the assumption of investor's perfect foresight might be impractical.

On the other hand, a majority of the listed firms in Korea are December-fiscal-year firms whose ex-dividend day falls on the first trading day of January in the next year.[3] In this case, a January effect can be doubted

---

3) In 2001, the ex-dividend day of a December-fiscal-year firm was moved to the second last trading day in December from the first trading day in January next year, implying a decrease in the possibility of contamination from the January effect after 2001.

as a cause of inefficient stock price adjustment around the ex-dividend day. Yoon, Kim and Chung (1998) investigated the ex-dividend day stock return of both December-fiscal-year firms and non-December-fiscal-year firms and found a positive abnormal return only for December-fiscal-year firms, implying the likelihood of the January effect on the ex-dividend stock price behavior of December-fiscal-year firms. Also their findings showed the average price- drop-to-dividend ratio (PDR) on the ex-dividend day calculated by using the actual dividend amount was 1.342, which was far greater than the theoretical ratio of 0.785 derived from Elton and Gruber's (1970) tax model. They argued that investors cannot predict exactly the upcoming current-period dividend amount resulting in inefficient stock price adjustment.

Kim and Kim (2004) re-examined the dividend announcement effect by using the sample of voluntary preannouncement events. With this sample, they can observe the information content of the dividend more clearly than previous studies since the preannounced date for the upcoming dividend payment was employed for the first time as the event date. Empirical results showed that the announcement effects of a cash or stock dividend was significantly positive around the announcement date.

Park and Park (2009) examined the abnormal stock returns around the ex-dividend day by using the non-December-fiscal-year firms in order to remove any January effect. They found that there was no tax clientele effect in Korea, and the opening stock prices fell by the amount of the current cash dividend per share before 2002, but it does not fall as much as the current dividend per share after 2001. They did not, however, investigate the causes as to why the structural break began around the year 2001.

2.2 Information Asymmetry and Signaling Theory

Miller and Modigliani's (1961) work sustains that, in a perfect capital market, a firm's value is independent of dividend policy. However, some years later, Bhattacharya (1979), John and Williams (1985) and Miller and Rock (1985) develop signaling theory, showing that, in a world of asymmetric information, better informed insiders use dividend policy as a costly signal to convey their firm's future prospect to less informed outsiders. So, the dividend increase signals an improvement on firm's performance, while a decrease suggests a worsening of its future profitability.

Consequently, the signaling explanation should consider the following two issues. First, a dividend increase (decrease) should be followed by an improvement (reduction) in a firm's profitability and earnings. Second, there should be a positive relationship between a dividend change and subsequent share price reaction.

2.2.1 Dividends Signaling Future Earnings

This issue is well summarized as follows: dividend change announcements are positively associated with future earnings. So many researchers have tested the relationship between dividends and earnings explicitly through the perspective of signaling theory. Oferand Siegel (1987) found that analysts revised their earnings projections on the basis of unexpected changes in dividend policy. Nissim and Ziv (2001) analyzed the case of dividend changes, concluding that there was a strong association between dividend changes and subsequent earnings.

On the other hand, Watts (1973) found no evidence supporting the relationship between the current unexpected dividend changes and future earning changes. Penman (1983) found a trivial relationship between the dividend and subsequent earnings after controlling for the earnings announcement effect. Benartzi, Michaely, and Thaler (1997) has also argued that there was a lagging correlation between dividends and earnings. Grullon, Michaely, and Swaminathan (2002) found a relationship between dividend changes and shifts in systematic risk, concluding that dividend changes are not useful in signaling future earnings (Grullon, Gustavo, Michaely, Bernartzi, and Thaler, 2005; Brav et al., 2005).

Nam (1991) examined the validity of signaling hypothesis in Korea. Using data from 1987 to 1988, he runs a regression of the change in EPS on the dividend, insider ownership and their interaction. He did not clarify the purpose of dividend signaling - whether the dividend increase signals an increase in future cash flow or a decrease in investment opportunity. He found that the changes in EPS were insignificantly associated with dividend changes, thus pointing out that dividend policy did not play a signaling role in Korea because the unclear ownership structure of Korean firms made the information unreliable. On the other hand, Park (2004) explicitly tested the hypothesis on the information content of the dividend that managers used dividend as a signal to the future earnings of firms in Korea. He used the change in ROA as the dependent variable and used the change in dividend payment as the independent variable in the empirical model with data from 1991 to 2002. The test results showed that the change in ROA had a positive relation with the change in dividend payment during the short-term period (one year). These findings support the idea that dividend has information content regarding the future profitability of firms.

2.2.2 Dividend Announcements and Stock Price Reactions

There have been a significant number of empirical tests showing that dividend change announcements are positively associated with stock returns in the days surrounding the dividend change announcement. Pettit (1972) found strong evidence that dividend change announcements conveyed information to the market. Similar results were obtained by several papers, such as by Aharony and Swary (1980), and Benesh, Keown and Pinkerton (1984) for dividend change announcements, by Asquith and Mullins (1983), and Michaely, Thaler, and Womack (1995) for dividend initiations.

Although there were empirical studies supporting the signaling model based on the positive relationship between dividend change announcements and the subsequent share price reactions, some studies did not support this view. Alternatively, the positive effect of a dividend announcement could be explained by the over investment opportunity decrease (Lang and Litzenberger, 1989), the risk reduction (Grullon et al., 2002 and 2005) and by the wealth transfer effect out of the bondholder (Dhillon and Johnson, 1994), rather than by the signaling effect of the firm's subsequent earning increase. Especially, Dhillon and Johnson (1994) investigated the information effect of dividend changes from the standpoint of bondholders. They did not support a signaling theory on the basis of negative bondholder returns associated with dividend increases. Because of this wealth expropriation from bondholder to shareholder, they concluded that signaling theory might play a less important role in discerning information content than it had previously.

Recently, Amihud and Li (2006) suggested that greater institutional holdings were related to lower informational content of dividends since the stock price of firms with high institutional ownership had already incorporated part of the information that the dividend announcement supposedly conveys. As a result, the larger the firm's institutional holdings are, the smaller the role of dividends is as a means of conveying information.

In Korea, Nam and Woo (1987) supported the information content hypothesis of dividends by finding a positive announcement abnormal return around the dividend announcement day.[4] However, Kim (1989) did not find the presence of an abnormal stock return using a different event day-the day of

---

4) It is the first day of public announcement on dividend information to the market.

the shareholders' annual meeting. Also Park, Lee and Lee (2003) analyzed the reaction of investors to the dividend announcement by controlling for other determinants of dividend policy in Korean firms. The empirical results showed that investors reacted differently to the announcements of dividends depending on firm characteristics such as the amount of free cash flows. Firms with a larger amount of free cash flows experienced significantly more positive investor reactions to the announcement of a dividend increase than firms with a smaller amount of free cash flows did. They interpreted this result to be consistent with the agency hypothesis of dividends in which dividends play an important role in reducing agency problems related to free cash flow.

2.3 Agency Costs and Free Cash Flow Hypothesis

According to Rozeff (1982), dividends are one way of mitigating the principal-agent problem. He argues that there is a dividend-payout ratio that maximizes the firm's value. A firm achieves the optimal dividend-payout ratio at the point where it minimizes the sum of the agency costs and transaction costs of financing. Agency costs decrease with dividends whereas transaction costs increase with dividends. The minimization of the sum of these costs then produces a unique optimal dividend payout ratio for the firm.

Agency relationships between various claim holders of the firm may offer another explanation for why firms pay dividends. Easter brook (1984) argues that a firm's dividend payments help reduce the agency costs between shareholders and managers because dividends are made by firms that rely more on the external financing market, resulting in exposure to outside monitoring. Jensen (1986) makes a similar argument based on the shareholder-manager agency relationship where managers pay dividends to reduce the firm's discretionary free cash flow that managers could use to fund suboptimal investments that benefit themselves but diminish shareholder wealth. Lang and Litzenberger

(1989) examine the stock market's reaction to corporate dividend changes for a sample of firms with Tobin's Q ratios greater than and less than 1.0 respectively. They interpret that the market particularly welcomes cash payouts by firms having Tobin's Q ratios less than 1.0 since it appears these firm shave no attractive investment opportunities. Allen, Bernardo, and Welch (2000) offer another agency argument for dividend payments. When institutional investors are relatively less taxed than individuals, dividends result in "ownership clientele" effects and high-dividend payers attract relatively more institutions which play an important role in monitoring.

LaPorta, Lopez-de-Silanes, Shleifer, and Vishny (2000) offer two competing hypotheses - outcome hypothesis and substitute hypothesis - as views in predicting the relationship between a firm's dividend policy and the strength of legal protection and shareholder rights. They support the outcome hypothesis that the firm will pay more dividends to minority shareholders in countries with stronger legal protection since firms use dividends as substitutes for legal protection. Jiraporn and Ning (2006) reported a positive relationship between the firms' G-Index used as corporate governance proxy and their dividend payout ratio, supporting the substitute hypothesis that firms extending lesser protection to minority shareholders pay higher dividends. Chae, Kim and Lee (2009) analyzed the effect of corporate governance on the payout policy when a firm has both agency problems and external financing constraints. They empirically tested whether strong corporate governance would lead to higher payout to minimize agency problems (outcome hypothesis), or to lower payout to avoid costly external financing (substitute hypothesis). They found that firms with higher (lower) external financing constraints tended to decrease (increase) the payout ratio with an improvement in their corporate governance. The results were consistent with their hypothesis that the relation between payout and corporate governance is reversed depending on the relative sizes of agency and external financing costs. Pinkowitz, Stulz, and Williamson (2006) tested an agency theory prediction that the value of corporate cash holdings is less in countries with poor investor protection because insiders are better able to extract private benefits in these countries. Consistent with agency theory, they found that the relationship between cash holdings and firm value was weaker in countries with poor protection and that the relationship between dividends and firm value was weaker in countries with stronger investor protection. Brockman and Unlu (2009) found that both the probability and amount of dividend payouts were significantly lower in countries with poor creditor rights. They also showed that the agency costs of debt played a more decisive role in determining dividend policies than the previously documented agency costs of equity.

Recently, the empirical studies based on life cycle theory have been vitalized since Grullon et al. (2002) argued that a firm signals its maturity through dividends (DeAngelo, DeAngelo, and Skinner, 2004 and 2006 Denis and Osobov, 2008). DeAngelo et al. (2006) elaborated the life cycle theory by testing the relationship between retained earnings and dividend payments. According to this theory, as firms grow into maturity, they initiate dividends or increase the dividend level because agency costs from free cash flow get higher.[5]

The former literature in Korea studying agency problems mainly focused on the effect of insider ownership on dividend policy before the Asian financial crisis in 1997 (Yook, 1989; Kim, 1996). Since 1997, two major issues have been discussed. One is the effect of foreign investors on dividend policy. The investment ceiling of foreign investors was completely abolished in May 1998. As a result, the ownership ratio of foreign investors in Korea stock market increased from 18.6% at the end of 1998 to 40.1%

---

5) In Korea, Shin and Song (2007) study empirically the dividend initiation decisions of IPO firms listed on Korea Securities Market and KOSDAQ Market. Most of the dividend initiation firms start paying dividends within two years from the IPO.

at the end of 2004, and decreased to 30% at the end of 2009 as shown in <Figure 2>. The other effect is that of corporate governance on dividend policy. Korea implemented various reform programs to overcome its economic crisis during the Asian financial crisis period in accordance with the suggestions of the World Bank and IMF. Programs were introduced to enhance transparency in corporate governance, to allow hostile takeovers, and to reform the board of enlisted Korean firms.

2.3.1 Corporate Governance

The term "Corporate Governance" has been used in Korea since the financial crisis in 1997 and the improvement of the corporate governance system of listed companies in Korea has emerged as an important issue. To enhance corporate governance, the business law and securities exchange act were revised, the "Committee for Corporate Governance Improvement" was established and the "Corporate Governance Best Practice" was enacted around the 1999. In 2002, The "Korea Corporate Governance Service (KCGS)" was established and has annually evaluated corporate governance. Also since 2002, the KCGS has released the "Corporate Governance Index (CGI)" each year and most empirical papers in Korea have examined the effect of corporate governance on dividend policy by using this index.

Using the CGI, Park, Park and Hwang (2005) found that firms with good governance practices were associated with both high firm value and high dividend payments. They support the outcome hypothesis that the insiders of firms with poor protection of minority shareholder rights are less likely to distribute corporate earnings to shareholders. However, Kim and Lee (2008) pointed out that the previous literature mostly focused on the direct relationship between agency costs and dividend payments without explicitly considering external financing constraints. Dividend payouts result in two counteracting effects: reducing agency problems by decreasing managers' expropriation while increasing expected external financing costs. Therefore, the company should consider these two aspects when deciding its optimal payout policy. For example, a company facing higher external financing costs may not want to pay high dividends even in the absence of agency problems. Thus, by conditioning on external financing constraints, Kim and Lee (2008) overcome the limitation and ambiguity in existing empirical papers that have focused on the simple relationship between corporate governance and dividend payments. They empirically tested whether an improvement in corporate governance would lead to higher dividend payments to minimize agency problems (outcome hypothesis), or alter natively whether it would lead to lower dividend payments to avoid costly external financing (substitute hypothesis).

They found that firms with higher external financing constraints tended to decrease dividends as their corporate governance improves, while the opposite is true for firms with lower external financing constraints. Their results were consistent with the substitute hypothesis that external financing costs affect corporate dividend decisions and that firms minimize financing costs by reducing dividend payouts when corporate governance improves. The empirical results showed that Korean firms seemed to be properly taking into consideration agency problems, external financing constraints, and growth opportunities when making their dividend policies.

2.3.2 Monitoring Role of Foreign Investors

After the Asian financial crisis in Korea, one major change has been the rise of the holdings of foreign investors, who collectively hold a dominant position among investors. Thus, previous papers in Korea tried to identify the causal relationship between foreign investors and dividend policy (Sul and Kim, 2006; Joo and Kang, 2007; Kim, Jung, and Chun, 2009; Ko and Joh, 2009). Sul and Kim (2006) made an empirical analysis on the impact of foreign

shareholders' ownership on a firm's dividend policy by using 110 listed firms over the sample periods of 2001 to 2003 in Korea. They found the amount of foreign investor-owned shares alone had little impact on raising dividends. However, foreign investors with more than 5% of a company's shares could make a significant impact on its dividend increase. In addition, those companies whose majority shareholders are foreign investors tend to pay higher dividends than others whose majority shareholders are domestic investors. On the other hand, Kim, Jung and Chun (2009) who employed various panel regression methodologies over a sample period of 1992 to 2005 found no evidence that the foreign investor's holdings induced an excessive dividend level in Korea firms. Joo and Kang (2007) also identified the interaction effect between the ownership ratio of foreign investors and the dividend yield to total asset ratio by analyzing the mutual relationship between them. They argue that the increase in foreign ownership is likely to induce firms to pay more dividends. Meanwhile, Ko and Joh (2009) divided investors with more than 5% ownership into two groups - the foreign investors and the domestic institutional investors- and compared the behavior of the two groups. The empirical results showed that there was a negative relationship between the ownership of the latter group and dividend yield, and a positive relationship with the ownership of the first group and dividend yield. Therefore, they argued that foreign investors played a monitoring role while domestic institutional investors were short-term traders.

The above studies in Korea have some limitations because they implicitly assume that foreign investors have more capability to monitor firms than domestic investors without explicitly investigating the monitoring role of the foreign investors as a way of reducing the agency problem. The importance of the monitoring role by foreign investors depended on various factors such as market situations and firm characteristics. For example, dividend reduction could be more desirable in a firm with more investment opportunities and high external financing costs (See Kim and Lee, 2008).

3. Dividend Types

3.1 Unequal Dividend

Dividends are distributed in proportion to the number of shares owned by shareholders, but there is an exception to this rule, which are unequal dividend payments in Korea. Korean companies have a unique unequal dividend policy unlike foreign countries, and it is to put discrimination on dividend payments between the major shareholders and minority shareholders. In other words, the major shareholders receive less dividend payment than minority shareholders do.

However, assuming that the major shareholders have a capacity to veto the unequal dividend policy, why do they allow such a policy to reduce their wealth? Kim and Jeong (1997) are the first to suggest two possible motivations for unequal dividend payments. The first came from the domestic tax regime, which put greater tax burden on the major shareholders, driving them to pay fewer dividends to themselves (marginal tax rate hypothesis). The second is the lack of earnings available for dividend payments, which forces firms to distribute dividend payments unequally between shareholders (dividend resources hypothesis). Their findings supported the above two hypotheses the higher the shareholder's marginal income tax rates and the smaller the size of the distributable earnings are, the more the unequal dividend payment is shown. Jung (1997) investigated further the motivation for the unequal dividend through the prerogative consumption hypothesis which expects that the higher the major shareholders have prerogative consumption, the more the companies tend to distribute unequal dividends. Kim (2000) investigated the motives of the unequal dividend payment by surveying the CEOs of the enlisted companies. He found that the most important motivation for the unequal dividend was the compensation for minority shareholders.

3.2 Stock Dividend

A stock dividend is a dividend payment made in the form of additional shares, rather than a cash payout. A common explanation for issuing stock dividends is that stock dividends are a temporary replacement for cash dividends although Lakonishok and Lev (1987) indicate that the rationale for regarding a stock dividend as a substitute is unclear.

Researchers offer many hypotheses to explain the positive reaction to stock dividends. These explanations include the retained-earnings hypothesis, trading-range hypothesis, attention hypothesis, increase-in-cash-dividends hypothesis, and signaling hypothesis. Among them, the retained-earnings hypothesis is proposed by Barker (1959), and Rankine and Stice (1997) suggest that paying a stock dividend requires firms to subtract the value of the newly distributed shares from retained earnings (earned surplus) and to add the amount to the firm's capital account. The attention hypothesis proposed by Grinblatt, Masulis, and Titman (1984) suggests that management of underpriced firms wants to bring attention to the firm in order to trigger reassessment by analysts on the firm's cash flows. Meanwhile Fama, Fisher, Jensen, and Roll (1969) identify a positive announcement effect but do not separately examine stock dividends and stock splits. Foster and Vickrey (1978), and Woolridge (1983) find the positive excess returns on the announcement date after isolating stock dividends.

Empirical findings of Kim and Shin (1993), and Woo and Shin (1996) in Korea showed a positive abnormal return around stock dividend announcement date.[6]

---

6) In Korea, stock dividend regulation, which allows companies to payout dividend in stocks less than 1/2 of aggregate dividend if approved at stockholders meeting, was first introduced in 1984. As the 'Act of Capital Market Development' was enacted in 1987, this regulation restricting the size of a stock dividend was abolished. Stock dividends have gained more attention since then.

⟨Table 4⟩ Summary of Major Findings on Dividends and Dividends Policy

Topics	Researcher	Data periods	Dependent variables	Main results
Tax and ex-dividend	Woo (1993)	1987 ~ 1992	Abnormal Stock Return	• Find the inefficient price adjustment around the ex-dividend day.
	Kim (1997)	1992 ~ 1994	Abnormal Stock Return	• Test the relationship between mispricing and the ex-dividend stock return. • Show that the Korean stock market is inefficient.
	Yoon, Kim and Chung (1998)	1992 ~ 1995	Price-Drop-to-Dividend Ratio	• Investigate the price-drop-to-dividend ratio (PDR) on the ex- dividend day. • Find the greater PDR than that derived from Elton and Gruber's (1970) tax model on the ex-dividend day.
	Kim and Kim (2004)	1998 ~ 2000	Abnormal Stock Return	• Make analysis by using the unique sample firm which preannounce the dividend level voluntarily before the ex-dividend day. • Identify the announcement effects of cash dividend is significant around the event date.
	Park and Park (2009)	1994 ~ 2007	Abnormal Stock Return	• Examine the abnormal stock return around the ex-dividend day. • Find a structural break of the abnormal stock return around the year 2001.
Dividend signaling future earnings	Nam (1991)	1974 ~ 1988	%Change in EPS	• Examine the signaling hypothesis in Korea. • Do not find signaling role of dividend because of the unclear ownership structure of Korean firms.
	Park (2004)	1991 ~ 2002	%Change in Ordinary Income and ROA	• Test explicitly that the dividend signals the future earning. • Find significantly positive relationship between dividend change and future profitability for one year.
Dividend announcement and stock price reaction	Nam and Woo (1987)	1975 ~ 1985	CAR	• Examine the CAR around the public dividend announcement day. • Support the hypothesis on information content of dividend.

〈Table 4〉 Continued

Topics	Researcher	Data periods	Dependent variables	Main results
	Kim (1989)	1982 ~ 1986	CAR	• Examine the CAR around the dividend confirmation day by the shareholders. • Do not support the hypothesis on information content of dividend.
	Park, Lee and Lee (2003)	1993 ~ 1999	CAR	• Analyze the CAR around the dividend announcement day after controlling dividend policy determinants. • Identify that firms with large free cash flow experience more positive market reactions to dividend increase announcement.
Corporate governance	Park, Park and Hwang (2005)	2003	Tobin Q, Dividend yield	• Find that firms with sound governance practices are associated with both high firm value and high dividend payments.
	Kim and Lee (2008)	2002 ~ 2004	Dividend yield, Payout yield	• Test the relationship between the corporate governance and dividend payment after adding the external financing constraints. • Support the substitute hypothesis that improvement in corporate governance lower dividends under higher external financingcost.
Monitoring role of foreign investors	Sul and Kim (2006)	2001 ~ 2003	Dividend ratio, Dividend yield	• Analyze the impact of foreign investors on dividend policy. • Find that foreign investors with more than 5% can exert significant impact on its dividend increase.
	Joo and Kang (2007)	1998 ~ 2003	Dividend ratio, Dividend yield, Dividend / Assets	• Examined the interaction effect between foreign ownership and dividend yield ratio. • Show that the foreign investors prefer high dividend.
	Kim, Jung and Chun (2009)	1998 ~ 2007	Dividend ratio, Dividend yield, Dividend / Assets	• Analyze the relationship between foreign investors and dividend by using the various methodologies. • Do not find that the foreign investor's holdings have induced the excessive dividend level in Korea firms.

Topics	Researcher	Data periods	Dependent variables	Main results
	Ko and Joh (2009)	1997~2006	Dividend ratio, Dividend yield, Dividend / Assets	• Compare the behavior on dividend after dividing the investors into foreign investors and domestic institutional investors. • Argue that foreign investors play a monitoring role and domestic institutional investors are short-term traders.
Unequal dividend	Kim and Jeong (1997)	1985~1994	Probability of unequal dividend	• Support the Dividend Resources hypothesis and the Marginal Tax Rate hypothesis for the reason of unequal dividend.
	Jung (1997)	1987~1996	Probability of unequal dividend	• Support the Investment Resources hypothesis and the Prerogative Consumption hypothesis.
	Kim (2000): Survey Studies	1998	-	• Show that the compensation for minority shareholders is the most important motivation for the unequal dividend.
Stock dividend	Kim and Shin (1993)	1990~1991	CAR	• Identify the CAR around the stock dividend announcement day.
	Woo and Shin (1996)	1990~1994	CAR	• Find the CAR around the stock dividend announcement day. • Support the retained earning hypothesis and the attention hypothesis for the reason of CAR.
Survey evidence on dividends and dividend policy	Woo (1988)	-	-	• Show that the external factors such as the previous dividend pattern, dividend practice of industry, and the government guide line interest rate determine the dividend level of Korean firms.
	Oh and Choi (1992)	-	-	• Find that the internal factors such as the future earnings, adjustment for optimal capital structure and cash flow level is becoming important in determining the dividend level of Korean firms.
	Won and Kim (1999)	-	-	• Identify that the internal factors such as the net income level, the earning level available for dividend and cash flow were recognized primarily in making decision on dividend.

Note: Dividend yield = Dividend ÷ Market value of equity, Dividend ratio = Dividend ÷ Net income. Payout yield = (Dividend + Share repurchase) ÷ Market value of equity.

Woo and Shin (1996) found evidence supporting both the retained-earning hypothesis and the attention hypothesis. <Table 4> summarizes the major findings of empirical evidence on dividends and dividend policy.

4. Survey Evidence on Dividends and Dividend Policy

Lintner (1956) and Brav et al. (2005) asked financial managers why they pay dividends in an attempt to infer why investors want dividends. Lintner (1956) found evidence that firms have long-run target dividend payout ratios that lead to a smoothing of dividend payments over time. Thus, firms tend to increase their dividends gradually toward a target payout ratio to avoid any sudden changes in dividends if the earnings increase should not be permanent. The dividend changes announced by firms follow shifts in long-run sustainable earnings because managers are hesitant to announce dividend increases that may later have to be reversed. Managers are also very reluctant to cut dividends unless adverse circumstances are likely to persist. Nearly 50 years after Lintner (1956), Brav et al. (2005) summarize survey responses from 384 financial executives. Their findings indicate that maintaining the dividend level is on par with investment decisions, while repurchases are made out of residual cash flow after investment spending. Perceived stability of future earnings still affects dividend policy as in Lintner (1956). Brav et al. (2005) found that the link between dividends and earnings had weakened. Many managers now favor repurchases because they are viewed as being more flexible than dividends and can be used in an attempt to time the equity market or to increase earnings per share. Executives believe that institutions are indifferent between dividends and repurchases and that payout policies have little impact on their investor clientele. In general, management views provide little support for agency, signaling, and clientele hypotheses of payout policy but taxes are indicated to be a second-order payout policy concern.

〈Table 5〉 Summary of the Ranks of the Major Factors affecting Dividend Policy in Korea based on the Survey Studies

Rank	Woo (1988)	Oh and Choi (1992)	Won and Kim (1999)
1	Dividend practice in industry	Future profit level	Current earning level
2	Previous dividend pattern	Maintenance of optimal capital structure	Earnings available for dividend
3	Government guided benchmark interest rate level	Dividend practice in industry	Cash requirement level for future usage
4	Change in future economic situation	Maintenance of stock price	Future profit level
5	Maintenance of optimal capital structure	Current cash flow level	Future business cycle
6	Management of stock price	Availability of profitable investment opportunity	Shareholder's preference for dividend
7	Future profit level	Previous dividend pattern	Maintenance of stock price

Woo (1988), Oh and Choi (1992), and Won and Kim (1999) surveyed the dividend policy for Korean firms in the pre-2000 period. During this period, the empirical tests using financial characteristic variables might have some limitations because of the immature capital markets and the regulatory environments in Korea. Instead, the above survey researches could be utilized as a complimentary tool to understand the dividend policy in Korea. According to Woo's (1988) survey, the dividend policy in Korean firms is more affected by external factors such as the dividend practice in industry, previous dividend patterns and the benchmark market interest rate, rather than internal factors such as future investment opportunities, optimal capital structure and future profit levels. Contrary to Woo (1988), Oh and Choi (1992) show that internal factors are becoming more important in dividend policy. Among the factors, future earnings, adjustment for optimal capital structure and cash flow level are highly ranked among others. Won and Kim (1999) show that there are fundamental changes in factors affecting dividend policy. The internal factors such as the current earning level, the earnings available for dividends and the cash requirement level for future usage are primarily recognized in deciding dividend amounts. These factors coincide consistently with the determinants embedded in the dividend policy. However, the external factors continue to be important for Korean firms' dividend policy. <Table 5> summarizes the major factors affecting dividend policy based on these survey results.

Ⅲ. Share Repurchases: Empirical Evidences

Share repurchase is the acquisition of their own stocks by listed companies through the open market with its own capital. Share repurchase had been principally prohibited by Korean Business Law due to reasons that companies may have difficulty in maintaining adequate levels of capital, and could cause inequality among shareholders, unfair control over companies and unfair transactions. However, the indirect share repurchase program or share repurchase fund was introduced on August 24, 1992 to revitalize the depressed stock market. The open market share repurchase was allowed in May 1994 to permit unfriendly mergers and acquisitions by foreign shareholders and to provide tools to defend corporate control and stock price management. For the KOSDAQ market, share repurchase was allowed from May 1999.[7]

The previous literature in Korea on share repurchase in pre-IMF era was initiated to empirically scrutinize the background of adopting indirect share repurchase funds and direct share repurchase programs, which were intended to stimulate the stock market and to stabilize stock volatility (Jung and Lee, 1996; Kim, 1997). After the share repurchase is permitted in 1998, various hypotheses were examined to explain whether the share repurchase increased shareholder wealth. Under the signaling hypothesis, the wealth effects of the repurchase are examined from both shareholders' (Jung and Lee, 1996 and 2003; Kim, 1997; Jung and Kim, 2007) and creditor's perspectives (Jung, 2005 and 2008). In addition, there are various ongoing empirical studies on share repurchases, including tests of free cash flow hypothesis (Shin and Lee, 2007), managerial incentive hypothesis (Jun and Kim, 2005), takeover deterrence hypothesis (Ko and Joh, 2009) and substitution hypothesis (Choi and Kim, 2004).[8]

---

7) In Korea, a firm can purchase its own stocks either directly or indirectly. Direct purchase means that a firm acquiresits treasury stocks at the open market with its own books. Indirect purchase means thatthe firm has a third party acquire the treasury stocks through treasury stock funds.
8) Dittmar (2000) enumerates the major motivations for share repurchases as follows: excess capital, under-valuation, optimal leverage ratio, managerial incentive, and takeover deterrence.

1. Asymmetric Information

1.1 Signaling on Shareholder's View

Signaling is the most widely studied motivation for share repurchases in the academic literature. The basis of signaling theory is that a firm's management is better informed about the company's true value than outside shareholders. Because of this informational asymmetry, prevailing stock prices may not reflect true value. Repurchasing shares of the firm's stock may signal that existing stock prices are below the stock's intrinsic value.

Much empirical evidence shows sizable share price reactions to share repurchase announcements (Masulis, 1980; Dann, 1981; Lakonishok and Vermaelen, 1990; Oded, 2005; Louis and White, 2007). Dann (1981) found significantly positive announcement returns for stockholders, convertible debt holders, and convertible preferred stockholders. Lakonishok and Vermaelen (1990) found excess returns of 8 percent for two years. Louis and White (2007) reported a significant three years of excess returns of 31 percent for fixed-price tender offers and 24.7 percent for Dutch-auction tender offers, respectively.

Jung and Lee (1996, 2003), Kim (1997), Sul and Kim (2005), and Jung and Kim (2007) empirically tested the signaling role of share repurchases. Their findings showed mixed results on the signaling effect of share repurchases.[9] Jung and Lee (1996) and Kim (1997) found that direct share repurchase was more effective to stabilize stock prices than indirect share repurchase. Jung (2005) found that the cumulative abnormal returns (CAR) around the announcement date of direct share repurchase was bigger than that of indirect share repurchase.

Sul and Kim (2005) found that the announcement of share repurchase

---

9) Jung and Lee (1996) expect the pre-announcement period cumulative return to be negative because share repurchase should signal stock undervaluation, but the results showed that only preferred stock shad significant negative return. Kim (1997) found no evidence to support signaling theory in both directs hare repurchase and indirect repurchase.

results in positive abnormal returns only when the motivation of share repurchase is to stabilize stock prices or retire shares,[10] whereas the market reacted negatively if treasury stocks are granted to executives and employees as incentives. Consistently, Jung and Kim (2007) found that abnormal announcement returns are more positive in the case of retirement than those in other cases. Further, the higher announcement returns for retirement-purposed repurchase are found only when the cash flow of the firms increased in the subsequent periods. This implies that the market can discern false signals provided by share repurchases.

On the other hand, the share repurchase might be used to give a 'false signal'. Fried (2005) explains that managers are currently able to use open market repurchases to cheat on other shareholders. Consistently, there is some evidence that Korean firms use share repurchase to boost up the right offering prices (Jung, 2004; Park, 2008).

1.2 Signaling on Bondholder's View

Financial decisions may have at least two distinct effects on the distribution of total firm value among different classes of securities. First, if claim holders are inadequately protected by me-first rules, a financing decision may result in wealth transfers among different classes of securities. Second, if the market processes imperfect information, a financing decision may signal information to the market concerning firm value and thereby influence the values of all security classes (Woolridge, 1983). Handjinicolaou and Kalay (1984) analyzed bond returns around dividend changes, whereas Brennan and Thakor (1990) and Maxwell and Stephens (2003) examined bond returns around the share repurchase announcement. Maxwell and Stephens (2003) found a significantly negative abnormal bond-price reaction to repurchase announce-

---

10) In Korea, firms can retire treasury stock forever or resell it later in the market.

ments. The magnitude was even more negative for larger repurchase programs and for firms with non-investment-grade debt. These findings indicated a wealth transfer from bondholders to stockholders. Interestingly, although the bond value decreases after the repurchase announcement, Maxwell and Stephens (2003) further reported that the positive announcement return for stockholders offset more than the negative wealth change for bondholders, resulting in a positive net change in firm value.

In Korea, Jung (2008) tests the relationship of share repurchases with bondholder's wealth change by adding the stock option holdings variable. The empirical results showed that in the case where managers hold stock options, the stockholders' wealth was increased less than in the case without stock options holdings by managers, and the bondholders' wealth was decreased. The correlation between stock returns and bond returns was found to be positive in the firm whose managers did not hold stockoptions, which supports the signaling hypothesis. On the other hand, the correlation is negative in the case that managers hold stock options, supporting the wealth transfer hypothesis.

2. Agency Costs and Free Cash Flow Hypothesis

As revealed in Brav et al. (2005), managers tend to use share repurchases to reduce excess cash holdings, representing agency cost concerns. In addition, firms are more likely to buy back shares when few good investment opportunities are available. Taken together, the existing evidence provides strong support for the free cash flow hypothesis. Dittmar (2000) investigates how a firm's level of cash flow affects its decision to repurchase stock and finds that, after controlling for investment opportunities, firms repurchase stock to distribute excess capital. Nohel and Tarhan (1998) find that the improvement of post-repurchase performance only occurs in low-growth (low-Tobin's-Q) firms. Consistent with the findings in Nohel and Tarhan (1998), Grullon and Michaely (2004) also show that repurchasing firms experience a decline in profitability and investment opportunity within three years after repurchases. Additionally, the average value of the repurchasing firms' cost of capital also decreases from 16 percent to about 14 percent in the three years following the year of the repurchase announcements.

In Korea, Shin and Lee (2007) tested empirically the free cash flows hypothesis on share repurchases by using the methodology of Jensen (1986), Nohel and Tarhan (1998), Jagannathan, Stephens and Weisbach (2003), and Grullon and Michaely (2004). Conclusively, their empirical results showed that, when firms experienced a decline in profitability, capital expenditures, cash reserves, systematic risk and cost of capital, they decided to repurchase stocks to reduce free cash flows, supporting the free cash flow hypothesis.

3. Managerial Incentive Hypothesis

Managers with insider information can utilize the share repurchase in order to obtain their own benefit at the expense of shareholders when there is asymmetric information between managers and shareholders (Fried, 2001). Executive stock options have the characteristics of call options with the underlying asset of common stock. Thus, managers with executive stock options have the incentive to use financial policy in a way that favorably affects the value of stock options. (Lambert, Lanen, and Larcker, 1989; Fenn and Liang, 2001; Kahle, 2002; Charles, Gerald, and John, 2009; Babenko, 2009). Lambert et al. (1989) found a correlation between the adoption of an executive stock option plan and a substantial reduction in the level of cash dividends. Fennand Liang (2001) show that higher managerial option holdings are associated with lower dividends and higher share repurchases. This finding is consistent with that of Lambert et al. (1989), which suggest that firms increase repurchases at the expense of dividends. Recently Babenko (2009) find that managers are more likely to engage in the opportunistic stock buy backs when employees collectively hold a large stake in the firm.

In Korea, Jun and Kim (2005) examined whether executive stock options affect the choice of a corporate payout policy. They empirically tested this hypothesis using the data of 516 non-financial firms listed on the Korean Stock Exchange over the period of 1998 through 2003. The results showed that firms with more executive stock options outstanding had the higher possibility of choosing share repurchases instead of cash dividends. And by further testing the effect of stock option maturity on the choice of payout policy, they found that options with a shorter maturity or vested stock options had higher prediction power in a firm's choice of payout policy.

4. Takeover Deterrence Hypothesis

Managers can use share repurchases to serve as a takeover repellent to an unwanted bid by signaling firm value or increasing the cost of purchasing the remaining shares outstanding. Harris and Raviv (1988) and Stulz (1988) model how firms issue debt and use the proceeds to repurchase shares to deter takeovers. In Bagnoli, Gordon, and Lipman (1989), share repurchases serve as a defense against takeover by signaling management's private information about firm value. While a large body of empirical evidence supports these theories in the case of tender offers, there is little evidence in relation to open market repurchases (Bagwell, 1991 and 1992; Brown and Ryngaert, 1992). Billett and Xue (2007) find a significantly positive relation between open market share repurchases and takeover probability.

In Korea, Ko and Joh (2009) investigate whether the ownership and the control rights of controlling shareholders are linked to corporate payout decisions. It has been widely recognized that there can be a discrepancy between the ownership rights (also known as cash flow rights) and the control rights of controlling shareholders. They find that firms of which controlling shareholders have greater ownership and control rights are more likely to choose cash dividends. In contrast, firms with lower ownership and control rights are more likely to adopt share repurchase programs. Thus they conclude that a firm's payout policy depends on ownership structure. Moreover, firms with weak ownership structures tend to adopt share repurchase programs to protect controlling shareholders from external threats.

5. Substitute Hypothesis

The survey results of Brav et al. (2005) suggest that share repurchases now play a more important role than cash dividends in a firm's payout policy. The prevalence of share repurchase programs is mainly attributable to their flexibility. Grullon and Michaely (2002) find that there is a substitution effect between dividends and share repurchases, and that large, dividend paying firms are repurchasing stock rather than increasing dividends. The evidence that dividends and repurchases are interchangeable payout methods is consistent with the undervaluation and free cash flow hypotheses. Skinner (2007) extends the findings of Grullon and Michaely (2002) by analyzing the evolution of the relationship among earnings, dividends, and repurchases at both the aggregate level and the firm level. He documents that the link between repurchases and earnings has strengthened over time in a manner suggesting that repurchases are replacing dividends. Jagannathan, Stephens, and Weisbach (2000) find that firms tend to select share repurchases over a dividend increase when 'temporary' non-operating income comprises a greater proportion of total income and when earnings tend to be more volatile. Guay and Harford (2000) also focus on the impact of the permanence of cash flow on the choice between dividends

⟨Table 6⟩ Summary of Major Findings on Share Repurchases

Topics	Researchers	Analysis periods	Dependent variables	Main results
Signaling on shareholder's view	Jung and Lee (1996)	1992 ~ 1994	CAR	• Show positive CAR after share repurchase announcement. • Support the signaling hypothesis.
	Kim (1997)	1994 ~ 1995	CAR	• Find no evidence to support signaling theory in both direct and indirect share repurchase.
	Jung and Lee (2003)	1994 ~ 1998	CAR	• Find positive long-term performance in traditional cumulative abnormal return approach. • Do not find positive CAR in the calendar-time portfolio approach.
	Byun (2004)	1994 ~ 2000	CAR	• Examine the possibility that the open-market repurchases announcement of firms send a false signal to investors. • Identify that the market reaction are less positive in case that firms with a relatively low cash flow because it is unlike to carry out actually repurchase.
	Jung (2004)	1994 ~ 2001	CAR	• Find that the time intervals between the indirect stock stabilization fund and the announcement dates of right offerings are significantly related with the cumulative abnormal rate of returns. • Suggest the possibilities of how indirect share repurchases can be regarded as one of unfair trading practices.
	Sul and Kim (2005)	2001 ~ 2003	CAR	• Find positive market response of share repurchase announcement when its motive is retirement of stock or stock stabilizing, and negative market response of share repurchase announcement when its motive is granting incentives to executives or employees.
	Jung and Kim (2007)	2001 ~ 2004	CAR	• Analyze the financial characteristics and the value of the firms which repurchased their stocks through open market repurchases for retirement purposes. • Show that the market responses to the firms' share repurchases announcement for stock retirement are higher than those of the repurchases for other motivation.
	Park (2008)	1994 ~ 2001	CAR	• Figure out that direct repurchase affect the price of new issues favorably. • Do not show the severer underperformance of both sample firms than equity offerings only firms.

⟨Table 6⟩ Continued

Topics	Researchers	Analysis periods	Dependent variables	Main results
Signaling on bondholder's view.	Jung (2005)	2000 ~ 2003	CAR	• Investigate the wealth effect of open market share repurchase on shareholders and bondholders. • Find that correlation between the shareholder's wealth and the bondholder's wealth is positive only in the firms with speculative grade debt.
	Jung (2008)	2001 ~ 2006	CAR	• Expand the previous research to test the relation of share repurchases with bondholder's wealth change by adding the shock option holdings variable. • Find that in the firm whose managers hold stock options, the stockholders' wealth increases less than firms without stock option holdings, and the bondholders' wealth even decreases.
Agency costs and free cash flow hypothesis	Shin and Lee (2007)	1994 ~ 2005	CAR, Drift	• Test empirically the free cash flows hypothesis on share repurchase. • Show that firms repurchase stocks to reduce free cash flows when experiencing a decline in profitability, capital expenditures and cash reserves, systematic risk and cost of capital. • Support the free cash flow hypothesis.
Managerial incentive hypothesis	Jun and Kim (2005)	1998 ~ 2003	Dividend yield, Share Repo. yield, Payout yield, Share Repo. % ratio as Total payout	• Examine whether executive stock options affect the choice of a corporate payout policy. • Identify that firms with more executive stock options outstanding have the higher possibility of choosing share repurchases instead of cash dividends.
Takeover deterrence hypothesis	Ko and Joh (2009)	1998 ~ 2005	Prob. of Dividend, Prob. of Share Repo.	• Investigate whether the ownership and the controlrights of controlling shareholders are linked to corporate payout decisions. • Find that firms with weak ownership structures tend to adopt share repurchase programs at the cost of other shareholders.
Substitute hypothesis	Choi and Kim (2004)	1990 ~ 2002	Dividend forecasting error	• Examine substitution hypothesis between dividends and share repurchases. • Figure out that share repurchase yield and dividend forecast error have a statistically significant positive correlation. • Do not support the substitute hypothesis.

and repurchases, and report similar conclusions in the United States. On the other hand, Dittmar and Dittmar (2004) examine how macroeconomic variables influence firms' payout policies and find that repurchases are indeed a way of distributing both transitory and permanent earnings, whereas dividends are a way of distributing only permanent earnings. They conclude that dividends and repurchases both substitute and complement each other.

Choi and Kim (2004) examine the substitution hypothesis between dividends and share repurchases in Korea. After estimating dividend forecast error by using Lintner's model, they run the cross-sectional regression analysis based on the Fama and MacBeth's (1973) control variables to investigate the relationship between dividend forecast error and share repurchases yield. If firms utilize share repurchases as a substitute for dividend payments, repurchase yield should have a negative relationship with dividend forecast error. The results show that share repurchase yield has a statistically positive relationship with dividend forecast error, as opposed to the substitution hypothesis between dividends and share repurchases, and finds out that dividends and share repurchases could be used rather as a supplemental method to each other in terms of a payout policy. <Table 6> summarizes the major findings of empirical evidence on share repurchases.

IV. Summary and Concluding Remarks

This paper reviews the empirical evidence on dividends and share repurchases over the last three decades in Korea. Some are creative whereas others have replicated for the Korean financial market former foreign studies. As shown in <Table 2>, it is interesting that dividend studies mostly focused on agency problems from 2004 onwards, while share repurchase studies have covered the signaling issue more than other issues. The empirical research on payout policy in Korea was not as abundant as foreign studies before the Asian financial crisis in 1997 since the payout policy was of little importance to Korean firms when making financial decisions during this period. This is due to the regulatory environment that suppressed dividend amounts, the lack of earnings to distribute to shareholders, and persistent excess demand for capital to invest in future profitable investment opportunities.

Bharath (2009) stated that "the theory finds support when its basic assumptions hold in the data, as should reasonably be expected of any theory." This viewpoint implies that it would be difficult to infer proper implications from the empirical results of studies done before the IMF financial crisis in Korea.

Until the Asian financial crisis in 1997, the Korean market had not experienced the appropriate conditions to test the various hypotheses based on the dividend theory because firms did not have an optimal dividend policy based on theirs needs and capability to maximize the firm's value. Instead, dividends were determined by the external factors such as the industry dividend level and government guidelines, or were completely disregarded by managers and even investors as an important indicator for investments. Thus, even though empirical papers in Korea contained empirical evidence to satisfy some dividend hypotheses, it seems difficult to accept them as true supporting evidence given these circumstances.

However, after 1997, the paradigm shift in the business environment brought about shareholder-value maximization management, transparency enhancement in corporate governance, and investor-favorable regulation changes, making the Korean market more qualified for sophisticated empirical tests.[11] Thus, some empirical evidence presented by recent studies

[11) Interim dividend policy was introduced as the Securities and Trading Act was amended in 1997, just after receiving bail-out funds from the IMF, and applied to companies listed on the stock exchange or registered on association. Also quarterly dividends, paying dividends every three months to shareholders, was allowed in April of 2004.

based on the free cash flow hypothesis to alleviate the agency problem, or the managerial incentive hypothesis of preferring share repurchases to dividend have become worthwhile research topics.

The empirical results in Korea show that companies have been actively considering share repurchases along with dividends as a part of their payout policy. This study suggests a further research area which includes an investigation of the optimal size and the timing of dividend payments and share repurchases, simultaneously to determine the optimal payout policy, considering financial characteristics of firms and external factors such as industry and financial market conditions.

Nevertheless, there are also several limitations to this research. First, only the main findings in each paper are introduced because we must categorize them into dividend theory and hypothesis, despite the fact that they have thoroughly examined various issues. Second, the details of previous studies have not been fully explained, for example, various methodologies and empirical results. Third, this study does not compare domestic and foreign research through one-to-one mapping because conducting this mapping without considering the different market situations in the US and Korea would possibly arouse controversy.

References

Aharony, J. and I. Swary, "Quarterly Dividend and Earnings Announcements and Stockholder's Returns: An Empirical Analysis", *Journal of Finance*, Vol. 35(1980), pp. 1-12.

Allen, F., A. Bernardo, and I. Welch, "A Theory of Dividends based on Tax Clientele", *Journal of Finance*, Vol. 55(2000), pp. 2499-2536.

Amihud, Y. A. and Li, K., "The Declining Information Content of Dividend Announcements and The Effect of Institutional Holdings", *Journal of Financial and Quantitative Analysis*, Vol. 41(2006), pp. 636-660.

Asquith, P. and D. Mullins, "The Impact of Initiating Dividend Payments on Shareholders'Wealth", *Journal of Business*, Vol. 56(1983), pp. 77-96.

Babenko, I., "Share Repurchases and Pay-Performance Sensitivity of Employee Compensation Contracts", *Journal of Finance*, Vol. 64(2009), pp. 117-151.

Bagnoli, M., R. Gordon, and B. Lipman, "Stock Repurchases as a Takeover Defense", *Review of Financial Studies*, Vol. 2(1989), pp. 423-443.

Bagwell, L. S., "Share Repurchase and Takeover Deterrence", *Rand Journal of Economics*, Vol. 22(1991), pp. 72-88.

Bagwell, L. S., "Dutch auction repurchases: An analysis of shareholder heterogeneity", *Journal of Finance*, Vol. 47(1992), pp. 71-106.

Barker, C. A., "Price Changes of Stock-Dividend Shares at Ex-dividend dates", *Journal of Finance*, Vol. 14(1959), pp. 373-378.

Baker, H. K., G. E. Powell, and E. T. Veit, "Revisiting the dividend puzzle: Do all of the pieces now fit?", *Review of Financial Economics*, Vol. 11(2002), pp. 241-261.

Benartzi, S., R. Michaely, and R. Thaler, "Do Changes in Dividends Signal the Future or the Past?", *Journal of Finance*, Vol. 52(1997), pp. 1007-1034.

Benesh, G. A., A. J. Keown, and J. M. Pinkerton, "An Examination of Market Reaction to Substantial Shifts in Dividend Policy", *Journal of Financial Research*, Vol. 7(1984), pp. 131-140.

Bharath, S. T., "Does Asymmetric Information Drive Capital Structure Decisions?", *Review of Financial Studies*, Vol. 22(2009), pp. 3211-3243.

Bhattacharya, S., "Imperfect Information, Dividend Policy, and 'the Bird in the Hand' Fallacy", *Bell Journal of Economics*, Vol. 10, No. 1(1979), pp. 259-270.

Billett, M. T. and H. Xue, "The Takeover Deterrent Effect of Open Market Share Repurchases", *Journal of Finance*, Vol. 62(2007), pp. 1827-1850.

Black, F. and M. Scholes, "The Effect of Dividend Yield and Dividend Policy on Common Stock Returns", *Journal of Financial Economics*, 1974, pp. 1-22.

Brav, A., J. R., Graham, C. R., Harvey, and R. Michaely, "Payout Policy in the 21st Century", *Journal of Financial Economics*, Vol. 77, No. 3 (2005), pp. 483-527.

Brennan, M. J., "Taxes, Market Valuation and Financial Policy", *National Tax Journal*, Vol. 23(1970), pp. 417-429.

Brennan, M. J. and A. V. Thakor, "Shareholder Preferences and Dividend Policy", *Journal of Finance*, Vol. 45(1990), pp. 993-1018.

Brockman, P. and E. Unlu, "Dividend Policy, Creditor Rights, and The Agency Costs of Debt", *Journal of Financial Economics*, Vol. 92(2009), pp. 276-299.

Brown, D. and M. Ryngaert, "The Determinants of Tendering Rates in Interfirm and Selftender Offers", *Journal of Business*, Vol. 65(1992), pp. 529-556.

Byun, J. H., "Signaling Effects and the Long-term Performance of False Signaling Firms: Eividence from the Under-variation Stock Repurchases", *Korean Journal of Financial Studies*, Vol. 33, No. 1(2004), pp. 207-248(in

Korean).

변진호, "저평가 자사주매입공시의 허위 정보 신호효과와 장기성과", 증권학회지, 제33권 제1호(2004), pp. 207-248.

Campbell, J. and A. Beranek, "Stock Price Behavior on Ex-Dividend Dates", *Journal of Finance*, Vol. 10(1955), pp. 425-429.

Charles J. C., S. M. Gerald, and J, P. John, "Stock Options and Total Payout", *Journal of Financial and Quantitative Analysis*, Vol. 44, No. 2(2009), pp. 391-410.

Chae, J., S. M. Kim, and E. J. Lee, "How Corporate Governance Affects Payout Policy under Agency Problems and External Financing Constraints", *Journal of Banking and Finance*, (2009), pp. 949-981.

Choi, D. S. and S. M. Kim, "Dividends, Share Repurchases and the Substitution Hypothesis", *KSA Meeting Presenting Paper*, No. 4(2004), pp. 1-28(in Korean).

최도성, 김성민, "배당과 자사주매입의 대체 가설에 관한 연구", 한국증권학회 학술대회 발표논문(2004년 제4차), pp. 1-28.

Choi, D. S. and S. M. Kim, *Dividend Policy in Korea: How Korean Firms Make Dividend Decisions*, Seoul National University Press, 2005(in Korean).

최도성, 김성민, 한국의 배당정책의 변화, 서울대학교출판부, 2005.

Dann, L. Y., "Common Stock Repurchase: An Analysis of Returns to Bondholders and Stockholders", *Journal of Financial Economics*, Vol. 9(1981), pp. 113-138.

DeAngelo, H., L. DeAngelo, and D. J. Skinner, "Special Dividends and the Evolution of Dividend Signaling", *Journal of Financial Economics*, Vol. 57, No. 3(2000), pp. 309-354.

DeAngelo, H., L. DeAngelo, and D. J. Skinner, "Are Dividends Disappearing? Dividend Concentration and the Consolidation of Earnings",

Journal of Financial Economics, Vol. 72, No. 3(2004), pp. 425-456.

DeAngelo, H., L. DeAngelo, and R. Stulz, "Dividend Policy and the Earned/ Contributed Capital Mix: A Test of The Lifecycle Theory", Journal of Financial Economics, Vol. 81(2006), pp. 227-254.

Denis, D. J. and I. Osobov, "Why Do Firms Pay Dividends? International Evidence on the Determinants of Dividend Policy", Journal of Financial Economics, Vol. 89(2008), pp. 62-82.

Dhillon, U. S. and H. Johnson, "The Effect of Dividend Changes on Stock and Bond Prices", Journal of Finance, Vol. 49(1994), pp. 281-289.

Dittmar, A., "Why Do Firms Repurchase Stock", Journal of Business, Vol. 73, No. 3(2000), pp. 331-355.

Dittmar, A. K. and R. F. Dittmar, "Stock Repurchase Waves: An Explanation of The Trends in Aggregate Corporate Payout Policy?", Working Paper, University of Michigan(2004).

Eades, K. M., P. J. Hess, and E. H. Kim, "On Interpreting Security Returns During the Ex-Dividend Period", Journal of Financial Economics, Vol. 13(1984), pp. 3-35.

Easterbrook, F. H., "Two Agency-Cost Explanations of Dividends", American Economic Review, Vol. 74(1984), pp. 650-659.

Elton, E. J. and M. J. Gruber, "Marginal Stockholder Tax Rates and The Clientele Effect", Review of Economics and Statistics, Vol. 52(1970), pp. 68-74.

Fama, E. F., L. Fisher, M. Jensen, and R. Roll, "The Adjustment of Stock Prices to New Information", International Economic Review, Vol. 10(1969), pp. 1-21.

Fama, E. F. and K. French, "Disappearing Dividend: Changing Firm Characteristics or Lower Propensity to Pay?", Journal of financial Economics, Vol. 60(2001), pp. 3-43.

Fama, E. F. and J. D. MacBeth, "Risk, Return, and Equilibrium: Empirical

Tests", *Journal of Political Economy*, Vol. 71(1973), pp. 607-636.

Fenn, G. and N. Liang, "Corporate Payout Policy and Managerial Stock Incentives", *Journal of Financial Economics*, Vol. 60(2001), pp. 45-72.

Foster, T. W. and Vickrey, D., "The Information Content of Stock Dividend Announcement", *Accounting Review*, Vol. 53(1978), pp. 360-370.

Fried, J. M., "Open Market Repurchases: Signaling or Managerial Opportunism?", *Theoretical Inquiries in Law*, Vol. 2(2001), pp. 865-894.

Fried. J. M., "Informed Trading and False Signaling with Open Market Repurchases", *California Law Review*, Vol. 93, No. 5(2005), pp. 1326-1386.

Grinblatt, M. S., R. W. Masulis, and S. Titman, "The Valuation Effects of Stock Splits and Stock Dividends", *Journal of Financial Economics*, Vol. 13(1984), pp. 461-490.

Grullon, G., Gustavo, R. Michaely, S. Bernartzi, and R. Thaler, "Dividend Changes Do Not Signal Changes in Future Profitability", *Journal of Business*, Vol. 78, No. 5(2005), pp. 1659-1682.

Grullon, G. and R. Michaely, "Dividends, Share Repurchases and the Substitution Hypothesis", *Journal of Finance*, Vol. 57, No. 4(2002), pp. 1649-1684.

Grullon, G. and R. Michaely, "The information Content of Share Repurchase Programs", *Journal of Finance*, Vol. 59, No. 2(2004), pp. 651-680.

Grullon, G., R. Michaely, and B. Swaminathan, "Are Dividend Changes a Sign of Firm Maturity?", *Journal of Business*, Vol. 75(2002), pp. 387-424.

Guay, W. and J. Harford, "The Cash Flow Permanence and Information Content of Dividend Increases vs. Repurchases", *Journal of Financial Economics*, Vol. 57(2000), pp. 385-415.

Handjinicolaou, G. and A. Kalay, "Wealth Redistributions or Changes in Firm Value: An Analysis of Returns to Bondholders and Stockholders around Dividend Announcements", *Journal of Financial Economics*,

Vol. 13(1984), pp. 35-63.

Harris, M. and A. Raviv, "Corporate Control Contests and Capital Structure", *Journal of Financial Economics*, Vol. 20(1988), pp. 55-86.

Jagannathan, M., C. Stephens, and M. Weisbach, "Financial Flexibility and the Choice between Dividends and Stock Repurchases", *Journal of Financial Economics*, Vol. 57(2000), pp. 355-384.

Jagannathan, M., C. Stephens, and M. Weisbach", Motives for Multiple Open-Market Repurchase Programs", *Financial Management*, Vol. 32(2003), pp. 71-91.

Jensen, M. C., "Agency Costs of Free Cash Flow, Corporate Finance and Takeovers", *American Economic Review*, Vol. 76, No. 2(1986), pp. 323-329.

Jiraporn, P. and Y. Ning, "Dividend Policy, Shareholder Rights, and Corporate Governance", *Journal of Applied Finance*, Vol. 16, No. 2(2006), pp. 24-36.

John, K. and J. Williams, "Dividend, Dilution and Taxes: A Signaling Equilibrium", *Journal of Finance*, (September 1985), pp. 1053-1070.

Joo, J. K. and K. H. Kang, "A Study on the Relationship between Dividends and Foreign Ownership", *KJF Meeting Presenting Paper*(2007), pp. 1-25(in Korean).
주재근, 강길환, "외국인 지분율과 배당변수의 관련성 연구", 5개학회 공동 학술발표회(2007), pp. 1-25.

Jun, S. G. and T. Kim, "The Effect of Executives Stock Options on the Choice of Payout Policy", *Korean Journal of Financial Studies*, Vol. 34, No. 1(2005), pp. 35-61(in Korean).
전상경, 김태수, "경영자의 스톡옵션 소유가 자사주매입과 배당금지불의 선택에 미치는 영향", 증권학회지, 제34권 제1호(2005), pp. 35-61.

Jung, K. H., "Understanding of Unequal Dividends in Korea", *Korean Journal of Financial Management*, Vol. 14, No. 3(1997), pp. 231-261(in Korean).

정균화, "우리나라 상장기업의 차등배당에 대한 이해", 재무관리연구, 제14
권 제3호(1997), pp. 231-261.

Jung, M. K., "The Wealth Effects of Stock Repurchase on Shareholder and
Bondholders", *Korean Journal of Finance*, Vol. 18, No. 2(2005), pp.
67-99(in Korean).
정무권, "자사주 매입선언에 따른 주주와 채권자의 부의 변화", 재무연구,
제18권 제2호(2005), pp. 67-99.

Jung, M. K., "The Effect of Stock Option Holdings on the Wealth Change
in Share Repurchases", *Asia-Pacific Journal of Financial Studies*, Vol. 37,
No. 3(2008), pp. 425-464(in Korean).
정무권, "스톡옵션보유가 자사주매입 공시에 따른 투자자 반응에 미친 영
향", 증권학회지, 제37권 제3호(2008), pp. 425-464.

Jung, S. C., "The Right Offerings and the Stock Repurchases Unfair Tradings
might be Possible", *Korean Journal of Financial Studies*, Vol. 33, No.
3(2004), pp. 123-156(in Korean).
정성창, "유상증자와 자사주 취득의 동기 : 불공정거래 가능성의 제기", 증
권학회지, 제33권 제3호(2004), pp. 123-156.

Jung, S. C. and Y. H. Kim, "Open Market Stock Repurchases for Retirement
Purposes and the Value of Firms", *Asia-Pacific Journal of Financial
Studies*, Vol. 36, No. 1(2007), pp. 33-75(in Korean).
정성창, 김영환, "이익소각목적의 자기주식취득과 기업가치", 증권학회지,
제36권 제1호(2007), pp. 33-75.

Jung, S. C. and Y. G. Lee, "A Study on Direct Share Repurchase and Indirect
Share Repurchase", *Korean Journal of Finance*, Vol. 9, No. 1(1996), pp.
241-371(in Korean).
정성창, 이용교, "자사주매입과 자사주펀드제도의 유효성 분석", 재무연구,
제9권(1996), pp. 241-371.

Jung, S. C. and Y. G. Lee, "The Long-Term Performance of Repurchase

Stocks", *Korean Journal of Finance*, Vol. 16, No. 2(2004), pp. 129-161(in Korean).

정성창, 이용교, "자사주 취득기업들의 장기성과에 관한 연구", 재무연구, 제16권 제2호(2003), pp. 129-161.

Kahle, K., "When a Buyback Isn't a Buyback: Open Market Repurchases and Employee Options", *Journal of Financial Economics*, Vol. 63(2002), pp. 235-261.

Kalay, A., "The Ex-Dividend Day Behavior of Stock Prices: A Re-Examination of The Clientele Effect", *Journal of Finance*, Vol. 37(1982), pp. 1059-1070.

Kalay, A. and R. Michaely, "Dividends and Taxes: A Re-Examination", *Financial Management*, Vol. 29(2000), pp. 55-75.

Kim, C. J., "Ownership Structure, Capital Structure and Dividend Policy", *Korean Journal of Financial Management*, Vol. 13, No. 1(1996), pp. 51-78(in Korean).

김철중, "소유권 구조, 자본조달정책 및 배당정책의 상호관련성에 관한 연구", 재무관리연구, 제13권 제1호(1996), pp. 51-78.

Kim, C. K., "Empirical Analysis of Korean Stock Market Reaction to Share Repurchase", *Korean Journal of Finance*, Vol. 13(1997), pp. 169-195(in Korean).

김철교, "자사주 관리가 한국 주식시장에 미치는 영향에 관한 연구", 재무연구, 제13권(1997), pp. 169-195.

Kim, D. W., "Empirical Study of Information Content of Dividend", *Korean Journal of Financial Management*, Vol. 6, No. 2(1989), pp. 97-112(in Korean).

김동욱, "배당의 정보효과에 관한 실증적 연구", 재무관리연구, 제6권 제2호(1989), pp. 97-112.

Kim, S. M., "The Stock Price Behavior around the Ex-Dividend Day: The

Case of Korea", *Korean Journal of Finance*, Vol. 14(1997), pp. 145-170(in Korean).

김성민, "배당락일의 주가행태에 관한 효율성 검증", 재무연구, 제14호 (1997), pp. 145-170.

Kim, S. M., "Manager's View on the Unequal Dividend of the Korean enlisted firms", *Korean Journal of Finance*, Vol. 13, No. 1(2000), pp. 63-98(in Korean).

김성민, "우리나라 상장기업의 차등배당에 관한 경영자의 인식", 재무연구, 제13권 제1호(2000), pp. 63-98.

Kim, S. M. and J. H. Jeong, "Why Do Korean Firms Pay Unequal Dividends Between Large and Small Shareholders", *Korean Journal of Financial Management*, Vol. 16, No. 3(1997), pp. 57-72(in Korean).

김성민, 정진호, "대주주와 소액주주의 차등배당을 실시하는 동기에 관한 연구", 재무관리연구, 제16권 제3호(1997), pp. 57-72.

Kim, S. M. and J. E. Kim, "Information Contents of Dividend and Ex-dividend Day Stock Returns", *Korean Journal of Financial Management*, Vol. 21, No. 1(2004), pp. 1-32(in Korean).

김성민, 김지은, "현금배당 사전공시기업의 정보효과 및 배당락일의 주식수익률", 재무관리연구, 제21권 제1호(2004), pp. 1-32.

Kim, S. M. and E. J. Lee, "Corporate Governance and Dividend Policy under External Financing Constraints and Agency Problems", *Asia-Pacific Journal of Financial Studies*, Vol. 37, No. 4(2008), pp. 949-981.

Kim, T. H. and Y. K. Shin, "The Announcement and Signaling Effect of Stock Dividend", *Korean Journal of Financial Studies*, Vol. 15(1993), pp. 79-109(in Korean).

김태혁, 신용길, "주식배당의 공시효과와 정보전달효과에 관한 연구", 증권학회지, 제15권(1993), pp. 79-109.

Kim, Y. H., S. C. Jung, and S. E. Chun, "Foreign Stock Investment and

Firms' Dividend Policy in Korea", *Korean Journal of Financial Management*, Vol. 26, No. 1(2009), pp. 1-29(in Korean).

김영환, 정성창, 전선애, "외국인투자자가 국내 유가증권시장 상장기업의 배당행태에 미치는 영향에 대한 연구 : 다양한 계량 경제모형의 적용", 재무관리연구, 제26권 제1호(2009), pp. 1-29.

Ko, Y. K. and S. W. Joh, "The Effect of Ownership Structure on Payout Policy", *Asian Review of Financial Research*, Vol. 22, No. 3(2009), pp. 36-72(in Korean).

고영경, 조성욱, "소유지배구조가 지급정책에 미치는 영향", 재무연구, 제22권 제3호(2009), pp. 36-72.

Lakonishok, J. and B. Lev, "Stock Splits and Stock Dividends: Why, Who, and When", *Journal of Finance*, Vol. 62(1987), pp. 913-932.

Lakonishok, J. and T. Vermaelen, "Tax Reform and Ex-Dividend Day Behavior", *Journal of Finance*, Vol. 38(1983), pp. 1157-1179.

Lakonishok, J. and T. Vermaelen, "Anomalous Price Behavior around Repurchase Tender Offers", *Journal of Finance*, Vol. 45(1990), pp. 455-478.

Lambert, R. A., W. N. Lanen, and D. F. Larcker, "Executive Stock Option Plans and Corporate Dividend Policy", *Journal of Financial and Quantitative Analysis*, Vol. 24, No. 4(1989), pp. 409-425.

Lang, L. and R. Litzenberger, "Dividend Announcements: Cash Flow Signaling vs. Free Cash Flow Hypothesis?", *Journal of Financial Economics*, Vol. 24(1989), pp. 181-191.

La Porta, R., F. Lopez-de-Silanes, A. Shleifer, and R. W. Vishny, "Agency Problems and Dividend Policies around the World", *Journal of Finance*, Vol. 55(2000), pp. 1-33.

Lease, R. C., K. John, A. Kalay, U. Loewenstein, and O. H. Sarig, "Dividend Policy: Its Impact on Firm Value", *Harvard Business School Press*, Boston, 2000.

Lintner, J., "Distribution of Incomes of Corporations among Dividends, Retained Earnings and Taxes", *American Economic Review*, Vol. 46, No. 2(1956), pp. 97-113.

Litzenberger, R. H. and K. Ramaswamy, "The Effects of Personal Taxes and Dividends on Capital Asset Prices: Theory and Empirical Evidence", *Journal of Financial Economics*, Vol. 7(1979), pp. 163-195.

Louis, H. and H. White, "Do Managers Intentionally Use Repurchase Tender Offers to Signal Private Information? Evidence from Firm Financial Reporting Behavior", *Journal of Financial Economics*, Vol. 85(2007), pp. 205-233.

Masulis, R. W., "The Effect of Capital Structure Change on Security Prices: A Study of Exchange Offers", *Journal of Financial Economics*, Vol. 8(1980), pp. 139-178.

Maxwell, W. and C. Stephens, "The Wealth Effect of Repurchase on Bondholders", *Journal of Finance*, Vol. 58(2003), pp. 895-919.

Michaely, R., R. Thaler, and K. Womack, "Price Reactions to Dividend Initiations and Omissions: Overreaction and Drift?", *Journal of Finance*, Vol. 50(1995), pp. 573-608.

Miller, M. H. and F. Modigliani, "Dividend Policy, Growth, and the Valuation of Shares", *Journal of Business*, Vol. 34, No. 4(1961), pp. 411-433.

Miller, M. H. and K. Rock, "Dividend Policy under Asymmetric Information", *Journal of Finance*, Vol. 40, No. 4(1985), pp. 1031-1051.

Nam, S. H., "Empirical Study of Signaling Effect of Dividend", *Korean Journal of Financial Management*, Vol. 8, No. 1(1991), pp. 43-67(in Korean).
남수현, "배당의 신호전달효과에 관한 실증 연구", 재무관리연구, 제8권 제1호(1991), pp. 43-67.

Nam, M. S. and C. S. Woo, "Empirical Test of Information Content of Dividend Policy", *Korean Journal of Financial Studies*, Vol. 9, No.

1(1987), pp. 257-308(in Korean).

남명수, 우춘식, "배당정책의 신호표시내용에 관한 실증적 검증", 증권학회지, 제9집 제1호(1987), pp. 257-308.

Nissim, D. and A. Ziv, "Dividend Changes and Future Profitability", *Journal of Finance*, Vol. 56, No. 6(2001), pp. 2111-2133.

Nohel, T. and V. Tarhan, "Share Repurchases and Firm Performance: New Evidence on the Agency Costs of Free Cash Flow", *Journal of Financial Economics*, Vol. 49, No. 2(1998), pp. 187-222.

Oded, J., "Why do Firms Announce Open-Market Stock Repurchase Programs", *Review of Financial Studies*, Vol. 18(2005), pp. 271-300.

Ofer, A. and R. Siegel, "Corporate Financial Policy, Information, and Market Expectations: An Empirical Investigation of Dividends", *Journal of Finance*, Vol. 42, No. 4(1987), pp. 889-911.

Oh, Y. S. and W. Y. Choi, "Study on Dividend Policy of Listed Companies in Korea", *The Korea Listed Companies Association*, Vol. 92, No. 4(1992) (in Korean).

오유선, 최운열, "한국 상장기업의 배당정책에 관한 연구", 연구보고서, 한국상장회사협의회, 제92-4호(1992).

Park, Y. K., "Does Dividend Change Predict Corporate Future Earnings?", *Korean Journal of Financial Studies*, Vol. 33, No. 4(2004), pp. 63-94(in Korean).

박영규, "배당변화를 통한 기업의 미래이익 예측가능성 연구", 증권학회지, 제33권 제4호(2004), pp. 63-94.

Park, Y. K., "The Signaling Effect of Stock Repurchase on Equity Offerings in Korea", *Korean Journal of Financial Management*, Vol. 25, No. 1(2008), pp. 51-84(in Korean).

박영규, "자기주식매입의 유상증자에 대한 신호 효과", 재무관리연구, 제25권 제1호(2008), pp. 51-84.

Park, C. and S, C. Park, "The Behavior of Stock Prices on Ex-Dividend Day in Korea", *Korean Journal of Financial Management*, Vol. 26, No. 1(2009), pp. 221-263(in Korean).

박 철, 박수철, "현금 배당락 전·후 차익거래와 거래량 변화 : 배당락일 이상 현상인가?", 재무관리연구, 제26권 제1호(2009), pp. 221-263.

Park, K. S., E. J. Lee, and I. M. Lee, "Determinants of Dividend Policy of Korean Firms", *Korean Journal of Finance*, Vol. 16(2003), pp. 195-229(in Korean).

박경서, 이은정, 이인무, "국내기업의 배당행태와 투자자의 반응에 관한 연구", 재무연구, 제16권(2003), pp. 195-229.

Park, K. W., R. S. Park, and L. S. Hwang, "Corporate Governance and The Distribution of Shareholder Wealth", *Korean Journal of Financial Studies*, Vol. 34(2005), pp. 149-188(in Korean).

박광우, 박래수, 황이석, "기업지배구조와 주주부의 배분에 관한 연구", 증권학회지, 제34권(2005), pp. 149-188.

Penman, S., "The Predictive Content of Earnings Forecasts and Dividends", *Journal of Finance*, (September 1983), pp. 1181-1199.

Pettit, R. R., "Dividend Announcements, Security Performance, and Capital Market Efficiency", *Journal of Finance*, Vol. 27, No. 5(1972), pp. 993-1007.

Pinkowitz, L., R. Stulz, and R. Williamson, "Does the Contribution of Corporate Cash Holdings and Dividends to Firm Value Depend on Governance? A Cross-Country Analysis", *Journal of Finance*, Vol. 61 (2006), pp. 2725-2751.

Rankine, G. P. and E. K. Stice, "The Market Reaction to the Choice of Accounting Method for Stock Splits and Large Stock Dividends", *Journal of Financial and Quantitative Analysis*, Vol. 32(1997), pp. 161-182.

Rozeff, M. S., "Growth, Beta and Agency Costs as Determinants of Dividend Payout Ratios", *Journal of Financial Research*, Vol. 5(1982), pp. 249-259.

Shin, M. S. and J. S. Lee, "The Tests of Free Cash Flows Hypothesis about Stock Repurchase", *Korean Journal of Financial Management*, Vol. 24, No. 1(2007), pp. 59-83(in Korean).
신민식, 이정숙, "자사주매입에 관한 잉여현금흐름 가설 검증", 재무관리연구, 제24권 제1호(2007), pp. 59-83.

Shin, M. S. and J. H. Song, "An Empirical Study on Dividend Initiation Decisions of Firms", *Korean Journal of Financial Management*, Vol. 24, No. 4(2007), pp. 135-161(in Korean).
신민식, 송준협, "기업의 배당개시결정에 관한 실증적 연구", 재무관리연구, 제24권 제4호(2007), pp. 135-161.

Skinner, D., "The evolving relation between earnings, dividends, and stock repurchases", *Journal of Financial Economics*, Vol. 87(2007), pp. 582-609.

Stulz, R., "Management Control of Voting Rights", *Journal of Financial Economics*, Vol. 20(1988), pp. 25-54.

Sul, W. S. and S. J. Kim, "The Announcement Effects of Stock Repurchase and Stock Dispositions on Shareholder Wealth", *Korean Journal of Financial Management*, Vol. 22, No. 1(2005), pp. 37-69(in Korean).
설원식, 김수정, "자기주식취득 및 처분공시가 주주의 부에 미치는 영향 : 취득 및 처분목적을 중심으로", 재무관리연구, 제22권 제1호(2005), pp. 37-69.

Sul, W. S. and S. J. Kim, "Impact of Foreign Investors on Firm's Dividend policy", *Korean Journal of Financial Studies*, Vol. 35, No. 1(2006), pp. 1-40(in Korean).
설원식, 김수정, "외국인 투자자가 기업의 배당에 미치는 영향", 증권학회지, 제35권 제1호(2006), pp. 1-40.

Watts, R., "The Information Content of Dividend", *Journal of Business*, Vol.

46, No. 1(1973), pp. 191-211.

Won, J. Y. and S. M. Kim, "Study of Manager's View on the Dividend Policy of Companies", *The Journal of Finance and Banking*, Vol. 5, No. 1(1999), pp. 131-158(in Korean).

원정연, 김성민, "기업의 배당정책에 관한 경영자 인식에 관한 연구", 증권·금융연구, 제5권 제1호(1999), pp. 131-158.

Woo, C. S., "Managers' View on the Determinants and the Effect of Dividend Policy", *Journal of Korea Investors Services*(Winter 1988), pp. 6-16(in Korean).

우춘식, "배당정책의 결정요인과 그 효과에 관한 경영자의 견해", 신평저널, 겨울호(1988), 한국신용평가주식회사, pp. 6-16.

Woo, C. S., "The Ex-Dividend Stock Price Behavior: An Empirical Analysis", *Korean Journal of Financial Studies*, Vol. 15(1993), pp. 215-241(in Korean).

우춘식, "배당락일의 주가조정행위에 관한 실증적 연구", 증권학회지, 제15권(1993), pp. 215-241.

Woo, C. S. and Y. K. Shin, "Empirical Study of Stock Dividend Announcement Effect", *Korean Journal of Financial Management*, Vol. 13, No. 1(1996), pp. 115-136(in Korean).

우춘식, 신용균, "주식배당의 공시효과에 관한 실증적 연구", 재무관리연구, 제13권 제1호(1996), pp. 115-136.

Woolridge, J. R., "Dividend Changes and Security Prices", *Journal of Finance*, Vol. 38, No. 5(1983), pp. 1607-1615.

Yook, K. H., "Empirical Study of Agency Problem between Shareholders and Managers, and Dividend Policy", *Korean Journal of Financial Studies*, Vol. 11, No. 1(1989), pp. 143-166(in Korean).

육근효, "주주-경영자 간의 대리문제에 관한 실증연구 : 배당정책을 중심으로", 증권학회지, 제11권 제1호(1989), pp. 143-166.

Yoon, P. S., J. K. Kim, and K. H. Chung, "The Ex-Dividend-Day Behavior of Stock Prices", *Korean Journal of Financial Management*, Vol. 22(1998), pp. 115-143(in Korean).

윤평식, 김정국, 정기호, "배당락일의 주가조정에 관한 연구", 증권학회지, 제22권(1998), pp. 115-143.

Any citation of this article must refer to the following: Yang, Chae-Yeol, "A Survey of the Korean Literature on Corporate Governance", Asian Review of Financial Research, Vol. 24 (2011), No. 3, pp. 909-951.

Chapter 9

A Survey of the Korean Literature on Corporate Governance

Chae-Yeol Yang* Professor, College of Business Administration, Chonnam National University

Abstract Finance is unique in that researchers question even the integrity of managers. Researchers in other disciplines in management sciences consider managers to be agents with good intentions. They focus on supplying good instruments for managers to put into practice, failing to question the intent of managers. But researchers in corporate finance equipped with agency theory question the more fundamental problems and ask what if managers are bad or if managers are plagued with agency problems? These kinds of questions are the topics of corporate governance. Researchers in corporate finance who have a way of seeing things differently have brought and will bring many spectacular achievements in both the academic and practical world.

This paper reviews the empirical literature on the corporate governance issues in the Korean capital market setting, where corporate governance issues are important because Korea's chaebols, family-owned conglomerates, are blamed for minority shareholder expropriation via unlawful inheritances and accounting fraud with all the success in international markets. This survey focuses on the effectiveness of internal governance and external markets to monitor and control managers. The topics covered in the following four sections are: (1) The effect of corporate governance structure on corporate policy, (2) Corporate governance and firm value, (3) Market discipline, and (4) Determinants of governance structure. Finally, the discussion and conclusion are presented in the last section.

Keywords Corporate Governance, Agency Cost, Market Discipline, Internal Market, Tunneling

* **Address:** Chonnam National University, 77 Yongbong-ro, Buk-gu, Gwangju 500-757, Korea;
E-mail: cyyang@chonnam.ac.kr; **Tel:** 82-62-530-1443.

This paper is prepared as a part of the 2010 knowledge database project by the Korean Finance Association (KFA), and financially supported by KFA. The author thanks Woochan Kim and another anonymous referee for their helpful suggestions. The author would like to express special thanks to Woochan Kim for his helpful suggestions and supplying lists of important articles to be included. All remaining errors are mine. I also thank You Kyung Kang and professor Sungho Choi for their kind help.

Ⅰ. Introduction

Corporate governance can be defined in many ways. According to Shleifer and Vishny (1997), "corporate governance deals with the ways in which suppliers of finance to corporations assure themselves of getting a return on their investment." And Gillan and Starks (1998) define corporate governance as "the system of laws, rules, and factors that control operations at a company." Gillan (2006) adopts a framework dividing governance into internal and external governances, which are further subdivided as shown in <Figure 1>.

<Figure 1> Gillan's Framework on Corporate Governance (Gillan 2006)

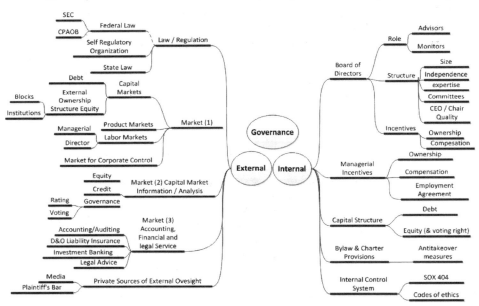

A useful framework for research questions is that of ECGN (European Corporate Governance Network) with regard to ownership and the voting power used in Gugler (2001). Gugler provides four quadrants based on dispersion-concentration of ownership and voting rights, with each quadrant having different research questions of its own. Some of the most important questions are: "Are owner-controlled firms more profitable than manager-controlled firms? Is there rent extraction by large shareholders? What are the effects of pyramiding?" In the Korean setting, the quadrant with low ownership and high voting rights may be the most relevant research area given the chaebol system.

This paper reviews mostly empirical papers on Korean corporate governance in the major Korean academic journals.[1] There will be more than one way to classify and organize papers. This paper classifies four research questions as follows. They will be covered in the next following four sections.

Q1. Does the corporate governance affect the policy of firms?

Q2. Does corporate governance affect the value of firms?

Q3. Do the external markets work properly to control managers?

Q4. What determines the corporate governance structure?

Corporate governance structure, especially managerial ownership, can affect firm policies and values because of the incentive/power effect of common stocks. Common stocks have two features affecting the incentives and power of stockholders. One is the residual claim on the firm's cash flow (cash flow right) and the other is the voting right regarding corporate decision making (voting right).

---

1) The articles covered in this survey are mostly from major Korean journals, written-in Korean. Here are papers reviewing Korean corporate governance in major international journals, which are suggested to be included by an anonymous referee. I thank the referee for helpful suggestions. For a general overview on Korean corporate governance after 1997 crisis, see Kim and Kim (2008). Papers concentrating on specific aspects of Korean governance include Chang (2003), Lim and Kim (2005) Kim, Lim, and Sung (2007) and Almeida, Park, Subrahmanyam, and Wolfenzon (2011) on ownership structure of chaebol, Ferris, Kim, and Kitsabunnarat (2003) on efficiency of investments of chaebol firms, Hong, Lee, and Lee (2007) Lee, Park, and Shin (2009) on internal capital market, Choi, Park, and Yoo (2007) and Black and Kim (forthcoming) on the effect of governance structure on firm values, Baek, Kang, Lee (2006) on tunneling, Lee and Park (2009) and Kim, Kim, and Kwon (2009) on shareholder activism, Kho, Stulz, and Warnock (2009) and Kim, Sung, and Wei (2011) and Bae and Goyal (2010) on foreign investors, Black, Jang, and Kim (2006) on the determinants of governance structure, Kato, Kim, and Lee (2007) on managerial compensation.

Considering the manager as a decision making unit, managerial ownership will have three effects on managers: interest alignment effect, diversification loss effect, and job security enhancement effect. Because common stocks are residual claims on the firm's cash flow, an increase in a manager's equity stake will make the manager more concerned about an increase in firm value by making the manager's wealth more sensitive to the change in firm value. This interest alignment effect will align the manager's interest more closely with those of shareholders, reducing agency costs of equity. Also due to the convexity of payoff to the levered equity (like a call option), managers may prefer increasing the riskiness of the firm (risk shifting) by taking on risky projects or increasing debt levels. The diversification loss effect comes from the fact that an increase in a manager's stake in a particular firm makes the managers' portfolio less diversified, increasing the manager's exposure to the firm's specific risk and making the manager more risk averse. The job security enhancement effect comes from the stock's voting right. An increase in a manager's voting power, via increased ownership, will make the manager less vulnerable to any attack on his tenure. This may lead to a less myopic behavior by making managers more long-term oriented, or it may lead to more managerial entrenchment.[2]

There are some reasons that make research on Korean corporate governance attractive. The first is the prevalence of chaebol firms in Korea, which are fertile ground for internal capital markets, self dealings, and economic entrenchment as addressed in Morck, Wolfenzon, and Yeung (2005). The second may be special regulations on corporate governance-Korea has unique corporate governance rules that apply only to large firms that make it possible to construct an instrument variable (Black, Jang, and Kim, 2006). Finally, data on ownership and governance structure are widely available

---

2) This paragraph is mostly from introduction of my dissertation, "Essays on Management Ownership: Its Implications For Corporate Policies And Market Reactions(Yang, 1994, Northwestern University)."

due to special filing regulations for chaebol firms.

There are some qualifications. First, since the effect of foreign investors and dividends are two separate areas covered by other articles, these topics are not directly covered here. Also, articles mostly dealing with the relations between governance structure and accounting information are not covered in this paper. Since many articles covered here try to answer more than one research question, some may be covered in more than one section.

II. The Effect of Corporate Governance Structure on Corporate Policy

Corporate governance structure will influence corporate policy through the incentives and constraints faced by decision makers. This section reviews papers that examine the effect of corporate governance structure on the way a firm is operated, namely managerial perquisite consumption, investment, cash holdings, innovation, and the issues of internal market.

Most empirical work in finance is usually in the form of regressions, where the Left Hand Side (LHS) variable is explained by the Right Hand Side (RHS) variables. So for research in this section, LHS variables are corporate policies and RHS variables are components of internal corporate governance structure.

1. Perquisite Consumption

One area where an agency problem can be directly identified is managerial perquisite consumptions. Managers with high agency costs may consume more perquisites, and firms with inappropriate governance structures cannot deter managers from consuming more perquisites. Park, Shin, and Choi (2004) use the entertainment expenses per sales as the proxy for agency costs, and find no relation between the equity holding of the largest share-holder and agency costs but find that the equity holdings of foreign invest-ors are negatively related to agency costs. Park and Kim (2006) measure the agency costs by the ratio of operating expenses to annual sales, and find agency costs are negatively related to the Corporate Governance Index. Kim and Park (2009) use entertainment and welfare expenses and R&D expenses normalized by sales as a measure of agency costs. They present evidence showing that firms with independent audit committees and in-dependent executive boards have smaller agency costs.

2. Investment

Investment affects the size and types of the assets that managers control, so investment decisions by the delegated manager may not necessarily fol-low the shareholder value maximization rule. According to Jensen's free cash flow theory (Jensen, 1986), managers with empire building motivation may prefer to have as much resources under their control as possible rather than to give back to the claimholders.

Kim (2006) reports, "large blockholders have a U-shaped relationship with balanced investments," and "foreign stock ownership is positively related to balanced investments."[3] Park and Cho (2002) focus on diversification deci-sions and find a negative relation between the level of diversification and in-sider ownership, meaning less agency problems as insider ownership increases.

The governance structure of the chaebol system may insulate chaebol firms from the discipline of the capital market and may show higher agen-

---

3) They come up with a new measure of investment, introducing the concept of "balanced score board per-spective to evaluate the managers' investment activities which supplements traditional financial measurers with criteria that measures performance from three additional perspectives those of customers, internal busi-ness processes. and learning and growth."

cy problems of free cash flow, leading to empire building. Shin and Park (1999) find "investment-cash flow sensitivity is low and insignificant for chaebol firms," and "chaebols invest more than non-chaebol firms despite their relatively poor growth opportunities," suggesting a greater empire building motive of chaebol firms.

Agency problems may affect the restructuring decisions after bad operating performances. Kang, Na, and Lee (2004) investigate whether a corporate governance structure affects restructuring activities following a sudden deterioration of operating performance. They find "chaebol firms with poor corporate governance systems are more likely to expand their businesses when their controlling shareholders' ownership is larger," suggesting "that ownership and corporate governance structures affect the nature of corporate reorganization activities and performance improvements following these activities."

3. R&D

Firms plagued with agency problems may show short-term oriented behaviors. As the agency problem is mitigated, the firm may invest in more long-term oriented investments. R&D investments are usually considered as long-term investments. Therefore, the severity of agency problems may affect the firm's R&D investments. Kim (2003) investigates the effect of corporate governance structure on R&D investments, and finds that CEO equity ownership and foreign equity ownership are positively related to R&D investments, confirming the agency explanation of R&D investments. Yoon (2005) finds that R&D investments decrease with the shareholdings of the controlling owner, in the case of chaebol firms, but not in independent firms. He also reports that R&D investments are negatively related to the disparity of separation of ownership and control.

4. Cash Holdings

Agency problems are also shown to affect the cash holdings of firms. This is because cash is the asset with the highest managerial discretion, which will be mostly preferred by managers if not deterred by an appropriate governance system. Park and Yon (2009) examine whether this agency theory explains the level of cash holdings. Using firm-level corporate governance scores from the Korea Corporate Governance Service (KCGS) for the RHS variable, they find that the corporate governance score is negatively related to the level of cash holdings. Shin and Kim (2010) also find that cash holdings are positively related to the large shareholder's equity holdings, the difference between first largest shareholder's and second largest shareholder's equity holdings, and the ownership concentration ratio. But managerial ownership displays a non-linear relation with cash holdings-N shape. They conclude that large shareholders extract private benefits from corporate resources at the expense of minority shareholders, supporting the expropriation hypothesis.

5. Wage Decisions

Park, Byun, and Lee (2009a) empirically confirm the disciplinary role of controlling ownership in wage decisions in firms. They find a negative relationship between controlling ownership and the wage level, confirming the monitoring role of controlling shareholders. They conclude "the overall results suggest that a professional manager with lower stock ownership would collude with his employees and allow them higher wages in order to secure his control over his firm. ⋯ On the other hand, any increase in the ownership by employees or their participation in a labor union tends to have an increasing effect on their wage level."

6. Chaebol and Internal Market: Tunneling/propping

The Korean economy is stylized by the chaebol system, so there are wide ranges of literature on the effectiveness of internal market and its dark side. The contentious issue is whether internal transactions among chaebol group firms are efficiency enhancing (propping) or manifestation of agency problems (tunneling). Internal markets can be a very effective means to improve the effectiveness of resource allocation among firms (propping), especially when external markets are not well developed. But internal transactions can be used to expropriate minority shareholders (tunneling).

Chang and Hong (2000) find "group-affiliated firms benefit from group membership through sharing intangible and financial resources with other member firms," and "various forms of internal business transactions, such as debt guarantee, equity investment, and internal trade, are extensively used for the purpose of cross-subsidization."

Bae, Kang, and Kim (2002) examine the soundness of the acquisitions of chaebol affiliated firms. They find that acquisitions by chaebol-affiliated firms are associated with a drop in stock prices. Further, they report "while minority shareholders of a chaebol-affiliated firm making an acquisition lose, the controlling shareholder of that firm on average benefits because the acquisition enhances the value of other firms in the group," supporting the tunneling hypothesis.

Yoon (2004) investigates the motives and the direction of intra-group fund transactions. He finds that "the group-affiliated firms in a chaebol with many investment opportunities, little free cash flow and a low degree of separation of ownership and control, are the funds-receiving firms." And he also finds "the intra-group fund transactions have been done not only to mitigate the information asymmetry in the external capital market, but also for the owner of chaebol to exploit the wealth of minority shareholders." He concludes that there exist both a bright side and dark side to intra-group fund transactions.

Kang, Park, and Jang (2006a) find "debt guarantees are mainly used for the purpose of propping up financially weak member firms, while illegal internal transactions are mainly used for the purpose of tunneling corporate wealth from minority shareholders to controlling shareholders," suggesting controlling shareholders are willing to suffer financial loss in the short run to support their member firms.

In a series of papers, Won Heum Lee investigates the efficiency of internal market transactions in chaebol firms. Lee (2005) tests whether related-party transactions are used as a means for controlling shareholders to expropriate minority shareholders. He finds "firms undertaking related-party transactions earn significantly negative excess returns at the initial announcement, non- group firms with weak corporate governance having the most severe negative returns," mostly supporting the tunneling hypothesis. But he finds no evidence to support the tunneling hypothesis for chaebol-affiliated firms with good governance and finds evidence of the propping hypothesis for non-group firms with good corporate governance.

Lee (2006) examines the effect of ownership structure and related-party transactions on their firm values, and finds "a significantly negative relation between the controlling shareholders and firm values proxied by Tobin's Q," and also finds "a significantly negative relation between related-party transactions and the firm values," supporting the expropriation hypothesis. Employing the piecewise regression analysis, he finds "a significant inverse U-shape pattern between the controlling shareholders ownership structure and firm values, quite different from the existing literatures that have usually reported a U-shape pattern."

Lee (2009a) also "examines the agency problems of the related party transactions between a listed company and its controlling shareholders by directly estimating the size of the agency costs of the firm," using a firm valuation model of value-based event study analysis (VESA) of his own. He observes that "the agency problems seem to occur in the internal capital market and also in the internal business market," and concludes "either the tunneling or propping hypothesis regarding to the related party transactions is equally well supported in both markets."

Lee (2009b) examines the agency problems of self-dealings in the business groups using value-based event study analysis. He does not find any evidence to support the tunneling hypothesis. Instead, he finds evidence to support the propping hypothesis. Comparing before and after components of firm values in VESA, he reports that self-dealings seem to decrease agency costs, but at the same time, decrease intrinsic value of firms, seemingly contradicting results.

7. Financing Decision

Jeong and Kwon (2006) investigate the effect of the ownership structure on the opportunistic behavior of a firm's financing decisions. They find that opportunistic financing only exists for equity issuing firms, but not in debt issuing firms. Furthermore, they find that the level of equity holding of large shareholders is negatively associated with the less opportunistic behavior.

III. Corporate Governance and Firm Value

If the agency problem influences the policy of a firm, it will eventually affect the value of the firm. Articles in this section investigate whether governance structure affects firm values. In the empirical model, LHS variables are some measures of firm value (Tobin's Q) and performance measures (ROA) while RHS variables are corporate governance structure (managerial ownership, board ownership, board structure etc.).

1. Ownership Structure and Firm Value with Ownership Measure as a LHS Variable

1.1 U: Quadratic Relationship

Kim and Lee (2000) find evidence of a U-shaped relation between the ownership of the largest blockholders and corporate value (put square term of ownership variable in the regressions and find a positive coefficient on square term), allegedly verifying the managerial entrenchment hypothesis at the lower level of equity ownership and the convergence of interest hypothesis at a high level of equity ownership. Similarly, Park (2002) finds that the relationship between insider ownership and Tobin's Q shows a curve convex to downwards.

1.2 Cubic Relationship

Some find that there is a cubic relationship between firm value and managerial ownership. Kim, B. H. (2002) finds evidence of a significant non-monotonic relationship in Tobin's Q, first increasing, then decreasing, and finally increasing again as ownership by the board of directors rises. However, Park (2007) reports a non-linear relationship between major shareholder's holdings and firm values, first decreasing, then increasing, and finally decreasing again.

1.3 No Relationship

Some find that there is no relationship between firm value and managerial ownership. Kim, C. S. (2006) finds no relationship between firm values and equity holdings of the largest stockholder (His focus is on the role of outside directors, though). Lee and Son (2009) also do not find any significant difference in Tobin's Q between the companies with good corporate governance and those with poor governance. They also find that companies that have good corporate governance displayed higher ROAs and higher EVAs. They use corporate governance rankings from Korea Corporate Governance Service (KCGS) as a RHS variable.

1.4 Negative Relationship

Lee (2006) reports a significant negative relation between the controlling shareholders ownership structure and firm values proxied by Tobin's Q. He reports "a significant inverse U-shape pattern between the controlling shareholders ownership structure and firm values." In a related work, Ryu and Joo (2007) find a negative relation between the firms' economic goodwill and the largest investor's shareholdings among KOSDAQ firms.

2. Ownership Structure and Firm Value with Corporate Governance Index as a LHS Variable

Instead of using managerial ownership for the RHS variable, many articles use some (combined) measure of good corporate governance practices. Most papers using corporate governance index find that good governance leads to good performance.

Lee (2009a) directly estimates the size of the agency costs of firms using his valuation model and examines the relations between the corporate governance level and the agency problems. He finds that good governance systems are associated with low agency costs.

Park and Lee (2004) investigate the relation between the corporate governance ranking supplied by the Corporate Governance Service (CSG) and firm values (as measured by Tobin's Q). They report a positive and significant correlation in manufacturing companies, although there are much weaker relations for financial institutions. They interpret the finding as the result of the effectiveness of the outside monitoring by supervisory authorities in financial institutions, supporting the complementary monitoring role of governance components. They also find that the equity ownership of the largest shareholders has a negative correlation with corporate governance ranking, suggesting a negative effect of the largest shareholder on corporate governance by resisting monitoring activities.

Similarly, using a constructed corporate governance index (KCGI) based on the Stock Exchange survey, Black, Jang, and Kim (2006) find a positive relationship between KCGI and firm values (Tobin's q, market/book, and market/sales).

Park and Kim (2007) analyze the effect of capital and R&D expenditures on firm values in association with corporate governance structure. They find a significant and positive correlation between the firm values (Tobin's q or industry-adjusted EV/EBITDA) and the capital and R&D investments for the group of firms with high corporate governance index or firms with high cash flow rights ratios.

3. Ownership Structure and Accounting Profitability

Several papers investigate the relationship between accounting performance and ownership structure. Kim, B. H. (2002) finds "no relationship between management ownership and accounting and security returns," the reason being that "the two variables are more likely to be influenced by short-term factors rather than management ownership."

Joh (2003) finds a positive relationship between firm profitability (ordinary income to assets and net income to assets) and ownership concentration of controlling shareholders.

Yoon and Oh (2005) find that the performance variables (ROA) are positively associated with firm's corporate governance index (CGI), in ordinary least squares regressions (OLS) and in the two-stage least squares regressions (2LS). But for the value variable (MV/BV), they find a positive association in OLS but not in 2LS. They also find that an investment strategy of buying high CGI-firms and shorting low CGI-firms obtains abnormal returns, indicating the information in corporate governance has not been fully reflected in the stock prices, seeming to contradict the efficient market hypothesis (EMH).

Also, Lee, and Son (2009) find companies with good corporate governance display higher ROA and higher EVA, using corporate governance rankings from Korea Corporate Governance Service (KCGS) as an RHS variable (But they find no significant difference in Tobin's Q according to the corporate governance).

4. Outside Director's Role, Blockholder's Holdings, etc.

Ownership stakes of managers (or controlling shareholder, or largest shareholders) are the most popular RHS variable in firm value determination regressions. However, there are additional dimensions in the internal governance mechanism - the ownership of outside directors, or board structure, which may hold managerial discretion in check.

Shin, Lee, and Chang (2004) find a positive relationship between firm values (Tobin's Q and MV/BV) and the existence of foreign block shareholders and foreign directors. Ryu and Joo (2007) also report a positive association between the foreign investors' shareholdings and the firms' economic goodwill.

However, Kim, C. S. (2006) does not find outside directors to have any impact on firm values. Park and Kim (2006) also do not find a strong positive relation between board composition and firm values.

But, Park (2007) finds a positive relation between the ratio of outside directors in the board and firm values. He also reports a non-linear relationship between the outside directors' ratio and firm values.

Park et al. (2004) report that foreign investors are efficient monitors and reduce entertainment and other like expenses. Kim and Park (2009) identify active monitoring role of independent audit committee in deducing managerial perk consumption. Choi and Bae (2009) also report active monitoring and controlling role of outside directors in replacing CEO with poor performance.

5. Distribution of Shares and Firm Value

Ownership structure has an additional dimension in addition to the equity holdings of some stockholders. One of these is distribution and the evenness of the distribution. Ahn (2009) reports, "a more equal distribution of the votes among large blockholders has a positive effect on firm value," particularly strong in family-controlled firms. He interprets this to be due to the fact that "founding families are more prone to private benefit extraction if they are not monitored by another strong blockholder."

6. Disparity and Firm Value and Related Issues

There is an issue of the disparity between control rights and ownership rights of shares. This is especially an important issue in Korea because of the pyramid ownership structure in Korean chaebols. The contentious issue is whether the disparity is good or bad for the firm and eventually for the economy.

Joh (2003) finds a negative relation between disparity and profitability of firms. She also finds that resource transfers among group firms are often wasted, suggesting tunneling. However, Kang, Shin, and Chang (2005) find no significantly negative relation between the disparity and the firm value proxied by the market-to-book ratio. Further, they do not find any significant relation between the disparity and operating performance.

Yoon S. M. (2005) investigates the effect of disparity on innovative activities of firms and finds that innovative activities are negatively associated with the disparity of separation of ownership and control in chaebol firms.

Ahn (2007) investigates how firm governance and control structure vary with a firm's accounting information transparency. He finds that discrepancy negatively affects accounting transparency (Here, accounting transparency is measured by the variability of discretionary accruals).

Ⅳ. Market Discipline

If investors know that corporate policies can be affected by agency problems, they can see through the managers' motivation and react to corporate events differently, according to the degree of suspicion of agency problems. If outside investors adjust their evaluation of firms according to the severity of agency problems, the market will take these factors into account and the price of the securities will reflect this information. Since shareholders will be the ultimate bearer of the agency costs, they will have incentive to reduce agency costs because of market discipline. Articles in this section explore whether the external markets properly discipline managers.

1. Discipline in Debt Market

Cheon, Choe, and Gil (2006) investigate whether market discipline works properly in bond rating markets. They find a positive association between the credit ratings of bonds and the ownership of owner-managers and ownership of foreign investors for firms listed in Korea stock exchange, but not for the firms in the KOSDAQ market.

Byun, H. (2007) finds that good corporate governance practices are negatively related to the cost of debt capital, confirming that good corporate governance mitigates agency problems and eventually leads to lower costs of debt capital for a firm.

2. Discipline in Managerial Labor Market

Many articles investigate whether the managerial labor market is working properly, specifically the replacement of poor performing managers and directors, and market reactions to the replacements, and so on.

Shin and Chang (2005) find "CEOs with poor firm performance are more likely to be replaced, but that owner CEOs are less likely to be replaced than professional CEOs."[4] They also examine the effect of business group affiliation and find "the CEO turnover of business group firms is not more sensitive to firm performance than that of non-group firms," suggesting ineffectiveness of a monitoring and controlling role of business group headquarters. Shin and Chang (2003) report "firms with CEO turnover underperform firms without CEO turnover prior to the CEO turnover," suggesting the proper working of managerial labor markets. They also find "the new CEO's identity - whether a professional or a relative of large blockholders - does not make a difference in performance improvement following the CEO turnover."

Choi and Bae (2009) find a connection between the outside director and outsider CEO turnover with poor performance, and the connection is stronger for firms with non-majority shareholders. The result seems to suggest that managerial labor market discipline is working properly for non-majority shareholder firms, but not for majority shareholder firms.

Kim and Baek (2005) investigate outside director turnovers and find neg-

---

4) They define owner CEO as CEO identified as the largest shareholder, his/her son, daughter, cousin, uncle, etc.

ative market reactions on the dismissal of outside directors, indicating an active monitoring role of outside directors in reducing agency problems. They also find that market reactions on the dismissal of outside directors are positively associated with the equity holdings of the largest shareholder, meaning that the negative effect is less severe for the firms with high equity holdings of the largest shareholder. Another important finding is that the market reaction is the most negative for chaebol firms with large equity ownership by controlling shareholders, suggesting that the outside directors of chaebol firms did a good job in monitoring and controlling managers before the dismissal.

3. Discipline in Product Market and M&A

Agency problems may cause managers to overinvest due to the empire building motivation. Jinn and Song (2003) investigate this overinvestment problem employing an event study method for the firms making equity investments. They find that market reactions to equity investments are negative, and the abnormal returns of equity investments for related diversification is greater than that of unrelated diversification. They also find that the equity holdings of controlling shareholders are significantly and negatively associated with abnormal returns, suggesting the controlling shareholder has a private motive for equity investments.

Bae, Kang, and Kim (2002) examine acquisitions by chaebol firms to test the tunneling hypothesis. They find that acquisitions by chaebol-affiliated firms are followed by negative abnormal returns to bidders. They also find that "the concentrated ownership by owner-managers in chaebol bidders is negatively related to bidder announcement returns, but is positively related to announcement returns of the value-weighted portfolio of other firms in the same group." They conclude that "minority shareholders of chaebol firms making acquisitions typically lose from the acquisitions, but the controlling shareholders of these firms gain from them," supporting the tunneling hypothesis.

Cho and Jun (2004) examine the stock performances of acquirers in the Korean Stock Exchange, and find that the ownership of outside active shareholders is positively correlated with the performance of acquirers, but the ownership of insiders, such as that of incumbent managers or major shareholders, does not have any significant effect on the performance of M&A's. Similarly, Cho and Jeong (2009) also examine the acquirer performance of mergers and acquisitions in the KOSDAQ Market and find similar results.

4. Discipline in Capital Market: Security Offerings

Kang and Baek (2003b) explore security transactions among chaebol firms to investigate whether security issues are used to transfer wealth among chaebol firms, expropriating minor shareholders. They find negative abnormal returns for non-issuing firms to the announcements of private equity issues by chaebol firms and a negative correlation between the returns of issuing chaebol firms and those of purchasing chaebol firms, confirming a wealth transfer from issuing to purchasing firms.

Kang and Baek (2003a) test the tunneling/propping hypothesis on the rights offering firms belonging to chaebol firms. For poorly performing issuers, they find that the announcement returns of rights offerings are significant and positive and that its return is significantly and negatively related to the abnormal returns for the value-weighted portfolio of other non-issuing firms in the same group, supporting the tunneling view for chaebols. In contrast, for the sample of firms excluding poor performing firms, there is a significant and positive return relation between issuing firms and non-issuing firms, supporting the propping view for chaebols. They also find that announcement returns for issuing firms are positively associated with the equity holdings of the largest shareholders but negative for chaebol firms, suggesting less agency costs for non-chaebol firms but higher agency costs for chaebol firms with high equity holdings.

Kang, Park, and Baek (2004) explore the long-run performance of issuers and acquirers following private placements of equity and find negative effects on firm values, suggesting that placement of private equity is used for private purposes rather than for the maximization of firm values. They also find "chaebol-affiliated issuers with high equity ownership by individual controlling shareholders experience a smaller decrease in long-run performance," suggesting lower agency costs.

Park and Baek (2003) investigate the effect of convertible debt issue on firm values employing event study methods. They find that issues of private convertible bonds by chaebol firms lead to significantly negative abnormal returns, and the reactions are more favorable as the ownership of the largest shareholder increases, that is, firms with higher than median ownership of the largest shareholder show positive market reactions but negative market reactions for firms with lower than medial ownership of the largest shareholder. Employing logit analysis, they also find that firms with lower equity ownership of the largest shareholder are likely to go for the private placement of convertible debts, indicating that convertible bond issues can be used as an expropriation tool for chaebol owner-managers.

5. Discipline in Insurance Markets

Lee and Choi (2006) investigate market discipline in insurance markets. They find a significantly negative relationship between director and officer insurance premiums and governance quality, meaning firms with good corporate governance pay low insurance premiums (They use managerial ownership, foreign investor ownership and establishment of audit committees as proxies for governance quality).

6. Distribution of Stock Returns

Bae and Lim (2003) examine "whether the insurance/risk-sharing function is reflected in the stock returns" of chaebol firms. If there is an implicit guarantee of bailout for the firms belonging to chaebols, the risk-sharing function will have a negative shock not so severe due to the risk-sharing function, causing higher conditional skewness in the stock returns. They indeed find that chaebol-affiliated firms show significantly higher conditional skewness, supporting a risk-sharing role of chaebol. But they also find that the conditional skewness is negatively associated with the holding of related firms in the chaebol, suggesting the wealth transfer hypothesis due to high agency costs.

Byun and Hwang (2007) examine whether sound corporate governance practices affect stock price synchronicity and stock return skewness. They find "sound corporate governance practices are negatively related to stock price synchronicity" because "sound corporate governance practices increase firm- specific information" and thus, reduce stock price synchronicity. They also find a negative association between corporate governance practices and stock return skewness, interpreting this to be the case that firms with good corporate governance and less agency costs have less need to use discretion to hide bad news, leading to lower return skewness.[5]

---

5) Note that this interpretation is different form the logic of Kee-Hong Bae, Chan-Woo Lim (2003), who interpret lower return skewness as a manifestation of agency costs (= bad corporate governance).

7. Governance Premium: Stock Returns

If good governance leads to good performance due to low agency costs, then firms with good governance will command a higher price (premium) in the market and a lower cost of capital, which is another way of saying low stock returns to the investors. Whether the information about corporate governance is utilized by investors and is reflected in stock prices is an empirical question that is needed to be tested.

Yoon and Oh (2005) examine the relation between corporate governance and a firm's performance and market returns. They find that "an investment strategy of buying high-CGI firms and shorting low-CGI firms yields excess returns of around 46.9% on an annual basis." And based on these empirical results, they conclude that "information on corporate governance has not been fully reflected in the stock prices in the Korean stock market," suggesting market inefficiencies. Park, Byun, and Lee (2009b) also draw similar results that show "purchasing the stocks of the firms with good corporate governance and selling those stocks with bad corporate governance results in abnormal returns," contradicting the efficient market hypothesis. Lee and Kim (2007) even assume that firms with good governance will have high stock returns, which is quite contradictory to the EMH, and find corporate governance is positively associated with stock returns.

However, Park, J. C. (2009) "investigates the stock market response to the announcement of excellent firm in corporate governance structure by the corporate governance service center (CGS)," and finds the announcement effects are not significantly different from zero. He concludes that firms with good governance are already recognized as superior firms by investors, therefore the information about governance is already reflected in stock prices, supporting the EMH.

Byun and Cho (2010) try to resolve the inconsistencies in previous literature on the effect of the corporate governance on firm values and stock returns. The articles in section 2.1, 'Ownership structure and firm value', mostly report positive associations between corporate governance and firm values, supporting the claim that good governance reduces agency costs and increases firm values by reducing the cost of capital. Additionally, Park, J. C. (2009) also claims that information about governance is already reflected in stock prices. However papers in this section - Yoon and Oh (2005), Park et al. (2009b), and Lee and Kim (2007) - present evidence that supports that "information on corporate governance has not been fully reflected in stock prices in the Korean stock market." They "reconcile these two contradictory findings by providing evidence that the realization of the effect of good corporate governance is contingent on the level of firms' information asymmetry." They find that investors do not really reflect the information only in case of higher information asymmetry.

Ⅴ. Determinants of Governance Structure

1. Managerial Compensation: Stock Options

Kim, C. S. (2004) examines the relations between corporate governance and performance of the firms that introduce stock options. Investigating the time series of stock price performances and the overreaction of the stock market to the stock option introduction, he suspects the possibility of market timing. He also finds a negative association between the performances after the stock option introduction and the shareholdings of the largest shareholder, but no relation for the firms with very high shareholdings of the largest shareholder. He interprets this as large shareholders playing the role of substitute to stock options. He also finds the substitutional role of shareholding of the second largest shareholder and foreigners.

Lee, Lee, and Park (2005) also find similar results. They find that "the significance of executives' stock options decreases as the extent of share holdings by the major owner and the management increases." It supports "the conflict of interests between shareholders and the management is diminished when share holdings by the management increases and that the controlling shareholders perform the monitoring function."

2. Share Ownership, Outside Directors, and Holding Company

Firms with lower managerial ownership are supposed to be associated with high agency costs, implying more need to monitor the managers. Consistent with this argument, Choi, Kim, and Kim (2003) find a negative association between the management's shareholding ratio and the ratio of outside directors, suggesting a substitutional role for outside directors and managerial ownership.

Ahn, Shin, and Chang (2005) examine the relationship between the foreign investors and information asymmetry, and find that "foreign ownership is significantly higher for firms with larger analyst coverage," suggesting that "the foreign investor prefers firms with lower information asymmetry."

Kang, Park, and Jang (2006b) test the hypothesis that "controlling families are as much interested in their controlling power as they are interested in firm performance." They find that control is a more important factor than firm value in the determination of ownership structure. "Controlling families prefer to own the shares of de facto holding companies that hold relatively larger ownerships of other affiliated firms in the group. ⋯ On the other hand, controlling families force their affiliated companies to own more shares of firms that provide the families with less of controlling power over other member firms."

Park, Lee, and Jang (2004) investigate the role of controlling shareholders in corporate governance. They find that "the controlling shareholder of a firm in general resists the introduction of governance mechanisms that strengthen the monitoring power of outside investors." They observe that "it suggests a necessity for regulatory intervention in setting corporate governance, and also for an active market for corporate control to complement internal governance."

Kim, Shin, and Goh (2009) investigate accounting practices around the chaebol transformation into holding companies, specifically, whether accounting transparency has improved after the transformation. They find that "business transparency does not improve under the governance of a holding company," and therefore, "capital market and government authorities should monitor holding companies more closely so that it can actually lead to improvement in corporate governance."

VI. Discussions and Conclusions

Existing work in corporate governance suggests that agency problems do exist and affect the policies and values of firms, and market discipline seems to be working to control managers to some extent. However, there are some discrepancies and inconsistencies in the empirical results. Some issues in empirical research design are covered in this section, followed by normative policy implications and suggested future research directions.

1. Problems in Research Design

First, there is the issue of the proper decision making unit in a firm. Researchers use managerial ownership as a proxy for agency costs, but it may be very difficult to properly identify who (or what) is the decision making unit of a firm. Is it a CEO, board of directors, controlling shareholders, or the largest shareholder? Still, there are additional dimensions to ownership structure: concentration ratio, degree of even distribution, and differences between the largest shareholder and second largest shareholder.

The second issue is about the proper relationships between variables in empirical test models. Is the relation between the two variables linear, square, or cubic? What about the piece-wise linear regression instead of OLS? Why not convert the ownership variables into category variables based on some range of the variable and use dummy variables instead?

The third issue is the handling of a pooled sample. Data are usually in the form of firm-year observations, mostly unbalanced panel. Most empirical tests are implemented using pooled OLS, considering all firm-observations as individual data points. One problem is "what if the corporate governance variables stays the same for many years, but other policies and performance measures vary each year?" (One solution might be the use of average figures.) Researchers need to check the stability or variability of variables.

The final issue is endogeneity problems. Instead of the RHS variables causing the LHS variables, there may be a reversed causality. This problem can be addressed properly if there is an instrument variable, which is exogenous but correlated with the potentially endogenous variable. Black, Jang, and Kim (2006) take advantage of the unique features of Korea's corporate governance rules to construct an instrument variable.[6]

---

6) Black, Jang, and Kim (2006) use an asset size dummy at 2 trillion won for an instrument for Korea corporate governance index (KCGI), because "several important Korean rules apply only to firms with assets of at least 2 trillion won (roughly US$2 billion)."

2. Normative Issues: Policy Implications

The efficiency of the chaebol system is one of the most important and contentious areas. On a micro-economic level, Joh (2003) finds a negative relation between ownership-control disparity and the profitability of firms. Yoon (2005) also reports the disparity is negatively associated with innovative activities, supporting the claim that the chaebol system is bad for the economy. On the other hand, Kang et al. (2005) find that large disparity does not hurt firm value (as measured by a market-to-book ratio) and operating performance. On a macro-economic level, Almeida and Wolfenzon (2006) note that "the role of the chaebols changed from being the driver of economic growth in the early stages of development to inhibiting development in its later stages ⋯ imposing negative externality to other small- and medium-sized firms by making it more difficult for good projects outside the conglomerate to raise funds." It may be the case that the effect of the chaebol system on the economy may be different on micro-level and macro-level.[7]

Controlling shareholders seem to exploit minority shareholders and "resist the introduction of governance mechanisms that strengthen the monitoring power of outside investors" (Park, Lee, and Jang, 2004). Furthermore, Morck et al. (2005) assert that "corporate control provides resources and power to influence institutional development. The whole body of economics suggests that such resources and power would be used to further the self-interest of those who wield them." Under this circumstance, regulatory intervention may be needed to set the governance rules, i.e., the rule-setting role of the government should be strengthened. But there is still the old dilemma of

---

7) Morck et al. (2005) observe that "concentrated control of a country's large corporations, as in family control pyramids, could serve important positive economic functions. It might help overcome market inefficiencies by facilitating monitoring, control, and capital allocation. But the concentrated control of a country"s large corporations might also induce microeconomic problems associated with entrenched management wielding control rights vastly disproportionate to their ownership stakes and macroeconomic resource misallocation."

"who monitors the monitor"; Government officials may also be plagued by agency problems.8) So a grand governance mechanism for the whole national system needs to be reviewed incorporating government officials (regulators) as players in a political economy game, employing the Virginia School's public choice approach.

3. Future Research Directions and Conclusion.

Investigation into the effect of disparity between cash flow rights and voting rights is one area where some discrepancies exist in existing research. Also, the efficiency of the chaebol system and the issue of tunneling are still unresolved areas. The Korean chaebol system may fit the category of oligarchic capitalism. Therefore, investigation into the topic of economic entrenchment seems to be a very important research topic.9)

The governance problem may be most prevalent in the area where the market is missing or not working properly, or where measuring performance is difficult. Non-profit organizations (NPO) and non-governmental organizations (NGO) seem to be promising areas where governance research is badly needed. Many irregularities in the administration of some private universities may be mostly due to agency problems, which can be analyzed with the analytical tools in corporate governance research. The methods and insights in corporate governance research can be applied out-

8) Claessensa et al. (2000) in explaining crony capitalism in East Asia, observe that "the concentration of corporate control in the hands of a few families creates powerful incentives and abilities to "lobby" government agencies and public officials for preferential treatment." and that "concentration of control might also have been a detriment to the evolution of the countries' legal systems." They conclude that "wealth concentration might have negatively affected the evolution of the legal and other institutional frameworks for corporate governance and the manner in which economic activity is conducted. It could be a formidable barrier to future policy reform."
9) Accdrding to Morch et al. (2005), "oligarchs wield their political influences to attain policies that preserve and expand their corporate governance power and thus sustain concentrated corporate control. This in turn preserves and expands the resources at their disposal for further political lobbying⋯. The concurrence of oligarchic capitalism, weak institutions, and slow growth in a stable, but Pareto-inferior, equilibrium, we call economic entrenchment."

side of the business area to identify inefficiencies and to suggest remedies due to agency problems. Like economic imperialism, it may be termed as "corporate governance imperialism." In these pursuits, interdisciplinary approaches-from political economy, law and economics, ethics, and cultural studies-will be useful in analyzing and explaining richer realities.

Researchers in corporate governance question even the integrity of managers instead of being satisfied with the role of just supplying instruments to managers as researchers in other disciplines in management sciences do. Researchers in corporate finance equipped with an agency theory think out of the box, asking the more fundamental problems. What if managers are bad? What if managers are plagued with agency problems? Researchers in corporate finance who have a way of seeing things differently have brought and will bring many spectacular achievements in both the academic and practical world.

Even with many discrepancies and conflicting results, there is some common ground. One of the most important prescriptions is that improvement in transparency is good. It makes market discipline possible, which is an effective antidote to agency problems without the side effects of corruption.[10] Further, achieving transparency in the modern world has become less costly with the development of information and telecommunications technology.

---

10) Djankov et al. (2008), observe that "countries with successful stock markets mandate that shareholders receive the information they need and the power to act on this information. There is no evidence that these countries rely heavily on fines and criminal sanctions." and that "to avoid self-dealing, however, it appears best to rely on extensive disclosure, approval by disinterested shareholders, and private enforcement."

References

Ahn, H. B., "The Study on the Relation of Firm Governance, Control Environment and Accounting Information Transparency", *Korea International Accounting Review*, Vol. 19(2007), pp. 109-137(in Korean).
안홍복, "기업지배구조, 통제환경 및 회계정보 투명성의 관련성 분석", 국제회계연구, 제19집(2007), pp. 109-137.

Ahn, H. B., "The Contestability of Multiple Shareholders in Governance and Firm's Value", *Korea International Accounting Review*, Vol. 25 (2009), pp. 91-111(in Korean).
안홍복, "기업지배구조에서 대주주간 경쟁가능성과 기업가치의 관련성 분석", 국제회계연구, 제25집(2009), pp. 91-111.

Ahn, Y. Y., H. H. Shin, and J. H. Chang, "The Relationship between the Foreign Investors And Information Asymmetry", *Korean Accounting Review*, Vol. 30, No. 4(2005), pp. 109-131(in Korean).
안윤영, 신현한, 장진호, "외국인 투자자와 정보비대칭 간의 관계", 회계학연구, 제30권 제4호(2005), pp. 109-131.

Almeida, H. and D. Wolfenzon, "Should business groups be dismantled? The equilibrium costs of efficient internal capital markets", *Journal of Financial Economics*, Vol. 79, No. 1(2006), pp. 99-144.

Bae, K. H., J. K. Kang, and J. M. Kim, "Tunneling or value added? evidence from mergers by Korean business groups", *Journal of Finance*, Vol. 57, No. 6(2002), pp. 2695-2740.

Bae, K. H. and C. W. Lim, "Why are Stock Returns of Business Groups Positively Skewed? Evidence from Korean Business Groups", *The Korean Journal of Finance*, Vol. 16, No. 1(2003), pp. 39-68(in Korean).
배기홍, 임찬우, "기업집단의 상호지원과 기업집단 소속 기업의 주가수익률 특성 : 조건부 왜도(conditional skewness)에 관한 실증적 연구", 재무연구,

제16권 제1호(2003) pp. 39-68.

Black, B. S., H. S. Jang, and W. C. Kim, "Does Corporate Governance Predict Firms' Market Values? Evidence from Korea", *Journal of Law, Economics, and Organization*, Vol. 22, No. 2(2006), pp. 366-413.

Black, B. S., H. S. Jang, and W. C. Kim, "Predicting Firm's Corporate Governance Choices: Evidence from Korea", *Journal of Corporate Finance*, Vol. 12, No. 3(2006), pp. 660-691.

Byun, H. S. and Y. H. Cho, "When Does the Information on Corporate Governance Affect Firm Values?: The Relationship Between Information Asymmetry and Cost of Capital", *Asian Review of Financial Research*, Vol. 23, No. 3(2010), pp. 213-248(in Korean).
변희섭, 조영현, "기업지배구조는 언제 기업가치에 영향을 미치는가? : 정보 비대칭과 자본비용의 관계", 재무연구, 제23권 제3호(2010), pp. 213-248.

Byun, H. Y., "The Cost of Debt Capital and Corporate Governance Practices", *Asia-Pacific Journal of Financial Studies*, Vol. 36, No. 5(2007), pp. 765-806.

Byun, H. Y. and L. S. Hwang, "Stock Price Synchronicity and Corporate Governance Practices", *Korean Management Review*, Vol. 36, No. 4(2007), pp. 939-979(in Korean).
변혜영, 황이석, "기업지배구조와 주가 동조화에 관한 연구", 경영학연구, 제36권 제4호(2007), pp. 939-979.

Chang, S. J. and J. B. Hong, "Economic performance of group affiliated companies in Korea: Intragroup resource sharing and internal business transaction", *Academy of Management Journal*, Vol. 43, No. 3(2000), pp. 429-448.

Cheon, Y. S., K. H. Choe, and H. Y. Gil, "How do managerial ownership and corporate governance affect the credit ratings of bonds?", *Korean Management Review*, Vol. 35, No. 5(2006), pp. 1393-1425(in Korean).

전영순, 최국현, 길형용, "기업의 소유지배구조가 무보증회사채의 신용등급 결정에 미치는 영향", 경영학연구, 제35권 제5호(2006), pp. 1393-1425.

Cho, J. H. and S. H. Jeong, "The Effect of Corporate Governance on Performance of Mergers and Acquisitions in KOSDAQ Market", *The Korean Journal of Financial Management*, Vol. 26, No. 2(2009), pp. 33-61(in Korean).
조지호, 정성훈, "코스닥시장에서 인수합병에 따른 성과와 소유구조", 재무관리연구, 제26권 제2호(2009), pp. 33-61.

Cho, J. H. and S. G. Jun, "The Effect of Corporate Governance on Performance of Mergers and Acquisitions", *The Korean Journal of Financial Management*, Vol. 21, No. 2(2004), pp. 1-25(in Korean).
조지호, 전상경, "기업지배구조가 인수합병의 성과에 미치는 영향", 재무관리연구, 제21권 제2호(2004), pp. 1-25.

Choi, J. H., S. J. Kim, and S. J. Kim, "An Empirical Study on the Agency Costs and Composition of Outside Directors to the Corporate Board", *Korean Accounting Journal*, Vol. 12, No. 2(2003), pp. 61-86(in Korean).
최정호, 김성진, 김성중, "대리인 비용과 사외이사 선임의 관련성에 관한 연구", 회계저널, 제12권 제2호(2003), pp. 61-86.

Choi, U. Y. and H. J. Bae, "The Effect of Corporate Governance on the Outsider CEO Turnover", *Accounting Information Review*, Vol. 27, No. 3(2009), pp. 95-124(in Korean).
최웅용, 배현정, "기업지배구조가 최고경영자 교체에 미치는 영향", 회계정보연구, 제27권 제3호(2009), pp. 95-124.

Gillan, S. L., "Recent Developments in Corporate Governance: An Overview", *Journal of Corporate Finance*, Vol. 12, No. 3(2006), pp. 381-402.

Gillan, S. L. and L. T. Starks, "A survey of shareholder activism: motivation and empirical evidence", *Contemporary Finance Digest*, Vol. 2, No. 3(1998), pp. 10-34.

Gugler, K., *Corporate Governance and Economic Performance*, Oxford University Press, 2001.

Jensen, M. C., "Agency Costs of Free Cash Flow, Corporate Finance, and Takeovers", *American Economic Review*, Vol. 76, No. 2(1986), pp. 323-329.

Jeong, J. H. and J. E. Kwon, "Large Shareholder Ownership and Opportunistic Behavior of Firm's Financing", *The Korean Journal of Finance*, Vol. 19, No. 2(2006), pp. 189-224(in Korean).

정진호, 권정은, "대주주 지분과 기회주의적 자본조달 행태에 관한 연구", 재무연구, 제19권 제2호(2006), pp. 189-224.

Jinn, T. H. and H. S. Song, "Valuation Effect of the equity Investment of Korean Firms", *The Korean Journal of Finance*, Vol. 16, No. 2(2003), pp. 163-193(in Korean).

진태홍, 송홍선, "기업 출자의 효율성에 관한 실증연구", 재무연구, 제16권 제2호(2003), pp. 163-193.

Joh, S. W., "Corporate governance and firm profitability: evidence from Korea before the economic crisis", *Journal of Financial Economics*, Vol. 68, No. 2(2003), pp. 287-322.

Kang, H. C., K. S. Park, and H. S. Jang, "Determinants of Internal Transactions among the Member firms of Korean Conglomerates", *The Korean Journal of Finance*, Vol. 19, No. 1(2006a), pp. 77-118(in Korean).

강형철, 박경서, 장하성, "기업집단의 계열사 간 거래의 결정요인", 재무연구, 제19권 제1호(2006a), pp. 77-118.

Kang, H. C., K. S. Park, and H. S. Jang, "Determinants of Family Ownerhsip: The Choice between Control and Performance", *Asia-Pacific Journal of Financial Studies*, Vol. 35, No. 6(2006b), pp. 39-75(in Korean).

강형철, 박경서, 장하성, "한국상장기업에 있어 지배주주 지분율의 결정요인 : 기업가치와 통제권간의 선택", 증권학회지, 제35권 제6호(2006b), pp. 39-75.

Kang, H. S., J. W. Park, and J. S. Baek, "Long-run Performance Following Private Placements of equity", *The Korean Journal of Finance*, Vol. 17, No. 2(2004), pp. 203-241(in Korean).

강효석, 박진우, 백재승, "사모주식발행의 장기성과 : 발행기업과 인수기업 주주의 부에 미친 영향을 중심으로", 재무연구, 제17권 제2호(2004), pp. 203-241.

Kang, J. K. and J. S. Baek, "The Efficiency of Business Group (Chaebol) and Shareholder Wealth Maximization: An Analysis of equity Issues", *The Korean Journal of Finance*, Vol. 15, No. 1(2003a), pp. 1-47(in Korean).

강준구, 백재승, "기업집단(재벌)의 효율성과 주주 부의 극대화 : 신주발행을 중심으로", 재무연구, 제15권 제1호(2003a), pp. 1-47.

Kang, J. K. and J. S. Baek, "The Study on the Efficiency of the Financing Decision in Korea: The Effect of Private equity Issues on Firm Value", *The Korean Journal of Finance*, Vol. 16, No. 1(2003b), pp. 69-113(in Korean).

강준구, 백재승, "국내기업 자본조달정책의 효율성에 관한 실증연구 : 기업집단의 사모주식발행과 기업가치", 재무연구, 제16권 제1호(2003b), pp. 69-113.

Kang, J. K., H. S. Na, and I. M. Lee, "Corporate Restructuring During Performance Declines: The Role of Ownership and Corporate Governance in Restructuring Activities and Post-Restructuring performance", *The Korean Journal of Financial*, Vol. 17, No. 2(2004), pp. 1-40(in Korean).

강준구, 나현승, 이인무, "영업성과 악화에 따른 기업의 대응방식과 이후의 성과 : 기업의 소유 및 지배구조 관점에서", 재무연구, 제17권 제2호(2004), pp. 1-40.

Kang, W., H. H. Shin, and J. H. Chang, "The Effect of a Disparity between

Cash Flow Right and Voting Right on Firm Value and Performance: The Case of Korean Large Business Groups", *The Korean Journal of Finance*, Vol. 18, No. 2(2005), pp. 1-39(in Korean).

강 원, 신현한, 장진호, "대규모기업집단의 지배-소유 괴리도와 기업가치 및 경영성과 간의 관계분석", 재무연구, 제18권 제2호(2005), pp. 1-39.

Kim, B. H., "Management Ownership and Valuation in the Korean Stock Market", *Asia-Pacific Journal of Financial Studies*, Vol. 30(2002), pp. 391-434(in Korean).

김병호, "기업의 소유구조와 기업가치 및 수익률에 대한 연구 : 임원지분율을 중심으로", 증권학회지, 제30권(2002), pp. 391-434.

Kim, C. S., "Stock Options and the Corporate Governance", *The Korean Journal of Financial*, Vol. 17, No. 1(2004), pp. 1-40(in Korean).

김창수, "스톡옵션과 기업지배구조", 재무연구, 제17권 제1호(2004), pp. 1-40.

Kim, C. S., "Outside Directors and Firm Value in Korea", *The Korean Journal of Finance*, Vol. 19, No. 2(2006), pp. 105-153(in Korean).

김창수, "한국의 사외이사제도 도입과 기업가치", 재무연구, 제19권 제2호(2006), pp. 105-153.

Kim, G. M., "Corporate Governance Structure and Innovation: The Influence of Ownership Structure on R&D Investment", *Korean Management Review*, Vol. 32, No. 6(2003), pp. 1799-1832(in Korean).

김경묵, "기업 지배구조와 혁신 : 소유구조가 연구개발 투자에 미치는 영향", 경영학연구, 제32권 제6호(2003), pp. 1799-1832.

Kim, G. M., "The orchestration of corporate governance structure: A balanced scorecard based evaluation of corporate governance structure", *Korean Management Review*, Vol. 35, No. 3(2006), pp. 899-934(in Korean).

김경묵, "기업 지배구조의 합주 : 균형성과표 개념 적용을 위한 기업 지배구조의 성과 분석", 경영학연구, 제35권 제3호(2006), pp. 899-934.

Kim, J. H., H. H. Shin, and J. M. Goh, "Transformation into Holding Company and Earnings Management", *Accounting Information Review*, Vol. 27, No. 4(2009), pp. 147-180(in Korean).

김치홍, 신현한, 고재민, "지주회사 전환이 이익조정에 미치는 영향", 회계정보연구, 제27권 제4호(2009), pp. 147-180.

Kim, M. H. and J. S. Baek, "Effects of Outside Directors Turnover on Firm Value", *Asia-Pacific Journal of Financial Studies*, Vol. 34, No. 2(2005), pp. 209-246(in Korean).

김문현, 백재승, "사외이사 해임정보가 기업가치에 미치는 영향", 증권학회지, 제34권 제2호(2005), pp. 209-246.

Kim, M. T. and G. Y. Park, "The Impacts of Audit Committees and Outside Directors on Managers' Perks and Efficiency Ratio", *Accounting Information Review*, Vol. 27, No. 2(2009), pp. 211-235(in Korean).

김문태, 박길영, "감사위원회와 사외이사가 경영자의 사적소비와 자산효율성에 미치는 영향", 회계정보연구, 제27권 제2호(2009), pp. 211-235.

Kim, Y. S. and J. C. Lee, "The Relationship between Corporate Value and Ownership Structure", *Asia-Pacific Journal of Financial Studies*, Vol. 26 (2000), pp. 173-197(in Korean).

김영숙, 이재춘, "기업가치와 기업소유구조와의 관련성", 증권학회지, 제26권(2000), pp. 173-197.

Lee, H. G. and Y. G. Son, "The Effect of Corporate Governance on Financial Performance and Firm Value", *Korean Journal of Accounting Research*, Vol. 14, No. 2(2009), pp. 317-339(in Korean).

이호갑, 손영건, "기업지배구조가 재무적 성과와 기업가치에 미치는 영향", 회계연구, 제14권 제2호(2009), pp. 317-339.

Lee, J. H. and Y. H. Kim, "The Effect of Corporate Governance on Stock Return", *Korean Journal of Accounting Research*, Vol. 12, No. 3(2007), pp. 57-80(in Korean).

이장희, 김연화, "기업지배구조가 주식수익률에 미치는 영향", 회계연구,

제12권 제3호(2007), pp. 57-80.

Lee, K. T. and J. W. Choi, "An Outside Assessment of the Corporate Governance Quality: The Directors' and Officers' Insurance Premium", *Korean Accounting Review*, Vol. 31, No. 4(2006), pp. 53-84(in Korean).
이경태, 최종원, "기업지배구조가 임원배상책임보험료에 미치는 영향", 회계학연구, 제31권 제4호(2006), pp. 53-84.

Lee, K. T., S. C. Lee, and A. Y. Park, "Effect of Ownership and Governance Structure on Executives' Stock Options", *Asia-Pacific Journal of Financial Studies*, Vol. 34, No. 3(2005), pp. 37-70(in Korean).
이경태, 이상철, 박애영, "소유 및 지배구조와 경영자 스톡옵션 보상", 증권학회지, 제34권 제3호(2005), pp. 37-70.

Lee, W. H., "A Study on Stock Price Response to Related-party Transactions", *Asia-Pacific Journal of Financial Studies*, Vol. 34, No. 4(2005), pp. 111-148(in Korean).
이원흠, "상장기업과 대주주와의 내부거래가 주가에 미치는 영향에 관한 실증연구", 증권학회지, 제34권 제4호(2005), pp. 111-148.

Lee, W. H., "The Effect of Controlling Shareholders and Related-Party Transactions on Firm Value", *The Korean Journal of Financial Management*, Vol. 23, No. 1(2006), pp. 69-100(in Korean).
이원흠, "대주주 소유구조 및 연계거래 여부가 기업가치에 미치는 영향에 관한 실증연구", 재무관리연구, 제23권 제1호(2006), pp. 69-100.

Lee, W. H., "A Valuation Model and Estimation of the Agency Costs", *Korean Journal of Financial Studies*, Vol. 38, No. 1(2009a), pp. 1-25(in Korean).
이원흠, "기업가치 평가모형과 대리인 비용의 추정에 관한 연구", 한국증권학회지, 제38권 제1호(2009a), pp. 1-25.

Lee, W. H., "Agency Costs of Related Party Transactions in the Internal Markets", *Korean Journal of Financial Studies*, Vol. 38, No. 2(2009b), pp. 257-288(in Korean).

이원흠, "대주주 연계거래의 대리인 비용에 관한 연구", 한국증권학회지, 제38권 제2호(2009b), pp. 257-288.

Lee, W. H., "Agency Costs of Self-Dealings in Korean Business Groups", *Korean Journal of Financial Studies*, Vol. 38, No. 4(2009c), pp. 454-477(in Korean).

이원흠, "대기업집단 내부거래의 대리인 가설 검정에 관한 연구", 한국증권학회지, 제38권 제4호(2009c), pp. 454-477.

Morck, R., D. Wolfenzon, and B. Yeung, "Corporate Governance, Economic Entrenchment, and Growth", *Journal of Economic Literature*, Vol. 43, No. 3(2005), pp. 655-720.

Park, B. J., "The Relationship between Ownership (and Outside Directors) and Firm Value in KOSDAQ", *The Korean Journal of Financial Management*, Vol. 24, No. 4(2007), pp. 45-73(in Korean).

박범진, "코스닥 상장법인의 소유구조 및 사외이사와 기업가치 간의 관련성 분석", 재무관리연구, 제24권 제4호(2007), pp. 45-73.

Park, H. J., H. H. Shin, and W. S. Choi, "The Korean Firms' Agency Costs and Firm Value: Role of Foreign Investors' Equity Ownership", *Korean Management Review*, Vol. 33, No. 2(2004), pp. 655-682(in Korean).

박헌준, 신현한, 최완수, "한국기업의 대리인 비용과 기업가치 : 외국인 지분의 역할", 경영학연구, 제33권 제2호(2004), pp. 655-682.

Park, J. C., "Market Response to the Announcement of Excellent Firm in Corporate Governance Structure by CGS", *Daehan Journal of business*, Vol. 22, No. 4(2009), pp. 2319-2337(in Korean).

박주철, "지배구조 우수기업 선정에 대한 시장반응", 대한경영학회지, 제22권 제4호(2009), pp. 2319-2337.

Park, J. I. and W. H. Kim, "The Relation between Board Composition and Firm Value", *Accounting Information Review*, Vol. 24, No. 1(2006), pp.

91-123(in Korean).

박종일, 김완희, "이사회 구성과 기업가치", 회계정보연구, 제24권 제1호 (2006), pp. 91-123.

Park, J. W. and J. S. Baek, "Corporate Governance and Shareholder Wealth Maximization: An Analysis of Convertible Bond Issues", *The Korean Journal of Financial Management*, Vol. 20, No. 2(2003), pp. 1-39(in Korean).

박진우, 백재승, "전환사채 발행과 주주 부의 극대화 : 기업지배구조와 관계를 중심으로", 재무관리연구, 제20권 제2호(2003), pp. 1-39.

Park, K. S., "Ownership Structure and Firm Value", *Asia-Pacific Journal of Financial Studies*, Vol. 30(2002), pp. 207-325(in Korean).

박기성, "소유구조와 기업의 회계적 성과 및 Tobin's Q의 관계에 관한 연구", 증권학회지, 제30권(2002), pp. 207-325.

Park, K. S., H. S. Byun, and E. J. Lee, "The Role of Controlling Shareholder in Corporate Management: Ownership Structure and Wage", *Asian Review of Financial Research*, Vol. 22, No. 4(2009a), pp. 1-32(in Korean).

박경서, 변희섭, 이은정, "지배주주의 존재가 기업경영에 미치는 영향 : 소유구조와 임금의 관계", 재무연구, 제22권 제4호(2009a), pp. 1-32.

Park, K. S., H. S. Byun, and E. J. Lee, "Do Ex Post Corporate Governance Premia Exist in the Korean Stock Market?", *Korean Journal of Financial Studies*, Vol. 38, No. 4(2009b), pp. 423-454(in Korean).

박경서, 변희섭, 이은정, "한국주식시장에 사후적 지배구조 프리미엄이 존재하는가?", 한국증권학회지, 제38권 제4호(2009b), pp. 423-454.

Park, K. S. and D. S. Cho, "Ownership Structure and Diversification Strategy", *Korean Management Review*, Vol. 31, No. 5(2002), pp. 1423-1443(in Korean).

박기성, 조동성, "소유 구조가 다각화 전략에 미치는 효과에 관한 연구", 경영학연구, 제31권 제5호(2002), pp. 1423-1443.

Park, K. S. and E. J. Lee, "How different is the effect of corporate governance

of financial institutions on corporate value? A comparison with manufacturing companies", *Korean Journal of Money and Finance*, Vol. 18,
No. 2(2004), pp. 129-155(in Korean).

박경서, 이은정, "기업지배구조가 기업가치에 미치는 영향에 있어 일반기업
과 금융기관 간 비교 연구", 금융연구, 제18권 제2호(2004), pp. 129-155.

Park, K. S., E. J. Lee, and H. S. Jang, 2004, "Role of Controlling Shareholders
in the Corporate Governance of Korean Firms", *The Korean Journal
of Finance*, Vol. 17, No. 2(2004), pp. 163-201(in Korean).

박경서, 이은정, 장하성, "대주주의 존재가 한국기업의 지배구조에 미치는
영향", 재무연구, 제17권 제2호(2004), pp. 163-201.

Park, S. H. and K. H. Yon, "The Effect of Corporate Governance on the
Level of a Firm's Cash Holdings", *Asian Review of Financial Research*,
Vol. 22, No. 2(2009), pp. 1-36(in Korean).

박순홍, 연강흠, "기업지배구조가 보유현금수준에 미치는 영향", 재무연구,
제22권 제2호(2009), pp. 1-36.

Park, Y. S. and N. G. Kim, "Corporate Governance and Firm Value: Agency
costs and efficiency of capital and R&D expenditures", *Korean Management Review*, Vol. 36, No. 5(2007), pp. 1203-1232(in Korean).

박영석, 김남곤, "기업지배구조와 기업가치 : 투자 효율성과 대리인 비용을
중심으로", 경영학연구, 제36권 제5호(2007), pp. 1203-1232.

Ryu, S. Y. and S. L. Joo, "The Factors of the Firms' Economic Goodwill
in KOSDAQ Market", *Korea International Accounting Review*, Vol.
20(2007), pp. 181-206(in Korean).

유성용, 주상룡, "코스닥 시장에서 경제적 영업권의 형성요인", 국제회계연
구, 제20집(2007), pp. 181-206.

Shin, H. H. and J. J. Chang, "Firm Performance Following CEO Turnover",
The Korean Journal of Finance, Vol. 16, No. 2(2003), pp. 231-256(in
Korean).

신현한, 장진호, "최고경영자의 교체에 따른 경영성과 변화", 재무연구, 제

16권 제2호(2003), pp. 231-256.

Shin, H. H. and J. J. Chang, "An Analysis of the Determinants of CEO Turnover: Firm Performance, Professional CEO, and Business Group", *Korean Management Review*, Vol. 34, No. 1(2005), pp. 289-311(in Korean).

신현한, 장진호, "최고경영자 교체에 영향을 미치는 요인분석 : 경영성과, 전문경영자, 대규모 기업집단", 경영학연구, 제34권 제1호(2005), pp. 289-311.

Shin, H. H., S. C. Lee, and J. J. Chang, "Outside Monitors and Firm Value", *The Korean Journal of Finance*, Vol. 17, No. 1(2004), pp. 41-72(in Korean).

신현한, 이상철, 장진호, "외부감시주체와 기업가치", 재무연구, 제17권 제1호(2004), pp. 41-72.

Shin, H. H. and Y. S. Park, "Financing Constraints and Internal Capital Markets: Evidence from Korean Chaebols", *Journal of Corporate Finance*, Vol. 5, No. 2(1999), pp. 169-191.

Shin, M. S. and S. E. Kim, "The Relations between Ownership Structure and Cash Holdings of Firms", *The Korean Journal of Financial Management*, Vol. 27, No. 1(2010), pp. 89-120(in Korean).

신민식, 김수은, "기업의 소유구조와 현금보유간의 관계", 재무관리연구, 제27권 제1호(2010), pp. 89-120.

Shleifer, A. and R. W. Vishny, "A survey of corporate governance", *Journal of Finance*, Vol. 52, No. 2(1997), pp. 737-783.

Yoon, B. H. and J. Y. Oh, "Korean Case Studies on Corporate Governance and Firm's Performance, Value and Market Returns", *Asia-Pacific Journal of Financial Studies*, Vol. 34, No. 1(2005), pp. 227-263(in Korean).

윤봉한, 오재영, "기업지배구조와 기업성과 및 기업가치 : 한국 상장기업에 대한 실증연구", 증권학회지, 제34권 제1호(2005), pp. 227-263.

Yoon, S. M., "Motives and Direction of Fund Transactions in the Internal Capital Market of Chaebol", *Asia-Pacific Journal of Financial Studies*, Vol. 33, No. 2(2004), pp. 45-82(in Korean).

윤성민, "재벌 내부자본시장에서의 자금거래 동기 및 지원방향", 증권학회지, 제33권 제2호(2004), pp. 45-82.

Yoon, S. M., "The Effects of Separation of Ownership and Control on Innovative Activity", *KyongJeHak YonGu*, Vol. 53, No. 1(2005), pp. 71-96(in Korean).

윤성민, "소유권-지배권 분리가 혁신활동에 미치는 영향", 경제학연구, 제53권 제1호(2005), pp. 71-96.

Any citation of this article must refer to the following: Kim, In Joon, "A Review of the Literature on Derivative Securities in Korea", Asian Review of Financial Research, Vol. 24 (2011), No. 4, pp. 1175-1230.

Chapter 10

A Review of the Literature on Derivative Securities in Korea

In Joon Kim*   Professor, School of Business, Yonsei University

Abstract

The main purpose of this paper is to review the literature on derivatives securities published in Korean finance and economics journals by focusing on three research areas: derivatives markets, the valuation of derivatives securities, and risk management. First, the literature on derivatives markets is reviewed in terms of four issues: the effects of launching the derivative securities on the underlying assets markets; the lead and lag effects between derivatives and the underlying assets markets, which have drawn substantial attention from academia; and the price discovery functions of derivatives markets as well as the expiration-day effects of options. In addition, papers analyzing arbitrage trading strategies with derivative securities are reviewed. Second, for the valuation of derivatives securities, we review papers presenting theoretical models for the pricing of futures, various types of options, and interest rate derivatives. Then, empirical papers on the valuation of derivative securities are reviewed. These papers examine empirically the distributions and stochastic processes of the underlying asset prices, as well as the behavior of volatilities in order to understand and overcome the limitations of the standard models. Third, we review the literature on risk management, which is regarded as one of the main functions of derivative securities. These papers investigated how to formulate effective hedging strategies using derivative securities. Finally, we make suggestions as to the next steps and directions for future research on derivative securities in Korea based on the review of the literature.

Keywords   Derivatives Markets, Futures, Options, Volatility, Hedge

---

* Hyundai Motors Distinguished Professor of Finance; **Address:** Yonsei University, 50 Yonsei-ro, Seodaemun-gu, Seoul 120-749, Korea; **E-mail:** ijkim728@yonsei.ac.kr; **Tel:** 82-2-2123-5489.

This paper is prepared as a part of the 2010 knowledge database project by the Korean Finance Association (KFA), and financially supported by KFA. The author thanks two referees, Jangkoo Kang and one anonymous referee for their helpful suggestions. The author would like to express special thanks to Sol Kim, Sun-Joong Yoon and Byung Jin Kang for the valuable comments and the useful suggestions, and Dong Haeng Lee and So Jung Kim for their assistance. All remaining errors are the author's own.

I. Introduction

The main economic function of derivative securities is to serve as tools to hedge financial risks and thereby to spread risks across economic agents. The early research on derivative securities in Korea focused on introducing the results of papers already published in the economics and finance journals of advanced countries.

The KOSPI 200 stock index futures and the KOSPI 200 stock index options were launched in May 1996 and July 1997 in Korea, respectively. The introduction of these new instruments represented the beginning of a new era in the history of the Korean financial markets. Since then, the trading volume of derivative securities in Korea has increased dramatically. The rapid expansion of these markets led to the development of various types of new derivative securities, generating substantial interest in original research on derivative securities in Korea. Additionally, the Capital Market Consolidation Act, implemented in February 2009, set to change the landscape of Korean financial markets in general and the derivatives markets in particular.

This paper attempts to review the literature on derivative securities published in Korean finance and economics journals in order to help readers understand the progress in research on derivative securities in Korea.

The rest of the paper is organized as follows. In the next section, we present a brief overview of the derivative security markets. We describe how derivatives markets have expanded globally as well as in Korea over the past decade. Next, we discuss the literature on derivative securities and their markets in Korea. The literature was divided into three research areas: derivatives markets, valuation of derivative securities, and risk management.

The literature on the derivatives markets is reviewed in terms of four issues: the effects of launching the derivative securities on the underlying assets markets; the lead and lag effects between derivatives and the underlying assets markets, which have drawn substantial attention from academia; and the price discovery functions of derivatives markets as well as the expiration day effects of options. In addition, papers analyzing arbitrage trading strategies with derivative securities are reviewed. The literature on the valuation of derivative securities is divided into two parts. First, we review papers focusing on theoretical pricing models for futures, various types of options, and interest rate derivatives. Then, empirical studies on the valuation of futures and options are reviewed. These papers examine the distributions and stochastic processes of the underlying asset prices as well as the behavior of volatilities in order to understand and overcome the limitations of the standard models. Next, we review research on risk management which is regarded as one of the main functions of derivative securities. The papers reviewed investigate how to formulate effective hedging strategies using derivative securities.

Finally, we summarize our discussions on the literature of derivative securities and the derivatives markets in Korea to draw concluding remarks on the current status of research. We also make suggestions as to the next steps and directions for future research on derivative securities in Korea based on the review of the literature.

II. A Brief Overview of the Derivative Securities Markets in Korea

We present a brief overview of the derivatives markets in Korea as background information necessary to understand the literature on derivative securities in Korea. The global derivatives markets have grown substantially over the last decade. Trading volume in terms of the notional amount outstanding at the end of 2009 was about 687 trillion dollars, up more than six times in the past 10 years. This figure amounted to approximately 12 times world GDP in 2009. According to the Bank for International Settlements (BIS), only around 10.6 percent of the notional amount outstanding was traded on the exchange markets at the end of 2009. The derivatives markets in terms of the notional amount outstanding have been growing at the rate of around 24 percent every year throughout the 2000s. The notional amount outstanding of the OTC markets, which accounted for more than 85 percent of the global derivatives markets, rose 24 percent per year over the previous decade. The exchange markets have grown as rapidly as the OTC markets, which increased 23 percent every year during the same period. But, the size of the exchange markets is much smaller than that of the OTC markets.

Global financial markets have expanded not only in terms of size, but also in the variety of products. Deregulation in global financial markets helped accelerate the development of complicated financial derivatives such as structured products, collateralized debt obligations (CDOs), credit default swaps (CDSs), and asset-backed securities (ABSs). The notional amount outstanding of CDSs reached 58.24 trillion dollars in December 2007, and has grown rapidly since being introduced in 1995 as a means to manage credit risk. These structured credit-linked securities and asset-backed securities were believed to trigger the global financial crises in 2007. The notional amount outstanding of credit-related derivatives such as CDSs, single name instruments and multi-name instruments, doubled each year since 2005, and was 116 trillion dollars in 2007, reaching to a record high. However, due to the global financial crises started in

2007, which were claimed to be caused by abuses of derivative securities, the size of the markets declined by 28.1 percent to 83.7 trillion dollars in 2008 and by 21.9 percent again to 65.3 trillion dollars in 2009. It is imperative to investigate what role derivative securities played in precipitating the global financial crisis.

In Korea, the KOSPI 200 index futures and the KOSPI 200 index options were introduced in May 1996 and in July 1997, respectively. The opening of the stock index futures and the options markets satisfied the diverse needs of market participants and furnished effective asset management tools such as risk hedging. In particular, the KOSPI 200 index options became the largest index options markets in the world. The Korean Exchange has listed a variety of derivatives instruments, but three products have been actively traded: the KOSPI 200 index derivatives, interest rate derivatives and foreign exchange derivatives.

As mentioned above, the global derivatives markets have grown dramatically in the 2000s as have the derivatives markets in Korea. During the same period, the total number of contracts traded in a month increased more than 13.3 times, and the trading values increased more than 8.3 times in the Korean derivatives markets. There were 43,849 thousand contracts with the contract value of 3,046,203 billion won traded in the KOSPI 200 index futures markets in 2005, but these figures increased to 83,117 thousand contracts with the contract value of 7,652,807 billion won in 2009. As for the KOSPI 200 index options, which are the world's most liquid equity index options, 2,535,202 thousand contracts with the contract value of 140,825 billion won exchanged hands monthly on average in 2005. The figure also increased to 2,920,991 thousand contracts with the contract value of 256,578 billion won in 2009. Korea has the most active exchange listing index futures and index options markets in the world. This is remarkable considering Korea's GDP level, and so it is worthwhile and interesting to investigate this curious phenomenon.

<Figure 1> Notional Amounts Outstanding on the Exchange and OTC Markets
(KRW trillion)

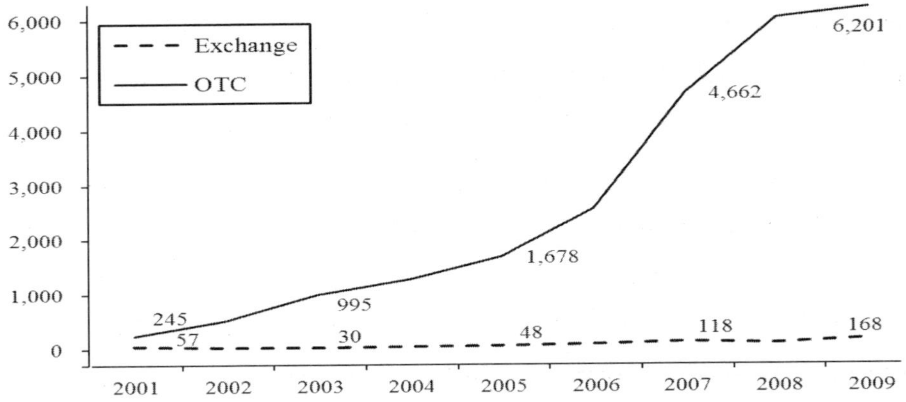

Source: Financial Supervisory Service.

According to the Financial Supervisory Service, the notional amounts outstanding in the exchange market steadily expanded to reach 118,239 billion won in December 2007. However, due to the global financial crisis, this amount declined 26.2 percent to 87,215 billion won in 2008, and rebounded to 168,257 billion won in 2009. The OTC markets have increased surprisingly. The notional amount outstanding in the OTC markets was 1,678,226 billion won in December 2005 and grew 3.7 times to 6,201,936 billion won in December 2009.

Although the market share of equity derivatives, 64.4 percent in 2009, was still dominant, interest rate and foreign exchange derivatives have increased their market shares in recent years. The trading volume of interest rate derivatives doubled from 3,037,340 billion won in 2006 to 6,757,807 billion won in 2009 and the trading volume of foreign exchange derivatives increased almost three times from 4,016,805 billion won to 11,548,033 billion won, respectively. Credit derivatives represented a minuscule portion, 5,377 billion won or 0.01% of the total trading value.

The Korean government enacted the Financial Investment Services and Capital Markets Act, commonly called the Capital Market Consolidation Act. The main purpose of the law is to spur competition among market participants and to encourage them to create more innovative financial products so as to foster the growth of capital markets in Korea. Since the act lowers the amount of capital that a financial institution is required to have in order to obtain a license to trade securities in the OTC markets, it is expected to increase the number of market participants. And the negative system under the act, which specifies the list of restricted financial products, will allow innovative derivatives with more diversified underlying assets, and induce market participants to trade aggressively in the markets. Therefore, we expect that the increasing number of market participants with innovative financial products will add more vitality to the Korean derivatives markets.

III. The Literature on Derivative Securities in Korea

1. The Derivative Securities Markets

Asset pricing theories were designed to present results that aid the understanding of the behavior and characteristics of equilibrium prices of securities. Most asset pricing models developed under the assumption of complete information; although these cannot explain how new information is reflected in securities prices or how investors' subjective expectations are revealed in the securities prices under an asymmetric information setting. Prices contain new information and investors' expectations in reality. The processes and consequences of trading assets under specified trading rules are examined in the studies on market microstructure. If two separate financial markets are efficient, two derivative securities in each market with the same underlying asset should respond identically when new information regarding the underlying asset is released.

To investigate such issues, the literature near to the introduction of the KOSPI 200 futures and options focused on behavior of the KOSPI 200 index. But, more recently many studies examine the influence of derivatives securities on entire stock markets, including stocks not represented in the stock index.

1.1 Effects on the Underlying Assets Markets

The earliest research on derivatives markets examines how the introduction of derivative securities influences the underlying assets markets. Even before derivative securities were introduced in Korea, research papers emerged to discuss the effects that derivative securities could bring to the underlying assets markets. As a matter of fact, the verification of such effects was useful in guiding us to design the markets when derivative securities were listed. The influence of stock index futures on the underlying stock markets has drawn more attention than that of the stock index options since the stock index futures markets were established a year before the stock index options markets.

Predating the opening of futures markets in Korea, Lee and Ohk (1992) examine the effects of the trades in stock index futures on stock market volatility and efficiency for the stock markets in Australia, Canada, Japan, Hong Kong, Sweden, the U.K., and the U.S. This study presents evidence indicating that the introduction of stock index futures led to an increase in stock market volatility. They also show that the futures markets can help to change the speed of stock index volatility absorption when shocks hit markets. Regarding volatility as information packets, decreasing the speed of absorption after introducing the stock index futures was interpreted as improvement of efficiency in the stock market, providing economic justification to introduce stock index futures contracts into Korea.

Many studies on these issues were carried out after the stock index derivative contracts were introduced into Korea. Kim, Kim and Park (1997) compare the KOSPI 200 and an alternative index that was not affected by stock index futures listing. They did not find any evidence that the start of trades in stock index futures increased stock index volatility. Kwon and Park (1997) compare the KOSPI 200 index return volatility to that of a matching set of stocks after controlling for cross-sectional differences in firm attributes known to affect volatility. They presented evidence showing that stock return volatility decreased after the KOSPI 200 index futures were listed. Although this study does not suggest what causes volatility to decrease, the KOSPI 200 index futures were shown to have effects on volatility that were different from those of previous studies. Also, Yang and Moon (1998), using the intervention analysis model, conclude that there was no intervention effects of the stock index futures contracts. However, using the KOSPI 200 data from 1990 to 2003, Ohk (2005) shows that KOSPI 200 index volatility and liquidity increased after the KOSPI 200 futures contracts were listed.

Before the introduction of index derivatives, their impact on the underlying asset markets had been debated; positive effects that the new financial products would enhance information efficiency and liquidity in the underlying asset markets and negative effects that they would increase volatility in the underlying assets markets due to increasing speculative transactions. Then, after opening of the derivatives markets, both effects were confirmed in empirical studies which have contributed to the development of the derivatives markets.

Kwon and Lee (2000) analyze the effects of the stock index futures and options trades on the volatility of the stock index, controlling firm characteristic factors and exchange rate premiums, to present evidence showing that trading of the derivative securities did not increase the volatility of the stock index. Ohk and Jang (2008) also examine the effects of the trading activity of the KOSPI 200 index options on the KOSPI 200 index volatility by classifying the types of the KOSPI 200 index options according to trading volume, open interests, information types, moneyness, and time to expiration. Their results showed that the trading volume of the KOSPI 200 index call options has a positive correlation with the volatility of the KOSPI 200 index for most cases. But, the correlation between trading volume and volatility of the KOSPI 200 index was ambiguous for the KOSPI 200 index put options, a result in contrast to that for the index call options.

In addition to stock index futures and options, the Korean Treasury Bonds (KTB) futures and the KTB futures options were introduced in 1999 and 2002. Kho and Kim (2002) examine the impacts of the KTB futures options on the intraday volatility of the KTB futures contracts to present the results indicating that volatility did not increase after controlling some relevant factors.

Summing up, whether or not volatility of the stock index increased due to listing of the stock index futures or options in Korean financial markets is inconclusive. Theoretically, financial futures contracts should not influence the underlying assets markets since financial futures contracts are redundant assets in perfect markets without frictions. In reality, however, frictions do exist and financial futures contracts provide means for hedging risk as well as for speculation with lower transaction costs than trading the underlying assets themselves. Options which are not redundant securities can be used for the same purposes.

Kim, Shin and Byun (1996) explore how dynamic trading strategies to hedge index options would influence the underlying assets markets. The Black-Scholes model represents a partial equilibrium model in which the stochastic process of the underlying asset would not be affected by dynamic trading strategies to hedge options. In reality, trading the underlying asset would influence the price of the underlying asset. They developed a model to examine the effects of dynamic trading strategies designed to achieve portfolio insurance on the underlying assets markets. The model allowed us to see why volatility in stock markets would go up if the payoff of index put options is synthesized by dynamic trading strategies which require buying the stock index if the stock index goes up and selling the stock index if the stock index goes down. The stock index would fluctuate more widely since dynamic trading strategies in this case have trend reinforcing effects on the stock index. Now, let us ask ourselves what would happen to the stock markets if more and more investors holding stock portfolios employ the same trading strategies? Eventually, it is not possible for every investor to execute the same trading strategies as volatility of the stock index goes up too high, precipitating a collapse of the financial markets. This is, we believe, what happened to the stock markets in the U.S. in October 1987.

1.2 Information Effects and Price Discovery

If investors have private information on the underlying assets or markets, derivative securities could be useful instruments to take advantage of such private information. The introduction of derivative securities, hence, allows new private information to be reflected in the prices of the underlying assets more efficiently through derivative markets. Such activities can increase the volatility of the prices as well as the liquidity of the underlying assets, and thereby improve the efficiency of the underlying assets markets. On the other hand, one can argue that stock market liquidity can be reduced with the introduction of the stock index futures and options as investors have alternative means to manage stock portfolios. Furthermore, since the positions in the stock index futures and options are highly levered, their prices can be relatively easily manipulated without a large amount of capital. Or, one can earn abnormally high returns on the positions in the stock index futures and options by manipulating the prices of the underlying assets. If these happen, the efficiency of the underlying assets markets would be sacrificed. This line of reasoning also suggests that an increase in volatility does not necessarily imply improvement of efficiency.

As mentioned above, theoretically, futures contracts on financial assets should not influence the underlying assets markets since financial futures contracts are redundant in perfect markets and information should be reflected simultaneously both in the financial futures markets as well as the underlying assets markets. In this case, we do not expect to find lead-lag relationships between financial futures markets and the underlying assets markets. In reality, however, information can be reflected more quickly in financial futures markets since higher leverage on futures contracts with lower transaction costs allows a higher return than the underlying assets for those with superior information. The same argument can be made for options.

Many studies were carried out to see if lead-lag relationships exist between the price of derivative securities and that of the underlying asset as well as between price and volume. Most studies on futures markets in other countries found that futures markets led the underlying assets markets, but studies on options markets did not provide consistent results. In Korea, the abundant data on the stock index, the stock index futures and the stock index options allowed many researchers to examine the lead-lag relationships in detail.

Lee and Min (1997), using the initial data for the four months after the KOSPI 200 index futures were listed in 1996, examine the lead-lag relationships between the KOSPI 200 markets and the KOSPI 200 index futures markets. They conclude that the KOSPI 200 index futures markets led the KOSPI 200 index markets. This paper had the limitation of relying on short-term data and could not pinpoint reasons for the lead-lag relationships. However, it provided useful results to facilitate the successful establishment of the future markets and helped to initiate research efforts to examine why the lead-lag relationships occurred. Other researchers such as Jeong and Seo (1999) examine the dynamic relationships between the stock index futures markets and the underlying index markets, by controlling non-synchronous trading. They found that the index futures markets changed more quickly than the underlying index markets because of the differences in transaction costs, leverage effect, liquidity, etc. Their study was useful to understand the meaningful lead-lag relationships by excluding those lead-lag relationships falsely observed due to non-synchronous trading. Kim and Kang (2000) shed additional light on the phenomenon that the index futures markets led the underlying cash markets. They argued that their results were attributable to the higher transaction costs and the short sales restriction in cash markets.

Lee and Hahn (2007) study the lead-lag relationships between the returns and the volume of the KOSPI 200 index markets and the KOSPI 200 index options markets in order to examine price discovery. The result indicated that the option volume might influence the stock returns indirectly via the option returns. Kim (2007) investigated the lead-lag relationships between the call-put options trading value ratio and the KOSPI 200 index returns, using the model proposed by Chen, Lung, and Tay (2005, 2006). The results show that the call-put options trading value ratios led the KOSPI 200 index returns. Kim and Hong (2004) compute implied stock prices based on the Black-Scholes model, and find that the implied prices were not significantly different from stock prices. Furthermore, they examine the lead-lag relationships between the implied stock prices and stock prices by using the vector autoregression (VAR) model, and reported bi-directional causality between options and stock markets.

Studies on the lead-lag relationships between markets are generally intended to see whether information is reflected simultaneously in derivatives markets and the underlying assets markets. A recent trend is to take the issues even further and to investigate how sensitive the reactions are for the given information and to examine price discovery functions of the derivative securities in more detail.

As the futures markets have grown over time, researchers became more interested in changes of price discovery and factors which influenced price discovery. Kim and Kim (2000) empirically examine price discovery of the KOSPI 200 index futures using the error correction model. They present results showing that the KOSPI 200 index futures markets led the KOSPI 200 index markets by approximately thirty-five minutes. This paper suggests that the lead-lag time decreased and the influence became stronger as the futures markets grew during the sample period. Kim and Ko (2000) examine the price and volume relationships between the KOSPI 200 index and the KOSPI 200 index futures by dividing the data set into two periods: pre-option listing and post-option listing. The analysis indicates that relationships between the KOSPI 200 index and the index futures strengthened with the passage of time and that the lead-lag time decreased; this was consistent with the results of Kim and Kim (2000). Using the data from 1997 to 2003, Lee (2006) estimates the contribution of the KOSPI 200 index futures on price discovery in the underlying index markets by the method suggested by Hasbrouck (1995). He shows that growth of the futures markets significantly contributed to the efficiency of the underlying asset markets and price discovery processes.

Unlike other studies, Kang, Lee and Park (2008) examine the information transmission processes between the KOSPI 200 futures markets and their underlying stock markets using the 10-second quote and trade data in order to avoid the bid-ask bounce effects. The results reveal that quote revisions through limit orders led trades through market orders and the futures markets tended to lead the stock markets in terms of quote revisions and trades.

As for the relationship between Equity Linked Warrants (ELWs) introduced in 2005 and their underlying assets, Yi (2007) investigates the price, volume, and volatility effects on the underlying stocks around the date of introducing ELWs. The study reports that the hedging effects on the price and volume of the underlying stocks increased on or prior to the date when the terms and conditions of ELWs were determined, and that short-term signaling effects on the price and volume of the underlying stocks increased one day after the introduction of ELWs. Ryu (2010) investigates the effects of introducing ELWs on the prices, trading volume, volatility, and systematic risk of the underlying stocks by using the event study methodology. The results showed no evidence of the hedging effects of issuers before the announcement dates and the information effects after the announcement dates. The results also indicated that short-sales restrictions became less binding as put ELWs provide investors with means to take short positions in the underlying stock.

Cho (2006) investigates whether the futures markets responded to the news more sensitively and used more diverse information than the underlying assets markets. This paper employs econometric analysis of information through an estimation of sensitivity and diversity. Both sensitivity and diversity were not significantly different in the two markets during the whole-period. Futures markets were more sensitive only in the most recent period, and were also more diverse only for the nearest-maturity contracts.

1.3 Expiration-Day Effects

How do the derivatives markets and the underlying assets markets behave on the expiration day of derivative securities? These phenomena are called "expiration-day effects." We expect that the volume and the volatility of both markets increase as derivatives positions are closed on the expiration day of derivative securities. Arbitragers using futures and options are exposed to risk if they do not close their positions before the derivative securities expire. Therefore, arbitragers need to trade the underlying assets to close positions during the period near the closing time of the underlying assets markets on the expiration day of derivative securities, forcing the volatility of the underlying assets to increase.

Many studies in other countries indicate that expiration-day effects were negligible, while some studies show that expiration-day effects were significant in the Korean financial markets. The significant expiration effects found in Korea might be due to speculative activities and arbitrage activities being more dominant than hedging activities in the derivatives markets.

With the help of the previously used six methodologies measuring volatility, Seo, Eom and Kang (1999) investigate the relationships among time to maturity, volume, and volatility using the price and volume data of the KOSPI 200 index futures from 1996 to 1998. They find that volume increases as the expiration date approaches. Even though volume and volatility had positive relationships, there was no evidence supporting expiration-day effects. Chay and Ryu (2006) analyze expiration-day effects of the KOSPI 200 futures and option contracts using the volume and volatility of the KOSPI 200 index from 1997 to 2004. They find expiration-day effects of the index futures and options and confirmed the presence of the abnormal returns on the index at the expiration day. They argued that the irregularity found on the expiration days of the index futures and options reflect the weakness of the Korean stock markets. Choe and Eom (2007) examine the expiration-day effects using the KOSPI 200 index and the non-KOSPI 200 index. They focus on individual stocks since the stock index could not reflect specific characteristics of individual stocks. The results support the finding that expiration-day effects exist in the index futures markets, although the expiration-day effects are not supported for the index options. Especially, the expiration-day effects in the Korean stock markets were evident in large capitalization stocks. This paper suggests that expiration-day effects were due to trading imbalances. The studies on the expiration-day effects in Korea do not provide consistent results. Presumably inconsistent results appear because the studies employed different methods using different time-period data.

As near-expiration options expire, next-to-near-expiration options become near-expiration options on the expiration day. In efficient markets, option prices should not be influenced by the rollover processes in which next to near-expiration options turn into near-expiration options. It is not unreasonable, however, to expect rollover effects since trading is most active for the near-expiration options in the KOSPI 200 index options markets. Kim, Lee and Cho (2005) analyze the rollover effects on the KOSPI 200 index option prices. Especially, they examine how the implied volatilities of next-to-near-expiration options change as they become near-expiration options. They present results confirming rollover effects, which lower the implied volatilities of the next-to-near-expiration KOSPI 200 index options.

1.4 Arbitrage Trading Strategies

We expect that the KOSPI 200 index futures, the KOSPI 200 index options and the KOSPI 200 index influence each other since the KOSPI 200 index futures and options contracts can be duplicated with the KOSPI 200 index. If any of them are mispriced, various arbitrage strategies can be implemented, eliminating mispricing.

Using data from 1996 to 1997, Tae (1997) examines whether futures prices are fairly determined in the KOSPI 200 index futures markets. The results showed that the KOSPI index futures prices were quite frequently underpriced in comparison with the theoretical price. Then, arbitrage opportunities on long futures and short underlying assets are presented. Kim and Lee (1998a) also find that arbitrage opportunities existed since the KOSPI 200 index futures were underpriced consistently and that price disparities were larger than those in 1997 as the KOSPI 200 index futures markets grew in volume. Chung (1999) also reports that there were frequent opportunities for institutional investors to make arbitrage profits and short index arbitrages occurred more often than long index arbitrages.

Lee (1998) examines the ex post arbitrage profitability, the ex ante arbitrage profitability, and profitability of early unwinding strategies. The ex ante arbitrage strategies did not bring significant profits even though the futures markets were considered to be inefficient in light of the ex post arbitrage opportunities. Also, the early unwinding strategies appear to be profitable for large institutional investors that can save transaction costs and execute arbitrage strategies using computerized systems.

Futures markets provide economic agents with vehicles to hedge the risk of the underlying assets. Long hedgers and short hedgers can eliminate uncertainty associated with the price at which they trade the underlying assets in the future by taking positions in the futures contracts. The long hedgers are able to eliminate risk of the underlying assets price going up by giving up the chance to buy the underlying assets at lower prices. The short hedgers are able to eliminate risk of the underlying assets' price going down by giving up the chance to sell the underlying assets at a higher price. Institutional investors and foreign investors who hold stock portfolios participate in the index futures markets as the short hedgers. Then, who are the long hedgers in the KOSPI 200 index futures markets? No definite answer can be given to this question. In other words, the KOSPI 200 index futures markets are dominated by the short hedgers, resulting in the underpricing of the futures contracts. Institutional investors taking short positions in the KOSPI 200 index futures for hedging purposes would not be interested in index arbitrage strategies.

Oh and Kim (2009) examine the implicit tax effects on the basis of KOSPI 200 index futures to explain the underpricing of futures contracts. The implicit taxes were expected to lower the before-tax rate of return on the synthetic bond and thus to shrink the size of the basis. The analysis indicates that implicit taxes were reflected and thus priced on the basis of the KOSPI 200 index futures.

Studies also were carried out to understand whether profits can be earned by individual investors from trading derivatives. Chung and Kim (2005) investigate the report of the Financial Supervisory Service to see if the behavior of the individual investors to buy the out-of-the-money options was excessively speculative. Using long period data covering six years, this paper reconfirms the huge losses of individual investors from the trading of options and find that a tendency of individual investors losing money from option trading persisted during the six-year period.

2. Valuation of Derivative Securities

2.1 Theoretical Valuation Models

Few papers have made a contribution to the literature on the theoretical models for option valuation. The Black-Scholes model, introduced in 1973, represents the backbone of the literature on derivative securities. The Black-Scholes model defines the value of options in a simple and closed-form equation with one unknown parameter, the volatility of gross returns. The underlying assumptions were relaxed in order to extend and generalize the Black-Scholes model. Kim (1992) relaxes the assumption of the constant interest rate, which implies the flat-term structure of the interest rates, and assumed stochastic interest rates to derive a closed-form equation defining the option values with one unknown parameter, the volatility of excess returns. The two models look alike except for the meaning of the single unknown parameter. Since the term structure of interest rates is not flat in reality, the valuation model used to compute implied volatility is not the Black-Scholes model but the model derived by Kim (1992). Furthermore, the implied volatility obtained is not volatility of gross returns, but volatility of excess returns.

Ki, Lee and Choi (2004) consider an option pricing model based on the assumption that stock returns have a leptokurtic distribution to examine the KOSPI 200 index options and find that market prices were closer to the option prices computed from the alternative model than those from the Black-Scholes model. Cho and Lee (2007) derive the Gerber-Shiu model with drift and jump components under the Levy process. They expand the Heston model by adopting a Gamma distribution that included jumps, and showed a better price-fitting performance of the model compared to that of the Black-Scholes.

American call options would be exercised early if the underlying asset pays dividends before the expiration. Roll (1977) derives a closed-form valuation equation for American call options under the assumptions of the constant interest rate and a single fixed amount of dividend from the underlying asset before expiration. Kim and Ryu (2000) employ the same concept in Kim (1992) to extend the valuation model of Roll (1977) to derive a closed-form valuation equation for American call options under the stochastic interest rates. American put options, which allow early exercise with or without dividends, do not lend themselves easily to closed-form solutions and can be valued by numerical methods. Song (1995) improved the accuracy of the analytic solution and expanded its application by comparing numerical methods in terms of computation speed as well as financial meaning.

Rhee and Chang (2004) develop a theoretical extension from the study of Dupire (1994) in order to derive a formula of local volatility surface when the stock price follows the geometric Levy processes. Ku, Eom and Jang (2007) examine an efficient way of implementing numerical analysis using characteristic function for pricing European options when the underlying asset price follows the Levy processes. They find that one can achieve the most efficient method when characteristic function is expressed in terms of the model in Bakshi and Madan (2000) and Gaussian quadrature numerical inversion method is employed at the same time.

Complexity of option structure has resulted in order to meet the diversified needs of consumers. Exotic options became more complicated and the closed-form pricing solutions were not available for them in many cases. As in the early literature on exotic options, Choi and Kim (1998) derive the closed-form valuation formulas from the outside double barrier options, 'knock-in' or 'knock-out' with two underlying variables.

The valuation of interest rate derivatives requires assumptions on the evolution of future interest rates. As an early study, Choi (1988) derives several pricing equations for interest rate futures, interest options, and options on interest futures under the assumption that the short interest rate follows the Ornstein-Uhlenbeck process. Rhee (2004) examines the pricing of interest rate derivatives such as caps and swaptions in which the underlying state variable is assumed to follow the general infinitely divisible Levy process. Ku, Eom and Ji (2006), under the stochastic interest rates assumption, derive closed or semi-closed-form solutions of the various types of barrier options in order to value equity linked products such as ELD (Equity Linked Deposit) and ELS (Equity Linked Securities).

The underlying asset for the KTB futures, which accounts for the largest portion of the interest rate derivatives markets in Korea, is an artificial bond with maturities of three years or five years and a face value of 100. There are two difficulties associated with computing the theoretical futures price. First, the underlying asset is a non-tradable hypothetical asset, even though the Korea Exchange has announced "theoretical" prices by using an ad hoc cost-of carry model. Second, the traditional cost-of-carry model is designed to explain the forward price which can be different from the futures price. Due to the daily resettlement of the futures contracts, differences between the forward and futures prices occur. Using an inappropriate model to compute the "theoretical" price of the KTB futures contracts can result in underpricing of the KTB futures contracts. To overcome these two difficulties, alternative models for pricing the KTB futures were proposed, such as the Black-Karasinski term structure model (Kang and Lee, 2002), and the Chan-Karolyi-Longstaff-Sanders (CKLS) model and the multifactor Vasicek model (Choi, Oh, and Seo, 2004).

2.2 Empirical Research on Valuation

The interest rate swap market in Korea developed after 2002 and has expanded rapidly since 2007. The swap rates were usually higher than the Treasury interest rates due to the liquidity and credit risk of interest rate swaps in most developed countries. However, since 2005, the negative swap spreads have persisted in the Korean fixed income markets. Choi, Ku and Eom (2010) document that the swap rates were significantly lower than its theoretical values estimated by the three factor affine term structure model. Then, they showed that the differences between the Korean won/American dollars currency swap rates and the interest rate swap rates had the most significant impact on the mispricing. Won (2010) argues that arbitrage transactions by foreigners in the interest rate swap market reduced the Korean swap rates more than the yields on the Korean Treasury bonds. Both of these papers were not able to fully explain why they persist in the Korean markets. It will be a challenging issue to investigate the persistency of negative swap spreads in the Korean interest rate swap market.

The Black-Scholes model with one parameter has been extensively used to analyze the derivative securities over the last 20 years, but empirical studies on the valuation models helped us realize the limitations of the assumption that the price of an underlying asset follows a geometric Brownian motion. The major differences between the assumption of the Black-Scholes model and the empirical results are as follows: the volatility of underlying assets is time-varying rather than constant and the distribution of stock returns is skewed, leptokurtic and/or fat-tailed instead of the normal distribution.

To reconcile the differences, jump processes and/or stochastic volatility were considered in the option valuation models, or alternative distribution for stock returns was assumed, or state density function was derived from option price data in the literature. Chang (1997) compares three models, a jump-diffusion model, a GARCH model, and a GARCH-jump model, and finds that there exists significant jump components even after taking account of the heteroscedasticity effects in financial markets. This approach generated more elaborate pricing models.

Wee, Wee, Tak and Lee (2006) examine statistical fitness of the option pricing model based on hyperbolic distribution for the KOSPI 200 index options and compare it with the Black-Scholes model. The results indicate that the hyperbolic model outperforms the Black-Scholes model. Recently, in order to explain the pricing errors, Kim (2006b) investigates whether skewness and kurtosis of the risk neutral distribution were relevant for the valuation of the KOSPI 200 index options, to obtain the results suggesting that skewness is an important parameter to be included in an option valuation model since skewness is related to the pricing errors with statistical significance. Han and Yun (2007) employ the stochastic volatility model introduced by Heston (1993) for the dynamic of the underlying assets and estimate the parameters of pricing kernel of the KOSPI 200 index options to find that the distribution had much higher skewness with thinner left and fatter right tails than the normal distribution.

Kim and Ryu (1993) examine whether the model derived by Kim (1992) showed better performance than the Black-Scholes model analyzing the data on the prices of the 5-years Scores. The main question in this study is whether volatility of gross returns is significantly different from volatility of excess returns. During the periods of stable interest rates, there were not significant differences between them.

Equilibrium prices of financial instruments are determined by demand and supply which are influenced by the degree of risk aversion and time preferences of market participants. The prices in the options markets allow us to infer the risk-neutral density functions introduced by Breeden and Litzenberger (1978), which in turn provide information on the state density function in underlying assets as well as investors' preferences. Lee and Lee (2005) carry out a comparative study of the risk-neutral implied distribution from the KOSPI 200 options markets, and compare it with a historical distribution, whose diffusion characteristic was estimated by a nonparametric kernel estimator. The diffusion term was estimated from the KOSPI 200 index data under the risk-neutral assumption and reflected into the future path via a Monte Carlo simulation resulting in a historically implied probability density distribution. The differences in the skewness and kurtosis between the two state price density distributions were regarded as a trading opportunity.

According to Bakshi and Madan (2006), the difference between the historical volatility and the risk-neutral volatility, termed volatility spreads, is determined by the risk aversion and the higher moments of return distribution. Based on this study, Byun, Yoon and Kang (2007) investigate the risk aversion implied in the KOSPI 200 options and explore relative importance between skewness and kurtosis. They find that the kurtosis of return distribution was relatively more important than the skewness on the KOSPI 200 option markets. In a subsequent study, Kang, Kim and Yoon (2008) directly assume the functional forms of investors' risk aversion in the KOSPI 200 options markets and discover that the estimated relative risk aversions sharply decrease across wealth levels. Byun, Yi and Kang (2010) examine the anomalies which were U-shaped patterns as a function of moneyness and negative values of implied risk aversion in the index options markets. They suggest that the phenomenon is caused by investors' heterogeneous beliefs. Kang, Kim, Ryu, and Yun (2008) estimate the pricing kernels implied by the KOSPI 200 index options. They find that the risk aversion implied by the estimated pricing kernels is time varying and has statistically significant relationships with the KOSPI 200 index returns and the lagged values of the risk aversion.

It has been reported that volatility sneers were observed for equity options in other countries. This phenomenon has also been observed in the KOSPI 200 options markets. Kwon and Lee (2008) compute the implied volatility for any given exercise price and time to expiration using the high frequency intraday data on the prices of the KOSPI 200 options to construct the implied volatility surface. They find sneer patterns in the KOSPI 200 options markets. Their findings were also supported by the early study by Moon and Kim (2001). The sneer phenomena in equity options markets also tends to show up in Korea.

The volatility smiles observed for options are not consistent with the implication of the Black-Scholes model. It is natural to ask what causes the volatility smiles. The volatility smiles have been taken as evidence that the Black-Scholes model cannot explain the market prices of options. In order to understand the volatility smiles, the Black-Scholes model has been extended by relaxing the assumption of the lognormal diffusion process for the evolution of the underlying asset price. Research efforts have concentrated on finding the stochastic processes for the evolution of the underlying asset price, which are consistent with the volatility smiles. We should ponder whether fruitful results were obtained from research in this direction which produced models with a large number of parameters. We do not have means to estimate those parameters from the time series data on the underlying asset prices. In this respect, it is useful to understand the results of Kim, Kim and Ziskind (1994) showing that volatility smiles could be explained by errors in option prices and the inverse of the vega. The in-the-money (ITM) options and the out-of-the-money (OTM) options tend to have positive pricing errors due to the upper and lower arbitrage bounds for options. The inverse of the vega measures a change in implied volatility due to a small error in option price. The inverse of the vega as a function of moneyness has the similar shape as volatility smiles. The positive pricing errors for the ITM options and the OTM options along with the U shape for the inverse of the vega can produce volatility smiles even if the market prices are generated by the Black-Scholes model.

If option markets are efficient and implied volatilities contain enough information about the underlying assets, the volatility index can be used as the anticipated future volatility values. Lee and Kwon (2001) and Lee and Chung (2006) derive a volatility index for the KOSPI 200 options markets and test its predictability. Eom, Ji, and Jang (2008) test whether the volatility index was an unbiased estimator of the future actual volatility. They show that the unbiasedness of the volatility index to the actual volatility is not rejected when some econometric issues are considered and that the volatility index had higher predictive power than those of other volatility measures such as historical volatilities.

Convertible bonds are hybrid securities, consisting of both bonds and options that can be converted into stocks and realize capital gains as stock price increases. Kim, Kim and Lee (2001) compute the theoretical prices of convertible bonds with resettable conversion prices and find that the convertible bonds were underpriced. They argue that the resettable feature is not helpful to prevent the convertible bonds from losing the value. In that sense, promising firms with high financial risk could raise capital with a lower coupon rate by utilizing convertible bonds with the resettable conversion prices.

Studies in exotic options usually draw attention when the instruments are introduced or debates regarding the exotic options are turned into a social issue in the markets. An example is the commercial papers (CP) with option features that caused liquidity risk for domestic credit card companies during the 2003 liquidity crisis in Korea. Won (2006) examines whether the CPs with option features were adequately priced by decomposing the CPs with option features into CPs and call options. Additionally, Ku, Eom and Ji (2007) examine the empirical implications of Ku et al. (2006) for the Equity Linked Securities (ELDs) by decomposing them into the straight bonds and equity options. They demonstrate that the stochastic interest rates assumption had little effect on the prices and the implied volatility model is a better fit than the historical one in explaining the issue prices of the ELDs.

Credit risk is an investor's risk of loss where a lender fails to make payments as promised in the event of the lender's default. As a way to hedge credit risk, investors can transfer credit risk through credit derivative securities which allow us to trade credit risk in the same way as market risk. Hence, we need to consider counterparty risks and default correlations between firms to estimate the accurate valuation. In that sense, the global financial crisis in 2007 ignited the literature on counterparty risk. Kim (2010) derives a pricing formula for a bond with counterparty risk based on the structural models instead of the reduced-form models. Kim (2009) also examines default correlation when the firm value is exposed to correlated jump risks. After extending the structural model of Merton (1974) to incorporate coskewness and cokurtosis between assets, Kim and Bae (2010) observe that the lower coskewness (or the higher cokurtosis) the larger default correlations. Instead of using multivariate Gaussian distribution of the asset returns to measure credit loss distribution, Choi and Min (2009) investigate whether the Gaussian model would be adequate even under the assumption that true distribution of the portfolio returns is non-normal other than the t-distribution, and show by a simulation analysis that the Gaussian model usually underestimated but sometimes overestimated the true values at risk (VaR).

Default correlation is an important element for a basket of credit derivative securities which are written on a bond portfolio. Credit risk is affected by a firm's specific factors and market factors. While the default risk of a firm is mostly dependent on systematic risk, it is also seriously correlated with the default risk of the other firms. This implies that the value of credit derivative securities needs to be evaluated in terms of portfolio risk rather than individual default risk. This is the reason why accurate default correlation is required to price credit derivatives securities such as CBO (Collateralized Bond Obligation), CLO (Collateralized Loan Obligation), CDS (Credit Default Swap). Through a study on credit derivatives valuation with default correlation, Kim, Byun and Park (2002) present a numerical procedure for pricing CBOs and analyze the impact of default correlations on the prices of CBOs by adopting the default correlation model of Zhou (2001) and the first passage time model of Black and Cox (1976). They compare the model prices with the CBO issue prices to find that no default correlation model overpriced the CBOs and the default correlation model underpriced the CBOs. Thus, their result highlights the role of default correlation in analyzing the CBOs.

Kim (2006a) uses a reduced-form model in order to price basket credit default swaps and synthetic CDOs, estimated default correlations depending on credit rating and industries, and investigates historical loss distribution of domestic firms using expected default frequency (EDF) data. The study demonstrates that multiple peaks were observed in the shape of a historical loss distribution, and this phenomenon could not be explained under the one factor Gaussian copula model. On the other hand, the stochastic correlation model with multiple systematic risk factors could be a candidate to explain multi-peak phenomenon.

Kang, Min and Lee (2010) demonstrate the usefulness of CDS spreads as a proxy for credit risk. They also realized that equity volatilities, leverage ratios, absolute bid-ask spreads, and CDS spreads on foreign exchange stabilization bonds issued by the Korean government were the most powerful variables in explaining CDS spreads of Korean corporations; they accounted for approximately 95% of CDS spreads and explained 21% of the differences in CDS spreads. Kim and Lee (2007) analyze the spreads obtained by the following two types of methods: one method used the market quotes of dollar-denominated CDSs issued by domestic firms; the other method used the credit spreads of won-denominated risky bonds. They find that the spreads of basket CDSs or single name CDSs with counterparty default risk has a negative relationship with asset return correlations.

3. Risk Management

One of the major economic functions of derivative securities is to hedge risk associated with the underlying assets. Empirical studies were conducted to compare hedging performance among various models that are designed to estimate hedging ratios. They are largely divided into naive or time-invariant models such as ordinary least square models (OLS) and vector error correction models (VECM), and time-varying hedge ratios models such as generalized autoregressive conditional heteroskedasticity (GARCH) models and exponential generalized autoregressive conditional heteroskedasticity (EGARCH) models during specified periods. Most studies conclude that there are no significant differences in hedging performance among these models for the KOSPI 200 index futures contracts (Lee and Jang, 2001; Hong and Moon, 2006), the KOSDAQ 50 index futures contracts (Moon and Hong, 2003), the KTB futures contracts (Jeong, Yim, and Won, 2002), and currency futures contracts (Kang, 2009).

These results are somewhat puzzling because periodic rebalancing of hedge portfolios using time varying hedge ratios resulted in no better hedging performance than the time-invariant hedge portfolios guided by the simple risk-minimization model. Here is our suggested explanation. First, hedging performance is affected by the special characteristics of the Korean futures markets. Most institutional investors in Korean financial markets who hold portfolios of the underlying assets take short positions to hedge risk associated with the underlying assets. Consequently, short hedgers are dominant in the futures markets. Speculators are willing to take long positions only if arbitrage opportunities arise. Thus, the futures markets experience imbalances of strong short positions, leading to the underpriced futures contracts for most of the time. Second, hedging performance has been affected by estimation errors of the models. The GARCH type models are required to estimate more parameters than OLS or VECM. Each parameter is prone to estimation errors. When there are many parameters, estimation errors of each parameter can interact inducing huge errors for the model as a whole. The greater errors due to more parameters could more than offset the higher accuracy achieved by the more elaborate GARCH type models.

Ohk (1997) draws our attention to a contrasting result which indicates that the time-varying hedge ratio models perform better that the simple models in formulating hedging strategies. He estimates the hedge ratios in two types of models considering transaction costs and tests the hedging performance directly using actual market prices. It is interesting to observe that hedge portfolios constructed based on the time-varying hedge ratio models yield higher returns than the simple model.

Many studies comparing the performance of pricing models indicate that more complex models generate values closer to market values than simple models such as the Black-Scholes model. However, in the case of comparing hedging performance, the studies show that the complex models do not always perform better than the simple one. Kang and Ryu (2009) examine the empirical performance of the standard GARCH-type models in terms of pricing and hedging options and find that the autoregressive conditional heteroskedasticity (ARCH) model shows generally good hedging performance. In other words, the elaborate models do not always allow better hedging performance than the simple model capturing the correlation structure between the path of the underlying asset returns and volatility, as well as describing the volatility clustering in the price data of the KOSPI 200 index options. Empirical findings suggest that the Black-Scholes model allows good hedging performance although there are some limitations as an option pricing model. This finding is strengthened by the study of Jung and Lee (2009) which compares the Black-Scholes model and the Heston model in terms of the hedging performance of dynamic hedging strategies using Monte Carlo simulation. They find that the performance of the Black-Scholes model was almost as good as that of the Heston model. What we can learn from these kinds of studies is that it is not necessarily desirable to develop complex models and to implement abstruse methodologies to explain phenomena in financial markets.

The risk of asset portfolios can be reduced in two ways. Unsystematic risk or idiosyncratic risk can be eliminated through diversification. On the other hand, systematic risk or market risk should be transferred to other economic agents through derivative securities. Since systematic risk arises due to uncertainty affecting an entire financial system or economy, the total amount of systematic risk is fixed. We can call it the "conservation law of systematic risk", and systematic risk cannot be eliminated from a financial system or an economy. The only way to reduce systematic risk is to transfer it to other economic agents as a risk premium. There are two ways to transfer systematic risk: static hedging strategies and dynamic hedging strategies.

Static hedging strategies permit us to maintain the positions in the derivative securities without adjusting hedge ratios in the hedge portfolios, while dynamic hedging strategies require adjusting the hedge ratios continuously to maintain delta neutral positions as the price of the underlying asset evolves stochastically. Dynamic hedging strategies rely on derivatives valuation theory such as the Black-Scholes model to compute hedge ratios. They are widely used in the risk management of financial assets including derivative securities. Portfolio insurance is a hedging strategy that is designed to make profits in bullish markets, but limit losses in bear markets. Portfolio insurance can be achieved by taking a long position in put options of the underlying asset or by following a dynamic trading strategy duplicating the payoff of the put options. To implement the dynamic trading strategy, one should purchase the shares of the underlying asset if the price goes up, and sell the shares of the underlying asset if the price goes down in order to maintain upside potential, but eliminate downside risk. Kim and Lee (1998b) compare and evaluate the performances of dynamic hedging strategies using the KOSPI 200 futures. They find that the portfolio loss was lower than the return of KOSPI 200 index during the period from May 1996 to June 1998 which included the Asian Financial Crisis of 1997. The strategies failed to adequately protect portfolio value in the bearish market.

Whereas stock index futures and options are extraordinarily liquid contracts, the trading volume of individual stock options is negligible in the Korean derivatives markets. This is one of the peculiar properties of emerging financial markets. ELSs and ELWs were introduced to substitute for individual stock options. If volatilities of individual stocks change with issuance and expiration of the ELS and ELW, the two products are regarded as individual stock options. Nam and Cho (2009) examine how issuance and expiration of ELSs and ELWs affect the volume as well as the volatility of the underlying asset. They present evidence that issuance of ELSs had significant positive effects on the volume and volatility of the underlying asset while ELWs did not have the same effects. These results can be interpreted that ELSs played the role of hedging vehicles, but ELWs as hedging vehicles for the underlying asset lacks evidence.

IV. Concluding Remarks

This paper intended to survey and review the literature on derivative securities and their markets as conducted and published in Korea over the past 25 years. The literature is too abundant to be covered by one paper. The focus of this paper is limited to a few issues of derivative securities and their markets. We feel that progress has been made in terms of the scope and size of the literature.

Derivative securities have been playing an important role in the Korean financial markets since the opening of the index futures markets in 1996, bringing strong interest in research on the related issues. The KOSPI 200 index futures and options markets have grown to the world's most liquid derivatives markets. We need to ask whether the trading volume in those markets is too large to be justified considering the economic fundamentals of Korea and what causes the substantial trading volume in those markets, how much of it represents hedging activities and how much of it comes from speculative activities. Further studies should be conducted in order to understand these puzzling phenomena. The main role of derivative securities is to reduce risk for individual economic agents and to spread risk among those agents in an economic system. We need to ask whether some derivative securities function against their intended purposes.

The derivatives markets cannot function without the underlying assets markets. Hence, it is important to understand how the derivatives markets interact with the underlying assets markets and what the outcomes of the interactions are. These are essential research issues for the derivatives markets. There appears some evidence indicating that the introduction of the stock index futures has tended to increase the volatility of the underlying stock index while the stock index options do not have the same effect. Empirical results were presented to imply that the stock index futures markets led the stock index markets while there was no definite evidence for the lead-lag relationships between the stock index options markets and the stock index markets. We need to understand how frictions interfere with information transmission among markets to have a better idea of the issues.

Too many efforts have been concentrated on developing alternative stochastic processes or distributions of the underlying asset prices to extend and generalize the Black-Scholes model which is inconsistent with the volatility smiles or sneers. The empirical validity of the alternative models which have many parameters has been examined by fitting the models to the data of option prices and the underlying asset prices. Pursuing research on valuation models in this direction would not be fruitful without considering the fundamental characteristics of the options markets and the basic properties of the option valuation models as indicated by Kim et al. (1994).

It is interesting to discover that hedging strategies with time-varying hedge ratios did not always perform better than the simple model with a constant hedging ratio and among the time-varying volatility models, the simplest ARCH model resulted in the best performance for hedging.

The Black-Scholes model, which is the simplest option valuation model, does not generate worse outcomes in terms of hedging performance than the stochastic volatility model of Heston. These results might imply that complex models are not always superior in explaining real world phenomena. Models with many parameters could have more explanatory power than those with fewer parameters. However, each parameter is subject to estimation errors which can adversely affect overall performances of the models. Furthermore, abstruse methodologies are required in order to estimate complex models. We need to consider the tradeoff between the explanatory power and the effects of estimation errors on performance in developing models.

Option pricing models, including the Black-Scholes model, are partial equilibrium models, assuming a stochastic process for the evolution of the underlying asset price as given exogenously. Dynamic hedging strategies to maintain delta neutral positions are assumed not to affect the stochastic process. In reality, however, the changes in the prices of derivative securities affect the movements in price and volatility of the underlying asset, and vice versa. This means that the derivatives markets and their underlying asset markets are affecting each other. Without a general equilibrium perspective, it is not possible to gain full understanding of what role derivative securities play in the financial markets.

The recent global financial crisis starting in 2007 differs from previous ones in which derivative securities were not a significant part of the financial markets. It is imperative to investigate how derivative securities precipitate global financial markets into crises. We point out how dynamic trading strategies for portfolio insurance can increase the volatility of the markets leading to market failure as more agents are drawn into the same trading strategies. What underlies these phenomena is the fallacy of composition. Portfolio insurance can be achieved by dynamic trading strategies from the view point of individual agents. If the same strategies are followed by every agent, however, no agent is able to achieve portfolio insurance. We introduce a concept called the "conservation law of systematic risk." Portfolio insurance by means of dynamic trading strategies is not a viable hedging method because it violates the "conservation law of systematic risk." It is an illusion to believe that any risk can be managed by dynamic trading strategies. Furthermore, overconfidence in the effectiveness of dynamic hedging strategies can encourage high risk investments, inducing instability in financial markets.

A large number of research works were reviewed in this paper to help understand the current status of the literature on derivative securities and their markets in Korea. This paper attempted to lay down the ground work for more fruitful future research by providing a critical assessment of some of the results in the literature and by emphasizing the more fundamental research issues.

References

Bakshi, G. and D. Madan, "Spanning and Derivative-Security Valuation", *Journal of Financial Economics*, Vol. 55(2000), pp. 205-238.

Bakshi, G. and D. Madan, "A Theory of Volatility Spreads", *Management Science*, Vol. 52(2006), pp. 1945-1956.

Black, F. and J. C. Cox, "Valuing Corporate Securities: Some Effects of Bond Indenture Provisions", *Journal of Finance*, Vol. 31(1976), pp. 351-367.

Black, F. and P. Karasinski, "Bond and Option Pricing When Short Rates Are Lognormal", *Financial Analysts Journal*, Vol. 47(1991), pp. 52-59.

Black, F. and M. Scholes, "The Pricing of Options and Corporate Liabilities", *Journal of Political Economy*, Vol. 81(1973), pp. 637-654.

Breeden, D. and R. Litzenberger, "Prices of State-Contingent Claims Implicit in Option Prices", *Journal of Business*, Vol. 51(1978), pp. 621-651.

Byun, Y. T., M. C. Yi, and T. H. Kang, "The Heterogeneity of Beliefs and Preferences Reflected in Implied Risk Aversion", *Korean Journal of Financial Management*, Vol. 27, No. 4(2010), pp. 175-205(in Korean).
변영태, 이명철, 강태훈, "내재위험회피도에 반영된 기대와 위험선호의 이질성", 재무관리연구, 제27권 제4호(2010), pp. 175-205.

Byun, S. J., S. J. Yoon, and B. J. Kang, "Volatility Spread on KOSPI 200 Index Options and Risk Aversion", *Korean Journal of Finance*, Vol. 20, No. 3(2007), pp. 97-126(in Korean).
변석준, 윤선중, 강병진, "KOSPI 200 지수 옵션 시장의 변동성 스프레드와 위험회피도", 재무연구, 제20권 제3호(2007), pp. 97-126.

Chan, K. C., G. A. Karolyi, F. A. Longstaff, and A. B. Sanders, "An Empirical Comparison of Alternative Models of the Short-Term Interest Rate", *Journal of Finance*, Vol. 47, No. 3(1992), pp. 1209- 1227.

Chang, K. H., "Jump Risks and Heteroscedasticity in Korean Financial Markets", *Asia-Pacific Journal of Financial Studies*, Vol. 20(1997), pp.

273-299(in Korean).

장국현, "한국 자본시장의 점프위험과 조건부 이분성에 관한 연구", 증권학회지, 제20권(1997), pp. 273-299.

Chay, J. B. and H. S. Ryu, "Expiration-day Effects of the KOSPI 200 Futures and Options", *Asia-Pacific Journal of Financial Studies*, Vol. 35, No. 1(2006), pp. 69-101(in Korean).

최종범, 류혁선, "KOSPI 200 선물 및 옵션의 만기일 효과", 증권학회지, 제35권 제1호(2006), pp. 69-101.

Chen, C., P. Lung, and N. Tay, "Information Flow between the Stock and Option Markets: Where do Informed Traders Trade?", *Review of Economics Studies*, Vol. 14(2005), pp. 1-23.

Chen, C., P. Lung, and N. Tay, "Informed Trading under Different Market Conditions and Moneyness: Evidence from TXO Options", *Working paper*, Western Kentucky University(2006).

Cho, D., "Do the Futures and Spot Markets Respond Differently to the News?: An Empirical Study of KOSPI 200 Futures Market", *Korean Journal of Financial Management*, Vol. 23, No. 2(2006), pp. 85-107(in Korean).

조 담, "선물 및 현물시장은 뉴스에 대해 동일하게 반응하는가? : 코스피200 선물시장에 대한 실증적 연구", 재무관리연구, 제23권 제2호(2006), pp. 85-107.

Cho, S. M. and P. S. Lee, "Option Pricing Models with Drift and Jumps under Levy Processes: Beyond the Gerber-Shiu Model", *Korean Journal of Financial Management*, Vol. 24, No. 4(2007), pp. 1-43(in Korean).

조승모, 이필상, "Levy 과정 하에서 추세와 도약이 있는 경우 옵션가격결정 모형 : Gerber-Shiu 모형을 중심으로", 재무관리연구, 제24권 제4호(2007), pp. 1-43.

Choe, H. and Y. S. Eom, "Expiration-day Effects: The Korean Evidence", *Korean Journal of Financial Management*, Vol. 24, No. 2(2007), pp.

41-79(in Korean).

최혁, 엄윤성, "주가지수 선물과 옵션의 만기일이 주식시장에 미치는 영향 : 개별 종목 분석을 중심으로", 재무관리연구, 제24권 제2호(2007), pp. 41-79.

Choi, H. B., B. I. Ku, and Y. H. Eom, "An Empirical Study of KRW Interest Rate Swap Market: Focused on 'Mispricing' Compared to Theoretical Fair IRS Rates and Arbitrage Opportunities", *Asia-Pacific Journal of Financial Studies*, Vol. 39, No. 1(2010), pp. 59-101(in Korean).

최한복, 구본일, 염영호, "원화스왑 시장에 대한 실증연구 : 이론 이자율 스왑 금리 대비 평가오차와 차익거래 유인 분석을 중심으로", 증권학회지, 제39권 제1호(2010), pp. 59-101.

Choi, H. S., "The Pricing of Interest Rate Securities: Interest Rate Futures, Interest Rate Option and Option on Interest Futures", *Korean Journal of Finance*, Vol. 1(1988) pp. 49-72(in Korean).

최흥식, "금리증권의 가격결정 : 선물, 옵션, 선물 옵션을 중심으로", 재무연구, 제1권(1988), pp. 49-72.

Choi, H. S. and S. H. Kim, "A Valuation for the Outside Double Barrier Options", *Asia-Pacific Journal of Financial Studies*, Vol. 22(1998), pp. 139-161(in Korean).

최흥식, 김상환, "Outside Double Barrier Options의 평가", 증권학회지, 제22권(1998), pp. 139-161.

Choi, P. S. and I. S. Min, "A Simulation Analysis for Gaussian Credit Risk Model", *Journal of Money and Finance*, Vol. 23, No. 1(2009), pp. 1-23(in Korean).

최필선, 민인식, "정규분포 신용리스크 모형의 추정 성과 시뮬레이션", 금융연구, 제23권 제1호(2009), pp. 1-23.

Choi, Y. S., S. J. Oh and J. Y. Seo, "Korean Treasury Bond Futures Pricing Model", *Korean Journal of Futures and Options*, Vol. 12, No. 1(2004), pp. 1-22(in Korean).

최영수, 오세진, 서재영, "국채선물 이론가격 결정모형", 선물연구, 제12권 제1호(2004), pp. 1-22.

Chung, J. M. and J. K. Kim, "The KOSPI 200 Index Option Trading Behavior and Performance of Individual Investors", *Korean Journal of Futures and Options*, Vol. 13, No. 1(2005), pp. 99-127(in Korean).
정재만, 김재근, "개인 투자자의 옵션 매매 성과와 행태", 선물연구, 제13권 제1호(2005), pp. 99-127.

Chung, M. K., "Examination of Intraday Behavior of KOSPI 200 Futures Mispricing Series: Focusing on the Arbitrage Profitability for Institutional Investors", *Asia-Pacific Journal of Financial Studies*, Vol. 24(1999), pp. 169-201(in Korean).
정문경, "KOSPI 200 지수선물가격의 일중괴리율 행태와 위탁자의 차익거래기회 분석", 증권학회지, 제24권(1999), pp. 169-201.

Dupire, B., "Pricing with a Smile", *Risk*, Vol. 7(1994), pp. 18-20.

Eom, Y. H., H. J. Ji, and W. W. Jang, "The Predictability of Volatility Index in KOSPI 200 Option Market", *Journal of Money and Finance*, Vol. 22, No. 3(2008), pp. 1-33(in Korean).
엄영호, 지현준, 장운욱, "변동성지수의 미래예측력에 대한 연구", 금융연구, 제22권 제3호(2008), pp. 1-33.

Financial Supervisory Service, "Trading Volume and Notional Amounts Outstanding of Korean Derivatives 2009", *Business Report*, Financial Supervisory Service, 2010(in Korean).
금융감독원, "2009년 금융회사의 파생상품 거래 및 2009년 말 잔액현황", 업무자료, 금융감독원, 2010.

Gerber, H. U. and E. S. W. Shiu, "Option Pricing by Esscher Transforms", *Transactions of Society of Actuaries*, Vol. 46(1994), pp. 99-140.

Han, S. I. and C. H. Yun, "The Estimation of Pricing Kernel of KOSPI 200 Options under Stochastic Volatility", *Korean Journal of Futures and Options*, Vol. 15, No. 1(2007), pp. 135-165(in Korean).
한상일, 윤창현, "확률변동성 구조하에서 KOSPI 200 옵션의 가격 커널 추정”, 선물연구, 제15권 제1호(2007), pp. 135-165.

Hasbrouck, J., "One Security, Many Markets: Determining the Contributions to Price Discovery", *Journal of Finance*, Vol. 50(1995), pp. 1175-1199.

Heston, S. L., "A Closed-Form Solution for Options with Stochastic Volatility with Applications to Bond and Currency Options", *Review of Financial Studies*, Vol. 6(1993), pp. 327-343.

Hong, C. H. and G. H. Moon, "A Study on the Cross Hedge Performance of KOSPI 200 Stock Index Futures", *Korean Journal of Financial Management*, Vol. 23, No. 1(2006), pp. 243-266(in Korean).
홍정효, 문규현, "코스피 200 주가지수선물을 이용한 교차헤지", 재무관리연구, 제23권 제1호(2006), pp. 243-266.

Jeong, J. H., B. J. Yim, and C. H. Won, "Estimation of the Optimal Hedging with the KTB Futures in Korean Bond Market", *Asia- Pacific Journal of Financial Studies*, Vol. 30(2002), pp. 163-188(in Korean).
정진호, 임병진, 원종현, "국채선물을 이용한 적정 헤지비율 추정에 관한 연구", 증권학회지, 제30권(2002), pp. 163-188.

Jeong, J. Y. and S. G. Seo, "Dynamic Relationships between the Stock Index Futures Market and the Cash Market", *Korean Journal of Financial Management*, Vol. 16, No. 2(1999), pp. 337-364(in Korean).
정재엽, 서상구, "주가지수 선물시장과 현물시장 간의 동적관련성에 관한 실증적 연구", 재무관리연구, 제16권 제2호(1999), pp. 337-364.

Jung, D. S. and S. W. Lee, "Dynamic Hedging Performance and Test of Options Model Specification", *Korean Journal of Financial Management*, Vol. 26, No. 3(2009), pp. 227-246(in Korean).
정도섭, 이상휘, "시뮬레이션을 이용한 동태적 헤지성과와 옵션 모형의 적격성 평가", 재무관리연구, 제26권 제3호(2009), pp. 227-246.

Kang, B. J., T. S. Kim, and S. J. Yoon, "Implied Risk Preferences from Option

Prices: Evidence from KOSPI 200 Index Options", *Korean Journal of Futures and Options*, Vol. 16, No. 2(2008), pp. 1-35(in Korean).
강병진, 김동석, 윤선중, "KOSPI 200 지수옵션 투자자들의 위험회피성향에 관한 실증연구", 선물연구, 제16호 제2권(2008), pp. 1-35.

Kang, J., B. C. Kim, D. J. Ryu, and J. S. Yun, "A Study on Empirical Pricing Kernels: A Case of the KOSPI 200 Options", *Korean Journal of Finance*, Vol. 21, No. 3(2008), pp. 91-137(in Korean).
강장구, 김병천, 류두진, 윤재선, "실증적 추계 할인율에 대한 연구 : KOSPI 200 옵션 시장을 중심으로", 재무연구, 제21권 제3호(2008), pp. 91-137.

Kang, J. and J. J. Lee, "Pricing KTB Futures: An Application of Black-Karasinski Model", *Korean Journal of Futures and Options*, Vol. 10, No. 2(2002), pp. 1-23(in Korean).
강장구, 이정진, "한국 선물거래소의 국채선물의 가격 추정 : Black-Karasinski 모형의 응용", 선물연구, 제10권 제2호(2002), pp. 1-23.

Kang, J., S. Lee, and H. J. Park, "Information Transmission between Cash and Futures Markets through Quote Revisions and Order Imbalances", *Korean Journal of Financial Management*, Vol. 25, No. 4(2008), pp. 117-144(in Korean).
강장구, 이순희, 박형진, "Information Transmission between Cash and Futures Markets through Quote Revisions and Order Imbalances", 재무관리연구, 제25권 제4호(2008), pp. 117-144.

Kang, J., J. H. Min, and C. J. Lee, "An Empirical Analysis on the Determinants of Credit Default Swap Spreads", *Journal of Money and Finance*, Vol. 24, No. 2(2010), pp. 99-128(in Korean).
강장구, 민준홍, 이창준, "CDS 스프레드의 결정요인에 대한 연구", 금융연구, 제24권 제2호(2010), pp. 99-128.

Kang, J. and D. J. Ryu, "A Study on the Empirical Performance of GARCH-type Models in the KOSPI 200 Options Market", *Asia-Pacific Journal of Financial Studies*, Vol. 38, No. 2(2009), pp. 137-176(in

Korean).

강장구, 류두진, "옵션 시장에서 GARCH 계열 모형들의 성과비교에 관한 연구", 증권학회지, 제38권 제2호(2009), pp. 137-176.

Kang, S. K., "The Analysis and Comparison of the Hedging Effectiveness for Currency Futures Markets: Emerging Currency versus Advanced Currency", *Korean Journal of Financial Management*, Vol. 26, No. 2 (2009), pp. 155-180(in Korean).

강석규, "통화선물 시장의 헤징유효성 비교 : 신흥통화 대 선진통화", 재무관리연구, 제26권 제2호(2009), pp. 155-180.

Kho, B. C. and J. W. Kim, "Intraday Price Change and Trading Volume in the KTB Futures and Futures Option Markets", *Korean Journal of Futures and Options*, Vol. 10, No. 2(2002), pp. 57-94(in Korean).

고봉찬, 김진우, "국채 선물 및 옵션 시장의 일중 가격변화와 거래량", 선물연구 제10권 제2권(2002), pp. 57-94.

Ki, H. S., M. Y. Lee, and B. W. Choi, "Option Pricing with Leptokurtic Feature", *Korean Journal of Financial Management*, Vol. 21, No. 2(2004), pp. 211-233(in Korean).

기호삼, 이미영, 최병욱, "급첨분포와 옵션 가격결정", 재무관리연구, 제21권 제2호(2004), pp. 211-233.

Kim, C. K. and H. Lee, "Arbitrage Opportunities of Stock Index Futures Market in Korea", *Korean Journal of Financial Management*, Vol. 15, No. 1(1998a), pp. 95-116(in Korean).

김철교, 이현, "국내 주가지수 선물시장에서의 차익거래기회", 재무관리연구, 제15권 제1호(1998a), pp. 95-116.

Kim, H. S., "The Effects of Correlated Jump Risks on Default Correlation", *Korean Journal of Futures and Options*, Vol. 17, No. 1(2009), pp. 1-20(in Korean).

김화성, "상관점프 위험이 부도상관관계에 미치는 영향", 선물연구, 제17권 제1호(2009), pp. 1-20.

Kim, H. S., "A Structural Model with Counterparty Risks", *Korean Journal of Futures and Options*, Vol. 18, No. 3(2010), pp. 25-40(in Korean).
김화성, "상대방 부도위험을 고려한 구조모형", 선물연구, 제18권 제3호 (2010), pp. 25-40.

Kim, H. S. and K. I. Bae, "Default Correlations in the Presence of Coskewness and Cokurtosis between Two Firm Values", *Korean Journal of Futures and Options*, Vol. 18, No. 2(2010), pp. 1-17(in Korean).
김화성, 배광일, "두 기업가치 간에 공왜도 및 공첨도가 존재할 경우 부도상 관관계", 선물연구, 제18권 제2호(2010), pp. 1-17.

Kim, I. J., "A Simple Approach to the Valuation of Options under Stochastic Interest Rates", *Korean Journal of Financial Management*, Vol. 9, No. 1(1992) pp. 25-33(in Korean).
김인준, "추계적 이자율 하에서 옵션평가를 위한 단순접근법", 재무관리연 구, 제9권 제1호(1992) pp. 25-33.

Kim, I. J., S. J. Byun, and Y. J. Park, "The Impact of Default Correlations on the Prices of Collateralized Bond Obligations", *Korean Journal of Futures and Options*, Vol. 10, No. 1(2002), pp. 113-142(in Korean).
김인준, 변석준, 박윤정, "부도 상관관계를 고려한 채권 담보부 증권(CBO) 가격결정의 실증연구", 선물연구, 제10권 제1호(2002), pp. 113-142.

Kim, I. J., T. S. Kim, and Y. Lee, "An Empirical Study on Valuation of Convertible Bonds with Adjustable Conversion Price", *Korean Journal of Futures and Options*, Vol. 9, No. 2(2001), pp. 195-216(in Korean).
김인준, 김동석, 이용, "전환가격 재조정이 포함된 전환사채의 가치평가에 관한 실증연구", 선물연구, 제9권 제2호(2001), pp. 1-23.

Kim, I. J., T. S. Kim, and G. Y. Park, "The Effects of Introducing Stock Index Futures on the Stock Market Volatility: An Empirical Evidence in Korea", *Korean Journal of Futures and Options*, Vol. 5, No. 1(1997), pp. 59-84(in Korean).
김인준, 김동석, 박건엽, "주가지수 선물거래 도입이 주식시장 분산성에 미

치는 영향 : 한국에서의 실증분석", 선물연구, 제5권 제1호(1997), pp. 59-84.

Kim, I. J., K. C. Kim and R. Ziskind, "On the Apparent Systematic Bias of Implied Volatility in the Black and Scholes Model", *Advances in Investment Analysis and Portfolio Management*, Vol. 2(1994), pp. 133-158.

Kim, I. J. and H. S. Ryu, "Stochastic Interest Rates and Implied Volatilities: An Empirical Study Using Scores", *Korean Journal of Finance*, Vol. 6(1993), pp. 137-153(in Korean).

김인준, 류혁선, "추계적 이자율과 암묵적 변동성 : Scores를 이용한 실증분석", 재무연구, 제6권(1993), pp. 137-153.

Kim, I. J. and J. H. Ryu, "Compound Option Pricing under Stochastic Interest Rates", *Korean Journal of Futures and Options*, Vol. 7(2000), pp. 1-19(in Korean).

김인준, 류정호, "추계적 이자율 하에서의 복합옵션 평가모형과 응용", 선물연구, 제7권(2000), pp. 1-19.

Kim, I. J., D. K. Shin and S. J. Byun, "A Study on the Relationship between Portfolio Insurance Strategies Using the Stock Index Futures and the Stock Market Volatility", *Korean Journal of Futures and Options*, Vol. 4(1996), pp. 45-68(in Korean).

김인준, 신동국, 변석준, "주가지수선물을 이용한 포트폴리오 보험전략과 주식시장 변동성의 관계에 관한 연구", 선물연구, 제4권(1996), pp. 45-68.

Kim, M. A., "Historical Credit Portfolio Loss Distribution: Using Expected Default Frequency", *Asia-Pacific Journal of Financial Studies*, Vol. 35, No. 5(2006a), pp. 109-136(in Korean).

김미애, "신용 포트폴리오의 역사적 손실분포 추정 : EDF를 이용하여", 증권학회지, 제35권 제5호(2006a), pp. 109-136.

Kim, M. A. and J. H. Lee, "A Study on Determining the Spreads of Won-Denominated Credit Default Swaps", *Korean Journal of Finance*,

Vol. 20, No. 1(2007), pp. 1-33(in Korean).

김미애, 이지현, "원화신용디폴트스왑의 스프레드 결정에 관한 연구", 재무연구, 제20권 제1호(2007), pp. 1-33.

Kim, S., "Which One is More Important Factor for Pricing Options, Skewness or Kurtosis?", *Korean Journal of Futures and Options*, Vol. 14, No. 2(2006b), pp. 25-50(in Korean).

김 솔, "위험중립분포 왜도, 첨도의 옵션 가격결정에 대한 영향력", 선물연구, 제14권 제2호(2006b), pp. 25-50.

Kim, S., "Information Contents of Call-Put Options Trading Value Ratio", *Korean Journal of Futures and Options*, Vol. 15, No. 2(2007), pp. 31-53(in Korean).

김 솔, "콜/풋옵션 거래금액 비율의 정보효과", 선물연구, 제15권 제2호(2007), pp. 31-53.

Kim, S. and T. S. Kim, "The Price Discovery Role of the Stock Index Futures and the Stock Index: A Cointegration Approach", *Korean Journal of Futures and Options*, Vol. 7(2000), pp. 87-115(in Korean).

김 솔, 김동석, "주가지수 선물과 주가지수의 가격발견기능에 관한 실증연구 : 공적분과 오차수정 모형", 선물연구, 제7권(2000), pp. 87-115.

Kim S. K. and C. H. Hong, "The Relationship between Stock and Option Markets: An Empirical Analysis Using Implied Stock Prices", *Asia-Pacific Journal of Financial Studies*, Vol. 33, No 3(2004), pp. 95-122(in Korean).

김서경, 홍정훈, "내재주가지수를 이용한 옵션 시장과 주식시장의 상호관계에 관한 실증연구", 증권학회지, 제33권 제3호(2004), pp. 95-122.

Kim, S. K. and K. S. Ko, "An Analysis of Transactions Data for The Relationship between Index and Index Futures", *Asia-Pacific Journal of Financial Studies*, Vol. 27(2000), pp. 101-137(in Korean).

김서경, 고광수, "주가지수와 주가지수 선물 관계의 일중 거래 자료 분석", 증권학회지, 제27권(2000), pp. 101-137.

Kim, S. Y. and H. I. Lee, "An Empirical Study on the Performance of Dynamic Hedging Strategy Using KOSPI 200 Futures", *Asia-Pacific Journal of Financial Studies*, Vol. 23(1998b), pp. 119-144(in Korean).
김석용, 이하일, "KOSPI 200 선물을 이용한 동적 헤징전략에 관한 실증적 연구", 증권학회지, 제23권(1998b), pp. 119-144.

Kim, T. H. and S. K. Kang, "A Study on the Linear Causality between KOSPI 200 Intraday Futures Returns and the Cash Returns", *Korean Journal of Financial Management*, Vol. 17, No. 1(2000), pp. 203-226(in Korean).
김태혁, 강석규, "KOSPI 200 하루 중 선물수익률과 현물수익률 간의 선형인 과성에 관한 연구", 재무관리연구, 제17권 제1호(2000), pp. 203-226.

Kim, T. Y., J. H. Lee, and J. W. Cho, "Rollover Effects on KOSPI 200 Index Option Prices", *Korean Journal of Financial Management*, Vol. 22, No. 1(2005), pp. 71-91(in Korean).
김태용, 이중호, 조진완, "KOSPI 200 지수 옵션 만기시 Rollover 효과에 관한 연구", 재무관리연구, 제22권 제1호(2005), pp. 71-91.

Korea Exchange, *KRX Fact Book 2009*, Korea Exchange, 2010.

Ku, B. I., Y. H. Eom, and W. W. Jang, "An Efficient Numerical Method for Pricing Levy Option Models: with Variance Gamma Process", *Korean Journal of Futures and Options*, Vol. 15, No. 2(2007), pp. 1-29(in Korean).
구본일, 엄영호, 장운욱, "Levy 옵션 모형의 효율적 수치방법 : Variance Gamma 과정을 중심으로", 선물연구, 제15권 제2호(2007), pp. 1-29.

Ku, B. I., Y. H. Eom, and H. J. Ji, "Pricing Barrier Options in a Stochastic Interest Rate Model", *Korean Journal of Finance*, Vol. 19, No. 1 (2006), pp. 155-186(in Korean).
구본일, 엄영호, 지현준, "확률적 이자율 모형 하에서의 베리어 옵션 가격결정", 재무연구, 제19권 제1호(2006), pp. 155-186.

Ku, B. I., Y. H. Eom, and H. J. Ji, "An Empirical Study on the Pricing

Model of Equity Linked Deposit", *Korean Journal of Finance*, Vol. 20, No. 1(2007), pp. 35-76(in Korean).

구본일, 엄영호, 지현준, "주가연계예금(Equity Linked Deposit) 가치평가모형에 대한 실증연구", 재무연구, 제20권 제1호(2007), pp. 35-76.

Kwon, S. S. and J. H. Lee, "The Function of Intraday Implied Volatility in the KOSPI 200 Options", *Asia-Pacific Journal of Financial Studies*, Vol. 37 No. 5(2008), pp. 913-948(in Korean).

권상수, 이재하, "KOSPI 200 옵션의 일중 변동성함수", 증권학회지, 제37권 제5호(2008), pp. 913-948.

Kwon, T. H. and H. M. Lee, "An Empirical Test of the Effect of KOSPI 200 Futures and Options Trading on Korean Stock Market Volatility", *Korean Journal of Finance*, Vol. 13, No. 2(2000), pp. 103-133(in Korean).

권택호, 이해문, "KOSPI 200 선물과 옵션 거래가 주식시장의 변동성에 미친 영향에 대한 실증분석", 재무연구, 제13권 제2호(2000), pp. 103-133.

Kwon, T. H. and J. W. Park, "The Effects of KOSPI 200 Futures Trading in the Spot Market's Volatility", *Korean Journal of Financial Management*, Vol. 14, No. 2(1997) pp. 57-81(in Korean).

권택호, 박종원, "KOSPI 200 선물거래가 현물시장의 변동성에 미치는 영향", 재무관리연구, 제14권 제2호(1997) pp. 57-81.

Lee, I. H. and J. H. Lee, "A Comparative Study on KOSPI 200 Index State Price Density", *Asia-Pacific Journal of Financial Studies*, Vol. 34, No. 2(2005), pp. 153-180(in Korean).

이인형, 이준행, "KOSPI 200 지수의 상태 가격 밀도 비교 분석", 증권학회지, 제34권 제2호(2005), pp. 153-180.

Lee, J. H., "The Intraday Ex-ante Profitability of Arbitrage between the KOSPI 200 Futures and Options and the Early Unwinding Strategy", *Asia-Pacific Journal of Financial Studies*, Vol. 23(1998), pp. 145-186(in Korean).

이재하, "KOSPI 200 선물과 옵션 간의 일중 사전적 차익거래 수익성 및 선종결전략", 증권학회지, 제23권(1998), pp. 145-186.

Lee, J. H. and J. R. Chung, "Derivation and Analysis of Volatility Index in the KOSPI 200 Options Market", *Asia-Pacific Journal of Financial Studies*, Vol. 35, No. 2(2006), pp. 109-138(in Korean).
이재하, 정제련, "KOSPI 200 옵션 시장에서의 변동성지수 산출 및 분석", 증권학회지, 제35권 제2호(2006), pp. 109-138.

Lee, J. H. and D. H. Hahn, "Lead-Lag Relationship between Return and Volume in the KOSPI 200 Spot and Option Markets", *Korean Journal of Futures and Options*, Vol. 15, No. 2(2007), pp. 121-143(in Korean).
이재하, 한덕희, "KOSPI 200 현물 및 옵션 시장에서의 수익률과 거래량 간의 선도·지연관계", 선물연구, 제15권 제2호(2007), pp. 121-143.

Lee, J. H. and G. Y. Jang, "Hedging Strategies with the KOSPI 200 Futures", *Asia-Pacific Journal of Financial Studies*, Vol. 28(2001), pp. 379-417(in Korean).
이재하, 장광열 "KOSPI 200 선물을 이용한 헤지전략", 증권학회지, 제28권(2001), pp. 379-417.

Lee, J. H. and S. S. Kwon, "The Predictability of Implied Volatility in KOSPI 200 Options", *Korean Journal of Futures and Options*, Vol. 9, No. 1(2001), pp. 25-50(in Korean).
이재하, 권상수, "KOSPI 200 옵션 내재변동성의 예측력", 선물연구, 제9권 제1호(2001), pp. 25-50.

Lee, P. S. and J. S. Min, "Relations for Day Trading Between Stock Index Futures Return and the Spot Return", *Korean Journal of Financial Management*, Vol. 14, No. 1(1997), pp. 141-169(in Korean).
이필상, 민준선, "주가지수 선물수익률과 현물수익률 간의 일중관계에 관한 연구", 재무관리연구, 제14권 제1호(1997), pp. 141-169.

Lee, S. B. and K. Y. Ohk, "Are Stock Index Futures Trading Increasing Stock Market Efficiency and the Dispersion?", *Asia-Pacific Journal of Financial Studies*, Vol. 14(1992), pp. 245-282(in Korean).

이상빈, 옥기율, "주가지수 선물의 거래는 주식시장의 분산성과 시장 효율성을 증가시키는가?", 증권학회지, 제14권(1992), pp. 245-282.

Lee, W. B., "An Empirical Analysis on Change in Price Discovery of KOSPI 200 Futures through Market Maturity Process", *Korean Journal of Futures and Options*, Vol. 14, No. 2(2006), pp. 51-77(in Korean).
이우백, "KOSPI 200 선물시장 성숙화에 따른 가격발견의 변화 분석", 선물연구, 제14권 제2호(2006), pp. 51-77.

Merton, R. C., "On The Pricing of Corporate Debt: the Risk Structure of Interest Rates", *Journal of Finance*, Vol 29, No. 2(1974), pp. 449-470.

Moon, G. H. and C. H. Hong, "Risk Management with KOSDAQ50 Index Futures Markets", *Korean Journal of Futures and Options*, Vol. 11, No. 2(2003), pp. 51-79(in Korean).
문규현, 홍정효, "코스닥시장의 가격변동 위험관리", 선물연구, 제11권 제2호(2003), pp. 51-79.

Moon, S. J. and D. H. Kim, "An Empirical Study on Price Gap and the Cause in KOSPI 200 Index Options", *Korean Journal of Finance*, Vol. 14, No. 1(2001), pp. 89-120(in Korean).
문성주, 김대호, "KOSPI 200 지수 옵션의 가격괴리 및 원인에 관한 실증연구", 재무연구, 제14권 제1호(2001), pp. 89-120.

Nam, K. T. and H. Cho, "Empirical Study of Volume and Volatility Effects Associated with ELS and ELW Issuance", *Korean Journal of Futures and Options*, Vol. 17, No. 3(2009), pp. 1-21(in Korean).
남경태, 조훈, "ELS와 ELW의 발행이 기초자산의 거래량 및 변동성에 미치는 영향에 관한 실증연구", 선물연구, 제17권 제3호(2009), pp. 1-21.

Oh, J. M. and W. H. Kim, "Tax Effects on the Basis of KOSPI200 Index Futures", *Korean Journal of Futures and Options*, Vol. 17, No. 4(2009), pp. 105-135(in Korean).
오종문, 김완희, "주가지수선물 베이시스에 대한 암묵세효과", 선물연구, 제17권 제4호(2009), pp. 105-135.

Ohk, K. Y., "An Empirical Study on the Asymmetric Effect of News on Volatility", *Asia-Pacific Journal of Financial Studies*, Vol. 21(1997), pp. 295-324(in Korean).

옥기율, "주가변동성의 비대칭적 반응에 관한 실증적 연구", 증권학회지, 제21권(1997), pp. 295-324.

Ohk, K. Y., "The Effect of Futures Trading on Spot Market Liquidity", *Korean Journal of Futures and Options*, Vol. 13, No. 1(2005), pp. 29-52(in Korean).

옥기율, "선물거래가 현물시장의 유동성에 미치는 영향에 관한 연구", 선물연구, 제13권 제1호(2005), pp. 29-52.

Ohk, K. Y. and W. A. Jang, "According to Time-moneyness in Option Market on Stock Price Volatility", *Korean Journal of Futures and Options*, Vol. 16, No. 2(2008), pp. 37-65(in Korean).

옥기율, 장우애, "만기-행사가격별 옵션 거래활동이 주가변동성에 미치는 영향", 선물연구, 제16권 제2호(2008), pp. 37-65.

Rhee, J. H., "Derivatives Pricing in the Positive Interest Rates", *Korean Journal of Futures and Options*, Vol. 12, No. 2(2004), pp. 157-179(in Korean).

이준희, "이자율 파생상품에 관한 연구", 선물연구, 제12권 제2호(2004), pp. 157-179.

Rhee, J. H. and K. H. Chang, "Volatility Smile Surface for Levy Option Pricing Model", *Korean Journal of Futures and Options*, Vol. 12, No. 1(2004), pp. 73-86(in Korean).

이준희, 장국현, "Levy 주가 옵션 모형에서의 Smile Surface", 선물연구, 제12권 제1호(2004), pp. 73-86.

Roll, R., "An Analytic Valuation Formula for Unprotected American Call Options On Stocks with Known Dividends", *Journal of Financial Economics*, Vol. 5(1977), pp. 251-258.

Ryu, D., "Effects of Introducing Equity-Linked Warrants on Stock Market

Behavior", *Korean Journal of Futures and Options*, Vol. 18, No. 4(2010), pp. 23-50(in Korean).

류두진, "주식워런트 증권 도입의 영향력에 대한 연구 : 주식시장의 행태를 중심으로", 선물연구, 제18권 제4호(2010), pp. 23-50.

Seo, S. G., C. J. Eom, and I. C. Kang, "An Empirical Test for the Relationship among Maturity, Volume and Volatility in the Korean Stock Index Futures Market", *Korean Journal of Financial Management*, Vol. 16, No. 1(1999), pp. 193-222(in Korean).

서상구, 엄철준, 강인철, "한국주가지수 선물 시장에 있어서 만기, 거래량, 그리고 변동성간의 관계에 관한 실증연구", 재무관리연구, 제16권 제1호 (1999), pp. 193-222.

Song, Y. H., "The Optimal Exercise Boundary of American-Style Options and Price Estimation Using the Numerical Method", *Korean Journal of Finance*, Vol. 10(1995), pp. 31-56(in Korean).

송영효, "수치해석 방법을 이용한 미국형 옵션의 최적 행사 경계 및 가격 추정", 재무연구, 제10권(1995), pp. 31-56.

Tae, S. J., "The Study on Arbitrage in the Korea Stock Index Futures Market", *Korean Journal of Financial Management*, Vol. 14, No. 3 (1997), pp. 289-318(in Korean).

태석준, "한국주가지수 선물시장에서의 차익거래에 관한 연구", 재무관리 연구, 제14권 제3호(1997), pp. 289-318.

Wee, I. S., J. B. Wee, R. H. Tak, and J. H. Lee, "Hyperbolic Pricing Model for Options on KOSPI 200", *Asia-Pacific Journal of Financial Studies*, Vol. 35, No. 2(2006), pp. 177-196(in Korean).

위인숙, 위정범, 탁래현, 이종현, "Hyperbolic pricing model for options on KOSPI 200", 증권학회지, 제35호 제2호(2006), pp. 177-196.

Won, S. Y., "Analysis on the Characteristics and Fair Value of 'Option CP'", *Korean Journal of Futures and Options*, Vol. 14, No. 1(2006), pp. 1-24(in Korean).

원승연, "옵션 CP의 성격과 적정가격에 대한 연구", 선물연구, 제14권 제1호 (2006), pp. 1-24.

Won, S. Y., "Covered Interest rate Arbitrage Trading and Negative Spreads of Interest Rate Swap in Korea", *Korean Journal of Futures and Options*, Vol. 18, No. 1(2010), pp. 43-75(in Korean).
원승연, "차익거래와 스왑스프레드의 역전현상", 선물연구, 제18권 제1호 (2010), pp. 43-75.

Yang, S. K. and S. J. Moon, "The Intervention Effects of Introducing Stock Index Futures on Stock Market", *Korean Journal of Financial Management*, Vol.15 No.1(1998), pp. 165-181(in Korean).
양성국, 문성주, "주가지수선물 도입이 주식시장에 미치는 개입효과", 재무관리연구, 제15권 제1호(1998), pp. 165-181.

Yi, J. S., "Introduction and Expiration Impacts of Equity Linked Warrant (ELW) on Underlying Assets", *Korean Journal of Finance*, Vol. 20, No. 3(2007), pp. 57-96(in Korean).
이준서, "ELW 상장 및 폐지가 기초자산에 미치는 영향", 재무연구, 제20권 제3호(2007), pp. 57-96.

Zhou, C., "An Analysis of Default Correlations and Multiple Defaults", *Review of Financial Studies*, Vol. 14(2001), pp. 555-576.

Any citation of this article must refer to the following: Park, Daekeun, "Empirical Studies in Exchange Rates and Foreign Exchange Markets: A Survey", Asian Review of Financial Research, Vol. 24 (2011), No. 3, pp. 851-908.

Chapter 11

Empirical Studies in Exchange Rates and Foreign Exchange Markets: A Survey

Daekeun Park*

Professor, Department of Economics and Finance, Hanyang University

Abstract

This paper presents a selective survey of the recent empirical research on exchange rates and foreign exchange markets in Korea. This paper focuses on four basic areas: purchasing power parity and real exchange rates, nominal exchange rate dynamics, foreign exchange market efficiency and market microstructure, and corporate finance issues of exchange rates including foreign exchange risk hedging. First of all, we introduce empirical studies that investigate whether the won/dollar exchange rate satisfies the purchasing power parity relationship in the long run and examine the determinants of short-run fluctuations in the won/dollar real exchange rate. Then, we introduce research about nominal exchange rate dynamics and exchange rate forecasting. Research based on the asset market approach is presented including those investigating the effect of "news" on nominal exchange rates. In addition, empirical studies about foreign exchange markets covering diverse topics such as market efficiency, foreign exchange market intervention and the market microstructure approach are discussed. Finally, studies that measure the foreign exchange exposure and identify the factors that determine the foreign exchange exposure of Korean firms are introduced together with studies that investigate the effect of foreign exchange risk on the return from international portfolio investment.

Keywords   Exchange Rate, Foreign Exchange Market, Survey, Empirical Studies

---

* **Address:** Hanyang University, 222 Wangsimni-ro, Seongdong-gu, Seoul 133-791, Korea;
E-mail: parkdk@hanyang.ac.kr; **Tel:** 82-2-2220-1033.

This survey paper was prepared as a part of the 2010 knowledge database project by the Korean Finance Association and was financially supported by the Korean Finance Association. The author thanks two anonymous referees and the editor, Hee-Joon Ahn, for helpful comments. All remaining errors are mine.

I. Introduction

This paper intends to present a selective survey of the recent empirical research on exchange rates and foreign exchange markets in Korea. Most of the empirical literature covered in this study includes articles from academic journals published in Korea. Naturally, most of the empirical literature covered in this study focuses on the won/dollar exchange rate and the foreign exchange market in Korea, though there are a few exceptions.

Empirical studies on exchange rates and foreign exchange markets may cover diverse topics. Among these, this paper focuses on four basic areas: purchasing power parity and real exchange rates, nominal exchange rate dynamics, foreign exchange market efficiency and market microstructure, and corporate finance issues of exchange rates.

This paper is organized as follows. Chapter II presents research on purchasing power parity and the equilibrium real exchange rate. According to purchasing power parity, the exchange rate between two currencies should revert to the level that reflects their relative purchasing power, which implies that the real exchange rate should also converge to a constant level in the long run. Empirical studies try to find if the won/dollar exchange rate satisfies purchasing power parity. Researchers and policy makers also use real exchange rates to determine if a currency is overvalued or not.

Chapter III introduces empirical studies that search for the determinants of nominal exchange rate dynamics. Research based on the asset market approach is presented including those investigating the effect of "news" on nominal exchange rates and those examining the explanatory power of the standard monetary models. In addition, this chapter compares and evaluates the performance of the various forecasting methods and models in predicting the won/dollar exchange rate.

In chapter IV, we introduce empirical studies about foreign exchange markets. We first discuss research that tries to find out if foreign exchange markets are efficient, that is, if all relevant available information is properly reflected in exchange rates. Then, we present studies on foreign exchange market interventions. These studies try to find answers to diverse questions relating to foreign exchange market interventions including whether they are effective, whether they are sterilized or not, and whether vocal interventions are effective. In addition, Chapter IV introduces studies based on the market microstructure approach. This approach attempts to explain the market phenomena that traditional macroeconomic models fail to explain primarily from the microeconomic perspective.

Since the Korean economy depends heavily on foreign trade, it is likely that Korean firms are exposed to foreign exchange risk. Chapter V introduces empirical studies that measure the foreign exchange exposure and identify the factors that determine the foreign exchange exposure of Korean firms. Chapter V also investigates if foreign exchange risk hedge by firms is effective in reducing their currency exposure and compares the hedge performance of various hedging instruments and models. In addition to firms, investors investing in foreign stocks are also exposed to foreign exchange risk. Chapter V also introduces studies that investigate the effect of the foreign exchange risk on the total risk and the expected return involved with international equity investment. Finally, Chapter VI concludes the paper by presenting a brief summary and by pointing out the limitations of this paper.

II. Purchasing Power Parity and Real Exchange Rates

Empirical studies on real exchange rates have been an important part of international finance literature for a variety of reasons. First of all, empirics as well as theories consistently demonstrate that the real exchange rate is one of the key determinants of current account balance. Secondly, the real exchange rate can be used as a guide to determine overvaluation of a currency. Researchers and policy makers determine whether exchange rates are over-valued or not by estimating it through an economic model the equilibrium level of a real exchange rate with the actual level of a real exchange rate. In addition, investigation of the behavior of real exchange rates can provide researchers with a means of testing purchasing power parity.

1. The Purchasing Power Parity

Purchasing power parity (hereafter PPP) represents the equilibrium relation-ship among the nominal exchange rate, the domestic price level and the foreign price level. Since PPP is one of the most important relations in international finance that most economic models adopt as the link between domestic and foreign goods markets, testing for PPP has naturally become one of the most popular topics of empirical literature on exchange rates. Earlier studies found that PPP does not hold except for periods of high inflation. Some researchers, however, paid attention to the fact that shocks to real exchange rates tend to dampen over time albeit very slowly. Such an observation implies that although PPP does not hold in the short run, it may hold in the long run in the sense that deviation from PPP is not permanent. Such an interpretation has lead to the concept of long-run PPP. In order to test long-run PPP, econo-mists usually adopt one of the following two approaches.

The first approach tests the null hypothesis that real exchange rates follow a random walk process against the alternative hypothesis that real exchange rates show mean reversion. The reason why we can test long-run PPP by investigating the behavior of real exchange rates should be clear.

The log of real exchange rate can be written as follows:

$$q_t = s_t - p_t - p_t^*$$ (1)

where s_t, p_t, and p_t^* stand for the log of nominal exchange rate, the log of the domestic price level, and the log of the foreign price level, respectively. If we look at equation (1), we can understand that q_t can be interpreted as the deviation of the log of an exchange rate from the level implied by PPP.

In practice, a couple of methods have been adopted in empirical studies to determine if the deviation from long-run PPP is permanent. The first one tests if the real exchange rate(q_t) given in equation (1) is stationary by applying unit root tests. The other method uses variance ratio tests to find if the real exchange rate(q_t) follows a random walk process.

The second approach to testing long-run PPP asks if there exists a co-integrating relation among the exchange rate, the domestic price level and the foreign price level. To be concrete, this approach tries to find if $s_t - \mu p_t - \mu^* p_t^*$ is stationary for any constants μ and μ^* using cointegration tests such as the Johansen test.

Both of these approaches have been adopted in attempts to find if the won/dollar exchange rate satisfies long-run PPP. Bahmani-Oskooee and Rhee (1992), for example, employ the Johansen cointegration test to determine there does not exist any cointegrating relation among the won/dollar exchange rate and the price level of Korea and the price level of the U.S. Rhee (1993) applies cointegration tests based on Engle and Granger (1987), Johansen (1988), and Johansen and Juselius (1990) but also finds that the won/dollar exchange rate does not satisfy long-run PPP.

The cointegration tests employed in the analysis of long-run PPP are often subject to the criticism that they do not have sufficient power to reject the null hypothesis, and as a result they are likely to accept the null hypothesis. The power problem arises because it is very hard to distinguish between a random walk process and a stochastic process that reverts to the mean very slowly. In order to increase the power of these tests, one should have a very large sample. In consequence, recent studies in long-run PPP try to increase the sample size by using a very long time series data covering hundreds of years or by using a multi-country panel data. Such a solution, however, is hardly applicable to the won/dollar exchange rate, for which only a limited length of time-series data is available.

In order to overcome the problem of limited test power in testing long-run PPP for the won/dollar exchange rate, Park (1995) uses a different approach of applying the J-test developed by Park (1990). This test differs from other cointegration tests in that it takes existence of a cointegrating relation as the null hypothesis. The test result, however, still confirms the findings of previous studies that the won/dollar exchange rate does not satisfy the long-run PPP. Kim (1998) applies a test based on the spectral density function as well as a cointegration test and finds both of these tests reject long-run PPP for the won/dollar exchange rate.

Another way to resolve the power of test problem is to increase the sample size by using multi-currency panel data. Lee (1996) applies the Johansen cointegration test to panel data consisting of the exchange rates of seven currencies against the USD and reports that long-run PPP does not hold in the whole sample and in most of the subsamples. In some subsamples where there exist cointegrating relations, the cointegrating vectors fail to satisfy the restrictions imposed by long-run PPP. Based on these findings, he concludes that the won/dollar exchange rate does not satisfy long-run PPP. Kim (2001) also tests long-run PPP using panel data consisting of the Pacific Rim countries. Estimation of a panel regression model by the GMM (generalized method of moment) demonstrates that the relative version of purchasing power parity hypothesis is not supported by his sample.

Kim and Park (2008), on the other hand, investigate if the wide-spread rejection of purchasing power parity in the empirical literature is due to slow adjustment to the long-run equilibrium or failure of the PPP hypothesis itself using an error correction model derived by Park-Ogaki transformation. Their approach is based on the decomposition of the nonstationarity in the transformed error correction model into two components: nonstationarity of the variables included in the model and nonstationarity of the disequilibrium error. Results from the yen/dollar exchange rate and the pound/dollar exchange rate reveal that slow adjustment to the long-run equilibrium is more likely to be the reason why PPP does not hold.

2. Equilibrium Real Exchange Rate

Policy makers are often interested in finding out whether a currency is overvalued or not. An answer to this question can be found by estimating and comparing the equilibrium level of real exchange rate with the actual level.

In order to calculate the equilibrium exchange rate to be used as the criterion for currency overvaluation, the concept of 'equilibrium' should be clearly defined. Williamson (1994) defines the equilibrium real exchange rate as the level of real exchange rate that is compatible with internal and external equilibrium of an economy. Such an equilibrium real exchange rate is usually termed as the FEER (fundamental equilibrium exchange rate). On the other hand, the BEER (behavioral equilibrium exchange rate) approach depends on estimation of econometric models that reflect the theoretical relation between a real exchange rate and macroeconomic fundamentals such as the difference in productivity and the terms of trade.

Park and Choi (2000) investigate if the Korean won was overvalued before the 1997 currency crisis using two criteria: real equilibrium exchange rate and current account sustainability. The real equilibrium exchange rate calculated by the BEER approach indicates that the won was overvalued by as much as 15% before the 1997 currency crisis while current account sustainability criterion points out that the current account deficit was not excessive except for the year 1996. Kang (2001) also examines if the Korean won was overvalued before the 1997 currency crisis by estimating the BEER. According to him, the Korean won was overvalued before the 1997 crisis and during the period of exchange rate turbulence in 2000.

Chun and Kim (2006) estimate a BEER-based measure of the equilibrium won/dollar real exchange rate using a multivariate cointegration method. The long-run equilibrium value of the Korean won derived from the estimated cointegrating equation reveals that the Korean won was overvalued during the year 1986 and during the period between 1988 and 1997.

Ahn (2006) uses the NATREX (natural real exchange rate) model to estimate the long-run equilibrium real exchange rate of the Korean won The results indicate that the Korean won shows cyclical movement of overvaluation and undervaluation in turn, rather than systematic misalignment in one direction. The results also show that, the Korean won was overvalued by 3.2% in the first quarter of 2006.

Ⅲ. Studies on Nominal Exchange Rates

1. Models of Nominal Exchange Rates

1.1 Monetary Models

After the breakdown of the Bretton Woods System and the shift of the foreign exchange regime of major countries to free floating, much of the international finance literature has focused on developing and exploring models to explain nominal exchange rate dynamics. The main theoretical approach to nominal exchange rate determination is the asset market approach. In this approach, the foreign exchange market is regarded as a market where the price is determined by expectations on the returns that can be generated by holding assets denominated in foreign currencies rather than a market where the flow supply and demand determine the equilibrium price.

A typical model adopted in the asset market approach is the standard monetary model that assumes that money market equilibrium, purchasing power parity and the uncovered interest rate parity hold at all times. Before long, however, empirical failure of the simple monetary models became apparent. Nominal exchange rates under the free floating exchange rate regime was simply too volatile to be explained by fundamental macroeconomic variables included in the monetary model alone.

In response, modified versions of the simple monetary model such as the overshooting model and the portfolio balance model have been suggested. Empirical research has naturally focused on estimating and exploring testable versions of these models.

In addition, economists have also tried to find if the monetary model is capable of explaining the movement of nominal exchange rates in the long run. Although the relationship between monetary fundamentals and nominal exchange rates does not appear to be close in the short run, they may share common long-run trends. Various versions of cointegration tests have been adopted for this endeavor. Rapach and Wohar (2002), for instance, test for linear cointegration in the monetary model using a century of nominal exchange rate data. They find evidence of cointegration in six of the ten countries examined. Lee and Strazicich (2009) extend this work to the nonlinear framework by performing a threshold cointegration test that allows for asymmetric adjustments in two different regimes. Overall, using a long-span data, they find stronger support for nominal models of exchange rate determination in the nonlinear framework.

Rhee (1997) examines if monetary models are capable of explaining the movement of the won/dollar exchange rate in the long run. Applying the Johansen-Juselius cointegration test, he finds that there exists a long-run stable relationship among real income, real quantity of money, interest rate differential between the U.S. and Korea and the won/dollar exchange rate. In particular, the Korean won appreciates against the U.S. dollar as her real income increases or as her real money supply decreases.

Jung (2009) uses a cointegration test based on ARDL (autoregressive distributed lag) to find if monetary models are capable of explaining the movement of the won/dollar exchange rate during the period from 1993 to 2008. He finds that all the fundamental variables included in the monetary model have a stable long-run equilibrium relationship among them and that all the fundamental variables except the U.S. money supply and U.S. stock prices have significant effects on the won/dollar exchange rate in the long run.

1.2 Bubbles and Herding

Previous attempts to understand nominal exchange rate dynamics have found that nominal exchange rates are simply too volatile to be explained by macroeconomic fundamentals alone. As a result, attempts have been made to explain short-run excess volatility of exchange rates that cannot be explained by macroeconomic fundamentals. One of these new approaches tries to determine if there exist speculative bubbles or herd behavior in the foreign exchange market.

Lee (2002), for example, investigates if speculative bubbles exist in the won/dollar exchange rate using a monetary model of exchange rate determination with rational speculative bubbles. Since the pioneering study on the German hyperinflation by Flood and Garber (1980), many attempts have been made to test for the existence of bubbles in financial markets. Since bubbles are not directly observable, these studies depended on indirect methods of detecting bubbles including variance bounds tests and tests for stability of the model parameters. For instance, Meese (1986), using a variance bounds test, demonstrates that bubbles exist in the USD/DM exchange rate and the GBP/USD exchange rate. Instead of using an indirect method, Lee (2002) directly estimates bubbles by estimating a state-space version of a monetary model through the Kalman filtering method. The results indicate that speculative bubbles existed in the won/dollar exchange rate for a substantial portion of the period between 1980 and 1999. In particular, he finds that the Korean Won was overvalued by as much as 40% in 1996 and 1997 because of bubbles.

Excessive volatility of foreign exchange rates can also be explained by the herd behavior of market participants. One of the reasons for the existence of herd behavior in financial markets is the information asymmetry caused by slow and insufficient transmission of information. Through a computer simulation based on the herding behavior model of Cont and Bouchaud (2000), Yoon and Kim (2005) observe that the return distribution of the won/dollar exchange rate has fat tails that tend to disappear as the time scale increases. Their observation supports one of the important implications of the Cont and Bouchaud model that extremely large movements in exchange rates are likely to happen as the time scale becomes smaller because herd behavior is more likely to appear during a small time period. Applying the same method, Yoon and Ryu (2007) show that the EUR/USD exchange rate is also affected by herd behavior.

2. The Effect of "News" on Nominal Exchange Rates

One of the implications of the asset market approach to nominal exchange rates is that economic and political news that signal possible future changes in the value of foreign currencies have the potential to explain fluctuations in nominal exchange rates. As a result, some empirical studies on exchange rate determination based upon the asset market approach paid attention to the prediction of the theory that unanticipated events should have qualitatively different effects on exchange rates from anticipated ones. Specifically, exchange rates should show a discrete change in response to the arrival of unanticipated relevant information. That means only gradual changes in exchange rates should be observed in the absence of news. As a result, empirical studies try to find if exchange rates show a discrete and large response to news.

One of the difficulties encountered in these studies is how to identify news, that is, arrival of unanticipated information. In order to identify "news", these studies adopt one of the following two approaches. The first one uses a statistical model like the ARiMA model to derive and estimate unanticipated changes in the fundamental determinants of exchange rates such as interest rate differentials and money supplies. The second approach compiles actual announcements of official statistics, policy changes and other relevant events from press releases and newspapers and observes the movement of exchange rates immediately before and after the announcement. We find that both of the methods have been adopted in the studies on the influence of news on the won/dollar exchange rate.

Lee (1999) examines the influence of foreign news on the won/dollar exchange rate using a unique method of identifying news. First, he calculates the daily rate of foreign exchange rate change in the foreign market as the log difference between the opening rate of day t+1 and the closing rate of day t in the Seoul foreign exchange market and the daily rate of foreign exchange rate change in the domestic market as the log difference between the closing rate and the opening rate of day t. Then, he estimates a vector ARMA model comprising these two variables and uses the unpredictable part of the rate of exchange rate change in the foreign market as the measure of foreign news. Using this measure, Lee estimates the effect of foreign news on the won/dollar exchange rate and finds that foreign news had almost no influence on the domestic foreign exchange market before the opening of the capital market in Korea, while they had critical influence on the domestic market after the opening of the capital market and especially after the 1997 currency crisis in Korea.

Song (2002), on the other hand, uses the search and compilation approach to identify news to investigate if large changes in the won/dollar exchange rate are related to the arrival of news. He finds that arrival of news had significant effects on the won/dollar exchange rate as well as Korean stock prices and that while a wide range of news, including stock market policies, corporate and financial restructuring, fundamental economic issues, sovereign and corporate rating events, had significant effects on the stock price, the won/dollar exchange rate only responded to news on sovereign and corporate rating events and foreign economic issues. The findings of Song (2002), however, has a limitation in that this study delves into the influence of news only for the period in which exchange rates or stock prices showed significant changes rather than using the entire sample period. In other words, this study does not analyze the unconditional influence of news and as a result, it is probable that the results of this study are biased toward accepting the hypothesis that exchange rates and stock prices are significantly influenced by news.

3. Exchange Rate Forecasting

Forecasting exchange rates is one the most popular research topics in international finance. Diverse techniques are utilized to predict exchange rates including time series models, regression models consisting of macroeconomic fundamentals, models that take advantage of information from forwards exchange rates and currency futures prices and technical analysis. Meese and Rogoff (1983), in one of the most influential studies on exchange rate forecasting, compare the out-of-sample forecasting performance of various kinds of forecasting models and find that no models can consistently outperform the simple random walk model. Since then, research in exchange rate forecasting has focused on finding a model that can consistently surpass the random walk model. These efforts, however, had only limited success. Some models display better forecasting performance than the random walk model depending on the forecasting horizon, the exchange rate to be forecast and the performance criterion. Yet it is impossible to find a model that can consistently outperform the random walk model at all times.

3.1 Forecasting the won/dollar Exchange Rate

Lee (1996) adopts as a performance measure the Henriksson-Merton test that measures a forecast's accuracy of the direction of the exchange rate movement in addition to the traditional RMSE (root mean squared error) to compare the predictive power of various time series models against the random walk model. He reports that measures of the random walk model with the end of the month effect has the best one-month predictive power under the RMSE criterion, whereas the AR (4) model is the best performer under the Henriksson-Merton criterion.

Jeong and Cha (1998), using the monthly data from March of 1990 to November of 1997, compare the forecasting ability of the random walk model and different versions of the monetary model under the Market Average Exchange Rate System. They find that the simple monetary model which does not include lagged variables shows better out-of-sample forecasting performance than the random walk model.

Oh and Lee (1999, 2000) using monthly won/dollar exchange rate data from March of 1990 to December of 1996, compare the short-term and the long-term forecasting ability of the asset market model, the random walk model, and the ARIMA model. According to their results, the random walk model demonstrates the best forecasting ability in short-term forecasting with one to three month horizons. On the other hand, the real interest differential model and the unified model show the best performance when the forecasting horizon is extended to 6 and 12 months.

Chun (1998) compares the quarterly forecasting performance of seven models using the won/dollar exchange rate data from the first quarter of 1980 to the fourth quarter of 1996 and finds out that most of the models with error correction terms show better performance than the random walk model in short-term forecasting with a horizon of less than one year.

Kim and Mo (2000) investigate the performance of monetary models specified in the error correction form in the prediction of the exchange rates of ten OECD countries including Korea. They report that monetary models have better forecasting ability than the random walk model except for short-term forecasting with the forecasting horizon of less than one month.

Chung (2004) finds that the vector error correction model that utilizes the information embodied in forward exchange rates has better forecasting capability than the random walk model. However, there is no significant difference between the vector error correction model and the random walk in forecasting performance with a forecasting horizon of less than 40 weeks.

Lee (2007) reports that while AR models show better performance for forecasting horizons of less than one year, simple time series models that include variables such as capital account balance and inflation rate differential between Korea and the US have relatively high forecasting power for forecasting horizons of over one year. This study, however, does not compare the forecasting performance of time series models with that of the random walk model.

As we have seen, domestic researches on forecasting the won/dollar exchange rate compare the performance of various models, including time series models and monetarist models, to that of the random walk model. According to these studies, time series models and structural models demonstrate higher out-of-sample forecasting power in long-term forecasting though they do not outperform the random walk model for short-term forecasting. Such findings are consistent with the findings of the foreign literature.

Meanwhile, it has been pointed out that the power of existing models in predicting the dynamic movement of the won/dollar exchange rate should be limited due to their linear nature. As a result, there have been attempts to utilize models with nonlinearity in exchange rate forecasting. Kim and Yu (2004), for example, use the Markov regime switching model to forecast the won/dollar exchange rate for the period from the first quarter of 1988 to the second quarter of 2003. They find, however, that the Markov switching model fails to outperform the random walk model.

Park (1997, 1998) demonstrates that the neural network regression quantiles model estimated by a genetic algorithm has greater predictive power compared to the standard neural network model or the ARMA model when it comes to predicting the yields from four currencies. Shin (1995) also applies neural network models to forecast foreign exchange rates. Kim (2000) compares the performance of diverse neural network models in forecasting the won/dollar exchange rate. Results from the weekly data show that neural network models have better predictive power than the random walk model. Results from the monthly data, however, show that performance of the models differs depending on the model specification.

3.2 Forecasting Exchange Rate Volatility

Researchers have also attempted to predict the volatility as well as the level of exchange rates. Choi and Hyung (2003) compare the performance of the EWMA (exponentially weighted moving average) model and various versions of the GARCH models in forecasting the volatility of the won/dollar exchange rate. They find that the EWMA shows better performance than the GARCH type time series models in short-term forecasting. For forecasting horizons of longer than a month, however, the FIGARCH (fractionally integrated GARCH) model, which is a GARCH model that can reflect long memory, shows the best performance.

Lee (2009) compare the out-of-sample forecasting performance of various volatility models using daily won/dollar exchange rate data from 1992 to 2008. He reports that the model with the lowest mean squared forecasting error and lowest VaR forecast error among the models considered is the EWMA (exponentially weighted moving average) model.

3.3 Forecasting the Won/Yen Exchange Rate

There have also been attempts to predict the won/yen exchange rate along with won/dollar exchange rate. The won/yen exchange rate is determined as the cross rate between the won/dollar exchange rate and the yen/dollar exchange rate. Lee (1997), using the won/yen exchange rate data from April 1985 to May 1996 compares the forecasting performance of different models for various forecasting horizons. In short-term forecasting, there is hardly any difference in their forecasting ability. In long-term forecasting, however, the AR model shows significantly better performance than the random walk model.

Ⅲ. Studies on Foreign Exchange Markets

1. Foreign Exchange Market Efficiency

The method that is most widely used in testing the efficiency of the foreign exchange market is to find if the forward exchange rate is an un-biased predictor of the future spot exchange rate. Tests of this unbiasedness hypothesis or also termed the unbiased forward rate hypothesis, however, are actually tests of the joint hypothesis that market participants form their expectation of future spot exchange rates rationally, that market partic-ipants are risk neutral and that foreign exchange markets are efficient. As a result, tests of the unbiasedness hypothesis are subject to the limitation that one cannot conclude that the foreign exchange market is inefficient even though the unbiasedness hypothesis is rejected by the tests. Despite this limitation, many attempts have been made to find if the Korean foreign exchange market is efficient by testing the unbiasedness hypothesis.

1.1 Testing the Unbiasedness Hypothesis

Sung and Kim (1999) use the won/dollar exchange rate data from the NDF (non-deliverable forward) market from March of 1997 to February of 1999 to test the unbiasedness hypothesis. Estimating an OLS model and an error correction model, they find evidence that the unbiasedness hypothesis does not hold. This study, however, has the limitation in that it uses overlapping samples to estimate the models.

Kim and Lee (2000) evaluate the efficiency of the onshore forward ex-change market in Korea by testing the unbiasedness hypothesis. In the case of one-week forwards, neither the test based on the ARCH model nor the one based on the OLS model can reject the unbiasedness hypothesis. When forward exchange rates with longer maturities such as one month, three months and six months are used, however, the unbiasedness hypothesis is rejected, implying that the onshore forward market is not efficient. Kim, Lim and Jung (1999) also test if the unbiasedness hypothesis holds in the onshore forward exchange market using one-month and three-month won/dollar forward exchange rate data. Applying the Johansen's co-integration test, they find that the unbiasedness hypothesis is rejected.

You and Han (2002) test the unbiased forward rate hypothesis in the won/dollar foreign exchange markets using the one-week forward exchange rate data from the offshore NDF market and the onshore forward exchange market. The sample covers the period from November 1994 to June 2000 so that comparison between the period before the 1997 Korean currency crisis and the period after the crisis can be made. They attempt to reconcile some conflicting results regarding the unbiased forward rate hypothesis in the won/dollar market by testing a diverse set of models including the change rate model (CRM), the error correction model (ECM), the GARCH-M CRM, and the GARCH-M ECM. They find that the unbiased forward rate hypothesis is rejected under the formulation of the CRM and the ECM most of the time but that the test results are highly sensitive to the choice of the sample period. They specifically point out that there was a structural change in the relationship between the won/dollar spot market and the forward market since the 1997 currency crisis. They also find evidence from the GARCH-M model that there exists a time-varying risk premium in the won/dollar forward exchange rate. Based on this finding, there argue that the existence of a time-varying risk premium is one of the major factors that can explain the failure of the unbiased forward rate hypothesis to hold after the currency crisis.

Meanwhile, studies have found that unlike the forward exchange markets, the unbiased hypothesis seems to hold in the won/dollar futures market. Kang and Kim (2005) test the unbiasedness hypothesis using the won/dollar currency futures price data from March 23, 1999 to August 16, 2004. Testing the restriction with the cointegrating equation imposed by the unbiasedness hypothesis, they conclude that the unbiasedness hypothesis holds in the currency futures market in Korea.

Kang (2006) tests the unbaisedness hypothesis using the forward exchange rates from the Singapore NDF market and the New York NDF market and the currency futures data from the Korea Exchange. Since all the exchange rate data are non-stationary, he adopts Johansen's cointegration test with parameter restriction as a test for the unbiasedness hypothesis. The result shows that while the unbiasedenss hypothesis is rejected in the Singapore NDF market and the New York NDF market, it cannot be rejected in the won/dollar futures market.

1.2 Testing Market Efficiency through Information Spillover

In order to overcome the limits of testing the unbiasedness hypothesis as a test for foreign exchange market efficiency, a few studies tried to see if there exists information spillover between the spot market and the forward market. Lee and Lim (2000) analyze information spillover between the offshore won/dollar NDF market and the domestic spot exchange market. Estimating an AR (1) model and a GARCH (1) model, they find that there is a simultaneous two-way flow of information between these markets rather than a one-way flow from one market to the other.

Kim and Lee (2003) delve into information spillover between the offshore NDF market and the domestic foreign exchange market using the NDF data with one-month and three-month maturities from September 1996 to August 2002. Estimating the AR (1)-GARCH (1, 1)-M model, they also find that information is reflected simultaneously in both of these markets and then flows in both directions rather than being reflected in one of the markets first and then spilling over to the other market.

Kang (2006) also observes that there exists two-way information spillover between the domestic spot exchange market and the won-dollar NDF market in New York. His findings confirm the existence of bi-directional information spillover found in previous studies.

1.3 Other Approaches to Market Efficiency

Mo and Kee (1996) pays attention to the fact that rejection of the unbiased forward rate hypothesis may result from the existence of risk premium in the forward exchange market. Thus, using an ARCH-M model and a GARCH-M model, they investigate if a forward risk premium exists in the foreign exchange market and analyze the characteristics of the forward risk premium. Analysis of the exchange rates of the currencies of Belgium, Canada, Germany, the United Kingdom, Japan and Switzerland against the U.S. dollar reveals that the unbiasedness hypothesis is rejected in all of the six currencies. However, they could not find a forward risk premium in four of the six currencies examined. Based on these findings, they conclude that the unbiasedness hypothesis is rejected not necessarily because of the risk premium but rather because of the inefficiency of the market.

Lee and Lim (2002), test efficiency of the won/dollar exchange market by exploring the existence of arbitrage opportunities between the won/dollar spot market and the currency futures markets. They assume that arbitrageurs can use either the money market or the swap market to buy and lend (or borrow and sell) dollars. According their findings, the won/dollar futures market appears to be somewhat inefficient on an ex post basis. However, they argue that the substantially reduced ex ante profits suggest that the won/dollar futures market is generally efficient despite its early stage of development.

Ahn (2008), on the other hand, tests market efficiency by examining the performance of filter rule profits in the won/dollar spot exchange market. Applying the predictive failure test of Pesaran-Timmermann to a daily spot exchange rate data during the *de facto* flexible exchange rate period of 1998～2007 in Korea, he shows that the technical filter trading rule cannot produce statistically significant profits with any filter size. Based on his finding, Ahn concludes that the won/dollar spot exchange market is efficient.

2. Foreign Exchange Market Intervention

The exchange rate regime in Korea shifted from a managed floating system named the Market Average Exchange Rate System to the current free floating system in December of 1997. In order to avoid abrupt changes in foreign exchange rates, however, the Bank of Korea intervened in the foreign exchange market under the free floating system as well as the managed floating system. Studies on the foreign exchange market intervention have attempted to find answers to questions such as whether foreign exchange market interventions are effective even if they are sterilized, whether the Bank of Korea sterilizes the change in money supply caused by foreign exchange market interventions, and whether vocal interventions are effective in managing the won/dollar exchange rate.

2.1 Purpose of FX Market Interventions

Ryou and Kim (1998) use a vector error correction model consisting of the current account balance, the capital account balance, the foreign exchange market intervention, the domestic credit and the inflation rate in Korea as well as the won/dollar exchange rate, to investigate the purpose of foreign exchange market interventions in Korea. They find that although the Bank of Korea intervened in the market to counter current account shocks as well as capital account shocks, the intensity of intervention was much greater in the case of capital account shocks. They interpret this finding as providing evidence that the foreign exchange market intervention in Korea put more emphasis on maintaining export competitiveness and preventing expansion of current account deficits.

Park (1998) investigates the pattern of foreign exchange market intervention in Korea using the exchange market pressure and the intervention index. The exchange market pressure and the intervention index are useful in grasping the short-term change in the intervention intensity and the intervention pattern. According to this analysis, the Bank of Korea mainly used the against-the-wind type intervention in order to stabilize the won/dollar exchange rate. However, there were cases in which dollars were bought through interventions even when there was pressure for appreciation of the won. Such interventions were usually made during the periods of yen depreciation in which the won/yen exchange rate increased. These observations imply that the won/yen exchange rate had an important affect on intervention policy in Korea and that sustaining export competitiveness was a significant factor in exchange market intervention.

2.2 Dynamic Effects of Foreign Exchange Market Interventions

Using a GARCH model, Lee, Rhee and Choi (1998) find that when the Bank of Korea intervenes in the foreign exchange market, the won/dollar exchange rate moves in the direction intended by the intervention. However, estimation of the impulse response function reveals that the effect of the intervention does not last long. Lee, Rhee and Choi argue that such a result can be obtained when there is expectation among market participants that the Bank of Korea will sterilize the change in the money supply caused by the intervention. Rhee (1997) also analyzes the short-term and the long-term effects of foreign exchange market interventions in Korea using a VAR model and finds that the impact of market interventions on the won/dollar exchange rate is short-lived.

2.3 Estimating the Sterilization Coefficient

Studies on foreign exchange market interventions in Korea have also tried to estimate to what degree changes in money supply caused by market interventions are sterilized. Most of these studies rely on estimating the sterilization coefficient in the money supply response function.

Kim (1991), through estimation of the money supply response function for the period from 1980 to 1989, comes up with an estimate of 0.87 for the sterilized coefficient. This means that the change in money supply caused by foreign exchange market interventions was not completely sterilized during this period. Using a VAR model, Choi (1995) examines the reaction of net domestic assets in the balance sheet of the Bank of Korea to the change in net foreign assets and draws the conclusion that foreign exchange market interventions are completely sterilized in the short run. In the long run, however, foreign exchange market interventions by the Bank of Korea are not completely sterilized, causing an increase in high powered money.

Lee and Yoon (1997) also find that the estimate of the sterilization coefficient becomes smaller in the long run. In addition, they observe that there was a structural change in the sterilization coefficient as the exchange rate regime shifted from the Currency Basket System to the Market Average Exchange Rate System in 1990. Unlike the Currency Basket System, the estimates for the short-run and the long-run sterilization coefficients under the Market Average Exchange Rate System are -0.12 and 0.01, respectively, which means that the change in the quantity of money caused by foreign exchange market interventions was hardly sterilized.

2.4 Effects of Vocal Interventions

Park and Song (2003) analyze the effects of vocal interventions by the Japanese government on the yen-dollar exchange rate. Using resources from newspapers, they find that vocal interventions are most effective when conducted simultaneously with actual interventions. They also find that vocal interventions are effective during normal times when exchange rates are stable and that they are hardly effective during times of turbulence.

Kang, Park and Byun (2006) examine the effects of the verbal interventions by the Bank of Korea on the forward and the spot won/dollar exchange rates using intraday trading data. They find that verbal interventions announced during the trading hours are effective in affecting the exchange rate level and in reducing the exchange rate volatility. On the contrary, verbal interventions announced after trading hours are hardly effective.

Research on exchange market interventions in Korea are faced with the limitation that they have to be undertaken without accurate data on the timing and the scale of interventions. This is because the Bank of Korea does not disclose data on foreign exchange market interventions. Due to this limitation, studies on foreign exchange market interventions in Korea rely on the alternative method of using the change in the net foreign assets of the Bank of Korea as the proxy for the size of the market intervention. However, the size of the market intervention cannot be estimated accurately by this method because foreign exchange reserves as well as net foreign assets are influenced not only by market interventions but also by other factors such as changes in the value of currencies held as reserves and the receipt of interest payments on assets held as reserves. In order to vitalize research into foreign exchange market interventions and improve their quality, it is desirable that the Bank of Korea disclose data on market interventions at least with a certain time lag.

3. Market Microstructure Approach

Empirical studies on nominal exchange rates based upon the traditional asset market approach have found little evidence that macroeconomic variables have strong and consistent explanatory power except during extraordinary circumstances such as periods of hyperinflation. Such findings have led economists to turn to the market microstructure approach that analyzes foreign exchange markets primarily from the microeconomic perspective.

One of the empirical puzzles in the foreign exchange market is the high trading volume. The asset market macroeconomic models predict an absence of trading in foreign exchanges for portfolio investment purposes. It is because, if all agents are identical and information is perfect, agents should form homogenous expectations about the future movement of exchange rates. Such prediction is inconsistent with the empirical reality of high daily transaction volume in foreign exchange markets. In addition, the market microstructure approach tries to evaluate the economic effects of foreign exchange market institutions such as the use of brokers, location of trading, transparency and decentralization.

The foreign exchange market in Korea provides ideal data for empirical studies of exchange rates based on the market microstructure approach. This is because a majority of transactions in the Seoul foreign exchange market are made through foreign exchange brokers and as a result actual trading data including the transaction price and volume is available on a minute-by-minute basis. Such an advantage in data availability may explain the relative abundance of empirical studies based on the market microstructure approach in Korea.

3.1 Trading Volume and Exchange Rate Volatility

One of the characteristics of foreign exchange markets is their high trading volume. The trading volume in foreign exchange markets dwarfs that of any other financial market. There are two opposing explanations for the high trading volume: the event uncertainty view and the hot potato view. According to the event uncertainty view, uninformed market makers infer arrival of new information from a higher trading volume and as a result a higher than normal trading volume results in higher exchange rate volatility. On the contrary, the hot potato view argues that a higher trading volume reflects changing hands among dealers for inventory adjustment purposes rather than the processing of new information. According to the hot potato view, a higher trading volume does not necessarily coincide with higher exchange rate volatility. Investigating the explanatory power of these two views is one of the major research topics for the market microstructure approach.

For example, Chung and Joo (1999) investigate if the trading volume in the foreign exchange market is useful in explaining the volatility of the won/dollar exchange rate. Using the t-GARCH model, they find that higher trading volume tends to increase foreign exchange volatility. Since exchange rate volatility changes over time, researchers have relied on GARCH models to measure and investigate foreign exchange volatility. GARCH models, however, have limitations in that the distribution of the error term should be specified as a normal or t distribution to make the estimation. In order to overcome this limitation, Park (2001) applies the quantile regression, a semi-parametric method that is capable of estimating GARCH models without specifying the distribution of the error term. Using the daily won/dollar spot exchange rate data, he finds that trading volume has positive effects on exchange rate volatility and that the positive effects get stronger under the free floating exchange rate regime Korea adopted after the 1997 currency crisis. His findings are in favor of the event uncertainty view. This study, however, has the limitation that it uses daily data rather than the intra-day data used by most of the empirical studies based on the market microstructure approach.

Seon and Eom (2006) also test the two opposing views by investigating the intra-day pattern of trading volume, exchange rate volatility and bid-ask spreads constructed from real-time transactions data and the two-minute-interval quotes data of inter-dealer trades brokered through Seoul Money Brokerage Services Ltd. from April 1 to May 30, 2003. They observe that the number of trades and the trading volume show U-shaped intra-day patterns while the volatility and the bid-ask spread exhibit inverse J-shaped intra-day patterns. They contend that observation of higher volatility and wider spreads when trading activities are higher is consistent with the prediction by the event uncertainty view. They also argue that private information does exist and plays an important role in the Seoul foreign exchange market. Applying a semi-nonparametric technique to the high frequency (two-minute interval) won/dollar exchange rate data from 2002 to 2005, Chung (2008) also finds that there exist private information effects as well as position adjustment effects in the Seoul foreign exchange market.

Lee and Chung (2007) also investigate the two opposing views using the two-minute interval, real-time transactions data of the Seoul foreign exchange market from January 2002 to October 2002. Investigating the trading volume and volatility for each thirty-minute interval, they find that the Seoul FX market shows higher volatility during the thirty-minute intervals at opening, after the lunch break, and before the closing of the market. But contrarily, they find that an extraordinary hike in trading volume can be observed during the thirty-minute interval at the close of the market only. Lee and Chung interpret the high trading volume at the close of the market is a reflection of the reluctance of foreign exchange dealers to carry their foreign exchange positions overnight. They conclude that their findings are consistent with the hot potato view.

In addition to investigating the intra-day pattern of trading volume and exchange rate volatility, Lee and Chung also investigate the event uncertainty view by testing the mixture of distribution hypothesis (MDH). The MDH states that the trading volume as well as the transaction price is affected by latent information variables that flow into financial markets. Since market participants respond immediately to new pieces of information that flow into financial markets, the trading volume and the volatility of exchange rates must show a contemporaneous relation. The contemporaneous relation between the trading volume and the exchange rate volatility in the MDH is usually tested through the following GARCH model:

$$r_t = \alpha + \sum_{k=1}^{p} \beta_k r_{t-k} + u_t \tag{2}$$

$$\sigma_t^2 = c + \sum_{i=1}^{q} \sigma_{t-i}^2 + \sum_{j=1}^{s} \delta_j u_{t-j}^2 + \eta V_t$$

where r_t denotes the rate of change in the won/dollar exchange rate, σ_t^2 is the time-varying conditional variance of u_t which is independently distributed with mean 0, and V_t is the trading volume at time t.

Investigating the MDH for each of the thirty minute intervals during the operating hours of foreign exchange brokers, Lee and Chung demonstrate that the MDH holds at the opening of the market and during most of the afternoon hours, which implies that excess volatility in the Seoul foreign exchange market is in part due to the inflow of new pieces of information. This result is consistent with the earlier finding of Chung (2006).

Empirical tests of the event uncertainty view using the MDH method are often subject to the criticism that the test results of different studies do not coincide with each other. Park (2007) contends that one of the reasons for the inconsistency of test results lies with erroneous specification and estimation of the conditional variance in the standard MDH method. According to him, empirical tests may get different results if normal information and surprise information have different effects on the relation between trading volume and exchange rate volatility. Specifically, while surprise information causes exchange rates to become more volatile, it may reduce the trading volume by narrowing the gaps in the views of market participants. In that case, researchers may get erroneous estimates for the conditional variance if they do not distinguish between surprise information and normal information in specifying their models. Park uses the won/dollar exchange rate data for every two minutes to estimate a GARCH model in which a dummy for surprise information is added to the equation for the conditional variance. In particular, he modifies the specification of the conditional variance in the GARCH model given in equation (2) as follows:

$$\sigma_t^2 = c + \sum_{i=1}^{q} \sigma_{t-i}^2 + \sum_{j=1}^{s} \delta_j u_{t-j}^2 + \eta V_t + \lambda D_t^S \tag{3}$$

In equation (3), D_t^S is the dummy variable standing for surprise information. The results verify his conjecture that the relation between trading volume and exchange rate volatility becomes weaker when there is an inflow of surprise information to the market.

Extending this study, Park (2008) introduces the SISV (surprise information stochastic volatility) model, which captures the nonlinear relationship between trading volume and exchange rate volatility which may result from the state change of volatility due to the inflow of surprise information. Using high frequency won/dollar exchange rate data, he finds a significant positive relationship between exchange rate volatility and trading volume, which was not observable in the traditional stochastic volatility models used in previous studies. Furthermore, he demonstrates that while the flow of surprise information increases the volatility of the won/dollar exchange rate, it has little effect on the trading volume.

3.2 Other Uses of the Market Microstructure Approach

The market microstructure approach is also useful in predicting exchange rates. Park and Jang (1999) identify the flows of private information and public information by estimating a structural VAR model using the won/dollar bid and ask rates in the foreign exchange market in Korea. They find that flows of private information can explain about 30% of the hourly changes in the won/dollar exchange rate and that their effects last for a significant amount of time. Based on these findings, Park and Jang attempt to forecast the won/dollar exchange rate using their estimates of the private information flow. It turns out that the private information model has a better out-of-sample forecasting power than the macroeconomic model and the random walk model in most of the forecasting horizons.

3.3 Market Anomalies

The market microstructure approach is also useful in explaining some of the anomalies observed in the foreign exchange market. One of the anomalies observed in the foreign exchange market in Korea is the synchronization of the Korean won and the Japanese yen. The won-yen synchronization refers to the phenomenon that the won/yen exchange rate shows very stable movement as the Korean won and the Japanese yen move synchronously against the U.S. dollar. The won/yen exchange rate is determined as the cross rate between the won/dollar exchange rate and the yen/dollar exchange. Very strong won-yen synchronization was observed between 1998 and 2005, when the won/yen exchange rate continuously stayed at around the level of 10.

Lee and Ko (2003) observe that synchronization of the won and the yen got stronger after the 1992 capital account liberalization and the 1997 currency crisis in Korea. They also find that while synchronization of the won and the yen can be observed mostly during the period of the yen depreciation before the 1997 currency crisis, such asymmetry disappears after the currency crisis. Based on these observations, they argue that synchronization of the two currencies can be explained by foreign exchange market interventions or market expectations of interventions rather than demand and supply of foreign exchange. Since the two countries have a similar trade structure and thereby compete with each other in the export market, market participants expect foreign exchange market interventions whenever the won/yen exchange shows a large fluctuation and the market expectation moves the won/dollar exchange rate in line with the yen/dollar exchange rate.

Park and Song (2006), using the transaction order data constructed from high frequency bid and ask rate data for the won/dollar exchange rate from July 2001 to January 2006, find that desynchronization of the won and the yen can be observed in about one third of the trading days included in the sample and that the volatility of the won/dollar exchange rate tends to increase when desynchronization appears. They also observe that the possibility of the won-yen synchronization tends to increase when the volatility of the yen/dollar exchange rate increases. They argue that their observations can be explained if foreign exchange market participants show stronger reactions when the volatility of the yen/dollar exchange rate increases.

V. Exchange Rates and Corporate Finance

1. Measuring and Managing Foreign Exchange Exposure of Firms

The Korean economy depends heavily on foreign trade. As a result, measuring and managing the foreign exchange exposure of Korean firms is an important topic for empirical studies on foreign exchange rates.

1.1 Measuring Foreign Exchange Exposure of Firms

There is a vast body of literature focusing on measuring foreign exchange exposure and identifying the factors that determine it. Most of these studies employ the following regression model:

$$R_{jt} = \alpha_j + \beta_j R_t^x + \beta_m R_t^m + e_{jt} \tag{4}$$

where R_{jt} is the return from holding the stock of firm j, R_t^m is the return from holding the market portfolio, and R_t^x is the rate of change of the exchange rate between the Korean won and a basket of foreign currencies including the U.S. dollar. The foreign exchange exposure of firm j is measured by β_j and the determinants of the foreign exchange exposure can be probed by regressing β_j against a set of variables that represent the characteristics of firm j. Contrary to common belief, most of these studies report that the proportion of domestic firms with foreign exchange exposure is rather small.

Kwon and Hwang (1999) investigate the characteristics of the foreign exchange exposure of 460 manufacturing companies in Korea. Using monthly data, they find that only 4.8% out of the 460 companies investigated are exposed to currency risk. In particular, they find that while depreciation of the Korean won has an immediate effect of increasing the value of Korean manufacturing firms, it eventually decreases its value in the long run. Regarding the determinants of foreign exchange exposure, they find the size of the firm is the only factor that consistently demonstrates a negative influence with statistical significance.

Lee (1999), using daily data, analyzes the patterns and the determinants of foreign exchange exposure of Korean firms. He observes that textile, paper, wholesale, transportation and lodging industries have significant exposure to the U.S. dollar. Regarding the determinants of foreign currency exposure, he finds that firm size and financial cost have significant effects, which is consistent with the findings of Kwon and Hwang (1999).

Bian, Park and Cho (2006) compare the foreign exchange exposure of Korean companies during the period before the 1997 currency crisis and the period after the currency crisis. Employing the empirical method developed by He and Ng (1998), they find that the foreign currency exposure of Korean firms decreased after the 1997 crisis although the volatility of the won/dollar exchange rate increased sharply with the adoption of the free floating exchange rate regime. Regarding the determinants of currency exposure, they also find that firm size has a negative effect on currency exposure. In addition, the book-to-market ratio, dividend yield and quick ratio have significant effects on the currency exposure of firms during the period before the currency crisis. The effect of these variables, however, becomes statistically insignificant after the currency crisis.

Most of the empirical studies to measure foreign exchange exposure companies in Korea find that the number of firms with a statistically significant level of foreign exchange exposure is quite small. This finding is surprising because the Korean economy is heavily dependent on foreign trade. Lee (2003) argues that if there exist asymmetries in the foreign exchange exposure of Korean firms, measuring the foreign exchange exposure without considering such asymmetries can result in insignificant estimates. Investigating asymmetry in the foreign exchange exposure of Korean firms, he concludes that a high proportion of Korean domestic firms face asymmetric foreign exchange exposure.

Lee (2004) analyzes the determinants for foreign exchange exposure of Korean firms under various return horizons of the U.S. dollar and the Japanese yen. This study also considers the possibility of asymmetric exposure to foreign exchange risk. According to the result of the study, exchange rate exposure exhibits significant time variation reflecting changes in cash flow sensitivities. The study also finds that the extent to which a firm is exposed to exchange rate fluctuations can be explained by the level of growth potential, firm size and leverage; that is, firms with higher growth potential tend to have higher exposure and larger firms tend to have lower exposure. The export ratio and leverage ratio, however, do not exhibit consistent influence on foreign exchange exposure. Kwon (2007) also observes that the foreign exchange exposure of Korean firms demonstrate asymmetry to appreciation and depreciation of the Korean won. In addition, this study shows that foreign currency denominated debt plays a significant role in intensifying asymmetry in foreign exchange exposure.

Instead of investigating the sensitivity of the returns from holding stocks, Kang (2009) measures the exposure of Korean firms to the currencies of major trading partner countries by probing the sensitivity of short-term cash flows to changes in exchange rates. The cash flow approach has the advantage of making it possible to analyze the operational performance of individual firm's hedging strategies. Using the data of listed firms from 2000 to 2008, he finds that more than 30% of the sample firms exhibit significant foreign exchange exposure. Kang also finds that firm size and leverage have significant effects on foreign currency exposure.

1.2 Managing Foreign Exchange Exposure of Firms

It is natural for firms with foreign exchange exposure to hedge foreign exchange risk by employing various hedging techniques and instruments. As a result, empirical studies have also tried to find out whether these hedging techniques are effective in reducing foreign exchange exposure.

Jung and Lee (2000) investigate the foreign exchange risk management strategy of Korean firms. Using the data acquired by a mail survey, they find that the ratio of foreign currency denominated debt to total debt has significantly negative effects on foreign exchange gains. They also observe that better exchange risk management practices such as a higher perception level of foreign exchange risk, accurate calculation of foreign exchange position, and intensive use of risk management tools enhance the business performance of firms.

Jung and Kwon (2007) analyze if the use of foreign currency derivatives in Korean manufacturing firms are effective in reducing their foreign exchange exposure. They find that use of currency derivatives are effective in reducing the foreign exchange exposure caused by foreign currency denominated debt. On the contrary, they also find that currency derivatives are not effective in reducing the exposure arising from exports.

Park, Kim and Bahng (2009) study how the hedging behavior of firms affects their foreign exchange exposure. They compare the effects of various hedging instruments including netting, financial hedging, and operational hedging and conclude that netting significantly decreases the foreign exchange exposure of Korean firms.

The foreign exchange exposure of firms can also be managed through international transactions within business groups. Using a sample of non-financial companies listed on the Korean Exchange, Kwon (2009) demonstrates that international transactions with domestic related firms reduce the foreign exchange exposure of firms and that the effect of internal transactions on the foreign exchange exposure is nearly independent of the use of foreign currency derivatives.

2. International Portfolio Investment and Foreign Exchange Risk

Exchange rate fluctuations not only affect the financial performance of companies but also affect the return from international portfolio investment. Eun and Resnick (1988) measure the size of foreign exchange risk involved with international equity investment under the floating exchange rate regime. They demonstrate that foreign exchange risk explains about 50% of the total risk arising from international equity investment. Contrarily, Yon (1996) finds that most of the risk faced by Korean investors who invest in foreign stocks arises from fluctuations in stock prices rather than fluctuations in exchange rates. One of the reasons for such an unusual result may be use of data from 1985 to 1994 during which the won/dollar exchange rate did not show much fluctuation.

Jang (2004) investigates the effect of foreign exchange risk on the performance of international equity investment from the perspective of Korean investors using data from 1992 to 2003, during which the won/dollar exchange rate showed higher volatility. The study finds that foreign exchange risk accounts for as much as 40% of the total risk borne by Korean investors who invest in foreign equities and that the correlation between foreign exchange return and foreign equity return is generally positive. Based on the findings of the study, Jang argues that Korean investors can improve their investment performance through international diversification but that appropriate hedging strategies are needed in order to achieve improved performance.

Alternatively, Park, Kwon and Lee (2008), investigate the effect of foreign exchange risk on foreign investors investing in the Korean stock market. Comparing the investment behavior of foreign investors and domestic investors, they find that foreign investors increase their sell orders and sell transactions when the change in the won/dollar exchange rate shows negative covariance with the change in stock prices on the previous day. Negative covariance occurs if the Korean won depreciates when the Korean stock prices go down, implying higher risk involved with investing in Korean stocks. They interpret such findings as a piece of evidence that foreign investors attempt to actively manage the foreign exchange risk in order to avoid declines in the value of their investment portfolio caused by depreciation of the Korean won.

The foreign exchange risk borne by firms and investors is reflected in the price of stocks and as a result in the returns from holding stocks. Park and Lee (2009) examine the intertemporal relation between risk and return in the Korean stock market and the foreign exchange market based on the two factor ICAPM framework. Applying the quasi-maximum likelihood estimation method and estimating the multivariate GARCH in mean model, they find that the expected stock returns are negatively related to the dynamic covariance between stock prices and the won/dollar exchange rate.

3. Optimal Hedge Ratio

Economic agents who get exposed to foreign exchange risk as a result of cross-border transactions try to employ diverse hedging techniques to manage the foreign exchange risk. One of the simplest hedging techniques is to take a position in the currency futures that is exactly opposite to their foreign exchange position. Such a simple hedging method, however, still leaves economic agents exposed to the basis risk because spot and forward exchange rates do not always show similar movements. In order to reduce the basis risk, economic agents should select the optimal hedge ratio by taking into consideration the movements of spot and forward exchange rates.

It can be shown that if the basis risk is the only source of risk, the optimal hedge ratio is the ratio of the conditional covariance between spot and forward exchange rates to the conditional variance of forward exchange rates. Consequently, studies on the optimal hedge ratio focus on determining which model, among the ones that can be used to estimate the conditional variance and covariance, can bring about the best hedging performance in terms of reducing the basis risk.

Lee (2002) compares the performance of diverse models including the OLS model, the error correction model and the CCC-GARCH(1, 1) model in hedging foreign exchange risk with won/dollar forward contracts. Adopting two different performance measures, mean-variance utility maximization and risk minimization, he finds that the error correction model with an ARCH (1) error structure outperforms other models in maximizing the mean-variance utility function while conventional models including the simple hedging model and the OLS model show relatively better performance in minimizing risk.

Hong and Moon (2004) examine hedge strategies that utilize won-dollar futures. In particular, they compare the hedge performance of the naive hedge model, the minimum variance hedge model and the bivariate ECT-ARCH (1) model using a sample from January 2, 2001 to December 31, 2002. They find there is no significant difference in the hedge ratio and the hedge performance between the minimum variance model and the bivariate ECT-ARCH (1) model that controls for the cointegration relationship between the won-dollar futures and the won/dollar spot exchange rate. Based on this finding, they advise that investors should use the simple minimum variance hedge model rather than complex and sophisticated models when they intend to hedge the won-dollar exchange rate risk with the won-dollar futures.

Yun and Ahn (2004) compare the hedge effectiveness of the domestic won/dollar futures and the offshore non-deliverable forwards (NDFs). They investigate three hedge strategies including the simple one-to-one hedge, the OLS model and the error correction model. The results verify that the domestic won/dollar futures demonstrate better hedge performance than the offshore NDFs no matter what strategy is used.

Yun (2007) compare the hedge performance of the yen futures and the euro futures listed in the Korea Exchange against that of the dollar futures. He investigates three strategies including the simple one-to-one hedge, the OSL model and the error correction model. He also applies diverse performance measures. The results show that if minimizing risk is the only performance criterion the dollar futures outperform the yen futures and the euro futures. However, the results are reversed when a performance criterion that takes in consideration the return as well as the risk is applied. Yun (2007) also delves into the hedge performance for different hedge horizons and finds that while hedge performance based on the risk only improves as the hedge horizon becomes longer, the result is reversed when the performance criterion is based on the return as well as the risk.

Kang (2009) estimates and compares the hedge effectiveness of currency futures in emerging economies and advanced economies. According to this study, there is hardly any difference in the hedging effectiveness among the simple hedging, the OLS model, the error correction model and the bivariate GARCH (1, 1) model. Irrespective of the hedging model and the hedging horizon, hedging with the won/dollar futures is capable of reducing currency risk by about 97%, which is the highest among the currencies examined in his study.

VI. Conclusion

This paper introduced empirical studies on the won/dollar exchange rate and the foreign exchange market in Korea. Empirical studies on diverse topics including purchasing power parity, the real exchange rate, models to explain nominal exchange rate dynamics, prediction of the won/dollar exchange rate, tests for foreign exchange market efficiency, foreign exchange market interventions, the market microstructure approach, and foreign exchange risk hedging have been presented and discussed. The discussions reveal that depending on the methods and the samples, empirical studies produce different results and conclusions. That implies that while trying to explore these topics with new data and new methods, researchers also need to make efforts to compare and reconcile the different results and conclusions.

Though this paper tries to cover a comprehensive array of topics regarding the won/dollar exchange rate and the foreign exchange markets in Korea, there still remains a vast literature that this paper fails to discuss.

First of all, there is a vast body of literature on the 1997 Korean currency crisis. This literature covers such topics as the cause of the currency crisis, the predictability of the currency crisis, the effectiveness of the IMF loan and conditionality in resolving the crisis, the contagion effect, the early warning system of currency crises, the self-fulfilling nature of the currency crisis, and so on. Coincidentally, there is also a burgeoning literature on the 2008 global financial crisis. Second, there is also a large literature on the co-movement among financial markets.

Survey of the literature on either of these topics deserves a separate full paper. We would like to leave it as a future task.

References

Ahn, C., "Natural Equilibrium Real Exchange Rate in Korea", *Journal of International Economic Studies*, Vol. 10, No. 2(2006), pp. 47-69(in Korean).

안창모, "한국의 장기 균형실질환율 : 장기 균형과 단기 균형이탈률 추정", 대외경제연구, 제10권 제2호(2006), pp. 47-69.

Ahn, C., "Is Filter Trading Rule Profitable in the USD/KRW Rates?: Evidence from De Facto Flexible Rate Period(1998~2007)", *Journal of Korean Economy Studies*, Vol. 22(2008), pp. 81-102(in Korean).

안창모, "원/달러 시장에서 필터 거래규칙이 수익을 낼 수 있는가? : 사실상의 자유변동환율 기간(1998~2007)을 중심으로", 한국경제연구, 제22권 (2008), pp. 81-102.

Bahmani-Oskooee, M. and H.-J. Rhee, "Testing for Long-Run Purchasing Power Parity: An Examination of Korean Won", *International Economic Journal*, Vol. 6(1992), pp. 93-103.

Bian, A., K-I. Park, and J.-W. Cho, "Exchange Rate Exposure of Korean Companies: Pre-and Post-Economic Crisis Analysis", *International Business Journal*, Vol. 17, No. 3(2006), pp. 1-22(in Korean).

변애련, 박경인, 조진완, "외환위기 전·후 한국기업의 환노출 비교 분석", 국제경영연구, 제17권 제3호(2006), pp. 1-22.

Choi, C. G., "Analysis of the Dynamic Effects of Sterilized Foreign Exchange Market Interventions", *Quarterly Economic Analysis*, Vol. 1, No. 2(1995), pp. 69-101(in Korean).

최창규, "불태화외환시장 개입의 동태적 효과 분석", 경제분석, 제1권 제2호 (1995), pp. 69-101.

Choi, S. R. and N. W. Hyung, "Comparing Exchange Rate Volatility Forecasting Models: the Case of KRW/USD", *International Business Journal*, Vol. 14, No. 1(2003), pp. 95-109(in Korean).

최생림, 형남원, "환율 변동성 예측 모형의 실증분석 : 원/달러 환율을 중심으로", 국제경영연구, 제14권 제1호(2003), pp. 95-109.

Chun, S. E., "Developing the Forecasting Model for the won/dollar Exchange Rate", *Proceedings of the 1998 Winter Academic Conference*, Korea International Economic Association(1998), pp. 441-461(in Korean).
전선애, "원/달러 환율예측 모형 개발", 1998년도 동계학술발표대회 논문집, 한국국제경제학회(1998), pp. 441-461.

Chun, S. E. and C. H. Kim, "Estimating Equilibrium won/dollar Real Exchange Rate: the BEER approach", *Korean Economic Journal*, Vol. 24, No. 2(2006), pp. 1-24(in Korean).
전선애, 김정한, "원/달러 실질균형환율의 추정 : 행태균형환율 접근법", 경제연구, 제24권 제2호(2006), pp. 1-24.

Chung, C. H., "Forecasting won/dollar Exchange Rates Using Information in the Forward Exchange Rates and Vector Error Correction Model", *POSRI Business Review*, Vol. 4, No. 1(2004), pp. 174-190(in Korean).
정철호, "선물환 환율을 이용한 원/달러 환율예측 : VECM 기법을 중심으로", POSRI 경영연구, 제4권 제1호(2004), pp. 174-190.

Chung, C.-S., "Exploring Empirical Relationship between Volatility and Transaction- Related Variables in KRS/USD Using High Frequency Data", *Kukje Kyungje Yongu*, Vol. 12, No. 1(2006), pp. 15-44(in Korean).
정재식, "원/달러 환율의 거래관련 정보와 변동성간의 관계 : 고빈도 실거래 자료를 중심으로", 국제경제연구, 제12권 제1호(2006), pp. 15-44.

Chung, C.-S., "The Role of Information in the Seoul Foreign Exchange Market", *Korean Journal of Money and Finance*, Vol. 22, No. 4(2008), pp. 159-184(in Korean).
정재식, "외환거래량을 이용한 정보모형의 비교 분석 : 서울외환시장을 중심으로", 금융학회지, 제22권 제4호(2008), pp. 159-184.

Chung, C.-S. and S. Joo, "Effects of Trading Volume on the Volatility of won/dollar Exchange Rates", *Kukje Kyungje Yongu*, Vol. 5, No. 3(1999), pp. 27-44(in Korean).

정재식, 주상영, "외환거래량이 원/달러 환율변동성에 미치는 영향", 국제경제연구, 제5권 제3호(1999), pp. 27-44.

Cont, R. and J. P. Bouchaud, "Herd Behavior and Aggregate Fluctuations in Financial Markets", *Macroeconomic Dynamics*, Vol. 4, No. 2(2000), pp. 170-196.

Engle, R. F. and C. W. J. Granger, "Co-integration and Error Correction: Representation, Estimation, and Testing", *Econometrica*, March(1987), pp. 251-276.

Eun, C. and B. Resnick, "Exchange Rate Uncertainty, Forward Contracts, and International Portfolio Selection", *Journal of Finance*, Vol. 43(1988), pp. 197-215.

Flood, R. P. and P. M. Garber, "Market Fundamentals Versus Price Level Bubbles: the first tests", *Journal of Political Economy*, Vol. 88(1980), pp. 745-770.

He, J. and L. K. Ng, "The Foreign Exchange Exposure of Japanese Multinational Corporations", *Journal of Finance*, Vol. 53(1998), pp. 733-753.

Hong, C.-H. and G-H. Moon, "Hedge Effectiveness in won-dollar Futures Markets", *The Korean Journal of Financial Management*, Vol. 21, No. 1(2004), pp. 231-253(in Korean).

홍정효, 문규현, "원/달러 선물시장을 이용한 헤지효과성", 재무관리연구, 제21권 제1호(2004), pp. 231-253.

Jang, H., "International Portfolio Investments and the Effects of Foreign Exchange Risk: a Perspective of Korean investors", *International Business Journal*, Vol. 15, No. 2(2004), pp. 61-83(in Korean).

장호윤, "한국 투자가의 관점에서 본 해외 주식투자와 환 위험의 헷징", 국제경영연구, 제15권 제2호(2004), pp. 61-83.

Jeong, C. W. and B. I. Cha, "Forecasting Performance of Monetary Exchange Rate Models: the Case of won/dollar Exchange Rates Under the Market Average Exchange Rate System", *Journal of Money and Finance*, Vol. 12, No. 1(1998), pp. 25-41(in Korean).

정찬우, 차인백, "원/달러 환율모형의 예측력 분석 : 시장평균환율제도 기간을 대상으로", 금융연구, 제12권 제1호(1998), pp. 25-41.

Johansen, S., "Statistical Analysis of Cointegration Vectors", *Journal of Economic Dynamics and Control*, Vol. 12(1988), pp. 231-254.

Johansen, S. and K. Juselius, "Maximum Likelihood Estimation and Inference on Cointergration with Application to the Demand for Money", *Oxford Bulletin of Economics and Statistics*, Vol. 52(1990), pp. 169-210.

Jung, S.-C. and T. H. Kwon, "Does the Use of Foreign Currency Derivatives in Korean Firms Reduce the Exchange Rate Exposure?", *International Business Journal*, Vol. 18, No. 4(2007), pp. 37-63(in Korean).

정성창, 권택호, "기업의 통화파생상품거래, 환노출을 감소시키는가?", 국제경영연구, 제18권 제4호(2007), pp. 37-63.

Jung, T. and K. Lee, "Foreign Exchange Risk Management Strategy of Korean Firms", *International Business Journal*, Vol. 11, No. 1(2000), pp. 57-86(in Korean).

정태영, 이광철, "한국기업의 환위험관리 전략에 관한 실증연구", 국제경영연구, 제11권 제1호(2000), pp. 57-86.

Jung, Y. S., "An Analysis on the Monetary Model of won-dollar Exchange Rate Determination: Using ARDL Method", *Korean Economic Journal*, Vol. 27, No. 4(2009), pp. 99-120(in Korean).

정용석, "원/달러 환율결정의 통화모형에 대한 분석 : ARDL 방식을 이용하여", 경제연구, 제27권 제4호(2009), pp. 99-120.

Kang, J. K., H. J. Park, and S. S. Byun, "On the Effects of Official Intervention Announcements on the Foreign Exchange Markets", *Korean Journal of Money and Finance*, Vol. 11, No. 2(2006), pp. 35-65(in

Korean).

강장구, 박형진, 변성섭, "외환시장의 구두개입 영향에 관한 실증분석", 금융학회지, 제11권 제2호(2006), pp. 35-65.

Kang, S. K., "A Study on the Efficiency in Korean Foreign Exchange Market", *Korean Journal of Futures and Options*, Vol. 14, No. 2(2006), pp. 79-108(in Korean).

강석규, "한국외환시장의 효율성에 관한 연구", 선물연구, 제14권 제2호(2006), pp. 79-108.

Kang, S. K., "The Analysis and Comparison of the Hedging Effectiveness for Currency Futures Markets: Emerging Currency Versus Advanced Currency", *The Korean Journal of Financial Management*, Vol. 26, No. 2(2009), pp. 155-180(in Korean).

강석규, "통화선물시장의 헤징유효성 비교 : 신흥통화 대 선진통화", 재무관리연구, 제26권 제2호(2009), pp. 155-180.

Kang, S. K. and T. H. Kim, "Unbiased Expectations Hypothesis and Price Discovery Performance in Korean Currency Futures Market", *Asia-Pacific Journal of Financial Studies*, Vol. 34, No. 4(2005), pp. 1-28(in Korean).

강석규, 김태혁, "한국 통화선물시장의 불편기대가설과 가격발견성과", 증권학회지, 제34권 제4호(2005), pp. 1-28.

Kang, S. M., "Analysis of Overvaluation of the Real Exchange Rate in Korea", *Korean Journal of Money and Finance*, Vol. 6, No. 2(2001), pp. 75-10(in Korean).

강삼모, "한국의 실질환율 고평가 분석", 금융학회지, 제6권 제2호(2001), pp. 75-100.

Kang, W., "Corporate Cash Flow Exposures to Foreign Exchange Rate and the Determinants: Korean Listed Non-Financial Firms", *The Korean Journal of Financial Management*, Vol. 26, No. 3(2009), pp. 31-64(in Korean).

강 원, "현금흐름의 단기 환노출과 결정요인에 관한 연구", 재무관리연구, 제26권 제3호(2009), pp. 31-64.

Kim, B. H. and M. S. Yu, "Forecasting Analysis of won/dollar Exchange Rate with Markov Switching Models", *Korean Economic Journal*, Vol. 43, No. 1-2(2004), pp. 269-286(in Korean).
김봉한, 유만식, "마코프 국면전환모형을 이용한 환율예측분석", 경제논집, 제43권 제1, 2호(2004), pp. 269-286.

Kim, C. B. and S. W. Mo, "Estimation and Forecasting of Exchange Rates Using Cointegration and Error Correction Model", *Journal of Industrial Economics and Business*, Vol. 13, No. 6(2000), pp. 479-489(in Korean).
김창범, 모수원, "공적분과 오차수정모형을 이용한 환율의 추정과 예측", 산업경제연구, 제13권 제6호(2000), pp. 479-489.

Kim, G. H., "A Study on the Effectiveness of the Intervention Policy in Korea", *Research in Finance and Economics*, Vol. 28(1991), pp. 139-175 (in Korean).
김규한, "개방경제하에서 우리나라 통화정책의 유효성에 관한 연구 : 불태화정책과 자본유출입에 대한 통화상쇄현상을 중심으로", 금융경제연구, 제28권(1991), pp. 139-175.

Kim, J. S., "Estimating the Equilibrium Exchange Rate: An Application to Korea", *Korean Journal of Money and Finance*, Vol. 3, No. 2(1998), pp. 139-175(in Korean).
김정식, "한국의 원/달러 균형 환율 추정", 금융학회지, 제3권 제2호(1998), pp. 139-175.

Kim, J.-O., "Purchasing Power Parity: Two-Country vs. Multi-Country Model", *Korean Journal of Money and Finance*, Vol. 6, No. 2(2001), pp. 101-119(in Korean).
김진옥, "구매력평가설 : 두 국가 대 다 국가 모형", 금융학회지, 제6권 제2호(2001), pp. 101-119.

Kim, K. W. and J. N. Lee, "Efficiency Test of Markets for Forward Exchange Rate in Korea", *The Korean Journal of Finance*, Vol. 13, No. 1(2000), pp. 187-214(in Korean).

김건우, 이재남, "한국선도환 시장의 효율성 검증", 재무연구, 제13권 제1호(2000), pp. 187-214.

Kim, S. H., "Analysis of the Specification and the Forecasting Performance of the Optimal Neural Network Model", *Journal of Money and Finance*, Vol. 14, No. 1(2000), pp. 57-85(in Korean).

김상환, "최적 인공신경망 모형의 설정과 환율예측성과분석", 금융연구, 제14권 제1호(2000), pp. 57-85.

Kim, S. T. and J. J. Lee, "A Study on the Informational Relationship between the NDF Market and the Domestic FX Market", *Korea Trade Review*, Vol. 28, No. 5(2003), pp. 185-214(in Korean).

김석태, 이정준, "역외 NDF 시장과 원/달러 현물 시장간의 시장정보 전이효과에 대한 연구", 무역학회지, 제28권 제5호(2003), pp. 185-214.

Kim, T.-Y., J.-S. Lim, and H.-D. Jung, "An Empirical Study on Efficiency of Foreign Exchange Market in Korea", *Journal of Korean Economy Studies*, Vol. 3(1999), pp. 5-22(in Korean).

김태열, 임종수, 정행득, "우리 나라 외환시장의 효율성에 관한 연구", 한국경제연구, 제3권(1999), pp. 5-22.

Kim, Y.-Y. and J. Y. Park, "Testing Purchasing Power Parity in Transformed ECM with Nonstationary Disequilibrium Error", *Quarterly Economic Analysis*, Vol. 14, No. 1(2008), pp. 42-63(in Korean).

김윤영, 박준용, "오차단위근을 고려한 구매력평가설 검정", 경제분석, 제14권 제1호(2008), pp. 42-63.

Kwon, T. H., "Asymmetric Exchange Rate Exposure and Foreign Currency Denominated Debt", *International Business Journal*, Vol. 18, No. 1(2007), pp. 87-110(in Korean).

권택호, "환노출의 비대칭성과 외화표시 부채", 국제경영연구, 제18권 제1호(2007), pp. 87-110.

Kwon, T. H., "Internal Transactions Within Business Group and Management of Foreign Exchange Exposure", *International Business Journal*, Vol. 20, No. 4(2009), pp. 79-103(in Korean).
권택호, "기업집단 내 내부거래와 환노출 관리", 국제경영연구, 제20권 제4호(2009), pp. 79-103.

Kwon, T. H. and H. K. Hwang, "The Characteristics of Currency Exposure in Korean Manufacturing Companies", *International Business Journal*, Vol. 9, No. 2(1999), pp. 35-63(in Korean).
권택호, 황희곤, "한국 제조기업의 환노출 특성 분석", 국제경영연구, 제9권 제2호(1999), pp. 35-63.

Lee, C. E., "Rational Bubbles in the won/dollar Exchange Rates", *Korean Journal of Money and Finance*, Vol. 7, No. 1(2002), pp. 25-50(in Korean).
이충언, "원/달러 환율에서의 합리적 거품", 금융학회지, 제7권 제1호(2002), pp. 25-50.

Lee, H., "Analysis of the Foreign Exchange Exposure and Its Relation with Firm Characteristics in Korean Firms and Industries", *The Korean Journal of Financial Management*, Vol. 16, No. 2(1999), pp. 383-404(in Korean).
이현석, "우리나라 기업 및 산업의 환노출", 재무관리연구, 제16권 제2호(1999), pp. 383-404.

Lee, H., "The Foreign Exchange Exposure and Asymmetries on Individual Firms", *The Korean Journal of Financial Management*, Vol. 20, No. 1(2003), pp. 305-329(in Korean).
이현석, "개별기업의 환노출과 비대칭성에 관한 연구", 재무관리연구, 제20권 제1호(2003), pp. 305-329.

Lee, H., "An Analysis of the Foreign Exchange Exposure and Determinants",

The Korean Journal of Financial Management, Vol. 21, No. 2(2004), pp. 65-99(in Korean).

이현석, "개별기업의 환노출과 결정요인에 관한 연구", 재무관리연구, 제21권 제2호(2004), pp. 65-99.

Lee, H.-J., "Out-of-sample Forecasting Performance of won/dollar Exchange Rate Return Volatility Model", *Journal of International Economic Studies*, Vol. 13, No. 1(2009), pp. 57-89.

Lee, J. and M. C. Strazicich, "Testing for Nonlinear Threshold Cointegration in the Monetary Model of Exchange Rates with a Century of Data", *KDI Journal of Economic Policy*, Vol. 31, No. 2(2009), pp. 2-13(in Korean).

이준수, M. C. Strazicich, "화폐모형에 의한 환율 결정 이론의 비선형 문턱 공적분 검정 : 100년간 자료를 중심으로", 한국개발연구, 제31권 제2호 (2009), pp. 2-13.

Lee, J. H. and S. G. Lim, "Causality between the Onshore won/dollar Forward Exchange Market and the Offshore NDF Market", *The Korean Journal of Financial Management*, Vol. 17, No. 2(2000), pp. 211-227(in Korean).

이재하, 임상규, "원/달러 역내현물환시장과 역외 NDF 시장 간의 인과관계", 재무관리연구, 제17권 제2호(2000), pp. 211-227.

Lee, J. H. and S. G. Lim, "The Intraday ex Ante Profitability of Arbitrage between won/dollar Spot and Futures", *Korean Journal of Financial Studies*, Vol. 30, No. 1(2002), pp. 267-296(in Korean).

이재하, 임상규, "원/달러 현물과 선물간의 일중 사전적 차익거래 수익성", 증권학회지, 제30권 제1호(2002), pp. 267-296.

Lee, K. Y., "A Study on Forecasting Performance of Weekly won-dollar Exchange Rate", *Korean Journal of Money and Finance*, Vol. 1, No. 2(1996), pp. 44-70(in Korean).

이근영, "주간 원/달러환율을 이용한 오차 및 방향 예측분석", 금융학회지,

제1권 제2호(1996), pp. 44-70.

Lee, K. Y., "A Study on won-yen Exchange Rate Forecasting Models", *Kukje Kyungje Yongu*, Vol. 3, No. 3(1997), pp. 109-127(in Korean).

이근영, "원/엔 환율 예측모형에 관한 연구", 국제경제연구, 제3권 제3호 (1997), pp. 109-127.

Lee, K. Y., "The Effects of Foreign News on the Domestic Foreign Exchange Market", *Korean Journal of Money and Finance*, Vol. 4, No. 2(1999), pp. 27-54(in Korean).

이근영, "해외뉴스가 국내 외환시장에 미치는 영향", 금융학회지, 제4권 제2 호(1999), pp. 27-54.

Lee, K. Y., "The Optimal Hedging Analysis with won/dollar Futures Exchange Rates", *Journal of Korean Economic Analysis*, Vol. 8, No. 2(2002), pp. 109-150(in Korean).

이근영, "원/달러 선물환율을 이용한 최적헤징분석", 한국경제의 분석, 제8 권 제2호(2002), pp. 109-150.

Lee, S. H. and C.-S. Chung, "Testing Information Flows in KRW/USD: Using High Frequency Real Transaction Data", *Korean Journal of Money and Finance*, Vol. 12, No. 2(2007), pp. 127-144(in Korean).

이승호, 정재식, "실거래 자료를 이용한 정보흐름 모형 검정 : 서울외환시장 을 중심으로", 금융학회지, 제12권 제2호(2007), pp. 127-144.

Lee, S. H., Y. S. Rhee, and C. K. Choi, "Foreign Exchange Intervention and Exchange Rate Stability in Korea", *Kukje Kyungje Yongu*, Vol. 4, No. 2(1998), pp. 49-68(in Korean).

이승호, 이영섭, 최장규, "외환시장개입의 환율안정효과", 국제경제연구, 제 4권 제2호(1998), pp. 49-68.

Lee, W. H. and K. S. Yoon, "The Analysis of the Behavior and the Effect of the Foreign Exchange Market Intervention in Korea", *Korea Trade Review*, Vol. 22, No. 1(1997), pp. 31-55(in Korean).

이환호, 윤경석, "우리나라의 외환시장개입의 행태 및 효과분석", 무역학회지, 제22권 제1호(1997), pp. 31-55.

Lee, Y. H. and J. T. Ko, "Synchronization of won/dollar Exchange Rate and yen/dollar Exchange Rate", *Journal of Korean Economic Analysis*, Vol. 9, No. 2(2003), pp. 1-52(in Korean).
이연호, 고정택, "원/달러 환율의 엔/달러 환율에 대한 동조화", 한국경제의 분석, 제9권 제2호(2003), pp. 1-52.

Lee, Y. S., "Does the Long-Run Relationship of Purchasing Power Parity Hold?", *Kukje Kyungje Yongu*, Vol. 2, No. 2(1996), pp. 205-224(in Korean).
이영식, "구매력평가의 장기균형관계는 성립하는가?", 국제경제연구, 제2권 제2호(1996), pp. 205-224.

Lee, Y. S., "A Study on the Predictability of the won/dollar Exchange Rate", *Financial Research Report*, Korea Institute of Finance, 2007(in Korean).
이윤석, "원/달러 환율 예측력 분석에 관한 연구", 금융조사보고서, 한국금융연구원, 2007.

Meese, R., "Testing for Bubbles in Exchange Markets: A Case of Sparkling Rate?", *Journal of Political Economy*, Vol. 94(1986), pp. 345-373.

Meese, R. and K. Rogoff, "Empirical Exchange Rate Models of the Seventies: Do They Fit Out of Sample?", *Journal of International Economics*, Vol. 14(1983), pp. 3-24.

Mo, S. W. and S. R. Kee, "Is the Forward Exchange Market Efficient?", *Kukje Kyungje Yongu*, Vol. 2, No. 2(1996), pp. 187-203(in Korean).
모수원, 기성래, "선물환시장은 효율적인가?", 국제경제연구, 제2권 제2호(1996), pp. 187-203.

Oh, M. S. and S. K. Lee, "The Comparison of Time Series Models to Forecast won/dollar Exchange Rate in Short-Term", *Korean Journal of Money and Finance*, Vol. 4, No. 1(1999), pp. 27-48(in Korean).
오문석, 이상근, "시계열모형에 의한 환율 단기예측력 비교", 금융학회지,

제4권 제1호(1999), pp. 27-48.

Oh, M. S. and S. K. Lee, "The Comparison with Exchange Rate Determinant Models to Forecast won/dollar Exchange Rate", *Korea Management Review*, Vol. 29, No. 4(2000), pp. 711-722(in Korean).
오문석, 이상근, "환율결정모형의 원/달러환율 예측력 비교", 경영학연구, 제29권 제4호(2000), pp. 711-722.

Park, B. J., "Robust Forecasts of Exchange Rates Using Neural Network Regression Quantiles", *KyongJeHak YonGu*, Vol. 45, No. 2(1997), pp. 31-60(in Korean).
박범조, "신경회로망 회귀위수를 이용한 환율예측", 경제학연구, 제45권 제2호(1997), pp. 31-60.

Park, B. J., "Neural Network Regression Quantiles Using a Genetic Algorithm and Their Applications in Forecasting Exchange Rates", *Kukje Kyungje Yongu*, Vol. 4, No. 3(1998), pp. 239-253(in Korean).
박범조, "유전적 알고리즘을 이용한 신경회로망 회귀위수와 외환예측" 국제경제연구, 제4권 제3호(1998), pp. 239-253.

Park, B. J., "The Impact of Surprise Information on the Relation between Volatility and Trading Volume in Exchange Rate Markets", *Quarterly Economic Analysis*, Vol. 13, No. 1(2007), pp. 56-87(in Korean).
박범조, "외환시장의 충격정보가 변동성과 거래량의 관계에 미치는 영향", 경제분석, 제13권 제1호(2007), pp. 56-87.

Park, B. J., "A study on the Relationship between Volatility and Trading Volumes Using a Surprising-Information-Stochastic-Volatility (SISV) Model", *Quarterly Economic Analysis*, Vol. 14, No. 4(2008), pp. 47-85(in Korean).
박범조, "외환시장의 변동성과 거래량의 관계 분석 : 충격정보 확률변동성 모형 이용", 경제분석, 제14권 제4호(2008), pp. 47-85.

Park, D., "An Empirical Test of the Deviation of won-dollar Exchange Rates form Long-Run Purchasing Power Parity", *Kukje Kyungje Yongu*, Vol.

1, No. 1(1995), pp. 141-163(in Korean).

박대근, "원/달러 환율의 장기구매력평가로부터의 이탈에 대한 실증분석", 국제경제연구, 제1권 제1호(1995), pp. 141-163.

Park, D., "The Effect of the won-yen Exchange Rate on the Foreign Exchange Market Intervention in Korea: an Exchange Market Pressure Approach", *Korean Journal of Money and Finance*, Vol. 3, No. 1(1998), pp. 67-97(in Korean).

박대근, "원/엔 환율과 외환시장 개입 : 외환시장압력을 중심으로", 금융학회지, 제3권 제1호(1998), pp. 67-97.

Park, D. and J. H. Choi, "Was the Korean Won Overvalued before the Currency Crisis?", *Korean Journal of Money and Finance*, Vol. 5, No. 1(2000), pp. 43-65(in Korean).

박대근, 최준혁, "외환위기 이전에 원화는 고평가되었는가?", 금융학회지, 제5권 제1호(2000), pp. 43-65.

Park, H. S. and W. C. Jang, "The Effect of Private Information on Short-Term Fluctuation of the Won/Dollar Exchange Rate", *Journal of International Economic Studies*, Vol. 3, No. 4(1999), pp. 35-75(in Korean).

박해식, 장원창, "사적정보를 이용한 원/달러 환율의 단기변동 분석", 대외경제연구, 제3권 제4호(1999), pp. 35-75.

Park, H. S. and C. Y. Song, "Vocal Intervention and Exchange Rate Volatility: The Case of Japan between 2000 and 2003", *Kukje Kyungje Yongu*, Vol. 9, No. 3(2003), pp. 1-27(in Korean).

박해식, 송치영, "엔/달러 외환시장에서의 구두개입 효과", 국제경제연구, 제9권 제3호(2003), pp. 1-27.

Park, H. S. and C. Y. Song, "Understanding the Synchronisation of the Movements of Korean Won and Japanese Yen form an FX Market Micro-Structural Approach", *Quarterly Economic Analysis*, Vol. 12, No. 4(2006), pp. 1-34(in Korean).

박해식, 송치영, "미시구조적 접근을 통한 원/엔 동조화의 이해", 경제분석,

제12권 제4호(2006), pp. 1-34.

Park, J.-G. and P.-S. Lee, "Relation Between Risk and Return in the Korean Stock Market and Foreign Exchange Market", *The Korean Journal of Financial Management*, Vol. 26, No. 3(2009), pp. 197-226(in Korean).
박재곤, 이필상, "주가와 환율의 위험-수익 관계에 대한 연구", 재무관리연구, 제26권 제3호(2009), pp. 197-226.

Park, J. W., T.-H. Kwon, and W.-B. Lee, "Foreign Investors Response to the Foreign Exchange Rate Risk in the Korean Stock Markets", *The Korean Journal of Financial Management*, Vol. 25, No. 4(2008), pp. 53-78(in Korean).
박종원, 권택호, 이우백, "한국 주식시장에서 환위험에 대한 외국인 투자자의 반응", 재무관리연구, 제25권 제4호(2008), pp. 53-78.

Park, J. Y., "Testing for Unit Roots and Cointegration by Variable Addition", in Fomby, T. B. and F. G. Rhodes Jr. (eds.) Advancesin Econometrics, Vol. 8(1990), pp. 107-134.

Park, S. W., H. H. Kim, and D. W. Bahng, "Netting and Hedging Effect on the Exchange Risk Exposure of the Korean Export Firms", *International Business Journal*, Vol. 20, No. 4(2009), pp. 1-28(in Korean).
박세운, 김희호, 방두완, "네팅과 헤지가 우리나라 수출기업의 환위험 노출계수에 미치는 효과", 국제경영연구, 제20권 제4호(2009), pp. 1-28.

Rapach, D. E. and M. E. Wohar, "Testing the Monetary Model of Exchange Rate Determination: New Evidence from a Century of Data", *Journal of International Economics*, Vol. 58(2002), pp. 359-385.

Rhee, H. J., "An Empirical Study on the Exchange Rate Determination between U. S. Dollar And Korean Won: New Results From Johansen's Cointegration Methodology", *Kukje Kyungje Yongu*, Vol. 3, No. 3(1997), pp. 129-151(in Korean).
이현재, "원화의 대미 환율결정에 관한 실증분석 : 공적분추정법에 의한 접근", 국제경제연구, 제3권 제3호(1997), pp. 129-151.

Rhee, Y. H., "A Cointegration Test of the Long-Run Purchasing Power Parity: The Case of the won/dollar Exchange Rate", *Working Paper*, Daewoo Economic Research Institute(1993) (in Korean).

이연호, "한국 원화환율의 장기구매력평가 관계분석", 조사월보, 대우경제연구소(1993).

Rhee, Y. S., "On the Effects of Foreign Exchange Market Intervention", *Korean Journal of Money and Finance*, Vol. 2, No. 1(1997), pp. 35-60(in Korean).

이영섭, "우리나라 외환시장개입에 장단기 효과 분석", 금융학회지, 제2권 제1호(1997), pp. 35-60.

Ryou, J. W. and T. J. Kim, "Balance of Payments Shocks and the Dynamics of Foreign Exchange Market Intervention", *Korean Journal of Money and Finance*, Vol. 3, No. 2(1998), pp. 95-137(in Korean).

유재원, 김태준, "국제수지 충격과 동태적 외환시장개입", 금융학회지, 제3권 제2호(1998), pp. 95-137.

Seon, J. and K. S. Eom, "Trading Intensity and Informational Effect of Trades in the won/dollar FX Market: Event Uncertainty Hypothesis vs. Hot Potato Hypothesis", *Asia-Pacific Journal of Financial Studies*, Vol. 35, No. 6(2006), pp. 77-102.

Shin, S. H., "An Evaluation of the Exchange Rate Forecasting Power of the Neural Network Model and the Moving Average Method", *Journal of Money and Finance*, Vol. 9, No. 1(1995), pp. 103-135(in Korean).

신성환, "인공신경망모형과 이동평균법의 환율예측력 평가", 금융연구, 제9권 제1호(1995), pp. 103-135.

Song, C.-Y., "News and Financial Prices", *Kukje Kyungje Yongu*, Vol. 8, No. 3(2002), pp. 1-34(in Korean).

송치영, "뉴스가 금융시장에 미치는 영향에 관한 연구", 국제경제연구, 제8권 제3호(2002), pp. 1-34.

Sung, B. Y. and E. R. Kim, "A Study of the Efficiency of the Non-Deliverable Forward Exchange Market", *Korea Trade Review*, Vol. 24, No. 1(1999), pp. 63-83(in Korean).

성범용, 김응래, "역외선물환시장의 효율성에 관한 연구", 무역학회지, 제24권 제1호(1999), pp. 63-83.

Williamson, J. (ed.), *Estimating Equilibrium Exchange Rates*, Institute for International Economics, Washington, 1994.

Yon, G.-H., "International Portfolio Investment and Currency Risk Hedging", *The Korean Journal of Financial*, Vol. 9, No. 2(1996), pp. 211-247(in Korean).

연강흠, "해외증권투자와 환위험의 헤징", 재무연구, 제9권 제2호(1996), pp. 211-247.

Yoon, S. M. and K. S. Kim, "Time Scale and the Efficiency of Foreign Exchange Market: Herd Behavior and Information Transmission", *KyongJeHak YonGu*, Vol. 53, No. 2(2005), pp. 145-168(in Korean).

윤성민, 김경식, "시간척도와 외환시장의 효율성 : 무리행동과 정보전달", 경제학연구, 제53권 제2호(2005), pp. 145-168.

Yoon, S. M. and S.-Y. Ryu, "Time-scale, Information Asymmetry and Herd Behavior", *Korean Journal of Money and Finance*, Vol. 12, No. 4(2007), pp. 229-256(in Korean).

윤성민, 류수열, "시간척도, 정보비대칭성, 무리행동", 금융학회지, 제12권 제4호(2007), pp. 229-256.

You, T. and K. S. Han, "Testing the Unbiased Forward Rate Hypothesis in the won/dollar Foreign Exchange Markets: Before and After the Korean Financial Crisis", *The Korean Journal of Finance*, Vol. 15, No. 1(2002), pp. 151-188(in Korean).

유태우, 한기수, "원/달러 환율에 대한 불편선물환가설 검증 : 외환위기 전후 비교", 재무연구, 제15권 제1호(2002), pp. 151-188.

Yun, W.-C., "Comparative Analysis on the Hedging Effectiveness Among Domestic Currency Futures Contracts", *Korean Journal of Futures and Options*, Vol. 15, No. 1(2007), pp. 41-72(in Korean).

윤원철, "국내 통화선물계약의 상대적 헤징효과 분석", 선물연구, 제15권 제1호(2007), pp. 41-72.

Yun, W.-C. and H.-J. Ahn, "A Comparative Analysis of Hedging Effectiveness of won/dollar Futures and NDF Contracts", *Korean Journal of Futures and Options*, Vol. 12, No. 2(2004), pp. 73-99(in Korean).

윤원철, 안현진, "원/달러 선물계약과 NDF 계약의 헤징효율성 비교", 선물연구, 제12권 제2호(2004), pp. 73-99.

AUTHOR INDEX

Acharya, V. V.   161

Adams, J. C.   352

Adkisson, J. A.   366

Affleck-Graves, J.   243, 301

Aggarwal, R.   293, 295, 297

Agrawal, A.   305

Agudelo, D. A.   83

Aharony, J.   473

Ahn, C. M.   136, 622, 635

Ahn, H. B.   532-533

Ahn, H. J. (Hee-Joon)   95-96, 165-166, 169

Ahn, H. J. (Hyun-Jin)   653

Ahn, S. L.   245

Ahn, Y. G.   152, 218-219, 226, 228, 230, 232, 249, 288, 290

Ahn, Y. Y.   541

Alexander, G. J.   344, 349

Aliber, R.   241

Allen, F.   119, 475

Almazan, A.   352

Almeida, H.   544

Amihud, Y.   34, 85, 108n; 121n; 151, 161, 163n; 167, 473

An, Y. H.   35

Anand, A.   115n

Anderson, R. M.   152-153

Ang, A.   18

Angel, J.   114

Asquith, P.   139, 300, 473

Avramov, D.   344

Babenko, I.   492-493

Bae, C. M.   222

Bae, H. J.   532, 534

Bae, J. B.   152

Bae, K. H.   79, 91, 114, 169, 244, 351, 525, 535, 538, 538n

Bae, K. I.   588

Bae, S. C.   169

Baek, J. S.   534, 536-537

Baek, Y. H.   239

Bagnoli, M.   493

Bagwell, L. S.   493

Bahmani-Oskooee, M.   619

Bahng, D. W.   650

Baik, Y. H.   37

Bailey, W.   84-85, 85n; 86

Baker, H. K.   467

Baker, M.   206n; 242-243, 245-246, 291

Baks, K. P.   342

Bakshi, G.   581, 585

Ball, R.   225

Ban, J. I.   380

Bandi, F. M.   148

Banz, R.   9, 274

Barber, B. M.   117, 236-237, 237n; 238, 345, 368

Barberis, N.   206n; 208, 221, 249, 251, 381

Barclay, M. J.   91, 114-115, 130, 350

Barker, C. A.   481

Barras, L.   343

Basu, S.   12

Beatty, R. P.   423-424

Bekaert, G.   64n; 70-72, 75, 77-78, 78n; 79, 81, 97

Benartzi, S.   209, 471

Benesh, G. A.   473

Ben-Rephael, A.   364

Benson, P. G.   349

Benveniste, L. M.   426, 439, 442n

Beranek, A.   468

Bergstresser, D.   346, 358

Berk, J. B.   346, 362

Berkman, H.   136

Bernardo, A.   475

Bernartzi, S.   472- 473

Berry, T. D.   122n

Bessembinder, H.   133

Bharath, S. T.   498

Bhargava, R.   356

Bhattacharya, S.   471

Biais, B.   109n; 130

Bian, A.   647

Billett, M. T.   493

Binh, K. B.   139, 139n; 140, 149-150, 150n

Black, B. S.   519n; 520, 530, 543, 543n

Black, F.   2, 5-6, 8, 15, 21, 468, 589

Blake, C. R.   340, 345, 359, 366-367

Blume M.   279
Bodie, Z.   359
Bodurtha, J. N.   364
Boehmer, E.   139, 141n
Bollen, N. P. B.   148n; 341-342, 345, 347, 374
Bollerslev, T.   155
Booth, J. R.   429, 439n
Bose, A.   356
Bouchaud, J. P.   625
Boudreaux, K. J.   361
Boyer, B.   347
Bradley, M.   363
Brauer, G. A.   361
Brav, A.   363, 458-459, 472, 485, 491, 494
Breeden, D.   3, 27, 585
Breen, W.   342
Brennan, M. J.   164, 468, 490
Brickley, J.   361
Bris, A.   344
Brockman, P.   476
Brown, D.   493
Brown, F. E.   339
Brown, K. C.   352, 357
Brown, N.   241
Brown, S. J.   342, 349, 351, 359
Bruner, R.   305
Burgess, R. C.   360
Busaba, W. Y.   439
Busse, J. A.   341-342, 345, 349, 357, 360, 364, 374
Byun, H. S. (Hyun Su)   233
Byun, H. S. (Hee Sub)   524, 539-540
Byun, H. Y.   534, 538
Byun, J. C.   156, 235
Byun, J. H.   234, 237, 239, 243-246
Byun, S. J.   571, 585, 589
Byun, S. S.   638
Byun, Y. H.   238
Byun, Y. T.   585

Cai, J.   341
Campbell, J. Y.   39, 41-42, 152, 158, 291-292, 468
Cao, C.   127-128
Carhart, M. M.   33, 342, 355-356, 360
Carlson, M.   352
Carpenter, J. N.   360
Carrieri, F.   64n; 73-74, 75n
Carter, R. B.   429

Cesari, R.   341
Cha, B. I.   628
Cha, H. J.   346
Cha, M. H.   377
Cha, M. J.   239
Chae, J.   33, 119, 230, 230n; 232, 475
Chakraborty, A.   119
Chakravarty, S.   114, 115n
Chalk, A.   294
Chalmers, J. M. R.   356, 358
Chambers, J.   131
Chamon, M.   84
Chan, K.   79, 368
Chan, K. C.   225
Chan, L. K. C.   349
Chan, M. C.   341
Chance, D. M.   344
Chang, U.   138n
Chang, E. C.   340
Chang, J. H.   433n; 434-435, 531-532, 534, 541, 544
Chang, K. C.   152, 248
Chang, K. H.   25, 144, 146, 157, 581, 584
Chang, S. J.   525
Chang, S. Y.   158
Chang, U.   373
Chang, Y. K.   123, 141n; 278
Charles J. C.   492
Chay, J. B.   169, 362, 576
Chen, C.   573
Chen, D. H.   79
Chen, G. M.   85, 85n
Chen, H. L.   343, 349, 354
Chen, J.   18, 344
Chen, L.   42
Chen, N.   30, 207n
Chen, Q.   347, 351
Chen, Y.   367
Cheon, Y. S.   533
Cheong, K.-W.   31, 156
Cherkes, M.   363
Chevalier, J.   343, 346, 353, 357
Chi, H. J.   31
Cho, D. (Dam)   24-25, 29, 373, 575
Cho, D. D.   136
Cho, D. S.   522
Cho, H.   594
Cho, J. H. (Ji-Ho)   222, 536

Cho, J. H. (Jaeho)   37, 39, 42, 42n; 374
Cho, J. W.   91, 577, 647
Cho, J. Y.   422, 427
Cho, S. M.   580
Cho, Y. H.   118n; 540
Choe, H.   34-35, 79, 81-82, 90, 115, 117-118,
    124-125, 127-128, 135, 138, 141, 162, 163n;
    164, 169, 215, 219, 380, 577
Choe, K. H.   533
Choi, B. W.   580
Choi, C. G.   638
Choi, C. K.   637
Choi, D. S.   458, 488, 497
Choi, H. B.   583
Choi, H. G.   36n
Choi, H. S. (Heung Sik)   14, 273, 281, 283, 287,
    581-582
Choi, H. S. (Hae Sool)   298, 429-430
Choi, I. C.   237, 239
Choi, J. H.   541, 621
Choi, J. J.   361
Choi, J. W.   537
Choi, J. Y.   153n; 158n
Choi, M. S.   233n; 298, 418-421, 423, 425, 425n;
    426-428, 437, 440, 440n; 441-443
Choi, P. S.   588
Choi, S. K.   88n
Choi, S. R.   631
Choi, U. Y.   532, 534
Choi, W. S.   157, 521, 532
Choi, W. Y.   19, 36, 214-217, 239, 459, 487
Choi, Y. S.   582
Chong, B.-U.   150n
Chopra, N.   207n
Chordia, T.   160-161, 161n; 344
Chou, P. H.   136
Christie, W. G.   148n
Christoffersen, S. E. K.   344, 367
Chua, L.   439n
Chui, A.   382, 252n
Chun, S. E.   478-479, 622, 629
Chung, C. H.   152, 227, 284
Chung, C. S.   169, 641-643
Chung, H. Y.   376
Chung, J.   131
Chung, J. M.   90, 115, 117-118, 130, 579
Chung, J. R.   587
Chung, J.-W.   433n; 434-435

Chung, K.   122n; 156n
Chung, K. H.   132-134, 472
Chung, M. K.   578
Cici, G.   344, 354-355
Clark, P. K.   154
Cochrane, J. H.   36n; 41-42
Cohen, K.   109n; 339
Cohen, L.   350
Cohen, R. B.   343
Coles, J. L.   363
Collins, S.   350
Comer, G.   367
Conrad, J.   285
Cont, R.   625
Cooper, M. J.   346
Coval, J. D.   215, 343, 347, 350
Covrig, V.   368
Cowles, A.   291
Cox, J. C.   589
Cremers, M.   343, 351
Cross, F.   282
Cumby, R. E.   341

Dahlquist, M.   87, 341
Dangl, T.   351
Daniel, K.   204, 222, 251, 252n; 276, 342, 376
Dann, L. Y.   363, 489
Das, S. R.   353
Dass, N.   353
Datar, V. T.   226
Davis, G. F.   352
Davis, J. L.   275-276
De Jong, F.   109n
DeAngelo, H.   458, 476
DeAngelo, L.   458, 476
DeBondt, W.   207, 218, 221, 223-224, 285-286, 288
Del Guercio, D.   359, 366
Deli, D. N.   352, 367
DeLong, J. B.   81, 208-209
Demsetz, H.   108n
Denis, D. J.   476
Dermine, J.   350
Derrien, F.   245
Desai, H.   234
Dhillon, U. S.   473
Diamond, W. D.   139
Dierkens, N.   300

Dittmar, A.   488n; 491, 497
Dittmar, R. F.   497
Domowitz, I.   85-86
Dreman, D.   241
Driessen, J.   351
Duarte, J.   35, 125-126, 126n; 164, 164n; 165
Dubofsky, D. A.   356
Dupire, B.   581
Dvorak, T.   92

Eades, K. M.   468-469
Easley, D.   35, 124n; 125, 164
Easterbrook, F. H.   474
Edelen, R. M.   131, 345, 356
Edwards, W.   221
Eger, C. E.   349
Ellison, G.   343, 346, 353, 357
Elton, E. J.   340, 345, 349, 359-360, 364, 367, 468, 470
Engle, R. F.   145, 155, 162n; 619
Engstrom, S.   341
Eom, C. J.   229, 232, 576
Eom, K. S.   34, 119-120, 126, 131, 133, 135n; 136, 141-143, 143n; 144-150, 150n; 152-153, 159, 161, 161n; 162-163, 163n; 165, 169, 641
Eom, Y. H.   11, 11n; 32, 32n; 33n; 34, 163-164, 278, 581-583, 587-588
Eom, Y. S.   94, 138n; 169, 215, 219, 230, 230n; 232, 577
Errunza, V.   64n; 73-74, 75n
Eun, C.   650
Evans, R. B.   354

Fabozzi, F. J.   348, 367
Faff, R. W.   366
Falkenstein, E. G.   365
Fama, E. F.   1, 9-10, 15-16, 21, 31-32, 39, 42, 73n; 163-164, 233, 235, 272-273, 275-276, 286, 291, 299, 306, 343, 440, 440n; 458, 481, 497
Farnsworth, H.   342
Fenn, G.   492
Ferris, S. P.   344
Ferson, W.   342, 343, 367
Financial Supervisory Service   84n; 566, 579
Firth, M.   369
Fisher, A. K.   294

Fisher, L.   151, 233, 481
Flood, R. P.   625
Foster, F. D.   125, 164
Foster, T. W.   481
Francis, J. C.   348, 367
Fraser, D. R.   366
Frazzini, A.   350, 364-365
French, K. R.   1, 9, 31-32, 39, 42, 73n; 123, 163-164, 272-273, 275-276, 282-283, 286, 291, 306, 343, 458
Fried, J. M.   490, 492
Friedman, M.   203, 206-207

Gale, D.   119
Gallagher, D. R.   356
Gallant, A. R.   155-156
Garber, P. M.   625
Gardner, P.   356
Garman, M.   108n
Gaspar, J. M.   355
Gatto, M. A.   367
Gemmill, G.   362
George, T. J.   33, 123, 154, 163n
Gerald, S. M.   492
Gervais, S.   354
Geske, R.   367
Ghosh, A.   84
Gibbons, M. R.   6, 283
Gibson, S.   344, 351, 354-355
Gil, H. Y.   533
Gil-Bazo, J.   345
Gillan, S. L.   518
Glen, J.   85-86, 341
Glosten, L.   35, 108, 109n; 156, 164
Goetzmann, W. N.   237, 342-343, 350-351, 356, 360, 365, 359
Goh, J. M.   542
Goldstein, I.   347, 351, 363
Golec, J.   349
Gong, J. S.   156-157
Goodhart, C. A. E.   109n; 154n
Gordon, R.   493
Gottesman, A. A.   167, 343
Goyal, A.   147, 147n
Graham, J. R.   2, 27, 242, 458-459, 472, 485, 491, 494
Grammig, J.   143, 150

Granger, C. W. J.   619
Green, R. C.   346
Green, T. C.   349
Greene, J. T.   356
Gremillion, L.   328
Gressis, N.   342
Griffin, J. M.   73n
Grinblatt, M.   93, 217-219, 251, 341-343, 365, 376, 481
Grossman, S. J.   158
Gruber, M. J.   340, 345, 347, 349, 359-360, 364, 367, 468, 470
Grullon, G.   471-473, 476, 492, 494
Guahk, S. Y.   227-228
Guay, W.   494
Guercio, D. D.   363
Gugler, K.   518
Guidolin, M.   368
Gulen, H.   344, 346
Gultekin, M. N.   280
Gultekin, N. B.   280
Gutierrez, V.   241

Ha, Y. J.   330n; 333, 374-375, 377, 379
Habermeier, K.   84
Habib, M. A.   431
Hahn, D. H.   573
Hahn, J.   94
Hahn, J. H.   11, 11n; 32, 32n; 33n; 34, 163-164, 278
Hahn, S. B.   92, 94, 138n; 143, 143n; 152-153, 161, 161n; 162, 169
Han, A. R.   250
Han, B.   217-219, 251
Han, D.
Han, K. S.   633
Han, M. Y.   238
Han, S. I.   27, 584
Handa, P.   20, 114
Handjinicolaou, G.   490
Hansch, O.   127-128
Hansen, L. P.   17, 24, 39, 41
Harford, J.   494
Harlow, W. V.   357
Harris, J. H.   127, 148n
Harris, L.   35, 109n; 114, 132-133, 138, 159, 164

Harris, M.   493
Harvey, C. R.   2, 24n; 27, 64n; 70-72, 75, 77-78, 78n; 79, 81, 97, 242, 458-459, 472, 485, 491, 494
Hasbrouck, J.   35, 108n; 114, 125, 128, 141, 148, 161-162, 164, 574
Hau, H.   92, 368
Hazelkorn, T.   305
He, J.   648
Heckman, J. J.   167
Heinkel, R.   301
Hendershott, T.   91
Hendricks, D.   342
Henriksson, R. D.   340
Henry, P. B.   64n; 78
Hentschel, L.   156
Heo, H. J.   233n
Herman, E. S.   344, 344n
Hertzel, M.   301
Hess, P. J.   283, 468-469
Heston, S. L.   584
Hietala, P.   85
Hillion, P.   130
Hiraki, T.   351
Hirshleifer, D.   204, 206n; 222, 247-249, 251, 252n
Hodges, C. W.   356
Hogan, K.   64n; 73-74, 75n
Hong, C. H.   169, 250, 574, 590, 653
Hong, D. H.   376
Hong, G. H.   241, 378
Hong, H.   222, 251, 344
Hong, J. B.   525
Hong, J. P.   379
Hong, K.   94
Horowitz, I.   339
Hortacsu, A.   361
Hou, K.   73
Howe, K. M.   122n
Huang, J.   346
Huang, M.   344
Huang, R.   125, 127
Huh, H. J.   298, 418-419, 421, 423, 440, 440n; 441
Huh, N.-S.   419, 425, 429-430
Hvidkjaer, S.   35, 125, 164
Hwang, C. Y.   154
Hwang, H. K.   647
Hwang, L. S.   477, 538

Hwang, S. K.   375, 379
Hwang, S. W.   6-8, 11, 11n; 224, 228
Hwang. S. H.   304
Hyung, N. W.   631

Ibbotson, R. G.   294, 359, 437-438
Ikenberry, D.   234
Ingersoll, J.   343
Ippolito, R. A.   340
Irvine, P. J.   342
Ivkovic, Z.   343, 347, 356

Jackson, D.   342
Jacoby, G.   167
Jaffe, J.   283, 305, 437-438
Jagannathan, M.   492, 494
Jagannathan, R.   25-26, 41-42, 156, 340, 342
Jagtiani, J.   85-86
Jain, P.   234, 346
Jang, B. S.   419, 433, 433n
Jang, G.   139, 139n; 140
Jang, G. Y.   590
Jang, H.   651
Jang, H. S.   14, 113-114, 117, 119, 121-122, 126,
    129, 136, 273, 283, 287, 519n; 520, 526, 530,
    541-543, 543n; 544
Jang, J. C.   29
Jang, J. Y.   304
Jang, S.   169
Jang, S.-S.   425, 429-430
Jang, W. A.   570
Jang, W. C.   644
Jang, W. W.   581, 587
Jarnecic, E.   156n
Jayaraman, N.   348
Jee, C.   31, 126, 130, 289-290
Jegadeesh, N.   216, 218, 221, 229, 284, 286-288,
    343
Jen, F. C.   339, 348
Jensen, M. C.   6, 15, 21, 233, 244, 339, 474, 481,
    492, 522
Jeong, C. W.   628
Jeong, H. J.   225, 288
Jeong, J. H.   480, 527, 590
Jeong, J. Y.   156, 158, 573

Jeong, S. H.   214-217, 219, 239, 536
Jeong, W. H.   158
Ji, H. J.   582, 587-588
Ji, S. G.   239
Jiang, G. J.   343
Jiang, W.   347, 351, 363
Jinn, T. H.   373, 535
Jiraporn, P.   475
Jo, H. H.   21n
Jo, J. I.   156, 235
Joh, K. S.   300
Joh, S. W.   420, 423, 433n; 436, 436n; 478-479,
    488, 493, 530, 532, 544
Johansen, S.   619
John, J, P.   492
John, K.   467, 471
Johnson, H.   473
Johnson, S. A.   362
Johnson, W. T.   356
Jones, C. S.   342
Jones, M. C.   139
Joo, H. K.   379
Joo, J. K.   478-479
Joo, S.   641
Joo, S. H.   379
Joo, S. L.   244, 418-419, 425, 529, 531
Jostova, G.   18
Joy, O. M.   342
Jun, S. G.   488, 493, 536
Jun, S. Y.   420, 428
Jung, D. S.   592
Jung, H.   11n; 12, 33n; 38-39, 42
Jung, H. C.   306
Jung, H. D.   632
Jung, J. R.   17
Jung, K. H.   480
Jung, K. Y.   243
Jung, M. K.   488-489, 491
Jung, S. C.   233-234, 243, 418-421, 425, 438,
    441-442, 478-479, 488-489, 489n; 490, 650
Jung, T.   649
Jung, Y. S.   624
Juselius, K.   619

Kacperczyk, M.   344, 355
Kadiyala, P.   344

Kadlec, G. B.   131, 356

Kahle, K.   492

Kahneman, D.   203, 207, 210, 220-221

Kalay, A.   300

Kalev, P. S.   156n

Kam, H. K.   11, 11n; 31-32, 276

Kan, R.   207n

Kandel, S.   8, 42, 364

Kang, B. H.   136n; 138n

Kang, B. J.   585

Kang, H. C.   91, 133, 135n; 526, 541

Kang, H. S.   11n; 12, 14, 136, 233-234, 273, 287,
    296, 307, 418-420, 422-423, 425, 427, 429, 537

Kang, I. C.   576

Kang, J. K. (Jun-Koo)   93, 244, 523, 535-536

Kang, J. K. (Jangkoo)   95-96, 132, 169, 376, 575,
    582, 585, 589, 592, 638

Kang, J. M.   19

Kang, K. H.   478-479

Kang, S. H.   156

Kang, S. K.   169, 573, 590, 633-634

Kang, S. M.   622

Kang, T. H.   585

Kang, W.   532, 544, 649, 654

Kaniel, R.   355-356

Karceski, J.   349

Karolyi, G. A.   64n; 73, 79, 82, 87, 94, 149n

Karpoff, J.   154n

Katz, L.   366

Kaul, G.   33, 123, 163n; 285

Kavajecz, K. A.   128

Kee, S. R.   635

Keim, D. B.   116, 279-280, 283, 291, 343

Kelley, E.   241

Keloharju, M.   93

Kempf, A.   357

Keown, A. J.   473

Keswani, A.   346

Khil, J.   82, 116, 122n; 136n; 152, 156n

Kho, B. C.   18, 73, 79, 81-82, 88, 90-91, 114,
    117-118, 156-157, 169, 229, 230n; 231-232,
    236, 289, 374, 570

Khorana, A.   344-345, 347-348, 351-352, 354, 363

Ki, H. S.   580

Kiefer, N. M.   124n

Kim, B. C.   585

Kim, B. G.   303

Kim, B. H. (Byoung Ho)   528, 530

Kim, B. H. (Bonghan)   630

Kim, B. J. (Byoung Joon)   225, 288

Kim, B. J. (Bong Jun)   39, 41-42, 42n; 374

Kim, C. B.   629

Kim, C. H.   622

Kim, C. J.   476

Kim, C. K.   489, 489n

Kim, C. S.   231-232, 378, 528, 531, 540

Kim, C. T.   278

Kim, D.   7, 8, 11, 11n; 12, 14-16, 18, 32, 33n; 35,
    38-39, 42

Kim, D. H. (Dong Hoe)   20, 152, 227, 284

Kim, D. H. (Dae-Ho)   586

Kim, D. S. (Dong-Soon)   12, 364

Kim, D. S. (Dae Sik)   250

Kim, D. W.   473

Kim, E. H.   64n; 78-79, 83, 352, 468-469

Kim, E. R.   632

Kim, G. H.   637

Kim, G. M.   522-523

Kim, H. A.   233, 243, 420, 425, 438, 441-442, 425

Kim, H. B.   379

Kim, H. C.   17

Kim, H. H.   650

Kim, H. J.   222

Kim, H. S. (Hwa-Sung)   588

Kim, H. S. (Hyun-Seok)   152

Kim, I. J.   569, 571, 580-581, 584, 586-587, 589,
    595

Kim, J. E.   470

Kim, J. H. (Jee Hong)   542

Kim, J. H. (Jae Hwi)   238

Kim, J. H. (Jin-Ho)   12

Kim, J. I.   420

Kim, J. K. (Jae Keun)   579

Kim, J. K. (Jeong Kuk)   471

Kim, J. K. (Jong-Kwon)   36n

Kim, J. M.   244, 525, 535

Kim, J. O. (Jong-Oh)   139n

Kim, J. O. (Jin-Ock)   620

Kim, J. S. (Jung Sik)   620

Kim, J. S. (Jin-Sun)   11n

Kim, J. S. (Joon-Seok)   132-134, 136

Kim, J. W. (Jin-Woo)   91, 169, 236, 374, 416,
    420-421, 423, 425, 433n; 435, 570

Kim, J. W. (Juwan)   35

Kim, J. Y. 11, 11n; 32, 277

Kim, K. A. 136

Kim, K. C. 586, 595

Kim, K. H. (Ki Ho) 14

Kim, K. H. (Kyung Hui) 19

Kim, K. H. (Kyuhyong) 378

Kim, K. J. (Kwon-Jung) 11n

Kim, K. J. (Kwang Jung) 136

Kim, K. S. (Kyungsik) 625

Kim, K. S. (Keun-Soo) 95, 243, 246

Kim, K. W. 632

Kim, K. Y. 11, 11n; 12, 248, 292

Kim, M. 123

Kim, M. A. 589-590

Kim, M. H. 534

Kim, M. S. 237, 239

Kim, M. T. 522, 532

Kim, N. G. 530

Kim, N. Y. 82

Kim, S. (Soon-Ho) 42

Kim, S. (Sol) 573-574, 584

Kim, S. B. 373

Kim, S. C. 11, 11n; 32, 233-234, 277

Kim, S. E. 524

Kim, S. H. 281, 581, 630

Kim, S. J. (Sung-Jung) 541

Kim, S. J. (Sung-Jin) 541

Kim, S. J. (Soojung) 478, 489

Kim, S. K. 213, 574

Kim, S. M. 299, 420, 423, 425, 433n; 434, 434n;
    437, 458, 464, 469-470, 475, 477-478, 480,
    487, 497

Kim, S. P. 11, 11n; 234, 277, 307

Kim, S. S. (Sungsin) 374

Kim, S. S. (Sungsoo) 290

Kim, S. T. 634

Kim, S. U. 276

Kim, S. W. (Sunwoong) 11n; 12, 14, 233, 273,
    283, 287

Kim, S. W. (Soowon) 241

Kim, S. W. 375

Kim, S. Y. 593

Kim, T. (Taesu) 488, 493

Kim, T. (Tye) 341

Kim, T. H. 39, 41-42, 42n; 229, 232, 481, 573,
    633

Kim, T. J. 636

Kim, T. S. (Tong Suk) 569, 574, 585, 587

Kim, T. Y. (Tae Yeol) 632

Kim, T. Y. (Tae Yong) 577

Kim, W. (Woochan) 82, 88-89

Kim, W. (Woojin) 88

Kim, W. C. 519n; 520, 530, 543, 543n

Kim, W. H. 522, 531, 579

Kim, W. K. 443

Kim, Y. B. 11, 11n; 12, 292

Kim, Y. C. 243

Kim, Y. G. 248

Kim, Y. H. (Yeon-Hwa) 539-540

Kim, Y. H. (Young-hye) 233n; 440n; 441, 443

Kim, Y. H. (Young-Hwan) 478-479, 488-490

Kim, Y. H. (Yong H.) 136

Kim, Y. K. 152, 233n; 440n; 441, 443

Kim, Y. M. (Yoo-Man) 374

Kim, Y. M. (Youngmin) 375

Kim, Y. S. 528

Kim, Y. Y. 621

Kindleberger, C. P. 241

King, M. R. 149n

Klibanoff, P. 362

Ko, J. T. 645

Ko, K. S. 95, 123, 131, 153-154, 330n; 333,
    374-375, 377, 379, 574

Ko, Y. K. 478-479, 488, 493

Koch, E. B. 348

Koh, G. S. 300

Kon, S. J. 339-340, 348

Kong, M. J. 303

Koo, B. Y. 8, 17, 30, 36, 36n

Koo, M. H. 19n

Kook, C. P. 27, 158

Korajczyk, R. A. 340

Korea Exchange 66n; 582

Koski, J. L. 367-368

Kosowski, R. 341

Kothari, S. P. 20, 225, 291, 341

Ku, B. I. 11, 11n; 32, 32n; 33n; 34, 121n; 152n;
    156-157, 160, 162n; 163-164, 278, 581-583,
    588

Kubik, J. D. 344

Kumar, A. 237

Kwak, J. S. 225, 228

Kwon, J. E. 527

Kwon, K. S. 88

Kwon, S. S. 586-587
Kwon, S. T. 300
Kwon, T. H. (Taek Ho) 33-34, 137, 163n; 169, 569-570, 647, 649-651
Kyle, A. S. 108, 114

LaPorta, R. 475
Laibson, D. 361
Lakonishok, J. 234, 241, 280, 349, 481, 489
Lambert, R. A. 492-493
Lamont, O. 38, 42, 362, 364
Lamoureux, C. 154
Lanen, W. N. 492-493
Lang, L. 473-474
Lanstein, R. 9, 275
Larcker, D. F. 492-493
Larrymore, N. 367
Lastrapes, W. 154
Lease, R. C. 467
Lee, B. S. (Bong-Soo) 85, 85n; 346
Lee, C. (Charles M. C.) 207, 218, 226, 245, 362, 364
Lee, C. (Cheng-Few) 340, 367
Lee, C. 207n
Lee, C. E. (Chung-Eun) 624-625
Lee, C. H. 25
Lee, C. J. 20, 376, 589
Lee, C. W. (Chae Woo) 227-228
Lee, C. W. (Chang Wook) 36n
Lee, D. H. 19
Lee, D. W. 91
Lee, E. J. 82, 91, 113-115, 117, 119-120, 129, 474-475, 477-478, 480, 524, 529, 539-540, 542, 544
Lee, G. G. J. 145
Lee, G. H. 29
Lee, G. S. 420, 425
Lee, H. (Hyonsok) 647-648
Lee, H. (Hyun) 578
Lee, H. D. 376
Lee, H. G. 529, 531
Lee, H. I. 593
Lee, H. J. (Han-Je) 11n; 12
Lee, H. J. (Hye Jin) 304
Lee, H.-J. (Ho-Jin) 631
Lee, H. J. (Hyun Jin) 149-150

Lee, H. M. 570
Lee, H. Y. 19
Lee, I. 301
Lee, I. H. 585
Lee, I. K. 6-8
Lee, I. M. 474, 523
Lee, J. 623
Lee, J. B. T. 136
Lee, J. C. 528
Lee, J. D. 19, 19n; 152, 226, 228, 230, 232, 288, 290
Lee, J. H. (Jang-Hee) 539-540
Lee, J. H. (Joo Hee) 17, 24-25
Lee, J. H. (Jae Ha) 379, 573, 578, 586-587, 590, 634-635
Lee, J. H. (Jaehyun) 116, 250
Lee, J. H. (Jong Hyun) 584
Lee, J. H. (Joonhaeng) 95, 124, 585
Lee, J. H. (Jung-Ho) 577
Lee, J. H. (Jihyun) 590
Lee, J. J. (Jeong-Joon) 634
Lee, J. J. (Jungjin) 582
Lee, J. K. (Joon Koo) 37
Lee, J. K. (Jin Keun) 7, 32, 32n; 33n; 277
Lee, J. N. 632
Lee, J. R. 21n; 416, 420-421, 423, 425, 433n; 435-436, 436n
Lee, J. S. 488, 492
Lee, K. 649
Lee, K. H. 419-421, 425, 429-430, 441
Lee, K. J. 222
Lee, K. K. 214-215
Lee, K. T. 537, 541
Lee, K. Y. 626, 628, 631, 652
Lee, M. Y. 376, 580
Lee, P. S. 29, 573, 580, 652
Lee, S. (Sanghyuk) 420, 423, 425, 433n; 434, 434n; 437
Lee, S. (Soonhee) 575
Lee, S. B. 123, 131, 136, 146-147, 568
Lee, S. C. 531, 541
Lee, S. H. 637, 642
Lee, S. K. (Sungkyu) 233n; 297-298, 425, 439, 441
Lee, S. K. (Seungkook) 21n
Lee, S. M. 367
Lee, S. W. 592

Lee, S. Y. (Seon Yoon)   234
Lee, S. Y. (Sang Youp)   380
Lee, W. B. (Woo-Baik)   90, 115, 127-128, 137, 141,
    574, 651
Lee, W. H. (Won Heum)   11n; 12, 14, 233, 273,
    287, 376, 526-527, 529
Lee, W. H. (Hwan Ho)   638
Lee, Y.   587
Lee, Y. G. (Yong-Gyo)   234, 488-489, 489n
Lee, Y. G. (Yoon-Goo)   379
Lee, Y. H. (Yeonho)   645
Lee, Y. H. (Yong Ho)   29
Lee, Y. H. (Young-Hwan)   281
Lee, Y. J.   135n
Lee, Y. S. (Young Shik)   620
Lee, Y. S. (Yoon-sok)   629
Lee, Y. T.   117
Lee, S. K.   629
Lehmann, B. N.   342
Lemmon, M. L.   353
Lerro, A. J.   367
Lev, B.   481
Levhari, D.   20
Levis, M.   296
Levy, H.   20
Lewellen, J.   292
Lewellen, W. G.   340
Li, K.   367, 473
Liang, N.   492
Lilien, D.   162n
Lim, B. K.   233n; 298, 419, 429, 441, 443
Lim, C. W.   538, 538n
Lim, J. S.   632
Lim, K. W.   373
Lim, S. G.   634-635
Lim, S. J.   420, 425, 431
Lim, T. I.   19
Lim, U. K.   233n; 297-298, 373, 422, 425, 427,
    439, 441
Lin, C.   369
Lin, J. C.   362
Lintner, J.   2, 458-459, 485
Lipman, B.   493
Litzenberger, R.   15, 367, 468, 473-474, 585
Liu, W.-M.   156n
Liu, Y. J.   117
Ljungqvist, A.   424, 426n; 428n; 431

Lo, A. W.   152, 154n; 227-228, 230, 232
Locke, P. R.   215
Loderer, C.   305
Loewenstein, U.   467
Lopez-de-Silanes, F.   475
Losq, E.   73
Loughran, T.   233, 243, 245, 301
Louis, H.   489
Lu, C.-Y.   79
Lucas, R.   3
Lumsdaine, R.   64n; 72
Lundblad, C. T.   64n; 70, 78n; 97
Lung, P.   573
Lynch, A. W.   346, 354, 360
Lyons, R. K.   109n

MacBeth, J. D.   10, 15-16, 21, 163, 497
Macey, J. R.   148n
Mack, P.   350
Mackinlay, A. C.   152, 227-228, 230, 232
Madan, D.   581, 585
Madhavan, A.   85-86, 95, 109, 109n; 116, 125, 141n;
    166
Madrian, B. C.   361
Maenhout, P.   351
Maier, S.   109n
Malkiel, B. G.   340
Malloy, C.   350
Mamaysky, H.   342
Manaster, S.   361, 429
Mandelker, G.   305
Mann, S. C.   215
Mansi, S. A.   352
Martin, K.   305
Massa, M.   344, 350, 353, 355, 360, 365, 368
Masulis, R. W.   481, 489
Matos, P.   355
Matvos, G.   369
Maxwell, W.   490-491
McDonald, J.   294, 341
McInish, T.   121
Meese, R.   625, 628
Melvin, M.   150
Mendelson, H.   85, 108n; 121n; 151, 161, 167
Merton, R. C.   3, 27, 37, 588
Metrick, A.   342

Meyer, J.   342

Michaely, R.   429, 458-459, 468, 471-473, 476, 485, 491-492, 494

Mikkelson, W. H.   300

Milgrom, P.   108

Miller, E.   139

Miller, M. H.   15, 207n; 467, 470-471

Miller, R.   295

Miller, T. W.   342

Min, B. K.   38

Min, I. S.   588

Min, J. H.   589

Min, J. S.   573

Min, S. K.   374, 377

Mitchell, M. I.   122n; 440

Mo, S. W.   629, 635

Modest, D. M.   342

Modigliani, F.   467, 470

Moeller, S. B.   244-245

Mola, S.   368

Moon, G. H.   169, 590, 653

Moon, S. J. (Seong Ju)   569, 586

Moon, S. J. (Seung Joo)   299

Morck, R.   520, 544, 544n

Moreno, D.   342

Morey, M. R.   343, 366

Morgenstern, O.   210

Moskowitz, T. J.   350

Moussawi, R.   354-355

Mulherin, J. H.   122n

Mullins, D.   300, 473

Musto, D. K.   346, 354-356, 360

Na, H. S.   523

Na, I. C.   153n; 158n

Naik, N.   226

Nam, J. H.   17, 24-25, 36n

Nam, K. T.   594

Nam, M. S.   122, 136, 473

Nam, S. H.   472

Nam, S. K.   34, 121, 139n; 145, 147, 162, 222

Nanda, V.   344, 355

Narayanan, M. P.   344

Neal, R.   364

Nelling, E.   348

Ng, A.   79, 81

Ng, L. K.   368, 648

Nijman, T. E.   360

Nimalendran, M.   33, 123, 163n

Ning, Y.   475

Nishikawa, T.   352

Nishiotis, G. P.   363

Nissim, D.   471

Nohel, T.   355, 491-492

Novy-Marx, R.   42

O'Dell, B. T.   360

O'Hara, M.   35, 108, 108n; 109n; 124n; 125, 148n; 154n; 155, 164

Odders-White, E. R.   128

Odean, T.   117, 214-217, 236-237, 237n; 238, 345, 369

Oded, J.   489

Ofer, A. R.   342, 471

Oh, G. T.   378

Oh, H. T.   306

Oh, J. M.   579

Oh, J. Y.   531, 539-540

Oh, M. S.   629

Oh, S. H.   92, 94, 138n; 169

Oh, S. J.   582

Oh, S. K.   11n; 12, 14, 233, 273, 287

Oh, Y. S.   459, 487

Ohk, K. Y.   138n; 156, 568-570, 591

Ok, J.   121, 126, 130, 141-142

Osobov, I.   476

Ostrovsky, M.   369

Ostry, J.   84

Otsuki, T.   351

Paek, M. Y.   374

Paek, W.   11-12

Panchapagesan, V.   127, 148n

Panetta, F.   341

Paperman, J.   124n

Park, A. Y.   541

Park, B. J. (Beum-Jo)   630, 643-644

Park, B. J. (Bum Jin)   374, 528, 531

Park, B. Y.   18

Park, C.   470

Park, C. B.   29

Park, C. W.   219
Park, D.   169, 620-621, 636
Park, G. Y. (Gun Youb)   569
Park, G. Y. (Gil Young)   522, 532
Park, H. B.   18
Park, H. J. (Hun-Joon)   521, 532
Park, H. J. (Hyoung-Jin)   169, 575, 638
Park, H. S.   638, 644, 646
Park, H. Y.   378
Park, J. (Jinwoo)   150-151
Park, J. (Joon)   222
Park, J. B.   136
Park, J. C.   539-540
Park, J. G. (Jae-Gon)   651
Park, J. G. (Jonggoo)   373
Park, J. H.   34-35, 121, 126, 131, 133, 136n; 139n;
     141-142, 145, 147-148, 148n; 149, 152-153,
     162, 165
Park, J. I. (Jong Il)   522, 531
Park, J. I. (Jung In)   19
Park, J. J.   34, 34n; 163, 163n; 165-167
Park, J. W. (Jong Won)   33-34, 137, 138n; 163n;
     169, 376, 569, 651
Park, J. W. (Jinwoo)   123, 537
Park, J. Y.   620-621
Park, K. H.   306
Park, K. I.   91, 289-290, 376, 647
Park, K. S. (Kyung Suh)   91, 113-114, 117, 118n;
     119-120, 129, 474, 524, 526, 529, 539-542, 544
Park, K. S. (Ki-Sung)   522, 528
Park, K. W.   420, 425, 431, 477
Park, R. S.   37, 420, 425, 432, 477
Park, S, C.   470
Park, S. B.   378
Park, S. H. (Soon Hong)   524
Park, S. H. (Seung-Ho)   248-249
Park, S. S. (Soon-Sik)   19, 218-219, 249
Park, S. S. (Sang Su)   376
Park, S. W.   650
Park, Y. J.   589
Park, Y. K.   158, 373, 375, 379-380, 472, 490
Park, Y. S. (Young S.)   116, 250, 523, 530
Partch, M. M.   300, 363
Parwada, J. T.   366, 368
Pastor, L.   161, 342-344
Patel, J.   342
Patgiri, R.   353

Pathak, A. P.   139
Patro, D. K.   363
Pearson, N. D.   350
Peavy J.   294, 361
Pedersen, L. H.   161
Penman, S.   471
Pennacchi, G. G.   354
Petajisto, A.   343
Peters, H.   367
Pettit, R. R.   472
Pham, P. K.   156n
Philipov, A.   18
Pinkerton, J. M.   473
Pinkowitz, L.   87, 476
Pinnuck, M.   341
Pitts, M.   154
Pogue, J. A.   339
Poh, H. L.   366
Pollet, J. M.   368
Pompilio, D.   148n
Pontiff, J.   361-362, 367-368
Porter, B.   84n
Porter, D. C.   141n
Porter, G. E.   363
Porter, R. B.   342
Poterba, J.   346, 367
Powell, G. E.   467
Pozen, R. C.   328
Pyo, M. K.   244

Qi, Y.   35
Qureshi, M.   84

Radcliffe, R.   226
Rahman, S.   340
Rakowski, D.   347
Ramaswamy, K.   15, 468
Rankine, G.   234
Rankine, G. P.   481
Rapach, D. E.   623
Rau, P. R.   344, 346
Raviv, A.   493
Reed, A. V.   355-356
Rehman, Z.   350
Reid, K.   9, 275

Reilly, F. 295
Reinganum, M. C. 9
Reinganum, M. R. 275, 279-280
Reinhardt, D. 84
Resnick, B. 650
Reuter, J. 358, 368
Rey, H. 368
Rhee, C. 169
Rhee, H. J. 619, 624
Rhee, J. H. 581-582
Rhee, S. G. 136
Rhee, Y. H. 619
Rhee, Y. S. 637
Richard, S. F. 38
Richardson, M. 95, 125, 166
Rindi, B. 109n
Ritter, J. 139, 233, 243, 245, 293-295, 297-298,
    301, 358, 423, 437-438
Rivoli, P. 293, 295, 297
Robins, R. 162n
Rock, K. 422, 471
Rodriguez, J. 367
Rodriguez, R. 342
Roenfeldt, R. L. 363
Rogalski, R. J. 283
Rogers, W. 142
Rogoff, K. 628
Roll, R. 5n; 6n; 29-30, 33, 123, 160-161, 161n;
    233, 244, 279, 481, 581
Roller, L. H. 350
Roomans, M. 95, 125, 166
Rosen, K. T. 366
Rosenberg, B. 9, 275
Ross, S. A. 2, 6, 27, 29-30, 359
Rossi, P. E. 155-156
Rouwenhorst, K. G. 286, 356
Rozeff, M. S. 234, 348, 474
Ruback, R. S. 206n; 242, 244-245
Rubinstein, M. 3
Ruenzi, S. 357
Rui, O. 85, 85n
Ruiz-Verdu, P. 345
Runkle, D. E. 156
Russell, J. R. 136, 148
Ruud, J. S. 433, 433n
Ryngaert, M. 493
Ryou, J. W. 636

Ryu, D. 20, 95-96, 169, 575, 585, 592
Ryu, H. S. 169, 576, 584
Ryu, J. H. 581
Ryu, S. Y. (Sung-Yong) 529, 531
Ryu, S. Y. (Su-Yeol) 625

Saar, G. 141n
Safieddine, A. 351
Sagi, J. 363
Santa-Clara, P. 147, 147n
Sapp, T. 346
Sarig, O. H. 467
Sarkissian, S. 344
Saunders Jr., E. M. 247-248
Scaillet, O. 343
Schadt, R. W. 343
Schallheim, J. S. 353, 361
Schiereck, D. D. 143
Schipper, K. 301
Schlag, C. 150
Schlingemann, F. P. 244-245
Scholes, M. 6, 15, 21, 468
Schwartz, E. 301
Schwartz, R. 109n; 114
Schwert, G. W. 276, 278, 280, 283, 287, 291
Seasholes, M. S. 93-94
Segal, D. 149n
Sensoy, B. A. 347
Seo, B. D. 306-307
Seo, J. H. 146-147
Seo, J. W. 88n
Seo, J. Y. 582
Seo, S. G. 573, 576
Seo, S. Y. 18
Seog, S. H. 213
Seon, J. 143, 143n; 144-146, 161, 161n; 162, 169,
    241, 641
Seppi, D. J. 161-162
Seru, A. 344
Servaes, H. 345, 347-348, 354
Sevick, M. 352
Shanken, J. 6, 8, 15-16, 16n; 21, 291, 342
Shapiro, J. E. 138
Sharpe, W. F. 2, 339, 365
Shaw, W. H. 429
Shefrin, H. 204-206, 206n; 207, 212-213

Shiller, R. J.   204
Shimrat, A.   300
Shin, B. S.   420, 425, 432
Shin, D. K.   571
Shin, H. (Hyun-Soo)   42
Shin, H. H. (Hyun-Han)   433n; 434-435, 521, 523, 531-532, 534, 541-542, 544
Shin, I.   94
Shin, J. S.   133-134
Shin, J. Y.   116, 248-249
Shin, K. C.   19
Shin, M. S.   19, 19n; 234, 476n; 488, 492, 524
Shin, S. H. (SungHwan)   169, 224, 228, 379, 630
Shin, S. H. (Seong-Ho)   7, 8, 14, 32, 33n; 35
Shin, Y. K. (Yong Kyun)   302, 481, 485
Shin, Y. K. (Yong Kil)   481
Shiraishi, N.   351
Shivdasani, A.   305
Shleifer, A.   81, 207, 207n; 208-209, 221, 241, 245, 249, 251, 362, 364, 475, 518
Shoven, J. B.   367
Shukla, R. K.   92
Shumway, T.   215, 247-249
Sialm, C.   344, 355
Sias R.   241, 241n
Sicherman, N. W.   363
Siegel, R.   471
Siegel, S.   64n; 70, 97
Sim, B. G.   18
Simonson, D. G.   367
Sin, D. S.   306-307
Singal, V.   64n; 78-79, 83
Singleton, K. J.   17, 39
Sirri, E. R.   345
Skinner, D. J.   458, 476, 494
Sloan, R. G.   235
Slovic, P.   206, 221
Smidt, S.   280
Smith, A.   301
Smith, R.   301, 429
Soderlind, P.   341
Sofianos, G.   138
Sohn, W.   94
Son, S. H.   39, 41-42, 42n
Son, Y. G.   529, 531
Song, C. S.   117-118, 123, 139n; 140n; 141n
Song, C. Y.   627, 638, 646

Song, H. S.   535
Song, J. H.   476n
Song, R. K.   362
Song, Y. C.   7, 11, 11n; 18, 32, 32n; 33n; 277, 373
Song, Y. H.   581
Song, Y. K.   18, 244
Sonu, S. H.   11n; 12, 14, 136, 233, 273, 283, 287
Sosin, H.   367
Spatt, C.   109n; 114, 130
Spiegel, M.   342
Spiess, D. K.   243, 301
Spindt, P. A.   426, 439, 442n
Stafford, E.   347, 440
Stambaugh, R. F.   21, 42, 161, 279, 283, 291, 342, 344
Stanton, R.   362-363
Starks, L. T.   349, 353, 357, 518
Statman, M.   204, 207, 212-213, 252
Stattman, D.   9, 275
Stein, J. C.   222, 245-246, 251
Stephens, C.   490-492, 494
Stice, E. K.   234, 481
Stiglitz, J.   64
Stolin, D.   346
Stoll, H.   108n; 109n; 125, 127, 154
Strazicich, M. C.   623
Stulz, R.   64n; 79, 81-82, 85-88, 90, 93, 243-245, 476, 493
Suay, J.   363
Subrahmanyam, A.   160-161, 161n; 164, 204, 222, 251, 252n
Suh, B. D.   376
Sul, W. S.   478, 489
Summers L.   81, 208-209
Sundaram, R. K.   353
Sung, B. Y.   632
Sung, S. Y.   420, 425, 431
Sung, T.   89
Sunwoo, S. H.   11n; 12, 14
Swaminathan, B.   218, 226, 362, 472-473, 476
Swan, P. L.   356
Swary, I.   473
Syverson, C.   361

Tae, S. J.   578

Tak, R. H.   584
Tarhan, V.   491-492
Tauchen, G.   154-156
Tay, N.   573
Teoh, S. H.   296
Ter Horst, J. R.   360
Thakor, A. V.   490
Thaler, R.   204, 206n; 207, 207n; 208, 211, 218, 221, 223-245, 285-286, 288, 362, 364, 381, 471-473
Thalerv, R.   209
Theissen, E.   143
Thiele, T.   357
Thomas, D. C.   362
Thornton, G.   145
Tiao, G. C.   136
Timmermann, A.   341
Titman, S.   216, 218, 221, 229, 252n; 276, 284, 286-288, 341-343, 351, 365, 376, 382, 481
Tiwari, A.   346
Tkac, P. A.   359, 366
Todd, S.   342
Torous, W.   291
Treussard, J.   359
Trombley, M. A.   247
Trzcinka, C. A.   362
Tsay, R.   136
Tufano, P.   345, 347, 352, 358
Tversky, A.   203, 207, 210, 220-221

Unlu, E.   476

Vagias, D.   83
Valkanov, R.   291
van Dijk, M. A.   83
van Inwegen, G. B.   92
Varma, R.   368
Vassalou, M.   38
Veit, E. T.   467
Verbeek, M.   360
Vermaelen, T.   234, 489
Verrecchia, E. R.   139
Vickers, D.   339
Vickrey, D.   481
Vishny, R.   208, 221, 241, 251, 475, 518

Viswanathan, S.   125, 164
Von Neumann, J.   210

Wachter, J.   342
Wahal, S.   354, 363
Waldmann, R.   81, 208-209
Wang, A. Y.   354
Wang, J.   154n; 158
Wang, X.   127-128
Wang, Y. P.   374
Wang, Z.   25-26, 42
Wang, Z. J.   355
Warner, J. B.   114-115, 130, 341, 345, 352
Warnock, F.   88
Warther, V. A.   344-345
Wasley, C.   20
Wasserfallen, W.   85-86
Watts, R.   471
Weaver, D. G.   141n
Wedge, L.   352, 354
Wee, J. B.   584
Wee, I. S.   584
Wei, K.   382
Wei, K.   241
Wei, K. C. J.   252n
Wei, K. D.   346
Wei, S. J.   82, 89
Weisbach, M.   350, 492, 494
Weisbenner, S.   347
Welch, I.   293, 296, 424, 475
Wermers, R.   241, 341-344, 365, 376
Werner, I. M.   148n
Westerfield, R.   283
Whaley, R.   154
Wheatley, S. M.   364
Whitcomb, D.   109n
White, H.   290, 341, 489
Wi, H. J.   227-228
Wilcox, R. T.   368
Wilhelm, W. J.   424, 426, 426n; 439
Williams, J.   471
Williamson, J.   621
Williamson, R.   87, 476
Wilson, M.   368
Wizman, T. A.   362
Wohar, M. E.   623

Wohl, A.   364
Wolfenzon, D.   520, 544, 544n
Womack, K.   473
Won, C. H.   590
Won, J. Y.   464, 487
Won, S. Y.   374, 583, 588
Wong, T. J.   296
Woo, C. S.   225, 228, 459, 473, 481, 485, 487
Woo, J. R.   373
Woo, M. C.   135
Woo, Y. H.   419, 433, 433n
Wood, R. A.   121
Woodbury, D.   363
Woolridge, J. R.   481, 490
Wruck, K. H.   301
Wu, J. S.   346, 352
Wu, Y.   352
Wurgler, J.   206n; 242-243, 245-246, 249, 291
Wylie, S.   365

Xue, H.   493

Yae, S. M.   18
Yamada, T.   341
Yan, H.   346
Yan, S.   291
Yan, X.   344
Yang, C. W.   33-35, 125, 160, 162, 163n; 164
Yang, C. Y.   378
Yang, J. J.   136
Yang, S. K.   569
Yao, T.   343
Yeung, B.   520, 544, 544n
Yi, J.   351
Yi, J. S.   139, 139n; 140, 575
Yi, K. Y.   376-379, 241
Yi, M. C.   419, 421, 425, 441, 586
Yilmaz, B.   119
Yim, B. J.   590
Yogo, M.   292
Yon, K. H.   147n; 425, 524, 650
Yoo, J.   136
Yoo, K. R.   378
Yoo, S. Y.   375, 379
Yook, K. H.   476
Yoon, B. H. (Bo Hyun)   39, 41-42, 42n

Yoon, B. H. (Bong-Han)   531, 539-540
Yoon, B. S.   419-420, 425, 429-430
Yoon, G. S.   29
Yoon, H. G.   281
Yoon, J. A.   148, 148n; 149, 159
Yoon, J. I.   290
Yoon, J. Y.   222
Yoon, K. S.   638
Yoon, P. S.   303, 470
Yoon, S. H.   138
Yoon, S. J.   585
Yoon, S. M. (Seong-Min)   156, 523, 525, 533, 544, 625
Yoon, Y. C.   378
Yoon, Y. K.   302
You, T.   633
Young, L.   35, 125-126, 126n; 164, 164n; 165
Yu, B. W.   19
Yu, I. S.   35, 35n
Yu, L.   141n
Yu, M. S.   630
Yu, T.   343
Yun, C. H.   584
Yun, J. S. (Jaesun)   585
Yun, J. S. (Jeongsun)   250
Yun, S. Y.   11, 11n; 32, 32n; 33n; 34, 163-164, 278
Yun, W. C.   653-654
Yun, Y. S.   12, 14, 273, 277-278, 283, 287

Zechner, J.   352
Zeckhauser, R.   342
Zender, J. F.   353
Zenner, M.   305, 363
Zhang, D.   358
Zhang, H.   342
Zhang, L.   42
Zhang, X.   139
Zhao, X.   348
Zheng, L.   344-347, 355, 368
Zhou, C.   589
Ziskind, R.   586, 595
Zitzewitz, E.   356, 368
Ziv, A.   471
Zou, H.   369

SUBJECT INDEX

12b-1 fee   344-345

accrual anomaly   235-236
accruals quality   35
active share   343
active shareholder   536
adjusted PIN (adjPIN)   125-126, 164-165
adverse selection cost   95-96, 166
affiliated mergers   307
aftermarket performance of IPOs   297-298, 418, 439, 442
age bias   366
agency costs   467-468, 474, 476-477, 491, 520-522, 527, 529, 533, 537-538, 538n; 539-541, 543
agency hypothesis of dividend   474
agency problem   87, 327, 335, 339, 351, 353, 357-358, 365, 373, 377, 380-381, 474-476, 478-479, 497, 499, 521-527, 529, 533-535, 542, 545-546
algorithm trading (algo)   114, 132, 168
American call option   581
American depositary receipt (ADR)   67n, 71-72, 75, 77, 149, 150
anchoring bias   245, 245n
anchoring effect   220
anomalies   9, 22, 31, 204, 206-207, 221, 232, 235-236, 247, 251, 272-277, 279-280, 282-283, 285, 291, 293-296, 308-311, 585, 645
anomalies in foreign exchange market   645-646
anonymity   110, 116, 142-143
AR model   629, 631
arbitrage   31, 140n; 206-209, 273, 329, 360, 362-363, 381, 469, 576, 578-579, 583, 587
arbitrage activities   209, 576
arbitrage opportunity   308, 379, 578, 591, 635
Arbitrage Pricing Theory (APT)   2-4, 27-31, 39, 43-44
arbitrage program trading   138
arbitrage trading strategy   379, 563, 578
ARCH/GARCH effect   155
ARCH/GARCH model   155
ARCH-M model   162n, 635
ARIMA model   626, 629

Asian financial crisis   73, 94, 137, 166, 459, 464, 476-477, 478, 498, 593
asset allocation effect   379
asset-backed securities (ABSs)   564
asymmetric effect of return volatility   156
asymmetric information   125-127, 151, 155, 159, 161n; 363, 417, 422, 424, 444, 471, 489, 492, 567
asymmetric information hypothesis   422
asymmetric information risk   110
asymmetric volatility puzzle   82
attention hypothesis   481
autoregressive conditional heteroskedasticity (ARCH) model   25, 30, 77, 592, 595, 632
autoregressive distributed lag (ARDL)   624
average cumulative abnormal return(ACAR)   287

backward pricing   332, 356, 377
barrier options   581-582
basis risk   652
behavioral equilibrium exchange rate (BEER)   621-622
beta   2, 5, 6n, 9-12, 14-22, 17n; 19n; 21n: 25-27, 30-32, 34, 36-37, 43, 117, 225, 249-250, 275-278, 288-289, 349, 375
bid-ask bounce effects   152, 575
bid-ask spread   118-119, 124, 132-133, 160, 209, 218, 590, 641
bi-directional causality   574
Black (1972) zero-beta CAPM   8
Black-Karasinski term structure model   582
Black-Scholes model   571, 574, 580, 583, 592, 595-596
block trading   110, 115-117, 116n
board structure   531
bonding hypothesis   149-150
bookbuilding process (method)   422, 426
book-to-market   9, 11-12, 14-15, 20, 22, 32-34, 39, 43-44, 95, 163-164, 207, 234, 272, 274-279, 292, 299-301, 303-304, 306, 310, 648
buy-and-hold abnormal returns (BHAR)   229, 233, 278, 299, 300, 303, 440, 441n

calendar month effect   281

calendar-time abnormal returns (CTAR)   299

Capital Asset Pricing Model (CAPM)   2-6, 6n; 8-12, 14, 16-17, 20-28, 31, 33, 36-37, 39, 41-44, 210, 272, 274-275, 278, 281, 349

capital market integration   65, 70

capital market liberalization   65, 76-77, 80

CAPM and GMM tests, conditional version of   21

CAPM, cross-sectional regression tests of   9

CAPM, time-series tests of   5

cash dividends   494

cash flow right   494, 519, 530, 545

cash holdings   476, 491, 521, 524

cash-flows-to-price ratio(C/P)   276

CCC-GARCH model   652

CDS spreads   589, 590

CEO turnover   534

certification effect   429-432, 445

chaebol   89, 519, 519n; 520, 522, 525-526, 532-533, 535-538, 542, 544-545

change rate model (CRM)   633

Chan-Karolyi-Longstaff-Sanders (CKLS) model   582

closed-end fund discounts   361-362

closed-end fund premium   361, 378

closed-end fund puzzle   378

closed-end funds   207, 207n; 245, 330, 335, 339, 361-364, 373, 378

cointegration tests   619-620, 623-624, 634

collateralized bond obligations (CBOs)   589

collateralized debt obligations (CDOs)   564

collateralized loan obligations (CLOs)   589

commercial papers (CPs)   587

Committee for Corporate Governance Improvement   477

compensation rate   352

competitive rational expectations equilibrium model   378

conservation law of systematic risk   592

conservatism   209, 221-222

Consumption-based CAPM (C-CAPM)   4, 36-37, 42

Cont and Bouchaud model   625

contagion effect   80-81, 655

contrarian premium   287-288

contrarian strategy   93, 118, 221-222, 224-227, 229-230, 285, 286, 288-290, 309

contrarian strategy, profitability of   222-229

controlling shareholders   87-88, 493-494, 523-527, 529-531, 535-537, 541-543

convertible bonds   537-587

Corporate Governance Best Practice   477

Corporate Governance Index (KCGI)   477, 522, 529-530, 543, 531

corporate governance rankings   529, 530, 531

cosmetic effects   347

cost-of-carry model   582

credit default swap (CDSs)   564, 589

cross-listing   110, 144, 149-150, 149n; 150n

cubic relationship   528

cum-dividend   469

cumulative abnormal return (CAR)   233, 250, 287, 299-300, 303, 306, 440, 441n; 489

Currency Basket System   638

daily price limit   420

day-of-the-week effect   160, 283-284

day-trading   110-111, 115, 117-120

defined contribution (DC)   358

delisting effect   249

depositary receipt (DR)   149

destabilization effect of foreign portfolio flows   80-81, 84, 97

direct market access (DMA)   132, 168

direct share repurchase program   488

director and officer insurance premium   537

discretionary accrual   296, 533

disparity of separation of ownership   533

disposition behavior   218

disposition effect   209, 213-219, 250-251, 365, 379

diversification loss effect   520

dividend announcement effect   470

dividend irrelevance theory   467-468

dividend policy   361-362, 458, 459, 464, 467-468, 471-472, 474-480, 485, 487, 498, 498n

dividend puzzle   467

dividend signaling   471-472

dollar-cost averaging investments   333, 379, 380

dynamic hedging strategy   593

dynamic trading strategy   571, 593, 596-597

earnings-to-price ratio (P/E)   276

economics of mutual funds   335

economies of scale, mutual fund   350

economies of scope, mutual fund   350

ECT-ARCH model   653

efficient market   81, 294, 296, 416-417, 443-445, 577

Efficient market hypothesis (EMH)   235, 249, 290, 340, 417, 433, 436, 531, 539

efficient market model   294

efficient market school   204

EIV-bias corrected t-statistic   16

empire building motivation   522, 535

endogeneity bias   431

endogeneity problem   133, 142, 543

equity carve-outs (ECO)   233, 301

equity linked deposit (ELDs)   582, 588

equity linked securities (ELSs)   582, 593-594

equity linked warrants (ELWs)   112n; 134-135, 575, 593-594

error correction model (ECM)   633, 653

errors-in-variables (EIV) Problem   15-16, 16n; 24, 43

European option   581

EVAs   529, 531

event study   86, 134, 138, 141-142, 233, 527, 535, 537, 575

event uncertainty view   640-643

ex ante uncertainty   423-425

excess-return Sharpe ratio   365

exchange rate forecasting   627-631

exotic options   581, 587

expected default frequency (EDF)   589

expected utility theory   210-212

expense ratio   344

expiration-day effect   576-577

exponential generalized autoregressive conditional heteroskedasticity (EGARCH) model   157, 590, 631

exponentially weighted moving average (EWMA) model   631

expropriation hypothesis   524, 526

Face-amount certificates   329

Fama and MacBeth two-pass methodology   30

Fama and MacBeth's control variables   497

Fama and MacBeth's CSR (cross-sectional regression) model   10, 42, 163, 275-276

Fama and MacBeth's CSR (cross-sectional regression) tests   16

family tournament   357

Financial Investment Services and Capital Markets Act (Capital Market Consolidation Act)   562, 567

FITC (full-information transaction cost)   148

five factor model   39, 41-42

flow-performance relationship   346, 357

foreign block shareholders   531

foreign directors   531

foreign exchange exposure of firms   646-650

foreign exchange market efficiency   616, 631, 634-635, 654

foreign exchange market interventions   617, 636-639, 645-646

foreign exchange market microstructure   616

foreign investment restrictions   84

foreign ownership limits   67-68, 67n; 72, 85-86, 85n

form of acquisition payment   307

forward exchange rate   632

forward pricing   332, 356, 377

fractionally integrated GARCH (FIGARCH) model   631

free cash flow   89, 245, 474, 476, 488, 491-492, 522-523, 525

free cash-flow hypothesis   474, 476, 488, 491-492, 494, 499

free floating exchange rate regime   623, 641

free floating system   623, 636, 641, 648

FreeBoard   144, 148-149, 148n

Friedman's paradigm of arbitrage   206

fund advisory compensation   363

fund flows   327, 345-347, 366, 374-376

fund rating   339, 365, 373, 381

fundamental equilibrium exchange rate (FEER)   621

fundamental risk   208-209

future spot exchange rate   632

GARCH-in-mean methodology   74, 652

GARCH-jump model   584

GARCH-M CRM   633

GARCH-M ECM   633

GARCH-M model   633, 635

Gaussian copula model   589

Gaussian distribution   588

Gaussian model   588

Gaussian quadrature numerical inversion method 581

gender differences   238

generalized autoregressive conditional heteroskedasticity (GARCH) model   71, 154, 156, 156n; 157-158, 584, 590-592, 631, 634, 637, 641, 643-644, 654

generalized least square model (GLS)   6n

generalized method of moment (GMM) method   6n, 17, 17n; 21, 24, 27, 30, 35, 43, 39, 620

geometric Brownian motion   583

geometric Levy process   581

Gerber-Shiu model   580

Gibbons, Ross, and Shanken (GRS) test   6-9, 7n; 16-17, 42

G-Index   475

global minimum variance portfolio (GMVP)   8

governance premium   539-540

growth manager   349

Hansen-Jagannathan distance (HJ distance)   41-42

Hasbrouck's pricing error   148

Henriksson-Merton test   628

herd behavior in foreign exchange market   624

herd behavior of mutual funds   364, 378

herding   79, 81-82, 240-242, 240n; 365, 378, 381, 624-625

Heston model   580, 592

heteroscedasticity effects   584

heuristic   209

high frequency trading (HFT)   132, 168

HML, Fama and French's   12, 32-33, 32n; 33n; 39, 163-164, 277-278, 286-287, 440n; 441n

holding companies   541-542

home bias   66, 368

home bias puzzle   78, 87, 89, 92

hot hands' results   342

hot issue markets   417, 435n, 437-439, 444-445

hot potato view   640, 642

hyperbolic distribution   584

idiosyncratic risk   28, 32, 592

idiosyncratic volatility   135-137, 147, 147n; 365

implementation costs   209

implicit tax effects   579

implied stock prices   574

implied volatility   577, 580, 586-588

implied volatility surface   586

incentive fees   345

incentive/power effect   519

increase-in-cash-dividends hypothesis   481

independent audit committees   522, 532

independent executive boards   522

index funds   340, 359-361, 377-378

indirect share repurchase fund   488

individual retirement accounts (IRAs)   358

industry price momentum   230, 232

ineligible security market index   74

information asymmetry   32, 34-35, 70, 89, 93, 111, 124-125, 137-138, 147n, 162, 164, 309, 418, 467, 489, 525, 540-541, 625

information content hypothesis   473

information extraction   426-428, 439

information hypothesis of block trading   116

information share   128, 141, 150, 424

information spillover   428, 428n; 438, 634

informed investors   222, 422-424

informed trader   95, 98, 114-115, 118, 133, 158-159, 166

initial public offerings (IPO)   358, 416

insider ownership   476, 522

instrumental variable   23-25, 23n; 41-42, 42n; 140, 167

integration index   74, 76

integration measure   71-72

interest alignment effect   520

international portfolio investment and foreign exchange risk   650

Intertemporal Capital Asset Pricing Model (I-CAPM)   3-4, 37-39, 44, 652

in-the-money (ITM) options   586-587

intraday price discovery   128

intrinsic pricing method   422

Investment Advisory Act of 1940   328

investment ceiling of foreign investors   476

Investment Company Act of 1940   328

investment selection change   239

investor relations (IR)   309

investor sentiment index   246

investor sentiment index, Korean version of   246

IPO anomalies   294-296

IPO underpricing   273, 418, 421-422, 424, 429, 432, 435, 435n; 442, 444-445

irrational manager's approach   244

January effect   14, 35, 273-274, 279-282, 310, 469, 469n; 470

Jensen's free cash flow theory   522

job security enhancement effect   520

Johansen cointegration test   619-620, 632-634

Johansen-Juselius cointegration test   624

jump-diffusion model   584

Kandel and Stambaugh R-square   42

KOFEX (the Korea Futures Exchange)   112

Korea Corporate Governance Service (KCGS)   477, 524, 529, 531

Korean Treasury Bonds (KTB) futures   92, 570, 582

KOSDAQ market   66n; 144, 147, 163, 282, 299, 421, 476n; 488, 534, 536

KOSPI 200 stock index futures   91-92, 162, 562, 565, 568-569, 573-576, 578-579, 590, 593-594

KOSPI 200 stock index options   95, 562, 565, 570, 573, 577-578, 580, 584-585, 592

KOSPI market   144, 163, 282-284

KRX (the Korea Exchange)   66-68, 66n; 83, 91, 94, 112, 112n; 115-116, 119-121, 125-126, 126n, 132-137, 139-144, 149-151, 163, 165, 243, 307, 435, 469

KSE (the Korea Stock Exchange)   34, 66n; 112-115, 119, 121-125, 121n; 127, 129-131, 129n; 133-134, 138, 138n; 139n; 140n; 144, 153, 153n; 156n; 158, 159n; 160-163, 161n; 166, 421, 423, 430, 435, 436

large shareholder   519, 524, 527, 541

lead-lag effect of trading volume   158

lead-lag relationship between derivatives price and underlying asset price   572

learning hypothesis   129-130

leverage   83, 156-157, 225, 276, 310, 488n: 572, 590, 648, 649

Levy process   580-582

life cycle theory   476

limit of arbitrage   206-207, 206n

limit order   112-113, 126-128, 133, 135, 139n; 144, 168, 575

liquidity factor   34, 41, 159, 161, 163-164

liquidity measure   34, 133, 159-160, 163n

liquidity premium   34

liquidity premium hypothesis   226

liquidity provider   90, 110, 112n; 119, 134

liquidity risk   34, 159, 163, 588

liquidity risk factor (IMV), Fama and French   163

liquidity risk premium   163, 226

liquidity, the commonality of   34, 159, 161-163

listing bias   277-278

listing effect   249

lognormal diffusion process   586

long hedgers   578-579

long-term performance reversal   234

long-term reversal effect   273, 285, 288, 290, 310

loss aversion   211

management companies   241-242, 329-330, 332-333, 352

manager style   349

managerial incentive hypothesis   488, 492, 499

managerial incentives   353, 381

managerial opportunism hypothesis   244

managerial ownership   354, 519

managerial perquisite consumptions   521

managerial replacement   351

market average exchange rate system   628, 636, 638

market beta, levered firm's   18

market beta, mis-specification in estimating   17

market efficiency   126, 139, 145, 149, 235, 272, 274, 310, 438

market impact cost   110, 115, 119-120, 124

market integration process   71

market macrostructure   110-111, 143-146, 167-168

market maker   112, 112n; 121, 121n; 134, 135n; 159, 161n; 215, 436, 640

market microstructure   108-111, 109n; 110n; 125, 132, 146, 151-152, 155, 159, 161, 165-169, 568, 616-617, 639-641, 644-645, 654

market order   112-114, 139n; 575

market portfolio   2, 5-6, 5n; 6n; 7n; 23-24, 26, 29, 30n; 32, 33n; 36n; 37, 39, 73, 78, 87, 299, 340-341, 647

market segmentation hypothesis   149-150

market timing   242-243, 246, 309, 340, 356, 367, 373, 376, 540

market timing ability   340, 367, 373-374, 376

market volatility   147, 156n; 219, 284, 289-290, 349, 568

market-to-limit order   113

Markov regime switching model   630

mean-variance efficiency   2, 5-8, 6n; 16-17, 17n; 29, 360

measure of individual investor sentiment   364

mental accounting   209, 211, 217, 245

mixture-of-distributions hypothesis (MDH) 154-155, 642-643

momentum effect   163, 284, 287-290, 342

momentum strategy   93, 227, 229-232, 230n; 286, 288-289, 290, 342, 365

momentum strategy, profitability of   229

money market fund (MMF)   329, 333

monitoring   88, 88n; 479, 524, 530, 532, 534, 535, 541, 542, 544, 544n

monitoring shareholders   88

Monte Carlo Reality Check   290

Monte Carlo simulation   585, 592

Morningstar's measure   365

multifactor Vasicek model   582

multi-peak phenomenon   589

mutual fund merger   348

mutual fund restrictions   352

mutual fund scandals   353, 356

mutual fund splits   348

mutual fund systematic risk   348

natural real exchange rate (NATREX)   622

negligible stock effect   273

net asset value (NAV)   131, 332, 334, 356, 362

new listing bias   277-278

no arbitrage   28, 39

noise hypothesis   129

noise trading   208

noisy rational expectations equilibrium (NREE)   159

nominal exchange rate dynamics   616, 623-624, 654

non-affiliated mergers   307

non-deliverable forward (NDF)   632, 653

non-normal distributions of stock returns   16

one factor Gaussian copula model   589

operating expenses of mutual funds   345

optimal dividend payout ratio   474

optimal hedge ratio   652-654

optimal portfolio selection   367

ordinary least square model (OLS)   6n; 16, 137, 292-293, 531, 543, 590-591, 632, 652-654

Ornstein-Uhlenbeck process   582

outcome hypothesis   475, 477-478

out-of-the-money (OTM) options   586-587

outside director turnover   534

outside directors   531

overconfidence   206, 209, 217, 222, 236-237, 239, 244, 252n, 597

overinvestment opportunity decrease effect   473

over-reaction   81, 206-207, 221, 223, 226, 232-233, 235-236, 250, 252, 285-286, 288, 540

overreaction hypothesis   250, 285

overshooting model   623

overshooting phenomenon   298

overweight of small probability   212

paid-in capital   301-304

partial adjustment hypothesis   426-428

partial equilibrium model   571, 596

partial price adjustment hypothesis   153

participation costs   346

PER (price-to-earnings ratio) effect   11n; 12, 14

performance evaluation   278, 326, 335, 339-343, 373, 376

performance evaluation techniques   339

performance persistence   339, 360, 374, 376, 379

performance-enhancing factors   339

portfolio balance model   623

portfolio pumping   356

post-merger performance   305, 348

predictability of trading volume   157

predictive failure test of Persaran-Timmermann   635

prerogative consumption hypothesis   480

pretrade transparency   140

price discovery   110-112, 126, 128-129, 131, 135-136, 138n; 139, 146, 150, 563, 571, 573-575

price limit system   110, 135, 135n; 137, 298

price momentum   216-219, 221-222, 229-232, 234, 250-252

price reversal   130, 207, 222-223, 225, 227-230, 250, 285

price stabilization   137, 417-418, 432-437, 433n, 442, 444-445

price-drop-to-dividend ratio (PDR)   470

private information risk   110, 120, 124-125, 151, 164-165

private placement of equity   537

probability of informed trading (PIN)   35, 124-126, 133, 164-165, 164n

proportion of gain realized (PGR)   214

proportion of loss realized (PLR)   214

propping hypothesis   526-527, 536

prospect theory   206, 207, 210-214, 216-217, 250

pseudo-DGTW method   373

purchasing power parity (PPP)   616, 618-621

pyramid ownership structure   532

quadratic relationship   528

R&D investment   523

random walk   83, 221, 290, 618-620, 628-631, 645

random walk hypothesis   83

random walk process   618-620

rational liquidity-based model of closed-end funds   363

real exchange rate   616-619, 621-622

reference-point bias   245

relative spread   133, 134, 160, 163, 163n; 166, 167

representativeness   209, 221-222

retained earnings   458, 476, 481, 485

retained-earnings hypothesis   481

return across time and securities (RATS)   299

return predictability   95, 110, 126, 127-128, 139n; 246, 251, 291, 359, 365

risk aversion   28, 73. 210, 211, 253, 584-586

risk reduction effect   473

risk seeking behavior   211

risk-sharing   76, 87, 538

ROA   443, 472, 528-529, 531

ROE   95, 443

rollover effects   577

Roll's "hubris" theory of acquisitions   244

root mean squared error (RMSE)   628

Russian default   73

seasonality in stock returns   14, 157, 280

seasoned equity offerings (SEOs)   300-304

seasoned offerings   297, 304

Securities Act of 1933   328

Securities Exchange Act of 1934   328

selection ability   340, 373-374, 376

share repurchase (stock repurchase)   234, 243-244, 246-247, 458n; 459, 464, 467, 487-494, 488n; 497, 499

Sharpe-Lintner-Black CAPM   2, 5, 9, 21

Sharpe's style analysis methodology   376

short hedgers   578-579, 591

short sales   110, 138-140, 573, 575

short-sale restrictions   575

sidecar   110, 137-138, 137n; 138n

signaling hypothesis   481, 488-491

signaling theory   470-472

size effect   9, 11, 16n; 19n; 207, 245, 273-278, 281, 299, 307, 310

smart money effect   158, 346, 374-375

SMB, Fama and French's   12, 32-34, 32n; 33n: 39, 163, 277-278, 286, 440n; 441n

smooth transition autoregressive (STAR) model   375

smoothing of dividend payments   458

sources of volatility   122-123

spectral density function   620

speculative activities   576

speculative behavior of mutual funds   367

speculative bubbles   624

speculators   73n, 80, 591

spoofing   110-111, 115, 119-120, 129

spoofing orders   119-120, 129

spread   19, 26, 31, 39, 42n; 95, 110, 118-121, 121n; 124-125, 128, 132-134, 137, 160, 163, 163n; 166-168, 209, 218, 291, 333, 351, 562, 583, 585, 589-590, 641

spread decomposition model, MRR   95, 125, 166

start-up bias   375, 382

static hedging strategy   593

stealth trading hypothesis   114-115, 115n

sterilized coefficient   638

stochastic correlation model   589

stochastic discount factor (SDF)   39-43

stochastic volatility model   584

stock dividend   481

stock options   115n, 491-493, 540-541, 593-594

structural VAR model   644

substitute hypothesis   475, 478, 494

substitution hypothesis   488, 497

surprise information stochastic volatility (SISV) model   644

survey evidence on dividends and dividend

policy   485
survivorship bias   224, 276-278, 359-360, 375
synthetic CDO   589
systematic risk   2, 4-5, 19, 21, 32, 140, 286, 288-289,
    348-349, 354, 472, 492, 575, 589, 592-593, 597

takeover deterrence hypothesis   488, 493
target dividend payout ratio   458, 485
tax-loss selling   279
tax-preference hypothesis   468
tax-timing option effect   378
t-GARCH model   641
three factor affine term structure model   583
three-factor model   32, 33-34, 41-42, 44, 73n; 95,
    163-164, 225, 228-229, 234, 272-273, 275-278,
    286-288, 299, 440n
tick size   110, 132-134, 132n: 348
time series analysis   37, 164, 277-278
time varying risk   152, 225, 229, 633
time-varying hedge ratio model   591
timing ability   340-341, 343, 351, 367, 373
timing performance   341
Tobin's Q   475, 526, 528
total asset turnover ratio   443
tournaments   353, 357, 377
trade and quote (TAQ) data   108, 124, 127, 130,
    133, 163n
trading costs of mutual funds   345
trading-range hypothesis   481
transfer hypothesis   491
tunneling hypothesis   519n; 525-527, 532, 535-536,
    545
tunneling tendency   89
turn-of-the-year effect (January effect)   274, 279-281
twin agency problems   87
two factor ICAPM   652
two-stage least square model (2SLS)   166

unbiased forward rate hypothesis (unbiasedness
    hypothesis)   632-635
under-reaction   131, 206, 218, 221, 232-233, 247,
    286, 365
unequal dividend   480-481
uninformed investors   222, 422-424
uninformed trader   158-159, 166
unit root tests   619

unit-investment trusts   329
unsystematic risk   140, 354, 592

Value at Risk (VaR)   589, 631
value manager   349
value premium effect   22, 33n; 274-275, 277-278
value-based event study analysis (VESA)   527
variance bound tests   625
variance ratio tests   619
vector ARIMA model   627
vector autoregression(VAR) model   72, 118, 140,
    158, 574, 637-638, 644
vector error correction model (VECM)   150,
    590-591, 629, 636
vector moving average (VMA)   150
venture-backed IPO   430
vocal intervention   617, 636, 638
volatility smile   586, 595
volatility sneers   586
volatility spillover   80, 136
volatility surface   581, 586
volatility timing   349, 373
volume-weighted average price (vwap)   90-91
voting behavior of mutual funds   352
voting right   518-520, 545

wage decision   524
wealth integration   210, 212
wealth relatives (WR)   295, 299-300, 440
wealth transfer   143, 377, 473, 490-491, 536,
weather effect   206, 247-249
weekend effect   273-274, 282-284
weighted price contribution (WPC)   91
Wilcoxon signed rank test   303
windows of opportunity hypothesis   244
winner's curse   244, 422-424
with-in-month effect   273
won-yen synchronization   645
world market portfolio (world float portfolio)   78,
    87

zero-beta portfolio   5, 25
zero-cost contrarian strategy   227
zero-investment portfolio   39, 440n; 441n
Z-sign test   303